Motivational Dynamics in Language Learning

MIX
Paper from
responsible sources
FSC® C014540
www.fsc.org

SECOND LANGUAGE ACQUISITION

Series Editor: Professor David Singleton, *University of Pannonia, Hungary* and Fellow Emeritus, *Trinity College, Dublin, Ireland*

This series brings together titles dealing with a variety of aspects of language acquisition and processing in situations where a language or languages other than the native language is involved. Second language is thus interpreted in its broadest possible sense. The volumes included in the series all offer in their different ways, on the one hand, exposition and discussion of empirical findings and, on the other, some degree of theoretical reflection. In this latter connection, no particular theoretical stance is privileged in the series; nor is any relevant perspective – sociolinguistic, psycholinguistic, neurolinguistic, etc. – deemed out of place. The intended readership of the series includes final-year undergraduates working on second language acquisition projects, postgraduate students involved in second language acquisition research, and researchers and teachers in general whose interests include a second language acquisition component.

Full details of all the books in this series and of all our other publications can be found on http://www.multilingual-matters.com, or by writing to Multilingual Matters, St Nicholas House, 31–34 High Street, Bristol BS1 2AW, UK.

Motivational Dynamics in Language Learning

Edited by
Zoltán Dörnyei, Peter D. MacIntyre and Alastair Henry

MULTILINGUAL MATTERS
Bristol • Buffalo • Toronto

Library of Congress Cataloging in Publication Data
Motivational Dynamics in Language Learning/Edited by Zoltán Dörnyei, Peter D. MacIntyre and Alastair Henry.
Second Language Acquisition: 81
Includes bibliographical references.
1. Second language acquisition. 2. Motivation in education. 3. Identity (Psychology) 4. Self. I. Dörnyei, Zoltán, editor. II. MacIntyre, Peter D., 1965- editor. III. Henry, Alastair.
P118.2.M677 2014
418.0071–dc23 2014019602

British Library Cataloguing in Publication Data
A catalogue entry for this book is available from the British Library.

ISBN-13: 978-1-78309-256-7 (hbk)
ISBN-13: 978-1-78309-255-0 (pbk)

Multilingual Matters
UK: St Nicholas House, 31–34 High Street, Bristol BS1 2AW, UK.
USA: UTP, 2250 Military Road, Tonawanda, NY 14150, USA.
Canada: UTP, 5201 Dufferin Street, North York, Ontario M3H 5T8, Canada.

Website: www.multilingual-matters.com
Twitter: Multi_Ling_Mat
Facebook: https://www.facebook.com/multilingualmatters
Blog: www.channelviewpublications.wordpress.com

The policy of Multilingual Matters/Channel View Publications is to use papers that are natural, renewable and recyclable products, made from wood grown in sustainable forests. In the manufacturing process of our books, and to further support our policy, preference is given to printers that have FSC and PEFC Chain of Custody certification. The FSC and/or PEFC logos will appear on those books where full certification has been granted to the printer concerned.

Typeset by Techset Composition India(P) Ltd., Bangalore and Chennai, India.
Printed and bound in Great Britain by Short Run Press Ltd.

Contents

Contributors

Ali H. Al-Hoorie is a Lecturer in the English Language Centre, Jubail Industrial College, Saudi Arabia. His interests include learning motivation, learning theories, complexity theory and research methodology. He is currently a PhD student at the University of Nottingham.

Kumiko Arano received her Master's Degree from the Graduate School of Foreign Language Education and Research at Kansai University in March 2013. Her research interests include the role of motivation in EFL and its application to teaching practice. She continues to pursue her interest in English teaching in her current position as an educator at a public high school in Japan.

Kyoko Baba is an Associate Professor at Kinjo Gakuin University in Nagoya, Japan, where she teaches undergraduate and MA courses. She completed her PhD at the Ontario Institute for Studies in Education at the University of Toronto in 2007. Her research interests include the learning of L2 writing skills (with a focus on the instructed context), the lexical features of L2 learners' language production and complexity theory.

Letty Chan is a Research Student in applied linguistics at the University of Nottingham. Her current research interests include the L2 Motivational Self System, faith and L2 identity, the use of imagery in the L2 classroom and Dynamic Systems Theory. She has taught academic English at both the University of Hong Kong and Nottingham Trent University. She has published papers on vision and imagery.

Kata Csizér holds a PhD in Language Pedagogy and works as a lecturer in the Department of English and Applied Linguistics at Eötvös University, Budapest, where she teaches various L2 motivation courses. Her main field of research interest focuses on the socio-psychological aspects of L2 learning and teaching, as well as second and foreign language motivation. She has published over 50 academic papers on various aspects of L2 motivation and has co-authored three books, including *Motivational Dynamics, Language Attitudes* *and Language Globalisation: A Hungarian Perspective* (2006, Multilingual Matters, with Zoltán Dörnyei and Nóra Németh).

Kees de Bot is Chair of Applied Linguistics at the University of Groningen in the Netherlands and research fellow at the University of the Free State in South Africa. His current research interests include the application of Dynamic Systems Theory in the study of Second Language Development, language attrition, the effectiveness of bilingual schools in the Netherlands and the history of Applied Linguistics (1980–2010).

Zoltán Dörnyei is Professor of Psycholinguistics at the School of English, University of Nottingham. He has published widely on various aspects of second language acquisition and language learning motivation, and he is the author of several books, including *Research Methods in Applied Linguistics* (2007, Oxford University Press), *The Psychology of Second Language Acquisition* (2009, Oxford University Press), *Teaching and Researching Motivation* (2nd edn, 2011, Longman, with Ema Ushioda), *Motivating Learning* (2013, Longman, with Jill Hadfield) and *Motivating Learners, Motivating Teachers: Building Vision in the Language Classroom* (2014, Cambridge University Press, with Magdalena Kubanyiova).

Tammy Gregersen is a Professor of TESOL at the University of Northern Iowa where she specializes in language teaching methodology. She taught English and trained teachers in Chile for 15 years and has also been involved in teacher education programs and conferences in Spain, Russia, Poland, United Arab Emirates, Italy, Portugal, France, Belgium and Austria. Her research interests include individual differences and nonverbal communication in applied linguistics. She is co-author of *Capitalizing on Language Learners' Individuality: From Premise to Practice* (2014, Multilingual Matters, with Peter MacIntyre).

Alastair Henry teaches at University West, Sweden, and has a PhD in Language Education from the University of Gothenburg. His research has focused on motivation in third language learning and gender differences in L2 motivation.

Phil Hiver is a Lecturer in the Department of English Language Teaching at the International Graduate School of English, Seoul, where he teaches courses in language pedagogy and materials development. His research interests include the broad areas of teacher motivation and development, and psychological constructs in instructed second language acquisition using DST and case-based methods.

Zana Ibrahim is a PhD Student Researcher in the School of English Studies, University of Nottingham. He is the recipient of a Fulbright Scholarship and obtained his Master's degree in TESOL from the Indiana University of Pennsylvania. He has worked in the field of foreign language teaching and translation. His research interests include Directed Motivational Currents, Dynamic Systems Theory and ESL syllabus design and materials development.

Kay Irie is a Professor at Gakushuin University, Tokyo where she is developing a CLIL-based English program. She also teaches in the Graduate College of Education at Temple University Japan. Her current research interests include learner autonomy and motivation in language education. She is a co-editor of *Realizing Autonomy: Practice and Reflection in Language Education Contexts* (2012, Palgrave Macmillan).

Diane Larsen-Freeman is Professor Emerita at the University of Michigan, Ann Arbor, and a Visiting Senior Fellow at the University of Pennsylvania. She is also a Distinguished Senior Faculty Fellow at the Graduate SIT Institute in Brattleboro, Vermont. Her interests include second language development, English grammar, language teaching and language teacher education.

Peter D. MacIntyre is a Professor of Psychology at Cape Breton University. His research focuses on the dynamic changes in emotion and cognition that take place as part of the psychology of communication. Recently, he co-authored *Capitalizing on Language Learners' Individuality: From Premise to Practice* (2014, Multilingual Matters, with Tammy Gregersen) as a guide to translating theory into classroom action. He teaches a variety of courses, including advanced research methods, human sexuality, personality, advanced social psychology, motivation and emotion, and positive psychology.

Sarah Mercer teaches at the University of Graz, Austria where she has been working since 1998. She has a PhD from the University of Lancaster and her research interests include all aspects of the psychology surrounding the foreign language learning experience, focusing in particular on the self. She is the author of *Towards an Understanding of Language Learner Self-Concept* (2011, Springer) and is co-editor of *Psychology for Language Learning* (2012, Palgrave MacMillan, with Stephen Ryan and Marion Williams) and *Multiple Perspectives on the Self* (2014, Multilingual Matters). She is also an associate editor at the journal *System*.

Christine Muir is a Postgraduate Teaching Fellow at the University of Nottingham and is currently completing her PhD under the supervision of Professor Zoltán Dörnyei. She graduated from the University of Edinburgh with an MSc in Language Teaching, having previously spent time teaching English in Russia, Finland, the Czech Republic and the UK. Her current research interests include Directed Motivational Currents, vision theory, time perspective and Dynamic Systems Theory.

Ryo Nitta is an Associate Professor at Nagoya Gakuin University, Japan, where he teaches second language acquisition in the Faculty of Foreign Studies. He received his PhD from the University of Warwick in 2007. His recent research focuses on changes in second language performance (both oral and written) and L2 motivation from a complex dynamic systems perspective.

Katalin Piniel is an Assistant Professor at the Department of English and Applied Linguistics at Eötvös University, Budapest, where she obtained her PhD in Language Pedagogy. She teaches courses in academic writing, research methodology, individual differences in language learning, language anxiety and language testing at both graduate and undergraduate levels. Her research interests include the interrelationship of individual differences in foreign language learning and language anxiety.

Stephen Ryan is a Professor in the School of Economics at Senshu University, Tokyo. His research and publications address a range of issues relating to the psychology of second language learning, with a recent interest in the motivational roles of narrative and the imagination in language learning. He is co-editor (with Sarah Mercer and Marion Williams) of *Psychology for Language Learning: Insights from Theory, Research and Practice* (2012, Palgrave Macmillan).

John H. Schumann is Distinguished Professor (Emeritus) of Applied Linguistics and former chair of the Department of Applied Linguistics and TESL at UCLA. His research includes language acquisition, the neurobiology of language, the neurobiology of learning and language evolution. He is co-author of *The Interactional Instinct: The Evolution and Acquisition of Language* (2009, OUP) and *The Neurobiology of Learning* (2004, Erlbaum). He is co-editor of *Exploring the Interactional Instinct* (2013, OUP). He is also the author of *The Neurobiology of Affect in Language* (1997, Blackwell).

Alicia Serroul is Student Researcher at Cape Breton University. Alicia is completing her honours degree in psychology (BA, 2014) on the topic of human–computer interaction regarding social stances.

Ema Ushioda is an Associate Professor and Director of Graduate Studies at the Centre for Applied Linguistics, University of Warwick, UK. Her research interests are motivation for language learning and intercultural engagement, learner autonomy, sociocultural theory and teacher development. Recent publications include *International Perspectives on Motivation: Language Learning and Professional Challenges* (2013, Palgrave Macmillan), *Teaching and Researching*

Motivation (2011, Longman, co-authored with Zoltán Dörnyei) and *Motivation, Language Identity and the L2 Self* (2009, Multilingual Matters, co-edited with Zoltán Dörnyei).

Marjolijn Verspoor gained her PhD in 1991 from The University of Leiden and is Associate Professor at the University of Groningen, Netherlands, and at the University of the Free State, South Africa. Her research is focused on second language development from a usage-based, dynamic systems perspective and on second language instruction drawing on dynamic usage-based principles.

Frea Waninge is a PhD student at the University of Nottingham, where she researches emotion and motivation and works as a teaching assistant and lab manager at the Centre of Research for Applied Linguistics. Her research interests include the interaction of emotion, motivation and cognition, the L2 learning experience and motivation in young language learners.

Tomoko Yashima is a Professor of Applied Linguistics and Intercultural Communication at Kansai University. Her research interests include L2 learning motivation, affect and language identity. Her studies have been published in journals such as *The Modern Language Journal*, *Language Learning*, *System* and *Psychological Reports*. She is the author of several books published in Japanese including *Motivation and Affect in Foreign Language Communication* (2004, Kansai University Press) and has published a Japanese translation of Zoltán Dörnyei's *Questionnaires in L2 Research*.

Chenjing (Julia) You is a PhD student in the School of English, University of Nottingham, where she also obtained her Master's degree. In China, she has worked as an Associate Professor in the field of foreign language teaching and has also taught English at several high schools for more than 10 years. Her research interests include second language motivation, vision and imagery, and Complex Dynamic Systems Theory.

Foreword

John H. Schumann

This book is a milestone in the study of motivation. It brings together several important advances. First it recognizes dynamic systems theory as the epistemological basis for conceptualizing motivation. It provides an extensive tutorial on dynamic systems. It introduces research methodologies that allow, on several timescales, the study of individual motivational trajectories in second language acquisition (SLA). The book challenges several assumptions about 'scientific' research in SLA. One is the assumption that truth is found in the study of inter-individual variability among large numbers of subjects. Another is that causal effects are either singular or few in number and that they operate linearly. An additional assumption is that categories and their labels refer to clearly identifiable entities in the world. The adoption of dynamic systems theory (DST) allows, indeed, compels us to eschew notions of single causes, linear causality, immutable categories and highly specified endpoints.

Traditional research on motivation in SLA consisted of studying large numbers of subjects using questionnaires that were administered at one time to large numbers of subjects. This research provided a freeze frame/snapshot perspective on motivation. However, it gave us no information about the individual learner and, as Molenaar (2004) has demonstrated, we cannot argue from groups to individuals except under very strict conditions (see also van Geert, 2011). These studies gave information about motivation at a particular moment in time. Nevertheless, they were often interpreted as providing information about what kind of motivation had brought the learner to this point and about what kind of motivation would carry him/her forward.

For some researchers, there has always been a concern for what was going on in the individual and how that changed over time. In the 1970s, colleagues and I undertook diary studies of individuals learning a second language (L2) in classrooms, in the environments where it was spoken or in a combination of both. Dozens of studies were done at UCLA and other institutions. Attempts were made to aggregate the results (Bailey, 1983, 1991), but commonalities were difficult to discern and no theory existed with which the individual variation could be explained.

In the 1990s, stimulus appraisal theory (Schumann, 1997) was applied to autobiographies of L2 learners. The categories of stimulus appraisal (novelty, pleasantness, goal/need significance, coping potential, and self and social image) were used to relate SLA motivation to underlying neural mechanisms, but also to analyze autobiographies of the L2 learners as a way of tracking the individual variables over longer periods. Thus, stimulus appraisal categories provided an organizational framework, but still an overall theory was lacking. This vacuum was filled by Diane Larsen-Freeman's (1997, 2002; Larsen-Freeman & Cameron, 2008) introduction of DST to our field and Zoltán Dörnyei's (2009) adoption of this perspective for his research on motivation.

DST allows researchers in L2 motivation to simultaneously abandon the notion of single and linear causality and frees them from the implicit demand in conventional research for large subject studies. As seen in this volume, DST provides a way to see motivation from the perspective of a general theory that applies to many phenomena. The individual is the entity of concern, and case studies become recognized as the appropriate level of granularity for understanding motivation trajectories in SLA. In this new work, it is wonderful to hear the learners' voices characterizing their motivation. In traditional research, these voices were silenced in statistical analyses, and the complex variation within individuals that characterizes SLA was hidden.

Several years ago at a conference, I asked a major motivation researcher when he thought his research on SLA motivation would be finished. This is part of a bigger question. When will we have sufficient knowledge of L2 motivation so that we can say our work is done? When will it no longer be necessary to do research on L2 motivation? Another question is whether any SLA motivation construct that has been proposed and studied has been wrong? I would suggest that none of them have been wrong. They may have been incomplete; they may have been extended too broadly or narrowly; research on the construct may have been inadequate owing to limitations on current technology or statistical procedures. The constructs may have been limited because of the lack of a larger theoretical framework in which to place them. So will we ever have the answer, and if not, why not?

Typical scientific research isolates an independent variable and a dependent variable, and then looks at the singular influence of the former on the latter. DST challenges this approach to understanding complex phenomena. Variation within and across individuals becomes central in a dynamic systems approach. But will thousands of longitudinal studies of individuals provide the final answer? Actually, I don't think so. The problem is that we are not dealing with physical phenomena. We are dealing with abstract constructs and conceptualizations. The terms we use to refer to these concepts are not mutually exclusive. In the neurobiological literature related to motivation, the following terms are frequent: intention, incentive, desire, goal, reward, approach, action tendency, wanting, liking, emotion, affect, arousal, valence, appraisal, reward. The Concise Oxford American Thesaurus (2006) under the heading motivation includes: motivating source, force, incentive, stimulus, stimulation, inspiration, inducement, spur, reason, drive, ambition, initiative, determination and enterprise. Other terms include enthusiasm, commitment, persistence, investment, engagement. Do all these terms refer to independent phenomena? Certainly not. They overlap; they capture slightly different perspectives on the issue. Are there any that we can do without? I suspect not. A prohibition on certain terms would create the same problem that Prohibition did – the proscribed words would be bootlegged. When we go beyond words and look at the labels for motivational constructs that have been explored in SLA, we find a similar proliferation. We see integrative motivation, instrumental motivation, self-determination theory, attribution theory, goal theories, situated motivation, task motivation, willingness to communicate, skill-challenge perspectives, value expectancy, the L2 Motivational Self System, identity theory, investment theory and the stimulus appraisal perspective.

Would we have the answer if we could find the definitive neurobiological mechanisms that produce motivation? Such reductionism is not a solution either. Even now we know a good deal about the biology that underlies motivation. It involves the amygdala, the orbitofrontal cortex, the anterior cingulate, the insula, the dopaminergic system, the opioid system, the endocrine system, the musculoskeletal system and the autonomic nervous system. But with even more detailed knowledge about how each of these systems contributes to motivation, we would not have a final answer because at the phenomenal level represented by the motivational constructs, there is so much more to understand and appreciate. And that list is not going to end. Different conceptualizations of SLA motivation will continue to be proposed and will continue to inform our notions of the phenomenon. In a species capable of generating symbolic nonmaterial constructs that cannot be isolated as physical entities but only as conceptualizations built out of other concepts, the number of possible formulations of the phenomena is potentially infinite.

This brings us to a discussion of how the field of SLA motivation research operates. Our field does not stand outside the realm of dynamic systems. In fact, it manifests all the processes that characterize such systems. Motivation became a focus of research in SLA in the late 1950s. Since then it has been pursued with varying degrees of intensity. If a professor takes an interest in this issue, he/she conducts some research often requiring a grant and graduate students as research assistants. The results of the research must be published in order to get the ideas known and to get the professor promoted. The students have to conduct research and publish in order to receive their degrees, secure a position and get tenure. These academics organize to present papers and colloquia at national and international conferences. The research reported at these colloquia is frequently published as collections or monographs. All this is done in order to accrue knowledge about motivation in SLA, but also for economic reasons. The fate of universities in various economies influences these dynamics. The variations in availability of resources affect hiring, student support, research funding, and hence how, where and with what intensity motivation gets studied. Interest in the phenomenon among SLA researchers waxes and wanes. As argued above, we are not likely to find the final answer as to how motivation affects L2 learning, but the field might just get tired of the issue, and its importance in applied linguistics could diminish. Indeed, there are areas of SLA research where motivation is not given much attention. Among some SLA cognitivists, motivation is seen as a minor intervening variable in L2 acquisition, but not central to the process.

The commitment to DST as a framework for studying motivation does not come automatically (Lewis, 2011). The human mind has evolved to view the world in terms of singular causes and single chains of causality. From an evolutionary perspective, we can assume that such cognition must have been very important for the survival of our species. The experimental method itself may be a manifestation of our tendency to isolate a single cause, to see averages as the truth and to dismiss variation as noise. Complicating the matter, is the fact that the search for a single causal variable often works and has often been very informative; we have learned a lot from this way of thinking. Thus, although case studies done within the framework of DST may be the best way to study intraindividual variation in L2, pressures of academic tradition could make many scholars retreat to the safer attractor – experimental studies of interindividual variation between groups of learners. All these issues play out in the dynamics of motivation research, leading into and out of attractor states and through conditions of considerable variation. Our field is studying the DST game while playing it.

So this volume marks an exciting new beginning. It provides a general theory for motivation in SLA and, I believe, for applied linguistics as a whole. It suggests new methods to do research within that theory. It prioritizes individual accounts over groups; values variation as strongly as states; it challenges historical ideologies; it forces us to rethink our conceptions about cause and categories; it makes us deal with the way the world actually works, not simply the way we all think it works; it allows us to see our research enterprise in terms of complex systems not just as the phenomenon of motivation; it permits us to question our assumptions about an eventual end state in our research; and leaves us open to the notion of investigation without an expectation of an ultimate answer. These are big contributions.

References

Bailey, K.M. (1983) Competitiveness and anxiety in adult second language learning: Looking at and through the diary studies. In H.W. Seliger and M.H. Long (eds) *Classroom Oriented Research in Second Language Acquisition* (pp. 67–102). Rowley, MA: Newbury House.

Bailey, K.M. (1991) Diary studies of language learning: The doubting game and the believing game. In E. Sadtono (ed.) *Language Acquisition and the Second/Foreign Language Classroom* (pp. 60–102). Singapore: SEAMEO RELC (Regional Language Centre).

Concise Oxford American Thesaurus (2006) London: Oxford University Press.

Dörnyei, Z. (2009) Individual differences: Interplay of learner characteristics and learning environment. *Language Learning* 59 (Suppl. 1), 230–248.

Larsen-Freeman, D. (1997) Chaos/complexity science and second language acquisition. *Applied Linguistics* 18, 141–165.

Larsen-Freeman, D. (2002) Language acquisition and language use from a chaos/complexity theory perspective. In C. Kramsch (ed.) *Language Acquisition in Language Socialization* (pp. 33–36). London: Continuum.

Larsen-Freeman, D. and Cameron, L. (2008) *Complex Systems and Applied Linguistics*. Oxford: Oxford University Press.

Lewis, M. (2011) Dynamic systems approaches: Cool enough? Hot enough? *Child Development Perspectives* 5 (4), 279–285.

Molenaar, P.C.M. (2004) A manifesto on psychology as idiographic science: Bringing the person back into scientific psychology, this time forever. *Interdisciplinary Research and Perspectives* 2 (4), 201–218.

Schumann, J.H. (1997) *The Neurobiology of Affect in Language*. Malden MA: Blackwell.

van Geert, P. (2011) The contribution of complex dynamic systems to development. *Child Development Perspectives* 5 (4), 273–278.

1 Introduction: Applying Complex Dynamic Systems Principles to Empirical Research on L2 Motivation

Zoltán Dörnyei, Peter D. MacIntyre and Alastair Henry

When nonlinear system dynamics was introduced into second language acquisition (SLA) research – under various rubrics such as chaos theory (Larsen-Freeman, 1997), emergentism (Ellis & Larsen-Freeman, 2006), dynamic systems theory (de Bot *et al.*, 2007) and complexity theory (Larsen-Freeman & Cameron, 2008) – the new approach, which may be seen as the 'dynamic turn' in SLA, resonated with many scholars because nonlinear system dynamics appeared to nicely describe several puzzling language learning phenomena. To offer but one illustration, the so-called 'butterfly effect' explained why language teaching input sometimes had considerable impact on the learners' progress, whereas at other times it led only to minimal, if any, uptake. The dynamic principles introduced also made intuitive sense research-wise. We have long known that the manifold issues and factors affecting SLA are interrelated, and the new paradigm represented a holistic approach that took into account the combined and interactive operation of a number of different elements/conditions relevant to specific situations, rather than following the more traditional practice of examining the relationship between well-defined variables in relative isolation.

Thus, proposals for a dynamic paradigm shift in the research community during the first decade of the new millennium were generally well received. However, by the end of the 2010s it had become noticeable that while there was a growing body of literature on complex dynamic systems within SLA contexts, very little of this work was empirical in nature. In other words, scholars spent much more time *talking* about research in a dynamic systems vein than actually *doing* it. Furthermore, even when dynamic principles were

1

referred to in data-based studies, this was often to explain away difficult-to-interpret results, stating in effect that such results occurred because of the unpredictable or 'emergentist' nature of the system. At the same time, in informal conversations at conferences, it was not at all uncommon to hear scholars privately express the sense of being at a loss as to how exactly to go about researching dynamic systems.

The Challenge of the New Paradigm

This growing uncertainty was to some extent understandable since – as Dörnyei (2009) summarised – at least three aspects of such an approach inevitably pushed researchers into unchartered territories (for a detailed overview, see Verspoor et al., 2011).

- Modelling *nonlinear change* (especially quantitatively); this has been succinctly summed up by de Bot and Larsen-Freeman (2011: 18) as follows: 'If the process is nonlinear, how is it possible to make any predictions that are likely to hold up?'
- Observing the operation of the *whole system* and the interaction of the parts, rather than focusing on specific units (e.g. variables) within it. In de Bot and Larsen-Freeman's (2011: 18) words: 'if everything is interconnected, how is it possible to study anything apart from everything else?'
- Finding *alternatives* to conventional quantitative research methodologies that, by and large, relied on statistical procedures to examine linear rather than dynamic relationships.

The combination of these three issues seriously questioned the feasibility of investigating cause–effect relations, the traditional basis of generalisable theories in the spirit of the 'scientific method' (see Dörnyei, 2007). As Byrne and Callaghan (2014: 173) put it:

> we cannot decompose the system into its elements and use control over discrete elements whilst varying just one of them, either directly or through the use of treatment and control groups, in order to establish causality in terms of the properties of those elements.

We should note here that the challenge that applied linguists and language psychologists have been facing is not merely having to master new research skills in order to find their bearings in a novel paradigm, but is related also to a much broader issue: the difficulty of transferring the nonlinear systems approach from the natural sciences – where dynamic systems theory has been flourishing in several areas (such as thermodynamics) – to the social sciences. In the natural sciences, where the main units of analysis are molecules or objects, it is possible to reconstruct the movement of a complex system by applying intricate mathematical modelling. However, in the social sciences, where the basic units of analysis are self-reflective human beings, dynamic situations tend to be so complex – and embedded in each other in such a multi-layered manner – that accurate mathematical modelling might be an unrealistic expectation. De Bot (2011) explains that the alternative to such hard-science-like attempts to adopt mathematics-based tools and models is a 'soft' approach, which simply imports dynamic *metaphors* from the natural sciences that are seen as useful in explaining observed phenomena in a qualitative and interpretive manner. While this second approach might appear more realistic, it still poses considerable paradigmatic challenges. Many of the core metaphors of complex dynamic systems theory – for example the central notion of 'attractor states' – originate in pure mathematics (Byrne & Callaghan, 2014), and it is questionable whether we can meaningfully deploy such metaphors by mapping them onto a social reality. For example, as Byrne and Callaghan (2014: 73) argue, attractor states can be described well by equations in abstracted topological spaces, while for social scientists they are 'real regions in real state spaces'. The social and the mathematical realms are not isomorphic, and therefore these scholars provocatively conclude:

> Frankly with some exceptions, almost all of which are spatially oriented, mathematical and computational social science remains at the level of the banal and trivial. This is not because the methods are at a very early state of development. It is because ... [they are] not a proper basis for the construction of accounts of complex realities which are made and remade in considerable part as a consequence of human social agency. Mathematics *can* be a useful tool for describing the reality but reality is its messy self, not a higher abstract order existing in mathematical form. (Byrne & Callaghan, 2014: 257)

Thus, when we started to think about the current anthology, the prevailing situation in the field of SLA was twofold. On the one hand, dynamic systems research was hailed as having a promising potential for a number of reasons:

- it was hoped to be able to capture the multi-faceted complexity of the SLA process;
- it treated learner-internal and learner-external factors in an integrated manner, thereby creating a socially grounded approach in which the context was seen as part of the system;
- it foregrounded individual-based research, thereby offering increased ecological validity and better insights into seemingly 'chaotic' occurrences;

- it offered a way of removing any qualitative/quantitative boundaries and merging the two approaches within some form of mixed methodology;
- it highlighted the significance of change and development in general – and thus longitudinal research in particular – which was more than welcome in a field that was, by definition, centred around 'acquisition'.

On the other hand, scholars interested in the approach found themselves not only without any templates or traditions they could rely on in producing workable and productive research designs, but also without a coherent set of new research metaphors to use. Consequently, although the approach was 'in the air', it became highly elusive when it came to operationalising it in concrete terms. The absence of established research tools and paradigms affected PhD students in particular, because for many of them, doing dynamic systems research seemed just too difficult and too risky.

Dynamic Systems Research and Motivation

Second language (L2) motivation research was initiated by social psychologists Robert Gardner and Wallace Lambert in Canada (Gardner & Lambert, 1959) by adopting a macro perspective that captured the overall language disposition of substantial learner samples on a large timescale. At this level of analysis, traditional statistical procedures that utilised linear relationships (such as correlation-based analyses) worked well. This situation, however, changed dramatically in the 1990s, when researchers' interests shifted to a more micro-level analysis of motivation, focusing on how motivation affected language learning behaviours and achievement in specific learning contexts such as L2 classrooms. When motivation was conceptualised in such a situated manner, one could not help noticing the considerable fluctuation in learners' motivational dispositions exhibited on an almost day-to-day basis, which led to attempts to reframe the concept in process-oriented terms (e.g. Dörnyei, 2000; Dörnyei & Ottó, 1998). However, process models that were based on cause-effect relationships failed to offer a realistic account of the motivational phenomena observed in real-life situations; the linear progression implied by a flow-chart diagram was not reflected in the seemingly random iterative processes that many learners described. Therefore, as Dörnyei (2009) stated, it was only a matter of time before scholars started to look for a more dynamic conceptualisation.

In 2011, Dörnyei and Ushioda prepared a book-length overview of L2 motivation research, which contained extensive arguments to support the theoretical validity of dynamic approaches. They extended this discussion to also include possible selves and Dörnyei's (2005, 2009) L2 Motivational Self System, which they saw as a dynamic 'motivation–cognition–emotion amalgam'. However, when it came to providing sample studies in Part III of their book, they could only identify a single paper in the literature that explicitly embodied dynamic principles: MacIntyre and Legatto's (2011) study, which employed an 'idiodynamic' methodology to capture the fluctuation of rapidly changing affect in relation to the participants' willingness to communicate. The paucity of dynamic systems research closely reflected the general trend in SLA research mentioned above, namely that while most of the cutting-edge theorising took it for granted that the future lay along the dynamic path, most of the actual empirical research followed traditional, non-dynamic research approaches.

The recognition of the absence of relevant empirical studies played a significant part in our decision to initiate a large-scale project exploring the researchability of dynamic systems. We believed that the topic of L2 motivation was an ideal content area for such an endeavour, partly because motivation, with its ups and downs and ebbs and flows, was an SLA phenomenon that seemed to lend itself to the application of dynamically informed research designs, and partly because the currently most established constructs in the field – the various L2 self-guides – are by nature inherently dynamic and would therefore be well suited targets for investigation using dynamic approaches. The challenge we set ourselves was thus fairly straightforward: we could either initiate a robust research project that takes well-established motivation constructs and, by applying dynamic principles to their investigation, produces convincing empirical evidence for the sustainability of the approach; or we would have to come to terms with the fact that the dynamic approach in SLA might be simply an attractive but ultimately unrealisable idea. The production of this volume was therefore intended to serve as the primary testing ground.

The Current Anthology

As a first step in our efforts, invitations to join the project were sent out to a large number of established researchers specialising in language learning motivation. The initial reception was very positive and over 40 scholars from three continents agreed to participate. At the same time, we succeeded in securing a contract for an anthology on the topic with Multilingual Matters, which allowed the planning to start taking concrete shape. Interested scholars first met at the 2013 convention of the American Association of Applied Linguistics in Dallas, Texas, where a well-attended colloquium was co-organised by Dörnyei and MacIntyre to showcase the goals that the project had set out to achieve. The conference also included several other papers on dynamic systems issues, many of them not in motivational areas, thus prompting the idea of adding a conceptual part to the volume in which some of the central themes and notions are discussed in a generic manner by experts in the field.

The eight months following the conference involved intensive activity as an increasing tide of initial manuscripts were submitted, edited and revised, resulting finally in 21 accepted papers. During this process we applied unusually strict selection criteria in the sense that we turned down several chapters that were of publishable quality (and will hopefully be in print soon in some other forum) because, in our judgement, they were not instantiating complex dynamic systems research, an issue to which we shall return in the Conclusion. (Also, we should mention, an unintended result of this process is that we are beginning to realise how many free drinks and meals it will take over the next few years to reconcile our friends whose work was deemed insufficiently dynamic...) As we have come to the end of a three-year journey, we can commend to the reader the collective fruit of a great deal of dedication and hard work on the part of all the contributors. This has not been an easy project to pursue for any of us, but it has definitely been a project of commitment and passion – which of course should always be the case with any book on motivation!

References

Byrne, D. and Callaghan, G. (2014) *Complexity Theory and the Social Sciences: The State of the Art*. Abingdon: Routledge.

de Bot, K. (2011) Researching second language development from a dynamic systems theory perspective. In M.H. Verspoor, K. de Bot and W. Lowie (eds) *Epilogue* (pp. 123–127). Amsterdam: John Benjamins.

de Bot, K. and Larsen-Freeman, D. (2011) Researching second language development from a dynamic systems theory perspective. In M.H. Verspoor, K. de Bot and W. Lowie (eds) *A Dynamic Approach to Second Language Development: Methods and Techniques* (pp. 5–23). Amsterdam: John Benjamins.

de Bot, K., Lowie, W. and Verspoor, M.H. (2007) A Dynamic Systems Theory approach to second language acquisition. *Bilingualism: Language and Cognition* 10 (1), 7–21.

Dörnyei, Z. (2000) Motivation in action: Towards a process-oriented conceptualisation of student motivation. *British Journal of Educational Psychology* 70, 519–538.

Dörnyei, Z. (2005) *The Psychology of the Language Learner: Individual Differences in Second Language Acquisition*. Mahwah, NJ: Lawrence Erlbaum.

Dörnyei, Z. (2007) *Research Methods in Applied Linguistics: Quantitative, Qualitative and Mixed Methodologies*. Oxford: Oxford University Press.

Dörnyei, Z. (2009) *The Psychology of Second Language Acquisition*. Oxford: Oxford University Press.

Dörnyei, Z. and Ottó, I. (1998) Motivation in action: A process model of L2 motivation. *Working Papers in Applied Linguistics (Thames Valley University, London)* 4, 43–69.

Dörnyei, Z. and Ushioda, E. (2011) *Teaching and Researching Motivation* (2nd edn). Harlow: Longman.

Ellis, N.C. and Larsen-Freeman, D. (2006) Language emergence: Implications for applied linguistics – Introduction to the special issue. *Applied Linguistics* 27 (4), 558–589.

Gardner, R.C. and Lambert, W.E. (1959) Motivational variables in second language acquisition. *Canadian Journal of Psychology* 13, 266–272.

Larsen-Freeman, D. (1997) Chaos/complexity science and second language acquisition. *Applied Linguistics* 18, 141–165.

Larsen-Freeman, D. and Cameron, L. (2008) *Complex Systems and Applied Linguistics.* Oxford: Oxford University Press.

MacIntyre, P.D. and Legatto, J.J. (2011) A dynamic system approach to willingness to communicate: Developing an idiodynamic method to capture rapidly changing affect. *Applied Linguistics* 32 (2), 149–171.

Verspoor, M.H., de Bot, K. and Lowie, W. (eds) (2011) *A Dynamic Approach to Second Language Development: Methods and Techniques.* Amsterdam: John Benjamins.

Part 1
Conceptual Summaries

2 Ten 'Lessons' from Complex Dynamic Systems Theory: What is on Offer

Diane Larsen-Freeman

In some ways, the fact that 'theory' is in the name of Complex Dynamic Systems Theory (CDST) is unfortunate. While the use of 'theory' is not incorrect, it tends to underestimate what is on offer. The purpose of this chapter is two-fold: First, to introduce ten lessons from CDST as I see them; and second, to make a convincing case that CDST has far-reaching consequences, beyond what one might normally expect with a new theory. The fact is that CDST has fundamentally challenged our goal for research and our way of conducting it. No longer can we be content with Newtonian reductionism, a Laplacian clockwork universe with its deterministic predictability, and the use of statistics to generalize from the behaviour of population samples to individuals. Given its potential for encouraging entirely new regimes of thought, it has been called a paradigm by some, by others a metatheory, and by still others a theoretical framework. The point is that its influence and its promise extend beyond that of most theories.

This is because CDST is transdisciplinary in two senses of the term. It is transdisciplinary in that it has been used in many different disciplines to investigate issues ranging from the spread of disease, to the contribution of diversity in ecologies, to the formation of ant colonies and to an explanation for the demise of an ancient Pueblo people. More important, it is transdisciplinary in the Hallidayan sense (Halliday & Burns, 2006) of redefining the structure of knowledge. Indeed, like other powerful cross-cutting themes, such as structuralism and evolution, which have contributed the ideas of 'organization' and 'the arrow of time', respectively, CDST introduces the themes of *dynamism* and *emergence* to modern scholarship. As for dynamism, CDST makes the study of *change* central. CDST also contributes the notion of emergence, 'the spontaneous occurrence of something new' (van Geert, 2008: 182) that arises from the interaction of the components of the system, just as a bird flock emerges from the interaction of individual birds. In brief, change and emergence are central to any understanding of complex dynamic systems.[1]

For the remainder of this chapter, I briefly outline 10 lessons of CDST as I see them. I attempt from time to time to relate them to the theme of this chapter – motivation – although the study of motivation in second language development (SLD) is not one for which I claim expertise. I leave it up to the authors of the chapters in this volume to apply the lessons to motivational research in ways that I do not. I conclude by suggesting that CDST holds the potential for reuniting the major streams of research in the field of SLD, bringing together an understanding of learning and learner.

Change

CDST interjects dynamicity into our 'objects' of concern. 'Essentially, nothing in its [a complex dynamic system] environment is fixed' (Waldrop, 1992: 145).

Clearly, this lesson looms large in this volume on motivational dynamics because it was not so long ago that the prevailing assumption of individual difference research was one of stasis. Although characterizing individual differences as static was never stated explicitly, it is a fact that most researchers aimed to find correlations between certain learner characteristics theorized to be influential in SLD and language learning success *at one time*.

Although the types of motivation were postulated with increasing sophistication, the fact remained that change was not part of the picture. Thus, this first lesson of CDST has far-reaching consequences, heightening our awareness that motivation is dynamic. Periods of stability may be reached, but motivation undeniably changes, sometimes often and certainly over time. If we really want to understand motivation, and other aspects of SLD for that matter, we must conceive of them more as processes than states. CDST is a theory of process not state; becoming not being (Gleick, 1987). Hence this volume, *motivational dynamics,* is aptly named.

Space

Not only is time foremost on a CDST agenda, so also is space. CDST uses topographical images. It helps us see time in spatial terms. With this shift in perspective, we gain a host of concepts to stretch our thinking in new directions. System change is seen as movement in a trajectory across a 'state space' or 'phase space'. As the learner's motivational system moves across state space, it is attracted to certain regions of state space, repelled by others. The former constitute attractors in space, places where the system settles, usually temporarily.

Another interesting characteristic of its state space is its fractal geometry. A fractal is a geometric figure that is self-similar at different levels of scale. For instance, a visual image of motivation over time might look like Figure 2.1.

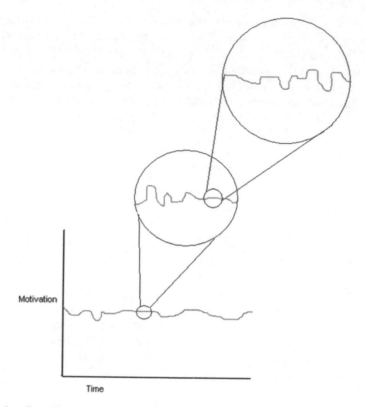

Figure 2.1 Example of a visual image of motivation over time at three different time-frames. (Figure courtesy of Frea Waninge)

If we compare the bottom line, say the time spent studying a modern language over a university semester, with the middle line, say a week in that semester, with the top line, say a lesson during the week, we see that each line displays periods of relative stability and periods of fluctuating motivation. We also see that what appear to be periods of stability at larger time-frames are made up of fluctuating motivation levels at shorter timeframes. Thus, another contribution of CDST is that it gives us a new set of images by which to describe motivation; ones that show scale independence, the structural dynamics of fractal geometry.

Complexity

As systems make their way through space/time, they display patterns – something novel – something that could not have been anticipated by probing their component parts one by one. An important concept in CDST, self-organization, 'refers to any set of processes in which order emerges from the interaction of the components of a system without direction from external factors and without a plan of the order embedded in an individual component' (Mitchell, 2003: 6). In contrast to preformationism ('the assumption that in order to build a complex structure you need to begin with a detailed plan or template' (Deacon, 2012: 50)), the novel behaviour of a complex system emerges through the self-organizing interaction of its components, be they elements in a weather system, agents in a social group or neurons in a neural network. Thus, CDST shifts the search for understanding from reductionism to understanding how patterns emerge from components interacting within the ecology in which they operate (van Lier, 2000: 246).

Relationship

What is important in a complex dynamic system is the interdependent relationship among the factors that comprise it. Again, from a CDST point of view, it is not sufficient to view factors one by one, and then to conduct a univariate analysis, such as a simple correlation between a factor and the language proficiency of the learner. This is not only owing to the mutability of the factor. It is also important to recognize that learner factors overlap and interact interdependently, with factors playing a larger role at certain times and not at others. It is not difficult to imagine, for instance, parents' ambition for their children to learn a language for instrumental purposes being a strong component of the children's motivation initially. However, as language study proceeds, the children's own sense of self-efficacy might determine their perseverance, and the parents' influence wanes. There is thus a reciprocal interaction. We cannot get a true measure of the influence of a factor if we isolate it from the others and examine it at one time.

Nonlinearity

As complex dynamic systems make their way through space/time, they can enter into periods of criticality or chaos, where predictions are not likely to be borne out. This is most often illustrated in terms of a sand pile (Bak, 1996). Bak explained that as grains of sand are added to a sand pile, the height of the pile increases until a certain critical level is reached. At that point, even the addition of one more grain will cause a different result – an avalanche of sand. In other words, the sand pile demonstrates nonlinearity: the effect, an avalanche, is not proportionate to the proximate cause, a single grain of sand. Complex dynamic systems that reach this critical state are unstable and unpredictable, in other words, chaotic. That an effect will follow a cause is certain, but predicting exactly when or to what extent the cause will have an effect is not. Thus, making predictions is appropriate for periods of linearity; I can predict that the sand pile will grow commensurately with each additional grain of sand, but when a system enters into nonlinearity, predicting an outcome is hopeless.

What this means for researchers is that commonly employed regression models are inadequate for the study of complex systems (Byrne & Callaghan, 2014: 6–7). We need all the tools in a complexity toolbox; therefore, the trick is to recognize indicators of criticality when systems become nonlinear, hence unpredictable. At this point, research in SLD is best carried out from a retrospective or retrodictive perspective (Dörnyei, 2014; Larsen-Freeman & Cameron, 2008). Retrodiction is predicting that one will find evidence of past events of which one at the time of retrodiction has no knowledge (Herdina, personal communication, 2013). One can explain behaviour after the fact, and one can anticipate behaviour based on general trends, but the reliability of a prediction is always subject to one of myriad factors unaccounted for.

CDSs Exhibit Sensitive Dependence on Initial Conditions

A slight change in initial conditions can have vast implications for future behaviour. It is, unfortunately, all too frequently the case that language learners terminate their study prematurely, convinced that they have no aptitude for study, based on an initial unsatisfactory experience. Moreover, there may be any one of a number of contributing factors that make the experience unsatisfactory: the time of day of the class, the teacher, the method, the grading, interaction with other students, etc. A change in any of these may restore the learner's motivation and lead to more salutary results.

In chaos theory, this concept has been popularized as 'the butterfly effect', the idea that a small influence in a nonlinear system can have a large effect at a later point in time, i.e. a butterfly flapping its wings in one part of the world will influence the weather in another. Perhaps an example that is easier to relate to is that of a rock at the top of a hill. Depending on its orientation when it is pushed, it will end up at the bottom of the hill in very different places. The point is that the systems with different initial conditions follow different trajectories, leading to divergent outcomes.

It is worthwhile pointing out that the term used, 'sensitive dependence on initial conditions', may give the impression that it is only the point at which a system commences where it is sensitive to minor disturbances. This is not the case. At any point in the evolving trajectory of a system, even a minor influence can lead the system in a different direction. This phenomenon has sometimes been referred to as 'the tipping point'. The point is, though, that a prior state influences a subsequent one, not always in a way that is anticipated, sometimes characterized as 'the law of unintended consequences'.

Openness and Nonfinality

As long as a complex system remains open, interacting with its environment, it will continue to evolve. It has no final state. Just as evolution is a process without a goal, a complex dynamic system has no foresight; it is not defined by its endpoint. Instead, a complex dynamic system is said to be autopoietic, self-modifying. Provided it is open to outside influences, it will continue to move and change. A complex dynamic system iterates in that it returns to the same state space repeatedly although its orbits never intersect. As it returns time and again, the system is built up, resulting in a hierarchical structure of nested levels.

Feedback Sensitivity/Adaptation

The order that complex dynamic systems exhibit is shaped by the fact that they are feedback sensitive. Feedback in SLD usually refers to the dynamic whereby the teacher gives, and the student receives, corrections. Positive feedback is seen as good, negative as bad. However, in CDST terms, feedback is seen more broadly in terms of cybernetics, where change in one instance results in either amplification (positive feedback) or dampening (negative feedback) of that change. A complex system adapts by changing in response to either type of feedback. In other words, an adaptive system changes in response to feedback from its changing environment. Therefore, adaptation is not a one-time process. 'A system is never optimally adapted to an environment since the process of evolution of the system will itself change the environment so that a new adaptation is needed, and so on' (Heylighen, 1989: 24). Thus, complex dynamic systems do not remain passive in light of changing events; they 'learn' or adapt to an ever-changing environment.

Context-Dependent

In CDST terms, it would be said that a person is coupled with his or her environment. Van Geert and Fischer (2009: 327) write that development applies to person–context assemblies across time. One theory in biology makes this a central point, i.e. that an organism and the environment are coupled, co-constructed and always in transition (Oyama, 2011). With the coupling of the learner and the learning environment, neither the learner nor the environment is seen as independent, and the environment is not seen as background to the main developmental drama.

It is not difficult to imagine how a person's being in one place at one time as opposed to others might affect motivational dynamics (Dörnyei, 2009). The important point is that context is not simply another 'variable'. A related point is that the observer/researcher does not occupy a position outside of the system that he or she is studying.

Complex Systems Also Have Non-Gaussian Distributions

A Gaussian distribution is one that is depicted by a bell curve, with the midpoint representing the average behaviour. It can be used with linear systems. Complex systems also have non-Gaussian distributions, often called 'heavy-tailed', which means that infrequent behaviour at the edge of a bell curve is much more common than it would be in a Gaussian distribution. It also means that computing the average behaviour does not tell us much about the behaviour of the components or agents that comprise the system (Larsen-Freeman, 2006).

A model based on samples of individuals does not automatically generalize to a model of individual processes. As van Geert puts it:

> Work on individual trajectory models has shown that such trajectories cannot be reduced to generic trajectory model trajectories based on sample information, plus or minus some random deviations. (van Geert, 2011: 274)

He adds '[Molenaar] and his collaborators have shown that the implicit step, so common in the behavioural sciences, from sample-based research to individual process statements is often demonstrably incorrect' (van Geert, 2011: 275). Indeed, one of Rogosa's (1995) myths is that 'The average growth curve informs about individual growth'. It clearly does not.

Of course, most researchers seek to generalize beyond the particulars of a given study. Foregoing the usual statistical means to generalize does not make this impossible in CDST. However, how this is to be achieved would be pursued in different ways. One way is to probe intraindividual variation of person-specific factors rather than interindividual variation at the level of population (Molenaar & Campbell, 2009). Individual case studies may not reveal much about the population of language learners, but they do have a direct bearing on theory (van Geert, 2011: 276).

A second way might be to discover particular configurations in state space. The possible configurations, at an abstract level, may be abundant, but not infinite. For instance, certain motivational archetypes might be identified, which would allow us to specify the signature dynamics of each archetype (Chan et al., this volume).

A third possibility is to search for new ways of understanding. 'The development of regression models is ... completely predicated on straightforward linear modelling ... The blunt point is that nonlinearity is the product of emergence. We need to start from emergence and develop a science that fits that crucial aspect of complex reality' (Byrne & Callaghan, 2014: 6–7). Methods that do just that are beginning to be developed. For instance, MacIntyre's idiodynamic method (2012) and others presented at the 2013 American Association of Applied Linguistics Colloquium on Motivational Dynamics, convened by Dörnyei and MacIntyre, and included in this volume, hold great promise to broaden our repertoire of research approaches in keeping with CDST.

Conclusion

I conclude by suggesting, as I wrote at the outset, that it is time to end the bifurcated research agenda in the second language acquisition field (Hatch, 1974), which has existed for almost 40 years. On the one side has stood the question of the nature of the process of second language (L2) acquisition. Is it similar to, or even identical to, L1 acquisition, albeit it with the important difference of knowledge of an L1 having already been established? The second side has focused on language learners, centred essentially on the differential success question, one in which 'individual differences' is the major topic of investigation. For almost 40 years, the two prongs of the research agenda have been pursued mostly independently.

While this is no indictment of either side, I have been concerned for many years (Larsen-Freeman, 1985) about efforts to characterize the learning process removed from context, under the assumption that the process is universal, and that once understood, learner factors can simply be added, making some allowances for slight deviations from the general process for individual differences. This way of thinking is misguided (Kramsch, 2002). I think that hope for the unification of the field rests in a situated view of learner and learning, using research methods that honour the ten lessons compiled for this chapter – in short, the broader view of research and understanding that is on offer from CDST.

Note

(1) 'Systems' is not being used in any special way. It means a set of interrelated components.

References

Bak, P. (1996) *How Nature Works: The Science of Self-organized Criticality*. New York: Copernicus.

Byrne, D. and Callaghan, G. (2014) *Complexity Theory and the Social Sciences. The State of the Art*. Oxon: Routledge.

Deacon, T. (2012) *Incomplete Nature*. New York: W. W. Norton & Company.

Dörnyei, Z. (2009) Individual differences: Interplay of learner characteristics and learning environment. *Language Learning* 59, 230–248.

Dörnyei, Z. (2014) Researching complex dynamic systems: 'Retrodictive qualitative mod-elling' in the language classroom. *Language Teaching* 47 (1), 80–91.

Gleick, J. (1987) *Chaos: Making a New Science*. New York: Penguin Books.

Halliday, M. and Burns, A. (2006) Applied linguistics: Thematic pursuits or disciplinary moorings? *Journal of Applied Linguistics* 3, 113–128.

Hatch, E. (1974) Second language learning—universals? *Working Papers on Bilingualism* 3, 1–17.

Heylighen, F. (1989) Self-organization, emergence, and the architecture of complexity. In *Proceedings of the European Congress on System Science* (pp. 23–32). Paris: AFCET.

Kramsch, C. (ed.) (2002) *Language Acquisition and Language Socialization: Ecological Perspectives*. London: Continuum.

Larsen-Freeman, D. (1985) State of the art on input in second language acquisition. In S. Gass and C. Madden (eds) *Input in Second Language Acquisition* (pp. 433–444). Rowley, MA: Newbury House.

Larsen-Freeman, D. (2006) The emergence of complexity, fluency, and accuracy in the oral and written production of five Chinese learners of English. *Applied Linguistics* 27, 590–619.

Larsen-Freeman, D. and Cameron, L. (2008) *Complex Systems and Applied Linguistics*. Oxford: Oxford University Press.

MacIntyre, P.D. (2012) The idiodynamic method: A closer look at the dynamics of com-munication traits. *Communication Research Reports* 29 (4), 361–367.

Mitchell, S.D. (2003) *Biological Complexity and Integrative Pluralism*. Cambridge: Cambridge University Press.

Molenaar, P. and Campbell, C. (2009) The new person-specific paradigm in psychology. *Current Directions in Psychological Science* 18 (2), 112–117.

Oyama, S. (2011) Development and evolution in a world without labels. In *The Future of the Embodied Mind Conference*, eSMCs Summer School, Donostia, San Sebastian, Spain.

Rogosa, D.R. (1995) Myths and methods: 'Myths about longitudinal research', plus sup-plemental questions. In J.M. Gottman (ed.) *The Analysis of Change* (pp. 3–65). Mahwah, NJ: Lawrence Erlbaum.

van Geert, P. (2008) The dynamic systems approach in the study of L1 and L2 acquisition: An introduction. *The Modern Language Journal* 92 (2), 179–199.

van Geert, P. (2011) The contribution of complex dynamic systems to development. *Child Development Perspectives* 5 (4), 273–278.

van Geert, P. and Fischer, K.W. (2009) Dynamic systems and the quest for individual-based models of change and development. In J.P. Spencer, M.S.C. Thomas and J.L. McClelland (eds) *Toward a Unified Theory of Development* (pp. 313–336). Oxford: Oxford University Press.

van Lier, L. (2000) From input to affordance: Social-interactive learning from an ecologi-cal perspective. In J. Lantolf (ed.) *Sociocultural Theory and Second Language Learning* (pp. 245–259). Oxford: Oxford University Press.

Waldrop, M. (1992) *Complexity: The Emerging Science at the Edge of Order and Chaos*. New York: Simon and Schuster.

3   Attractor States

Phil Hiver

The human existence is unmistakably varied but, just as patterns materialise in natural and human-made systems — one language class is 'dead' but the next one is 'engaged', global weather patterns such as 'El Niño' affect the climate for months at a time and the latest sports car is 'fast and fun to drive' — it is the norm rather than the exception to see stable patterns in human behaviour. These stable *tendencies, solutions* or *outcomes* for dynamic systems are called *attractor states*, and they are essential in understanding most physical and human phenomena (Prigogine & Stengers, 1984). The goal of this chapter is to provide unambiguous definitions of some of the central concepts in dynamic systems theories and, using straightforward examples and analogies, to enable motivation researchers new to this field to conceptualise attractor states and apply them in their research designs.

What Are Attractor States?

Let us take a first-year class of high school second language (L2) learners as an example of a dynamic system. We might expect to see an initial period of transition in which individuals establish their respective roles and collectively formulate principles or norms to guide their behaviour and interactions. This provides the starting idea of a number of variables at work in the system: the number of learners all with individual ability levels, desires and orientations that make them unique, the teacher who has either a stronger or weaker influence on the class, and the school culture and the education system in which it is located, all have some role to play inside the classroom. Any system behaviour or group outcome can be influenced by internal and external forces and events, such as the involvement of parents or threats to group cohesiveness. Despite all this complexity, we would in most cases expect to see the class stabilise into a cohesive group and a discernible pattern of behaviour emerge. This patterned outcome is called an attractor state.

An *attractor state* – a critical value, pattern, solution or outcome towards which a system settles down or approaches over time. (Newman, 2009)

A patterned outcome of self-organisation represents a pocket of stability for the dynamic system, and it can emerge without anyone purposely directing or engineering it into existence (Johnson, 2009). This closely mirrors what we observe across many phenomena in the field of second language acquisition (SLA) where dynamic collections of variables spontaneously self-organise into attractor states that represent higher-order patterns of equilibrium (Larsen-Freeman & Cameron, 2008). Of course, the state which the system settles in over time does not have to be described numerically. It is, among other things, often categorical, theoretical, circumstantial or phenomenological (Goldstein, 2011).

The simplest type of attractor state is a *fixed-point attractor state*. The fixed point of this state refers to a unique point of equilibrium that the system tends to settle in over time (Haken, 2006). An example of this might be observed in the tendency for the learners in our high school class to refuse to participate voluntarily and instead remain relatively silent when given the opportunity to interact in the L2. In reality, because of the immense complexity of life, systems that only tend to settle into a single fixed-point attractor state are rarer than we might think (Byrne, 1998).

How Do Attractor States Work?

While we have said that attractor states are critical outcomes that a system evolves toward or approaches over time, it is important to recognise that attractors do not actually exert a pulling force of attraction in the way that gravity or magnets do (Haken, 2006). The term *attractor state* is simply a convenient way to describe the behaviour of a dynamic system as it moves towards some, and away from other, critical patterns (Holland, 1995). While in the complexity literature both terms are used in an interchangeable manner, in order to avoid the tempting – and misleading – collocation that attractors *attract*, it would perhaps be better to refer unilaterally to attractors as 'attractor states'. It also is worth mentioning that attractor states are not necessarily perceived as pleasant or desirable states that a person wishes to be in, as we can see in Gregersen and MacIntyre's (this volume) description of the internal conflict between in-service language teachers' 'teacher' and 'learner' selves.

Self-organisation

Dynamic systems do not, of course, magically end up in attractor states. Attractor states are assumed as a result of the *system dynamics* self-organising (Juarrero, 1999).

> *System/signature dynamics* – the unique causal behaviour and change in the system's state that results from the interactions between the system variables/components. (Kelso, 2002)

Self-organisation is a process so central to dynamic systems theory (DST) that we often take for granted the clearly recognisable patterns it leads to in the world around us (Strogatz, 2003). In the biological sphere, the growth of the body, its structures (bones, organs, blood vessels, etc.), its systems (circulatory, digestive, neurological, etc.) and its cycles (sleep, hunger, menstrual, etc.) are all examples of self-organisation. When the system dynamics form a novel outcome without any agent in the system directing change towards the new pattern, we refer to this as *self-organisation* (Banzhaf, 2009). Looking back to our example of a dynamic system, if we see the high school class begin to settle into a pattern of supportive, inclusive and goal-oriented group learning behaviour, it is because the system dynamics are self-organising into this attractor state. Indeed we might even hear a teacher remark that 'things are falling into place', or 'things just seem to click'. We can then extend this observation by examining the unique system dynamics that will explain how and why it has self-organised into this particular attractor state.

Feedback is at the heart of all self-organisation, and it plays a role in how a dynamic system moves towards or away from an attractor (Boschetti *et al.*, 2011). While feedback often comes from an external source, such as the environment or another dynamic system, it may also originate from interaction between the system's components. Negative feedback is the most common type of feedback associated with how attractor states influence systems (Banzhaf, 2009). Negative feedback should not be interpreted as unpleasant; its role is simply to minimise variance from the attractor state. In a language lesson, the teacher of our high school class reminding the learners why using the L2 is more desirable while on-task is likely to shift the class away from using the L1. Conversely, iterations of positive feedback can amplify perturbations to the system, creating unstable patterns of movement that can spread erratically throughout a system and, if the pattern is strong enough, push it into another attractor state (Manson, 2001). A common example of positive feedback is when a microphone picks up its own signal from a loudspeaker, making an increasingly loud and unpleasant noise in the sound system. If the learners in our high school class repeatedly perform poorly, confirming their already low self-efficacy beliefs, they may choose to exert even less effort, impacting further on their language learning results. Positive feedback generates patterns that are sometimes identified as a vicious cycle – or its happier counterpart, a virtuous cycle. Consistent positive feedback may trap students in a state of learned helplessness wherein they give up altogether.

Attractor states offer a location of relative stability for a dynamic system. However, as these systems are by definition open, they constantly experience a range of inputs (Juarrero, 1999). Along with feedback, one of the most common types of inputs is a *perturbation* – a disturbing force that can jolt a system out of one attractor state and into a different direction (Kra, 2009). Early on in a school week, our high school class may be settled in a lethargic, 'why-should-I-care' pattern, when the sudden news of an unexpected language exam (i.e. a perturbation) causes the learners to shift into a high-intensity frenzy of preparation. The subsequent poor test results (i.e. another perturbation) may result in the learners becoming demoralised and expending less effort in the L2 learning process in the short term (see for example Henry, Chapter 19, this volume). The teacher's decision, following these events, to use an extrinsic reward or prize (i.e. yet another perturbation) may be able to budge the class out of this attractor state of general demotivation into a novel pattern of increased participation and cooperation. Ultimately, we cannot overlook the contextual and nonlinear nature of inputs. At times, large disturbances may have little or no effect on outcomes, while at other times relatively small perturbations may result in disproportionate or explosive effects (Byrne, 1998).

The state space

The *state space* is the metaphorical area in which we can find a system's attractor states, and it represents all combined possible positions or outcomes for the dynamic system (Johnson, 2009). Because a dynamic system could potentially settle into almost any outcome or location in the state space over time (a dimension of the state space), we might be tempted to think that all of the state space qualifies as an attractor state. In reality though, because of the dynamics of self-organisation, only a handful of salient patterns or outcomes exist for a system.

> *State/phase space* – the landscape of total possible outcome configurations that a system can be found in at any given time, within which a system can transition along a unique trajectory. (Kauffman, 1995)

To illustrate how we might conceptualise this topographical environment, let me use a parallel analogy from outside of SLA. Think of a system's state space as a golf course that consists of a teeing ground, a fairway, the rough, water hazards, sand traps and a putting green with a hole. Here the dynamic system is 'the game of golf being played' and the attractor state is reached when 'the ball stops rolling'. The hole, sand traps, water hazards and dips in the fairway all are potential attractor states where the system might settle – where the ball stops rolling.

The hole may be the main attractor or ultimate goal for the system, and will have a large influence on how a game of golf is played. There are, however, other constraints on the system's behaviour that make the system dynamics and patterns of change not simply random. A particular set of regulations guide the fairness of the game, the pace of play, scoring and when penalties must be given. For instance, the ball can be hit in specific ways using a handful of approved clubs (but not in other ways), and scoring the game follows a strict protocol. These principles that guide the way a system can move in its state space from one attractor state to the next are called *system parameters* (Haken, 2006).

> *System/control parameters* – the specific principles, constraints or rules which govern the interactions between system components and the patterns of change that take place. (Bak, 1996)

Awareness of the system parameters can allow us to better describe how and why a system came to settle into a certain pattern or outcome. The rules of golf are written in a rule book; the rules of language acquisition are still under construction. Relevant parameters are likely to include various attributes of the teacher, students, classroom setup, interpersonal relationships and cultural context, to name but a few. In brief, a system will tend to settle in one or another attractor state that can be more effectively understood and described by referencing a set of system parameters (Kelso, 2002). An engaged L2 classroom might be described with parameters such as an active and creative teacher, motivated non-anxious students, variety in classroom activities, positive relationships among students and support for the language in the local culture.

Metaphorically speaking, attractor states differ with respect to two properties: their 'width', which represents the range of the attractor state's reach, and their 'depth', which represents the strength of an attractor state on the dynamic system (Haken, 2006). The feature in state space that allows us to describe both the range and strength of an attractor state is the basin of attraction (Nowak *et al.*, 2005).

> An *attractor basin* – the set of all initial conditions that allow a dynamic system to evolve to a given attractor state. (Abraham & Shaw, 1992)

A wider basin of attraction means that a more varied range of initial conditions (see Verspoor, this volume), events or ideas can easily propel a dynamic system into the attractor state, whereas a deeper basin of attraction offers an outcome of greater stability for the dynamic system and provides an indication of the amount of force needed to shift or transition the system out of this attractor state (Kauffman, 1995). In golf, it is easier to hit the wide water hazard than it is to hit the narrow hole, even though both are deep enough to stop a rolling ball. These two properties are relevant to the stability of a dynamic system's current state. For instance, despite being reminded repeatedly of how and why effort attributions are more productive in the long term, the learners in our high school class seem to have a habit of falling back on ability attributions to explain their language learning difficulties and setbacks. From this observation we could reasonably conclude that these learners are in a particularly strong attractor state (i.e. one with a deep basin of attraction) and need a sustained or vigorous force of some kind to dislodge them from it.

Attractor States and Variables

Attractor states allow us to classify or categorise the kind of thing a dynamic system is, but they must not be confused with variables as we normally use the term (Byrne, 2002, 2009; Byrne & Callaghan, 2014). Instead, the closest thing in DST to the cross-sectional, quantitative meaning of a variable is a system component (Harvey, 2009). An attractor state, on the other hand, simply describes what a system is doing right now or how it is currently acting, and the outcome or pattern it has fallen into through self-organisation. While motivational outcomes such as apathy, flow and learned helplessness could be considered variables in the traditional sense, in keeping with recent developments in SLA research we may need to conceptualise states like these as emergent, dynamic and context-dependent rather than as absolute. Because they are all categorical patterns that L2 learners can settle into (when casing one or more L2 learners as the dynamic system), they can be considered as attractor states. However, while these may be attractor states for individual L2 learners, they may also be cased as dynamic systems themselves if instead we shift our focus to the common dimensions among people, where theory explicates the processes and components that constitute them. Think for instance of language aptitude as an intervening variable between personality and L2 achievement. Language aptitude can be specified as a system component of the learner who is cased as the system because it is one of the many parts that make up the dynamic system. When we study the self-organised outcome for the L2 learner, we may also find that this component/variable has a causal influence on the system dynamics.

There is one existing alternative: we can use the term 'variable' to refer to a condition of a self-organised pattern (Byrne, 2002, 2009). If we leave aside L2 learners and instead examine L2 achievement as the dynamic system, then personality and language aptitude can be conceptualised as conditions/variables that impact on any contextual outcome of the system dynamics. Determining whether to refer either to (1) a system component; or (2) a condition for self-organised patterns as 'variables', will depend on carefully operationalising the characteristics and boundaries of the dynamic system, and specifying the level and timescale (e.g. micro, meso, macro) on which we are observing it (dc Bot, this volume). For clarity in dynamic systems motivational research, it is critically important to define the system being considered.

Other Types of Attractor States

Periodic attractor states are one step up in complexity because they provide more possibilities for variations in system behaviour than is the case for fixed-point attractor states. A periodic attractor state – also known as a *limit-cycle attractor state* – represents two or more values that the system cycles back and forth between in a periodic loop. Patterns emerge when events or behaviours repeat themselves at regular intervals (Abraham & Shaw, 1992). Examples of periodic attractor states can be seen when the students in our high school class begin a school year with a high level of enthusiasm and expectancy of success, but as the semester progresses the class loses its edge as the familiar routine turns to a monotonous grind and, towards the final weeks of the semester, the students contract the so-called 'senioritis' virus, are repeatedly absent and have a generally dismissive and apathetic attitude – a pattern that seems to repeat itself year in and year out. Within a particular language lesson we might also see these students starting a task using only the L2, then gradually getting carried away until they are all mainly using the L1 on-task, before eventually reverting back to the L2 once they are reminded to do so by the teacher.

Strange attractor states – also known as *chaotic attractor states* – represent values that a system tends to approach over time but never quite reaches (Strogatz, 1994). The motion of a system in a strange attractor state is called *chaotic*, because the dynamics trace a somewhat erratic or irregular pattern that never quite repeats itself, although these systems do in fact show complex forms of organisation that can be understood after the fact (Gleick, 2008). Weather patterns that we experience from day to day are an excellent example of this. The weather can be difficult to predict with precision, but we can always look back on the movement and interactions among weather systems to explain the weather that occurred (e.g. why a tornado formed, why a hurricane veered away from land or how ocean currents affect a summer day). In SLA, the L2 Self System (and the Ideal L2 Self in particular) might be considered a strange attractor state. The competing motivational forces acting simultaneously on the learner will draw the learner's attitudes and behaviours into a dynamic pattern that never exactly repeats itself. The Ideal L2 Self can be something of a moving target as progress is made toward goals and new, more challenging goals are constructed (see Henry, Chapter 9, this volume). Likewise, as motives and expectations from the Ought-to L2 Self are internalised, they feed into the Ideal L2 Self and vary the attention and deliberate effort invested by the learner in learning the L2. Strange attractor states are the most complex, but also the most common type in the world around us (Kelso, 2002).

Conclusion

Many of life's events can be described as a synergy between an open collection of variables or components. Add to this the range of feedback and other inputs we experience and it is clear that human behaviour constantly changes and self-organises in ways that defy exact prediction. The schemata we rely on in our everyday existence in a variety of social contexts are, in part, a function of the existence of attractor states; on a bus, we expect the throng of fellow commuters to behave in certain typical ways, while at a large family reunion we may expect certain habitual patterns of interaction. But even when the systems do not behave as expected – a cause for surprise, awkwardness or even consternation – they do settle into a solution of some sort. Attractor states, then, are the compelling tendencies and patterns that we recognise around us, and indeed come to expect throughout life. Personality dispositions (e.g. optimistic, empathetic), cherished holidays and traditions (e.g. weekly worship services, Lunar New Year), SLA phenomena (e.g. unwillingness to communicate, error fossilisation), common health issues (e.g. insomnia, postpartum depression) and socio-political events (e.g. economic recession, political polarisation) are all attractor states. In short, attractor states enable us to understand how stability and predictability are the natural outcomes of complexity.

Acknowledgement

I would like to thank all three editors of this volume for their insightful feedback on earlier drafts of this chapter, and Diane Larsen-Freeman, Kees de Bot and David Byrne for the exchange of ideas they contributed to it.

References

Abraham, R. and Shaw, D. (1992) *Dynamics: The Geometry of Behavior* (2nd edn). Redwood City, CA: Addison-Wesley.
Bak, P. (1996) *How Nature Works: The Science of Self-organized Criticality*. New York: Springer-Verlag.
Banzhaf, W. (2009) Self-organizing systems. In R. Meyers (ed.) *Encyclopedia of Complexity and Systems Science* (pp. 8040–8050). New York: Springer.

Boschetti, F., Hardy, P.Y., Grigg, N. and Horowitz, P. (2011) Can we learn how complex systems work? *Emergence: Complexity & Organization* 13 (4), 47–62.

Byrne, D. (1998) *Complexity Theory and the Social Sciences – An Introduction*. New York: Routledge.

Byrne, D. (2002) *Interpreting Quantitative Research*. Thousand Oaks, CA: SAGE.

Byrne, D. (2009) Case-based methods: Why we need them; what they are; how to do them. In D. Byrne and C.C. Ragin (eds) *The SAGE Handbook of Case-Based Methods* (pp. 1–13). Thousand Oaks, CA: SAGE.

Byrne, D. and Callaghan, G. (2014) *Complexity Theory and the Social Sciences: The State of the Art*. New York: Routledge.

Gleick, J. (2008) *Chaos: Making a New Science*. New York: Penguin Books.

Goldstein, J. (2011) Probing the nature of complex systems: Parameters, modeling, interventions. *Emergence: Complexity & Organization* 13 (3), 94–121.

Haken, H. (2006) *Information and Self-organization: A Macroscopic Approach to Complex Systems* (3rd edn). New York: Springer.

Harvey, D. (2009) Complexity and case. In D. Byrne and C.C. Ragin (eds) *The SAGE Handbook of Case-Based Methods* (pp. 16–38). Thousand Oaks, CA: SAGE.

Holland, J.H. (1995) *Hidden Order*. Cambridge, MA: MIT Press.

Johnson, N. (2009) *Simply Complexity: A Clear Guide to Complexity Theory*. Oxford: Oneworld Publications

Juarrero, A. (1999) *Dynamics in Action: Intentional Behavior as a Complex System*. Cambridge, MA: MIT Press.

Kauffman, S. (1995) *At Home in the Universe: The Search for the Laws of Complexity*. Oxford: OUP.

Kelso, J.A.S. (2002) Self-organizing dynamical systems. In N. Smelser and P. Baltes (eds) *International Encyclopedia of the Social and Behavioral Sciences* (pp. 13844–13850). Oxford: Elsevier.

Kra, B. (2009) Introduction to ergodic theory. In R. Meyers (ed.) *Encyclopedia of Complexity and Systems Science* (pp. 3053–3055). New York: Springer.

Larsen-Freeman, D. and Cameron, L. (2008) *Complex Systems and Applied Linguistics*. Oxford: OUP.

Manson, S. (2001) Simplifying complexity: A review of complexity theory. *Geoforum* 32, 405–414.

Newman, L. (2009) Human–environment interactions: Complex systems approaches for dynamic sustainable development. In R. Meyers (ed.) *Encyclopedia of Complexity and Systems Science* (pp. 4631–4643). New York: Springer.

Nowak, A., Vallacher, R.R. and Zochowski, M. (2005) The emergence of personality: Dynamic foundations of individual variation. *Developmental Review* 25, 351–385.

Prigogine, I. and Stengers, I. (1984) *Order Out of Chaos*. New York: Shambhala.

Strogatz, S. (1994) *Nonlinear Dynamics and Chaos: With Applications to Physics, Biology, Chemistry, and Engineering*. Cambridge, MA: Westview Press.

Strogatz, S. (2003) *Sync: How Order Emerges from Chaos in the Universe, Nature, and Daily Life*. New York: Hyperion.

4 Rates of Change: Timescales in Second Language Development

Kees de Bot

In this contribution it will be argued that language development takes place at different, interacting timescales ranging from the decades of the life span to the milliseconds of brain activity. Because these timescales interact, looking at phenomena at only one timescale may lead to spurious results. At the same time, it is impossible to include all possible timescales in the study of second language development (SLD). A compromise would be to look at the timescale that is of primary interest, for example the learning of words over a two-week period, along with two adjacent relevant timescales, for example lexical development over a three-month period and lexical development on a day-by-day scale.

Timescales

What time is, remains elusive. We talk about losing time, buying time, saving time, forgetting time, that it heals all wounds and so on. It is seen as a commodity, something we 'have'. In philosophers' views, time plays a different role. According to Newton, absolute time exists independently of any perceiver and progresses at a consistent pace throughout the universe. Humans are only capable of perceiving relative time, which is a measurement of perceivable objects in motion (like the moon or sun). From these movements, we infer the passage of time. Unlike relative time, however, Newton believed absolute time was imperceptible and could only be understood mathematically.

Here we will be concerned with time in developmental processes, so the focus is on relative rather than absolute time. We tend to think of timescales as naturally given. While some timescales are defined by external changes, like the seasons and years, or day and night, other timescales, like

Table 4.1 Timescales (adapted from Lemke 2000)

Typical process	Timescale (s)	Duration	Reference events
Chemical synthesis	10^{-5}		Neurotransmitter synthesis.
Membrane process	10^{-4}		Ligand binding.
Neural firings	10^{-3}		Neuron process.
Neuronal patterns	10^{-2}		Multi-neuron process.
Vocal articulation	10^{-1}		Edge of awareness.
Utterance	1–10		Word, holophrase, short monologue; in context.
Exchange	$2–10^2$	Seconds to minutes	Dialogue; interpersonal relations; developing situation.
Episode	10^3	15 minutes	Thematic, functional unit; speech genre, educative.
Lesson	$10^3–10^4$	Hour	Curriculum genre.
Lesson sequence	10^4	2.75 hours	Macro curriculum genre.
School day	10^5	Day	['seamless day'].
Unit	10^6	11.5 days	Thematic, functional unit. Unit sequence [rare].
Semester/year curriculum	10^7	4 months	Organizational level; unit in next scale.
Multi-year curriculum	10^8	3.2 years	Organizational level; limit of institutional planning.
Lifespan educational develop.	10^9	32 years	Biographical timescale; identity change
Educational system change	10^{10}	320 years	Historical timescale; new institutions.

months, weeks, hours, minutes and seconds, are cultural inventions with no 'objective' reference. For instance, the definition of a second as ratified in 1976 is: 'the duration of 9,192,631,770 periods of the radiation corresponding to the transition between the two hyperfine levels of the ground state of the caesium-133 atom' (Guinot & Seidelmann, 1988). Lombardi (2007) provides an interesting overview of the history of timescales and argues that the division of the time between sunrise and sunset into 12 hours and the year in 12 months results from the Egyptians' use of a duodecimal counting system. The 7-day week was common in Babylonia and was taken over by

Judaism and Christianity following the description of the creation in the book of Genesis, but it has no natural basis. 'Unlike the day and the year, the week is an artificial rhythm that was created by human beings totally independent of any natural periodicity' (Zerubavel, 1989: 4). The fact that some timescales are socially constructed does not make them less stable; attempts in 18th century France, and early 20th century attempts, to shorten or lengthen the week (respectively) failed, mainly because the weekly rhythm was linked to religious practices and traditional peasant life (Zerubavel, 1989). Minutes became units with the invention of mechanical clocks in the 16th century. There are 60 seconds in a minute for no other reason than a parallelism with 60 minutes in an hour. Even finer timescales, like milliseconds came into existence only when there were devices invented to actually measure them.

For the study of human development, only a small part of the range of timescales is relevant. Lemke provides a useful overview of timescales (Table 4.1) showing that humans live on timescales between 10^{-5} seconds and 10^9 seconds.

Lemke looked at timescales and how they combine and interact in a school learning setting. For this the scales from 10^{-1}–10^7 are especially relevant.

A distinction should be made between timescales and *time windows*. Timescales refer to the granularity of the developmental process; we can take a very global perspective and look at changes over the life span, sampling many moments of time. Time windows refer to the period of time studied. For example, in a study of a person's life, the time window spans the whole period of the lifetime and the timescale might be used in examining changes from one decade to another. In another study, we might look at the phonological development of learners over a period of two years (time window), but measure their performance every week (timescale).

The Fractal Nature of Time

As discussed elsewhere (de Bot, 2012), the sub-systems of the language system develop on all timescales during the human life span. The nature of time is fractal in the sense that it is scale-free. This means that although we can look at the year scale or millisecond scale and all scales in between, there is no scale that is *the* scale for language development, or even for components of it. Through the methodology used to gather data on specific behaviour we define the timescale we are using. A longitudinal study that takes place over a two-year window with monthly observations may take place on the month timescale, and the year timescale, and all timescales between them (half year, two months and so on). A five-minute lexical decision experiment, with measurements at 300 millisecond intervals, takes place at the 5 minute and 300 millisecond scale and all scales in between. But that does not mean that development takes place only at the timescale used for the measurements. Language development in that sense also is scale-free, even when the focus is on one particular timescale.

Language Development on Different Timescales

There is no research that covers language development on the life-span level. No individual, as far as we know, has been followed from crib to coffin. Language development is a complex process that takes place on many interacting timescales, and the timescale chosen will have an impact on the selection and interpretation of the data. The same holds for the time window used. There is no timescale or window that gives a full picture of the total process of development. Development on one scale is influenced by what happens on smaller and larger scales. Development processes at various levels will have an impact on what happens on the timescale in focus. Trinh (2011) provides an interesting example of research showing the need to consider both the timescale and time window in order to draw conclusions on development. Considering the writings of a language expert over a 35-year period, Trinh found that lexical complexity and syntactic complexity show variation over time as there are periods in which they decline or grow. While on timescales of fine granularity the data may suggest slight decline, that change may actually be part of a pattern of growth on a scale that has a lower granularity and a longer time window.

Research on language attrition tends to be done on larger timescales than research on language acquisition. Attrition and acquisition typically have different rates of change; while acquisition may happen in terms of hours and days, language attrition takes much more time to materialize, typically decades. As the overview by Schmid (2011) shows, there is some research that looks at longer language attrition timescales. An example is the 16-year longitudinal study of first language attrition among Dutch migrants in Australia (de Bot & Clyne, 1994). Though the total period between the two measurements was 16 years, we do not know when and at what timescale the attrition actually took place. To define the curve of development, a large number of measurements over time would be needed. However, such measurements might lead to problems because the repeated testing may lead to learning.

Subsystems and Their Timescales

In a skills acquisition approach, SLD is the development of sub-skills with different levels of control. Higher level skills, such as conceptual processing, take more attentional resources than highly automatized skills, like lexical access and articulation. Lower level processing is typically automatized in order to free attentional resources for higher level processes

(Lyster & Sato, 2013). If smaller systems are embedded within larger systems, and subcomponents have their own timescale and rate of change, the question arises as to how far we can decompose systems into more and more layers or embedded subsystems. How deep we want to go will depend on our research question and the data available. If we are interested in code-switching in 17th century dialects round the city of Rotterdam in the Netherlands, we may be restricted by what written records can tell us about code switching. There might be a rich collection of source materials, but further refinement of analyses would be limited by the nature of the data.

In the skills acquisition approach, language, and therefore language development, can be decomposed into skills, these into sub-skills and sub-sub-skills, and so on. Whereas it could be argued that the sum of the development of these skills is what constitutes development, from a dynamic systems theory (DST) perspective it is not the sum of these components, but their mutual influence on each other over time that is the core of development. This is in line with the view expressed by Newell *et al.*:

> Traditionally, the study of behaviour has been categorized into particular kinds of tasks, such as perceptual, cognitive, motor and communicative. These task categories, however, are more reflections of an emphasis of particular processes than they are of mutually distinct processes in the organization of human behaviour. It should not be surprising, therefore, to find that the learning curves for tasks in different behavioural domains hold some similarities. (Newell *et al.*, 2001: 77)

Rates of Change

Development at different timescales typically is expressed in terms of functions of different shapes, the plot of outcomes of learning or change. So while pragmatic development may show a gradually rising function on the scale of years, no change would be visible on the minutes or seconds scale, for intonation learning there may be a sudden jump or discontinuity. 'The time scale of learning is expressed as the rate (exponent within a function) with which learning takes place over time' (Newell *et al.*, 2001: 64). The change function may take various shapes, with linear development as the exception rather than the rule. The typical learning curve is S-shaped, with little development at the beginning, followed by a jump that gradually levels off. This shape reflects the interaction between the characteristics of the learning system and the interaction with the environment. In the earlier phases there is plenty to be learned from environmental input, but the system has to store partly unrelated information in memory. The upper part of the function describing the learning curve is defined by the limitations of the input. If the environmental input remains more or less the same, the learning system will gradually absorb that information, leaving little left to acquire. Examples of this process include the learning rate of vocabulary in studies on the effectiveness of bilingual schooling in Dutch secondary education, as reported on by Huibregtse (2001) and Verspoor *et al.* (2011). While the learners in the bilingual classes show a levelling off of their learning curve, the control group continues to grow. Apparently the learners in the bilingual classes already have their vocabulary developed to such an extent that there are fewer and fewer new words in the input they receive, which results in a slowing down of their acquisitional rate. As early as 1919, Thurstone had already pointed out that the limitations of the environment of learning (e.g. the range of vocabulary in daily speech for learning new words) lead to a decreased effect of practice on the rate of learning. This is what van Geert (2008) refers to as the carrying capacity of an organism to learn. Because of the limitations of the environment, learning curves typically asymptote over time. Thus, there may not be a single learning curve for different organisms, or environments: 'A particular set of interactions of an organism, environment, and task over time can engender a particular function or change of type of learning curve at the task level' (Newell *et al.*, 2001: 58).

In research on motor learning and motor development, a distinction is made between persistent and transitory properties of change. Persistent change takes place at long timescales and the knowledge acquired tends to stabilize. Transitory properties are visible at shorter timescales. An example could be the development of the tense and aspect system in learners of French. While the development of a part of the system, for example the *Imparfait*, may show a gradual increase in correct use in tasks over time, a particular learner may at some point realize that there is something like the *Passé Simple* and will apply that new knowledge indiscriminately for a while, till the use of that tense also stabilizes. The overuse and wrong use of that tense would show greater variation on a shorter timescale than that of the *Imparfait* and would be transitory rather than persistent.

Timescales in the Brain

There may be a neurological basis for the processing of information at different timescales. Harrison *et al.* (2011) present evidence that different parts of the brain are working on different timescales:

> (the) primary visual cortex responds to rapid perturbations in the environment, while frontal cortices involved in executive control encode the longer term contexts within which these perturbations occur. (...) Many aspects of brain function can be understood in terms of a hierarchy of temporal scales at which representations of the environment evolve. The lowest level of this hierarchy corresponds to fast fluctuations associated

with sensory processing, whereas the highest levels encode slow contextual changes in the environment, under which faster representations unfold. (Harrison *et al.*, 2001)

Klebel *et al.* (2008: 7) point out that there is no theory that explains how the large-scale organization of the human brain can be related to our environment. 'Here, we propose that the brain models the entire environment as a collection of hierarchical, dynamical systems, where slower environmental changes provide the context for faster changes'. In other words, the brain processes input from the environment depending on the timescale on which it acts. Fast fluctuations in sensory processing are embedded in slower fluctuations in the environment. So, the brain is, to a certain extent, organized to process information at these different timescales and integrate it.

The Interaction of Timescales

To what extent do timescales interact? Following the principles of DST (Byrne & Callaghan, 2014), all timescales interact; there are however clear limits to that interaction. Lemke (2000: 279) refers to the adiabatic principle which proposes that 'very slowly varying processes appear as a stable background on the timescale of faster ones. (. . .) a very fast and a relatively much slower material process cannot efficiently communicate with one another, cannot efficiently transfer energy'. For example, my running has no effect on the rotation speed of the earth. In order to interact, processes should be close enough to impact on each other. An example could be that the development of advanced motor skills in soccer players has little impact on their linguistic skills; it is simply so that the systems have too little in common to exchange energy or information.

Lemke (2000: 285) also refers to the notion of Heterochrony, defined as 'A long timescale process producing an effect in a much shorter timescale activity or the other way around'. Examples could be changes in the global climate (long timescale) that reach a critical point for a particular habitat to survive (short timescale), or the effect of a volcanic eruption (short timescale) on the global climate (long timescale). A linguistic example might be when a learner of a language discovers that animacy plays a role in sentence processing within the developing language, even though the concept of animacy is absent in her mother tongue.

Combining Timescales

It could be argued that the 'now' is the resultant of changes on all possible timescales up to this point. Just as we cannot 'unscramble' an egg (that is, undo the interaction of variables over time), we cannot undo the interaction between timescales and study phenomena on one timescale without taking into account other timescales. But can we do research at all if we must include all possible timescales? There is a practical solution to this problem.

What is possible on the focal timescale, N, and the kinds of interactions that can happen, depends on the kinds of processes and participants at the levels immediately below it, i.e. level $N - 1$, and what happens at the next level, $N + 1$. Processes at level $N - 1$ are constitutive of processes at level N, providing the affordances for activity at level N. So what happens at level N is restricted by what happens at level $N - 1$ and influences what is possible at level $N + 1$ (Lemke, 1995). For example, if we take utterances as the N level, then what happens at that level limits what can happen on $N - 1$, the level of lexical selection and syntactic procedures. It would also be the case that what happens at level $N + 1$, the level of interaction or monologue, limits what happens at level N. For practical purposes it seems reasonable to limit ourselves to these three levels or timescales when doing research.

Timescales and Motivation

Why is all of this relevant for the present collection of papers and research on motivation and other individual differences more generally? The aim of this contribution was to show that processes can take place at different timescales and that timescales interact. It was also argued that looking at one timescale only may block our view on the larger picture of phenomena on different timescales. As MacIntyre and Serroul (this volume) and Waninge et al. (2015) demonstrate, motivation to learn a foreign language can vary from one moment to another and may be influenced by different types of motivation on different timescales. Long term motivation may come from career plans, shorter term motivation from the wish to pass an exam, an even shorter term motivation from expressing a view in class. The motivation at different timescales interacts with other processes and may vary in strength over time. In order to study motivation in a particular setting, for example in a classroom, data from different timescales have to be gathered and combined to get the full picture.

References

Byrne, D. and Callaghan, G. (2014) *Complexity Theory and the Social Sciences,* London: Routledge.

de Bot, K. (2012) Time scales in second language development. *Dutch Journal of Applied Linguistics* 1 (1), 143–149.

de Bot, K. and Clyne, M. (1994) A 16-year longitudinal study of language attrition in Dutch immigrants in Australia. *Journal of Multilingual and Multicultural Development* 15 (1), 17–28.

Guinot, B. and Seidelmann, P. (1988) Time scales – Their history, definition and interpretation. *Astronomy and Astrophysics* 194 (1–2), 304–308.

Harrison, L., Bestmann, S., Rosa, M., Penny, W. and Green, G. (2011) Time scales of representation in the human brain: Weighing past information to predict future events. *Frontiers in Human Neuroscience* 5, 37.

Huibregtse, I. (2001) *Effecten en Didactiek van Tweetalig Voortgezet Onderwijs in Nederland.* Utrecht: University of Utrecht.

Klebel, S., Daunizeau, J. and Friston, K. (2008) A hierarchy of time-scales and the brain. *PLoS Computational Biology* 4 (11), e1000209.

Lemke, J. (1995) *Textual Politics: Discourse and Social Dynamics.* London: Taylor and Francis.

Lemke, J. (2000) Across the scales of time: Artefacts, activities and meaning in ecosocial systems. *Mind, Culture and Activity* 7 (4), 273–290.

Lombardi, M. (2007) Why is a minute divided into 60 seconds, an hour into 60 minutes and there are only 24 hours in a day? *Scientific American.* See http://www.scientificamerican.com/article/experts-time-division-days-hours-minutes/ (accessed 5 March 2007).

Lyster, R. and Sato, M. (2013) Skill acquisition theory and the role of practice in L2 development. In M. Garcia Mayo, J. Gutierrez Mangado and M. Adrian (eds) *Contemporary Approaches to Second Language Acquisition* (pp. 93–110). Amsterdam: John Benjamins.

Newell, K., Liu, Y. and Mayer-Kress, G. (2001) Time scales in motor learning and development. *Psychological Review* 108 (1), 57–82.

Schmid, M. (2011) *Language Attrition.* Cambridge: Cambridge University Press.

Thurstone, J. (1919) *The Learning Curve Equation.* Princeton, NJ: Psychological Review Company.

Trinh, T.G.T. (2011) An Adult's Language Variability and Development. Unpublished MA thesis. University of Groningen.

van Geert, P. (2008) The dynamic systems approach in the study of L1 and L2 acquisition: An introduction. *Modern Language Journal* 92, 179–199.

Verspoor, M., de Bot, K. and van Rein, E. (2011) English as a foreign language: The role of out-of-school language input. In A. De Houwer and A. Wilton (eds) *English in Europe Today: Sociocultural and Educational Perspectives* (pp. 147–166). Amsterdam/Philadelphia: John Benjamins.

Waninge, F., Dörnyei, Z. and de Bot, K. (2015) Motivational dynamics in language learning: Change, stability and context. *The Modern Language Journal.*

Zerubavel, E. (1989) *The Seven Day Cycle: The History and Meaning of the Week.* Chicago: University of Chicago Press.

5 Initial Conditions

Marjolijn Verspoor

The term 'initial conditions' in dynamic systems theory (DST) is intricately linked to the so-called 'butterfly effect' initially discovered by Lorenz (1963). Using a numerical computer model to rerun a weather prediction, he had rounded off 0.506127 to 0.506, which resulted in a completely different weather scenario. It showed that in a nonlinear complex system such as the weather, a small change in one sub-system at one time may lead to large differences in a later state. In other words, in a complex dynamic system, in which many kinds of sub-systems interact over time, small differences in sub-systems at one point of time may have an impact on the eventual outcome.

When though, are conditions 'initial conditions'? In his rerun of the weather prediction, Lorenz must have had a number of other sub-systems (or variables) already in place, and only one variable was changed. In his case, the 'initial conditions' were set at the time when he 'tweaked' one of the variables and started measuring. As MacIntyre and Gregersen (2013) make clear, 'initial conditions' can therefore be defined as the state of the various sub-systems at the time one starts measuring.

DST is grounded in mathematics, computer models and simulations. In its basic form, a dynamic system is defined as a means of describing how one state (of a system) develops or changes into another state over the course of time (Weisstein, 1999). A dynamic system traces a particular (1) trajectory (i.e. a sequence of states) (2) over time (3) in the state space. The emergence of such a trajectory is based on the fact that a dynamic system describes iterative processes; take the first state to produce the second, take the second to produce the third, take the third to produce the fourth, and so forth for as many successive states as are needed to describe the system's time course. The iterative nature of the processes involved is central to the notion of development, where the next 'state' of development is a function of the preceding state and a condition for the next state. Iterative processes have very interesting properties, but they are also very difficult to imagine. Therefore, the best way of studying what they can do is by simulating them on a computer, and that is why computer simulation of iterative processes, based on developmental models, is of such crucial importance for our understanding of developmental processes (van Geert, 1994).

However, the problem with measuring human development is that we cannot always directly apply the computer metaphor because we cannot (re) tweak the system at an earlier state and then 'rerun' a program to see what the new outcome might be. The only way to rerun the empirical data is in computer simulations. To do so, dense, longitudinal, numerical data is needed. However, not all language developmental research or data lends itself to such a methodology. But even without the computer simulations, we can keep dynamic principles in mind, and I would suggest that we talk in terms of a dynamic approach (rather than a DST approach) to language development.

The following sections will relate the notion of initial conditions to predictions, attractor states, variability and variation to show their intricate interrelationships.

Predictions

One of the main principles to be kept in mind is that differences in initial conditions among individuals lead to differences among them. As each human is unique, not only genetically but also in actual experiences over time, we should expect variation and accept that exact predictions of development of any kind are not possible. On the other hand, we may also accept that there are predictable tendencies in human development, usually referred to as 'stages'. For example, a common sequence in motor development is sitting up, standing up, crawling and eventually walking. However, as de Bot (this volume) points out, the patterns we may find all depend on the timescale we examine. For example, when measured in years, children tend to walk at the same age, but what is not predictable, though, is exactly on what day, or which week or even month, the child first sits up or learns to walk. Each child has to go through his or her own trial and error process (resulting in variability) to reach the next stages. What's more, between 'stages' variability is especially large. During periods of development, the learner explores and tries out new strategies or modes of behaviour that are not always successful and may, therefore, alternate with old strategies or modes of behaviour (Thelen & Smith, 1994).

Therefore, I would like to argue that in language developmental research 'initial conditions' for each sub-system under investigation are intricately related to whether that particular sub-system is in transition, showing a great deal of variability, or has reached an attractor state where it is rather stable. The notions of time periods with 'a great deal of variability', 'some variability' or a high degree of 'stability' can be illustrated with the three possible states that sub-systems may have in Figure 5.1. The ball represents any sub-system, such as motivation, willingness-to-communicate, self-confidence, L1 proficiency, L2 proficiency, either at a short-term scale in the here and now (e.g. someone is in a bad mood and is not motivated to pay attention) or at a longer term scale (e.g. someone is on the whole a motivated learner), and will always

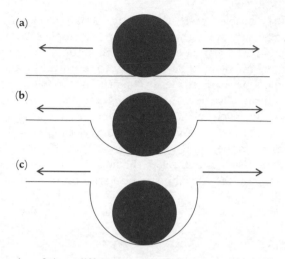

Figure 5.1 Examples of three different states a sub-system (the ball) can be in

show some level of variability, i.e. the ball will always be moving a bit from left to right. In Figure 5.1a, the flat line represents a rather neutral sub-system and with just the slightest force the ball could move either left (negative) or right (positive). For example, an L2 learner of Hungarian who enters her first lesson may be totally neutral as to whether she likes the language or likes the teacher; nevertheless all the early impressions may sway her attitude towards the language or the teacher, to the right or to the left.

Let us say she likes the way the language sounds and the teacher is enthusiastic, has humour and makes her feel the language is worth studying. The ball will be vacillating on the positive side of the line and start making an indentation there, resulting in a shallow basin, which represents a weak attractor (Figure 5.1b). Even though this indentation will 'attract' the ball, it may not be so difficult to move the ball out of this particular state. Suppose our enthusiastic learner, after a few weeks of class, has a new stressful job and is too tired to go to class, her positive attitude (first weak attractor) may temporarily change to a negative attitude (negative weak attractor). The longer the ball remains in a particular attractor, the deeper the attractor state becomes and the more difficult it is to move it out of that particular attractor (Figure 1c). The three states in Figure 5.1 are only some examples of possible states, but the point is that sub-systems may become more and more entrenched and, the more entrenched they become, the less likely they are to change much.

Attractors and Variability

On the developmental timescale, the notion of an attractor is reminiscent of the classical developmental notion of a stage, suggesting that development is a process creating a sequence of attractors. Even though language acquisition is typically described in the form of a sequence of such stages, the naïve notion of stage as a kind of universal staircase is hardly reconcilable with the empirical evidence. According to Siegler (2000), the traditional stage theorists' staircase metaphor of cognitive development (e.g. Piaget, 1950) neglected the extensive variability during and between stages of development (Slavin, 2005). Hence, the focus is on the number and ratio of different strategies that a learner uses at any stage, rather than on which specific strategy is used most during a particular stage. Siegler's theory is based on the assumptions that, when solving a problem, learners typically employ several strategies and ways of thinking rather than merely one, that the various strategies and ways of thinking coexist over long intervals (not only during short transition periods) and that experience manifests changes in learner's relative reliance on current strategies and ways of thinking and initiates more advanced approaches. Thus, viewed from a dynamic perspective, stability is a special case of variation in which a dynamic system seeks an equilibrium state or approaches an attractor (Fogel, 1993; Thelen & Smith, 1998; van der Maas & Molenaar, 1992; van Geert, 1998). In other words, 'stability reflects order within the extensive variations in a changing dynamic system rather than a relatively fixed characteristic, as assumed by concepts of both individual difference and fixed norm or mean' (Yan & Fischer, 2002: 144).

A good example of variability and subsequent stability can be found in the figure from Brown's famous L1 acquisition studies (1973), where he considered a morpheme acquired when there was a 90% accuracy rate. Figure 5.2, which shows Eve's first 12 data samples of 'in' and 'on', clearly

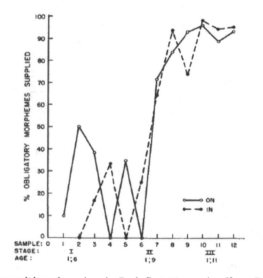

Figure 5.2 The prepositions *in* and *on* in Eve's first 12 samples (from Brown, 1973: 263)

shows the high level of variability initially when the two sub-systems are developing (reminiscent of the state in Figure 5.1a) and then a sudden and acute rise at sample point 7 (similar to state in Figure 5.1b) with a levelling off of the variability – an attractor state – (similar to the state in Figure 5.1c) towards the end of the figure. Obviously, if we start measuring from data point 1, when these subsystems are just emerging, and we consider them 'initial conditions', we should expect a high degree of variability for a while. However, if we start measuring from data point 10 when the two sub-systems have reached 'maturity', in DST terms an attractor state, we should expect much less variability.

The application of the notion of attractor to a developmental system implies that the system will evolve towards a particular state if it is under a particular set of conditions. More precisely, once the sub-system is in an attractor state and gets perturbed, it will probably return to the attractor state, unless counteracted very strongly by some external force. Such stability usually involves the coordination of different subsystems, in this case the two prepositions 'in' and 'on'. Any stability in behaviour requires the real-time coordination of a great many components. For example, the reading of words by a beginner reader involves many functional brain centres, motor processes, sensory processes, perception-action loops and each of these components represents a particular range of variation. If these components are not or only poorly coordinated, they may vary independently over time. However, functional behaviour requires a coordination of these components, for instance between eye movements and text processing in reading, or between articulatory motor processes and processes governing word order. Coordination implies that the components no longer behave independently of one another, and this mutual dependency corresponds with a reduction in the number of dimensions required to specify the behaviour of the system. In other words, once sub-systems are coordinated, a new sub-system at a higher level has emerged, which is more than the sum of its parts. A beautiful audio example of how different sub-systems behave independently and then eventually coordinate can be found in Deb Roy's (2011) Ted Talk 'The birth of a word' where he presents a time-lapsed audio of how his son learned the word 'water'. The careful listener will detect that at first the boy uses 'gaga' a lot, then, in each new occurrence of the word, he seems to practice a different sub-system, such as the different consonants and vowels of the word and the stress pattern. Early on, there is a great deal of variability, going from 'gaga' to almost perfect 'water', but quickly reverting back to 'gaga' and then at one time near the end he uses a strong aspirated 't' instead of a 'd', suggesting he is practicing the dental plosive, but now has a problem with voicing. But then at the end, the boy says 'water' fluidly as one whole unit. It sounds as if the different sub-systems have become coordinated and there are no longer separable sub-systems recognizable. In other words, the word that has emerged is greater than the sum of all its parts.

Again, this example illustrates that if 'initial conditions' are defined as the moment one starts measuring, the amount of variability one can expect can be quite different depending on where in the developmental process we start measuring. If the (sub) system is just developing, variability is expected. Once the different sub-systems have stabilized and coordinated, and a new 'stage' has been reached, we do not expect much change in this particular sub-system.

Variation

In a dynamic approach it is important to look at individual trajectories over time. However, many researchers will argue that despite varying initial conditions among individuals, there are general group trends and, at a very general scale, this is true as most children learn to walk and talk, and L2 learners become more proficient over time. However, we must also remember that even then development is an individual trial and error trajectory and, if we observe closely, no individual will develop in exactly the same manner. Verspoor *et al.* (2011) illustrate this with data from Cancino *et al.* (1978), who studied the development of the negative verb phrase system in six different L1 Spanish learners of English, all of whom had been in the US for less than three months and were followed every two weeks for about 10 months. There were two 5-year-olds, two 12–13-year-olds and two adults. In Figures 5.3 and 5.4, the percentage of *'don't'* uses are plotted. *Don't* is a target form, but early on it is overgeneralized and occurs instead of analysed forms of *do* (such as *didn't* and *doesn't*). In Figure 5.3, the dots show that no individual member develops in exactly the same manner and even if we take the two teenagers who are similar in age (Juan and Jorge), we see that they do not develop in exactly the same manner.

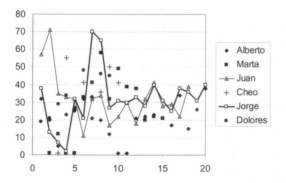

Figure 5.3 The use of *don't* + verb (expressed as the percentage used in all negative expressions uttered) by six Spanish L1 learners of English over the course of three months

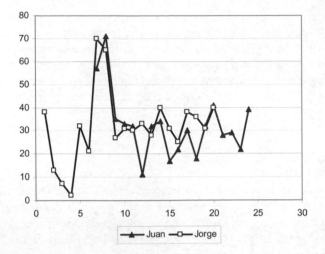

Figure 5.4 The use of *don't* + verb by Juan and Jorge with Juan's data moved to the right by seven data points

However, a closer scrutiny of the data does show some surprising similarities between the two teenagers. In Figure 5.4, we see that both Juan and
Jorge show peaks of 70% *don't* in the data, peaks that are higher than those
of the other learners, and if we move the peak in Juan's data from data point
2 to data point 7 (see Figure 5.4), we actually see that the development of
don't in the two learners has a very similar (but not identical) trajectory. It is
possible that Juan just learned faster (the overuse of *don't* took place earlier).
However, it is far more likely that he had been in the US longer than Jorge
when the researchers first started collecting their data. In other words, his
'initial conditions' for this particular sub-system were quite different and
had an effect on the results.

It is true, therefore, that despite the different initial conditions in this
particular sub-system, both learners eventually stabilized with a 20%–40%
use of *don't* in the data. However, among the group of the six learners, the
two younger ones developed the negative system at a much slower rate with
lower peaks; nevertheless the assumption is that they eventually acquired
the full negative system. The two adults, especially Alberto, never acquired
the negative system fully. If, though, we really are interested in the developmental process (and not just the end product), the averaging out of the individuals in this study would have concealed some of the more interesting
developmental patterns.

Therefore, researchers who want to take a dynamic approach to L2 development should study individual trajectories and consider the initial conditions of all relevant variables. And when considering initial conditions, the
researcher should make an educated guess at the level of entrenchment of the

sub-systems to be studied. Suppose one wants to know how well a group of students improves in general proficiency in a study abroad programme. As we already know from a great deal of previous research, relevant variables would have to do with the individual's personality type (how likely they are to seek opportunities to interact with speakers of the target language), the level of proficiency at the beginning of the study abroad programme (which may determine how successful and pleasant interactions with native speakers are), context variables such as where the student lives (an international house with little target language interaction) and of course attitudes and motivation, which are most likely to have greater variability earlier on than later.

For example, the attitude towards an L2 at the beginning of a study-abroad year may be high, but still very vulnerable and likely to vacillate early on, depending on the immediate positive or negative experiences with the language and its speakers. One strong negative experience early on may have a large effect and move the learner's attitude towards an attractor of a negative attitude, whereas that same negative experience at the end of a positive experience, with an entrenched positive attitude, will probably have only a temporary effect. Of course, even two novice learners might react differently to such a strong negative event with a native speaker, one feeling discouraged and the other more determined to learn than ever before, based on differences in their personality profiles.

In other words, the researcher who would like to take a dynamic approach to the effects of a study-abroad programme will have to consider the initial conditions of all the relevant sub-systems involved and measure them very frequently (probably daily) in the first few weeks, as the emotional sub-systems especially are likely to show considerable variability early on. However, after a month or so, the systems should have settled and then measuring once a month should suffice.

Conclusion

To summarize, initial conditions can be defined as the conditions sub-systems are in when the researcher starts measuring. Because not all human sub-systems can be measured adequately or frequently enough to take a mathematical DST approach, a dynamic approach that takes dynamic principles as given may be warranted. In such an approach it is important to know whether the sub-systems that are focused on are in a more variable or more stable state at the moment one starts measuring. A learner who has been highly motivated to learn a language over the course of a few years is not likely to change much, even if he has a negative experience with that language during the course of the study. On the other hand, a learner who is highly motivated to study an L2, but is still at the early stages of his study, may be completely discouraged after one strong negative event.

References

Brown, R. (1973) *A First Language*. Cambridge, MA: Harvard University Press.
Cancino, H., Rosansky, E. and Schumann, J. (1978) The acquisition of English negatives and interrogatives by native Spanish speakers. In E.M. Hatch (ed.) *Second Language Acquisition: A Book of Readings* (pp. 207–230). Rowley, MA: Newbury House.
Fogel, A. (1993) *Developing Through Relationships: Origins of Communication, Self, and Culture*. Chicago: University of Chicago Press.
Lorenz, E.N. (1963) Deterministic nonperiodic flow. *Journal of the Atmospheric Sciences* 20 (2), 130–141.
MacIntyre, P.D. and Gregersen, T. (2013) *An Idiodynamic Approach to Studying Language Learning and Use*. Paper presented at the American Association of Applied Linguistics annual conference, Dallas, TX.
Piaget, J. (1950) *Introduction à l' Épistémologie Génétique; I. La Pensée Mathématique. – II. La Pensée Physique. – III. La Pensée Biologique, la Pensée Psychologique et la Pensée Sociologique*. Paris: Presses Universitaires de France.
Roy, D. (2011) *The Birth of a Word*. Ted Talk. See http://www.youtube.com/watch?v=RE4ce4mexrU (accessed 21 November 2013).
Siegler, R.S. (2000) The rebirth of children's learning. *Child Development* 71, 26–35.
Slavin, E.S. (2005) *Educational Psychology; Theory and Practice* (8th edn) Boston, MA: Allyn and Bacon.
Thelen, E. and Smith, L.B. (1994) *A Dynamic Systems Approach to The Development of Cognition and Action*. Cambridge, MA: Bradford/MIT Press.
Thelen, E. and Smith, L.B. (1998) Dynamic systems theories. In R.M. Lerner (ed.) *Handbook of Child Psychology* (Vol. 1): *Theoretical Models of Human Development* (5th edn) (pp. 561–634). New York: Wiley.
van der Maas, H.L.J. and Molenaar, P.C. (1992) Stagewise cognitive development: An application of catastrophe theory. *Psychological Review* 99 (3), 395–417.
van Geert, P. (1994) Vygotskian dynamics of development. *Human Development* 37, 346–365.
van Geert, P.L.C. (1998) A dynamic systems model of basic developmental mechanisms: Piaget, Vygotsky and beyond. *Psychological Review* 105 (4), 634–677.
Verspoor, M., de Bot, K. and Lowie, W. (eds) (2011) *A Dynamic Approach to Second Language Development: Methods and Techniques*. Amsterdam: John Benjamins.
Weisstein, E.W. (1999) *CRC Concise Encyclopaedia of Mathematics*. Boca Raton/New York: CRC Press.
Yan, Z. and Fischer, K. (2002) Always under construction. *Human Development* 45 (3), 141–160.

6 Context and Complex Dynamic Systems Theory

Ema Ushioda

Learner–Context Relations as Ecosystems

A major challenge when it comes to researching complex dynamic systems theory (CDST) is how to define, delimit and empirically capture what is meant by context. Within second language acquisition (SLA) research, contexts have historically been characterized in fairly generic terms, such as cultural or linguistic setting, type of learning environment (e.g. formal versus informal, home versus study abroad), or input and instructional conditions (e.g. focus-on-form, task-based learning). Learners are thus located in particular types of contexts, and these contexts function as independent external variables that may have certain influences on learner-internal variables such as motivation, second language (L2) development or performance. In short, according to this traditional view, contexts and learners are treated as distinct and separate entities, and it is usually contexts that act upon learners.

Yet we do not need to venture into the realm of CDST to realize that the relationship between context and learner is far from one-directional. For example, if we think about language input as a feature of context in L2 learning (e.g. see the collection of studies in Howard *et al.*, 2011), we recognize that learners act upon their contexts, such as the high input generators characterized many years ago by Seliger (1977). We also recognize that learners contribute to shaping their contexts through how they interact with input. After all, the ways in which language learners orient and respond to language input will affect the content, quantity and quality of further input in the developing context of the interaction. In this sense, there is a dynamically evolving relationship between learner and context, as each responds and adapts to the other.

Moreover, through this process of co-adaptation, the learner necessarily becomes an integral part of the unfolding context of the interaction. The learner actively participates in shaping the developing linguistic interaction, and the learner also constitutes part of the dynamic physical, historical, social and cultural context within which the interaction is taking place. One could imagine, for example, exophoric references in an interaction to visible features of the immediate physical context, such as the learner's clothes, facial expressions or body language. One might also imagine references to previous conversations that form part of the historical context of the interaction, or references to shared memories or practices that form part of the social or cultural context of the interaction. In short, learners are not simply located in particular contexts, but inseparably constitute part of these contexts. Learners shape and are shaped by context. Through this mutually constitutive and co-adaptive relationship, changes emerge organically both within the learner and within the context or environment (Dörnyei, 2009: 229).

Among complex systems, ecological systems in the environmental sciences provide perhaps the most useful metaphor for describing this symbiotic co-adaptive relationship between learner and context, and the organic interconnectedness of social, psychological and environmental processes. The metaphor of an ecosystem is certainly a strong feature of recent discussions of CDST in our field (e.g. de Bot et al., 2007). Ecological perspectives on language learning and use have been helpful in capturing holistically the complex processes that take place within learners and between learners and their sociocultural environments (e.g. see the collection of studies and discussion papers in Kramsch, 2002a; also van Lier, 2004).

Defining and Delimiting 'Context' in Relation to the Learner

If learners and contexts are inseparable pieces shaping a metaphorical ecosystem, what does this mean in conceptual and empirical terms for how we define, circumscribe and capture the elements of 'context' in a CDST approach? There are essentially two interrelated problems here.

First, there is the technical problem of trying to separate 'learner' from 'context' for purposes of analysis and research inquiry. Kramsch (2002b) puts it metaphorically, quoting the poet W.B. Yeats in asking whether it makes sense to separate the 'dancer from the dance'. If learners are 'persons-in-context' (Ushioda, 2009) who are inherently part of, act upon and contribute to shaping the social, cultural and physical environments with which they interact, how do we differentiate meaningfully between learner and context when examining these evolving interactions? Moreover, how do we deal with psychological and historical elements of the evolving context that are *internal* to the learner, such as memories and experiences?

Second, there is the major problem of trying to define and circumscribe the external, internal and temporal boundaries of 'context' that may be relevant to the analysis of a particular learner–context ecosystem. For example, if, as in this volume, our empirical concern is with processes of motivation, how do we identify and delimit the multiple contextual elements that are empirically relevant to motivational development? How narrowly or widely should we focus our contextual lens? Should it encompass, for example, a whole study abroad experience, a single language lesson or a specific interactional encounter? Should we consider cultural context in the sense of national culture, or local institutional culture, or the 'small culture' (Holliday, 1999) of a particular classroom? Across these possible nested (Bronfenbrenner, 1989) contexts and sub-contexts, how do we then identify those elements that interact directly or indirectly with processes of motivation, as opposed to those that do not? Moreover, returning to the first stated problem above, how far do we integrate psychological and historical elements of context that are internal to the learner before we decide that we are dealing with learner characteristics rather than contextual characteristics?

There do not appear to be any straightforward solutions to these (and other related) questions. To make our research manageable, we are obliged to make certain pragmatic decisions about the contextual elements to be included and excluded, and pragmatic choices about the nested levels of analysis to focus on (e.g. see de Bot, this volume, on nested timescales; also Mercer, Chapter 12, this volume, on a nested approach to the self system). For example, a classroom study of motivation from a CDST perspective might entail a richly grounded ethnographic description of the physical and social setting of the classroom with detailed analyses of teacher and learner participants' linguistic and multimodal interactions, relations and behaviours in this setting, for a specified period of time or number of lessons. This would mean limiting the inquiry to those features of the immediate context that are directly observable and that can be recorded (i.e. captured in textual, image, audio or video form), as well as non-observable features of context that are invoked verbally by participants (such as references to people, events or cultural practices in the world outside or in the shared history of the participants).

In order to understand which contextual elements may be relevant to motivation in a given classroom, it would be necessary also to explore participants' own perspectives through various forms of introspection, such as stimulated recall interviews. These participant perspectives would help identify aspects of context that seem salient to particular individuals, and thus help constrain the multitude of potential contextual factors to be considered in the analysis. However, a limitation of introspective methods is that they cannot really shed light on contextual factors that are below the level of reflexive awareness and yet may be relevant to the development of motivation. These might include, for example, unanalysed memories, experiences or subliminal influences. Their significance may not impinge on the individual's consciousness, but such factors may, in interaction with other contextual and internal factors, contribute to the organic ebb and flow of motivation. From a methodological point of view, much will depend here on the skill of the researcher in carefully probing participants' perceptions during the stimulated recall interview, so that attention is drawn to possibly relevant features of context that have not been verbalized. In addition, a fruitful strategy may be to go back to participants at a later date, after preliminary analysis of the data, to conduct follow-up interviews or respondent validation (i.e. inviting participants to look through and comment on a summary report on their data). This may help bring about reflexive awareness of contextual factors not considered previously, as participants re-evaluate events from the perspective of current experience and hindsight.

Context and Complex Sub-systems Within the Learner

References in this chapter to learners' reflexive awareness point to another set of issues within the notion of context in CDST. So far in this discussion, the broad focus has been on contexts in relation to learners – that is, on the symbiotic and mutually constitutive relationship between contexts and language learners, as captured in the metaphor of a learner–context ecosystem. Given our core concern with issues of motivation in this volume, a focus on this particular ecosystem certainly makes sense. After all, we are interested in the processes of human intentionality, reflexive awareness and agency (see Al-Hoorie, this volume) that shape the relations between language learner and context. We are interested also in how learners act upon, engage with and respond to the contextual affordances (van Lier, 2004) in their surrounding environment.

Yet we might note that, according to CDST, processes of learner intentionality, reflexivity, awareness, agency, engagement and action may be said to constitute interacting components within their own internal complex system. We might conceptualize this complex system as the 'language learner', comprising a dynamic constellation of cognitive, affective, motivational and behavioural characteristics in constant evolving interaction with one another, such as described by Dörnyei (2009). We might also think of interconnecting complex sub-systems within the language learner, such as a 'cognitive ecosystem' as characterized by de Bot et al. (2007), or the complex adaptive systems of L2 development and use (e.g. Beckner et al., 2009; Ellis & Larsen-Freeman, 2009), or of possible selves (see Henry, Chapter 9, this volume). In other words, having highlighted earlier the problem of how to deal with psychological and historical elements of context that are *internal* to the learner, such as memories and experiences, we find we must also contend with the complexity of interacting dynamic sub-systems that are located *within* the learner, and consider what might be meant by 'context' within, and in relation, to these multiple internal ecosystems.

At one level, of course, from the perspective of complex sub-systems within the learner, context may refer simply to features of the environment that are external to the learner. For example, these might be features of the linguistic and social environment, such as L2 input, classroom instruction or peer group relations. Such features will be in dynamic interaction with various components within the learner's cognitive, language development or self-and-identity complex systems. Broadly speaking, this is no different from the concept of 'external' context already considered in relation to learner–context ecosystems. This concept of external context brings the same complications concerning how to define and delimit relevant contextual characteristics in this surrounding environment, and how to distinguish between contextual and learner-internal elements when these are interconnected and mutually constitutive. In this latter respect, for example, we might think of the learner's multiple social identities evolving within a self-and-identity complex system. While theoretically located within (or attributed to) the learner, these varying social identities are defined, negotiated or contested (e.g. Norton & Toohey, 2011) relationally in interaction with other people's social identities in the surrounding context. In the case of social identity, there is a mutually constitutive and co-adaptive relationship between internal and social-environmental processes. Identity both moulds and is moulded by shifting relations and social networks (on social networks and CDST, see Mercer, Chapter 8, this volume, for an example of a study that has dealt successfully with this issue).

Whereas social identity is a good example of a learner characteristic that is organically connected to the external surrounding context, it clearly also interplays with many other cognitive and affective sub-systems within the learner, such as processes of motivation, agency or self-esteem. Learner characteristics and systems constitute an internal ecology or co-adaptive environment with which social identity processes interact. In short, at this internal micro level, when our attention turns to specific components of complex sub-systems within the learner, the notion of what we mean by context or environment seems to transform in scale. As Larsen-Freeman and Cameron (2008: 230) explain, when we focus on a particular aspect of a complex system, 'other aspects or systems are taken as the environment in which the focal aspect or system changes'. This means that, depending on where we point our lens (e.g. willingness to communicate in the L2, such as in Mac-Intyre & Legatto, 2011), context may come to refer to various background systemic elements within the language learner (e.g. cognitive, affective and linguistic characteristics, such as motivation, self-confidence, anxiety, need, intentionality, linguistic competence, agency) with which the focal elements interact and co-adapt. As our analytical lens shifts (e.g. to speaking anxiety or linguistic competence), originally foregrounded elements may merge with contextual background systemic elements in this internal ecology. At the same time, if we broaden the focus of our lens, context will refer also to the wider ecology of external social and environmental conditions (e.g. social setting, communication topic, task difficulty, relationship with inter-locutors), which are in organic interaction with these learner-internal systemic processes.

Concluding Remarks

This shifting sense, scale and scope of what is meant by context in relation to the particular components, sub-systems or systems under focus raises enormous challenges for research in our field. On one hand, a pragmatic strategy may be to constrain the research inquiry to a select range of contextual features within a single ecosystem and to investigate their dynamic interplay with the focal elements. On the other hand, leading theorists (e.g. de Bot *et al.*, 2007; Larsen-Freeman & Cameron, 2008) argue that only by integrating all potentially relevant features of context (internal and external) in relation to this and other relevant interconnected systems can we hope to capture the true dynamic complexity of the processes in which we are interested. Yet clearly, an 'all or nothing' approach is hardly practicable. We need therefore to make certain decisions about which interconnected systems to consider and which contextual features within each system to include, while acknowledging that our empirical analysis will offer only a partial picture of the contexts and systems under focus.

For example, we may wish to explore how language learners' motivation to engage in a group work task shapes, and is shaped by, their interactions and social relations with other group members in this task. The primary learner–context ecosystem under focus here comprises the interplay among members of the group (the social context) in relation to the assigned work (the task context). This ecosystem could be examined by analysing a video recording of the interactions among group members as they engage in the task, and exploring how motivational processes are verbalized and evolve during these interactions and shape task engagement. Within the ecosystem of the group, participants will bring individual motivations and attitudes in relation to the immediate task context (e.g. interest or sense of challenge) as well as the social context (e.g. familiarity or friendship with particular group members). These context-oriented individual motivations will be in interaction with other cognitive and affective characteristics within each learner's internal ecosystem, such as feelings of self-efficacy or anxiety, and in interaction with other underlying motivational sub-systems, such as motivation for language learning or motivation for learning in general. To investigate these learner-internal motivations and contextual interactions, we would need to complement the video data with qualitative self-report data from group participants. These personal perspectives might be elicited through, for example, stimulated recall interviews (as described earlier) or structured forms of reflective writing.

In this example, our analysis would thus incorporate evolving motivational interactions among learners-in-context (where context refers to the task and the social group), and motivational interactions with learner-internal contextual characteristics. In this way, we may choose to confine our focus to the group and learner ecosystems for the depth and richness of insight to be gained, while recognizing that these are nested in, and interconnected with, the wider ecosystems of the classroom and sociocultural environment at large.

Ultimately, what seems important in light of all the above considerations, is to ensure that, when we try to conceptualize 'context' in relation to the language learner within a CDST approach, we endeavour to think big and small at the same time. Or to put it another way, we shuttle between learner-external and learner-internal contextual processes, as our analytical lens shifts from looking globally at particular learners engaging with the surrounding environment, to homing in on particular psychological or behavioural processes within the person. The research challenge is to describe interactions among internal contextual processes as well as contextual processes in the external environment. As our analytical perspective shifts from the external context (e.g. observing a student's behaviour in class and trying to interpret this in light of the classroom social dynamics) and drills down into the internal context (e.g. interviewing the student afterwards to explore their motivations, perceptions and history), we deepen our understanding of the person, their motivation and their behaviour, and the interconnected contextual factors involved.

References

Beckner, C., Blythe, R., Bybee, J., Christiansen, M.H., Croft, W., Ellis, N.C., Holland, J., Ke, J., Larsen-Freeman, D. and Schoenemann, T. (2009) Language is a complex adaptive system: Position paper. *Language Learning* 59 (Suppl. 1), 1–26.

Bronfenbrenner, U. (1989) Ecological systems theory. *Annals of Child Development* 6, 187–251.

de Bot, K., Lowie, W. and Verspoor, M. (2007) A dynamic systems theory approach to second language acquisition. *Bilingualism: Language and Cognition* 10 (1), 7–21.

Dörnyei, Z. (2009) *The Psychology of Second Language Acquisition*. Oxford: Oxford University Press.

Ellis, N.C. and Larsen-Freeman, D. (eds) (2009) *Language as a Complex Adaptive System*. Oxford: Wiley-Blackwell.

Holliday, A. (1999) Small cultures. *Applied Linguistics* 20 (2), 237–264.

Howard, M., Ó Laoire, M. and Singleton, D. (eds) (2011) Input and Learning Context in Second Language Acquisition. Special Issue of *International Review of Applied Linguistics in Language Teaching* 49 (2).

Kramsch, C. (ed.) (2002a) *Language Acquisition and Language Socialization: Ecological Perspectives*. London: Continuum.

Kramsch, C. (2002b) Introduction: How can we tell the dancer from the dance? In C. Kramsch (ed.) *Language Acquisition and Language Socialization: Ecological Perspectives* (pp. 1–30). London: Continuum.

Larsen-Freeman, D. and Cameron, L. (2008) *Complex Systems and Applied Linguistics*. Oxford: Oxford University Press.

MacIntyre, P.D. and Legatto, J.J. (2011) A dynamic system approach to willingness to communicate: Developing an idiodynamic method to capture rapidly changing affect. *Applied Linguistics* 32 (2), 149–171.

Norton, B. and Toohey, K. (2011) Identity, language learning, and social change. *Language Teaching* 44 (4), 412–446.

Seliger, H.W. (1977) Does practice make perfect? A study of interaction patterns and L2 competence. *Language Learning* 27 (2), 263–278.

Ushioda, E. (2009) A person-in-context relational view of emergent motivation, self and identity. In Z. Dörnyei and E. Ushioda (eds) *Motivation, Language Identity and the L2 Self* (pp. 215–228). Bristol: Multilingual Matters.

van Lier, L. (2004) *The Ecology and Semiotics of Language Learning: A Sociocultural Perspective*. Boston, MA: Kluwer.

7 Human Agency: Does the Beach Ball Have Free Will?

Ali H. Al-Hoorie

The fundamental difference between the hard sciences and the social sciences may not lie in the complexity of the latter, since it is possible to conceive of immensely complex situations in the hard sciences as well. Instead, the uniqueness of the social sciences might lie in people's ability to choose how to behave. Particles and molecules do not make choices, as their behaviour is predetermined and predictable by physical and chemical laws. That such precise predictability is absent in human behaviour is a strong argument for our ability to exercise free will through rational thought. In fact, it is the human ability to think and make rational choices that underlies ethical and moral judgments, for example deeming humans worthy of praise and reward for good behaviour, and answerable for wrongdoing.

As intuitive as it might be, the above reasoning has not gone unchallenged over the years. On the one hand, advances in quantum mechanics show that precise prediction is not possible *even in principle*. The position and the momentum of a particle, for example, cannot be precisely determined simultaneously; the more precisely one is known, the less precisely the other can be determined. On the other hand, several studies have questioned the extent to which humans are in control of their actions and thoughts. As a preliminary illustration, one of the most striking findings in this respect has come from neuroscience, where one study found that the outcome of a decision could be detected in brain activity up to ten seconds before it entered awareness, suggesting that it might be possible to predict people's behaviour prior to their conscious decision to behave (Soon *et al.*, 2008). Findings in a number of different theoretical and research paradigms have pointed to similar conclusions, leading some scholars to view our free will as a mere illusion (e.g. Wegner, 2002) and our behaviour as largely determined by unconscious, automatic processes, not by our conscious deliberation (e.g. Bargh & Williams, 2006). Other researchers have attempted to combine quantum indeterminacy with social sciences to account for human free will

(Glimcher, 2005; Kane, 1996). The applicability of insights from quantum mechanics to our behaviour is, however, disputed (Juarrero, 1999; Lau, 2009; Nahmias, 2010).

Regarding the main theme of the current edited volume, a recent approach to understanding human behaviour has turned to complexity theory to find explanations for human behaviour (cf. Larsen-Freeman & Cameron, 2008). Complexity theory raises interesting questions regarding agency and whether the individual is capable of exercising free will by choosing how to behave. This is because one of the most common metaphors in complexity nomenclature is 'the beach ball', which suggests that the behaviour of the individual tends to be a function of the terrain and its attractors, thus controlled by external factors; the beach ball does not have free will. Because multiple, combined and integrated forces constantly affect behaviour, making it almost never in equilibrium, it is easy to overlook the 'agent' and whether one can be in charge of his/her own behaviour. This reinforces the beach-ball view of the individual. Although most complexity theorists may not consciously embrace such a deterministic view, clearly this question has not received due attention. However, when we intend to apply complexity theory to human motivation, it becomes a crucial issue to examine whether the beach ball can have a will of its own. Can the beach ball, for example, make a decision to go against the flow?

Looking at the literature in general, scholars tend to agree on general principles on the relationship between the individual and the environment; beyond that the issue is 'oddly divisive' (Dörnyei, 2009: 236). Within complexity theroy in particular, Larsen-Freeman and Cameron (2008: 76) conclude that 'it remains to some extent an open question as to how far complexity theory can accommodate deliberate decision-making'. Indeed, complexity theory has made substantial strides in analysing the terrain of the system and its attractors, with much more work to be done to consider the extent to which behaviour is governed by the various system parameters and attractors. After all, the ultimate goal is not merely to describe the terrain features but to understand their effect on behaviour. In Albert Bandura's (1997: 7) words, 'Agency causation involves the ability to behave differently from what environmental forces dictate rather than inevitably yield to them'.

The question of human agency and free will has been the subject of bitter debates and sharp disputes, stimulating the thought of intellectuals belonging to diverse disciplines including Albert Einstein, Samuel Johnson, Immanuel Kant, John Stuart Mill, Jean-Paul Sartre and Percy Bysshe Shelley. This chapter builds on Larsen-Freeman and Cameron's (2008) discussion of this subject by presenting an overview of a number of theoretical paradigms that have challenged the independence of human agency, followed by a summary of the main arguments used by agency proponents to respond to these challenges.

Agency Under Attack

Early challenges

The first attempt to strip from humans the agency of their rational thought is represented in the *psychodynamic paradigm*. Sigmund Freud was the first scientist to offer a systematic analysis of unconscious motives and to conclude that the conflict between conscious and unconscious is not exclusive to those suffering from mental illness, but a general structure of the human mind, and that only a minority of our actions are based on rational thought (*cf.* Rennison, 2001). Many critics disapproved of Freud's theory because it was considered an 'insult' to deeply held beliefs about the self and reason, a standpoint that Freud himself acknowledged, but interpreted as 'resistance' and another defence mechanism not to accept this embarrassing truth (Robinson, 1993). According to the psychodynamic view, our conscious mind is only the tip of the iceberg, and our behaviour is primarily motivated by early childhood experiences that lead to an unconscious battle between the id, ego and super-ego, a battle fuelled by the pleasure, the reality and later the death principles (Heller, 2005; Thurschwell, 2000). It is worth noting, though, that at the heart of the psychodynamic paradigm is the fundamental assumption that we *can* exercise control over our behaviour, albeit indirectly, through the tools of psychoanalysis, such as studying dreams, free associations and Freudian slips (Sherman, 2000).

Psychoanalysis was replaced by the positivist empiricism of the *behaviouristic paradigm*. Following David Hume's (1921/1748) emphasis on the external nature of constant conjunction, Watson's methodological behaviourism rejected inner life because it is not directly observable and requires the unreliable method of introspection (Watson, 1913). B.F. Skinner's radical behaviourism went one step further by contending that the mind was no more than an imaginary invention, like all cognitive constructs, such as thinking, intention and knowledge (Skinner, 1961). Our phenomenological feelings were interpreted as 'collateral effects of the causes' (Skinner, 1989: 18), mere by-products of three kinds of selection by consequences: natural selection (genes), operant conditioning (reinforcement) and the social environment (Skinner, 1981). In his reply to Chomsky's (1959) review of *Verbal Behavior* (Skinner, 1957), Skinner (1972) claimed that creativity, whether in generative grammar or in poetry, is no more remarkable or less inevitable than a hen laying an egg![1] The belief that humans control their behaviour was compared with the belief that the wind controls its movement or that the farmer controls which type of fruit the plant will produce (Skinner, 1978). Skinner opposed the agentic mind so forcefully that in a speech just one day before his death he equated the effect of cognitive science on psychology with that of creationism on science (Skinner, 1990). Skinner accepted all corollaries of his position, rejecting free will, punishment for transgressions and even human dignity (Skinner, 1973).

Modern challenges

Today, the assumptions of Freud and Skinner that challenge our agency still persist in various guises. One is the *behaviour genetic paradigm*, first systematically utilized in 1875 by Sir Francis Galton (Burbridge, 2001). The most powerful design to extract genetic influences is 'twins-reared-apart' comparisons, limitations of which are compensated for by 'adoptees-reared-together' comparisons to examine environmental effects in the absence of genetic similarity and by non-human selective breeding to allow for randomization (Plomin, 1990; Plomin *et al.*, 2001). In 1979, the Minnesota Study of Identical Twins Reared Apart was initiated (see Segal, 2012) and found that 'genetic variation is an important feature of virtually every human psychological trait' (Bouchard, 2008: 69). To cite just a few figures, according to Bouchard (2004), heredity accounts for a substantial proportion of the variation in key human attributes, such as mental ability (around 80%), personality (40%–50%), psychological interests (36%) and social attitudes (65% for males and 45% for females), while environmental influences play a far smaller role, sometimes even decreasing with age. Although genetic influences do not usually account for more than 50% of the variance (Plomin, 1990), this magnitude is still remarkable considering that it constitutes a *single source* (Bouchard & McGue, 2003), thus leaving all other influences to share the remaining variance. These results support Skinner's argument that a substantial proportion of our behaviour is shaped by natural selection.

Further support to Skinner's theory comes from the *social paradigm*, specifically from the structure vs. agency debate in sociology. In one extreme, Emile Durkheim (Durkheim & Lukes, 1982/1895) challenged Karl Marx's philosophy and advocated the structuralist position that views human behaviour as passively and unidirectionally determined by social structure. The other extreme, the voluntarist position, shifts the focus to the individual, construing social structure as a result of human's purposeful autonomy, a position held by Max Weber (Weber *et al.*, 1978/1922) and recently by Baert and da Silva (2010). A compromise between these two extremes was later reached in Anthony Giddens's (1984) structuration theory and Pierre Bourdieu's (1977/1972) theory of practice. This position sees structure and agency as having a dialectical relationship in an iterative process where the system is 'recursively organized' (Giddens, 1984: 25). In this duality of structure, agents act reflexively to three sources of constraint (and enablement) represented in ability limitations, sanctions by powerful others and structural contexts that limit the agent's options. To draw an analogy, football players are constrained by rules, but these rules also give players the freedom to compete in a fair game that does not descend into complete anarchy.

Some sociocultural theorists in the second language (L2) field have expressed similar views (e.g. Duff, 2012; Lantolf & Thorne, 2006; van Lier, 2013), while others adopted a realist position (Gao, 2010; Sealey & Carter, 2004) arguing that agency and structure are independent and that their interaction produces emergent properties. Social psychologists working within Henri Tajfel and his student John Turner's social identity theory (Tajfel & Turner, 1986) have similarly demonstrated that group affiliation has a significant impact on a wide range of issues, including stereotyping and prejudice (Brown, 2010), crowd behaviour (Reicher, 2001), attitude and attitude change (Crano & Prislin, 2008), judgment and conformity (Jetten & Hornsey, 2012) and group motivation (Hogg & Abrams, 1993; Hogg et al., 2004). In addition to structure and agency, psychologist Albert Bandura (1986) adds a third component in his triadic reciprocal causation model, namely behaviour. In addition to influencing the environment, behaviour, once it has occurred can, in turn, have an influence back on the individual. Even the story influences the storyteller (McAdams & Pals, 2006).

In other words, 'there is no chance that … [our decisions] can be disconnected from the social-political-historical-moral-cultural influences of our time' (Larsen-Freeman & Cameron, 2008: 76). That one has to constantly navigate through all these influences indicates that human agency cannot be understood by looking into the individual, but, paradoxically, by looking into the social context (Dreier, 2008), as individuals cannot be completely autonomous (Ahearn, 2001). In fact, 'conditioning' is still accepted as an explanation of environmental effects by some sociologists (see Archer, 2000) and social psychologists (Bohner & Dickel, 2011), while frequency of stimulus is seen as a key determinant of L2 acquisition at all levels of analysis, including phonology, morphology, syntax, discourse and orthography (Ellis, 2002). This magnitude of environmental effects lends support to Skinner's argument that a large extent of our behaviour is shaped by the environment.

In the 1950s, the cognitive revolution supplanted behaviourism (Miller, 2003). The *cognitive paradigm* was largely inspired by Edward Chace Tolman's (1951/1932) purposive behaviourism and was a major step in reinstating the role of mental life in human behaviour. Cognitive psychology has subsequently split into two routes: the microanalysis of brain functions and the macroanalysis of the socially situated individual's goals, expectations and aspirations (Bandura, 2001). Proponents of both of these research avenues agree that, contrary to behaviourism, external stimuli do not influence the individual *directly*, but through how they are consciously perceived, thus restoring the individual's role in the causal chain. However, new strands within cognitive psychology have started to challenge this view. Originally, Thomas Henry Huxley (2011/1894) proposed the 'steam whistle hypothesis', wherein behaviour is caused by molecular changes in the brain while consciousness[2] is a by-product without a causal effect. Replacing 'conditioning' with 'automaticity', but accepting internal processes, advocates of this view explicitly state that they have 'reopened the behaviorists' hypothesis that the higher order responses of the human being can be *directly* put in motion by environmental stimuli' (Bargh & Ferguson, 2000: 928; emphasis added). Empirical studies, utilizing conscious and unconscious priming techniques (for methodological reviews, see Bargh & Chartrand, 2000; Neely, 1991), have confirmed that situational contexts have significant unintended effects:

- cognitively – information-processing goals can be primed (e.g. memorise vs. evaluate; Chartrand & Bargh, 1996);
- affectively – primes influence enjoyment and self-determination (i.e. intrinsic vs. extrinsic; Séguin Lévesque, 1999), attitudes towards goals (Ferguson & Bargh, 2004), goal-facilitating objects (Ferguson, 2008) and goal-facilitating people (Fitzsimons & Shah, 2009), as well as affect following success and failure (Moore *et al.*, 2011) and emotion regulation during anger provocation (Mauss *et al.*, 2007);
- behaviourally – priming increases the probability of goal pursuit and effort exertion (Aarts *et al.*, 2008; Holland *et al.*, 2009) and of resumption after interruption and persistence after setbacks (Bargh *et al.*, 2001);
- socially – automaticity extends to behavioural contagion (Chartrand & Bargh, 1999) and even moral judgment (Agerström & Björklund, 2009).

These unconscious effects can be activated by things as simple as chair softness (Ackerman *et al.*, 2010) or coffee temperature (Williams & Bargh, 2008). They also occur through the same brain regions (Pessiglione *et al.*, 2007) and working memory capacity (Hassin, 2008) as conscious effects.

In sum, automaticity is seen as 'a staple and indispensable construct for the explanation and prediction of almost all psychological phenomena' (Bargh *et al.*, 2012: 593), accounting for 99.44% of behaviour (Bargh, 1997: 243), while consciousness has 'no role' (Dijksterhuis *et al.*, 2007: 52) and 'has been vastly overrated; instead, it is often a post-hoc explanation of responses that emanated from the adaptive unconscious' (Wilson, 2002: 107). What about our phenomenological feeling of agency? These scholars consider self-knowledge a poor, unreliable measure, citing studies on confabulation, choice blindness and misattribution of agency (e.g. Bar-Anan *et al.*, 2010; Hall *et al.*, 2010; Johansson *et al.*, 2005; Wegner, 2002). The magnitude of empirical evidence supporting the effect of unconscious processes on behaviour left some wondering whether Freud is really dead (Westen, 1999) and whether the cognitive revolution would just be a detour to behaviourism (Mischel, 1997).

Our exercise of agency has further been challenged by other paradigms as well. For example, random events are said to 'rule our lives' (Mlodinow, 2008), where accidental occurrences can become life-changing occasions. Our free will is also constrained by hormones and other biological factors, such as the effect of testosterone level on generosity (Zak *et al.*, 2009) and social dominance (Terburg *et al.*, 2012), or the impact of diet on depression

(Akbaraly *et al.*, 2009; Sánchez-Villegas *et al.*, 2009) and on cognitive ability in childhood (von Stumm, 2012) and adulthood (Kesse-Guyot *et al.*, 2012). The effects in all of these cases operate below the threshold of consciousness, and therefore we are unable to control them directly. However, as discussed below, some scholars argue that we can still exert indirect, second-order control (Bandura, 2008) by learning about these effects and behaving adaptively. Researching these issues is therefore an instance of exercising agency.

Neuroscientific confirmation

A recent, powerful confirmation to the arguments against direct agency comes from the *neuroscientific paradigm*. Initially, German researchers Hans H. Kornhuber and Lüder Deecke (1965) discovered that voluntary action is preceded by bio-electrical activation in the brain, which they termed *Bereitschaftspotential*, or readiness potential (RP). This finding did not seem particularly remarkable until 20 years later when Benjamin Libet and colleagues (1983) found 'somewhat puzzlingly' (Larsen-Freeman & Cameron, 2008: 76) that RP precedes even the conscious intention to act. They concluded that 'voluntary' action is actually initiated unconsciously. Threatening as it is to free will, this conclusion attracted severe criticism on methodological (Klemm, 2010) and philosophical (Dennett, 2004; Mele, 2009) grounds. Experiments also questioned whether RP represents a decision to act (Trevena & Miller, 2010) and whether introspection is a reliable measure of decision time (Banks & Isham, 2009). Nonetheless, more refined replications confirmed the original findings (Haggard & Eimer, 1999; Matsuhashi & Hallett, 2008). Other studies predicted which hand the participant would move 10 seconds before this decision enters awareness (Soon *et al.*, 2008) and used direct recordings from single neurons with more than 80% predictive accuracy (Fried *et al.*, 2011), the latter being the most accurate approach in contemporary neuroscience (Haggard, 2011). In all of these cases, the participants' decisions were predicted before the participants themselves were aware they would make those decisions, leading some to conclude that we confuse correlation with causation in the relationship between our sense of agency and our actions (Wegner, 2002), and that full awareness of agency may even be 'postdicted' by the individual *after* action has been unconsciously initiated (Guggisberg *et al.*, 2008). Neuroscientist John-Dylan Haynes wonders, 'How can I call a will "mine" if I don't even know when it occurred and what it has decided to do?' (cited by Smith, 2011: 24). Further, transcranial magnetic stimulation can induce participants, unbeknownst to them, to choose which hand to move (Ammon & Gandevia, 1990) and, recently, this non-invasive brain stimulation was found to improve numerical competence (Cohen Kadosh *et al.*, 2010) and other arithmetic skills (Snowball *et al.*, 2013) with effects observed as long as six months later!

On the negative side, disruption to brain functions can have unwanted behavioural consequences. In addition to the famous Phineas Gage, whose personality reportedly changed after a freak accident that destroyed part of his brain (see Fleischman, 2002; Macmillan, 2000), brain tumours have been blamed for criminal behaviour, such as indecent conduct (Goldberg, 2001) and paedophilia (Burns & Swerdlow, 2003; see also Mobbs et al., 2009), as well as more extreme disorders, such as the alien hand syndrome (e.g. Assal et al., 2007). These findings raise the question of whether our behaviour is controlled unconsciously by our neurons. Yet, it is argued, we can exercise agency through consciously 'vetoing' the execution of impulses initiated unconsciously (Libet, 2003, 2004; though see Lau, 2009) by implementing a 'neural brake' mechanism (Filevich et al., 2012). Furthermore, this process, dubbed 'free won't', is not the only function of consciousness, because consciousness is an emergent property that also exerts top-down influence, complementing the unconscious bottom-up influence (Bandura, 2008; Gazzaniga, 2012). Finally, this counterargument assumes that the unconscious initiation of action discovered by Libet is generalizable from the simple finger movement examined in those laboratory studies to all human behaviour, and cannot be explained away by skill automation (Bandura, 2008).

Agency Fights Back

The previous sections have presented in some detail a range of powerful arguments and positions that go against the grain of traditional motivation research by claiming that the antecedent of human behaviour is not 'motivation' conceived as an attribute of which people are always aware. We have seen some potential counterarguments, and in the following such arguments will be further explored in an attempt to suggest some possible interim positions. Generally, those who adopt pro-agency views argue that the agent, given the same present situation and the same past events, 'could have done otherwise'. They are usually open to accept that certain factors may play a role in our behavioural choices, but maintain that these factors merely *influence* them, as opposed to *entirely produce* them (Nichols, 2008). 'Your genes, your upbringing, and your circumstances may predispose certain behaviour tendencies. But ultimately it is you who decides and who bears responsibility' (Myers, 2008: 32–33).

In an attempt to address the issue of agency head on, Baumeister et al. (2011) embarked on the task of answering what at first seems an obvious question: do conscious thoughts cause behaviour? In order to establish causality, these scholars reviewed various carefully selected lines of research that involve random assignment to experimental manipulations, such as imagining, mental practice, implementation intentions and anticipation. In support of the agency view, their results showed that conscious causation of behaviour is 'profound, extensive, adaptive, multifaceted, and empirically strong' (Baumeister *et al.*, 2011: 351). Agency proponents will certainly be delighted by this conclusion, but the disparity between this pro-agency conclusion and the wide range of anti-agency findings outlined above raises several questions.

First of all, these two viewpoints need to be reconciled. In their article, Baumeister *et al.* (2011) realised that the role of conscious thought is not as direct as might be intuitively assumed, but offline and indirect: 'Nothing indicated motivations *originating* in consciousness – instead, conscious thoughts interacted with existing motivations' (Baumeister *et al.*, 2011: 351, emphasis added). Put differently, in many situations, our agency seems to be represented not in our direct control of behaviour, but in our ability to resist an unconscious impulse or to select from multiple competing impulses. These resistant and selective roles of conscious behaviour still affirm our agency, and by extension our moral responsibility, albeit in an indirect fashion (*cf.* Juarrero, 1999; Larsen-Freeman & Cameron, 2008). This indirect view of agency supports a duality within human nature; while on the one hand the terrain with its multiple influences disposes behaviour towards one direction, on the other hand agentic behaviour requires conscious evaluation of these tendencies and vetoing what is deemed maladaptive.

The second question raised by the disparity of the agency-related findings is how consciousness can exercise its agentic role. That is, even if we accept the mediating influence of consciousness, we still need to explain the mechanism by which this agentic capacity is achieved. As Bargh and Ferguson (2000) argue, construing consciousness as an 'uncaused cause' reverts to a Cartesian dualism, which maintains that the mind is a non-physical entity (e.g. a soul) that is excluded from the causal order governing the body; in order to study consciousness scientifically, we must presuppose that it follows the physical laws of our universe. Complexity theory offers one solution that explains conscious free will without violating physical laws. Philosopher Alicia Juarrero (1999) maintains that modern philosophy is based on Aristotle's (mistaken) contention that cause must be external to its effect. Instead, Juarrero asserts that an alternative to external cause is 'self-cause'. That is, complex systems allow emergent properties, and these properties can have qualitatively different functions. Consciousness is seen as an emergent property that exerts top-down control on behaviour.

The third question concerns who can have this agentic ability. Is everybody capable of it? There seem to be at least two essential prerequisites. The first prerequisite is that one needs to believe in free will (Csikszentmihalyi, 2006). For example, research suggests that belief in determinism can lead to unethical behaviour through yielding to enticement (Vohs & Schooler, 2008). Contrary to philosophers who are interested in the abstract concept of free will and its existence, Dweck and Molden (2008) also argue that what people believe constitutes a psychological question whose answers construct differential psychological realties. This is because the laws of our universe referred to above also include human nature and how people view themselves, and this is at least partly self-constructed. To support their view, Dweck and Molden (2008) review diverse lines of research showing that self-theories – as fixed or malleable – have a direct and unequivocal effect on behaviour, attitudes and motivation. They conclude that 'personality is, in many ways, a highly dynamic system in which (changeable) beliefs can create a network of motivation and action' (Dweck & Molden, 2008: 58) and that 'people's self-theories have a cascade of effects on their personal motivation, as well as on the ways they judge and treat others' (Dweck & Molden, 2008: 47).

The second prerequisite is that agentic capacity requires becoming cognisant of the factors that influence one's behaviour. Awareness of the effects of unconscious primes may override and disrupt unconscious impulses (Bargh & Chartrand, 2000; Wegner & Bargh, 1998). Group affiliation, for example, may lead to prejudice automatically, but the realisation of this susceptibility would help one monitor one's behaviour and hopefully avoid the prejudice trap. People may shape their own destiny by learning about the factors that influence them. Agentic exercise of conscious thought can thus have a causal impact on behaviour (for a review, see Baumeister *et al.*, 2011) and, therefore, it is a false dichotomy to ask whether conscious or unconscious thought causes behaviour; it is the interplay between the two (Baumeister & Masicampo, 2010; Nordgren *et al.*, 2011). For this reason, psychological experiments typically involve an element of deception for fear of nullifying the independent variables under examination; allowing the participants to be conscious of the actual hypothesis prior to the study is considered 'a scientific prohibition' (Bandura, 2007: 655). Even covert, nonverbal communication from the experimenter can bias the participants' performance (Rosenthal, 2003).

In other words, the emergent nature of consciousness seems to allow one to exercise agency by recycling and reprocessing one's knowledge of the system in order to reshape the boundaries of the system and change its trajectory. This illustrates the nonlinearity of the system; the same situational input (the terrain) can have divergent outputs depending on one's expertise and attentiveness to input particulars. This conceptualisation is compatible with the First Law of Thermodynamics (*cf.* Juarrero, 1999), which states that energy is always conserved, cannot be created or destroyed, and can only be converted from one form into another. That is, consciousness does not have to be an uncaused cause, but a reorganisation of existing knowledge. Fate, we may argue, is not dictated by the terrain, but by whether one resists, or yields to, it. In fact, it is probably this capacity to resist attractive attractors that makes humans unique. If our behaviour were solely a product of the terrain, looking back and feeling proud about one's achievements would become meaningless.

An example of this agentic achievement should make the point clearer. A vivid illustration comes from research on psychological resilience.

Resilience is defined as 'the maintenance of positive adaptation by individuals despite experiences of significant adversity' (Luthar et al., 2000: 543). That is, some individuals are able to sustain normal functioning in situations of extreme stress, significant threat, severe adversity and trauma (Cicchetti, 2010), and can actually thrive after these aversive events (Bonanno, 2004). Such cases might be more interesting than cases where an individual follows the expected trajectory by succumbing to a negative attractor basin and consequently developing, say, mental disorders or other psychopathologies. Initially, theorists assumed that such cases are exceptional, but recent empirical studies have shown that resilience is actually *the most common* response to potential trauma (Bonanno, 2005). Although it might be tempting to think of resilience as an individual difference trait, resilience researchers have forcefully challenged such a view. These researchers argue that resilience is not 'in' the person (Masten, 2012: 208) or something that an individual 'has' (Cicchetti, 2010: 146). Instead, they stress that resilience emerges from the dynamic interaction of multiple factors, internal and external to the individual, that have differential effects depending on time and context.

Furthermore, like in so many other areas, researchers have been able to discover specific genes that appear associated with resilience. Kendler (2006) argues, however, that the expression 'X is a gene for Y' is misleading, because it implies a causal relationship that is strong, clear and direct, while in fact genes play a contributory role working in concert with a host of other factors. Indeed, recent findings dispute the direct causal role of genes suggesting that:

> there is much more scope for a single gene to have multiple diverse actions. But, even more basically, this dynamic process forces one to reconceptualize just what is meant by a gene. These new findings in no way undermine the evidence of the crucial pervasive importance of genes but they do undermine any notion that genes are determinative in a simplistic fashion ... (Rutter, 2006: 151)

Conclusion

Going back to the original question of whether the beach ball has free will, the above overview is consistent with Larsen-Freeman and Cameron's (2008: 76) assertion that 'we can marshal some substantial support for a positive answer to this question' and with Juarrero's conclusion that 'We are not passive products of either the environment or external forces. In a very real sense *we* contribute to the circumstances that will constrain us later on' (Juarrero, 1999: 253, emphasis added). This position is moderately optimistic as it rejects both the extreme view that we have absolute control over our behaviour, and the other extreme that our behaviour is entirely ruled by unconscious processes and external factors. Although past research has confirmed several behaviourist claims, investigations also point to our ability to exercise agency indirectly through top-down control (e.g. Baumeister *et al.*, 2011; Windmann, 2005). This conclusion, however, also compels us to make an important distinction between the beach ball and the individual in relation to attractors. While the ball gravitates towards various attractors, individuals can agentically repel themselves from certain others. As demonstrated in resilience research, this ironic process – repelling from attractors – is not uncommon and requires ordinary rather than extraordinary abilities, hence its nickname 'ordinary magic' (Masten, 2001). Motivational theorising within a complexity framework has paid little attention to this repellent process to date and has instead focused on the expected trajectory of individuals gravitating towards attractors. However, potentially introducing agency into the genes–environment debate, conscious repellent processes certainly deserve more attention in future research.

Acknowledgements

I would like to thank Zoltán Dörnyei for his extensive discussion and feedback on this topic. I also thank Diane Larsen-Freeman, Peter MacIntyre and William C. Peterson for their comments on an earlier draft.

Notes

(1)   In explaining his late reply, Skinner (1972: 345–346) stated, 'Let me tell you about Chomsky. I published *Verbal Behavior* in 1957. In 1958 I received a 55-page typewritten review by someone I had never heard of named Noam Chomsky. I read half a dozen pages, saw that it missed the point of my book, and went no further. In 1959, I received a reprint from the journal *Language*. It was the review I had seen, now reduced to 32 pages in type, and again I put it aside. But then, of course, Chomsky's star began to rise'.
(2)   Although they are not strictly the same, consciousness and rational thinking are treated in the same way in this context.

References

Aarts, H., Custers, R. and Marien, H. (2008) Preparing and motivating behavior outside of awareness. *Science* 319 (5870), 1639.
Ackerman, J.M., Nocera, C.C. and Bargh, J.A. (2010) Incidental haptic sensations influence social judgments and decisions. *Science* 328 (5986), 1712–1715.
Agerström, J. and Björklund, F. (2009) Moral concerns are greater for temporally distant events and are moderated by value strength. *Social Cognition* 27 (2), 261–282.
Ahearn, L.M. (2001) Language and agency. *Annual Review of Anthropology* 30 (1), 109–137.
Akbaraly, T.N., Brunner, E.J., Ferrie, J.E., Marmot, M.G., Kivimaki, M. and Singh-Manoux, A. (2009) Dietary pattern and depressive symptoms in middle age. *The British Journal of Psychiatry* 195 (5), 408–413.

Ammon, K. and Gandevia, S.C. (1990) Transcranial magnetic stimulation can influence the selection of motor programmes. *Journal of Neurology, Neurosurgery & Psychiatry* 53 (8), 705–707.

Archer, M.S. (2000) *Being Human: The Problem of Agency*. Cambridge: Cambridge University Press.

Assal, F., Schwartz, S. and Vuilleumier, P. (2007) Moving with or without will: Functional neural correlates of alien hand syndrome. *Annals of Neurology* 62 (3), 301–306.

Baert, P. and da Silva, F.C. (2010) *Social Theory in the Twentieth Century and Beyond* (2nd edn). Cambridge: Polity.

Bandura, A. (1986) *Social Foundations of Thought and Action: A Social Cognitive Theory*. Englewood Cliffs, NJ: Prentice-Hall.

Bandura, A. (1997) *Self-Efficacy: The Exercise of Control*. New York: Freeman.

Bandura, A. (2001) Social cognitive theory: An agentic perspective. *Annual Review of Psychology* 52, 1–26.

Bandura, A. (2007) Much ado over a faulty conception of perceived self-efficacy grounded in faulty experimentation. *Journal of Social and Clinical Psychology* 26 (6), 641–658.

Bandura, A. (2008) Reconstrual of 'free will' from the agentic perspective of social cognitive theory. In J. Baer, J.C. Kaufman and R.F. Baumeister (eds) *Are We Free? Psychology and Free Will* (pp. 86–127). Oxford: Oxford University Press.

Banks, W.P. and Isham, E.A. (2009) We infer rather than perceive the moment we decided to act. *Psychological Science* 20 (1), 17–21.

Bar-Anan, Y., Wilson, T.D. and Hassin, R.R. (2010) Inaccurate self-knowledge formation as a result of automatic behavior. *Journal of Experimental Social Psychology* 46 (6), 884–894.

Bargh, J.A. (1997) Reply to the commentaries. In R.S. Wyer (ed.) *The Automaticity of Everyday Life* (pp. 231–246). Mahwah, NJ: Lawrence Erlbaum.

Bargh, J.A. and Chartrand, T.L. (2000) The mind in the middle: A practical guide to priming and automaticity research. In H.T. Reis and C.M. Judd (eds) *Handbook of Research Methods in Social and Personality Psychology* (pp. 253–285). New York: Cambridge University Press.

Bargh, J.A. and Ferguson, M.J. (2000) Beyond behaviorism: On the automaticity of higher mental processes. *Psychological Bulletin* 126 (6), 925–945.

Bargh, J.A. and Williams, E.L. (2006) The automaticity of social life. *Current Directions in Psychological Science* 15 (1), 1–4.

Bargh, J.A., Gollwitzer, P.M., Lee-Chai, A., Barndollar, K. and Trötschel, R. (2001) The automated will: Nonconscious activation and pursuit of behavioural goals. *Journal of Personality and Social Psychology* 81 (6), 1014–1027.

Bargh, J.A., Schwader, K.L., Hailey, S.E., Dyer, R.L. and Boothby, E.J. (2012) Automaticity in social-cognitive processes. *Trends in Cognitive Sciences* 16 (12), 593–605.

Baumeister, R.F. and Masicampo, E.J. (2010) Conscious thought is for facilitating social and cultural interactions: How mental simulations serve the animal–culture interface. *Psychological Review* 117 (3), 945–971.

Baumeister, R.F., Masicampo, E.J. and Vohs, K.D. (2011) Do conscious thoughts cause behavior? *Annual Review of Psychology* 62 (1), 331–361.

Bohner, G. and Dickel, N. (2011) Attitudes and attitude change. *Annual Review of Psychology* 62 (1), 391–417.

Bonanno, G.A. (2004) Loss, trauma, and human resilience: Have we underestimated the human capacity to thrive after extremely aversive events? *American Psychologist* 59 (1), 20–28.

Bonanno, G.A. (2005) Resilience in the face of potential trauma. *Current Directions in Psychological Science* 14 (3), 135–138.

Bouchard, Jr. T.J. (2004) Genetic influence on human psychological traits: A survey. *Current Directions in Psychological Science* 13 (4), 148–151.

Bouchard, Jr. T.J. (2008) Genes and human psychological traits. In P. Carruthers, S. Laurence and S.P. Stich (eds) *The Innate Mind, Volume 3: Foundations and the Future* (pp. 69–89). New York: Oxford University Press.

Bouchard, Jr. T.J. and McGue, M. (2003) Genetic and environmental influences on human psychological differences. *Journal of Neurobiology* 54 (1), 4–45.

Bourdieu, P. (1977) *Outline of A Theory of Practice*. Cambridge: Cambridge University Press (original work published 1972).

Brown, R. (2010) *Prejudice: Its Social Psychology* (2nd edn). Oxford: Wiley-Blackwell.

Burbridge, D. (2001) Francis Galton on twins, heredity and social class. *The British Journal for the History of Science* 34 (3), 323–340.

Burns, J.M. and Swerdlow, R.H. (2003) Right orbitofrontal tumor with pedophilia symptom and constructional apraxia sign. *Archives of Neurology* 60 (3), 437–440.

Chartrand, T.L. and Bargh, J.A. (1996) Automatic activation of impression formation and memorization goals: Nonconscious goal priming reproduces effects of explicit task instructions. *Journal of Personality and Social Psychology* 71 (3), 464–478.

Chartrand, T.L. and Bargh, J.A. (1999) The chameleon effect: The perception–behavior link and social interaction. *Journal of Personality and Social Psychology* 76 (6), 893–910.

Chomsky, N. (1959) A review of BF Skinner's Verbal Behaviour. *Language* 35 (1), 26–58.

Cicchetti, D. (2010) Resilience under conditions of extreme stress: A multilevel perspective. *World Psychiatry* 9 (3), 145–154.

Cohen Kadosh, R., Soskic, S., Iuculano, T., Kanai, R. and Walsh, V. (2010) Modulating neuronal activity produces specific and long-lasting changes in numerical competence. *Current Biology* 20 (22), 2016–2020.

Crano, W.D. and Prislin, R. (2008) *Attitudes and Attitude Change*. New York: Psychology Press.

Csikszentmihalyi, M. (2006) Introduction. In M. Csikszentmihalyi and I.S. Csikszentmihalyi (eds) *A Life Worth Living: Contributions to Positive Psychology* (pp. 3–14). Oxford: Oxford University Press.

Dennett, D.C. (2004) *Freedom Evolves*. London: Penguin.

Dijksterhuis, A., Chartrand, T.L. and Aarts, H. (2007) Effects of priming and perception on social behavior and goal pursuit. In J.A. Bargh (ed.) *Social Psychology and the Unconscious: The Automaticity of Higher Mental Processes* (pp. 51–132). New York: Psychology Press.

Dörnyei, Z. (2009) Individual differences: Interplay of learner characteristics and learning environment. In N.C. Ellis and D. Larsen-Freeman (eds) *Language as a Complex Adaptive System* (pp. 230–248). Chichester: Wiley-Blackwell.

Dreier, O. (2008) *Psychotherapy in Everyday Life*. Cambridge: Cambridge University Press.

Duff, P.A. (2012) Identity, agency, and second language acquisition. In S.M. Gass and A. Mackey (eds) *The Routledge Handbook of Second Language Acquisition* (pp. 410–426). London: Routledge.

Durkheim, E. and Lukes, S. (1982) *The Rules of Sociological Method*. New York: Free Press (original work published 1895).

Dweck, C.S. and Molden, D.C. (2008) Self-theories: The construction of free will. In J. Baer, J.C. Kaufman and R.F. Baumeister (eds) *Are We Free? Psychology and Free Will* (pp. 44–64). Oxford: Oxford University Press.

Ellis, N.C. (2002) Frequency effects in language processing: A review with implications for theories of implicit and explicit language acquisition. *Studies in Second Language Acquisition* 24 (2), 143–188.

Ferguson, M.J. (2008) On becoming ready to pursue a goal you don't know you have: Effects of nonconscious goals on evaluative readiness. *Journal of Personality and Social Psychology* 95 (6), 1268–1294.

Ferguson, M.J. and Bargh, J.A. (2004) Liking is for doing: The effects of goal pursuit on automatic evaluation. *Journal of Personality and Social Psychology* 87 (5), 557–572.

Filevich, E., Kuhn, S. and Haggard, P. (2012) Intentional inhibition in human action: The power of 'no'. *Neuroscience & Biobehavioral Reviews* 36 (4), 1107–1118.

Fitzsimons, G.M. and Shah, J.Y. (2009) Confusing one instrumental other for another: Goal effects on social categorization. *Psychological Science* 20 (12), 1468–1472.

Fleischman, J. (2002) *Phineas Gage: A Gruesome but True Story about Brain Science*. Boston: Houghton Mifflin.

Fried, I., Mukamel, R. and Kreiman, G. (2011) Internally generated preactivation of single neurons in human medial frontal cortex predicts volition. *Neuron* 69 (3), 548–562.

Gao, X. (2010) *Strategic Language Learning: The Roles of Agency and Context*. Bristol: Multilingual Matters.

Gazzaniga, M.S. (2012) *Who's in Charge? Free Will and the Science of the Brain*. New York: HarperCollins.

Giddens, A. (1984) *The Constitution of Society: Outline of the Theory of Structuration*. Cambridge: Polity.

Glimcher, P.W. (2005) Indeterminacy in brain and behavior. *Annual Review of Psychology* 56, 25–56.

Goldberg, E. (2001) *The Executive Brain: Frontal Lobes and the Civilized Mind*. Oxford: Oxford University Press.

Guggisberg, A.G., Dalal, S.S., Findlay, A.M. and Nagarajan, S.S. (2008) High-frequency oscillations in distributed neural networks reveal the dynamics of human decision making. *Frontiers in Human Neuroscience* 1, 14.

Haggard, P. (2011) Decision time for free will. *Neuron* 69 (3), 404–406.

Haggard, P. and Eimer, M. (1999) On the relation between brain potentials and the awareness of voluntary movements. *Experimental Brain Research* 126 (1), 128–133.

Hall, L., Johansson, P., Tärning, B., Sikström, S. and Deutgen, T. (2010) Magic at the marketplace: Choice blindness for the taste of jam and the smell of tea. *Cognition* 117 (1), 54–61.

Hassin, R.R. (2008) Being open minded without knowing why: Evidence from nonconscious goal pursuit. *Social Cognition* 26 (5), 578–592.

Heller, S. (2005) *Freud A to Z*. Hoboken, NJ: Wiley.

Hogg, M.A. and Abrams, D. (1993) *Group Motivation: Social Psychological Perspectives*. New York: Harvester Wheatsheaf.

Hogg, M.A., Abrams, D., Otten, S. and Hinkle, S. (2004) The social identity perspective: Intergroup relations, self-conception, and small groups. *Small Group Research* 35 (3), 246–276.

Holland, R.W., Wennekers, A.M., Bijlstra, G., Jongenelen, M.M. and van Knippenberg, A. (2009) Self-symbols as implicit motivators. *Social Cognition* 27 (4), 579–600.

Hume, D. (1921) *An Enquiry Concerning Human Understanding*. Chicago: Open Court (original work published 1748).

Huxley, T.H. (2011) *Collected Essays*. Cambridge: Cambridge University Press (original work published 1894).

Jetten, J. and Hornsey, M.J. (2012) Conformity: Revisiting Asch's line-judgment studies. In J.R. Smith and S.A. Haslam (eds) *Social Psychology: Revisiting the Classic Studies* (pp. 76–90). London: SAGE.

Johansson, P., Hall, L., Sikström, S. and Olsson, A. (2005) Failure to detect mismatches between intention and outcome in a simple decision task. *Science* 310 (5745), 116–119.

Juarrero, A. (1999) *Dynamics in Action: Intentional Behavior as a Complex System*. Cambridge, MA: MIT Press.

Kane, R. (1996) *The Significance of Free Will*. New York: Oxford University Press.

Kendler, K.S. (2006) 'A gene for . . .': The nature of gene action in psychiatric disorders. *FOCUS: The Journal of Lifelong Learning in Psychiatry* 4 (3), 391–400.

Kesse-Guyot, E., Andreeva, V.A., Jeandel, C., Ferry, M., Hercberg, S. and Galan, P. (2012) A healthy dietary pattern at midlife is associated with subsequent cognitive performance. *The Journal of Nutrition* 142 (5), 909–915.

Klemm, W.R. (2010) Free will debates: Simple experiments are not so simple. *Advances in Cognitive Psychology* 6 (6), 47–65.

Kornhuber, H. and Deecke, L. (1965) Hirnpotentialänderungen bei Willkürbewegungen und passiven Bewegungen des Menschen: Bereitschaftspotential und reafferente Potentiale. *Pflüger's Archiv für die gesamte Physiologie des Menschen und der Tiere* 284 (1), 1–17.

Lantolf, J.P. and Thorne, S.L. (2006) *Sociocultural Theory and the Genesis of Second Language Development*. Oxford: Oxford University Press.

Larsen-Freeman, D. and Cameron, L. (2008) *Complex Systems and Applied Linguistics*. Oxford: Oxford University Press.

Lau, H.C. (2009) Volition and the function of consciousness. In N. Murphy, G.F.R. Ellis and T. O'Connor (eds) *Downward Causation and the Neurobiology of Free Will* (pp. 153–169). Berlin, Germany: Springer-Verlag.

Libet, B. (2003) Can conscious experience affect brain activity? *Journal of Consciousness Studies* 10 (12), 24–28.

Libet, B. (2004) *Mind Time: The Temporal Factor in Consciousness*. Boston, MA: Harvard University Press.

Libet, B., Gleason, C.A., Wright, E.W. and Pearl, D.K. (1983) Time of conscious intention to act in relation to onset of cerebral activity (readiness-potential): The unconscious initiation of a freely voluntary act. *Brain* 106 (3), 623–642.

Luthar, S.S., Cicchetti, D. and Becker, B. (2000) The construct of resilience: A critical evaluation and guidelines for future work. *Child Development* 71 (3), 543–562.

Macmillan, M. (2000) *An Odd Kind of Fame: Stories of Phineas Gage*. Cambridge, MA: MIT Press.

Masten, A.S. (2001) Ordinary magic: Resilience processes in development. *American Psychologist* 56 (3), 227–238.

Masten, A.S. (2012) Resilience in children: Vintage Rutter and beyond. In P.C. Quinn and A. Slater (eds) *Developmental Psychology: Revisiting the Classic Studies* (pp. 204–221). London: SAGE.

Matsuhashi, M. and Hallett, M. (2008) The timing of the conscious intention to move. *European Journal of Neuroscience* 28 (11), 2344–2351.

Mauss, I.B., Cook, C.L. and Gross, J.J. (2007) Automatic emotion regulation during anger provocation. *Journal of Experimental Social Psychology* 43 (5), 698–711.

McAdams, D.P. and Pals, J.L. (2006) A new Big Five: Fundamental principles for an integrative science of personality. *American Psychologist* 61 (3), 204–217.

Mele, A.R. (2009) *Effective Intentions: The Power of Conscious Will*. Oxford: Oxford University Press.

Miller, G.A. (2003) The cognitive revolution: A historical perspective. *Trends in Cognitive Sciences* 7 (3), 141–144.

Mischel, W. (1997) Was the cognitive revolution just a detour on the road to behaviorism? On the need to reconcile situational control and personal control. In R.S. Wyer (ed.) *The Automaticity of Everyday Life* (pp. 181–186). Mahwah, NJ: Lawrence Erlbaum.

Mlodinow, L. (2008) *The Drunkard's Walk: How Randomness Rules Our Lives*. London: Allen Lane.

Mobbs, D., Lau, H.C., Jones, O.D. and Frith, C.D. (2009) Law, responsibility, and the brain. In N.C. Murphy, G.F.R. Ellis and T. O'Connor (eds) *Downward Causation and the Neurobiology of Free Will* (pp. 243–260). Berlin, Germany: Springer-Verlag.

Moore, S.G., Ferguson, M.J. and Chartrand, T.L. (2011) Affect in the aftermath: How goal pursuit influences implicit evaluations. *Cognition & Emotion* 25 (3), 453–465.

Myers, D.G. (2008) Determined and free. In J. Baer, J.C. Kaufman and R.F. Baumeister (eds) *Are We Free? Psychology and Free Will* (pp. 32–43). Oxford: Oxford University Press.

Nahmias, E. (2010) Scientific challenges to free will. In T. O'Connor and C. Sandis (eds) *A Companion to the Philosophy of Action* (pp. 345–356). Wiley-Blackwell.

Neely, J.H. (1991) Semantic priming effects in visual word recognition: A selective review of current findings and theories. In D. Besner and G.W. Humphreys (eds) *Basic Processes in Reading: Visual Word Recognition* (pp. 264–336). Hillsdale, NJ: Lawrence Erlbaum.

Nichols, S. (2008) How can psychology contribute to the free will debate? In J. Baer, J.C. Kaufman and R.F. Baumeister (eds) *Are We Free? Psychology and Free Will* (pp. 10–31). Oxford: Oxford University Press.

Nordgren, L.F., Bos, M.W. and Dijksterhuis, A. (2011) The best of both worlds: Integrating conscious and unconscious thought best solves complex decisions. *Journal of Experimental Social Psychology* 47 (2), 509–511.

Pessiglione, M., Schmidt, L., Draganski, B., Kalisch, R., Lau, H.C., Dolan, R.J. and Frith, C.D. (2007) How the brain translates money into force: A neuroimaging study of subliminal motivation. *Science* 316 (5826), 904–906.

Plomin, R. (1990) The role of inheritance in behavior. *Science* 248 (4952), 183–188.

Plomin, R., deFries, J.C., McClearn, G.E. and McGuffin, P. (2001) *Behavioral Genetics* (4th edn). New York: Worth.

Reicher, S. (2001) The psychology of crowd dynamics. In M.A. Hogg and R.S. Tindale (eds) *Blackwell Handbook of Social Psychology: Group Processes* (pp. 182–208). Oxford: Blackwell.

Rennison, N. (2001) *Freud & Psychoanalysis*. Harpenden: Pocket Essentials.

Robinson, P.A. (1993) *Freud and His Critics*. Berkeley: University of California Press.

Rosenthal, R. (2003) Covert communication in laboratories, classrooms, and the truly real world. *Current Directions in Psychological Science* 12 (5), 151–154.

Rutter, M. (2006) *Genes and Behavior: Nature–Nurture Interplay Explained*. Malden, MA: Blackwell.

Sánchez-Villegas, A., Delgado-Rodriguez, M., Alonso, A., Schlatter, J., Lahortiga, F., Serra Majem, L. and Martinez-Gonzalez, M.A. (2009) Association of the Mediterranean dietary pattern with the incidence of depression: The Seguimiento Universidad de Navarra/University of Navarra follow-up (SUN) cohort. *Archives of General Psychiatry* 66 (10), 1090–1098.

Sealey, A. and Carter, B. (2004) *Applied Linguistics as Social Science*. London: Continuum.

Segal, N.L. (2012) *Born Together—Reared Apart: The Landmark Minnesota Twin Study*. Cambridge, MA: Harvard University Press.

Séguin Lévesque, C. (1999) On the existence and the consequences of automatically activated motivation. PhD thesis, University of Ottawa, USA.

Sherman, N. (2000) Emotional agents. In M.P. Levine (ed.) *The Analytic Freud: Philosophy and Psychoanalysis* (pp. 154–176). London: Routledge.

Skinner, B.F. (1957) *Verbal Behavior*. Englewood Cliffs, NJ: Prentice-Hall.

Skinner, B.F. (1961) A critique of psychoanalytic concepts and theories. In B.F. Skinner (ed.) *Cumulative Record* (enlarged ed., pp. 185–194). East Norwalk, CT, US: Appleton-Century-Crofts.

Skinner, B.F. (1972) A lecture on 'having' a poem. In B.F. Skinner (ed.) *Cumulative Record* (3rd edn) (pp. 345–355). New York: Appleton-Century-Crofts.

Skinner, B.F. (1973) *Beyond Freedom and Dignity*. Harmondsworth, Middlesex: Penguin.

Skinner, B.F. (1978) *Reflections on Behaviorism and Society.* Englewood Cliffs, NJ: Prentice-Hall.

Skinner, B.F. (1981) Selection by consequences. *Science* 213 (4507), 501–504.

Skinner, B.F. (1989) The origins of cognitive thought. *American Psychologist* 44 (1), 13–18.

Skinner, B.F. (1990) Can psychology be a science of mind? *American Psychologist* 45 (11), 1206–1210.

Smith, K. (2011) Neuroscience vs. philosophy: Taking aim at free will. *Nature* 477, 23–25.

Snowball, A., Tachtsidis, I., Popescu, T., Thompson, J., Delazer, M., Zamarian, L., Zhu, T. and Cohen Kadosh, R. (2013) Long-term enhancement of brain function and cognition using cognitive training and brain stimulation. *Current Biology* 23 (11), 987–992.

Soon, C.S., Brass, M., Heinze, H.J. and Haynes, J.D. (2008) Unconscious determinants of free decisions in the human brain. *Nature Neuroscience* 11 (5), 543–545.

Tajfel, H. and Turner, J.C. (1986) The social identity theory of intergroup behaviour. In W.G. Austin and S. Worchel (eds) *Psychology of Intergroup Relations* (pp. 7–24). Chicago, IL: Nelson-Hall.

Terburg, D., Aarts, H. and van Honk, J. (2012) Testosterone affects gaze aversion from angry faces outside of conscious awareness. *Psychological Science* 23 (5), 459–463.

Thurschwell, P. (2000) *Sigmund Freud.* London: Routledge.

Tolman, E.C. (1951) *Purposive Behavior in Animals and Men.* Berkeley: University of California Press (original work published 1932).

Trevena, J. and Miller, J. (2010) Brain preparation before a voluntary action: Evidence against unconscious movement initiation. *Consciousness and Cognition* 19 (1), 447–456.

van Lier, L. (2013) Control and initiative: The dynamics of agency in the language classroom. In J. Arnold and T. Murphey (eds) *Meaningful Action: Earl Stevick's Influence on Language Teaching* (pp. 241–251). Cambridge: Cambridge University Press.

Vohs, K.D. and Schooler, J.W. (2008) The value of believing in free will: Encouraging a belief in determinism increases cheating. *Psychological Science* 19 (1), 49–54.

von Stumm, S. (2012) You are what you eat? Meal type, socio-economic status and cognitive ability in childhood. *Intelligence* 40 (6), 576–583.

Watson, J.B. (1913) Psychology as the behaviorist views it. *Psychological Review* 20 (2), 158–177.

Weber, M., Roth, G. and Wittich, C. (1978). *Economy and Society: An Outline of Interpretative Sociology.* Berkeley: University of California Press (original work published 1922).

Wegner, D.M. (2002) *The Illusion of Conscious Will.* Cambridge, MA: MIT Press.

Wegner, D.M. and Bargh, J.A. (1998) Control and automaticity in social life. In D.T. Gilbert, S.T. Fiske and G. Lindzey (eds) *The Handbook of Social Psychology* (4th edn) (pp. 446–496). Boston: McGraw-Hill.

Westen, D. (1999) The scientific status of unconscious processes: Is Freud really dead? *Journal of the American Psychoanalytic Association* 47 (4), 1061–1106.

Williams, L.E. and Bargh, J.A. (2008) Experiencing physical warmth promotes interpersonal warmth. *Science* 322 (5901), 606–607.

Wilson, T.D. (2002) *Strangers to Ourselves: Discovering the Adaptive Unconscious.* Cambridge, MA: Belknap Press of Harvard University Press.

Windmann, S. (2005) What you see is never what you get: Dissociating top-down driven biases in perception and memory from bottom-up processes. In A. Columbus (ed.) *Advances in Psychology Research, Volume 35* (pp. 1–27). New York: Nova Science Publishers.

Zak, P.J., Kurzban, R., Ahmadi, S., Swerdloff, R.S., Park, J., Efremidze, L., Redwine, K., Morgan, K. and Matzner, W. (2009) Testosterone administration decreases generosity in the ultimatum game. *PLoS One* 4 (12), e8330.

8 Social Network Analysis and Complex Dynamic Systems

Sarah Mercer

Complexity theories represent an important development in attempting to interconnect internal, personal attributes and external, contextual factors into one integrated model indicating their mutually defining relationships as integral parts of the same complex dynamic system. In this way, complexity perspectives highlight how we are fundamentally social beings embedded in multiple layers of contexts and social relationships stretching across time and place. The challenge for researchers is to find ways of capturing this socially embedded complexity of individuals within a dynamic systems framework in an empirically researchable way.

One suggestion of how to make any complex dynamic system more amenable for research is to conceptualise it as a network. Indeed, one of the leading researchers in the field of network theory, Barabási (2003: 238), goes so far as to suggest that, 'networks are the prerequisite for describing any complex system, indicating that complexity theory must invariably stand on the shoulders of network theory'. Essentially, 'networks provide useful maps for disentangling complex and interwoven systems' (Caldarelli & Catanzaro, 2012: 41) and 'the network paradigm offers a powerful lens and methodology with which to model these complex systems' (Borgatti & Ofem, 2010: 29). However, network theory does not represent one single approach and there are many ways of understanding its theoretical framework and application. Research using network theory has been employed, for example, to examine a diverse range of topics, such as the spread of diseases, the use and flow of information in the internet, economic structures and global financial developments, as well as electrical and molecular networks (cf. Carolan, 2014). A particular form of network theory that concentrates on social connectivity and embeddedness of humans is social network theory.

Given the inherently social dimension of second language acquisition (SLA) and our interest in this volume in learner motivation and psychology, this chapter will focus on social networks; however, many aspects of the discussions will also be relevant for other forms of network analysis. An important point to clarify at the outset is that social networks do not exclusively refer to online networks of relationships, although it can include such a setting. Instead, the term refers more broadly to a way of understanding the nature of social structures and their interrelations in the form of a networked structure. It is fundamentally a socially situated form of contextualisation that recognises the interconnectedness of individuals in both formal and informal social structures (cf. Daly, 2010).

Characteristics of Networks

A useful way of explaining social network theory is to focus on some of the key characteristics of social networks and consider their perceived relevance for SLA. In the most basic terms, networks are concerned with relationships between things (actors or nodes). An actor or a node in a network can essentially be 'any type of entity that is capable of having some sort of relationship with another entity' (Borgatti & Ofem, 2010: 19). The social network perspective, as Carolan (2014: 7) explains, 'is concerned with the structure of relations and the implications this structure has on individual or group behaviour and attitudes'. It represents a key shift in focus away from focusing on individuals as a set of attributes and isolated, independent beings, towards looking at individuals as fundamentally social and relational beings. Social network theory examines individuals as interdependent actors (the term preferred in sociology to refer to individuals in social networks) situated within the complex dynamic system of their relational contexts. Social network theory investigates not only the individual and/or groups and their relationships with each other, but, as a focus of analysis, it also explores the network structure of these relationships, which can tell us something about patterns of behaviours and the nature of relationships and their development. In other words, the actor's relationships in themselves are influential, but also the larger network structure and the actor's position within it also dictate the nature of relationships.

Given the focus on relationships in Social Network Analysis (SNA), it is important to understand the different types of relationships in a network. One defining characteristic of relationships in any network concerns their directionality and whether a relationship is uni- or bi-directional. In SNA, bi-directional relationships are often referred to as 'edges' or 'relations', and relationships that are not necessarily reciprocated are known as 'arcs' or 'ties' (cf. Carolan, 2014 – although note that terminology appears to be used differently in different disciplines). Another crucial characteristic of a relationship is whether the link between two actors is composed of more than one type of relationship. The term 'multiplexity' is used to refer to those relationships between two actors that involve more than one role or function. These ties are naturally stronger than uniplex relationships, which consist of only one strand of connection. In social network terms, for example, a uniplex relationship could refer to a link between a teacher and student who only know each other within their educational social relationship; a multiplex relationship between a teacher and student could exist when they are also neighbours and the student is friends out of school with the teacher's own son or daughter. This would mean the relationship between the student and teacher in this case is multiplex, being composed of the teacher, neighbour and parent-of-friend roles. Other distinctions in types of relationships can also be generated as appropriate for the particular study, so for example, in the workplace, a difference has been made between 'expressive relationships', which generally refer to 'natural social and friendship-based affinities' and 'instrumental relationships', which are those that exist 'for a particular purpose related to the professional context' (Cole & Weinbaum, 2010: 81). An understanding of these different kinds and qualities of relationships viewed within the context of a social network can help researchers (and participants themselves) to recognise power structures, pathways of information and resources, as well as opportunities for growth and cooperation.

A crucial dimension of SNA is not only to focus on the types, numbers and qualities of relationships in a social network, but also to concentrate on the typography and architecture of the network itself. Very often, social networks are visualised in graphic form (e.g. using sociograms or network graphs), in which a network can be represented by nodes connected by lines. The emergent structure that forms when the lines and nodes are interconnected in a network is referred to as the network's structure or architecture (Kadushin, 2012). The emergent typology of the network is crucial to understanding how the network functions, where its weak points are, where the central points of influence (hubs) are, where possible 'structural holes' in the network exist, where dense clusters of highly interconnected actors may form, etc. (see below Figure 8.1 for an example of an illustration of a network).

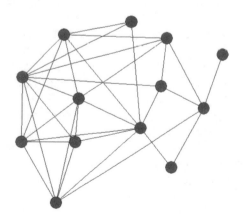

Figure 8.1 A basic illustrative example of a network structure (Generated with sociogram software (Lewejohann, 2005))

The structural foundations of a network represent the relational patterns within it and the nature and landscape of this structure can reveal a lot about the behaviour of the network, points of influence and role of actors within it.

When looking at the structure of a network, it is often possible to observe actors who are more connected to others and these are known as being more 'central'. In contrast, actors who may have fewer or no connections to the rest of the network are referred to as being 'peripheral'. Another way of discussing the network structure itself is in terms of the 'density' of connections in particular parts of the network, with dense areas being those where there are a high proportion of ties out of the total possible number of ties. There is also a tendency for clusters, zones or regions in a network, which represent more tightly interconnected and linked areas. One reason for this clustering and an important concept in network theory is 'homophily', which stems from the Greek meaning 'love of the same' (Kadushin, 2012: 18). This refers to the tendency for people to interact with others who share similar attributes, characteristics or attitudes, following the adage 'birds of a feather flock together' (Carolan, 2014; Kadushin, 2012). In strong cases, clusters in a network can even become closed off to other parts of the networks and relatively self-contained regions of the network (Carolan, 2014). In a classroom, these clusters of relationships could, for example, represent cliques of students. If parts of a network interact very little with each other, then these form 'structural holes' in the network and it can be useful for teachers in a class to identify these and work explicitly on filling those gaps and thereby enhancing overall group dynamics and group identity.

Another key concept in SNA is 'social capital'. Social capital is a metaphor that refers to advantages certain individuals or groups have because of their position in the social network structure (Burt, 2000). Burt (2000: 347) explains that social capital is 'the contextual complement to human capital' and that certain individuals or groups do better simply because they are better connected. In other words, the topographical network structure implies social capital (structuralist view), although the nature of the relationships themselves and access to resources can also contribute to any individual's social capital (connectionist view; see Gallagher, 2011: 48 for a discussion). This means that there is value in relationships themselves and the access to resources they may facilitate, but also the position of an actor within the network structure contributes to their potential social capital (Carolan, 2014). In the context of language education, and given the inherently social nature of language, social capital could be a crucially important concept to understand. It poses the question of what social resources a learner has for learning and using the language, inside and outside the classroom setting.

A final characteristic of networks related to its architecture concerns how the network is structured to facilitate the 'flow' of something (tangible or symbolic) around the network, and here ideas of 'contagion' and 'diffusion' are relevant (Carolan, 2014). In relation to social capital, the structure can facilitate, for example, the flow of knowledge, ensuring that certain members are better informed than others, or it can affect the flow of, and access to, material resources. In the context of this book, the structure of networks could be examined for the extent to which they facilitate or hinder the flow of knowledge, tools, resources, attitudes, emotions, motivation, etc. The principles of flow in networks will be familiar from concepts discussed in the media concerning the spread of diseases and epidemics, as well as 'cascading failures', such as in power or computer networks or global financial markets. In SNA, 'cascading behaviour in a network is sometimes referred to as "social contagion" because it spreads from one person to another in the style of a biological epidemic' (Easley & Kleinberg, 2010: 16). They stress that although there are fundamental differences given human agency and the ability to reflect and behave strategically, there are still similar network dynamics evident across different types of networks.

Methodological Issues

Within SNA, there are several key issues a researcher needs to address when planning a study based on this framework. While it is beyond the scope of this chapter to cover these fully, a basic outline of some key decisions is presented. For excellent practical advice, the interested reader is referred to Avila de Lima (2010), Carolan (2014) and Scott (2012).

A key primary decision in SNA concerns the focus of analysis. Essentially, there are two main types of social network studies: 'egocentric network' studies, which focus on one person's social environment; or 'complete-network' studies, which measure the relationships between actors in some defined social group (Carolan, 2014: 68). In principle, SNA can be applied to multiple levels of analysis. As Borgatti and Ofem (2010: 18) explain, 'the network lens can be applied to individuals, teams, and organizations, making it possible to examine nearly any type of social system characterized by relations between entities'. In an educational setting, different levels of networks could include, for example, a school class of learners as a network, an individual learner's language use network, a teacher's network of professional contacts, a regional, national or international network of schools, or even the global Foreign Language Teaching (FLT) network (cf. Easley & Kleinberg, 2010). In complete network studies, the boundaries of the social group can typically be formally defined (students in one class) in ways similar to the concept of a bounded case in case study research. However, an important word of warning in this respect is sounded by Avila de Lima (2010: 246), who cautions against automatically assuming that natural boundaries are the actual boundaries of a network. Rainie and Wellman (2012: 6) argue that rather than viewing individuals as embedded neatly within contexts, it is more useful to understand them as 'networked individuals'. In this way, traditional social boundaries may no longer be representative and, instead, we need to think in terms of 'networked individualism' (Rainie & Wellman, 2012), in which each actor forms their own unique network of social ties that may defy and extend beyond traditional boundaries. Other strategies for boundary specification can be positional (selecting a population based on some common attribute or criteria), relational (through the relations among actors) and event-based (all those who took part in an 'event' at a specific time and place) (Carolan, 2014: 68–73). Similar decisions concern the choice of actors to study in ego-network studies, although representative sampling is typically advocated given the more quantitative orientation of this approach (Carolan, 2014).

Network data are very often generated through questionnaires and possibly interviews and/or observations to establish a person's social relationships. In questionnaire design for SNA, there are several specific issues to consider, such as whether to use 'recognition', in which a person is presented a list of names to nominate ties from, or whether names are elicited with 'free recall', in which respondents are simply asked to recall from memory people and types of relationships (Avila de Lima, 2010: 250). Another important consideration is whether to fix the maximum number of people a person can nominate (many sociogram studies in sociology in schooling contexts typically ask participants to name three friends they like to work with), or leave the choice of how many to nominate open (Avila de Lima, 2010). Obviously, a major problem for SNA is that sampling in a group is problematic, as it typically leaves 'holes' in the network and, thus, its architecture becomes impossible to reconstruct. Given the importance of the network structure, missing and incomplete data sets pose a particular problem for SNA (Avila de Lima, 2010).

In addition to the basic information about the number of relationships and between whom (in a complete network study, this implies also directionality), researchers may also gather further information about the qualities of these relationships, for example, in terms of value (intensity of the relationship), multiplicity (whether it is a multiplex or uniplex relationship) and sign (the positivity or negativity of a relationship) (Scott, 2012). If the focus of the study is on the flow of some information or resource, data on that will naturally be required too. Once network data have been generated, the next steps can be to create a matrix to work with the data and potentially to use visualisation software to create graphs or sociograms of the network and its properties. Carolan (2014: 13) explains that 'images of networks, both static snapshots as well as their evolution over time, are commonly created to develop structural insights and to clearly communicate these insights to others'. An exciting potential of SNA is its capacity to examine dynamic processes and using longitudinal data and simulation software to examine how networks may develop over time. In this way, SNA dynamic analyses may be able to search for patterns and not just describe complex social networks and the flow within them, but explain and partially predict processes (Carolan, 2014). Several software packages exist (UCINET, NetMiner, MultiNet; Carolan, 2014: 277–283) for data analysis and visualisation, as well as packages for specialised network data collection (e.g. Network Genie).

Applications in SLA

What are the specific potentials of SNA for the field of SLA? It has already begun to receive considerable attention within disciplines related to SLA, such as other areas of the social sciences, political science, sociology, natural sciences, social psychology and, more recently, in education (e.g. Carolan, 2014; Daly, 2010; Deal *et al.*, 2009). It is likely to be of particular relevance in SLA given that language use and meaning-making through language is inherently social and interactional in nature (Byrnes, 2013: 225), thus implying that it is fundamentally relational in nature too. Within the area of sociolinguistics and in studies of bilingualism, there have already been some studies employing a social network view, including a special issue of the journal *The International Journal of the Sociology of Language* edited by de Bot and Stoessel in 2002. There has also been some initial work within foreign language learning (Ferenz, 2005; Gallagher, 2011; Isabelli-Garcia, 2006; Kurata, 2007, 2011); however, as yet, SNA remains a relatively uncommon conceptual and analytical framework, although given the growth of interest in complexity perspectives, this is likely to change.

Most obviously, social network theory can help us to understand the social interaction of individuals and groups. For example, it can cast light on individuals and their in- and out-of-class language use, their contact with users of the target language and their 'social capital' in terms of language use and learning opportunities. It can help us to better understand group dynamics in classrooms, and how people interact and identify with the class group as a whole. It can also be employed to examine teacher relationships with each other (within and across school settings) and explore their attitudes and their responses to educational reforms (Daly, 2010). SNA can also prompt us to reflect on the nature of teacher and learner motivation by switching our attention from solely looking at the internal processes of individuals, to instead looking at social motivation and how groups and individuals cooperate and generate collective forms of social motivation (cf. Tyler, 2011). It can also be adapted and used creatively as a conceptual, descriptive or metaphorical tool to understand other aspects of SLA, such as in the context of this book, learner psychology. Recently, for example, I have been keen to take a more holistic view of learners' sense of self and have found it useful to envisage the learners' language learning selves as comprised of a network of relationships (Mercer, 2014). This means conceptualising learners' self-descriptions in terms of the cognitive and affective relationships that they form with people, as well as to objects, ideas, places and concepts (past, present and future) surrounding their language learning and use experiences. Employing network thinking in these kinds of ways can push our conceptualisations of language learning psychology beyond reductionist, individualist frames and challenge us to engage with new complex, contextualised, relational perspectives on familiar constructs.

Conclusion

To conclude, SNA is likely to prove to be a useful methodological and/or conceptual tool for furthering our thinking about the complex dynamic systems involved in foreign language learning. However, we must remember that humans are unique in terms of their ability to reflect and subjectively interact with their environments, exercising their agency in complex and, at times, unpredictable ways (Vallacher & Nowak, 2009). Any models or methods we therefore choose to adopt, also need to adequately account for these unique and defining characteristics of human existence. As Easley and Kleinberg (2010) emphasise, 'models of networked behaviour must take strategic behaviour and strategic reasoning into account' and sufficiently account for the cognitive, affective and motivational character of human agency (Robins & Kashima, 2008). Therefore, a rounded, comprehensive picture of learners, teachers and settings will most likely be best achieved through a combination of SNA alongside other approaches and tools. No single research method or theoretical framework can answer all the complex questions posed by the field of SLA.

However, if SLA continues to develop a more complexity-informed approach to the study of learners, teachers and learning environments, then SNA will have much to offer. Given perhaps one of the key characteristics of complex dynamic systems are interrelations between component parts of the system, SNA is ideally suited to investigating the relational aspects of a particular system. It represents a way of retaining a holistic, interconnected, situated perspective on any complex dynamic system, yet enables a degree of simplification, which makes researching the system, especially the dynamics of the system and the relationships within it, more empirically manageable. Thus, any aspect of SLA that investigates complex systems of relationships could potentially benefit from adopting an SNA approach. Trueit and Doll (2010: 136) argue, 'the new found importance of relations and interactions in complex systems signals the limits of the concept of *individualism*' (emphasis in the original). In the context of this collection of papers, this raises questions about how research into learner psychology and motivation in SLA may benefit from moving beyond researching isolated individuals, to exploring more explicitly relational perspectives on learners and for this, SNA promises to be an invaluable tool.

References

Avila de Lima, J. (2010) Studies of networks in education: Methods for collecting and managing high-quality data. In A.J. Daly (ed.) *Social Network Theory and Educational Change* (pp. 243–258). Cambridge, MA: Harvard Education Press.

Barabási, A.L. (2003) *Linked: How Everything is Connected to Everything Else and What it Means for Business and Everyday Life*. London: Plume Books.

Borgatti, S.P. and Ofem, B. (2010) Overview: Social network theory and analysis. In A.J. Daly (ed.) *Social Network Theory and Educational Change* (pp. 17–29). Cambridge, MA: Harvard Education Press.

Burt, R.S. (2000) The network structure of social capital. *Research in Organizational Behaviour* 22, 345–423.

Byrnes, H. (2013) Renting language in the ownership society. Reflections on language use and language learning in a multilingual world. In J. Arnold and T. Murphey (eds) *Meaningful Action: Earl Stevick's Influence on Language Teaching* (pp. 222–240). Cambridge: Cambridge University Press.

Caldarelli, G. and Catanzaro, M. (2012) *Networks: A Very Short Introduction*. Oxford: Oxford University Press.

Carolan, B.V. (2014) *Social Network Analysis and Education Theory, Methods and Applications*. Thousand Oaks: SAGE Publications.

Cole, R.P. and Weinbaum, E.H. (2010) Changes in attitude: Peer influence in high school reform. In A.J. Daly (ed.) *Social Network Theory and Educational Change* (pp. 77–95). Cambridge, MA: Harvard Education Press.

Daly, A.J. (2010) (ed.) *Social Network Theory and Educational Change*. Cambridge, MA: Harvard Education Press.

Deal, T.E., Purinton, T. and Waetjen, D.C. (2009) *Making Sense of Social Networks in Schools*. Thousand Oaks, CA: Corwin Press.

Easley, D. and Kleinberg, J. (2010) *Networks, Crowds, and Markets Reasoning about a Highly Connected World*. New York: Cambridge University Press.

Ferenz, O. (2005) EFL writers' social networks: Impact on advanced academic literacy development. *Journal of English for Academic Purposes* 4, 229–351.

Gallagher, H.C. (2011) In the loop: A social network approach to the willingness to communicate in the L2 (L2 WTC). Unpublished doctoral thesis, University of Nottingham. Available at: http://etheses.nottingham.ac.uk/2407/ (accessed 13 June 2014).

Isabelli-García, C. (2006) Study abroad social networks, motivation and attitudes: Implications for second language acquisition. In E. Churchill and M. DuFon (eds) *Language Learners in Study Abroad Contexts* (pp. 231–258). Clevedon: Multilingual Matters.

Kadushin, C. (2012) *Understanding Social Networks: Theories, Concepts, and Findings*. New York: Oxford University Press.

Kurata, N. (2007) Language choice and second language learning opportunities in learners' social networks. A case study of an Australian learner of Japanese. *Australian Review of Applied Linguistics* 30 (1), 05.1–05.18.

Kurata, N. (2011) *Foreign Language Learning and Use: Interaction in Informal Social Networks*. London: Continuum.

Lewejohann, L. (2005) Sociogram (Version 1.0). [Computer software]. http://www.phenotyping.com/sociogram/ (accessed 13 June 2014).

Mercer, S. (2014) Re-imagining the self as a network of relationships. In K. Csizér and M. Magid (eds) *The Impact of Self-concept on Language Learning*. Bristol: Multilingual Matters.

Rainie, L. and Wellman, B. (2012) *Networked: The New Social Operating System*. Cambridge: MIT Press.

Robins, G. and Kashima, Y. (2008) Social psychology and social networks: Individuals and social systems. *Asian Journal of Social Psychology* 11, 1–12.

Scott, J. (2012) *What is Social Network Analysis?* London: Bloomsbury Academic.

Trueit, D. and Doll, W.E. (2010) Thinking complexity: Being-in-relation. In D. Osberg and G. Biesta (eds) *Complexity Theory and the Politics of Education* (pp. 135–151). Rotterdam: Sense Publishers.

Tyler, T.R. (2011) *Why People Cooperate: The Role of Social Motivations*. Princeton: Princeton University Press.

Vallacher, R.R. and Nowak, A. (2009) The dynamics of human experience: Fundamentals of dynamical social psychology. In S. J. Guastello, M. Koopmans and D. Pincus (eds) *Chaos and Complexity in Psychology: The Theory of Nonlinear Dynamical Systems* (pp. 370–401). Cambridge: Cambridge University Press.

9 The Dynamics of Possible Selves

Alastair Henry

At the minimum, it can be assumed that each time a particular conception of the self is activated, it will change, however slightly, by the conditions and circumstances of the processing.
Markus and Kunda, 1986

Dörnyei's recasting of second language (L2) motivation as a process of self-discrepancy has not only generated scores of journal articles and book chapters focusing on the motivational effects of L2 self-guides, but through practitioner-oriented publications (Dörnyei & Kubanyiova, 2014; Gregersen & MacIntyre, 2014; Hadfield & Dörnyei, 2013) the Ideal L2 Self is beginning to find its way into motivational practices in the classroom. Widely recognised as potentially powerful generators of motivation, ideal L2 selves risk, however, being conceptualised as static constructs, fixed 'targets' that the individual strives to achieve or live up to. Such a view does not fit easily with the current trend in second language acquisition (SLA) towards the application of dynamic approaches. For this reason, an elaboration of the dynamics of possible selves seems timely.

In this chapter I explore two important dynamic processes. First I look at the ways in which ideal L2 selves are upwardly and downwardly revised as a result of assessments of the likelihood of their achievement. I then consider processes in which changes in language speaking/using self-guides are triggered as a consequence of interactions with other self-concepts. While the identification of this first type of dynamic stems from the notion that, during a period of learning (long or short), the learner's goalposts are likely to shift, the second is a development of the long-held recognition that motivated behaviours do not take place in relative isolation, but are shaped by the other ongoing activities in which the learner is engaged (Dörnyei, 2005; Ushioda, this volume). Before looking at these two processes, I begin by outlining three aspects of complex dynamic systems (CDS) of particular importance in developing an understanding of self-guide dynamics. These are, respectively, changes to attractor states, system connectedness and timescales.

Three Important CDS Principles

Changes to attractor states

Even though on a day-to-day basis we are exposed to a mass of varying information relevant to inter- and intrapersonal functioning – much of which has the potential to bring about changes in the conceptions we hold about ourselves – generally speaking people are able to maintain relatively stable platforms for thought and action (Nowak et al., 2005). This also applies to possible selves. Because they represent people's enduring hopes and dreams, possible selves tend to be resistant to change, in many cases demonstrating preferences for stability. Stability, as Nowak et al. (2005) explain, is a function of processes where, over time, flows of thought and action tend to converge into a range of clearly defined *fixed-point attractors* (see also Hiver, this volume, Chapter 3). When a system is lodged in a part of the state space governed by a fixed-point attractor, cognitive, affective and behavioural coherence pertains. However, even though a motivational system might remain anchored in an attractor state, this does not mean that changes are not taking place to the attractor state itself. As I will argue, changes in the Ideal L2 Self are likely to be taking place all the time, the qualities of these changes having an effect on the system's overall resilience to change. It is these dynamics that I focus on here and a type that CDS researchers may have in mind when speaking of complex systems as being 'dynamically stable' (Larsen-Freeman & Cameron, 2008; Nowak et al., 2005).

System connectedness

The study of a system's dynamics involves the investigation of the connectedness of the system's constituent components, and the links between these components and those of other systems (de Bot, 2011; Larsen-Freeman & Cameron, 2008). This means that the researcher needs to map out the system under investigation, identify its focal components, take note of other systems operating simultaneously and plot the relationships they might have with the focal system. All the while, the researcher is considering how focal components are interacting and changing. Some particular aspect(s) or subsystem(s) need to be singled out for closer scrutiny. This, as Larsen-Freeman and Cameron (2008) explain, involves achieving a balance between *foreground* and *background*. Although necessary, not least for practical reasons, to limit focal scope by foregrounding particular elements and dynamic relationships, it is important not to lose sight of the fact that there is always a background of other systems, system components and relationships that are likely to impact on the chosen objects of study. Consequently, the trick is to allow the background to 'continue to be dynamic while we focus on the foreground activity' (Larsen-Freeman & Cameron, 2008: 230). When considering the dynamics of L2 self-guides, we need to be aware that they do not operate in isolation. Rather, they are part of a permanently shifting 'background' of self-concepts and self-knowledge that are embedded in other systems. When competing self-concepts from these other 'background' systems become activate in cognition changes can take place.

Timescales

The final CDS principle that we need to keep in mind when looking at the dynamics of possible selves is the concept of timescales (de Bot, 2012 and this volume). Specifically, when conceptualising changes to a language-using/speaking self-guide, we need to consider whether we are talking about changes that might take place in the few minutes during which a task is carried out, or whether we are interested in changes across progressively longer timescales, such as lessons, weeks, terms/semesters, entire programs of study or, indeed, a portion of the lifespan.

Shifting Goalposts: Changes in the Ideal L2 Self

When first introducing the concept of possible selves, Markus and Nurius (1986) emphasised that, being *future*-oriented self-conceptions, they are more susceptible to external influences than other forms of self-knowledge:

> Because possible selves are not well-anchored in social experience, they comprise the self-knowledge that is most vulnerable and responsive to changes in the environment. They are the first elements of the self-concept to absorb and reveal such change. As representations of potential, possible selves will thus be particularly sensitive to those situations that communicate new or inconsistent information about the self. (Markus & Nurius, 1986: 956)

Further, although in his theory of self-discrepancy Higgins (1987) does not emphasise sensitivity to contextual factors in the same way, he nevertheless makes the point that the accessibility of self-guides will vary considerably from one set of circumstances to another. It is therefore interesting that, even though in these original papers (see also Markus & Kunda, 1986; Markus & Wurf, 1987) self-guides are conceived as highly dynamic, in empirical study the overwhelming tendency has been to examine ideal and ought-to self guides as static constructs, that is to say fixed 'targets' that the individual strives to achieve or live up to. A mode of thinking where the ideal self is conceptualised as a static entity is perhaps easy to fall into; the methods that have been used to study the impact of self guides lend themselves to this way of thinking. Quantitative procedures adopted in prior studies almost invariably require respondents to provide numerical ratings to allow the discrepancy between current and ideal selves to be calculated (MacIntyre, personal communication). Taking a dynamic approach, conceptualising and studying a reified possible self may be easier to avoid.

In his discussions of the L2 Motivational System model, Dörnyei (2005, 2009) has emphasised that possible L2 selves are phenomenologically constructed. Construction processes are dependent on people's varying capacity to develop vivid mental imagery (Dörnyei & Chan, 2013) and their diverse social experiences. The main argument I want to make here is that, in order to avoid a static conceptualisation of the Ideal L2 Self, to these primary 'individual differences' we need to add a further *dynamic* dimension. Simply put, as the individual finds her/himself in different situations, the ability to construct and (once cognitively activated) maintain a possible self is likely to change. This can take place across both shorter and longer timescales, a function of both contextual conditions and the learner's evolving mindset.

Because possible selves are 'particularly sensitive to those situations that communicate new or inconsistent information about the self' (Markus & Nurius, 1986: 956), an Ideal L2 Self is likely to be subtly reformulated and revised every time it is activated. For example, changes could be triggered by comparisons with encountered others (in real life or virtually) who share certain characteristics of the individual's ideal self, thus providing opportunities for future selves to become more *elaborated* and *tangible* (Lockwood & Kunda, 1997). Similarly, the sensory qualities of an Ideal L2 Self are also likely to be affected by exposure to phenomenologically relevant teaching materials or target-language experiences (see e.g. Dörnyei & Chan, 2013; You & Chan, this volume). Possible selves are also dynamic in the sense that the power they exert is situationally determined. In particular, two aspects of a self-guide, its *availability* (the ease with which it can be imagined) and its *accessibility* (the ease with which it can be brought into awareness), will be highly dependent on factors such as the activities currently engaged in and the state of mind of the individual at a particular point in time. Consequently the functionality of possible selves in generating self-regulated behaviour will be dynamic, differing from one particular instant in time to another (Norman & Aron, 2003).

Possible selves can also change as a consequence of the individual's awareness of the distance between an *actual* and an *ideal* self. As Carroll and his associates (Carroll *et al.*, 2009; Carroll *et al.*, 2006) have suggested, when self-relevant situations alter expectations about the *likelihood* of achieving a desired possible self, the collection of possible selves may also change. Re-evaluations of the chances of achieving a desired future self – either more or less likely – are prompted by salient events, experiences, and implicit/explicit feedback relating to the development of target language skills.

Revisions in this respect can be both upward and downward. Regarding the former, if people perceive that they are close to realising the desired end-state of a particular ideal self, rather than signalling an end to self-regulated behaviour – a resting upon one's laurels so to speak – they may revise or 'upgrade' the ideal self in ways that enable it to continue to serve as a motivational source (Ogilvie, 1987). Positive learning experiences or engaging with the target language (TL) can trigger such reassessments, resulting in the enhancement of the Ideal L2 Self. In such processes of revision, the mental clothing of the desired self is likely to encompass images of increasingly sophisticated language use, hoped-for cross-cultural encounters and experiences, and even interaction with desirable interlocutors. Nevertheless, because desired possible selves tend, by nature, to take the form of best-case outcomes (people being generally optimistic about the future), the consequences of such positively perceived indicators of success may not have the same self-changing effects as their negative counterparts, the indicators of (partial) failure. When an individual experiences indications that progress towards the ideal self is not going as well as anticipated, doubts can be created as to the credibility – or 'possibility' – of the desired possible self. Such feedback (implicit or explicit) can mean, as a consequence, that an alternative, less desirable, but perhaps more realistic 'ideal' self may appear as more attractive. This downward revision involves changes in the mental imagery of future use, shifting the ideal self closer to the actual self, thereby reducing the discrepancy to a more manageable level (Carroll et al., 2009). This process can be likened to moving the goalpost nearer when it is perceived to be too far away (see for example You & Chan, this volume).

Shifting goalposts conceptualised as changes in attractor state geometries

Attractors may vary in strength, so that certain attractors are more likely than others to capture and maintain the dynamics of a person's functioning. (Nowak et al., 2005: 356)

For someone learning another language, whether in a formal or an informal setting, day-to-day events can be interpreted as indicative of the nature of the discrepancy between actual and ideal L2 selves. Whether struggling with verb tenses in the classroom or engaged in everyday social interaction in L2 settings, people are prompted to reflect not just on long-term aspirations – the person with the desired language skills they want in the future to be – but also on the likelihood of becoming such a person. In CDS terms, changes in the vision of the Ideal L2 Self (Dörnyei & Chan, 2013; You & Chan, this volume) and changes in the distance between it and the actual self, can be conceptualised as changes in attractor state *geometries*. A phenomenologically less vivid, less robust ideal self or a revision that shifts it in a direction closer to the actual self, would imply that the attractor state may not be quite as *deep* as before. Similarly, the *width of its basin of attraction* may have narrowed, meaning that the array of similar values in the vicinity of the attractor state might have decreased. The *shape* of the attractor state – representing the ability of the system to react to various deviations from its attractor and the strength with which each deviating state will be pulled back – may also change (Nowak *et al.*, 2005). Any of these changes in the nature of the attractor state will mean that the system is likely to be less stable or robust than before, making movement out of an attractor state more likely.

The importance of timescales

When considering changes of this sort, we need to be particularly aware of the timescale in which they may be taking place. An everyday event in the course of learning a language – the comment of a teacher, the response of another learner or an experience of frustration when using the TL in a communicative situation – can prompt reflection on the ultimate goal of becoming a proficient TL-speaker/user. While across *longer timescales* the cumulative effects of such reflections can result in changes to the phenomenology of the ideal self, possibly shifting it closer to the actual self, across a *shorter timescale* the same events could have the opposite effect. Specifically, this type of reflection could trigger compensatory processes as a consequence of which, momentarily at least, the desired self is reaffirmed and phenomenologically enhanced, thus putting a stop to any shift in the direction of the actual self. In fact, such reactions are not unusual, people tending to react in ways that have a protective function. Thus, a negatively construed event can trigger compensatory processes that insulate the desired self from the potential threat (Markus & Kunda, 1986). Indeed, such processes can be so effective that they can even result in a temporary enhancement of the desired self (Carroll *et al.*, 2009; Markus & Kunda, 1986). For example, in Henry's (2011) study of the impact of L2 English on L3 motivation, one of the students interviewed described how, following a threat to his ideal L3 self triggered by a negative comparison with his ideal L2 self, he simply refocused his energy on the task in hand, developing a strategy to protect the L3 self-concept and, consequently, maintain self-esteem. In the next section I continue the focus on shorter timescales, moving on to the second set of dynamics discussed in the chapter; the ways in which, within the self-concept, L2 self-guides interact with other self-concepts and relevant self-knowledge.

Interactions with Other Cognitive Systems

Systems may be coupled, with one acting as dynamic context for the other. (Larsen-Freeman & Cameron, 2008: 73)

A basic principle of CDS theory is that, rather than a static backdrop, social, cultural and cognitive contextual factors form part of the system under investigation. This means that when researching a complex system we need to take account of its interconnectedness with other dynamic systems, to be alert to between-system interactions and to be aware of the dyadic processes involved when systems *co-adapt* (Larsen-Freeman & Cameron, 2008). When investigating L2 motivation, this demands consideration not just of the dynamic processes at play when the system's components change (as in the above examples), but also the ways in which these components interact with those of *other systems*. As in the above example, where an L2 self appears to have an impact on its L3 counterpart (Henry, 2011), one useful way of examining between-system interactions is to broaden the focus by looking at the individual's overall self-concept, considering in particular the effects that components from different systems concurrently active in cognition might have on L2 selves.

The dynamic self-concept

The self-concept is a multidimensional, multifaceted structure that researchers define variously in terms of hierarchies, prototypes, networks and spaces (Markus & Wurf, 1987). More than simply a passive receptacle for self-relevant information, it is a dynamic structure, comprising collections of self-schemas (generalisations about the self) generated from previous experiences (Markus, 1977; Markus & Sentis, 1982). The role of these self-schemas is to mediate intra- and interpersonal processes, functioning in ways that *represent* the self as both 'the knower' and 'the known' (Markus & Wurf, 1987). Representations of the self differ in terms of elaboration, valence and whether they are focused on experiences from the here-and-now, the past or those that are anticipated. Representations also differ in terms of focus; that is to say in relation to what the self actually *is*, what in best case scenarios it *could ideally be*, what it *ought to be* or what, in undesired scenarios it *might become*. Through social interaction these self-representations change, their evolutionary paths altered both by information received about the self – through self-perception, social comparison and self-appraisal – as well as through the individual's cognitive processing of such self-conceptions. As they change, so too does the nature and composition of the self-concept (Markus & Wurf, 1987).

Like any dynamic system, the changes that take place in the self-concept will be a function of the timescale. While across shorter timescales rapid fluctuations can occur, over longer timescales more enduring trajectories may evolve. Thus, the self-concept can be highly stable, yet simultaneously responsive and malleable (Markus & Kunda, 1986). This, as Stein and Markus (1996: 354) explain, can mean that the same individual 'who consistently, over a period of years, endorses a set of personality attributes as a self-descriptive can demonstrate remarkable fluctuations in her self-view over the period of a few days'. This seemingly contradictory picture of the self – as both stable and dynamic – can be understood in the sense that while the self-concept constitutes a more or less stable collection of self-conceptions, because of its multidimensionality, not all of these will be cognitively active at any given time (Markus & Nurius, 1986; Stein & Markus, 1996). Consequently, attempts to understand changes in motivated behaviour that focus on the self-concept as a single 'lump-like' entity (Markus & Wurf, 1987: 301) are simply not feasible. Instead, focus needs to be directed to the self-concept's active ingredients, that is to say, the self-concept as it appears at any particular instant in time, the so-called 'working self-concept' (Markus & Kunda, 1986; Markus & Wurf, 1987).

Describing the dynamic nature of the working self-concept, Markus and Nurius (1986) emphasise how, as a result of interaction with other constituents, self-guides undergo change. Self-guides will only have an impact on self-regulated behaviour when cognitively activated. Consequently, as Markus and Nurius (1986: 957) point out, 'the value of considering the nature and function of possible selves is most apparent if we examine not *the* self-concept, which is typically regarded as a single, generalized view of the self, but rather the current or *working* self-concept' (emphasis in the original). Whenever activated in working cognition, possible selves are unlikely to remain in an entirely stable or unchanged form. In the social events and person-to-person interaction of an unfolding situation, different cognitive/affective systems are activated. This means that, at any particular point in time, the working self-concept will contain the totality of the active elements of these different systems. It is in this constantly shifting environment that changes to a possible self may take place, for example as a result of contact with another, competing possible self (Oyserman & James, 2009).

A CDS conceptualisation

Using Markus and Nurius' (1986) description of the functioning of the working self-concept as an example, Nowak and colleagues (2005: 355) explain how, in CDS, 'different and even conflicting goals, self-views, and behavior patterns' are conceptualised as multiple fixed-point attractors. When elements of different systems converge, or when the state space of a system contains competing attractors, the path the system takes will be a function of the strength of the attractor state in which it is currently lodged and the capacity of a competing attractor state to capture and maintain the dynamics of cognitive, emotional and social functioning (Nowak et al., 2005). As we have seen, the strength of an attractor state can be understood in terms of its geometrical characteristics. When an attractor state in which the system currently resides is deep-sided, where its basin of attraction is wide, and when it is shaped in a way that deviating states tend to be pulled back, any instability generated by a competing attractor state is unlikely to be enduring. However, if the geometry of a competing attractor state is such that the system is drawn away from the position previously occupied, a *phase shift* will take place, the system *self-organising* into a new pattern of behaviour (Larsen-Freeman & Cameron, 2008).

Across shorter timescales – for example when the learner is working with a task, engaged in a particular activity, or shows commitment over the course of a lesson – the cognitive context in which L2 self-guides operate is likely to be populated by a range of other self-knowledge. Although some self-concepts may be complementary to currently active L2 self-guides (e.g. the academic self-concept, or a conception of the self as a team-player or a supportive friend), others may compete. While complementary self-concepts/self-guides can function to create relative stability around a broad basin of attraction surrounding an ideal or ought-to L2 self attractor state, those that are discordant can create periods of instability.

The effect of the activation in working cognition of self-knowledge that does not readily align with already active TL self-guides has, for example, been demonstrated in studies with a focus on the simultaneous learning of more than one language. Henry (2011, 2014) described how, when learning foreign languages such as French, German and Spanish, students use L2 English as a source of support, meaning that they can become aware of an English-speaking/using self-concept during L3 lessons. The appearance of the L2 self in working cognition seems to have a negative impact on L3-speaking/using self-concepts. While for some of the students in Henry's (2011) study the instability to the system engendered by the intrusion of a competing attractor state (the L2 English self) could be enduring (the ability of the L3 attractor state to pull the system back progressively weakened after each such intrusion), for others the period of flux caused by a shift in the direction of the competing attractor state was followed by an almost immediate return of the system to the original attractor state as a result of the compensatory processes previously described.

The interaction of language speaking/using self-guides with the components of other cognitive systems is important in the dynamic processes that affect the self. Even in situations where learners experience the type of sustained and goal-directed motivational flow that Dörnyei *et al.* (Chapter 10, this volume) call a 'directed motivational current', language learning activities are never self-contained or hermetically sealed. Rather, over the course of any language learning sequence, priorities change, new priorities emerge and, at any time, new and potentially competing self-concepts can become active in working cognition. For example, a change of working partner can trigger the activation of very different social self-concepts, while the theme of a text, or of a conversation taking place parallel to the work going on, can radically alter the composition of working cognition.

A Tentative Model of Possible Self Dynamics

As sketched out in Figure 9.1, three dynamic processes appear to be of importance when considering the ways in which, across shorter timescales, L2 self-guides may change. Two of these, *the up- and downward revisions of the Ideal L2 Self,* and *changes triggered by interaction with other self-concepts* I have discussed here. Readers interested in the third, *changes in the vividness and elaboration of the image at the heart of L2 selves and in the availability and accessibility of the Ideal L2 Self* are referred to You and Chan (this volume) who explore the impact of L2 imagery on future self-guides. For each of these three processes, CDS theories provide a conceptual toolkit with the potential to shed light on the complex interactions taking place, and to generate insights into the system-level effects these changes can trigger.

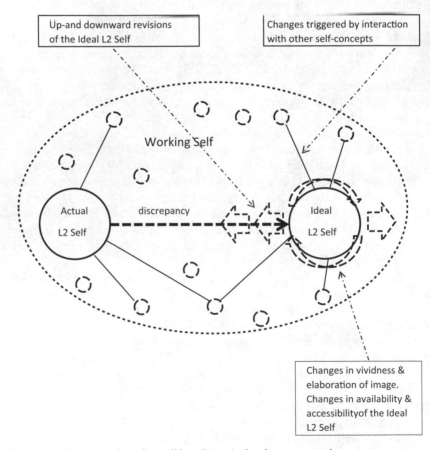

Figure 9.1 The dynamics of possible selves: A visual representation

Conclusion

Adopting complexity approaches in the investigation of L2 motivational processes presents very real challenges. In addition to the need to embrace what, at times, can appear to be a highly abstract conceptual apparatus, CDS tools, devices and concepts need to be integrated into a research paradigm that is itself continuing to emerge, grow and branch out in new directions. In an attempt to generate novel insights into the motivational functioning of language speaking/using self-guides by using a CDS approach, the purpose of this chapter has been to identify changes that are likely to take place in ideal L2 selves and to consider the system-level effects than can ensue. Although this represents an initial attempt to conceptualise a new and rather uncharted area (the account offered here being neither comprehensive nor definitive), there are compelling reasons for re-thinking the way we conceive of possible selves. Although from the outset Markus and her colleagues emphasised the *dynamic* nature and *multifaceted* qualities of possible selves (Markus & Kunda, 1986; Markus & Nurius, 1986; Markus & Wurf, 1987), because of the use of experimental and questionnaire-oriented methodologies, research in both mainstream psychology and in our own field has tended to 'freeze' current and ideal selves, presenting them as photographic stills rather than moving pictures. Moving away from the 'static target' understandings that these methodologies inevitably produce, language speaking/using self-guides are better regarded as *dynamic* structures, the phenomenological qualities of which can be highly variable, that are subject to revision (in both up- and downward directions), and which undergo constant transformation in interaction with other self-concepts.

References

Carroll, P.J., Shepperd, J.A. and Arkin, R.M. (2009) Downward self-revision: Erasing possible selves. *Social Cognition* 27, 550–578.

Carroll, P.J., Sweeny, K. and Shepperd, J.A. (2006) Forsaking optimism. *Review of General Psychology* 10, 56–73.

de Bot, K. (2011) Epilogue. In M.H. Verspoor, K. de Bot and W. Lowie (eds) *A Dynamic Approach to Second Language Development: Methods and Techniques* (pp. 123–127). Amsterdam/Philadelphia: John Benjamins.

de Bot, K. (2012) Timescales in second language development. *Dutch Journal of Applied Linguistics* 1, 143–149.

Dörnyei, Z. (2005) *The Psychology of the Language Learner: Individual Differences in Second Language Acquisition.* Mahwah, NJ: Lawrence Erlbaum.

Dörnyei, Z. (2009) The L2 motivational self system. In Z. Dörnyei and E. Ushioda (eds) *Motivation, Language Identity and the L2 Self* (pp. 9–42). Bristol: Multilingual Matters.

Dörnyei, Z. and Chan, L. (2013) Motivation and vision: An analysis of future L2 self images, sensory styles, and imagery capacity across two target languages. *Language Learning* 63, 437–462.

Dörnyei, Z. and Kubanyiova, M. (2014) *Motivating Learners, Motivating Teachers: Building Vision in the Language Classroom.* Cambridge: Cambridge University Press.

Gregersen, T. and MacIntyre, P. (2014) *Capitalizing on Language Learners' Individuality: From Premise to Practice.* Bristol: Multilingual Matters.

Hadfield, L. and Dörnyei, Z. (2013) *From Theory to Practice: Motivation and the Ideal Language Self.* London: Longman.

Henry, A. (2011) Examining the impact of L2 English on L3 selves: A case study. *International Journal of Multilingualism* 8, 235–255.

Henry, A. (2014) The motivational effects of crosslinguistic awareness: Developing third language pedagogies to address the negative impact of the L2 on the L3 self-concept. *Innovation in Language Teaching and Learning* 8 (1), 1–19.

Higgins, E.T. (1987) Self-discrepancy: A theory relating self and affect. *Psychological Review* 94, 319–340.

Larsen-Freeman, D. and Cameron, L. (2008) *Complex Systems and Applied Linguistics.* Oxford: Oxford University Press.

Lockwood, P. and Kunda, Z. (1997) Superstars and me: Predicting the impact of role models on the self. *Journal of Personality and Social Psychology* 73, 91–103.

Markus, H.R. (1977) Self-schemata and processing information about the self. *Journal of Personality and Social Psychology* 35, 63–78.

Markus, H.R. and Kunda, Z. (1986) Stability and malleability of the self-concept. *Journal of Personality and Social Psychology* 51, 858–866.

Markus, H.R. and Nurius, P. (1986) Possible selves. *American Psychologist* 41, 954–969.

Markus, H.R. and Sentis, K. (1982) The self in social information processing. In J. Suls (ed.) *Psychological Perspectives on the Self* (Vol. 1) (pp. 41–70). Hillsdale, NJ: Lawrence Erlbaum.

Markus, H.R. and Wurf, E. (1987) The dynamic self-concept: A social psychological perspective. *Annual Review of Psychology* 38, 299–337.

Nowak, A., Vallacher, R. and Zochowski, M. (2005) The emergence of personality: Dynamic foundations of individual variation. *Developmental Review* 25, 351–385.

Norman, C. and Aron, A. (2003) Aspects of possible self that predict motivation to achieve or avoid it. *Journal of Experimental Social Psychology* 39, 500–550.

Ogilvie, D. (1987) The undesired self: A neglected variable in personality research. *Journal of Personality and Social Psychology* 52, 379–385.

Oyserman, D. and James, L. (2009) Possible selves: From content to process. In K. Markman, W. Klein and J. Suhr (eds) *Handbook of Imagination and Mental Simulation* (pp. 373–394). New York: Psychology Press.

Stein, K.F. and Markus, H.R. (1996) The role of the self in behavioural change. *Journal of Psychotherapy Integration* 6, 349–384.

10 'Directed Motivational Currents': Regulating Complex Dynamic Systems through Motivational Surges

Zoltán Dörnyei, Zana Ibrahim and Christine Muir

Most people will, at some point or other, have come across a curious phenomenon whereby somebody suddenly embarks on a project, invests a great deal of time and energy in it for a period of time and, as a result, often achieves something quite remarkable. Take, for example, an overweight university professor (specialised in motivation), who is coming to terms with the fact that all the time spent sitting in front of his computer, as well as attending delicious business lunches and sumptuous conference dinners, has been causing a very noticeable increase in his waistline, until one day something changes: his friends and family are surprised to see that he has enrolled in a gym, his evening pudding has turned into a single yoghurt, and at conference buffet lunches he does not go back for seconds (and even his first plate contains an uncharacteristic amount of vegetables). As a result, he loses over 20 pounds over a period of three months. Alternatively, consider for example a second language (L2)-related situation when someone decides to start learning a foreign language in preparation for an extended foreign trip, and becomes embroiled in the process to such an extent that she spends virtually all her free time studying the language, while also purchasing dictionaries and computer software to direct her learning, as well as voraciously reading guidebooks and surfing L2 websites to familiarise herself with the L2 culture and environment. In an extreme case she might bore family and friends rigid by talking of the trip and the language incessantly, may dream of the journey at night and cannot help but rehearse the language even while lying in bed. It is as if a new world had opened up for her and, up until the journey, her pursuit of this newly found vision becomes one of the most significant parts of her life.

These and similar occurrences have undeniable relevance to motivation research as they represent motivational surges that powerfully transport an individual from one state to another, but how are they related to complex dynamic systems? In this chapter, we argue that the reason why such heightened motivational periods (which we have labelled *directed motivational currents*) can be so effective is because they have the capacity to override or modify the multiple pushes and pulls that people experience in their busy lives. In other words, directed motivational currents (DMCs) have the capacity to align the diverse factors that are simultaneously at work in a complex system, thereby acting as a regulatory force. This regulatory potential has considerable practical value because – as we shall see later in detail – it allows people to achieve goals that they may previously have seen as too distant or unmanageable. In addition, and what is particularly important from the perspective of the current book, this regulatory force has significant theoretical and empirical relevance in the light of the challenges posed by the potential unpredictability in researching complex systems.

As expressed in several papers within this anthology, the problem of unpredictability is one of the key issues at the heart of the ongoing struggle to find viable templates for researching complex dynamic systems (cf. Dörnyei, 2014; Lemke & Sabelli, 2008). Once a system's behaviour is deemed to be unpredictable, any methodical investigation of it carries the danger of being considered pointless; after all, what general principles can be deduced from an unpredictable situation? A key tenet of complex dynamic systems (CDS) theory encapsulates this predicament by stating that because systems differ in their initial conditions (see Verspoor, this volume), their future behaviour cannot be consistently predicted on the basis of prior experiences or other similar practices. In other words, we cannot rely on analogies or replicability as guiding principles when trying to deduce how a situation will unfold or what impact a certain factor will cause. Sometimes the overall operation and movement of the system will follow the direction that we would expect as based on past practices, but at other times the fluctuation of system behaviour and the manifold interferences among the system components will result in unique, unexpected patterns and produce indeterminate future outcomes (Larsen-Freeman & Cameron, 2008; Verspoor, this volume).

In an attempt to offer a solution to this potential limitation for research, Dörnyei (2014) has outlined three possible pathways that may allow for the meaningful and systematic study of motivational dynamics: (a) focusing on strong attractor-governed phenomena that regulate the system, (b) focusing on conglomerates of system components in the system's attractor basin that act as wholes and have a pervasive impact, and (c) analysing typical outcome patters in a retrodictive manner (i.e. 'retrodictive qualitative modelling'; see Chan *et al.*, this volume). The rationale for including the current chapter among the conceptual discussions in this book is our belief that the notion of a DMC is associated with a further area where system behaviour is predictable enough to provide a window of opportunity for meaningful research to take place. In order to demonstrate this potential utilisation of DMCs, let us begin by offering a description of their make-up and theoretical underpinnings.

The Unique Nature of Directed Motivational Currents

A DMC is a unique phenomenon; individuals experiencing a DMC are often aware that they are functioning at a heightened state of productivity and are able to perform with increased intensity, over and above what they may have believed possible (for more comprehensive summaries of this novel motivational concept, see Dörnyei et al., 2014; Muir & Dörnyei, 2013).Once a motivational current is initiated, it can transport an individual forward towards a goal at a startling velocity, not unlike the Gulf Stream or the East Australian Current (the latter vividly portrayed in the animated film *Finding Nemo* as an oceanic 'superhighway'). The contrast between the dependable flow of such underlying currents and the inherently temporary nature of waves in an ocean has been described by Peter MacIntyre (2012) as follows:

> The power and beauty of the Atlantic provide two key concepts, waves and currents, that I hope will be useful metaphors for understanding individual differences among language learners. On the one hand, waves roll along, rising and falling seemingly at random, cresting and crashing on the shore, only to retreat and be replaced by the next wave. On the other hand, currents exist beneath the surface of the water; the warm waters of the Gulf Stream, always moving dependably up the Atlantic seaboard from the eastern coast of Florida, help to moderate the climate for Cape Breton Island. (MacIntyre, 2012: 12)

Thus, currents differ from the 'surface variability' of the waves, which are 'here and then they are gone' (MacIntyre, 2012: 13), as the former represent 'long-lasting, deep-running, broad pathways of movement' (MacIntyre, 2012). It is important to note at this point, however, that we do not equate a DMC with any motivational current or trait in general; we conceive it as a unique period of heightened motivation that is set into motion by the combination of a number of factors in the pursuit of a specific goal or vision (see below). It is for this reason we apply the modifier '*directed*' to this motivational current. The concept is in some ways akin to Csikszentmihalyi's (1988) 'flow experience' but differs from this state of total absorption in several key features, most notably in that flow focuses on a person's involvement in a single task that is intrinsically rewarding (autotelic), whereas a

DMC involves a prolonged process of engagement in a series of tasks that are rewarding primarily because they transport the individual towards a highly valued end (a point we shall come back to later). Although DMCs are not particularly frequent, most people are likely to be able to identify occurrences of DMCs in their own history, or in that of a family member or friend, who may, for example, have become devoted to an activity and, in order to achieve a clear objective, acquired a reasonable level of expertise in a surprisingly short length of time. In educational settings, a DMC may be found within a high-school student's intense preparation for a maths competition, in a group of students' deciding to put on a drama performance at school and giving the rehearsals top priority in their lives, or in the initiation of a school campaign to support a charity or other public cause. All these instances involve the establishing of a momentum towards a goal that becomes dominant in the participants' life for a period of time, and which allows both self and observers to clearly sense the presence of a powerful drive pushing action forwards.

As we shall describe in more detail, the power of a DMC is created through the combination of a clear *vision* and a matching *action structure*, the latter involving a powerful launch and subsequent steady onward progression. This progression is scaffolded by sets of *behavioural routines* (e.g. regular amounts of time spent on a task) and *proximal subgoals* (i.e. shorter-term targets that structure action and cause satisfaction when achieved). In a DMC, the combination of these factors fuels the motivational current and enables it to become almost self-propelling, with people adapting their daily life to accommodate the surge as they become caught up in the wealth of possibilities suddenly on offer.

From a CDS perspective, the alignment of various personal and contextual factors in the directional current of a DMC offers a window for systematic research into motivational dynamics. Of course, in line with the principles of dynamic systems behaviour, no matter how powerful a DMC is, it cannot offer perfect predictability. Once the main goal has been achieved the current will cease, sometimes with a decrease of energy towards the end owing to an understanding that the goal is within one's grasp (cf. Locke, 1996), or with a final flurry to complete the mission before time is up. Although there remains a long way for future research to go in describing what causes DMCs to occur and on what factors their strength and duration depend, certain key elements of the process can be delineated; let us look more closely at four of the main components; *generating parameters, goal/vision-orientedness*, the *salient facilitative structure* and *positive emotionality*.

Generating parameters

A DMC occurs when a combination of contextual, personal and time factors come together in a unique and highly productive manner, resulting in the *launch* of the process. There is anecdotal evidence to suggest that sometimes the absence of a seemingly minor element might hold up the launch of a DMC, which is often only realised when the element materialises and suddenly the whole scheme comes to life. In many cases, specific *triggering stimuli* play an important role in initiating the launch, such as an opportunity for action (e.g. an event or a race), a piece of new information (e.g. an offer from the local gym) or a specific call (e.g. a campaign call or the setting of a school assignment). The effectiveness of any trigger depends on the interplay of a whole host of relevant factors involved in the system; this is a recognised phenomenon in CDS theories, the fact that even a small action can potentially initiate a disproportionately large effect often referred to as the 'butterfly effect'.

From a pedagogical perspective, we believe that the practical significance of a DMC lies in the fact that the motivational surge can also be intentionally generated through the provision of a framework and a set of conditions that can function as a facilitative blueprint. In educational settings, organisational frameworks of this type can include well-designed language learning tasks, longer-term projects or even study-abroad experiences. A successful language learning task (e.g. Ellis, 2003), when involving personalised goals and being pursued with vigorous motivation, can be seen as the simplest form of a DMC. A well-designed project (e.g. Stoller, 2002) can also act as a trigger owing to the fact that projects are inherently directed towards distinct outcomes and provide opportunities for ongoing autonomous – that is, student-owned – involvement along the way. Finally, a period of study abroad (e.g. Freed, 1995) can exemplify an instance of a prolonged DMC, characterised by strong dedication over time around an elaborately structured framework.

Goal/vision-orientedness

The most salient feature of a DMC is its *directional nature*; such a powerful motivational drive cannot happen without a well-defined goal, target or outcome that can provide cohesion for one's efforts and help focus energy on final goal achievement. The directional nature of a DMC is clearly manifested throughout its entire duration, a characteristic that distinguishes it from other actions displaying high motivation that are pursued not so much to reach a specific end-goal, as for the sake of enjoyment. The directional aspect also explains why *vision* constitutes a key factor in DMCs. Technically speaking, goals and vision represent similar directional intentions to reach future states; however there is a fundamental difference between the two concepts. Dörnyei and Kubanyiova (2014) explain that a vision, unlike a goal, includes a strong sensory element in the form of tangible images related to goal achievement. Thus, for example, the vision to become a doctor is made up of the goal of obtaining a medical degree *plus* the (imaginary) sensory experience of *being* a doctor, both accompanied by potent anticipatory emotions primed by this future state (cf. MacIntyre & Gregersen, 2012). We believe that the intensity of a DMC is dependent on the addition of this visionary aspect to the guiding goal.

Salient, facilitative structure

A DMC has a distinctive structure that plays a crucial role in facilitating the progress of motivated behaviour. Broadly speaking, the success of a DMC depends on the successful match of a targeted goal/vision with an adequately tailored pathway, allowing the individual to envisage a clear route to success. What, however, does 'adequately tailored' mean in this context? To begin, a critical first phase of the DMC structure is its *starting point*; a DMC cannot simply drift into being, but must be consciously and explicitly launched. Once this launch has occurred, the 'current' of the DMC takes over, and continued motivated behaviour is sustained through the inclusion of a number of regular *subgoals*, serving both as proxy targets and as criteria to evaluate and confirm progress. This represents the second required component of a successful DMC pathway: a series of regular *progress checks* offering affirmative feedback, such as the daily stepping on the scales during a strictly controlled diet, or the recurring self-assessment task in an online language learning programme. These subgoals divide long-term progression into 'digestible chunks', the successful completion of which both marks progress and, importantly, fuels further action.

A third criterion for adequacy is the existence of recurring *behavioural routines*, that is to say regular, fixed divisions of action, such as the going to the gym every evening or the learning of ten new vocabulary items every day. These behavioural routines create a sort of 'motivational autopilot' – they become an integral part of the DMC experience owing to the fact that each step is performed without exercising volitional control; in fact, not following this new routine would seem odd, and potentially even lead to feelings of dissatisfaction or guilt.

In sum, the salient structure of a DMC is more than merely a framework for progress; it is tailored for a specific individual in pursuit of a specific vision and, if successful, it becomes instrumental in generating and maintaining a great deal of the energy involved in fuelling action. In other words, the structure takes an active and procedural role in keeping the current flowing and, thus, forms an integral part of the motivational core of a DMC. In this sense, the behavioural outworking of a DMC – that is, the actual pathway that channels the initial momentum into action – becomes an integral part of the theoretical construct. This represents a marked difference from most motivational concepts described in the literature, which do not have an integrated behavioural dimension. Accordingly, we suggest that understanding the key structural elements of this pathway – as well as the impact of any variation within it – will form a crucial future research area into DMCs.

Positive emotionality

As discussed earlier, a DMC is characterised by a clear perception of prog-ress towards a desired target, with the resulting sense of fulfilment leading to positive emotionality associated with the process. However, this latter enjoy-ment is not necessarily intrinsic in the sense that the sheer performance of the behaviours involved in the task is perceived as pleasurable. Rather, the enjoyment is projected from the overall emotional loading of the target vision; it is as if each step along the way reproduces – or becomes permeated with – some of the joy linked to the overall journey. An illustration of this would be the explorer who finds every new step into the unknown thrilling in spite of the often considerable physical challenges. In this sense, the positive emotion-ality characterising DMCs is related to 'eudaimonic well-being' (e.g. Ryan & Deci, 2001; Ryff, 2013), a term that was first introduced by Aristotle and which is currently used widely in positive psychology to refer to personal wellness as distinct from happiness per se. It is linked to a sense of actualis-ing one's potential or the fulfilment of one's mission, as opposed to a simple giddy state of happiness or the experience of pleasure. Because a DMC always involves a personal journey that is central to the sense of self, it can activate and utilise this deeper meaning of eudaimonic satisfaction and joy.

As a consequence of this radiated positive disposition, activities that a person previously considered boring or tedious can suddenly become pleasant and enjoyable when part of the DMC process; because they are perceived as being conducive to the accomplishment of the higher purpose, they are thus seen as congruent with one's deep-seated values. At times like this, as Waterman (1993) summarises, the eudaimonic experiences of an activity are associated with:

> (a) an unusually intense involvement in an undertaking, (b) a feeling of a special fit or meshing with an activity that is not characteristic of most daily tasks, (c) a feeling of intensely being alive, (d) a feeling of being complete or fulfilled while engaged in an activity, (e) an impression that this is what the person was meant to do, and (f) a feeling that this is who one really is. (Waterman, 1993: 679)

As Waterman continues, particularly those activities will give rise to eudaimonic feelings in which the individual realises personal potential 'in the form of the development of one's skills and talents, the advancement of one's purposes in living, or both' (Waterman, 1993: 679). These are exactly the primary domains where DMCs operate, and the fact that DMCs have the capacity to project positive emotionality to all the stages of the progress they represent is a particularly powerful feature; it serves, in effect, as a regu-lator of affect as it eliminates unpredictable shifts in behaviour caused by emotional fluctuation.

DMCs as a New Motivational Framework

As already mentioned, a DMC is a novel conceptualisation. The reason why such a potent phenomenon has not been explicitly recognised in past research is chiefly related to the limited temporal focus of most established motivation constructs. For example, a lot has been written about the impact of various goal related dispositions on human action, but no mainstream motivation theory has taken the step of linking such dispositions with specific behavioural processes *over time* in an attempt to examine how optimal combinations of certain structural features of the behavioural pathway can amplify the overall motivational energy released. Yet, although the concept has not been previously identified, discrete elements of the DMC phenomenon have been the subject of extensive theorising. Four of the most prominent theoretical links in this respect include the following.

- *Goal-setting theory.* We have already discussed the fact that the goal-setting process (Latham & Locke, 1991) is a necessary element for any DMC, and that the DMC pathway requires a series of regular *subgoals* to serve as both proxy targets (Latham & Seijts, 1999) and a source of affirmative feedback. Goal-setting theory also provides a meaningful account of the mechanism by which goals affect overall performance in terms of focused direction and effort, persistence and strategy development. Furthermore, satisfaction in goal-setting theory is not seen as the outcome of engagement itself, but as the result of successful progress made towards goals; this is evident in the DMC mechanism of perceiving on-task engagement as being rewarding irrespective of the nature of the activity.
- *Flow theory.* Similar to DMCs, Csikszentmihalyi's (1988) flow experience features directed concentration, full engagement, high interest, clear feedback and goal-orientedness. However, whereas flow is mainly concerned with absorption in short-term, single tasks, the duration of a DMC can span longer – yet still finite – periods of time. In some ways, therefore, DMCs can be seen as the temporal expansion of the flow mechanism through the addition of a sustainable temporal and behavioural structure to the one-off flow experience. It is crucial to note, however, that the two processes display a fundamental difference in addition to the temporal issue; the enjoyment in flow is solely intrinsic, whereas, as discussed above, the positive emotional loading in a DMC does not necessarily stem from the enjoyment in the activity per se, but rather from the awareness that the targeted goal is being approached. This is, however, not to say that flow experiences may not occur while a DMC is in progress.
- *Future time perspective.* This theoretical approach in mainstream psychology (e.g. Zimbardo & Boyd, 1999) has gained increasing momentum over the past decade. It concerns an individual's general disposition towards,

and their personal understanding of, time; more specifically, it concerns whether one's thinking tends to focus on the past, the present or the future. Temporal focus is particularly relevant for DMCs, as it has been repeatedly shown that future-oriented students – that is, students who ascribe higher valence to goals in the distant future – tend to be more persistent and obtain better academic results in the present (e.g. Kauffman & Husman, 2004). This tendency of future-oriented individuals to look ahead and set future goals in order to overcome the complexities of their present learning environment is a valuable link with the DMC process.

- *Self-determination theory.* While we believe that DMCs may be externally facilitated, the generation of a DMC is only possible if an individual takes full ownership of the targeted goal and the action sequence that leads to it. This creates a strong link with self-determination theory (Deci & Ryan, 1985), which states that any meaningful engagement with an activity must be self-regulated, self-determined and autonomous (Ryan & Deci, 2000; cf. Murray *et al.*, 2011). The theory offers a detailed discussion of autonomous engagement with tasks as well as of the psychological nutrients that the social context of the task needs to supply, which is invaluable for our understanding of what is needed in order for a DMC to occur. In addition, the question of how extrinsic motives can be internalised by the learner – which has become an important aspect of self-determination theory – has special relevance for the designing of conditions whereby a DMC may be artificially induced.

Conclusion

A DMC is a potent motivational surge that emerges from the alignment of a number of personal, temporal and contextual factors/parameters, creating momentum to pursue an individually defined future goal/vision that is personally significant and emotionally satisfying. The experience of a DMC carries with it the excitement of journeying down a 'motivational highway' towards new pastures; thus, it can be seen as vision-led self-regulation along a fitting, made-to-measure pathway that augments and sustains exerted effort. Most people will have encountered a DMC at some point in their lives – the phenomenon occurs in numerous guises within the social world. DMCs have been used to transform individuals, groups and situations that have lost their 'zest' or lacked a clear future vision, by offering a pathway of intensive motivated action. If a DMC is successfully launched, people – and even organisations – can become caught up in it and can move on to new levels of existence or operation.

From the perspective of researching CDS, the significance of the generated motivational surge of a DMC lies in its capacity to align diverse factors, to override various obstacles and to regulate emotional fluctuation. Once a DMC has commenced, the main parameters of its movement and its aimed-for outcomes become, to a large extent, predictable. This is not unlike the launch of a rocket that, after take-off, will follow a set path as determined by the conditions surroundings its launch. It is in this sense that a DMC can function as a regulator of human motivation and activity; it has the potential, if only for a limited time, to override the complexity and chaos of the surrounding world and to channel behaviour down a goal-specific course of action. The resultant steadfast stream of system behaviour can be described in a systematic manner, providing a vital opportunity for research. In other words, DMCs offer us not only the possibility to tap into vast hidden resources of motivational power, but also a window for systematic research in our chaotic world.

Of course, every silver lining is linked to a cloud. Owing to the emergent nature of DMCs, it may not be an easy task for researchers to identify such processes at their inception, or as they develop, and thus be able to 'ride along with the wave' as the DMC progresses up until the point where the energy dissipates. The more practical solution may be conducting post hoc investigations, which, however, raises the question of how far we can go by relying exclusively on retrospective accounts. A viable alternative would be to induce DMCs in laboratory conditions, but an obvious drawback of this option is that such experiments usually involve short-term action, which would seriously restrict the length and type of DMCs examined. Admittedly, we face challenges, but there is also a lot to gain – the DMC phenomenon might turn out to be a basic ingredient in understanding human motivation and achievement in general.

References

Csikszentmihalyi, M. (1988) Introduction. In M. Csikszentmihalyi and I.S. Csikszentmihalyi (eds) *Optimal Experience: Psychological Studies of Flow in Consciousness* (pp. 3–14). Cambridge: Cambridge University Press.

Deci, E.L. and Ryan, R.M. (1985) *Intrinsic Motivation and Self-determination in Human Behaviour.* New York: Plenum.

Dörnyei, Z. (2014) Researching complex dynamic systems: 'Retrodictive qualitative modelling' in the language classroom. *Language Teaching* 47 (1) 80–91.

Dörnyei, Z. and Kubanyiova, M. (2014) *Motivating Learners, Motivating Teachers: Building Vision in the Language Classroom.* Cambridge: Cambridge University Press.

Dörnyei, Z., Muir, C. and Ibrahim, Z. (2014) 'Directed motivational currents': Energising language learning through creating intense motivational pathways. In D. Lasagabaster, A. Doiz and J.M. Sierra (eds) *Motivation and Second Language Learning: From Theory to Practice* (pp. 10–42). Amsterdam: John Benjamins.

Ellis, R. (2003) *Task-based Language Learning and Teaching.* Oxford: Oxford University Press.

Freed, B.F. (1995) Introduction: Language learning and study abroad. In B.F. Freed (ed.) *Second Language Acquisition in a Study Abroad Context* (pp. 1–33). Amsterdam: John Benjamins Publishing.

Kauffman, D.F. and Husman, J. (2004) Effects of time perspective on student motivation: Introduction to a special issue. *Educational Psychology Review* 16 (1), 1–7.

Larsen-Freeman, D. and Cameron, L. (2008) *Complex Systems and Applied Linguistics.* Oxford: Oxford University Press.

Latham, G.P. and Locke, E.A. (1991) Self-regulation through goal setting. *Organizational behavior and human decision processes* 50 (2), 212–247.

Latham, G.P. and Seijts, G.H. (1999) The effects of proximal and distal goals on performance on a moderately complex task. *Journal of Organizational Behavior* 20 (4), 421–429.

Lemke, J.L. and Sabelli, N.H. (2008) Complex systems and educational change: Towards a new research agenda. *Educational Philosophy and Theory* 40 (1), 118–129.

Locke, E.A. (1996) Motivation through conscious goal setting. *Applied and Preventive Psychology* 5 (2), 117–124.

MacIntyre, P.D. (2012) Currents and waves: Examining willingness to communicate on multiple timescales. *Contact (TESL Ontario) Magazine* 38 (2), 12–22.

MacIntyre, P.D. and Gregersen, T. (2012) Emotions that facilitate language learning: The positive-broadening power of the imagination. *Studies in Second Language Learning and Teaching* 2 (2), 193–213.

Muir, C. and Dörnyei, Z. (2013) Directed motivational currents: Using vision to create effective motivational pathways. *Studies in Second Language Learning and Teaching* 3 (3), 357–375.

Murray, G., Gao, X. and Lamb, T. (eds) (2011) *Identity, Motivation and Autonomy in Language Learning.* Bristol: Multilingual Matters.

Ryan, R.M. and Deci, E.L. (2000) Self-determination theory and the facilitation of intrinsic motivation, social development, and well-being. *American Psychologist* 55 (1), 68–78.

Ryan, R.M. and Deci, E.L. (2001) On happiness and human potentials: A review of research on hedonic and eudaimonic well-being. *Annual Review of Psychology* 52 (1), 141–166.

Ryff, C.D. (2013) Eudaimonic well-being and health: Mapping consequences of self-realization. In A.S. Waterman (ed.) *The Best Within Us: Positive Psychology Perspectives on Eudaimonia* (pp. 77–89). Washington, DC: American Psychological Association.

Stoller, F.L. (2002) Project work: A means to promote language and content. In J.C. Richards and W.A. Renandya (eds) *Methodology in Language Teaching: An Anthology of Current Practice* (pp. 107–118). Cambridge: Cambridge University Press.

Waterman, A.S. (1993) Two conceptions of happiness: Contrast of personal expressiveness (eudaimonia) and hedonic enjoyment. *Journal of Personality and Social Psychology* 64 (4), 678–691.

Zimbardo, P.G. and Boyd, J.N. (1999) Putting time in perspective: A valid, reliable, individual-differences metric. *Journal of Personality and Social Psychology* 77 (6), 1271–1288.

Part 2
Empirical Studies

11 Motivation on a Per-Second Timescale: Examining Approach–Avoidance Motivation During L2 Task Performance

Peter D. MacIntyre and Alicia Serroul

Examining motivation from a dynamic perspective just might be an *embarrasse de riches*. There certainly are a number of conceptual and methodological challenges presented by a dynamic perspective (de Bot *et al.*, 2007; Howe & Lewis, 2005; Poupore, 2013); the chapters in this volume show that research is beginning to work out some problems even as other challenges reveal themselves. New understandings of motivation processes can be gained by examining real people interacting with language in real time. The dynamic approach taken in the present study looks at the motivation process up-close, as it unfolds within a set of language tasks. If prior research has taken a snapshot of the effects of motivation in order to examine relationships among variables (see Dörnyei, 2005; Gardner, 1985, 2010), the present method is more like studying a series of short films, where actors improvise their performances while being recorded on video (MacIntyre, 2012). Our approach in the present study uses a novel, idiodynamic methodology to capture fluctuations in approach/avoidance tendencies that lie at the core of motivation.

In general, motivation can be defined as the force that gives behaviour its energy and direction (Reeve, 2009). Perhaps the most basic motivational tendency is to either approach or to avoid an object, another person or an activity (Eder *et al.*, 2013). The strength of particular approach and avoidance trajectories varies over time as both the person and the circumstances change, but basic tendencies to either approach or avoid can be found in low level brain-based processes (Gray, 1982; Gray & McNaughton, 2000; Gray *et al.*, 2000). The neurobiological physiology of the individual is reflected in activation of the behavioural inhibition system (BIS), which puts the brakes on behaviour in certain types of situations. The BIS functions to restrain action by increasing sensitivity to punishment (Amodio *et al.*, 2008; Carver & White, 1994; Gray & McNaughton, 2000). The behavioural activation system (BAS) has the opposite function, easing restraints on action and moving the person toward desirable goals, heightening the sensitivity to various types of rewards. Both systems influence ongoing behaviour, with approach and avoidance tendencies operating in concert, but somewhat independently, as behaviour unfolds in real time (see for example the Epstein & Fenz (1965) classic study of skydivers). The ongoing negotiation between the relative strengths of the approach and avoidance tendencies gives motivation its phenomenological quality (such as 'This task sounds interesting' vs. 'I don't want any part of this task') We tend to approach people, objects and situations that are interesting, desirable, attractive, enjoyable and so on; we tend to avoid threats, signs of danger and items that are unpleasant. (There also is a vast array of items that are ignored because they do not activate either an approach or avoidance system). We feel a conflicted state of ambivalence when both approach and avoidance tendencies are strong at the same time (see MacIntyre, 2007). Research in the literature on second language acquisition (SLA) has yet to consider motivation from such a nitty-gritty perspective.

Much of the previous research on motivation in SLA has been associated with either (1) Gardner's Integrative Motive or (2) Dörnyei's second language (L2) Self System. The integrative motive generally proposes that language learning is energized by positive attitudes toward the target language group, emotional engagement and a willingness to invest effort in learning (Gardner, 1985, 2010; MacIntyre *et al.*, 2009; Masgoret & Gardner, 2003). The other principal conceptual scheme is the L2 Motivational Self System, composed of: the ideal L2 self, the ought-to L2 self and the L2 learning experience (Dörnyei, 2005). The ideal self reflects a future-oriented vision of what a learner might like to be, including speaking a new language and interacting with others who also speak the language, and has consistently been shown to correlate with measures of language learning (see Csizér & Kormos, 2009; Dörnyei & Chan, 2013; Henry, 2009; Magid & Chan, 2012). The ought-to self 'concerns the attributes that one believes one ought to possess to meet expectations and to avoid possible negative outcomes' (Dörnyei, 2009a: 29), but correlations with language learning criterion variables have been inconsistent and difficult to interpret (Dörnyei, 2009a). The third dimension of the L2 self system, L2 learning experience, is conceptualized at a different level than the other two components (Dörnyei, 2005). L2 learning experience reflects situated, executive control over behaviour in a specific situation. Of the three components of the L2 self-system, L2 learning experience is the least well studied (Dörnyei, 2009a; Dörnyei & Chan, 2013) but likely the most relevant to ongoing task performance (see Waninge, this volume) and to the call for studies of motivation in language education (Crookes & Schmidt, 1991; Dörnyei, 1990). In the present study, we will examine whether respondents mention thinking about integrative motives or components of the L2 self system during task performance.

In general, dynamic fluctuations in motivation during a task occur as a response to a variety of cognitive, metacognitive and affective experiences related to the context, familiarity and situational demands of the task (Poupore, 2013). Features of the situation trigger the person's level of interest or boredom in the task (Ainley *et al.*, 2002). Curiosity about missing elements (Litman, 2005), surprising events and new information (Teigen & Keren, 2002) also can trigger increasing interest in the task. Not surprisingly, feeling motivated to continue effort at a task or to conclude the task has been associated with how confident or satisfied individuals feel about the correctness of their response (Efklides, 2002). Vohs *et al.* (2013) found that self-affirmation along with the experience of failure lead to demotivation and effort reduction, not only on current tasks, but also on new but related tasks. The sequencing of task-related success or failure might be especially relevant to changing levels of motivation as a series of tasks unfolds over time.

Dörnyei's (2009b) proposal to consider a dynamic systems account of task motivation eschews prior conceptualization of task motives as a combination of general and situation-specific (Julkunen, 1989, 2001; Tremblay *et al.*, 1995). Instead, building prior research into the dynamics of task motivation, Dörnyei (2009b: 1) suggested that each task 'activates a number of different motivational contingencies, resulting in dynamic motivational processes underlying task completion'. At the core of a dynamic account of task motivation are appraisal processes. Dörnyei and Tseng (2009: 119) define task appraisal as 'the learner's continuous processing of the multitude of contextual stimuli regarding one's progress, including comparisons with predicted or hoped-for progress or with performance that alternative action sequences would offer'. Appraisals have been well established in the literature on the cognitive processes underlying motivation (Arnold, 1960; Frijda, 1986; Lazarus, 1991, 1999; Lazarus & Folkman, 1987). Lazarus and Folkman (1987) identify a primary appraisal of 'what is at stake' that generates a basic approach or avoidance tendency, which is modified by secondary appraisals of one's coping ability. Schumann's (1999) more elaborate model considers five dimensions of appraisals: novelty, pleasantness, significance of goals/needs, coping potential and self/social image. Appraisals are ongoing, continuous processes that are modified on a second-by-second timescale and are a key process in generating emotional reactions.

Timescales in Motivation

Adopting a dynamic approach to motivation means directly and explicitly addressing the issue of timescales (see de Bot, this volume). Dörnyei (2003: 18) commented:

> I have now come to believe that many of the controversies and disagreements in L2 motivation research go back to an insufficient temporal awareness ... that different or even contradictory theories do not exclude one another, but may simply be related to different phases of the motivated behavioural process.

The two most prevalent concepts in the existing literature on SLA motivation adopt a timescale of months and years. The integrative motive (Gardner, 1985, 2010) can be considered a long-term motive reflecting the learner's willingness to approach the target language group, meet and communicate with members of the group and take on characteristics associated with them, including the language they speak. This process can take years to fully engage as one builds the linguistic competence to communicate in authentic situations. Similarly, the L2 self (Dörnyei, 2005, 2009a) reflects the learner's aspirations for language learning in the form of long-term future-oriented visions of personal achievement, possible experiences and sustained trends in identity development. In addition, Dörnyei's ought-to L2 self has been used to suggest a motive emerging from a long-term sense of obligation (for example, obligations to parents and teachers, Henry, 2009; Papi, 2010). But it is also possible to add a new timescale to the conceptualization of the ought-to L2 self. Specifically the ought-to L2 self might refer to a near-term obligation to perform actions related to language learning, especially those that are not intrinsically interesting, and a metacognitive appraisal of what one should be able to do in a given situation. This more immediate sense of the ought-to self can be linked more closely to task motives (see Julkunen, 2001) than has been done in past research (see Poupore, 2013), reflecting ways in which motivation rises or falls as different types of tasks are appraised on an ongoing basis.

Motivation, Emotion and Cognition on a Second-by-second Timescale

Despite calls for a dynamic approach to the study of motivation in general, and task motivation in particular, it is notable that studies have not examined the moment-by-moment fluctuations of motivation in the here-and-now. Dörnyei (2002: 156) suggested that 'motivation is never static but is constantly increasing or decreasing depending on the various social influences surrounding action, the learner's appraisal of these influences and the action control operations the learner carries out on such motivational content'. Unfortunately, motivation itself was not measured dynamically by Dörnyei (2002). Indeed, previous SLA research offers little concept of how motivation changes on a second-by-second timescale, or how to study those changes. Dörnyei and Tseng (2009) suggest that research should explore the links among L2 task motivation, noticing and the self-evaluation process.

Concepts in complex dynamic systems (CDS) theory present a toolbox with which to examine task motivation on a second-by-second timescale. The emphasis in CDS theories is on nonlinearity as systems interact and influence one another, for example as various systems are recruited to respond to a specific communication task (Fogel, 2006). With native language communication, the ongoing process of listening to another person, thinking, choosing vocabulary and assembling grammatical utterances are integrated rather seamlessly most of the time. In L2 learning and communication situations, cultural variations and developing language skills present a long list of additional challenges to the communication process. Sudden loss of meaning can create a jarring effect on both learning and communication. When one does not understand what another person is saying, or cannot recall the vocabulary or grammar to say what's on one's mind, the sense-appropriate timing of oral communication is disrupted. Such situations can be considered repeller states that a person will seek to escape quickly; Gudykunst (1995) called them 'catastrophe points' in L2 communication. As communicative difficulties unfold over a few seconds or less, the cognitive systems engage to search for words and meaning while affective systems also engage emotional reactions (such as anxiety) that can interfere with the cognitive system (Eysenck, 1979; MacIntyre & Gardner, 1991, 1994). As seemingly endless seconds pass, the personality tendencies of the learner – that predispose her/him to persevere (such as conscientiousness, Goldberg, 1992) or to give up (such as volatility, Kuhl, 1991) – interact with social systems of conversation that include politeness and face-saving strategies that can hold a leaner in place for an uncomfortable length of time. These situations can create a brief 'soft assembly' of contradictory cognitions and emotions that would not be thought of as compatible most of the time (MacIntyre & Legatto, 2011). High levels of motivation, plus high anxiety, plus intense effort, plus frustration is not a sustainable state in the long run.

The emergent phenomenological quality of communicative difficulties is uncomfortable and avoidant – rarely do people want to struggle in this way. But there is a general acceptance that language learners must communicate in the L2, to talk in order to learn (MacIntyre et al., 2003; Skehan, 1989), using a tongue that is not their own (MacIntyre, 2007). Therefore, ambivalent situations occur in SLA and are both tolerated and expected by learners. The literature on motivation in SLA has not dealt well with ambivalence, possibly because it has not integrated motivation, emotion and ongoing cognition on a dynamic basis.

Adopting a dynamic perspective allows us to draw the concept of motivation closer to a key cognitive process underlying communication: choosing what to say and how to say it. In the literature on native language communication, Greene (1984, 1989, 1997, 2006; Greene & Cappella, 1986; Greene et al., 2000) proposed action assembly theory to explain how individuals generate and produce both verbal and nonverbal behaviours. The theory proposes that two key processes underlie how we choose what we say: activation and assembly. The activation process makes use of procedural records, cognitive representations of action, and outcome and situational features that vary in level of abstraction. Procedural records are stored in long-term memory, offering information about what to expect in specific situational contexts, based on experience. Procedural records of action and situational features will be activated if they are relevant and are strong enough to exceed a threshold. Following activation, the assembly process begins. This process organizes the activated procedural records into a larger behavioural complex, where the specifications for action are created. Features are activated and assembled into a complex form called an output representation (Greene, 1995), which includes procedural records matching the relevant goal and situational context of the individual. Procedural records are enacted if they are appropriate in context, decaying back to a baseline state if not enacted. The cognitive process of assembly usually runs smoothly and in the background. However, problems can and do arise when action features do not fit well together. This is especially likely to occur in situations where a person is using a non-native language that has not yet been mastered.

In second-generation action assembly theory, Greene (1997) introduced the idea of coalition formation. Coalition formation is the term given to the process whereby appropriate features are joined together to produce action; similar to the assembly process in the original action assembly theory (Greene, 1997; Greene et al., 2000). The processes of activation and coalition formation run in parallel, meaning that a number of features are activated, while at the same time a number of coalitions are operating. It takes only a fraction of a second for action features to be activated and to decay back to their resting level (Greene, 1997; Greene et al., 2000). If the ongoing assessment of competence during a communication event is considered in conjunction with the action assembly process, research may be better able to examine the links between communicative performance on the one hand and dynamic (rising and falling) perceptions of approach/avoidance motivation on the other hand, in real time.

We propose here that part of the process that modifies coalitions as we talk with other people is a self-assessment process, essentially a check on how well we are doing as events quickly unfold. Gray (1982) described the operation of the septo-hippocampal circuit in the brain as a check on whether events surrounding us are unfolding as expected ('okay-mode') or not unfolding as expected ('not-okay mode'). In the not-okay mode, the hippocampus triggers an arousal reaction that leads to coping. In part, this reaction can be perceived as anxiety or apprehension that 'something is wrong'. McNaughton and Corr show that the decisions associated with coping responses occur extremely quickly:

> It should also be noted that the time course for decision making will be very swift, of the order of tens of milliseconds, while that for arousal is necessarily slow with autonomic and hormonal actions having latencies of the order of seconds. (McNaughton & Corr, 2004: 299)

In this way, the ongoing checking on whether events are 'okay' or 'not-okay' complements the action assembly process wherein coalitions (the wording of utterances and how to perform them) are built.

If L2 communication takes an unexpected, not-okay turn, the focus rapidly shifts to coping efforts and assembly of new coalitions, under a building sense of time pressure. Within a few seconds, if the communication has not been repaired in a manner that returns the speaker to the okay-state, one would expect emotional arousal to increase and avoidance motivation to engage. In this manner, cognitive difficulties in the L2 activate the physiological fight-flight-or-freeze response (McNaughton & Corr, 2004), generating distracting, self-related cognition. Thoughts associated with avoidant motivation in this context will be evidenced by face-saving attempts to cope with difficulties to keep communication going, such as nonverbal displays to compensate for missing vocabulary, or ways to escape from the L2, such as temporarily code switching to the L1, or finally disengaging from the communication topic. The underlying process of cognition, emotion and adaptation can have a profound effect on interpersonal communication because it disrupts the exchange of information and the exquisite timing of speech (Allen, 1973; Boutsen et al., 2000). Perhaps it goes without saying, but from a motivation perspective, the 'not-okay' mode is closely related to avoidance and the 'okay' mode to approach tendencies.

The present study uses an idiodynamic approach to examine the degree of fluctuation in approach/avoidance motivation as time moves along and L2 communication task demands change. The idiodynamic method (MacIntyre, 2012; MacIntyre & Legatto, 2011) is a recently developed mixed methods approach to studying communication processes by recording a series of communication tasks and asking the respondent to rate and explain fluctuations in his or her affective reactions. Eight specific L2 communication tasks, in the form of an oral interview, allow us to dynamically examine motivation. Prior to undertaking the tasks, participants completed a questionnaire measure of personality traits, integrative motivation and the can-do measure of expected task performance. In a laboratory setting, eight of the can-do tasks were completed in the L2 as the respondent was videotaped. Following the responses, the respondent watched and rated their video for changes in motivation. Immediately after ratings were completed, respondents were interviewed and asked to describe the reasons for peaks and valleys in their ratings of motivation during the eight tasks.

The focus of this study is intra-individual, with a goal of building toward a tentative model of relevant interacting cognitive and affective components that contribute to the L2 communication system. In doing so, this procedure will address three specific research questions:

> RQ1: Do participants have a generally positive or negative reaction to the tasks and is there much variability in the idiodynamic ratings of motivation across the tasks? If so, what factors are associated with increasing and decreasing motivation?
>
> RQ2: At the individual level of analysis, do pre-test approach/avoidance ratings for specific tasks show any correlation with idiodynamically recorded approach/avoidance ratings as the corresponding task unfolds?
>
> RQ3: In the qualitative analysis of the interviews, do the respondents discuss fluctuations in their motivation using concepts related to integrative motivation (Gardner, 2010), task motivation (Julkunen, 2001), the ideal self, the ought-to self, L2 learning experience (Dörnyei, 2009a) and/or motivation from the unique experimental situation?

Method

Participants

The sample consisted of 12 undergraduate students from Cape Breton University. Half of the participants reported considering themselves 'French speakers' and none of them spoke languages other than English and French. Only one of the participants previously had lived in a French community. All of the participants had taken regular French classes and nine of the 12 had French immersion education experience. There were nine females and three males who participated in this study. The ages of participants varied from 19 to 22 years.

Materials

Can-do

Participants were asked to rate their French proficiency using a modified version of the can-do scales developed by Clark (1981). They were given 21 items in total and asked to use a 10-point Likert scale (–5 to +5) to rate how willing they would be to approach or avoid each item.

L2 tasks

Participants were asked to complete the same eight communicative tasks used by MacIntyre and Legatto (2011). The questions were presented by the research assistant orally (in English, their L1) and respondents were asked to reply in French (L2).

(T1) Describe what you are wearing.
(T2) Discuss the education system of your home province in some detail.
(T3) Discuss the role of Parliament in the Canadian system of government.
(T4) Order a complete meal as if in a restaurant.
(T5) Describe your hobbies.
(T6) Describe what you see happening in this painting.
(T7) Count to 100 by 10s.
(T8) Give directions to [a local] shopping mall.

The tasks were presented in one of two orders. Order 1 consisted of a mixture of both difficult and easy tasks. Order 2 consisted of tasks that became progressively more difficult.

Vocabulary sheets

For each task, a 10-item vocabulary sheet was developed. The items on the sheet included vocabulary words that the respondents might choose to use in their responses. In each case, the vocabulary items were presented as English–French pairs.

Dynamic motivation ratings

The ratings of approach and avoidance motivation were collected using Windows-based software that was written specifically for collecting idiodynamic ratings (MacIntyre, 2012). The computer mouse was clicked to raise or lower the level of motivation that was shown on the screen. The software allowed for ratings to range from +5 to –5; positive ratings indicated how strong the approach tendency was, negative ratings indicated the strength of the avoidance tendency. The software features an 'auto-zero' function that returns the level of the respondent's rating toward zero at the rate of one point per second if there is no response from the user. This feature requires active responses from the user, unless the user's motivation is equal to zero. The output from the software consisted of both a bitmap graph showing the dynamic Willingness to Communicate (WTC) ratings and an Excel spreadsheet with WTC and time data. The software is available from the website: http://faculty.cbu.ca/pmacintyre/ and is free of charge.

Procedure

After giving informed consent, participants completed a questionnaire that included demographics and the can-do measures.

When the questionnaire was completed, the respondent was presented with eight oral tasks. One of two possible task orders was randomly assigned before the tasks began. The research assistant administering the tasks offered the respondent a vocabulary sheet if communication began to break down. Each participant was videotaped as they completed the tasks. Immediately after completing the last of the tasks, the respondent's video was loaded into the idiodynamic software. Participants completed their idiodynamic ratings by watching the video of their task performance and using the software to rate their approach–avoidance on a second-by-second basis. A click of the left mouse button caused the 'approach' rating to rise to a maximum of +5. A click of the right mouse button lowered the 'avoid' rating toward a score of –5. When complete, a graph of the ratings was printed and handed to the respondent. The research assistant then re-started the video in order to interview each respondent. Using the graph as a point of reference, participants were asked to describe and explain moments in their task performance when their approach or avoidance tendency changed, that is, to explain the peaks and valleys in the graphs. Either the participant or the research assistant could stop the video when the graph showed a noticeable change in dynamic motivation ratings. Each participant's interview was also videotaped and transcribed for coding.

Coding procedures

To address RQ3, two pairs of two research assistants rated the videos and transcripts of the respondents' post-task interview for specific motivation concepts. Coding was done using the definitions of integrative motivation (Gardner, 2010), task motivation (Julkunen, 2001), ideal L2 self, ought-to L2 self and L2 learning experience (Dörnyei, 2009a), with an additional category of references to the experimental situation (called local motives). More specifically, integrative motivation was defined by references to the L2 group, French-speakers in the present case. The ideal L2 self was reflected in references to future goals of the learner, or the person that the participant would like to become. The ought-to L2 self was identified when participants made comments about what she or he should be or ought-to be able to do. L2 learning experience was defined by respondents' references to their own language experience or training in the L2. Task motivation was evidenced by references to the structure of the task or general knowledge related to the task. Finally, local motives include reference to the experimental situation, such as the presence of a video camera or research assistant.

In scoring respondents' explanations for variations in their idiodynamic ratings, the following rubric was employed.

0 = the respondent made no reference to the concept.
1 = a single reference to the concept.

2 = more than a single reference but the concept was not presented as dominant in the rationale.

3 = the concept was offered by the participant as the main reason for fluctuations in idiodynamic ratings.

Scores across the eight tasks and between the raters were combined and averaged to keep the distribution of scores on the 0–3 scale.

Results and Discussion

This section will integrate the presentation of the results and discussion. Each of the four research questions will be addressed in turn.

Research Question 1: Mean and variability of idiodynamic ratings

The first research question (RQ1) asks whether the reaction to the tasks can be classified as generally approach-oriented or avoidance-oriented, and whether there is much variability in motivation during the tasks. Three-quarters of the sample showed mean ratings on the avoidant side of the ledger (a negative mean rating), indicating a somewhat aversive reaction to the eight tasks as a group. However, when attention is directed to the changes in motivation, a diversity of patterns emerges. Results show a high level of variability across the idiodynamic ratings of motivation. Table 11.1 shows a summary of the data for each of the 12 participants' idiodynamic ratings. Variability in the ratings is shown in two ways. First, the standard deviation of the idiodynamic ratings is presented, with higher standard deviation values indicating greater variability. Second, following Gregersen et al. (2014) we calculated the number of spikes and dips in the ratings for each person, where a spike or dip was defined as an uninterrupted increase or decrease (respectively) of five or more points.

Overall, the patterns of all 12 participants appear to cluster around four types (see Figures 11.1–11.4). One response pattern showed a rollercoaster of swings between approach and avoidant motivation during the tasks (for example, see Participant 2). A second pattern showed very little variability and a fairly steady, unaroused motivational state (see Participant 9). A third pattern showed a generally positive, approach reaction (see Participant 10) to the sequence of tasks that is countered by a fourth pattern of mostly negative, avoidant reactions (see Participant 5).

In these results we see that examining the data on a per-second and individual basis shows a great deal of variability for some and steadiness for others in their levels of motivation. In this dynamic system, even the

Table 11.1 Individual level data

Part-icipant	Can do-21	Can do-8	Dyn. mean	Dyn. SD	# of spikes	# of dips	Integ-rative	Ideal	O + E	Situ	Task
1, F	38	21	-1.69	2.33	4	6	0	0	0.33	0.44	2.87
2, F	2	-2	-1.53	3.18	13	15	0	0	0.33	0.62	2.62
3, F	25	7	-0.75	2.89	8	11	0	0	0	0.75	2.31
4, F	13	-2	-1.84	2.76	3	4	0	0	0.67	0.12	2.5
5, M	-44	-15	-1.38	1.75	3	5	0	0	0	0.62	2.56
6, F	-7	0	-0.67	1.85	13	13	0	0	0	0.5	2.5
7, F	27	-3	-0.53	0.53	3	1	0	0	1.33	0.25	2.62
8, M	37	17	0.24	0.24	6	7	0	0	0	0.5	2.25
9, F	7	9	-0.55	0.55	1	1	0	0	1	0	2.25
10, F	46	22	0.63	0.63	5	5	0	0	0	0	2.62
11, M	20	-2	-0.31	0.31	7	5	0	0	0.33	0.19	2.81
12, F	-6	-3	0.004	2.40	4	2	0	0	1.33	0	2.62

Notes: Participant sex (M = Male, F = Female) is indicated in the first column, Can do-21 = total of all can do scores, Can do-8 = ratings of eight can-do items used as tasks, Dyn = idiodynamic ratings, Rating O + E = combined ratings of Ought-to self and L2 learning experience, Situ = ratings of situational motivation, Task = ratings of task motivation.

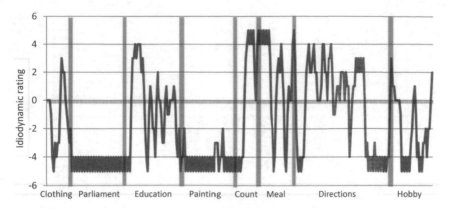

Figure 11.1 A roller coaster pattern (Participant 2, see also Appendix 11.1)

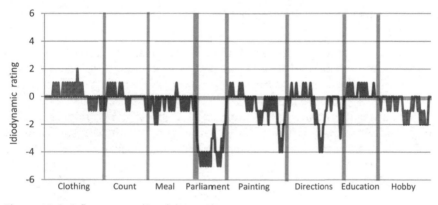

Figure 11.2 A flat pattern (Participant 9)

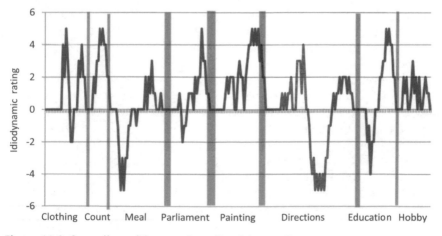

Figure 11.3 Generally positive reactions (Participant 10)

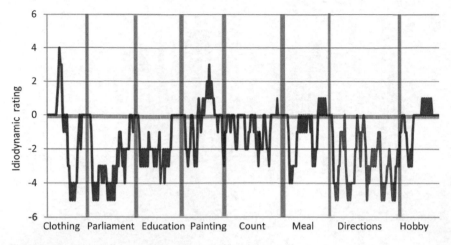

Figure 11.4 Generally negative reactions (Participant 5)

degree of variability shows variability! From a research perspective, this is good news indeed. Directing interest toward explanations of variability is not only an issue for dynamic systems theory, it is at the heart of traditional statistical procedures as well. Both analysis of variance (on which *t*-tests and ANOVAs are based) and correlation (on which regression and related analyses rest) partition and account for variability, so the focus on variation is appropriate and consistent with past research. The analytic strategy for RQ1 differs from prior research by reporting quantitative data for individuals and not using group comparisons or correlations for the group of participants. These data strongly support Dörnyei's (2002) suggestion that motivation is not static but fluctuates owing to a variety of factors. With a great deal of variability available for analysis, the search can begin for the most relevant influences. We turn to the interview component of the idiodynamic method for respondents' explanations of fluctuations in the ratings, accounting for the so-called spikes and dips on the graph.

The interview data shed light on drivers of change in the idiodynamic ratings, reflecting the most relevant appraisals from the respondents' point of view. Direct quotes from the participants' interviews will be presented below in italics. Respondents most often felt avoidance when tasks required knowledge or specialized vocabulary that they did not feel they possessed. The question about the Canadian system of government was especially difficult, despite all participants being Canadians, born and raised. The question is open ended and phrased in an unusual way, but could be approached from a variety of starting points (discussing elections, politicians, law-making, the economy, taxation, public policy, etc.). The lack of direction implied in the question makes the process of answering in the L2 more challenging. Participant 1 explained a dip in motivation by saying *'I definitely didn't have the vocabulary and ... I didn't know where to start, especially with no vocabulary'*. The theme of avoidance motivation coupled with a failure in the action assembly processes, specifically not retrieving appropriate vocabulary, was repeated across all of the interviews. For example, *'My answer was no good ... I didn't know any words and I just wanted it to be done'* (Participant 7). The task that required analysis of a painting also presented a challenge to initiating an appropriate response, *'I had so much to say I just couldn't get it out, I just couldn't think of the words'* (Participant 8).

Approach motivation was associated with success in the action assembly process, especially on questions perceived to be easier and more straightforward in the requirements for an acceptable answer. In response to the item 'Describe what you are wearing today', Participant 2 explained a spike in motivation occurred as she *'was remembering words, slowly I think (laughs)'*. Participant 3 explained a similar spike, *'because I knew what I was talking about'*. Another relatively simple task, order a meal, produced similar success in retrieving vocabulary with relative ease. Participant 11 explained an increase in approach motivation, *'I knew what I was talking about, I wanted ice cream'*. Table 11.2 presents the explanations for all of the spikes and dips for one person, Participant 4.

In general, fluctuation in motivation seemed to be strongly associated with the quality of the action assembly process. The vocabulary and grammatical demands of the different tasks were considered by respondents to be the key factor driving the variability in idiodynamic motivation ratings. But there is more going on than their introspective eye can see. When L2 communicators struggle to find vocabulary items, a series of coordinated cognitive and affective reactions take place. Some respondents, such as Participant 4 and Participant 1, indicated frustration and anxiety during the tasks that seemed to negatively influence their responses as the study went along. Focusing on Participant 4, a sense of frustration emerged during task performance that seemed to lower her motivation to respond to tasks that she thought, in advance, might be approachable. The phenomenological quality of the individual learner's affective response to struggling with the task is complex, implicating approach and avoidance motivation, anxiety, perceived competence and willingness to communicate. In the case of Participant 4, an unexpected, mounting sense of frustration as the study proceeded likely reduced the correlation between can-do ratings made in advance of the tasks and mean idiodynamic ratings during the tasks (see the next section). Participant 1 experienced a similar sequence of events and mounting frustration that affected the quality of her responses. For the other participants, the task performance (good and poor) was pretty much as expected and the correlations between idiodynamic ratings and can-do ratings are strong.

Table 11.2 Participant 4's rationale for spikes and dips in idiodynamic ratings

Question, Participant 4's Scores	Trend	Participant 4's explanation for spikes and dips
Government Can do = –5 Idio (M) = –3.9	Dip	'because I don't know very much at all about parliament or government. 'It's all just very bad.'
Education Can do = –5 Idio (M) = –4.5	Dip	'I guess if the question was more specific then I would have said more specific things … In English, I don't think the answer would have been any better.'
Painting Can do = –5 Idio (M) = 1.1	Spike	'it went up because I could think of specific French words to say … *not* because I like describing paintings! … oh also, this may be irrelevant but I was excited that I remembered the word 'peche' cause it was fishing because that's like the main thing in the painting. I was like oh good I know that!'
Counting Can do = 5 Idio (M) = 3.6	Spike	'oh that's definitely the numbers one … just because I know all of them … I knew every word- yay! That's why.
Order a Meal Can do = 5 Idio (M) = –3.0	Dip	'even the vocabulary is not what I think I would say in French if I was ordering food, for example I wanted a specific pasta but there wasn't [points to the vocabulary list] … you know what I mean? … I didn't feel comfortable.' 'I was thinking about how I just wouldn't say "I want chicken".'
Directions Can do = 3 Idio (M) = –3.2	Dip	'I could think of specific things to say right away but then like leaving CBU, like that was just really hard to describe in French. So like initially I was like "yay- driot et gauche" but then later I was like "I don't know what to say".'
Hobby Can do = 4 Idio (M) = –0.1	Spike	'it's because I could think of the 3 specific words I wanted to say.'

Note: The participant did not show a spike or dip for the question on clothing. Can do = rating for the task on the Can do pre-test, Idio (M) = mean idiodynamic rating for the task.

Research Question 2: Correspondence between can-do and idiodynamic ratings

The second research question (RQ2) addressed the degree to which there is a relationship between pre-test assessment of respondents' approach/ avoidance motivation for specific tasks (based on the can-do test) and their later reactions to actually performing those tasks. To assess the

Table 11.3 Participant 2's ratings for each of the eight tasks

Participant 2	Task							
	Cloth.	Parl.	Educ.	Paint.	Count	Meal	Direct.	Hobby
Can-do rating	1	−5	1	−3	4	0	3	−3
Mean idiodyn.*	−1.6	−4.5	−0.6	−4.3	1.9	0.8	−0.4	−2.43

Note: *Mean of the idiodynamic ratings made during each task.

correspondence between the two sets of ratings, a within-person correlation coefficient was computed for each of the 12 participants between the can-do scores and the mean idiodynamic rating within each task. The scores on all eight tasks for Participant 2 are provided in Table 11.3 to show how the correlations were calculated; Table 11.4 shows the correlations for all participants. The correlations ranged from a low of 0.28 (for Participant 4) to a high of 0.89 (for Participant 12), with a median correlation of 0.67, showing a strong relationship between the two sets of scores. Overall, these correlations indicate that participants had very good anticipation of their reactions to tasks before attempting them.

The strong correlations between can-do ratings and the mean idiodynamic score also can be taken as a test of the validity of the idiodynamic ratings themselves. This relatively new method produces patterns of quantitative ratings closely tied to qualitative interpretations of the ratings. The validity of those scores also is supported by previous studies (e.g. Gregersen

Table 11.4 Correlation between idiodynamic and can-do ratings for each participant

Participant	Correlation
1	0.30
2	0.88*
3	0.57*
4	0.28
5	0.71*
6	0.81*
7	0.61*
8	0.67*
9	0.87*
10	0.66*
11	0.64*
12	0.89*

*$p < 0.05$ if assessed by conventional hypothesis testing with six degrees of freedom.

et al., 2014; MacIntyre & Legatto, 2011; Mercer, Chapter 12, this volume). Similar to results reported by Poupore (2013), changes in motivation were associated with significant communicative events, such as forgetting words and lack of knowledge on a subject for avoidance, succeeding in vocabulary retrieval and smoothly flowing conversation for approach motivation. The correlations between can-do scores, reflecting expected levels of motivation, and actual mean idiodynamic ratings on the same task are impressive considering that there are only eight pairs of data points available for each participant. This lends support to the meaningfulness of the quantitative idiodynamic ratings. The correspondence between spikes and dips in the ratings and events that affect communication provides additional qualitative support for the meaningfulness of the ratings.

In the case of the two smallest correlations (Participants 1 and 4), both learners expressed concern and confusion with how the questions ought to be interpreted. Discrepancies between their pre-test expectations and actual performance appear to be largely owing to how broadly or specifically the questions should be interpreted, their confidence in their knowledge of each topic and their growing uncertainty in what the researcher expected from their responses. Participant 1 describes his uncertainty with the researcher's expectations for duration of the response which led to a drop in the ratings: *'I just didn't know what else to say. I wanted to make it a little longer but I just started making stuff up I think'*. Participant 4 said *'I guess if the question was more specific then I would have said more specific things ... In English, I don't think the answer would have been any better'*. She seemed frustrated that her response was affected by a lack of knowledge on the subject and the ambiguity of the question, rather than a lack of experience speaking French. She likely felt unable to demonstrate her French-speaking skill under such conditions, a sense of frustration that mounted as the study went along.

Research Question 3: Is there evidence of key motivational concepts in the interview data?

In addressing the third research question, (RQ3), the qualitative analysis of the interviews coded for evidence of situated motivation, integrative motivation, task motivation, the ideal L2 self, the ought-to L2 self and the effect of L2 learning experience. This research question addresses the concepts considered most relevant to task motivation by the learners themselves. As shown in Table 11.1, there is no evidence that the respondents were thinking about long term motives, such as the ideal self or the integrative motive, as they explained spikes and dips in their idiodynamic ratings. Perhaps this is not surprising on such a limited timescale. This must not be taken as evidence that integrative motivation or the ideal L2 self are irrelevant to motivation in SLA in general or to task motivation in particular. It seems more likely that the ideal L2 self and integrative motive simply were not activated by questions and related events during the study. Had respondents been choosing courses, deliberating about careers or places to travel, had they been developing friendships or thinking about international adventures, ideal selves and thoughts consistent with the integrative motive seem likely to arise. Future research might use the idiodynamic method to examine, in greater detail, the ways in which activating either of these motives affects task performance (see Dörnyei & Tseng, 2009; Gardner & MacIntyre, 1993; Gardner *et al.*, 1992).

The most prevalent type of motivation, by a long shot, was task-related. Within range of 0–3, every participant showed a task motivation score above 2.3. Perhaps this result also is not surprising given the timescale used in the present study. The interview data reinforce the close connection between the action assembly process and the experience of fluctuations in approach and avoidance motivation, where references to finding or losing the flow of vocabulary and grammatical items (that is, coalition formation) was *the* most prominent explanation for changes in motivation. de Bot (this volume) has suggested that dynamic systems research examine one timescale up (N + 1) and one timescale down (N − 1) from the process being studied. This advice has been most helpful for the present study. We see that the shorter timescale (N − 1) involves the 'okay'/'not-okay' checking of the BIS and BAS, semantic processing, L2 vocabulary retrieval and coalition formation, all of which are relevant to the ongoing assessment of approach and avoidance. The next longer timescale (N + 1) captures the approach or avoidance quality of the task, reflected in the can-do ratings.

The coding process revealed another interesting development, relevant to the L2 self system. An interpretive disagreement was noted on three occasions between raters' classifications of ought-to self and L2 learning experience motivation. These differences, rather than being easily resolved through discussion among the researchers, appeared to us to reveal a need to examine more closely the operation of the L2 self system on this timescale (see Table 11.4). Discussing disagreements between raters revealed that each was responding with a different emphasis to the same co-occurring process, a dynamic interaction between ought-to self and L2 learning experience. Essentially, one coder called heads and the other tails as a two-sided coin was examined.

Both the ought-to self and L2 learning experience were being accessed simultaneously by the participants, creating an interaction between them that made coding either one or the other concept challenging, and somewhat artificial. For example, in the case of Participant 2 (see Table 11.5), the discrepancy between coders appears to be owing to a difficulty differentiating between an inability to begin an answer and the risk of a negative impression being created because of the inability to answer. This coding challenge can be produced if, in apprising one's ongoing L2 communication, the respondent generates ought-to expectancies based on prior experience. The fusion of the two parts of the self is reflected by comments that take the form 'GIVEN

Table 11.5 Simultaneous occurrences of ought-to and L2 learning experience

P.	Transcript excerpt	Category	Coder's rationale (from notes written during the coding process)
#2	**P2:** U-mm (I don't even like, is that horrible that I don't even know) umm like what am I supposed to talk about?	L2 learning experience	Participant does not know enough about topic to discuss, receives no peer support and gives up on current question but increases motivation for next question
	Researcher: (h) (shrugs) **P2:** Okay umm, I dunno I dunno (I'll do good on the next one I promise)	Ought-to self	Participant is trying to avoid a negative self-representation to the researcher. Externally motivated/trying to reduce discrepancy/compensate
#7	**P7:** Oh (.2) ahh (it's been a while (.2) what am I ordering?) (.2) as if I was in a restaurant okay (.6) (I can't think of a food now) (.3)	L2 learning experience	Participant is not in the proper setting to think of food or the participant has forgotten the words for food
		Ought-to self	Makes reference to time; that the length of time since speaking French (an extrinsic factor) is important. Participant feels expected to be able to speak French and that is the primary motivator
#12	**P12:** discuss the role played by parliament, I don't even (.2) Can we pass? **Researcher:** Yeah if you want	L2 learning experience	Participant does not know enough about topic to discuss even with the vocabulary sheet
	P12: I don't even know what I would say honestly I'm not very good my poli-sci is not good ***** (h)	Ought-to self	Chose to 'pass' in order to avoid negative outcomes. Aware of an inability to perform at a level consistent with their expectations (i.e. they claim to be 'not very good' at political science)

my learning experience I OUGHT TO be able to answer this question'. Kim (2009), in explaining previous inconsistent results for the ought-to L2 self, argued that external expectations must be internalized in order to be relevant to motivation. We suggest that, based on the joint operation of ought-to self and L2 learning experience, prior learning experience itself creates an internalization of expectancies. This internalization process generates a metacognitive sense of what one ought-to be able to do on a per-second timescale, helping to resolve the dilemma posed by Kim (2009). This speculation remains to be confirmed by future research.

Discussion

Putting it all together – The four horsemen of avoidance motivation

An initial model of the ongoing, dynamic process of avoidance motivation among L2 speakers is beginning to take shape. It is too early to offer a definitive account of the process, given the absence of research that uses this timescale. Yet it is possible to offer an account of multiple interacting processes co-occurring within the time frame of seconds and minutes that focuses directly on the situated complexity of the L2 motivation process (Ushioda, this volume; Ushioda & Dörnyei, 2012). Larsen-Freeman and Cameron (2008) have argued that a developing L2 incorporates a complex, dynamic, emergent, open, self-organizing and adaptive system. The model below reflects an attempt to meet all of those criteria in explaining what participants encountered during the task performance.

The emerging model suggests that if the action assembly process (Greene, 2006) of deciding what to say and how to say it is under-developed in the L2, then L2 coalitions might not form readily and sometimes not at all. Coalition failure presents a serious communication problem. The lack of coalition formation creates difficulties with the timing of discourse, as the speaker searches for vocabulary items and appropriate grammatical structures. As the communication process becomes disturbed, the person transitions from the 'okay' to the 'not-okay' checking mode, the BIS kicks in (Gray & McNaughton, 2000). Activation of the 'not-okay' mode is similar in character to encountering a perceived (potential) threat because it indicates that the situation is not meeting one's expectations – things are not as they should be. The reaction of the interlocutor(s) is monitored intensely for signs of understanding, approval and encouragement, or for signs of misunderstanding, disapproval and a chance to escape the conversation. With attention focused elsewhere, the process of noticing relevant linguistic material and paying attention to language use is diminished (Dörnyei & Tseng, 2009; Gass & Mackey, 2006). There is a threat to the sense of self (including self-esteem and the L2 self system) and possibly social position, as the speaker's inability to use language can mark her or him as an outsider in the group (Norton, 1995). Beneath the surface, the L2 self system engages a coordination of the expectancies consistent with the ought-to self and L2 learning experiences that indicates whether the individual should be able to use the L2 in the present situation. If the answer is 'no', then some of the emotional pressure is alleviated because the person is not responsible for the communication failure. If the answer is 'yes' and the person feels that she or he ought to be able to respond successfully, but cannot, then the emotional stakes are raised yet again in a potentially vicious cycle.

The threat to both a positive view of the self and to one's social position further increases the arousal of the individual's motivational and emotional systems; coping efforts begin. Initial coping efforts might be successful in recovering smooth communication and the okay checking mode, restoring approach motivation and reducing negative affect. However, if coping efforts are perceived to be unsuccessful and the communication difficulties persist for more than a few moments, the speaker is likely to experience an emerging anxiety reaction, along with increasing avoidance motivation, lower perceived competence and declining willingness to communicate. The arousal of anxiety in this context places increasing pressure on the action assembly process to come up with something to say, arousal that (ironically) also adds to the cognitive difficulty by initiating a fight-flight-or-freeze response in the sympathetic nervous system. With this response comes both the familiar physiological arousal (increasing heart rate, red face, perspiration, a sinking feeling in the stomach) and distracting, often self-deprecating cognition (such as: 'I should know this', 'what's wrong with me', 'I look like an idiot').

If activation of this arousal system continues, the person begins to contemplate escape strategies as a coping response that further consumes cognitive resources and makes L2 coalition formation even more difficult. Instead of appropriate L2 coalitions, alternative types of coalitions begin to be formed, this time with a goal of avoiding negative consequences (if possible) or escaping the situation in a way that saves face. Saving face further activates the expectancies represented in the ought-to self, as it applies in the situation. A lack of L2 learning experience in the area of the task can relieve the individual's sense of misadventure or even failure during communication task difficulties; it might be called self-forgiveness. But unfulfilled ought-to expectancies that are undeniable because of past learning experience can exert a powerful effect on the emotion and motivation systems; these moments can be enormously frustrating for the L2 speaker.

Increasing avoidance motivation and anxiety, along with lowering perceptions of competence and willingness to communicate, might be called 'the four horsemen' of communication difficulties. This is not a state in which the person will tend to remain; it is a repeller state for the interpersonal communication system. There are a number of verbal and nonverbal coping strategies that might resolve the difficulties. Code switching to another language, changing the topic, using nonverbal behaviour such as gestures, or face saving humour can extract a person from a difficult situation, and possibly restore or increase levels of approach motivation. Some persons are highly adept at using strategies and some language teachers will choose to teach them, as a way of keeping conversation going (Gregersen & MacIntyre, 2014).

Approach motivation likely works in a more subtle way, in the sense that it arouses less intense emotion. If the action assembly process unfolds as expected, and the communication process is smooth, then approach motivation is maintained or increased. Approach motivation is associated with the ability to quickly generate at least a few potentially acceptable coalitions. With coalitions forming, a person experiences confidence that she or he is likely to be able to respond successfully and to keep the response going in conversation. Unless anxiety or another factor is holding the person back, willingness to communicate increases past a threshold and the person approaches the exchange, initiating communication. On occasion, during the L2 communication process, a novel, unexpected or especially successful utterance might occur. For example, the speaker might try new vocabulary, an idiom or a grammatical structure for the first time. If the interlocutor responds appropriately, then approach motivation rises. Over time, the magnitude of this jolt of confidence and positivity declines as vocabulary, idioms, grammar rules, etc. become routinized, so approach motivation based on L2 coalition success might be considered less intense than avoidance motivation over the long run (see Epstein & Fenz, 1965 for an example of novice versus experienced parachutists). In the case of bilinguals, for example, approach motivation likely would depend on situational factors rather than success at coalition formation. Novice and experts experience the results of the appraisal process differently (Dörnyei & Tseng, 2009; Schumann, 1999).

The idiodynamic data in the present study generally support this emerging model. The tendency toward negative idiodynamic scores indicate avoidance motivation and our sample certainly struggled with the action assembly process. This was to be expected, as correlations between pre-test can-do items and mean idiodynamic ratings on the corresponding task showed participants have a strong metacognitive ability to anticipate future motivational states. Yet shifts from approach to avoidance motivation (the spikes and dips) occurred throughout the sample; some individual's motivational states were especially volatile. The post-task interviews were filled with nervous laughter, strained facial expressions and self-deprecating humour, which are indicative of an anxiety reaction. Incidents of code switching from French to English and back again were frequent during responses to the tasks, as were face-saving strategies such as claiming a lack of knowledge about politics or even saving face by explicitly promising the interviewer to do better on the next task. The present data are remarkably similar to MacIntyre and Legatto's (2011) data on willingness to communicate, both studies showing the critical importance of the process of retrieving L2 vocabulary and forming appropriate coalitions. With limited experience, generating L2 coalitions that lead to acceptable utterances is a significant challenge for the action assembly process.

There is a long list of additional and alternative ways to analyse the data that would shed light on the multiple interacting processes in play. Research could use the idiodynamic method to focus on the linguistic structures used by participants, their nonverbal behaviour and how the two interact. The method would be well suited to capture examples of multilingual persons' code switching, along with the reasons for switching among three or more languages in situations where a range of codes are possible. A discourse analysis could consider the role of the research assistant and how the vocabulary sheet was integrated into the conversation. The contrast between the affective displays during task performance and the affect displayed and reported verbally in the interview might reveal how participants managed anxiety and other emotions on the fly. Future research also might further test each of the so-called 'four horsemen': motivation, anxiety, perceived competence and willingness to communicate. It would be especially interesting to take these factors in pairs to examine the idiodynamic interactions among them in greater detail. One glaring need for future research is to integrate the L2 comprehension process on a continuing basis along with the action assembly process, as in a natural conversation rather than the question and answer format used in the present study. Compared with L1 ability, L2 skills and experience are far more variable, potentially ranging from persons with no experience at all to fluent bilinguals.

All of these ideas, and ones not yet contemplated, provide fertile ground for research on the dynamics within the interrelated language acquisition and communication processes. The analysis of this per-second timescale shows the processes that unfold as participants consciously experience events. The longer term timescales that have been the subject of prior research, based on summative evaluations of experience, tend to show a high degree of stability in their findings (see Dörnyei, 2005; Gardner, 1985, 2010). Longer timescales permit generalizations, such as 'motivation is positively correlated with perceptions of competence and willingness to communicate, but negatively correlated with anxiety'. These longer term timescales tend to cancel out the vibrations in motivation as it unfolds in real time. At the per-second timescale, research must exercise some caution in separating the signal from the noise (for a series of interesting examples of complex processes, from baseball statistics to weather patterns, see Silver, 2012). We believe that the idea of the four horsemen (motivation, anxiety, perceptions of competence and willingness to communicate) riding in formation allows for both typical patterns (consistent with prior research) as well as soft-assembled, unconventional patterns that do not last for long periods of time, but which might leave a lasting psychological impression.

Larsen-Freeman (2007: 783) has said, '(i)t is not that you learn something and then you use it; neither is it that you use something and then you learn it. Instead, it is in the using that you learn—they are inseparable'. The nitty-gritty detail of this complex process, observed as it unfolds in idiodynamic studies of the L2 learning and communication process, provides an *embarrasse de riches* that hopefully will motivate future research.

Acknowledgements

The authors would like to thank Brittany Morrison and Dougal Nolan for their many contributions to the study, including recruiting the participants, conducting the testing and preliminary data analyses. The research was funded by grants from Cape Breton University and the Social Science and Humanities Research Council of Canada.

References

Ainley, M., Hidi, S. and Berndorff, D. (2002) Interest, learning, and the psychological processes that mediate their relationship. *Journal of Educational Psychology* 94 (3), 545–561.

Allen, G.D. (1973) Segmental timing control in speech production. *Journal of Phonetics* 1, 219–237.

Amodio, D.M., Master, S.L., Yee, C.M. and Taylor, S.E. (2008) Neurocognitive components of the behavioural inhibition and activation systems: Implications for theories of self-regulation. *Psychophysiology* 45 (1), 11–19.

Arnold, M.B. (1960) Emotion and personality (Volume I). *Psychological Aspects.* Oxford England: Columbia University Press.

Boutsen, F.R., Brutten, G.J. and Watts, C.R. (2000) Timing and intensity variability in the metronomic speech of stuttering and nonstuttering speakers. *Journal of Speech, Language, and Hearing Research* 43, 513–520.

Carver, C.S. and White, T.L. (1994) Behavioral inhibition, behavioural activation, and affective responses to impending reward and punishment: The BIS/BAS scales. *Journal of Personality & Social Psychology* 67, 319–333.

Clark, J.L.D. (1981) Language. In T.S. Barrows (ed.) *A Survey of Global Understanding: Final Report* (pp. 25–35). New Rochelle, NY: Change Magazine Press.

Crookes, G. and Schmidt, R.W. (1991) Motivation: Reopening the research agenda. *Language Learning* 41, 469–512.

Csizér, K. and Kormos, J. (2009) Modeling the role of inter-cultural contact in the motivation of learning English as a foreign language. *Applied Linguistics* 30 (2), 166–185.

de Bot, K., Lowie, W. and Verspoor, M. (2007) A dynamic systems theory approach to second language acquisition. *Bilingualism: Language and Cognition* 10 (1), 7–21.

Dörnyei, Z. (1990) Conceptualizing motivation in foreign-language learning. *Language Learning* 40, 45–78.

Dörnyei, Z. (2002) The motivational basis of language learning tasks. In P. Robinson (ed.) *Individual Differences and Instructed Language Learning* (pp. 137–158). Amsterdam: John Benjamins Publishing Company.

Dörnyei, Z. (2003) Attitudes, orientations, and motivations in language learning: Advances in theory, research, and applications. *Language Learning* 53, 3–32.

Dörnyei, Z. (2005) *The Psychology of the Language Learner; Individual Differences in Second Language Acquisition.* Mahwah, NJ: Lawrence Erlbaum Associates.

Dörnyei, Z. (2009a) Individual differences: Interplay of learner characteristics and learning environment. *Language Learning* 59, 230–248.

Dörnyei, Z. (2009b) *The Antecedents of Task Behaviour: A Dynamic Systems Account of Task Motivation.* See http://www.lancaster.ac.uk/fass/events/tblt2009/presentations/DÖRNYEI _handout.pdf (accessed 7 November 2013).

Dörnyei, Z. and Chan, L. (2013) Motivation and vision: an analysis of future L2 self images, sensory styles, and imagery capacity across two target languages. *Language Learning* 63 (3), 437–462.

Dörnyei, Z. and Tseng, W.T. (2009) Motivational processing in interactional tasks. In A. Mackey and C. Polio (eds) *Multiple Perspectives on Interaction: Second Language Research in Honor of Susan M. Gass* (pp. 117–134). London, Routledge.

Eder, A.B., Elliot, A.J. and Harmon-Jones, E. (2013) Approach and avoidance motivation: Issues and advances. *Emotion Review* 5 (3), 227–229.

Efklides, A. (2002) Feelings and judgments as subjective evaluations of cognitive processing: How reliable are they? *Psychology: The Journal of the Hellenic Psychological Society* 9 (2), 163–184.

Epstein, S. and Fenz, W.D. (1965) Steepness of approach and avoidance gradient in humans as a function of experience: Theory and experiment. *Journal of Experimental Psychology* 70 (1), 1–12.

Eysenck, M.W. (1979) Depth, elaboration, and distinctiveness. In L. Cermak and F.I.M. Craik (eds) *Levels of Processing. An Approach to Memory.* Hillsdale, NJ: Lawrence Erlbaum.

Fogel, A. (2006) Dynamic systems research on inter-individual communication: The transformation of meaning-making. *Journal of Developmental Processes* 1, 7–30.

Frijda, N.H. (1986) *The Emotions.* New York: Cambridge University Press.

Gardner, R.C. (1985) *Social Psychology and Second Language Learning: The Role of Attitudes and Motivation.* Maryland, USA: Arnold London and Baltimore.

Gardner, R.C. (2010) *Motivation and Second Language Acquisition: The Socio-Educational Model.* New York: Peter Lang Publishing.

Gardner, R.C. and MacIntyre, P.D. (1993) On the measurement of affective variables in second language learning. *Language Learning* 43 (2), 157–194.

Gardner, R.C., Day, J.B. and MacIntyre, P.D. (1992) Integrative motivation, induced anxiety, and language learning in a controlled environment. *Studies in Second Language Acquisition* 14 (2), 197–214.

Gass, S.M. and Mackey, A. (2006) Input, interaction, and output. *AILA Review* 19, 3–17.

Goldberg, L.R. (1992) The development of markers for the big-five factor structure. *Psychological Assessment* 4, 26–42.

Gray, J.A. (1982) *The Neuropsychology of Anxiety: An Enquiry into the Functions of the Septo Hippocampal System.* New York: Clarendon Press/Oxford University Press.

Gray, J.A. and McNaughton, N. (2000) *The Neuropsychology of Anxiety* (2nd edn). Oxford: Oxford: University Press.

Gray, J.A., Gable, L.S., Reis, T.J. and Elliot, J.A. (2000) Behavioral activation and inhibition in everyday life. *Journal of Personality and Social Psychology* 78, 1135–1149.

Greene, J.O. (1984) Speech preparation processes and verbal fluency. *Human Communication Research* 11 (1), 61–84.

Greene, J.O. (1989) The stability of nonverbal behaviour: An action-production approach to problems of cross-situational consistency and discriminativeness. *Journal of Language and Social Psychology* 8 (3–4), 193–220.

Greene, J.O. (1995) An action-assembly perspective on verbal and nonverbal message production: A dancer's message unveiled. In D.E. Hewes (ed.) *The Cognitive Bases of Interpersonal Communication* (pp. 51–85). Hillsdale, NJ: Lawrence Erlbaum Associates, Inc.

Greene, J.O. (1997) *Message Production: Advances in Communication Theory.* Mahwah, NJ: Lawrence Erlbaum Associates Publishers.

Greene, J.O. (2006) Have I got something to tell you: Ideational dynamics and message production. *Journal of Language and Social Psychology* 25 (1), 64–75.

Greene, J.O. and Cappella, J.N. (1986) Cognition and talk: The relationship of semantic units to temporal patterns of fluency in spontaneous speech. *Language and Speech* 29 (2), 141–157.

Greene, J.O., Kirch, M.W. and Grady, C.S. (2000) Cognitive foundations of message encoding: An investigation of message production as coalition formation. *Communication Quarterly* 48, 256–271.

Gregersen, T. and MacIntyre, P.D. (2014) *Capitalizing on Language Learners' Individuality: From Premise to Practice.* Bristol: Multilingual Matters.

Gregersen, T., MacIntyre, P.D. and Meza, M. (2014) The motion of emotion. *Modern Language Journal* 98, 574–588. DOI: 10.1111/j.1540-4781.2014.120s4.x

Gudykunst, W.B. (1995) Anxiety/uncertainty management (AUM) theory: Current status. In R.L. Wiseman (ed.) *Intercultural Communication Theory* (pp. 8–58). Thousand Oaks, CA: SAGE.

Henry, A. (2009) Gender differences in compulsory school pupils' L2 self-concepts: A longitudinal study. *System* 37 (2), 177–193.

Howe, M.L. and Lewis, M.D. (2005) The importance of dynamic systems approaches for understanding development. *Developmental Review* 25 (3–4), 247–251.

Julkunen, K. (1989) *Situation and Task Specific Motivation in Foreign Language Learning and Teaching (Publications in Education No. 6).* Joensuu, Finland: University of Joensuu.

Julkunen, K. (2001) Situation- and task-specific motivation in foreign language learning. *Motivation and Second Language Acquisition* 23, 29–41.

Kim, T.Y. (2009) The dynamics of L2 self and L2 learning motivational qualitative case study of Korean ESL elementary school students' perceptual learning style, ideal L2 self, and motivated behavior. *Korean Journal of English Language and Linguistics* 9, 261–286.

Kuhl, P.K. (1991) Human adults and human infants show a 'perceptual magnet effect' for the prototypes of speech categories, monkeys do not. *Perception & Psychophysics* 50 (2), 93–107.

Larsen-Freeman, D. (2007) Reflecting on the cognitive–social debate in second language acquisition. *The Modern Language Journal* 91(1), 773–787.

Larsen-Freeman, D. and Cameron, L. (2008) *Complex Systems and Applied Linguistics.* New York: Oxford.

Lazarus, R.S. (1991) Cognition and motivation in emotion. *American Psychologist* 46 (4), 352–367.

Lazarus, R.S. (1999) The cognition–emotion debate: A bit of history. In T. Dalgleish and M.J. Power (eds) *Handbook of Cognition and Emotion* (pp. 3–19). New York: John Wiley & Sons Ltd.

Lazarus, R.S. and Folkman, S. (1987) Transactional theory and research on emotions and coping. *European Journal of Personality* 1 (3), 141–169.

Litman, J.A. (2005) Curiosity and the pleasures of learning: Wanting and liking new information. *Cognition and Emotion* 19 (6), 793–814.

MacIntyre, P.D. (2007) Willingness to communicate in the second language: Understanding the decision to speak as a volitional process. *Modern Language Journal* 91 (4), 564–576.

MacIntyre, P.D. (2012) The idiodynamic method: A closer look at the dynamics of communication traits. *Communication Research Reports* 29 (4), 361–367.

MacIntyre P.D. and Gardner, R.C. (1991) Language anxiety: Its relationship to other anxieties and to processing in native and second languages. *Language Learning* 41 (4), 513–534.

MacIntyre, P.D. and Gardner, R.C. (1994) The subtle effects of language anxiety on cognitive processing in the second language. *Language Learning* 44 (2), 283–305.

MacIntyre, P.D. and Legatto, J. (2011) A dynamic system approach to willingness to communicate: Developing an idiodynamic method to capture rapidly changing affect. *Applied Linguistics* 32 (2), 149–171.

MacIntyre, P.D., Baker, S., Clément, R. and Donovan, L.A. (2003) Talking in order to learn: Willingness to communicate and intensive language programs. *Canadian Modern Language Review* 59, 589–607.

MacIntyre, P.D., Mackinnon, S.P. and Clément, R. (2009) The baby, the bath water, and the future of language learning motivation research. In Z. Dörnyei and E. Ushioda (eds) *Motivation, Language Identity and the L2 Self* (pp. 43–65). Bristol: Multilingual Matters.

Magid, M. and Chan, L. (2012) Motivating English learners by helping them visualise their ideal L2 self: lessons from two motivational programmes. *Innovation in Language Learning and Teaching* 6 (2), 113–125.

Masgoret, A. and Gardner, R.C. (2003) Attitudes, motivation, and second language learning: A meta-analysis of studies conducted by Gardner and associates. *Language Learning* 53, 167–210.

McNaughton, N. and Corr, P.J. (2004) A two-dimensional neuropsychology of defence: Fear/anxiety and defensive distance. *Neuroscience and Biobehavioral Reviews* 28 (3), 285–305.

Norton, B. (1995) Social identity, investment, and language learning. *TESOL Quarterly* 29, 9–31.

Papi, M. (2010) The L2 motivational self system, L2 anxiety, and motivated behavior: A structural equation modeling approach. *System* 38, 467–479.

Poupore, G. (2013) Task motivation in process: A complex systems perspective. *Canadian Modern Language Review* 69 (1), 91–116.

Reeve, J. (2009) *Understanding Motivation and Emotion* (5th edn). Toronto: Wiley.

Silver, N. (2012) *The Signal and the Noise: Why So Many Predictions Fail – But Some Don't.* New York: Penguin Press.

Schumann, J.H. (1999). A neurobiological basis for decision making in language pragmatics. *Pragmatics & Cognition* 7, 283–311.

Skehan, P. (1989) *Individual Differences in Second Language Learning.* London: Edward Arnold.

Teigen, K.H. and Keren, G. (2002) Surprises: low probabilities or high contrasts? *Cognition* 87 (2), 55–71.

Tremblay, P.F., Goldberg, M.P. and Gardner, R.C. (1995) Trait and state motivation and the acquisition of Hebrew vocabulary. *Canadian Journal of Behavioural Science/Revue Canadienne des Sciences du Comportement* 27 (3), 356–370.

Ushioda, E. and Dörnyei, Z. (2012) Motivation. In S. Gass and A. Mackey (eds) *The Routledge Handbook of Second Language Acquisition* (pp. 396–409). New York: Routledge.

Vohs, K.D., Park, J. and Schmeichel, B.J. (2013) Self-affirmation can enable goal disengagement. *Journal of Personality and Social Psychology* 104 (1), 14–27.

Appendix 11.1

Complete transcript for Participant 2 task performance

Participant 2 is a 21-year-old female, with French immersion experience as well as taking regular core French classes, starting in grade 3. Before beginning the tasks, she mentioned to the interviewer that her French skills were 'very rusty'. This participant showed close to neutral can-do scores, indicating an ambivalent approach/avoidance profile. Her idiodynamic data show the greatest degree of fluctuation in the sample.

Coding: (h) = hesitation; Underlining = emphasis in the speaker's voice.

Researcher:	Alright question one: describe what you are wearing today
P2:	Um(h)m maintenant je port un chemise bleu et blanche et les shorts bleu(.)ish (h) yeah that's it (h)
Researcher:	Discuss the role played by parliament in the Canadian system of government.
P2:	Je n'ai aucune idée (h) parce que je suis <u>stupid</u> avec les politiques (h)
Researcher:	(h)
P2:	Alors oui (h)
Researcher:	Veux-tu le vocabulaire?
P2:	Umm okay
Researcher:	Essaye peut-être
P2:	U-<u>mm</u> (I don't even like is that horrible that I don't even know) umm like what am I supposed to talk about?
Researcher:	(h) (shrugs)
P2:	Okay umm >I dunno I dunno (I'll do good on the next one I promise) <
Researcher:	Alright, describe the education system in your home province
P2:	umm okay en Nouvel écosse umm nous ont ahh école comme nous sommes quand nous ont nous avons cinq ans Ahh à l'école primaire? (no) a puis après ca on va a l'école <secondaire peut-être> et puis après <u>ca</u> on va en universitaire et si on veut continue les études on va au grad school et yeah et c'est expensive
Researcher:	()(h)
P2:	Oui et ca c'est toute =.hh, hh =
Researcher:	=C'est toute= alright describe this painting right here
P2:	C'est (.) vocabulaire? Thank you umm Il y a un petite bateau et les homes la et ahh some belles arbres
Researcher:	(h)
P2:	(h) wow <u>et</u> <u>ahh</u> ils sont en train de faire du (.4) fishing (h)
Researcher:	(h)

P2:   And yeah that's about it (oh my god)
Researcher: C'est toute?
P2:   Ca c'est toute
Researcher: Alrigh = count= to 100 by tens.
P2:   =(<u>ahh</u>) =
                    Dix, vingt, trente, quarante, cinquante, soixante, soixante-dix, soixante-vingt?
                    NO quatre-vingt, quatre-vingt-dix, et cent.
Researcher: C'est toute?
P2:   C'est toute
Researcher: Alright order a meal as if you were in a restaurant.
P2:   Ahh est-ce que je peut avoir un pièce de pizza (h) e(h)t u(h)ne boisson gazeuse (peut-etre)
                    <u>et un salade</u> je veut un salade aussi yea(h)h
Researcher: c'est toute?
P2:   Et ca c'est toute
Researcher: C'est toute alright give directions to the May Flower Mall starting from this room
P2:   Umm on quitte cette chambre et marche a doigte et continue (h)
                    et puis il y a un autre corridor et les escaliers (I'm not sure down) (h)
Researcher: (h)
P2:   Umm après ca on va umm sortie les (.) (doors?) (h) et (rush) au auto et puis umm conduire a (.5) (I don't even know) ahh out of the parking lot et a la street et prend un gauche et continue de conduit a jusque au umm traffic light? Et on prend un autre gauche et vous être a la May Flower Mall
Researcher: C'est toute?
P2:   Ca c'est toute
Researcher: Alright describe one of your hobbies
P2:   One of my hobbies okay umm (.3)(I dunno) ahh je j'aime fait la yoga et c'est très relaxant et umm on a beaucoup de focus sur la breathe (h)t on fait beaucoup des stretches et yeah that's it
Researcher: c'est toute?
P2:   C'est toute
Researcher: Alright.

12 Dynamics of the Self: A Multilevel Nested Systems Approach

Sarah Mercer

Interest in the self has grown exponentially in second language acquisition (SLA) in recent years and this has been accompanied by an increase in the range of self-related terms and differing theoretical constructs being examined (Mercer & Williams, 2014). In this chapter, I propose that a useful way of integrating differing self constructs into a more holistic model is to conceptualise the different facets of the self as part of a larger complex dynamic system (Mercer, 2014). One of the most defining characteristics of a complex dynamic system is, as its name suggests, its dynamism and one of the most disputed characteristics of the self is the extent to which it is believed to be stable or dynamic. Therefore, examining the dynamics of the self from a complexity perspective may be able to generate fresh insights. This chapter reports on research that seeks to examine the dynamism of different facets of the self across different timescales based on nested systems view of the self.

Self as a Complex Dynamic System

In the field of individual differences in SLA, Dörnyei (2010) has suggested that contemporary research should seek to focus on particular conglomerates or constellations where cognition, affect and motivation function together as wholes. A perfect example of such a cluster would be the self, which is composed of a multitude of interrelated cognitions, affects and motives, which interact in ways that are often difficult to predict. The self reflects many characteristics similar to those of a complex dynamic system, such as its composition of multiple components that are completely interconnected, the embedded integral character of contexts into the system, its dependence on initial conditions, its nonlinear development, its continually emergent and self-organising character and the fact that as a whole it represents more than the sum of its parts (see also Mercer, 2011a, 2014). In this chapter, I will focus my discussion on one of the most salient characteristics of a complex dynamic system, namely, its dynamism. Interestingly, in the field of self research, this aspect of the self has proved to be one of the most controversial areas and difficult to resolve (e.g. Harter, 1999; Kernis & Goldman, 2003; Markus & Kunda, 1986; Markus & Wurf, 1987; Mercer, 2011b; Onorato & Turner, 2004). There are two possible issues, among others, contributing to the contradictory findings. First, problems can arise from discussing the dynamics of the self in binary terms – is it stable or dynamic? Paradoxically, '[T]he notion of personality implies some form of stability in thought, emotion and action. At the same time, human experience is inherently dynamic and constantly evolving in response to external circumstances and events' (Nowak *et al.*, 2005: 378). Humans are known to strive for stability and coherence in their sense of self, as suggested by work in self-verification (e.g. Swann, 1997), self-serving bias (e.g. Campbell & Sedikides, 1999) or self-esteem maintenance (Tesser, 1988). Thus, although we may talk of multiple selves and their dynamism, especially across contexts, there appears to also be a commensurate need for humans to feel coherence, rather than fragmentation, in regard to their sense of self. In this respect, it can be useful to conceive of the self as a complex dynamic system, which can be simultaneously stable, dynamic and/or dynamically stable.

The second problem in respect to dynamics may stem from the quagmire of terms and constructs that beset the field. It is beyond the scope of this chapter to discuss the problems surrounding self terms (see Mercer & Williams, 2014). However, a basic set of distinctions can be drawn as to whether a self construct is narrowly defined and understood in close connection to a specific context, or whether a self term is more globally conceived and less immediately context bound. Regarding the dynamism of the self, different constructs are likely to display different degrees and forms of dynamism depending on how they are understood, their relationships to contexts and the typical timescales across which these constructs function. As such, confusion may result if researchers compare findings from studies potentially investigating different constructs that may have different dynamic qualities. Therefore, any research on self dynamics needs to consider what type of construct is being looked at, how closely it is connected to what types of context and what the timespan is across which it typically functions.

A useful approach to exploring these dynamics may be to conceptualise the self as a series of nested systems of different layers of the self (see Figure 12.1 below). While it may essentially be impossible to create boundaries between separate layers of self, Davis and Sumara (2006: 29) propose that one way of distinguishing aspects of a complex dynamic system can be according to their relative 'size' and 'scope', as well as to different 'pace of their evolution'. Adapting this idea to the self, we can conceptualise the self as a series of nested systems of self constructs that differ in size as well as timescales of their dynamics. Considering established self constructs, we could talk, for example, about self-efficacy (typically defined as someone's expectancy belief about their ability to complete a particular task) as being limited in scope and size and tightly bound with contexts and thus typically evolving over timescales in terms of minutes rather than years. Similarly, we could conceptualise self-esteem (often defined as what one thinks and feels about one's self generally) as being broad in scope and size and as evolving over the many years of the person's lifespan. Therefore, a nested selves model can be thought of as comprising multiple layers of the self that differ in scope, evolve over different timescales and are interconnected with different types or levels of contexts. Nevertheless, it is worth reiterating that the boundaries between layers in such nested systems are not concrete but are permeable and, as the nested character implies, the overall system of the self emerges from the interaction of these nested systems and different levels of context that reciprocally influence each other (cf. van Geert's circular causality model, 2009).

This model of the self forms the basis for the research design proposed in this small-scale exploratory study, which seeks to examine different layers of the self in different contexts and on different timescales, with the aim of gaining a better understanding of the dynamics of the self as a complex dynamic system. Existing self constructs are, to some extent, reflected in this model as illustrated in the discussion above; however, it was decided to employ self constructs that reflect more closely the features of this particular

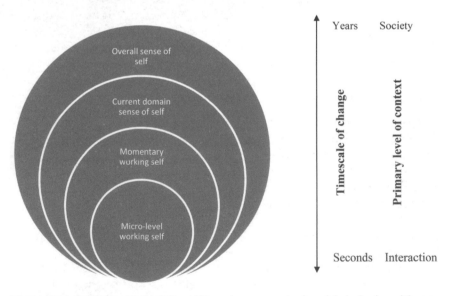

Figure 12.1 Nested systems of the self based on conceptual models in Davis and Sumara (2006)

model in this specific context, rather than seeking to force existent constructs into the model and particular timeframes used in this study. Instead, the conceptual framework of the self used is defined primarily by the respective time aspect and contextual specifics salient in the particular setting of data collection (cf. Lichtwarck-Aschoff *et al.*, 2008). However, as Lichtwarck-Aschoff *et al.* (2008: 375) caution, the boundaries between layers and timescales are 'fuzzy, not crisp' and the qualitative differences in different facets of the self need to be allowed to emerge, as will become apparent in the study that follows.

Methodological Design

Researching dynamics

Dynamics cannot meaningfully be understood merely by examining two fixed points in time, but rather we need to explore processes of changing, looking not at 'from-till' but at 'from-through' (Saldaña, 2003: 8). As MacIntyre (2012: 364) explains, only looking at fixed end-point data means that the 'intervening process is not studied directly as it unfolds; therefore the key drivers of change can be difficult to identify'. Indeed, van Dijk *et al.* (2011: 62) argue, 'if we really want to know how an individual (or group) develops over time we need data that is dense (i.e. collected at many regular measurement points), longitudinal (i.e. collected over a longer period of time), and individual (i.e. for one persona at a time and not averaged out)'. Therefore, in this study, it was decided to generate data according to the nested selves model at different levels of the self across different timescales, focusing in depth on individual learner's trajectories, in order to generate a detailed, composite picture of their self dynamics.

Data collection tools

Data were generated on four timescales using four different forms of data collection. Different levels of the self are focused on depending on the timescale being investigated. As explained in respect to the nested selves model above, the focus on eliciting data at each level was on aspects of the self salient on that timescale in the context of the study. Therefore, on the more macro levels, more global, holistic constructs with a focus on the field of English as a foreign language (EFL) and their studies generally were used. In the in-class data, the emphasis was placed on how confident they felt in using their English at that precise moment in time, mindful of the fact they were often working in different skill domains during sessions. In the idiodynamic data, students were asked specifically to report on their EFL speaking self-confidence as this was the most salient aspect of the self in that context and also represented an accessible term for communication with the

Table 12.1 Data collection matrix

Level of self anticipated and communicated to learners	Timescale	Data collection tool	Spacing of data collection	Number of data collection occasions
EFL sense of self/ academic self (Level 4)	Months	Interviews and multimodal narratives	Approximately 6 weeks apart	3
EFL sense of self/ academic self (Level 3)	Weeks	Journal	Every week	15–17
Working EFL self (Level 2)	Minutes	Questionnaire	Every 5 minutes within one session	3
Micro-level self: Speaking EFL confidence (Level 1)	Seconds	Idiodynamic tools	Every second	1

learners. Table 12.1 outlines the different data collection tools, the time spacing for data collection, the level of self focused upon and its primary timescale of dynamics.

The most macro-level (Level 4) set of data collected were generated through a series of open-ended interviews conducted in English and spaced at three roughly equal points, at the start, mid-way and at the end of the 15-week semester. Before the first interview, the students prepared a language learning self-description narrative in whatever form of media they preferred. These formed the basis for the first interview along with open-ended questions aimed at gaining a holistic view of the learner, while focusing on their language learning experiences and self perceptions.

The next level of data were generated (Level 3) in the form of weekly journal entries. In the past, experience had shown the danger of students simply reporting a list of activities with no level of reflection, so to avoid this, it was decided to provide loose guidelines for the writing. These stated, 'You should write about your feelings, thoughts, motivation, the way you feel about yourself as a language learner and any experiences of relevance'. No specific length was set and the volunteer students sent them via email every week. While cautious about influencing their writing too much, I also chose to respond specifically to their entries, given past experiences in which learners complained at my lack of response. In retrospect, I now feel this ongoing dialogue has been a vital component in building up our rapport and ensuring fuller reflections both in the journal and during the interviews.

The next layer of data (Level 2) were collected in the form of in-class pen and paper questionnaires, which contained several nine-point Likert scales on which the students were asked to rate how confident they felt in using their English in the class at five-minute intervals. There was space at the end of each scale for students to add additional comments. The lessons were audio-recorded to help match up potential peaks and troughs with what was happening in class. Every 5 minutes a bell would ring and the students would have a minute or two to complete the scale and add any comments before the lesson continued as normal. This was done in three separate lessons spaced three weeks apart and the first session using these took place in the fourth week of teaching once the group was more settled.

The final micro-level form of data collection (Level 1) involved the use of the idiodynamic software (MacIntyre & Legatto, 2010). Approximately around the mid-point of the course, the two volunteer students were invited to meet out of class time. Together they worked on two different speaking tasks for approximately 10 minutes in total. The first task required students to introduce themselves to each other based on prompt questions such as 'what book or film or TV show has your partner enjoyed recently?' This was deliberately open-ended and personal to help put learners at ease and to get to know each other. The second task was more challenging and required cooperation and agreement about perceived priorities regarding problems in the city where they live. While they worked on these speaking tasks together, they were video recorded. Immediately following the tasks, each participant was interviewed separately with two different interviewers, both of whom had worked with the software previously and who followed the same semi-structured interview protocols. The interviews were conducted concurrently to reduce the time lag for each participant from the event to the discussion of it. Each student was shown the video and asked to evaluate and mark with a computer mouse on a scale of +/–5 their feelings of English speaking self-confidence during the tasks. The idiodynamic software then generated an output graph (as a .jpg file and in Excel format) of their perceived highs and lows. An interview was then conducted in which students again watched the video, compared their graphs and discussed in more detail any rises or falls in their self-confidence, their perceived reasons for this and their general feelings and thoughts while completing the tasks. This stimulated recall interview was then followed by a general interview following the similar format to the one at the outset and the one at the end of the course as a mid-way marker.

Participants and context

This study was conducted with advanced, tertiary-level, EFL learners attending an integrated English language skills course at a university in Austria. One of the problems with this design is the considerable time commitment that it involves from the participants. Therefore, it is necessary to work with volunteers who, it is hoped, also felt it beneficial to take part. In the class, students were provided with a written outline of what the study would involve in terms of data collection and time commitment, as well as the main aims of the study. Three female students volunteered to take part. The students met with me at the end of one of the sessions and were told orally in more detail what participation in the project would involve. The data of two comparable learners are analysed in this chapter. At the time of the study, both were at the same stage in their studies (second year of studying), studying the same subjects to become a teacher (English and German – their mother tongue), from the same cultural and educational backgrounds (both Austrian) and of the same gender and level of competence (approximately B2/C1). To protect their identities, I have assigned them pseudonyms (Anita and Monika) and changed specific place names and other identifying markers in the reporting of the data. Anita was 21 years old and Monika was 20 years old at the time of the study[1].

During the data collection, I was also their teacher. In the information sheet about the study, it explicitly states that taking part or not taking part will not affect their grades in any way and reiterates that participation is entirely voluntary. Nevertheless, I am aware that my dual role does potentially affect the data and places me in an undesired position of power in relation to the learners. However, I would argue that I was able to build an open, positive rapport with the learners, show sensitivity to their contexts and concerns, and thereby work with them to generate a richer quality of data and reflection. Interestingly, in the interview transcripts, it is possible to see instances when I slip into 'teacher role' and offer reassurances or advice, and, indeed, I developed a specific code for these sections. Naturally, in analysing and writing about the data, caution needs to be exercised in interpreting learner statements and possible effects of my responses. I have tried to be conscious of, and careful to identify, my influence on the data. However, in my interactions with these committed and generous learners, I cannot remove myself from my identity and role as teacher; to do so would be to deny our common reality and shared relationship. Working with these learners and, in turn, with their data, requires attentiveness on my part to my responsibilities and role, but ultimately I feel that it has been beneficial to developing a positive basis on which to generate detailed and nuanced data.

Analysis

As necessary, all of the qualitative data were transcribed and digitalised for analysis using the data management software, Atlas.ti. The data were coded first in an open, grounded manner, coding line-by-line to allow all aspects of the data to be considered and to ensure potentially unexpected features were included in the analysis. In the following rounds of coding, codes were combined or expanded until categories began to form. During the coding, an essential stage is the memo writing that is especially important in longitudinal work in tracking possible hypotheses and developments. An additional strategy to facilitate an understanding of possible long-term dynamics on the more macro-levels involved the construction of a word document as a matrix organised both chronologically and thematically for both the journal and interview data as suggested by Saldaña (2003). The codes, categories, memos and matrices were then examined specifically with complex dynamic systems theory in mind, with a focus on characteristics of complex dynamic systems, their interrelations and dynamics. This process was done separately for each learner – focusing on each individual and developing their profile before moving on to the next. Finally, after the individual level of analyses, the data were examined for possible patterns and interactions across each level and for both learners.

Findings

Anita's data

Micro-level idiodynamic data – EFL speaking self-confidence (Level 1)
Anita's idiodynamic data were notably negative with her making 191 negative clicks in total compared with a total of only 49 positive clicks (see Figures 12.2 and 12.3 below). One possible reason for such strong negativity is that Anita reported having been unaware that she would be filmed while doing the tasks. Unfortunately, the written information sheet about the study as a whole does not explicitly state that the tasks would be filmed, although this was discussed orally and the other student appears to have been aware of this. Nevertheless, I should have ensured beforehand that this was absolutely clear to her. Before filming began, the students were asked to complete an additional consent form specifically about the filming and they were given the choice not to take part in this aspect of the study. However, both agreed and reported positively on the experiences in the interviews that followed, with Anita also specifically commenting in her journal how interesting she found the whole experience.

One notable aspect of all of Anita's data is what appear to be tendencies towards perfectionism as outlined by Gregersen and Horwitz (2002), such as extremely high performance standards, procrastination (postponing exam dates), notable concern over mistakes and accuracy, and fear of evaluation. As a result, it is likely that filming and 'being observed' might be especially difficult and anxiety-inducing for Anita. Additionally, Anita is highly self-critical, as she herself recognises in the idiodynamic interview: 'I'm very critical by myself, and every task I'm doing and every homework and every exercise and every paper ...'. Thus, I would suggest that it would be difficult

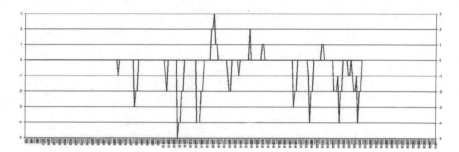

Figure 12.2 Anita idiodynamic graph Task 1

for her to observe herself and not be negative, potentially whatever the setting. However, being filmed and my presence as an observer appear to have accentuated the degree of negativity she experienced while completing these tasks.

Other aspects that she reported as contributing to her negative evaluation were occasions when she felt she had no ideas what to say, found the topic difficult, or was missing vocabulary (MacIntyre & Serroul, this volume, report similar results on this timescale). Perhaps most salient in the data is her lack of familiarity with her partner. As will be seen elsewhere in her data, the idea of familiarity with people and contexts seems to be highly important for Anita's sense of comfort and confidence. In this speaking task, Anita explains specifically how strange it was to talk to Monika as they did not know each other despite being in the same class. However, one of the rare, and indeed the largest set of positive peaks, comes in a cluster towards the end of Graph 2 in the final 37 seconds of the second task (see Figure 12.3 below). She explains this positive block as follows:

Anita: I think at the end it was getting better, so …
Interviewer: And why do you think it is getting better?
Anita: I just felt more comfortable with it
(Idiodynamic interview)

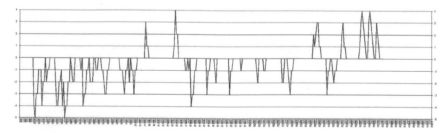

Figure 12.3 Anita idiodynamic graph Task 2

Table 12.2 Summary of Anita's idiodynamic data

Anita	Task 1	Task 2
Number of positive clicks	+14	+35
Number of negative clicks	−82	−109
Highest positive	+3	+4
Lowest negative	−5	−5
Total switches from positive/negative	5	5

The dynamics of her speaking confidence during these tasks are summarised in Table 12.2 of her idiodynamic data including the total number of positive/negative clicks, the range of her maximum peaks and troughs, as well as the number of times her graph switches from a negative to a positive phase or vice versa (cf. Fink, 2013).

What is striking about Anita's data, besides its obvious negativity in this context, is its relative consistency in remaining within the negative domain and rare switches to the positive side of the scale. From a dynamic systems perspective, it is especially interesting to note that there is, in fact, very little variation in positivity and her evaluation remains rather consistently negative throughout. Naturally, there is dynamism within the negative domain with certain aspects and incidents extenuating the extent of the negativity as one would expect on such a timescale of seconds with its heightened sensitivity to change.

In-class data – working EFL self (Level 2)

In contrast to the negativity experienced during the idiodynamic task, Anita reports much more positive levels of confidence during the in-class tasks as she consistently had values of between 2–3 on average[2], and, indeed, she never has a rating in the negative band although she has two single ratings on the neutral middle point. As in the idiodynamic data, she has no ratings on the most positive extreme on the scale at 1. Generally, the minor range of fluctuations in her self-confidence in this setting only stretch between 2–5 (see Figure 12.4 below). Anita did not comment explicitly on the reasons for her high levels of confidence in this setting, but it is perhaps worth noting that it was possible for her to work with the same set of people every week, sit in the same area of the classroom and nobody was ever called on in class as participation was entirely voluntary. Given her fear of evaluation and her desire for familiarity, these factors could have contributed positively to her degree of in-class comfort and confidence. Again, the most notable aspect of her data is its relative stability with her only dynamics taking place at the outset of the first two classes and then settling by the third session into a solid line of unchanging positivity, again possibly indicating the importance for Anita of clear expectations and familiarity. In this way, Anita's self-confidence in using her English in class remained fairly

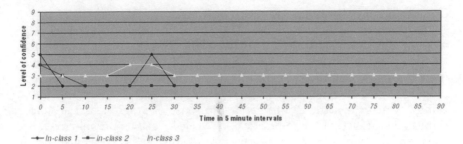

Figure 12.4 Anita in-class data (1 = high EFL self-confidence; 9 = low EFL self-confidence)

positive and stable within each session as well as across the semester as a whole in this setting.

Weekly journal data – EFL self (Level 3)

Obviously, the content of what Anita chose to report upon in her journals varied in its specifics each week, but two notable themes reoccurred throughout these data, as well as the interview data. The first and highly salient theme concerns her pronunciation. In her very first journal entry, Anita writes:

> My main worry this semester is my pronunciation. In school we never learnt anything about it and now I feel very unsure. But I decided to work very hard on it. I hope I will feel more secure and confident after this semester. (Journal entry 1)

Again, she seems to stress the idea that this is a new area with which she is unfamiliar and has no experience. Throughout all of her journal and interview data, Anita repeatedly stresses her belief in the importance of hard work and, as she indicates here, she is relatively optimistic that she can change and improve her pronunciation as long as she has a metacognitive knowledge of strategies of how to work on this. A strongly related second theme concerns planning, strategies and making lists of what to do. This sense of being organised and having a plan is very important for Anita to feel a sense of control and confidence. Indeed, her data are marked by a strong future-oriented perspective, as she repeatedly looks ahead, plans, organises and devises strategies for studying and improving.

Throughout the journal data, the more nuanced ups and downs of her experiences with her pronunciation are noticeable, although the general tone remains one of optimism, albeit mixed with considerable uncertainty and anxiety. She repeatedly expresses at various points how 'very insecure in this regard' she feels (e.g. Journal entry 3). In Week 7, she reports a critical incident in which a tutor advises her not to take the exam yet, as s/he predicts Anita would fail. Anita, unfortunately, then receives conflicting feedback from various people, leaving her even more uncertain and frustrated. In Week 10, she has a mock exam with her course tutor and everything seems to go well. At this point, she writes, 'I felt very relieved and I was happy that all the practice seems to be worth all the effort in the end. Now I feel much more secure and capable of passing this course'. However, in Week 14, directly before her pronunciation exam, she is once again full of doubt and uncertainty, which she attributes to having no sense of progress and an uncertainty about exactly how to practice. In Week 15, she reports having failed the pronunciation exam and how very disappointed she is. Yet, in the penultimate entry, she once again writes optimistically about a plan to work with a new strategy that she is hopeful will improve her pronunciation, namely, listening to audio books.

Interestingly, in terms of levels of the self, the journal data are less illuminating about the dynamics of Anita's overall sense of self in the EFL domain as she rarely makes reference to this level of self on this timescale. Instead she tends to write about specific skill domain areas, focusing strongly on her pronunciation, writing about this in eight of the 17 journal entries.

Macro-level interview data – EFL self (Level 4)

Anita's interview data share many themes that came up in her other data sets, namely, the importance of familiarity, and the need for metacognitive knowledge to feel a sense of agency, empowerment and confidence. On a more global level, Anita herself feels that her self-confidence generally fluctuates over the semester as she explains, 'I don't have a static confidence so it is always ... going up and down'. However, I would suggest that this confidence may fluctuate primarily across settings, as seen with the contrast in positivity across the in-class and idiodynamic data. Essentially, Anita does not express any negative self views but her data are marked by repeated expressions of uncertainty, as well as anxiety, which may make the positivity of her sense of self particularly susceptible to change across contexts. However, in the interview data across the semester as a whole, Anita gradually seems to gain an increased sense of certainty and confidence about her EFL abilities. In the final interview, she reports a sense of progress and states that her sense of self in English has become 'more stable'. Given the emphasis she has placed throughout on familiarity, this could be partly owing to it being now the end of her second year of studies, as well as the fact that she was highly successful (Grade A) in the course in which these data were collected.

A striking feature of Anita's data on the macro-level is her tendency to discuss her sense of self in respect to specific EFL domains, such as pronunciation, speaking or writing. Much of the interview data mirrored the journal entries regarding her pronunciation. She repeatedly explains how this area was new to her, but how with the right amount of practice and strategies, she feels that she will be able to improve. At the mid-term interview, she explains feeling a sense of progress in this area now that she can notice and hear a difference in how things are pronounced. Unsurprisingly, in the final interview after having failed the exam, she is again more uncertain and anxious.

In respect to speaking generally, in Interview 1, she says how uncertain she feels, 'when speaking sometimes I'm unsure and then I notice that I'm making mistakes and then I feel embarrassed'. However, in the final interview, she expresses more confidence saying, 'I feel more comfortable in talking and more fluent, but my pronunciation worries me' and 'I was always very scared at first when talking, and now it's better'. What is especially interesting is how she appears to isolate her pronunciation as separate from her speaking skills generally. This could be an example of 'compartmentalization' (Showers, 1992), in which a person protects their overall sense of self in a domain by 'isolating' an element that might affect its overall positivity.

One element that she remains consistently uncertain about throughout all her data is how she sees herself as a future language teacher and whether this is the right career path for her. For example, in the first interview, she says, 'I sometimes doubt if I want to be a teacher'. As with other domains in her sense of self, there are similar patterns in terms of the factors that are important for her in regard to this facet of her self, namely, the degree of familiarity, amount of experience and knowledge of strategies. An extract from her final interview illustrates this:

> I have times when I don't feel that I want to do it, when I don't feel that I'm suitable, or I don't know yet, I can't really tell it now because I haven't done the *Schulpraktikum* [practical experience] yet. Yes, there is always some struggle, but I think I can say if it fits when I stand in the class and really experience it, but, on the other hand, I think it's something you're getting into it with the years of teaching and then you develop own ideas and own plans and own strategies to deal with something. (Final interview)

In the context of her university studies, this 'teacher self' domain appears to be an integral part and subdomain of her overall EFL self.

Monika's data

Micro-level idiodynamic data – EFL speaking self-confidence (Level 1)

Monika's micro-level data is characterised by both positive (108 clicks) and negative (62 clicks) evaluations, but with an overall more positive tendency. Table 12.3 summarises the range and degrees of movement in her graphs (See Figures 12.5 and 12.6 below).

As can be seen, she does not use the full range of the scales, which never go below –2, but extend up to +4 on the positive band, again reinforcing the

Table 12.3 Summary of Monika's idiodynamic data

Monika	Task 1	Task 2
Number of positive clicks	+39	+69
Number of negative clicks	−20	−42
Highest positive	+4	+3
Lowest negative	−2	−2
Total switches from positive/negative	13	31

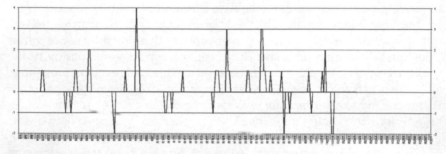

Figure 12.5 Monika idiodynamic graph Task 1

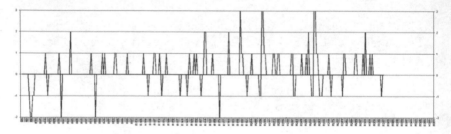

Figure 12.6 Monika idiodynamic graph Task 2

overall positive impression in her evaluation. An especially interesting characteristic of her idiodynamic data is that she switches frequently between the positive and negative bands, albeit often only crossing a minimal band range, in other words from either +1 to −1. Therefore, although her sense of self may fluctuate strongly across the band of positivity and exhibits considerable dynamism, the extent and magnitude of those changes is, on the whole, not especially large.

When discussing influences on her English speaking self-confidence during these tasks, she notes some of the same factors that Anita did, such as familiarity with the setting, topics, searching for words and ideas. In contrast to Anita, she explicitly noted that the filming did not affect her sense of self. The salient characteristic feature of Monika's data in this context is how closely her sense of self appears to be interdependent with how she believes Anita is feeling, behaving and evaluating the experience. For example, she explains, 'that's when I feel confident because things like ... when she is laughing, she understands me as well' (Idiodynamic interview). However, it is not only in an evaluative sense, but generally her interactions with Anita seem to be connected with various peaks and troughs. For example, she explains, 'There I felt confident because I helped her' (Idiodynamic interview). She summarises by saying about one particular peak, 'I think it is easier for her to talk, too, so it's going to affect me too' (Idiodynamic interview). In other words, how she feels during the tasks and how she rates her own speaking confidence appears highly interconnected with her beliefs about, and interpretation of, her partner's behaviours, experiences and thoughts. This suggests that Monika's EFL speaking self-confidence for this task is not only affected by internal factors, such as her access to necessary vocabulary, ideas and interest in the topic, but it also appears to be strongly dependent on how she views her interlocutor as well.

In-class data – working EFL self (Level 2)

Monika's in-class dynamics also indicate considerably more variation than Anita's and stretch across the full range of the scales, including the extremes of 1 and 9. Her ratings also oscillate across the positive and negative sides of the scale in every session: seven times in the first, four in the second and six in the final (see Figure 12.7 below).

The graphs for the first two in-class sessions are, overall, much more notably positive, as can be seen in Table 12.4; however, her ratings in the final in-class session reflect more of a balance between negative and positive ratings.

Unfortunately, Monika did not offer any possible reasons for this move towards more negative ratings in the final in-class session. One possible reason could be that the work in that class involved direct preparation for the upcoming written exam that was due to take place a week later. In the first

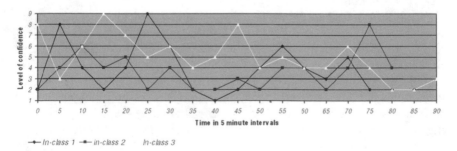

Figure 12.7 Monika in-class data (1 = high EFL self-confidence; 9 = low EFL self-confidence)

Table 12.4 Monika in-class positive and negative rating points

Monika in-class	Number of positive ratings	Number of negative ratings	Number of neutral ratings (point 5)
In-class 1	13	4	1
In-class 2	14	2	1
In-class 3	9	7	3

interview, Monika reports being anxious about exams generally, and thus the anticipation of the upcoming exams could have led to her more negative in-class ratings compared with the other two sessions. However, perhaps a more likely reason for this relative negativity can be deduced from her journal entry for that same week. The day before the class in question, she reports having had a negative experience, that the interviews later reveal is a falling out with a friend with whom she uses English socially. She explains in the journal how this experience negatively impacted her feelings towards English and willingness to use it.

> On Monday, I got confronted with a very unpleasant feeling and a disturbing view of English. I do not want to mention the event that brought me to these thoughts; however, this negative event has had a negative impact on my English ... all of a sudden, I did not want to use English anymore. (Journal entry 13)

In this way, it is possible to see how her out-of-university experiences with English, especially such social relationships and contact with other people, could potentially have an impact on her in-class EFL self, despite the fact the experience takes place beyond this immediate setting. This highlights the interconnections across levels of the self, domains and settings for Monika.

Weekly journal data – EFL self (Level 3)

Monika's journal entry was also detailed and varied, although its content was quite different to Anita's. For Monika, several themes were salient throughout her journals and the interview data. The most notable theme that reoccurs throughout is Monika's feeling that her sense of self in English and German (her L1 but also her second subject at university) are highly interconnected. She talks about having a 'double personality' with one for each language. She repeatedly discusses the challenges she faces in attempting not to mix the two languages. She refers to these issues in nine out of the 15 entries, sometimes with frustration (e.g. Journal entry 1 or 5) and, on other occasions, with humour (e.g. Journal entry 6). In Journal entry 10, she claims a feeling of progress in keeping the languages separate and says, 'At least, this "split" personality problem has become a little bit easier for me now'. She then starts to refer to it less, returning to it only in the final two entries. She then describes 'trying to maintain the balance between the two', rather than problematising their relationship. Therefore, across the semester, there seems to be a gradual improvement in how she perceives the relationship between these two aspects of her self.

Related to her perceived 'dual personality' are repeated statements in which Monika expresses delight when people do not recognise that she is a German speaker when using English, both in writing and speaking, for example, 'Something good: people seem to notice where I am from less and less' (Journal entry 6). Indeed, one of the things that characterises her data is the importance that she assigns to other people when discussing her sense of self, not only in an evaluative manner, but quite simply in terms of her social contact with other people in relation to the language. Monika expresses astute insight when she says in Journal entry 13, 'All people influence me, how I see myself and how I feel about my skills in general'. Many of the incidents she reports in her diaries involve other people in some way, either in terms of their feedback or opinion, their position as connections to the language or through social comparisons. These instances are often then associated with more positive or negative affective statements accordingly.

A particularly defining aspect of Monika's journal entries is that she writes much more on a global level about her sense of self. While she does mention skill domains, notably in respect to vocabulary, grammar and speaking, on the whole, she tends to refer more to her overall sense of self in English or as a student or a language learner generally. This structural difference in whether a person conceives of their sense of self in more domain-specific terms or more holistically may represent an important feature of a learner' sense of self and its effects on its dynamism, as will be discussed below.

A final notable element to her reported sense of self in these data is that it appears to be quite oriented to the past. For Monika, her past experiences seem to represent an important gauge for her present sense of self and she frequently compares aspects of, and experiences in, the present to the past, which often also gives her a positive sense of progress, e.g. 'I think that I have gained more self-confidence during the past few years (especially at university)' (Journal entry 8).

Macro-level interview data – EFL self (Level 4)

Many of the themes apparent in Monika's other data sets also appear in her interview data, such as her strong past-orientation, the competing nature of her L1/German and English selves, her more holistically defined sense of self and her reference to other people in various roles. However, Monika also makes some more domain-specific references to her sense of self in these data. One particularly interesting aspect, notable across the three interviews,

Table 12.5 Monika interview data extracts

Interview 1	Interview 2	Interview 3
Interviewer: ... what your strengths are?	Interviewer: And what would you say are the things you would say you feel most confident about, about your English at this stage?	I feel confident in talking, but in writing it's different
Monika: Probably writing, I'm writing a lot, also I'm kind of getting better at talking		
	Monika: Actually talking. And I think I have also become better in writing, so it's getting better.	

concerns her evaluations regarding her speaking and writing skills in English, which fluctuate from interview to interview as can be seen from the data extracts in Table 12.5.

An interesting dimension to these fluctuations between the skill domains is how Monika appears to view all these aspects of her English as highly interconnected:

> ... I don't know, probably writing every week in English, because writing is somehow more difficult because you need more vocabulary, and I think it had also an impact on my spoken English ... Yeah, I was also confident in writing, so I must be in speaking too. (Final interview 3)

This could imply that her EFL self could also be more sensitive to influences from all perceived EFL-related domains as she does not appear to separate and compartmentalise skill domains, or possibly even languages, but rather views them more holistically and as interconnected. Indeed, in the idiodynamic interview, she reveals how her experiences in English are also linked to her self in German, as she explains that being successful in a foreign language must give you confidence that you cannot fail in what is essentially your mother tongue:

> Probably mastering English a little bit more ... When you are good at something as big as a foreign language, then you know you can't fail in your own mother tongue. (Idiodynamic interview 2)

She also discusses other aspects of her studies, as was evident in her mind-map language learner narrative for the first interview, in which she sees her

English self as connected to her academic self and her sense of self in her courses, such as literature, linguistics and teacher training. In the final interview, she comments that her overall sense of self-confidence generally and academically has been positively affected by her successes in English. As she states, 'mastering a foreign language, at least to some extent, it has an improvement on my self'.

Overall, her interview data also reflect an upward tendency as implied in the journal data. Indeed, in the final interview she concludes, 'now I feel *way* more confident' (italics added for emphasis), which suggests also a strength of perceived change. In the same interview, she comments that her confidence is becoming more stable, in her words, 'like a rock'. However, as has also been seen in the other data sets, Monika's sense of self appears to be able to fluctuate quite considerably, even while maintaining an overall more positive character. Therefore, a problem facing all longitudinal research is that, at present, it is impossible to judge to what extent any changes to her sense of self may remain and endure after the end of this study.

Discussion

Both sets of data are quite different in terms of their content and their dynamics, despite the learners' similarities in terms of their stage and choice of studies, age, educational background, level of proficiency (both gained Grade A on completing this course) and even gender. These differences highlight the uniqueness of individuals, their reported sense of self and the inherent complexity of self systems. An interesting difference in the two learners was, despite responding to the same questions and research guidelines, that they chose to discuss very different forms and levels of self, possibly suggesting a different structure and conceptualisation of self, at least on the more macro-level. Lichtwarck-Aschoff *et al.* (2008) suggest a qualitative difference in identity between the 'expression of identity', which functions on micro-level timescales and is linked to real-time experiences of self, and the 'reflection on identity', which is aggregated across time and tends to be reported on a more abstract, generalised level through explicit reflection. This distinction may prove useful in future studies as both learners differed strongly on the macro-levels of self in terms of the content and focus of what they reported, but the more micro-level selves have a tighter 'scope and size' and are reported in real-time creating perhaps less potential for individual variation in content.

On the macro levels, Monika, for example, was generally more holistic in describing her self, referring to herself more as a language learner and EFL learner as a whole. She also made clear connections between all domains of her self giving the impression of a more interconnected system. In contrast, Anita reported a much more fragmented, domain-specific sense of self, barely

discussing herself as a language or even EFL learner, instead referring to specific skill domains, including reference to herself as a future language teacher
in line with her general future-orientation. This structural variation in the
learners' sense of self raises interesting questions about the potential influence of different system structures on the dynamics of the system. From
these data, the question arises about whether a more holistic and strongly
interconnected sense of self may make the self more susceptible to change
given the close connections between different facets and domains of the self
and their overall structure (see also Linville's (1985) idea of dynamism
depending on degrees of self-complexity). In contrast, a more complex,
domain-specific sense of self might allow for more 'buffering' between
domains and the chance to isolate or compartmentalise (Showers, 1992) any
area in which the learner may have negative experiences. Compartment-
alisation could also lead the learner to experience more potential 'conflicts'
between different areas of the self, perhaps leading to a lack of certainty in
the self (see discussions of self-concept clarity, Campbell, 1990; Campbell
et al., 1996; and self-esteem fragility/security, Kernis *et al.*, 2000). Indeed, it
was notable that Anita tended to refer more to her self-beliefs in terms of
certainty, whereas Monika tended to discuss her sense of self more in terms
of positivity and in affective terms. Such defining characteristics of a learner's self system could well impact on the types and degrees of changes in a
learner's self over time and place.

In terms of the drivers of change in each learner's self system, different
factors appeared to be important for each individual. This suggests that the
defining parameters and the most significant motors of change in the self
system are also not universal but vary across individuals. A key feature of
these individual drivers of change was the notable patterns across the levels
of the system for each learner. For Anita, her sense of self was driven by factors, such as her degree of familiarity, metacognitive knowledge and experiences of success or progress. Interestingly, these drivers of change were
fundamentally the same on each level of self, just expressed in different
ways. Thus, for example, on the idiodynamic level, it was her familiarity
with her interlocutor that affected her most strongly. In the more macro
levels of the journals and interviews, she repeatedly referred to changes in
expectations and frames of reference in the university setting, as well as
specifically her unfamiliarity with the field of pronunciation. One suggestion
in discussions of the dynamics of the self made by Mischel (2004) concerns
'IF ... THEN' signature dynamics. This means IF certain situations and factors come together, THEN I usually or typically feel or behave a certain way.
In other words, self dynamics may be governed by certain control parameters implying that intra-learner variation may not necessarily be random,
but there could be patterns to the system's behaviour, which could reveal
underlying characteristics of the self system. Such signature dynamics could
be important to understand in complexity research, given the search for

patterns in the dynamics of the system (Dörnyei & Ushioda, 2011). For Anita, it might be possible to express these signature dynamics as, 'IF Anita is familiar with a context (whatever level), feels she has metacognitive strategies to cope with the setting and its demands, and if she senses a degree of progress and success, THEN she is able to feel more confident in her sense of self (at that level)'.

In contrast, for Monika, her most important drivers of change are clearly interpersonal factors, as well as a sense of progress gained from a comparison of the present and the past. Again, these same drivers of change are apparent at different levels of her self system. In the idiodynamic data, for example, they are reflected in her strong focus on Anita's reactions and, in the interview and journal data, in her affective responses to her experiences with others. For Monika, these signature dynamics could be expressed as, 'IF Monika feels positive interpersonal dynamics and relationships (whatever level), as well as a positive sense of progress compared to past experiences, THEN she is able to feel more confident in her sense of self (at that level)'.

In terms of the dynamics for each learner, there also seems to be a number of parallels in the types and forms of dynamics across the levels of the systems. For example, for Anita, there is a high degree of relative stability within a certain timeframe, even if the positivity was noted to change dramatically across settings. Naturally, there are more visible fluctuations on the idiodynamic level, as one would expect given the timescale. Yet the predominant impression was one of relative consistency and more dynamic stability once a certain state was entered – such as the negative state in the idiodynamic data, and the positive state in the in-class data, mindful that these nevertheless remain 'snapshots' of moments in time. On the more macro levels, there were fewer fluctuations across time, but gradual changes not necessarily in terms of positivity but in terms of feelings of control, comfort and the degree of certainty with which she holds a certain self belief. Considering these characteristics in terms of dynamic systems theory, I would suggest Anita's uncertainty on each level of her self system makes the system relatively unstable, particularly in respect to contextual factors. Thus, when parameters change (such as when contextual familiarity varies), her sense of self can enter a deep basin of positivity or negativity, e.g. the change of positivity between the idiodynamic and the in-class data. The depth of the basins in her landscape of her self system reflect the character of the data that, once her self system has entered a specific basin, it remains relatively stable in that setting until the parameters change again, such as when she becomes more familiar and thus more certain in that setting, or she encounters an entirely new unfamiliar setting.

For Monika, there is a high degree of dynamism in her self system at all levels, especially in terms of changes in positivity/negativity, despite also an overriding sense of positivity throughout. On the more macro levels, her data also reflect considerable dynamism depending on specific events and interactions with people and yet she also perceived a gradual progression towards more stability and increased positivity. Monika's self dynamics seem to be marked by more short, sharp, quick changes. As such, Monika's self landscape seems to be defined by potentially a greater number of shallower attractor basins than Anita's. This suggests her sense of self is in a greater state of fluctuation all the time as it is affected by a broad range of parameters, such as interactional and social relationships of all kinds, as well as the relative holistic nature and the strongly interconnected facets of her self implying that changes in one part can easily affect other parts. However, the landscape structure also implies shallow basins, which means that her sense of self can more easily switch to another basin, rather than settling within one state making it generally more dynamic (for other discussions of self dynamics in terms of attractor states, see Vallacher & Nowak, 2009).

These data thus seem to suggest that each learner's self system has a different fundamental landscape. The parameters of each system are defined by different key drivers of change unique to the individual learner. A surprising finding in these data is the strong patterns of similarity in terms of the nature of the dynamics across the different levels of the system, as well as patterns across levels in terms of the same fundamental key drivers of change. It is worth considering whether these patterns in dynamics across the nested systems implies that fractalisation of the self (cf. Sade, 2009) could refer not only to the components of the system and their interrelations at each level, but potentially also to the structure and landscape of nested systems and consequently their dynamics and drivers of change (cf. de Bot et al., 2013).

Conclusion

It is hoped that this chapter has shown a potentially rich methodological approach to investigating the dynamics of a learner's self system. Each layer of data collected in this study could have been exploited in considerably more detail on its own. However, nuanced, wider-reaching insights have hopefully been gained by creating a composite picture of the dynamics of these learners' sense of self on multiple levels across different timescales. The findings have highlighted the highly individual nature of each learner's self system, not only in terms of its composition and structure but also in terms of its key drivers of change as well as its patterns of dynamics. It is hoped that the chapter has also illustrated the potential offered by complexity perspectives in generating exciting insights into self dynamics in ways that may integrate many other, sometimes conflicting, findings from the field. Future research is now needed to extend this work learning from the experiences in this study and exploring some of the hypotheses generated. Questions that I feel are particularly worthy of investigation are:

(1) the extent to which a nested systems model of the self attending to different levels and timescales proves useful for guiding empirical research, especially regarding dynamics;
(2) whether 'IF . . . THEN' signature dynamics (Mischel, 2004) might enable us to recognise patterns in complex dynamic systems, such as the self, and avoid the criticism that complexity theories offer nothing but chaos and unpredictability; and
(3) the question about whether fractalisation might function in multiple respects across different levels of the self, again aiding our search for potential patterns in the midst of interconnected complex dynamic systems (cf. Dörnyei & Ushioda, 2011).

Ultimately, we are only still at the beginning of our journey to understand the potential offered by complexity perspectives in conceptual, empirical and methodological terms in respect to the self in SLA. However, given that complexity theories are grounded in, rather than abstracted from, reality (cf. Byrne & Callaghan, 2014), such perspectives will doubtless have a vital role to play in helping us to understand the truly unique, situated, complex, dynamic self systems of real-world language learners.

Notes

(1) The data from the third student were omitted from the analysis reported on in this chapter. Her profile as a mature, visiting student was considerably different and it was decided to focus on two comparable students for the purposes of this chapter.
(2) 1 = highest level of confidence; 9 = lowest level

References

Byrne, D. and Callaghan. G. (2014) *Complexity Theory and the Social Sciences: The State of the Art*. London: Routledge.

Campbell, J.D. (1990) Self-esteem and clarity of the self-concept. *Journal of Personality and Social Psychology* 59 (3), 538–549.

Campbell, K.W. and Sedikides, C. (1999) Self-threat magnifies the self-serving bias: A meta-analytic integration. *Review of General Psychology* 3 (1), 23–43.

Campbell, J.D., Trapnell, P.D., Heine, S.J., Katz, I.M., Lavallee, L.F. and Lehman, D.R. (1996) Self-concept clarity: Measurement, personality correlates, and cultural boundaries. *Journal of Personality and Social Psychology* 70 (1), 141–156.

Davis, B. and Sumara, D. (2006) *Complexity and Education: Inquiries into Learning, Teaching, and Research*. New York: Routledge.

de Bot, K., Lowie, W., Thorne, S.L. and Verspoor, M. (2013) Dynamic systems theory as a comprehensive theory of second language development. In M. Mayo, M. Gutierrez-Mangado and M. Adrián (eds) *Contemporary Approaches to Second Language Acquisition* (pp. 199–220). Amsterdam: John Benjamins.

Dörnyei, Z. (2010) The relationship between language aptitude and language learning motivation: individual differences from a dynamic systems perspective. In E. Macaro (ed.) *Continuum Companion to Second Language Acquisition* (pp. 247–267). London: Continuum.

Dörnyei, Z. and Ushioda, E. (2011) *Teaching and Researching Motivation* (2nd edn). Harlow: Longman.

Fink, S. (2013) An exploration of the dynamic processes affecting EFL learners' willingness to communicate during speaking activities. Unpublished Master's thesis. University of Graz, Austria.

Gregersen, T. and Horwitz, E.K. (2002) Language learning and perfectionism: Anxious and non-anxious language learners' reactions to their own oral performance. *The Modern Language Journal* 86 (4), 562–570.

Harter, S. (1999) *The Construction of the Self: A Developmental Perspective*. New York: Guildford Press.

Kernis, M.H. and Goldman, B.M. (2003) Stability and variability in self-concept and self-esteem. In M.R. Leary and J.P. Tangney (eds) *Handbook of Self and Identity* (pp. 106–127). New York: The Guildford Press.

Kernis, M.H., Paradise, A.W., Whitaker, D.J., Wheatman, S.R. and Goldman, B.N. (2000) Master of one's psychological domain? Not likely if one's self-esteem is unstable. *Personality and Social Psychology Bulletin* 26 (10), 1297–1305.

Lichtwarck-Aschoff, A., van Geert, P., Bosma, H. and Kunnen, S. (2008) Time and identity: A framework for research and theory formation. *Developmental Review* 28 (3), 370–400.

Linville, P.W. (1985) Self-complexity and affective extremity: Don't put all of your eggs in one cognitive basket. *Social Cognition* 3 (1), 94–120.

MacIntyre, P.D. (2012) The idiodynamic method: A closer look at the dynamics of communication traits. *Communication Research Reports* 29 (4), 361–367.

MacIntyre, P.D. and Legatto, J.J. (2011) A dynamic system approach to willingness to communicate: Developing an idiodynamic method to capture rapidly changing affect. *Applied Linguistics* 32 (2), 149–171.

Markus, H. and Kunda, Z. (1986) Stability and malleability of the self-concept. *Journal of Personality and Social Psychology* 51 (4), 858–866.

Markus, H and Wurf, E. (1987) The dynamic self-concept: A social psychological perspective. *Annual Review of Psychology* 38 (1), 299–337.

Mercer, S. (2011a) The self as a complex dynamic system. *Studies in Second Language Learning and Teaching* 1 (1), 57–82.

Mercer, S. (2011b) Language learner self-concept: Complexity, continuity and change. *System* 39 (3), 335–346.

Mercer, S. (2014) The self from a complexity perspective. In S. Mercer and M. Williams (eds) *Multiple Perspectives on the Self in SLA* (pp. 160–176). Bristol: Multilingual Matters.

Mercer, S. and Williams, M. (eds) (2014) *Multiple Perspectives on the Self in SLA*. Bristol: Multilingual Matters.

Mischel, W. (2004) Toward an integrative science of the person. *Annual Review of Psychology* 55 (1), 1–22.

Nowak, A., Vallacher, R.R. and Zochowski, M. (2005) The emergence of personality: Dynamic foundations of individual variation. *Developmental Review* 25 (3–4), 351–385.

Onorato, R.S. and Turner, J. C. (2004) Fluidity in the self-concept: the shift from personal to social identity. *European Journal of Social Psychology* 34 (3), 257–278.

Sade, L.A. (2009) Complexity and identity reconstruction in second language acquisition. *RBLA* 9 (2), 515–537.

Saldaña, J. (2003) *Longitudinal Qualitative Research: Analyzing Change through Time*. Walnut Creek, CA: AltaMira Press.

Showers, C. (1992) Compartmentalization of positive and negative self-knowledge: Keeping bad apples out of the bunch. *Journal of Personality and Social Psychology* 62 (6), 1036–1049.

Swann, W.B. (1997) The trouble with change: Self-verification and allegiance to the self. *Psychological Science* 8 (3), 177–180.

Tesser, A. (1988) Towards a self-evaluation maintenance model of social behaviour. In L. Berkowitz (ed.) *Advances in Experimental Social Psychology* (Vol. 21) (pp. 181–227). New York. Academic Press.

van Dijk, M., Verspoor, M. and Lowie, W. (2011) Variability and DST. In M. Verspoor, K. De Bot and W. Lowie (eds) *A Dynamic Approach to Second Language Development Methods and Techniques* (pp. 55–84). Amsterdam: John Benjamins.

Vallacher, R.R. and Nowak, A. (2009) The dynamics of human experience: Fundamentals of dynamical social psychology. In S.J. Guastello, M. Koopmans and D. Pincus (eds) *Chaos and Complexity in Psychology: The Theory of Nonlinear Dynamical Systems* (pp. 370– 401). Cambridge: Cambridge University Press.

van Geert, P. (2009) Nonlinear complex dynamical systems in developmental psychology. In S.J. Guastello, M. Koopmans and D. Pincus (eds) *Chaos and Complexity in Psychology: The Theory of Nonlinear Dynamical Systems* (pp. 242–281). Cambridge: Cambridge University Press.

13 Changes in Motivation, Anxiety and Self-efficacy During the Course of an Academic Writing Seminar

Katalin Piniel and Kata Csizér

Describing and understanding change in issues pertaining to language learning have been increasingly important (Cameron, 2003; Dörnyei, 2005; Larsen-Freeman, 1997; Larsen-Freeman & Cameron, 2008). In order to map change and test less often used longitudinal statistical procedures, we have designed a study to analyse the ways in which the variables representing Dörnyei and Tseng's (2009) motivation–affect–cognition framework (i.e. motivation, anxiety and self-efficacy) change during the course of a university academic writing seminar. We opted for a sequential mixed methods design (Tashakkori & Teddlie, 2003) and collected both qualitative and quantitative data in a popular undergraduate programme in Budapest, Hungary. Our data were analysed in multiple stages. First, we used latent growth curve models to detect overall change and then carried out longitudinal clustering to define distinct groups of students with various trajectories. Qualitative data were used to give voice to the measured changes. Variability and correlation analyses were also conducted to investigate the change and the interrelationship of the above-mentioned individual variables. In the following chapter, we describe the theoretical background to the study, offer a short summary of the methods used and describe changes in motivation, anxiety and self-efficacy beliefs.

Dynamic Systems

Recently, in applied linguistics research, the description and investigation of various constructs as interrelated and interconnected parts of complex dynamic systems (DSs) have gained ground. Van Geert (1994: 50) defines a DS as 'a set of variables that mutually affect each other's changes over time'.

In this vein, Dörnyei (2009, 2010) and DeKeyser (2012) have begun to advocate the study of individual differences (IDs) variables in language learning through a DSs perspective, where the focus is on change, interaction and variability rather than merely observing isolated relationships between variables in the hope of formulating generalizations. With that in mind, Dörnyei (2009, 2010) proposes the existence of a higher-order amalgam of learner characteristics that encompasses an emerging self-organized combination of cognitive, affective and motivational factors. This amalgam can be considered as a subsystem, nested in the complex DS of the language learner. In the present study, motivation, writing anxiety and writing self-efficacy will be viewed as constituents of a DS, where these factors are interrelated and are observed to interact through time.

Scholars advocating a DSs approach in second language (L2) acquisition research have listed the fundamental features of DSs (de Bot *et al.*, 2007: 7; de Bot & Larsen-Freeman, 2011: 9), which include sensitive dependence on initial conditions, interconnectedness, nonlinear development, emergent characteristics, intra-individual variation, inter-individual variation, dependence on internal as well as external resources and change owing to interaction with the environment and internal re-organization.

These characteristics suggest that studies on IDs in language learning from a DS perspective likewise necessitate the study of the interrelationship(s) of variables with the help of longitudinal developmental data on inter-individual, as well as intra-individual variation (van Dijk *et al.*, 2011). This research approach is thought to be useful in uncovering dynamic principles for two reasons. First, truly longitudinal data (Menard, 2002) lends itself to analysis of temporal change in a non-retrospective time setting. Second, while we agree with Dörnyei's (2007: 79) contention that 'longitudinal research is rather underutilized in our field', it is also important to add that L2 acquisition research has been even less forthcoming in employing sophisticated procedures to analyse truly longitudinal data.

The L2 Motivational Self System and its Subcomponents

Although the majority of the synchronic studies have provided a better understanding of variability in language learning success, longitudinal studies are believed to be more fruitful in shedding light on how these individual variables interact through time and exert their influence on one another and on language learning success (DeKeyser, 2012; Dörnyei, 2009, 2010). One of the key variables affecting the process of language learning is perceived to be L2 motivation (Dörnyei & Ushioda, 2011; Gardner, 2010) in that it explains the amount of effort invested into, and general persistence towards, language learning. Despite the fact that researchers acknowledge the changing nature of motivation, longitudinal empirical studies have remained scarce in the field; one notable exception is the work of Ushioda (1998), who, using qualitative data, investigated how the passing of time affected students' motivational dispositions.

The L2 Motivational Self System (Dörnyei, 2005; see also Dörnyei & Ushioda, 2011) forms one of the main theoretical underpinnings of the present study. This theory hypothesizes that students' motivated learning behaviour, that is their choices, effort and persistence, will be largely affected by three variables: (a) their ideal L2 self, that is the extent to which students can imagine themselves as highly proficient users of the given foreign language; (b) their ought-to L2 self, which encompasses the outside pressures students acknowledge throughout the learning process that make them invest energy in language learning; and (c) the language learning experience, which involves attitudes to classroom processes (Dörnyei, 2005, 2009; Dörnyei & Ushioda, 2011).

Writing Anxiety

Another prominent variable that has received considerable research attention in IDs studies is foreign language anxiety, a variable that emerged in the 1970s (Kleinmann, 1977; Scovel, 1978). As far as its relevance to language learning is concerned, researchers have mostly focused on its negative aspect (e.g. Horwitz et al., 1986; MacIntyre, 1999), even though it is generally accepted in psychology that both debilitating and facilitating types of anxiety exist (Kleinmann, 1977).

Besides differentiating between the adverse and favourable effects of anxiety, scholars also distinguish between trait, state and situation-specific types of anxiety (MacIntyre, 1999). Language anxiety or foreign language classroom anxiety have been described as situation-specific anxiety, in other words, repeated momentary experiences of anxiety (state anxiety) linked to the context of language learning in particular. Yet another classification of language anxiety related to feelings of inhibition linked to different language learning skills includes speaking, listening, reading and writing anxiety (Cheng et al., 1999; Piniel, 2014). Recently, Pae (2012) has also argued for using the skills approach when investigating foreign language anxiety: Pae found that the types of anxiety experienced pertaining to the particular skills in language learning can be clearly distinguished from one another, but at the same time have been found to contribute significantly to the global construct of foreign language classroom anxiety.

The diversity of approaches exploring the effects of language anxiety, however, mainly rests on studies using cross-sectional designs. Longitudinal inquiries specifically addressing the change in levels of language anxiety are lacking. There are, however, a few exceptions where task-specific language anxiety and its influence on cognition (e.g. MacIntyre, 1994) have been investigated. Also, studies of change in willingness to communicate seem, by definition, to include an indirect link to change in anxiety (especially speaking anxiety) levels (e.g. MacIntyre & Legatto, 2010). Hence, in the present study, for the purposes of mapping the change in levels of anxiety throughout an academic writing course in English, we included state alongside situation-specific measures for both writing anxiety and facilitating anxiety (Piniel, 2014).

Writing Self-efficacy

For the cognitive component of the framework, in the present study we also decided to investigate self-efficacy. Self-efficacy beliefs include individuals' own dispositions towards what they think they are able to do and what tasks they can accomplish in the process of learning (Bandura, 1993, 1997, 2006; Valentine et al., 2004). Bandura (1993) hypothesized that self-efficacy beliefs affect students' goals, their motivation and anxiety; therefore, in a study focusing on changes in motivation and anxiety, it seems crucial to also tap into possible changes in learners' self-efficacy levels.

Research into self-efficacy and foreign language learning has started to flourish with pioneering work by Mills (2009), Mills and Perón (2009) and Mills et al. (2007). In their overview of self-efficacy research in the context of L2 learning, Raoofi et al. (2012) assert that most studies have focused on the relationship of self-efficacy and language learning strategies, language anxiety and achievement using correlational designs. They also point out that the ways in which self-efficacy develops has scarcely been examined.

One aspect of self-efficacy that is relevant to the present discussion, writing self-efficacy, has been investigated by Pajares (2003), who suggests several ways of operationalizing writing self-efficacy. In line with these proposals, in the present study we conceptualize writing self-efficacy as 'assessing the confidence that students have to complete writing tasks' (Pajares, 2003: 143). Previous research has shown writing efficacy to be positively linked with learners' interest and expanded effort, as well as with performance (Pajares, 2003; Pajares & Johnson, 1994; Schunk, 2003), and negatively associated with writing anxiety (McCarthy et al., 1985).

Two exceptional studies that have begun to fill the gap in research on writing self-efficacy and its development over time are those by Mills (2009) and Mills and Perón (2009). Using an experimental design, Mills (2009) found that false beginner French students' self-efficacy improved significantly in view of the five goal areas of the Standards of Foreign Language Learning after having taken part in project-based learning. Mills and Perón (2009) also investigated the change of learners' self-efficacy by targeting L2 writing in an intermediate French class using global simulation. The results of pre-tests and post-tests revealed that learners' sense of self-efficacy specifically related to composition writing sub-skills in a foreign language (e.g. using appropriate vocabulary, correct use of grammatical structures, etc.) increased in the global simulation classroom, but that their overall self-efficacy beliefs about their abilities to complete writing tasks did not change. Although through these studies we may gain insight into how writing self-efficacy in a foreign language can change, a research niche presents itself for longitudinal investigations that tap into this process.

Dynamic Relationship of Anxiety, Self-efficacy and Motivation

One of the IDs amalgams Dörnyei (2010) suggests investigating in a DS vein is the tripartite of motivation–affect–cognition. His idea coincides with social and cognitive psychologists who in the past decades have started emphasizing the interrelationship of affect and cognitive processing (Linnenbrink & Pintrich, 2004). According to Linnenbrink and Pintrich (2004), there are two distinguishable types of theories focusing on this inter-relationship: appraisal theories and cognitivist theories. In the present study it is the former we will use as a frame for studying motivation–affect–cognition. This is motivated by two reasons. First, the cognitive component in these theories (e.g. Lazarus, 1991; Scherer, 2001) is present in the form of appraisal (evaluation of the individual's resources to cope with the negative emotion; see Lazarus, 1991), a notion that in fact is very similar to self-efficacy (Zimmerman, 2000) as defined by motivational theories built on a cognitive framework; 'self-efficacy theory postulates that individuals' beliefs about their ability to produce successful outcomes and attain designated goals are critical to their achievement motivation' (Hidi et al., 2004: 90). Second, anxiety appears in appraisal theories as an affective factor that individuals will attempt to alleviate by way of problem focused (approach) or emotion focused (avoidance) coping mechanisms (Lazarus, 1991). Thus, it follows that situation-specific emotional experiences also influence motivational processes via self-efficacy beliefs (Hidi et al., 2004), which in turn renders the language learning anxiety–self-efficacy–language learning motivation triad a meaningful subsystem of investigation.

Research Questions

On the basis of the literature review presented above, we propose to investigate the following research questions: (1) How can we characterize changes concerning motivation, anxiety and self-efficacy throughout an academic writing course?; (2) Are there any typical trajectories in the obtained results?; (3) How can these trajectories be characterized?; (4) What character-izes the interrelationship of motivation, anxiety and self-efficacy throughout the academic writing course?

Method

Our study was guided by the above considerations and the notion that 'development is not always gradual (but is not always a matter of qualitative shifts, either) and development is clearly different between individuals, but also shows general patterns or prototypical trajectories' (van Geert, 1994: 14). Therefore, for our DS approach to investigating the subsystem of motiva-tion, writing anxiety and writing self-efficacy in the English-for-Academic-Purposes classroom, we used a longitudinal (sequential) mixed methods design (Tashakkori & Teddlie, 2003) with which we could draw a general picture of the participants, observe the general development of the sample, identify prototypical developmental trajectories the students went through (as well as their variability) and investigate the interrelationship of the selected IDs variables. This approach is close to what Byrne (2005) describes as a simplistic-complexity approach, where micro-social phenomena are under scrutiny with the possibility of drawing macro-social implications. The micro-social aspect of our study is the academic writing course in English at a large Hungarian university, while the macro-social component is comprised of curriculum and programme design, as well as the inclusion of international students in higher education in Hungary (Tankó & Csizér, in press).

Setting and participants

As Byrne (2005) has pointed out, complexity-based knowledge is essen-tially local; therefore, we decided to investigate a single setting involving Hungarian freshman students pursuing a BA in English language and litera-ture. The single setting design was also seen to be important in order to decrease possible contextual influences. The selected university is one of the oldest and most prestigious in Hungary as well as one of the most popular. The yearly intake of students is around 300, and all students entering the BA programme have to complete both compulsory and elective courses in order to obtain a degree. Courses offered cover a wide range of topics, including language development, theoretical and applied linguistics, as well as British and American literature and history. Despite the eminence of the school and the wide range of topics covered in the three-year BA track, students' disposi-tions towards its English programme can best be described as ambiguous (Kormos & Csizér, 2012; Kormos et al., 2008) as many students have com-plained about not being interested in all aspects of their study, not receiving enough guidance from tutors and receiving too little language instruction.

As for the participants in the present study, longitudinal data pertaining to 21 students are analysed. Of the participating students six were male and 15 female. The students' average age was 20.5 years; the youngest participants being 19 years old and the oldest 35 years old. Their average age of starting to learn English was eight. All these students were freshman BA students majoring in English, and all of them were completing the second of the two compulsory courses on academic writing (a course on English for Academic Purposes with a special focus on writing, entitled Academic Skills 2). In March, all students had to sit for a centrally administered and assessed Academic Skills Test, which covered the material learned in Academic Skills 1 as well as the beginning of Academic Skills 2, which constituted 50% of their final course grades for the latter. Based on the Common European Framework (Council of Europe, 2001), the students' level of English knowledge was between B2–C2. Many of the participants reported learning other foreign languages in addition to English, most often German, French or Italian.

Instruments

There were several data collection instruments used in the study to collect both quantitative and qualitative data. We collected data with the help of: (a) questionnaires mapping students' general (situation-specific) disposition and, at six points in time, current states of motivation, anxiety and self-efficacy within an academic semester; (b) grades of an academic writing test (the lowest i.e. failing grade is 1, the highest obtainable grade is 5) administered to students in the middle of the term, as well as their course grades, both of which are intended to reflect their performance; and (c) student essays (short, descriptive) written at the end of the semester concerning possible changes in dispositions towards the course and changes in experiences during the semester.

Two versions of the questionnaire were completed by the students, a longer version about participants' general dispositions concerning motivation, anxiety and self-efficacy, and a shorter version of the same instrument intended to measure state motivation, state anxiety, state self-efficacy and facilitating anxiety. The same items appeared in both questionnaires, but the instructions differed. Apart from collecting biographical information on the students, the following constructs were measured with the help of a five-point Likert-type scale, where 1 indicated the negative and 5 the positive end of the scale.

(1) Motivated learning behaviour (5 items; Cronbach's alpha = 0.78) describes how much effort students are willing to invest in language learning. Sample item: I do my best to learn English as well as possible. (Kormos & Csizér, 2008; Ryan, 2005)

(2) Ideal L2 self (4 items; Cronbach's alpha = 0.74) measures students' vision about their future language use. Sample item: When I think of my future career, I imagine being able to use English on a near native level. (Kormos & Csizér, 2008; Ryan, 2005)

(3) Ought-to L2 self (7 items; Cronbach's alpha = 0.76) asks about external pressures concerning learning English. Sample item: I feel that I am expected to speak English like a native. (Kormos & Csizér, 2008; Ryan, 2005)

(4) Language learning experience (4 items; Cronbach's alpha = 0.86) inquires about participants' past experience concerning learning English. Sample item: I always liked the tasks we did in English classes at my secondary school. (Kormos & Csizér, 2008; Ryan, 2005)

(5) Writing anxiety (8 items; Cronbach's alpha = 0.82) includes statements about students' anxiety concerning writing tasks at the university. Sample item: When I hand in a written assignment, I am anxious about my tutor's opinion. (Piniel, 2014)

(6) Writing self-efficacy (9 items; Cronbach's alpha = 0.91) measures to what extent students think that they are able to complete their writing assignments with self-confidence and ease. Sample item: I am sure that I can complete any writing task in English. (Bandura, 2006)

(7) Facilitating anxiety (for writing) (only appeared in the short version of the questionnaire; therefore, no Cronbach's alpha can be given) measures anxiety tied to the English for Academic purposes class and a result of which the learner invests more effort into performing well. Sample item: The more important a writing task is, the better I perform. (Piniel, 2014)

As for the qualitative data, students were asked to complete a short-essay task. The instructions of this task read as follows: 'Write a short descriptive essay of 200 words on the topic of how your attitudes and feelings towards academic essays have changed throughout the Academic Skills 2 course. Use specific reasons and examples to illustrate your point. Elaborate on how you felt at the beginning, before the Academic Skills Test, after the Test, and towards the end of the course'.

Data collection

Data was collected during the spring term of 2012, which lasted for 14 weeks. The term started in mid-February with an intensive preparation for the high-stakes test in mid-March. Owing to the fact that two instructors corrected each test, it took almost a month for the students to receive their test results. As the grade obtained in the test accounted for 50% of their final grade, once their results were published, the students had limited opportunities to influence their final grade. Prior to the semester, instructors were contacted and permission was obtained to collect data in six groups.

Data collection was scheduled in a way to cause minimum obstruction in teaching. Participation was voluntary, and anonymity was guaranteed for all the participants. Data were matched with the help of a code system that was not inputted into the data file.

After a pilot study with 79 students in the autumn term of 2011 (Csizér, 2012), the full version of the situation-specific questionnaire was completed at the end of March 2012. Further quantitative data was obtained on six different occasions during the semester with the help of a shorter, state-specific version of the previous instrument. The questionnaire was administered twice prior to the Academic Skills Test (Week 4) and four times after the test in equal intervals. Finally, qualitative data in the form of short essays were collected at the end of the semester.

Data analysis

Quantitative data were computer coded using SPSS for Windows 16. Following descriptive analyses, latent growth curve modelling (Byrne & Crombie, 2003) and longitudinal cluster analysis, variability analysis and correlation analysis were employed to shed light on change, possible trajectories and the interrelationship of the individual variables under investigation, following the approach of Verspoor and van Dijk (2011).

Larsen-Freeman and Cameron (2008) suggest using longitudinal approaches for the investigation of nonlinearity and variability in dynamic systems theory (DST) research, and among others they mention the possibility of adopting such analytical techniques as growth curve analysis (also known as latent growth curve modelling). Latent growth curve modelling (LGM) is an analytical tool based on the methodology of structural equation modelling (for a brief overview see Byrne, 2010); consequently, it employs regression models to test the hypotheses of expected change through time in individual trajectories regarding a measured variable (Byrne, 2010; Preacher et al., 2008). More precisely, the latent growth curve model depicts the average growth curve of all individuals. It involves the analysis of means, variances, covariances and estimations of models that include the 'regression of observed scores onto the slope and intercept factors' (Byrne, 2010: 306), where the slope factor indicates the rate of change and the intercept the difference between individuals' initial states in view of the observed variable. In its simplest form, LGM is suitable to test hypotheses of linear change, but it can also be used to detect nonlinear trajectories of a more systematic character (e.g. quadratic, logistic relationships) as well as those involving fluctuations, stoppings and unequal magnitudes of change (McArdle & Epstein, 1987) (for a detailed guide see Duncan et al., 2011). Thus, LGM has innumerable extensions (McArdle & Kadlec, 2013), one of which is the single-factor LGM, a variation of the two-factor model where, instead of including both the slope and the intercept as latent variables, only the slope is incorporated 'allow[ing] the curve basis to take on a form dictated by the empirical data' (McArdle & Kadlec, 2013: 310) rather than constraining the curvature into a particular shape. In the present case, the single-factor model was opted for to see whether the fluctuation in each of the observed variables is indicative of statistically significant change.

Another complex multivariate statistical technique used in the present study is longitudinal clustering. Cluster analysis is an exploratory technique to investigate possible subgroups in a sample. Cluster analysis was carried out in several steps in this study based on the algorithm provided by Csizér and Jamieson (2013). In order to account for the longitudinal nature of the data, from the second wave of data collection, the initial cluster centres employed were the final cluster centres of the preceding wave. The results of cluster analysis were transformed into typical trajectories. The difference between cluster groups and trajectories can be described as follows; each cluster group includes students who scored similar at one point in time. Similarly to cluster memberships, the trajectories were made up of groups of students, but these groups were based on the cluster memberships throughout the semester. The trajectories, in turn, were analysed both qualitatively and quantitatively.

Variability analysis of the longitudinal data gathered in six points in time (i.e. six waves) closely followed van Dijk et al.'s (2011) suggestion of data visualization based on which hypotheses can be set up. These hypotheses are then tested using reshuffling techniques and Monte Carlo analysis with the help of Excel. Van Dijk et al. (2011) contend that using a smoothing technique allows the researcher to see (or visualize) the general developmental pattern. For these purposes we created polynomial trend lines to the fourth order in Excel: 'the higher the order of the polynomial function, the more closely the trend line fits the curve, but the less smoothing is applied' (Van Dijk et al., 2011: 73). This allowed us to obtain a general view of the data gathered and, as explained below, based on this smoothing technique we could set up a hypothesis regarding the differences in variability regards two trajectories. As the next step, we used reshuffling and Monte Carlo techniques in order to test the hypothesis of the differences in variability. Again following the same authors' guidelines, we looked at variability in terms of the 'distance between two consecutive observations' (van Dijk et al., 2011: 78). We calculated the averages of these differences for the two trajectories regarding the variables that seemed to vary generally according to the LGM results. The difference between the average distances in the two trajectories was used as the test criterion in a resampling model. We tested the null hypothesis according to which the differences of two observations come from one sample, not two. For this the distances were reshuffled and the new average distances were calculated. With the help of Monte Carlo analysis we could check whether these distances reshuffled 5000 times would yield a similar difference in the average distances as calculated based on our data. We calculated the p-value 'by dividing the number of times the newly calculated distances was the same or greater than the testing criterion divided by the number of iterations' (van Dijk *et al.*, 2011: 80). If this number is below 5%, we can state that there is a less than 5% frequency with which the original difference between the two trajectories could be replicated, if we hypothesize that the differences come from the same distribution. Thus, we can reject the null hypothesis and claim that the difference of the average of the distances between two consecutive observations is distinct in the two trajectories; in other words, one trajectory is more variable than the other (for a step-by-step description of such an analysis see Verspoor *et al.*, 2011).

In terms of the quality of these differences in the variability of trajectories, we analysed the qualitative data using the qualitative software MAXQDA. First, the short essays were analysed independently for emerging categories. Then, categories were established, defined and recorded in a coding scheme. In the first phase, data were unitized, and 39 categories emerged that could be linked to the seven major themes of the constructs under investigation. After the saturation of categories, some were merged with others, resulting in 18 final categories, four of which reflected change in the factors under investigation (i e learner motivation, learners' ought-to L2 self, writing anxiety and self-efficacy). The coding scheme was finalized and, to check dependability, both researchers separately carried out the coding. The final coding scheme can be found in Appendix 13.1.

Results

A data set of this magnitude lends itself to a wide range of analyses. We opted, on the one hand, to proceed from the cross-sectional towards longitudinal in order to be able to characterize change and, on the other, to proceed from quantitative to qualitative to obtain depth, detail and voice in the analysis.

Results in Table 13.1 show that students are generally motivated to enhance their English language knowledge (M = 4.53 on a five-point scale), despite the fact that one might argue that language majors are language users and not language learners (Kormos *et al.*, 2008). Students' ideal L2 self seems to be well developed (M = 4.08 on a five-point scale), which is no surprise as deciding what to major in at tertiary level includes future-related considerations. The mean value concerning the scale measuring the ought-to L2 self is considerably lower than that of the ideal L2 self. This might indicate that these students have either internalized external expectations or are not really bothered by expectations for various reasons (e.g. expectations are unrealistic). These students do not seem to be anxious and possess a medium level of self-efficacy, which indicates that they feel somewhat comfortable in their positions at the university, but they do not think that they are in full possession of the repertoire needed to succeed in their studies.

Table 13.1 Descriptive statistics on the cross-sectional data

Scales	Mean*	SD
Motivated learning behaviour	4.53	0.33
Language learning experience	4.08	1.08
Ideal L2 self	4.54	0.42
Ought-to L2 self	3.62	0.61
Writing anxiety	2.78	0.56
Self-efficacy	3.73	0.77

Note: *Five-point scales were used in the study: 1 is the negative end of the scale, while 5 is the positive end.

The next step of the analysis was to investigate temporal changes over the period of 14 weeks. As an introductory step, we compared the obtained mean values of the scales for each wave of data collection with the help of repeated measures of analysis of varience. The results show that the majority of the mean values depict no significant differences (see Appendix 13.2), apart from self-efficacy, which decreased over time in a linear way. In order to investigate nonlinear differences, we employed latent growth curve modelling. Latent growth curve models were fitted to the data with the intention of checking for nonlinear fluctuations in the dataset. The most important requirement for this type of analysis is for the data to be the result of repeated observations on the same variables with the participation of the same subjects (McArdle & Epstein, 1987). We chose to apply the single-factor LGM, where the slope values were left free. This means that the growth model was left open to depict any type of change and was not constrained to be linear, cubic, quadratic or logistic (Kenny, 2011; Kenny, personal communication; McArdle & Epstein, 1987). In other words, the shape and direction of the changes the growth models represent were not predetermined but could take any shape or curvature depending on the rate or degree of change (Preacher *et al.*, 2008) (e.g. could freely go up from Wave 1 to Wave 2, slightly down for Wave 3, up again in Waves 4 and 5, and drastically down in Wave 6).

Scholars may argue that latent growth curve models require larger sample sizes than the current one ($N = 21$); however, in latent growth curve modelling, what seems to be of key importance in model estimation and statistical power is 'the total number of person-by-time observations' (Curran *et al.*, 2010: 125), in the present case six observations for 21 participants, rather than merely the sample size. Curran *et al.* (2010) provide the example of Huttenlocher *et al.*'s (1991) study, where latent growth curve modelling was successfully used to compare the vocabulary growth trajectories of two groups of 11 participants (which included six waves of data collection for the first group and three waves of data collection for the second group). Consequently, 'what constitutes "adequate" cannot be unambiguously stated, because this depends in part on other characteristics of the research design (e.g., complexity of the growth model, amount of variance explained by the model)' (Curran *et al.*, 2010: 125), also on the type of growth models fitted to the data and the methods of estimation in view of the data (Curran *et al.*, 2010). Although the present study does not involve the generally preferred sample size of minimum 100, we have decided to include latent curve models (a separate one for each variable) primarily to demonstrate how such analysis can help detect change in a DS and provide basis for further investigations.

According to our results, out of the seven variables measured, three showed a significant level of nonlinear change: language learning experience, ought-to L2 self and writing anxiety (Table 13.2; for the fit indices see Table 13.3).

Table 13.2 Curvilinear trends of language learning experience, ought-to L2 self and writing anxiety

	Time 1	Time 2	Time 3	Time 4	Time 5	Time 6	Slope mean	Slope variance
Learning experience	1.00	1.01	0.98	0.99	0.95	0.99	3.99	0.46
Ought-to L2 self	1.00	0.97	0.96	0.97	0.93	0.94	4.29	0.41
Writing anxiety	1.00	0.99	0.98	0.99	0.97	0.95	3.31	0.76

Note: The mean-related differences are reported in Appendix 13.2.

Table 13.3 Model fit of nonlinear change

	χ^2 (p)	CMIN/DF	CFI	TLI	RMSEA
Learning experience	19.4 (0.43)	1.021	0.996	0.997	0.033
Ought-to L2 self	20.56 (0.36)	1.082	0.983	0.987	0.064
Writing anxiety	18.06 (0.52)	0.95	1.00	1.008	<0.001
Recommended cut-off values (Byrne, 2010)	–	2.00	0.95	0.95	0.08

Note: For additional information of recommended cut-off points see: Browne and Cudeck (1993), Fan *et al.* (1999) and Hu and Bentler (1999).

Abbreviations: χ^2(p), significance value associated with the chi-square; CMIN/DF, chi-square value divided by the degrees of freedom; CFI, Comparative fit index; TLI, Tucker-Lewis index; RMSEA, Root mean square error of approximation.

The overall change in motivation (more specifically concerning language learning experience and the ought-to L2 self dimensions of the motivation construct) and writing anxiety are relatively small but statistically significant. Moreover, as it may be seen from the standardized coefficients of the latent growth curve models, these changes are minimally nonlinear, that is, the lines are slightly curved.

In order to answer Research Questions 2 and 3 concerning typical trajectories in our sample, we conducted a two-step analysis. First, we conducted longitudinal clustering, which meant that the clustering at each point in time took into consideration the cluster membership of the previous point in time, parallel to the logic of the development of DSs where the properties of the subsequent state depends on the characteristics of the previous state. Cluster 1 includes those students who scored higher than average on the motivation and self-efficacy scales and lower than average on the anxiety scale, while students scoring lower than the mean values concerning motivation and self-efficacy and higher than average on anxiety scale belong to Cluster 2. Based on the results, we proposed five trajectories (for details see Appendix 13.3). In order to provide further insight into these trajectories, we selected two characteristic paths to investigate qualitatively. One of them illustrates a trajectory of a group in an attractor state with relatively little variability (Figure 13.1); the other shows a trajectory of a group with more variability (Figure 13.2).

Both qualitative and quantitative data concerning Trajectory 1 indicate that these students are highly motivated to learn to write and genuinely enjoy the process (the quotes from student essays provided here verbatim): 'I was excited to take this course in the second semester, as I expected to have as

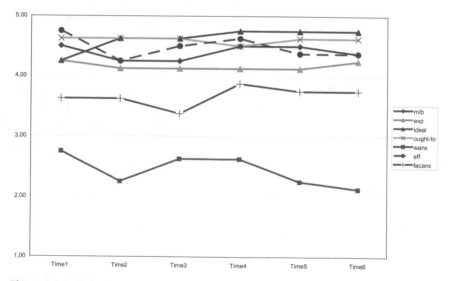

Figure 13.1 Trajectory 1, combined data from eight students

much fun as before' (Trajectory 1, 7/21); moreover, they reported having invested a lot of effort into completing the course requirements ('I'm a persistent student, and although my final grade will probably not as good as I wish I still think I have done everything I could' (Trajectory 1, 18/21)). In addition, while the quantitative data indicate little fluctuation in their anxiety and self-efficacy, in their short essays, learners in Trajectory 1 were very verbal about the fact that they felt that their writing anxiety decreased. For example: 'I definitely grew more confident based on the thorough and firm knowledge provided for us' (Trajectory 1, 4/21). At the same time their self-efficacy grew stronger: 'I could feel a rapid development in my writing style' (Trajectory 1, 18/21). With regard to achievement, the students in this trajectory had the highest grades on the Academic Skills Test (mean = 3.71, range 2 –4) and the highest course grades (mean = 4.50, range 4–5). Nevertheless, four out of the eight participants in this trajectory felt that assessment of their performance was not in sync with their own judgment (e.g. 'I thought I had done a great job, but actually I had not' (Trajectory 1, 18/21); 'The result wasn't as good as I wanted it to be' (Trajectory 1, 21/21); 'Unfortunately, the grade I received on it was not satisfactory for me' (Trajectory 1, 7/21)). They also praised their teachers and attributed their own positive attitudes towards the classes to their teachers' efforts and personality: 'For me the personality of the teacher is absolutely important, and luckily I happen to work with one of the best, friendliest, most qualified teachers, which gave me a great motivation to do my best throughout the semester' (Trajectory 1, 6/21).

Data of Trajectory 1 (Figure 13.1) provide empirical support for the general hypotheses that high levels of motivation, positive learning experiences,

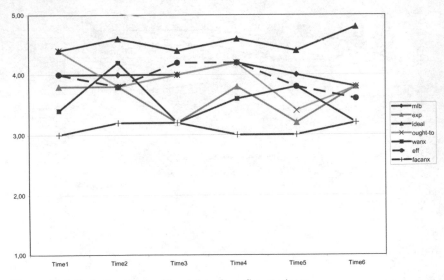

Figure 13.2 Trajectory 5, combined data from five students

strong ideal and ought-to L2 selves are linked with low levels of (debilitating) anxiety and a high sense of self-efficacy. Although this trajectory included the largest number of students, it is not an overwhelming majority, which leaves room for further hypotheses about the various patterns of relationships among these variables and other typical states and trajectories.

Trajectory 5 can be characterized by students who had relatively high motivation and reported a change in attitudes through the course (Figure 13.2): 'At the beginning of the semester my feeling and attitudes were different towards writing academic essays' (Trajectory 5, 8/21); 'At the beginning I felt myself a little bit bored but after two classes it definitely changed' (Trajectory 5, 13/21). Students in this trajectory also reported increasing self-efficacy levels with respect to the beginning of the course: 'I think that not only my writing has improved, but also my reading and text comprehension' (Trajectory 5, 20/21); 'my academic writing skills became better' (Trajectory 5, 8/21). As for the Academic Skills Test, they described being nervous around the time of the test but becoming more confident later: 'I was quite anxious before the test' (Trajectory 5, 3/21); 'I realized that academic writing is not so horrible and it is not impossible to get a good mark' (Trajectory 5, 3/21). Interestingly, the students in this trajectory obtained the widest range of grades on the test (mean = 3.20, range 1–4) and at the end of the course (mean = 3.60, range 2–5).

Based on the guiding decisions of the longitudinal cluster analysis, we tested whether indeed Trajectory 1 and Trajectory 5 differ in variability regards the IDs factors under investigation. First, literature suggests applying smoothing techniques or drawing trendlines when visualizing the data (Lowie *et al.*, 2011). Here, we opted for drawing polynomial trendlines using Excel. The two graphs with the trendlines for four of the variables seem to depict qualitatively different fluctuations (see Figures 13.3 and 13.4).

With the help of Monte Carlo Analysis, we found support for the notion that the variability of learning experience ($p = 0.042$), ideal L2 self ($p = 0.043$), ought-to L2 self ($p = 0.003$) and writing anxiety ($p = 0.047$) in Trajectory 5 is not only visually (as depicted by the graphs) but also statistically (as depicted by the level of statistical significance) higher than in Trajectory 1.

The qualitative data, with respect to frequency counts, provides further insight into the variability detected in the quantitative data. Table 13.4 summarizes the thematic results of the short essays reflecting change in Trajectories 1 and 5. As can be seen, the majority of learners in Trajectory 5 referred to change in their attitudes, self-efficacy and writing anxiety, while in Trajectory 1 the majority reflected on change only in connection with their sense of self-efficacy.

Nevertheless, it is also interesting to note that many participants commented on their improved self-efficacy concerning writing, which is in contrast with the linear decrease reflected in the quantitative data. This discrepancy might shed light on possible measurement differences in terms of investigating self-efficacy in real time and retrospectively. As the

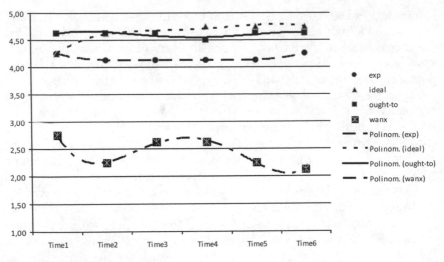

Figure 13.3 Trajectory 1

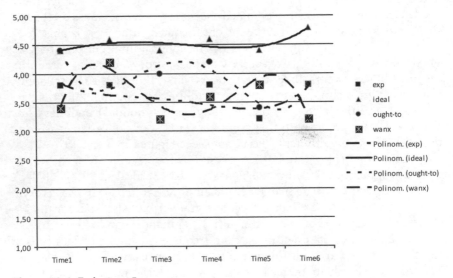

Figure 13.4 Trajectory 5

longitudinal data at each point of data collection asked students – in real time – whether or not they felt capable of completing the writing tasks, it did not take into account the fact that both students' knowledge and task difficulty increased over the duration of the course. This might have masked the students' overall improved self-efficacy; hence, when looking back at the semester, students reported that their overall self-efficacy feelings had developed.

Table 13.4 The number of participants indicating change regarding particular ID factors in Trajectories 1 and 5 based on qualitative data

Change in	Trajectory 1 (n = 8)	Trajectory 5 (n = 5)
Attitude	4	3
Motivation	2	1
Self-efficacy	5	3
Writing anxiety	1	3

Finally, we will turn to the elaboration of the interrelationship of the measured IDs, and how it changed through the course of the semester. Because of the sample size, we calculated Spearman's correlation coefficients for the six data collection points. Concerning the ought-to L2 self we could detect a number of statistically significant relationships (see Table 13.5), which are worthwhile summarizing.

Of the motivation constructs, the ought-to L2 self seems to be the most mysterious, as revealed by the ambiguous results of previous research in the Hungarian context (Kormos & Csizér, 2008). In the present study, through the course of the semester, we can see that towards the beginning of the course, the ought-to L2 self was not linked to other motivational factors, but from the middle of the term onwards it could be associated with the ideal L2 self.

For a closer look at the association of the two constructs, the ought-to and ideal L2 self, the data of the sample were smoothed and their correlations were plotted on a graph. The visualization of the two factors (Figure 13.5) already suggests that initially the relationship of the two variables is negative, or is not strong, and then changes to becoming positive. This is underpinned by the non-significant correlation coefficients in Time 1 and Time 2, and the significant positive correlation coefficients in Time 3 onwards (Figure 13.6). Therefore, we can state that considering the given sample, at

Table 13.5 Changes in the relationship of ought-to L2 self and other individual variables

	Time 1	Time 2	Time 3	Time 4	Time 5	Time 6
Motivated learning behaviour	0.18	0.38	0.35	0.42	0.47*	0.33
Learning experience	0.42	0.32	0.26	0.20	0.62*	0.38
Ideal L2 self	0.22	0.16	0.49*	0.65*	0.65*	0.55*
Writing anxiety	−0.26	−0.26	−0.10	0.08	−0.50*	−0.39
Self-efficacy	0.17	0.20	0.37	0.19	0.30	0.44*

Note: *Significant at $p < 0.05$ level.

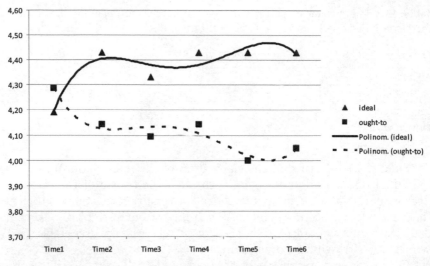

Figure 13.5 Smoothed data of ought-to L2 self and ideal self

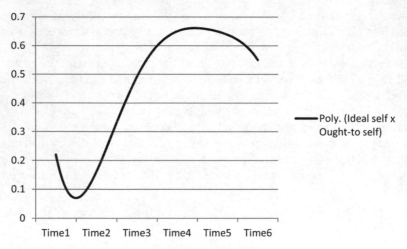

Figure 13.6 Values of correlations of ought-to L2 self and ideal L2 self from Time 1 to Time 6

first the two variables were in a negative pre-conditional relation where the ought-to L2 self decreased and the ideal L2 self strengthened. The relationship of the ought-to self and ideal L2 self had to be of a particular level before from Time 3 onwards, the two variables entered into a supportive relationship and continued to grow together (cf. Verspoor & van Dijk, 2011).

From this we could hypothesize that students have begun to internalize the expectations of the course, they have started to appreciate its usefulness (10 of the 21 participants mentioned this in their short essays) and thought they would use the knowledge gained here later in their careers (eight of the 21 participants explicitly mentioned this in their short essays). They had entered into an attractor state, 'a relatively stable phase' (de Bot, 2008: 167). This seemed to be the characteristic of the most populous trajectory (Trajectory 1) in the present study. Students' perceptions of their own and others' expectations towards them could be most positively linked with motivated learning behaviour, learning experience and the ideal L2 self, while they were negatively linked with writing anxiety.

Discussion

The results of our study lead to a number of points to discuss. First, to summarize our data, we need to point out that, generally, change affected the investigated variables to different degrees. When mean-based linear changes were investigated, only one scale showed significant results; thus, it seems that students' self-efficacy decreased throughout the semester, probably owing to the increased difficulty of the tasks. When our data were tested for curvilinear changes, we found evidence of significant nonlinear overall change in three of our scales: language learning experience, the ought-to L2 self and writing anxiety, whereas the remaining scales proved to remain stable over time.

The lack of change in most of the factors under investigation might be explained by the compulsory nature of the seminar the students attended; in order to advance in their studies, regardless of motivational and anxiety issues, they have to push themselves through the semester. Therefore, it can be said that the English majors participating in our study were generally motivated to advance their knowledge of writing academic texts in English and seemed to have developed their ideal L2 selves to complete tasks at the university. Developing and sustaining vivid ideal L2 selves arc seen to be an integral part of students' motivation (Dörnyei & Ushioda, 2011); therefore, it is a welcome fact that these language majors indeed have future visions of how to proceed with their learning. As a result, our measurement did not show any change, even when students were facing difficulties (in the form of a high stakes examination).

On the other hand, learners' ought-to L2 self and language learning experience, as well as their writing-related anxiety (owing to the various home assignments and the exam) linked to outside expectations and pressures did change as the semester proceeded. We assume that the more internalized parts of the selves are more resistant to change, even in contexts where change would be expected. Three issues need, however, to be taken into account in relation to this assumption. First, we do not know of any research that has investigated temporal issues related to motivational change, that is, how much time is needed to implement positive motivational changes. Perhaps the limited time frame of the present research was not sufficient to initiate these transformations. Second, the role of contextual issues helping or thwarting change (see Ushioda, this volume) need to be investigated in more detail in order to assess how external pressures might modify students' dispositions. Third, despite the fact that Dörnyei's L2 Motivational Self System has undergone regular testing in recent years (Dörnyei & Ushioda, 2009), we do not know of any studies that looked into how the interrelationships among the components of the proposed theory might change over time. While we found that the relationship between students' ideal and ought-to L2 selves strengthened over time, we have no regression results to test how these strengthening relationships modify motivated learning behaviour.

When zooming in on inter-individual variability, two points must be highlighted in connection with the differences between groups of students (Trajectory 1 vs. Trajectory 5). First of all, the observation of relative stability in one group as opposed to relative instability (i.e. variability) in the other suggests that, in terms of language learning motivation (especially concerning language learning experience, the ideal L2 self and the ought-to self) and writing anxiety, the first group must be in a more stable attractor state, whereas the other has not yet stabilized and thus is more susceptible to change. With reference to motivational variables, it seems that the higher level of internalization of the self/attitudes discussed above was more the characteristic of the subsample in Trajectory 1, whereas slight developmental changes still seemed to have been taking place in Trajectory 5 (van Dijk et al., 2011).

The second point worth highlighting concerns the interrelationship of motivation and anxiety. Numerous empirical studies have established significant, but not very strong, linear relationships between these two variables (e.g. Liu & Huang, 2011). From our results we could see that, besides the theoretically underpinned co-occurrence of high motivation and low anxiety levels (see Trajectory 1), there is another path (albeit somewhat less typical and more variable) learners are likely to take with the characteristic of high motivation and high anxiety levels.

In order to evaluate the methods used here for future DS studies, there are several lessons to be learnt. First, while longitudinal clustering and subsequent trajectories work well with and can provide insightful results on smaller samples, in order to produce robust quantitative results on change with the help of LGM, larger samples are necessary (Duncan et al., 2011). In terms of quantitative results, we also have to call the reader's attention to the fact that change can be either linear or nonlinear; based on relevant theory, researchers need to test for both. Second, when we decided to use a mixed-method study, we did not anticipate differences between quantitative and qualitative data. It seems that retrospective data can better account for overall change in time when students have the chance to reflect on their experience.

To summarize our methodological considerations, we have to admit that a larger sample with a fully crossed dataset might have provided more robust results. Moreover, a longer period of investigation with more points of data collection would have yielded a more intricate picture of change. In addition, long retrospective interviews could have added value to the results. As a consequence, for future research directions, however time-consuming and labour-intensive they might be, we propose large-scale longitudinal data collections with regular fieldwork on participants' dispositions concerning motivation as well as their views on change.

Conclusion

The aim of the present study was to map changes during the course of an academic semester in order to investigate how motivation, anxiety and self-efficacy might change and interact, as well as what characterizes typical student trajectories. Our most important results indicate that, despite the fact that these students majored in English, and they are motivated to learn more about the language, their motivation, anxiety and self-efficacy tend to show small fluctuations over the period of a relatively demanding course. In addition, we have evidence that change is not uniform concerning the variables investigated; that is, motivation, anxiety and self-efficacy changed in different ways. The motivational components most susceptible to change were learning experience and the ought-to L2 self, while the ideal L2 self and motivated learning behaviour remained stable; that is, these students seemed to have a strong, internalized vision of themselves as users of English in the future, but this vision did not entirely shield them from outside expectations and negative learning experiences. In addition, writing anxiety was also a less stable variable, revealing, as one would expect, that these students were relatively anxiety free. Interestingly enough, self-efficacy proved to be a variable for which we see a discrepancy between qualitative and quantitative data.

To offer possible guidance to future research on change, we hypothesize that change, or the lack thereof, is related to the level of internationalization of the various dispositions and selves, that is, more internalized notions tend to withstand change, while issues that are less internalized might fluctuate more easily. As a consequence, motivational training and anxiety reducing techniques will only work in the long run if students can manage to internalize the imposed dispositions, which thus calls for long and thorough training for them.

Notes

(1) The study was supported by OTKA 83243.
(2) We would like to express our gratitude to the instructors who helped us collect data in their classes.
(3) We would like to thank the work of our editors with our chapter.

References

Bandura, A. (1993) Perceived self-efficacy in cognitive development and functioning. *Educational Psychologist* 28, 117–148.

Bandura, A. (1997) *Self-efficacy: The Exercise of Control*. New York, Freeman.

Bandura, A. (2006) Guide to the construction of self-efficacy scales. In F. Pajares and T. Urdan (eds) *Self-efficacy Beliefs of Adolescents* (Vol. 5) (pp. 307–337). Greenwich, CT: Information Age Publishing.

Browne, M.W. and Cudeck, R. (1993) Alternative ways of assessing model fit. In K.A. Bollen and J.S. Long (eds) *Testing Structural Models* (pp. 136–162). Newbury Park, CA: SAGE Publications.

Byrne, D. (2005) Complexity, configurations and cases. *Theory Culture Society* 22 (5), 95–111.

Byrne, B.M. (2010) *Structural Equation Modeling with Amos: Basic Concepts, Applications, and Programming* (2nd edn). New York: Taylor & Francis/Routledge.

Byrne, B.M. and Crombie, G. (2003) Modelling and testing change: An introduction to the Latent Growth Curve Model. *Understanding Statistics* 2, 177–203.

Cameron, L. (2003) *Metaphor in Educational Discourse*. London: Continuum.

Cheng, Y., Horwitz, E.K. and Schallert, D.L. (1999) Language anxiety: Differentiating writing and speaking components. *Language Learning* 49, 417–446.

Council of Europe (2001) *Common European Framework of Reference for Languages: Learning, Teaching, Assessment*. Cambridge: Cambridge University Press.

Csizér, K. (2012) The role of the L2 Motivational Self System, self-regulation and self-efficacy beliefs in language learning: The results of a questionnaire study among English majors [In Hungarian]. *Iskolakultúra* 22 (11), 42–51.

Csizér, K. and Jamieson, J. (2013) Cluster analysis. In C.A. Chapell (ed.) *The Encyclopedia of Applied Linguistics*. Blackwell Publishing Ltd. DOI: 10.1002/9781405198431.wbeal0138.

Curran, P.J., Obeidat, K. and Losardo, D. (2010) Twelve frequently asked questions about growth curve modeling. *Journal of Cognition and Development* 11, 121–136.

de Bot, K. (2008) Introduction: Second language development as a dynamic process. *The Modern Language Journal* 92, 166–178. DOI: 10.1111/j.1540-4781.2008.00712. x

de Bot, K. and Larsen-Freeman, D. (2011) Researching second language development from a Dynamic Systems Theory perspective. In M.H. Verspoor, K. de Bot and W. Lowie (eds) *A Dynamic Approach to Second Language Development* (pp. 5–24). Amsterdam: John Benjamins Publishing Company.

de Bot, K., Lowie, W. and Verspoor, M. (2007) A Dynamic Systems Theory approach to second language acquisition. *Bilingualism: Language and Cognition* 10 (1), 7–21.

DeKeyser, R. (2012) Interactions between individual differences, treatments, and structures in SLA. *Language Learning* 62 (2), 189–200.

Dörnyei, Z. (2005) *The Psychology of the Language Learner: Individual Differences in Second Language Acquisition*. Mahwah, NJ: Lawrence Erlbaum.

Dörnyei, Z. (2007). *Research Methods in Applied Linguistics: Quantitative, Qualitative and Mixed Methodologies*. Oxford: Oxford University Press.

Dörnyei, Z. (2009) *The Psychology of Second Language Acquisition*. Oxford: Oxford University Press.

Dörnyei, Z. (2010) The relationship between language aptitude and language learning motivation: Individual differences from a dynamic systems perspective. In E. Macaro (ed.) *Continuum Companion to Second Language Acquisition* (pp. 247–267). London: Continuum.

Dörnyei, Z. and Tseng, W.T. (2009) Motivational processing in interactional tasks. In A. Mackey and C. Polio (eds) *Multiple Perspectives on Interaction: Second Language Research in Honor of Susan M. Gass* (pp. 117–134). London: Routledge.

Dörnyei, Z. and Ushioda, E. (eds) (2009) *Motivation, Language Identity and the L2 Self.* Bristol: Multilingual Matters.

Dörnyei, Z. and Ushioda, E. (2011) *Teaching and Researching Motivation* (2nd edn). Harlow: Longman.

Duncan, T.E., Duncan, S.C. and Strycker, L.A. (2011) *An Introduction to Latent Variable Growth Curve Modeling: Concepts, Issues, and Application* (2nd edn). New York: Psychology Press.

Fan, X., Thomson, B. and Wang L. (1999) Effects of sample size, estimation methods, model specification on structural modelling fit indexes. *Structural Equation Modelling: A Multidisciplinary Journal* 6, 56–83.

Gardner, R.C. (2010) *Motivation and Second Language Acquisition: The Socio-educational Model.* New York: Peter Lang.

Hidi, S., Renninger, A. and Krapp, A. (2004) Interest, a motivational variable that combines affective and cognitive functioning. In D.Y. Dai and R.J. Sternberg (eds) *Motivation, Emotion, and Cognition: Integrative Perspectives on Intellectual Functioning and Development* (pp. 89–118). Mahwah, NJ: Lawrence Erlbaum.

Horwitz, E.K., Horwitz, M.B. and Cope, J. (1986) Foreign language classroom anxiety. *The Modern Language Journal* 70, 125–132.

Hu, L.T. and Bentler, P.M. (1999) Cut-off criteria for indexes in covariance structure analysis: Conventional criteria versus new alternatives. *Structural Equation Modelling: A Multidisciplinary Journal* 6, 1–55.

Huttenlocher, J., Haight, W., Bryk, A., Seltzer, M. and Lyons, T. (1991) Early vocabulary growth: Relation to language input and gender. *Developmental Psychology* 27, 236–248.

Kenny, D.A. (2011) Growth curve models. See http://www.google.com/url?sa=t&rct=j& q=&esrc=s&source=web&cd=1&ved=0CDAQFjAA&url=http%3A%2F%2Fdavidake nny.net%2Fcm%2Fgcm.ppt&ei=C90xUtLQNITOsgaw9ICABA&usg=AFQjCNFDO tC4rlnfsO_zNUl2xiifTdg78w&sig2=-x4Mm22jEF4I9NUg2ykmAg&bvm=bv.52109 249,d.Yms (accessed 27 January 2013).

Kleinmann, H.H. (1977) Avoidance behaviour in adult second language acquisition. *Language Learning* 27, 93–107.

Kormos, J. and Csizér, K. (2008) Age-related differences in the motivation of learning English as a foreign language: attitudes, selves and motivated learning behaviour. *Language Learning* 58, 327–355.

Kormos, J. and Csizér, K. (2012) Language learning autonomy: an investigation of English majors. In É. Illés and T. Eitler (eds) *Studies in Applied Linguistics in Honor of Edit H. Kontra* (pp. 75–84). Budapest, Hungary: ELTE BTK.

Kormos, J., Csizér, K., Menyhárt, A. and Török, D. (2008) "Great expectations": The motivational profile of Hungarian English majors. *Arts & Humanities in Higher Education* 7 (1), 63–80.

Larsen-Freeman, D. (1997) Chaos/complexity science and second language acquisition. *Applied Linguistics* 18, 141–165.

Larsen-Freeman, D. and Cameron, L. (2008) Research methodology on language development from a complex systems perspective. *The Modern Language Journal* 92, 200–213.

Lazarus, R.S. (1991) *Emotion and Adaptation.* New York: Oxford University Press.

Linnenbrink, E.A. and Pintrich, P.R. (2004) Role of affect in cognitive processing in academic contexts. In D.Y. Dai and R.J. Sternberg (eds) *Motivation, Emotion, and Cognition: Integrative Perspectives on Intellectual Functioning and Development* (pp. 57–88). Mahwah, NJ: Lawrence Erlbaum.

Liu, M. and Huang, W. (2011) An exploration of foreign language anxiety and English language motivation. *Education Research International*. 2011, 8. http://dx.doi.org/10.1155/2011/493167.

Lowie, W., Caspi, T., van Geer, P. and Steenbeck, H. (2011) Modeling development and change. In M.H. Verspoor, K. de Bot and W. Lowie (eds) *A Dynamic Approach to Second Language Development* (pp. 99–122). Amsterdam: John Benjamins Publishing Company.

MacIntyre, P.D. (1994) Variables underlying willingness to communicate: A causal analysis. *Communication Research Reports* 11, 135–142.

MacIntyre, P.D. (1999) Language anxiety: A review of the research for language teachers. In D.J. Young (ed.) *Affect in Foreign Language and Second Language Learning: A Practical Guide to Creating a Low Anxiety Classroom Atmosphere* (pp. 24–45). Boston, MA: McGraw-Hill College.

MacIntyre, P.D. and Legatto, J.J. (2010) A dynamic system approach to willingness to communicate: Developing an idiodynamic method to capture rapidly changing affect. *Applied Linguistics* 32, 149–171.

McArdle, J.J. and Epstein, D. (1987) Latent growth curves with developmental structural equation models. *Child Development* 58, 110–133.

McArdle, J.J. and Kadleck, K.M. (2013) Structural equation models. In T.D. Little (ed.) *The Oxford Handbook of Quantitative Methods, Vol. 2, Statistical Analysis*. New York: Oxford University Press.

McCarthy, P., Meier, S. and Rinderer, R. (1985) Self-efficacy and writing. *College Composition and Communication* 36, 465–471.

Menard, S. (2002) *Longitudinal Research*. London, UK: SAGE Publications.

Mills, N.A. (2009) A guide du routard simulation: Increasing self-efficacy in the standards through project-based learning. *Foreign Language Annals* 42 (4), 607–639.

Mills, N.A. and Péron, M. (2009) Global simulation and writing self-beliefs of college intermediate French students. *International Journal of Applied Linguistics* 156, 239–273.

Mills, N., Pajares, F. and Herron, C. (2007) Self-efficacy of college intermediate French students: Relation to achievement and motivation. *Language Learning* 57, 417–442.

Pae, T.I. (2012) Skill-based L2 anxieties revisited: their intra-relations and the inter-relations with general foreign language anxiety. *Applied Linguistics* 34, 232–252

Pajares, F. (2003) Self-efficacy beliefs, motivation, and achievement in writing: A review of the literature. *Reading & Writing Quarterly: Overcoming Learning Difficulties* 19, 139–158.

Pajares, F. and Johnson, M.J. (1994) Confidence and competence in writing: The role of self-efficacy outcome expectancy, and apprehension. *Research in the Teaching of English* 28, 313–331.

Piniel, K. (2014) Language anxiety and the four skills. Paper presented at the *Matters of the Mind: Psychology and Language Learning Conference*, Graz, Austria.

Preacher, K.J. Wichman, A.L., MacCallum, R.C. and Briggs, N.E. (2008) *Latent Growth Curve Modeling*. Thousand Oaks, CA: SAGE Publications.

Raoofi, S., Tan, B.H. and Chan, S.H. (2012) Self-efficacy in second/foreign language learning contexts. *English Language Teaching* 5 (11), 60–73.

Ryan, S. (2005) *Motivational Factors Questionnaire*. Nottingham: School of English Studies, University of Nottingham.

Scherer, K.R. (2001). Appraisal considered as a process of multilevel sequential checking. In K.R. Scherer, A. Schorr and T. Johnstone (eds) *Appraisal Processes in Emotion: Theory, Methods, Research* (pp. 92–120). New York, Oxford University Press.

Schunk, D.H. (2003) Self-efficacy for reading and writing: Influence of modeling, goal setting and self-evaluation. *Reading and Writing Quarterly: Overcoming Learning Difficulties* 19 (2), 159–172.

Scovel, T. (1978) The effect of affect on foreign language learning: A review of the anxiety research. *Language Learning* 28, 129–142.

Tankó, G. and Csizér, K. (in press) Investigating English majors' individual differences through their argumentative writing processes. In J. Friedrich (ed.) *HUSSE Proceedings 2013.* Budapest, Hungary: ELTE BTK.

Tashakkori, A. and Teddlie, C. (2003) *Handbook of Mixed Methods in Social and Behavioral Research.* London: SAGE Publications.

Ushioda, E. (1998) Effective motivational thinking: A cognitive theoretical approach to the study of language learning motivation. In E.A. Soler and V.C. Espurz (eds) *Current Issues in English Language Methodology* (pp. 77– 89). Castelló de la Plana, Spain: Universitat Jaume I.

van Dijk, M., Verspoor, M. and Lowie, W. (2011) Variability and DST. In M.H. Verspoor, K. de Bot and W. Lowie (eds) *A Dynamic Approach to Second Language Development* (pp. 55–84). Amsterdam: John Benjamins Publishing Company.

van Geert, P. (1994) *Dynamic Systems of Development: Change between Complexity and Chaos.* Hertfordshire: Harvester Wheatsheaf.

Valentine, J.C., DuBois, D.L. and Cooper, H. (2004) The relation between self-beliefs and academic achievement: A meta-analytic review. *Educational Psychologist* 39 (2), 111–133.

Verspoor, M. and van Dijk, M. (2011) Visualizing interaction between variables. In M.H. Verspoor, K. de Bot and W. Lowie (eds) *A Dynamic Approach to Second Language Development* (pp. 85–98). Amsterdam: John Benjamins Publishing Company.

Verspoor, M., Lowie, W., van Geert, P., van Dijk, M. and Schmid, M.S. (2011) How to sections. In M.H. Verspoor, K. de Bot and W. Lowie (eds) *A Dynamic Approach to Second Language Development* (pp. 129–199). Amsterdam: John Benjamins Publishing Company.

Zimmerman, B.J. (2000) Self-efficacy: An essential motive to learn. *Contemporary Educational Psychology* 25, 82–91.

Appendix 13.1

Final coding scheme

Factors the categories can be linked to	Category codes	Definition	Examples
Motivated learner behaviour	1. Attitudes towards writing	Dispositions (positive or negative) towards writing in English	'I was excited when we were given the task to write a proper essay with sources' (Trajectory 1, 21/21)
	2. Invested effort	Any reference to practicing a lot, investing a lot of work and doing one's best	'I tried my best to succeed' (Trajectory 1, 7/21)
	3. Change in motivation	Any reference to change in enthusiasm	'I messed up everything and in the end I gave up fighting it' (Trajectory 3, 19/21)
	4. Change in attitudes	Any reference to change in attitudes towards the course (positive/negative)	'Her attitude changed my attitude as well' (Trajectory 5, 13/21)
Ideal L2 self	5. Future	Any reference to the usefulness of the skills learnt in the future	'(I learned a lot about academic writing) and I plan to carry on with the process' (Trajectory 4, 15/21)
Ought-to L2 self	6. Importance	Reference to the necessity to learn English as a foreign language	'Since this course is based on writing, I find it really important to attend the classes with attention' (Trajectory 4, 9/21)

	7. Discrepancy	Reference to actual and ought-to self-discrepancy	'Although my Academic Skills Test didn't turn out to be the best – even though I had high expectations of myself – at least I know in what kind of things I need more practice' (Trajectory 4, 9/21)
	8. Change in ought-to self	Reference to change in ought-to L2 self	'After the Test I wanted to prove that I was good at writing and put a lot of effort in finding sources and writing a well-organized excellent essay' (Trajectory 3, 19/21)
Experience	9. Positive experiences	Any reference to positive/good experiences concerning the academic writing course	'I really enjoyed learning how to write essays' (Trajectory 5, 13/21)
	10. Negative experiences	Any reference to negative/bad experiences concerning the academic writing course	'I have to admit that it is quite a boring course' (Trajectory 2, 2/21)
	11. Teacher-related (positive) experiences	Any positive experiences of the academic writing course linked explicitly to the teacher	'My teacher's work significantly contributed to the positive attitude that I had during the course' (Trajectory 4, 15/21)
Self-efficacy	12. Negative percieved self-efficacy	Any reference to finding difficulty in completing the tasks relevant to the academic writing course	'… sometimes it was difficult to get used to the strict rules, we have to obey while writing …' (Trajectory 5, 12/21)
	13. Positive perceived self-efficacy	Any reference to being able to complete tasks relevant to the academic writing course	'Towards the end of the course I felt much more confident about my writing skills' (Trajectory 3, 1/21)

(Continued)

Factors the categories can be linked to	Category codes	Definition	Examples
	14. Change in self-efficacy	Any change experienced in connection with the ability to complete tasks related to the academic writing course	'My writing skills have of course improved' (Trajectory 1, 17/21)
Writing anxiety	15. Experiences of writing anxiety	Reference to feelings of inhibition concerning academic writing	'I was also a bit frightened by the thought of writing about academic issues' (Trajectory 4, 15/21)
	16. Lack of anxiety	Explicit mention of not being nervous	'I wasn't very nervous about the test because I knew what was expected from me.' (Trajectory 1, 21/21)
	17. Change in anxiety	Reference to changing (increased or decreased) feelings of anxiety	'Before the Academic Skills Test I was 'excited', because without it the course can [not] be finished, and I heard opposite opinions, experiences about it. Although we practiced a lot, I wasn't really confident, because it seemed difficult. After the Test I was satisfied with my work' (Trajectory 3, 10/21)
Facilitating anxiety	18. Facilitating anxiety	Reference to anxiety that pushes the learner towards doing better	'After the Test I wanted to prove that I was good at academic writing and put a lot of effort in finding sources and writing a well-organized excellent essay, and I could manage it quite well' (Trajectory 3, 19/21)

Appendix 13.2

Mean values of the variables measured at six different points in time throughout the course

Variable	$Mean_{Time1}$	$Mean_{Time2}$	$Mean_{Time3}$	$Mean_{Time4}$	$Mean_{Time5}$	$Mean_{Time6}$	$F(\eta^2)$	Differences
Motivated learning behaviour	4.19	4.00	4.05	4.19	4.14	4.05	0.028 (0.001)	–
Learning experience	4.00	4.05	3.90	3.95	3.76	3.90	2.569 (0.125)	–
Ideal L2 self	4.19	4.43	4.33	4.43	4.43	4.43	0.721 (0.035)	–
Ought-to L2 self	4.29	4.14	4.10	4.14	4.00	4.05	2.707 (0.119)	–
Writing anxiety	3.33	3.24	3.29	3.29	3.19	3.10	1.827 (0.084)	–
Self-efficacy	4.29	3.95	4.10	4.14	3.90	3.90	5.957 (0.23)	T1 > T2; T1 > T5; T1 > T6
Facilitating anxiety	3.14	3.05	2.95	3.19	3.14	3.29	1.512 (0.70)	–

Appendix 13.3

The most important pieces of information on the defined trajectories

	Temporal stability	N	Short description
Trajectory 1	Stable	8	Students remained in Cluster 1 throughout the semester
Trajectory 2	Stable	2	Students remained in Cluster 2 throughout the semester
Trajectory 3	Some fluctuation	3	Students were in Cluster 1 at the beginning of the semester, but after the first data collection, they were grouped within Cluster 2.
Trajectory 4	Some fluctuation	3	Students started in Cluster 1 at the beginning, but either after the second or the third data collection, they ended up in Cluster 2.
Trajectory 5	Some fluctuation	5	Students changed cluster memberships more than twice within the investigated period of time.

14 Motivation, Emotion and Cognition: Attractor States in the Classroom

Frea Waninge

A dynamic approach to motivation is – as this book demonstrates – becoming well-established in the current landscape of applied linguistics. The recent focus on a range of new issues and notions, such as variability, stability, context, self, vision and emotion, makes for a more full-fledged representation of language learning motivation. Whereas extensive research has been carried out to validate and research the dynamics of the ideal second language (L2) self, this chapter aims to introduce a dynamic approach to researching another aspect of the L2 self system: the *L2 Learning Experience* (Dörnyei, 2005, 2009; Dörnyei & Ushioda, 2009). In this chapter I will first briefly situate the concept in the overall field of L2 motivation, then introduce the use of attractor states in this area and finally outline a promising approach to studying learning experience.

Motivation and Dynamics

One of the key characteristics of motivation as a dynamic system is that it displays ongoing change on the one hand, while it is also characterised by occasional states of stability on the other. Motivation has been demonstrated to fluctuate over time (e.g. MacIntyre & Serroul, this volume), yet it also tends to self-organise and settle into relatively stable *attractor states* like an ideal L2 self (e.g. Hiver, Chapter 3, this volume). Even while a student's overall motivational profile is susceptible to change (Campbell & Storch, 2011; Koizumi & Matsuo, 1993), this change is more frequently found in short-term motivation, relating to the here-and-now of students' in-class experiences (Pawlak, 2012; Poupore, 2013). A study by Hotho (2000: 326) demonstrated that, even when students' overall motivation is stable over the course of a semester, 'teachers may sense changes or fluctuations from week to week, as a result, perhaps, of a piece of homework, a test, or a class that was particularly inspiring or noninspiring'. Furthermore, even when a relatively stable concept such as a student's ideal L2 self (Dörnyei, 2005; Dörnyei & Ushioda, 2009) shows signs of change, those changes are often related to classroom experiences, as demonstrated by Campbell and Storch (2011: 185), who found that for learners of Chinese at an Australian university 'aspects of motivation most likely to change were those associated with the language learning environment'.

The interaction between the different *timescales* of motivation (see de Bot, this volume) is of interest to teachers and researchers alike, especially concerning the interaction between the episodic elements of the learning experience and a language learner's overall motivational profile. In a recent study, Nitta (2013: 268) has explored this interaction and concluded that 'classroom experiences promote the emergence of higher-order student motivation over time through the reciprocal feedback between the motivational components'.

Conglomerates of Motivational, Emotional and Cognitive Factors

Whereas motivation has traditionally been labelled an 'affective' variable in applied linguistics, the overall approach towards the topic has mostly been cognitive in nature. Recently, both the fields of psychology and applied linguistics have witnessed an increased awareness of the importance of affect in learning situations (Ainley, 2006, 2007; Hidi *et al.*, 2004; Schutz & Pekrun, 2007; Swain, 2013). Nevertheless, it has largely remained an unresolved issue as to how to take into account the interaction of motivation, cognition and affect – sometimes referred to as the *trilogy of mind* – either theoretically or in empirical investigations.

A possible solution lies in the use of *conglomerates* to refer to the integrated operation of several different forces such as – in this case – affect, cognition and motivation. Within the context of the psychology of second language acquisition, the concept was first proposed by Dörnyei (2009), although the complementary interrelationship of these three primary dimensions of mental functioning has been a long-established subject of research in psychology. Dörnyei has proposed that conglomerates of certain learner characteristics can create salient attractor states that act as integrated wholes, thereby resulting in relative system stability. Examples of such conglomerates on a longer-term timescale include the ideal L2 self (Dörnyei, 2009) or personality traits such as extraversion and introversion (Matthews & Zeidner, 2004) and, on shorter timescales, interest (cf. Ainley, 2006; Dörnyei, 2009; Hidi *et al.*, 2004).

Unravelling the Dynamics of Learning Experience

In the light of the two themes introduced above, namely a dynamic perspective on motivation and the concept of conglomerates, we can view L2 learning experiences as representing affective–cognitive–motivational conglomerates on a relatively short-term timescale in the overall context of a classroom. These transient states are central to understanding a learner's overall motivational profile.

Theoretically, a context as diverse as a classroom setting could lead to an endless variety of possible states for learners to experience. However, the self-organisation process within dynamic systems helps to provide order and consistency, so it follows that we are likely to find a number of states occurring more frequently than others in educational contexts. The first step towards understanding the nature of the learning experience is to identify these recurring attractor states towards which the system tends to gravitate. The literature gives us a set of possible candidates, four of which will be examined here.

One state that can be described is *engagement*. Often mentioned as being a subset of Csikszentmihalyi's (1990) concept of *flow*, engagement means that the student is immersed in and focused on the task (Mercedes & Rodrigo, 2011). Whereas there is certainly an overlap between engagement and flow (e.g. D'Mello & Graesser (2012) combine the two into one classroom-state, using the term 'engagement/flow'), it is important to note that one can be engaged without experiencing flow proper, for example when it is accompanied by anxiousness when studying to avoid a negative outcome like failing an exam. During a time period in which a learner experiences flow – the culmination of concentration, interest and enjoyment – there is an added layer of experience, namely a loss of self-consciousness and distortion of time (Shernoff et al., 2003). However in regular language classroom learning: 'such intense flow experiences would be welcome, but are rare' (D'Mello & Graesser, 2012: 146).

A closely related attractor state is *interest*. Interest is often named a motivational variable in the educational context (Ainley, 2007; Hidi et al., 2004). It also features in Gardner's (2004) Attitude/Motivation Test Battery in the form of 'interest in foreign languages' and according to Ainley (2007) it is a key component of engagement in academic tasks. Although it is sometimes labelled as an emotion (Silvia, 2005) and is even placed among the first-order emotions together with fear, disgust, enjoyment and sadness (Izard, 2011), its exact definition is still open for discussion. Recently, rather than classifying interest as either an affective, motivational or cognitive state, there has been a tendency to describe the phenomenon as a conglomerate of affective, cognitive and motivational processes (Ainley, 2007; Dörnyei, 2009). This approach, in fact, has a long history, as over a century ago Dewey also described 'interested' as a *complex affective-cognitive structure* (Dewey, 1913: 1). Later theories depict interest as a motivational variable that combines affective and cognitive functioning (Hidi *et al.*, 2004), and similarly, Ainley suggests that interest is a combined effect of cognition, emotion and motivation: 'The general point is that there are functional combinations of affective and cognitive processes, which persist across time as organized processing structures' (Ainley, 2007: 159).

A third state can be called *anxiety*, one of the traditional individual difference variables in applied linguistics. It is, as Dörnyei (2009) calls it, 'a curious variable'. First of all, anxiety has been examined both as a stable personality trait and as a transient state (Dewaele *et al.*, 2008). Second, whereas it has been related negatively to language learning and language processing (MacIntyre & Gardner, 1994), if the level of arousal is not too high for the individual student it can also increase effort and can thus have a positive effect on learning outcomes (MacIntyre, 2002). Like interest, anxiety seems to have affective, motivational and cognitive components: it is related to one of the basic emotions (i.e. fear) (Izard, 2011), it features in theories of motivation and self-confidence (Gardner, 2004; MacIntyre *et al.*, 1998), as well as cognitive appraisals (Pekrun *et al.*, 2002) and worry (see Dörnyei, 2005).

A fourth state might be called *boredom*. Although familiar to both teachers and students, boredom has received less research attention than the states mentioned above. Most recent research into boredom has been done by Pekrun and colleagues (Pekrun *et al.*, 2002, 2010), who regard boredom as one of the 'achievement emotions'. These scholars summarise boredom as a state composed of unpleasant feelings, a lack of cognitive stimulation and low physiological arousal, a sense of time passing slower than usual and a tendency to disengage from the activity – once again combining affective, cognitive and motivational characteristics into one state. Some studies suggest that boredom is the most enduring of any states in a classroom environment, whereas engagement, confusion and frustration seem to be relatively shorter lived (D'Mello & Graesser, 2012; Mercedes & Rodrigo, 2011). Boredom was originally thought to be caused by a lack of challenge; when ability is high and demands are low, boredom is elicited. However, research also suggests that students who are overwhelmed with information and feel unable to solve the task presented, or cannot follow the on-going discussion, are also likely to be bored or to 'zone out' (Lee Do & Schallert, 2004; Pekrun *et al.*, 2010).

The aim of this study is to identify the main attractor states that make up the learning experiences in a language classroom and then to explore the development of these states. The research questions addressed are as follows.

(1) What are the main attractor states that make up the learning experience?
(2) What are the main forces forming the attractor basin?

Based on a review of the literature on motivation and learning experience, we can put forward the following hypotheses.

(1)   The states are expected to include engagement, interest, anxiety, boredom, with variations and/or combinations thereof.
(2)   The states are most likely caused by a combination of motivational, cognitive and affective elements.

Methodology

Dynamic systems theory and methodology

The research design of this study was geared towards identifying attractor states in the participants' past learning experiences. If we assume that a few salient attractor states dominate the learning experience, we can expect these attractor states to be salient and therefore to surface in the data (cf. Dörnyei & Ushioda, 2011). Thus, through a content analysis of a good sample of focused qualitative interviews, we might expect to be able to identify the attractor states that make up the majority of the learning experience. In order to increase the effectiveness of this procedure, the interviews are kept deliberately short because it is reasonable to assume that a dominant attractor state will emerge in the first few minutes of an interview. Further, if such an attractor state is sufficiently powerful, it is likely to be experienced across boundaries of age, gender or culture, although idiosyncratic nuances may characterise certain groups of people. Therefore, the research design involved a sampling approach aimed at generating a heterogeneous group of interviewees (for details, see below under the various phases of the project).

Phase 1: Attractor states

The first phase of the study focused on eliciting possible states that students experienced in a learning environment. A combination of sampling methods was used to yield participants for this study. Half of the data were gathered interviewing second year students of English at a British university that were enrolled in a language development module. These students were relatively homogeneous in terms of age and educational background. The other half of the participants was selected in order to achieve a varied sample of different ages, nationalities, professions and educational background. The total number of participants for the first phase of the interview was 56, with an average age of 22.

Data were gathered by means of short, semi-structured interviews. Participants were informed that the study focused on classroom experience and were asked to list as many states they remembered experiencing in classroom settings in the past. In order to prevent biased answers, no examples of such states were provided, and the words 'affect', 'cognition' and 'motivation' (and their equivalents *feeling, thinking* and *wanting*) were also avoided in the questions. Some participants struggled with the term 'state', indicating uncertainty as to its meaning, but in the end only two participants were unable to answer the question without being given specific examples of possible states such as 'bored' and 'interested' (and these two were excluded from the analysis).

In case participants indicated they had experienced different states in different phases of education (e.g. secondary school and university education) they were encouraged to list the states for these phases separately and to indicate possible causes for these differences.

Interviews were digitally recorded and then transcribed. All the references to states were extracted from the transcripts and listed in a separate file before being categorised. The actual analysis involved assigning codes to the states mentioned, then grouping the codes into larger clusters according to similar concept domains (e.g. 'nervous', 'anxious' and 'unconfident' were placed together into one concept). This process of classification resulted in four different broad state categories.

Phase 2: Attractor basins

In order to fully understand the nature of the most frequent states in student learning experience by outlining the attractor basin related to them, a follow-up phase was included in the research design in order to explore the most frequently elicited state – *interest* – a state that also had the most salient motivational connotation. For this second phase of the study, 45 participants (with an average age of 26) were interviewed, the sampling method being identical as that used in Phase 1. Participants were asked to elaborate on their interest in school and classroom situations, how this interest emerged and how it further developed. Interviews varied from 7 to 19 minutes in length and they were processed using the same content analytical approach as before.

Results

Phase 1

In this phase of the study, a total of 89 different terms was used to describe the diversity of states students had experienced, although many of the terms overlapped. From the content analyses of these states four distinct categories emerged: *interest, boredom, neutral attention* and *anxiety*.

Interest

This category is a combination of the following descriptions: 'interested', 'engaged', 'curious', 'active' and 'enjoyment'. These terms were often mentioned together, participants using one to explain or to elaborate another. Aspects of interest were mentioned by 80% of the participants. From these data, the concept can be summarised as active engagement and enjoyment combined, leading to more active participation in the on-going learning activities. An example of how enjoyment, interest and active attention converged is illustrated in the following quote:

> If it was something that I'd enjoy then I'd be more interested and more willing to participate and that sort of thing. If it's something that I'm not interested in I'm not really paying a lot of attention. (Participant 25)

As early as 1913, Dewey, in his book on effort and interest in education, drew attention to the importance of interest and, specifically, to the relation between interest and attention. The explanation of Participant 25, above, closely echoes Dewey's words:

> If we can secure interest in a given set of facts or ideas, we may be perfectly sure that the pupil will direct his energies toward mastering them; (...) if we have not secured interest, we have no safeguard as to what will be done in any given case. (Dewey, 1913: 1)

Interest, being the most frequently mentioned state, is therefore an important attractor state in the learning experience, and its significance is not only owing to its overall frequency, but also to its link to learners' active engagement and future motivational intention in the classroom. Therefore, we explored the concept further in Phase 2.

Boredom

Another state mentioned by nearly 80% of the participants was, with some variation, *boredom*. Frequently heard descriptions were 'zoning out', being 'distracted', being 'sleepy' and 'not paying attention'. Boredom, in many ways, seems to be the polar opposite of interest. Whereas interest revolves around active participation and positive affect, boredom is passive and has no direct positive affective dimension. An example of a participant's elaboration of boredom can be seen in the following extract: '... day-dreaming, going off a tangent and going into my own world, you know, forgetting what's going on, you're not really there' (Participant 3). Many participants explained how their level of boredom and interest varied from subject to subject, some subjects being perceived as boring, whereas others were regarded as interesting:

> It definitely varied how bored I was, certain subjects like maths and stuff that was really boring and I'd watch the clock tick by, while with English when we were reading a book and you'd get absorbed in the

book and often there'd be a lot of work that you were meant to have done and often I hadn't so that was the overwhelming, sort of 'aaah'. (Participant 34)

This and similar quotes indicate a fairly settled state of boredom or, alternatively, interest for a particular subject, but in accordance with the characteristics of dynamic systems, even within these stable phases we find variation; several participants described their transition from being interested to being bored within a lesson, indicating that although some subjects may be more interesting than others, their state is still susceptible to change within a lesson:

Ehm, probably when I first go in, (...) I'm quite eager to learn and then as the lesson progresses you sort of get distracted especially when people are talking, it gets to the point of just sitting there and just boredom, because the teachers seem to be talking at you and you're not interacting or anything. (Participant 21)

Our data about the frequency of boredom are consistent with findings reported in the literature. Along with 'interested' and 'neutral', boredom is among the most commonly reported states in on-task measurements of emotions (Ainley, 2007) and has been linked negatively to academic achievement and classroom engagement (Baker et al., 2010; Dewaele, 2011; Pekrun et al., 2010).

Neutral attention

A third state many participants mentioned experiencing was, surprisingly, neither boredom nor interest, but rather a state somewhere in between the two; neutral, or passive, attention. A little over 40% of participants described variants of this state in their interviews. Neutral attention is the type of situation where a learner is still paying attention in class, but is not necessarily actively engaging with the material, nor does he or she have any particularly intense affective reaction to the situation. This is exemplified in the two quotes below:

Mainly just, you're just there, listening like, you pay attention to the stuff you absolutely need to, the rest you just ignore, well, don't ignore it but you kind of zone out. (Participant 5)

I think during lectures the tendency is just to sit there and sort of scribble down as much as I can hear and see on the PowerPoint. So that's a sort of reduced state of being, you're like passive, while in seminars you will actively pay attention to what your classmates and your tutors are saying, you're much more energized in seminars. (Participant 14)

Participant 5's quote demonstrates the difference between neutral attention and boredom; a learner is still paying attention, as opposed to being bored where zoning out is a frequent occurrence. The quote of Participant 14 shows the fine line between neutral attention and interest; while a learner might be paying attention, he/she will not process as much, or engage as actively, as during a state of interest where there is more energy.

Not all participants however, reported on neutral attention as lacking positive affect. As shown in the following quote, a state of neutral attention can still include a positive disposition without mentioning any active engagement associated with interest: '... but most of the time I was just quite neutral; I was just quite happy and pleasantly sitting there learning' (Participant 43).

Although this state was not among the hypothesised attractor states mentioned in the introduction to this chapter, it is not a foreign concept in the literature. A neutral state was also mentioned as one of the most frequently reported states in academic tasks in Ainley's (2007) study, and Baker *et al.* (2010) also found that in some learning environments a neutral state was most frequently observed.

Anxiety

The fourth state in terms of frequency was some form of anxiety. This term was mentioned by just under 40% of the participants and includes terms such as 'nervous', 'inferior', 'stressed' and, on one occasion, even 'terror'. Although less frequent than boredom, this state has the possibility to be more detrimental for learning. A classic example of this state can be read in the quote from Participant 2: 'Mathematics I found impossible because I couldn't understand it and I got very anxious and panicky about it. If I couldn't understand I would mentally beat myself up for not understanding' (Participant 2).

Another element of this particular state is confusion stemming from not understanding the material, as well as frustration stemming from this, examples of which are shown below:

> ... where the discussion is something that you don't understand but you're too nervous to just say, so you're just like sitting there not participating and a bit confused. (Participant 27)

> ... frustration to an extent, er, kind of annoyed, I think, that I didn't understand. (Participant 30)

Nervousness, anxiety, confusion and frustration were consistently mentioned together in the data; participants would often use one to explain the other, hence their appearance in the same category. Similar to engagement and boredom, participants indicated that there were some subjects for which anxiety was almost a 'default state', indicating a stable level of anxiety. For others, anxiety seemed to wax and wane during lessons, for instance when a participant had to present something in front of a group:

> I absolutely hate standing up in front of a group of people and having to talk to a large group of people and I was forced to do that on a lot of occasions in my master's degree and my undergraduate degree. And standing up in front of a lot of people and doing that still frightens me more than anything else. (Participant 6)

Phase 2

For the purpose of further analysis that involves the outlining of the attractor basin related to a learning state, interest was selected from the four categories elicited in Phase 1, partly because of its frequent occurrence in the interview data and partly because of its motivational relevance in that interest has been shown to be most related to the quality of classroom experiences (Schiefele & Csikszentmihalyi, 1994). The content analysis of the interview data produced four broad clusters related to *cognitive, motivational, affective* and *contextual* factors.

Cognitive factors

The cognitive element is represented in the students' experience of 'being good at' a certain subject. Over 60% of the participants mentioned this as a main factor for the initial generation and subsequent growth of interest:

> I always had a really good grasp of kind of vocab and grammar without necessarily learning it just 'cause I'd come into contact with it by reading, so I guess I found it easier, than some other people. When you're learning about stuff, and when you're good at something you do enjoy it more I think. So I guess that factors into it. (Participant 26)

Similarly, a (perceived) lack of competence sometimes had an opposite effect, making the student lose interest in a subject altogether:

> [I wasn't interested] because I couldn't do it. I wasn't good at it. I struggled to get a 40. I found doing languages miserable, I mean, I liked learning a new language or culture, but it cost me too much effort. The output that I got was not proportional to my input. I put in lots of effort and didn't get results. (Participant 29)

In terms of causality, participants indicate that the relationship between interest and cognition is very much a two-way influence; perceived competence increases interest, which then increases one's learning effort and thus makes it more likely that competence will further increase. According to the interview data, this cycle can be initiated by both interest (see the following quote by Participant 33 on studying law) and competence/cognition (e.g. Participant 30 on music), indicating that there is not a simple cause–effect relation here:

> It doesn't really have my interest that much, so I don't remember it well. I find it difficult to look for things in a law-book or er, I find that difficult. It's not my material, it doesn't stick. If I find something interesting then I retain it more as well. (Participant 33)

> Well, it wasn't because I had a good teacher, because I definitely didn't have that... It was because, and I've always found that very funny, it was because I was the best. Because I had played the recorder before, so when I started with the sax I was the best, I was way ahead of everyone because they were all struggling with the notes and I could already do that. It was just very easy at the start so I became the best, and then it was supercool to practice for that. And it was also really nice that- then you are appreciated. I was always struggling with social things, and the people in saxophone class they really admired me, and they told me that I was the best. Then you feel valued so you get a kind of positive trigger in your brain: if you play sax you are appreciated, that's how that happened. (Participant 30)

A final interesting point is made by Participant 37, who mentioned how it can be a conscious decision for a student to invest in a certain topic in order to become better at it: 'This is gonna sound like I really up myself, but I was very good at everything in school, so, ehm, so it was more about I suppose picking the thing that I *wanted* to be good at' (Participant 37).

Motivational factors

Another one of the forces influencing the students' state of interest is related to motivation; over 30% of the participants indicated aspects of goal-orientation in this area. Similarly to the cognitive element, the interaction between motivation and interest is a bidirectional one. While some participants stated that they were interested in a certain topic because of a pre-existing goal is associated with it (see Participant 38's quote below), others developed a goal later on, their interest already well established (e.g. Participant 37).

> I used to love chemistry ehm and biology and Spanish. Chemistry and biology because I've always *always* wanted to be a doctor since the age of five (...) When I was five a family friend for my birthday gave me this plastic doctor's kit and gave me the promise that when I was older

I would be able to chop people's legs off [laughs] but the idea of becoming a doctor really just stayed with me and I really enjoy the science side of it as well as the potential to help people if I get fully qualified. (Participant 38)

I think that came because I wanted to do physics, so I decided physics first and then decided yeah I wanna do physics as a career. (Participant 37)

From the quotes above it is obvious that goal-specific motivational factors impact on the participants' overall interest in a certain subject. Significantly, even though this motivational dimension is concerned with long-term plans, it can have a certain amount of impact on the actual interest-levels in the classroom, as illustrated by Participant 7:

I do enjoy the classes but sometimes you don't sometimes you're having a day when it's still hard work and a struggle but knowing what you want to do in the future knowing you want to go into writing or publishing knowing this is what I need to do, have to get in order to progress to that level. (Participant 7)

However, many of the participants indicated that their interests were not directly related or influenced by future plans or goal-orientation, even though they were passionate about what they did:

I think a lot of English is more about providing a platform upon a platform, giving you the stimulus to do something else. I don't know if in this instance I find the stuff I find interesting is directly related to my future. (Participant 20).

Affective factors

Factors related to affect are among the most frequently mentioned in relation to interest. While over 50% of the participants indicated their interest was related to affective factors, curiously, the specific nature of these factors proved difficult for many participants to define. What is clear though is that it is linked to positive affective experiences, such as enjoyment, and ties into what Dörnyei and Kubanyiova (2014) have called 'transportable identities', a type of personal identity that is relatively independent of the situation:

the person's core or master identity that subsumes such fundamental features as one's sex, age, race as key components as well as other central personal characteristics that the individual transports from one situation to the other (e.g. art enthusiasm, conservative worldview, high-tech geek). (Dörnyei & Kubanyiova, 2014: 110)

The common struggle to explain this effect is well illustrated in the following interview extract:

Participant 1:   I have a very art brain, so my interests were music-related, art-related or English-related, possibly history. Whereas I know people who have a science brain are more interested in science or maths.

Interviewer: What do you mean by art brain?

Participant 1:   Like, of the arts, more inclined towards the arts, you know, like English, languages, music kind of that type of stuff (...) er, stuff that I enjoy doing. I don't enjoy doing an equation more than I do reading a book.

Interviewer: Do you know why that is?

Participant 1:   I don't know, maybe when I was younger, I've always been doing reading when I was young so maybe that just carried on, it's just what I prefer I think. I played the piano when I was young so maybe that helped with how I enjoy, and kind of the leisure activities that I enjoy link with more art stuff, I don't kind of really enjoy doing experiments in my own time I like to go to the theatre or to see a concert, and that's kind of linked I suppose, or read a book

Similarly, when a certain subject does not link to anything the student enjoys or can relate to, such as for example chemistry for Participant 3 (see following excerpt), there is likely to be little to no interest:

> I was totally disinterested in stuff like chemistry. I just found them [humanities] far more relatable to like your life, personal experiences, whereas I didn't see any point in me studying chemistry, I didn't see any point to it, I didn't see what I would, obviously I would learn those you know the periodic table, or the specific things but I wouldn't see how I could use it to further myself. (...) And in general, because my mind doesn't really work with numbers, stuff like that I just don't find them interesting. (Participant 3)

Apart from the obvious divide between academic subjects that activate a learners' transportable identity and those that do not, there is also variation within a subject; the degree to which a student relates to the subject can change dramatically over time, as happened to Participant 35 in her history class:

Participant 35:   At the beginning [of secondary school] I found history mega-interesting, and I was quite good at it (...). In the

	final year I didn't enjoy history at all anymore, I didn't care about it at all. We were constantly repeating WW2 stuff, Vietnam, and in year one we got like ancient history, that I really enjoyed. That last bit, I didn't enjoy it at all, what do I care about the Golden Age?!
Interviewer:	Why didn't you?
Participant 35:	Well that last bit it is less long ago, and just lots of years and names to remember and lots of political structures, but I really enjoy digging things up and archaeology and stuff.
Interviewer:	Why was that?
Participant 35:	I don't know, I always wanted to be an archaeologist in primary school and in my first year.
Interviewer:	What made you want to be an archaeologist?
Participant 35:	At primary school I really enjoyed history, digging sites, bog bodies, that kind of things. I always really enjoyed prehistory things back then, as in, that book, the bog witch[1], it was super interesting to see how things were back then. And it was always like, for example my great great grandfather he found two of those bog bodies[2], I found that really interesting. And otherwise, I've always been interested in how people used to live, not necessarily prehistorically, but always like the Archeon[3], that was fantastic. But with history, in the end it was no longer how people lived, but just war and politics, and I didn't enjoy it at all.

In addition to the excerpt above, the rest of the interview also confirms the impression that history was an integral part of this respondent's transportable identity. Her family regularly visited museums and historical sites during holidays, and her grandfather, who she greatly admired, was a history enthusiast (he had several fossils displayed in his house, and was an excellent storyteller): 'Most of his stories began with "When I lived with the nomads five hundred years ago …"' (Participant 35). When she went to secondary school, history as a subject – with its focus on early history and daily life – clearly tied in with this particular transportable identity. However, when the content diverged from this familiar domain, her initial interest did not hold and, in her final year, she failed the subject in her exams, scoring just 4.5 out of 10.

Contextual factors

A fourth set of factors supporting the construct of interest in learners is the context in which the learning takes place. The influence of the teacher, the dynamics of the group and even the time of day are but a few of the relevant factors mentioned in the interviews. Over 45% of the participants related some contextual variable to their interest development. The following quote by Participant 16 highlights the teacher's impact in this area, including their approach, methods and even their delivery:

> I think when I judge if a class is interesting or not I will pay more atten-
> tion to the lecturer. If the teacher has a very particular method of teaching
> I will pay more attention. Most of it depends on the teacher. (…) I think
> many parts can constitute to the teacher, like the accent, I'm really bored
> in one of my classes because the teacher's accent is so slow and no pitch
> and er, so I can't pay my attention to him. And the second I think is the
> method. One of my teachers in the business course, his method is very
> new and interesting, and we should not pay attention more on the books
> he has his own methods so that's really interesting. He really has his own
> method of teaching and his class is really interesting. (Participant 16)

In the following account by Participant 19, we can see how contextual factors, when they are sufficiently strong, can trigger the development of a whole new interest for a learner:

> Basically so I eh when I went to my secondary school I went into this sort
> of massive environment and I went into a new course I'd never really done
> before: art. I'd never really done it, I'd never really shown any interest in
> it, I wasn't, I wasn't very good at it. We go in and there are paintings on
> the wall that are unbelievable, they sort of caught my eye. So we had our
> first class and the teachers there were unbelievable: they'd look after you,
> they'd really focus on you on a one to one level they'd say 'This is what
> you're doing wrong, improve this way', and they were just so inspiring
> you know, they'd say 'These are the artists of the past, learn from them'
> and they'd teach us and they'd really sort of inspire you to work. And I
> enjoyed that class because I felt like I really, like I wanted to do it because
> I enjoyed their company in a sort of like a very almost a friendly way. I
> wanted to go to the art room and I looked forward to it. Whereas going
> to another class where I was berated by another teacher you know it
> wasn't, it was 'oh I've got to go to politics now' rather than 'can't wait to
> get to art', so that was different I think. I think the way teachers interact
> with you I think is a really important thing. (Participant 19)

The importance of a facilitating context for the short-term development and subsequent maintenance of interest comes through clearly in the data. However, the influence of the environment stretches further than the here and now of a particular classroom. As reflected in the comment by Participant 7, a teacher can shape a student's interest beyond the scope of the direct classroom context: 'I had a maths teacher I didn't like so that affected it as well, and a physics teacher I didn't like, and that affected the, past teachers I've had affected how I paid attention in future lessons' (Participant 7).

Apart from the teacher, the overall dynamics of the classroom also affected the development of interest and the data indicate that many different factors can make a difference, from the way a task was presented and the enthusiasm of fellow students to the set-up of the room in either neat rows of three or in circles. An interesting spin on this issue is given by Participant 22:

> And I think if you've got negative experiences in a certain environment that gets stuck in the back of your head, so when you're next in that environment you'll have those past experiences affecting how you think about it, for example if I say I enjoy English, because I enjoy that subject, and let's say we move classroom, and we were in a science lab, because of the experience I've had were negative in that environment before, they would make the English in that environment less enjoyable. I think your experiences- if you have negative experiences in a certain area of environment, I think that sticks in the back of your mind and will be relevant whenever you're back in that environment, so it's a kind of a contextual factor. (Participant 22)

To sum up, the data collected in this phase of the study revealed that the three factors earlier referred to as key parts of effective conglomerates – cognition, affect and motivation – were all mentioned consistently as forces influencing the participants' development of interest. They frequently work in combination with one another and with the immediate learning context, which is the fourth decisive factor appearing frequently in the data. The specific combination and weighting of cognition, affect, motivation and context differs from one learner to another. While some participants reported strong affective and motivational elements underlying their interest, others indicated that contextual factors alone were sufficient to sustain it, and some participants mentioned the presence of all four factors at some point in the development of interest. It is important to note that not all of these forces need to be part of the attractor basin for interest to develop as an attractor state. However the more factors that work together, the more *momentum* a learner's interest is likely to have, and the less likely it is to disappear completely.

From the data it seems that interest can be initially triggered by any of the four different forces. For example, Participant 30 indicated her interest in music had started after she discovered she was good at playing the saxophone. Participant 19's interest in art started because of the positive context he encountered in art class. This initial trigger is then often joined by other forces such as, for Participant 30, deciding to want to do a music degree, thus adding a motivational force to her interest development, or for Participant 19, who found out that he was really good at art, thereby combining cognitive and contextual elements.

Discussion and Conclusion

In this study we have seen that something as seemingly multi-faceted and unpredictable as the learning experience can in fact be studied systematically using a relatively simple dynamic systems-based research design. Focusing on identifying attractor states that are expected to emerge in a self-organising system, the variation in students' learning experience has been narrowed down to four main types; interest, boredom, neutral attention and anxiety. These states are frequently mentioned in the literature in educational psychology and second language acquisition (SLA), although they have mostly been treated from individual differences, rather than a dynamic systems perspective.

Although some learners report that they may switch from one state to the other within a single lesson, which is indicative of variability on a short-term time scale, there is consistent data that point to relatively stable 'default states' characterising certain subjects, as reflected for example in learners' comments on how they were always interested in French,or were always really bored in English classes.

The underlying attractor basin, causing the occurrence of a certain attractor state, is a combination of cognitive, motivational, affective and contextual elements. Although the different factors were mentioned separately, an important finding arising from the analysis of learners' narratives is the almost inseparable nature of cognition, motivation, affect and context (see Ushioda, this volume). This combination of factors often surfaces together in the learners' accounts, supporting or undermining a student's interest by the way they interact and reinforce one another, thereby making it difficult to separate their influence and pinpoint any straightforward causality. This finding is in accordance with the observations of other researchers who have emphasised the inseparability of emotion and cognition (e.g. Lewis, 2005; Swain, 2013), or of motivation, emotion and cognition (e.g. Dai & Sternberg, 2004).

Further research into the interaction of motivation, cognition, affect and context might uncover attractor patterns in the learning experience in general and interest specifically. A potentially promising strand of research would be the situated longitudinal micro-mapping of different states within the learning environment (see e.g. Nitta, 2013; Pawlak, 2012; Waninge et al., 2014) as a means of analysing the variability of the learning experience, its relation to the context and its implications for the overall learner experience on a larger timescale.

Notes

(1) A book given to the participant at age 10, telling the story of a famous bog-body dug up in her region and displayed in the local museum.
(2) Two famous bog bodies from the Iron Age displayed in the same museum.
(3) A history-themed park where life through the ages is represented and re-enacted. She visited this park at age 11.

References

Ainley, M. (2006) Connecting with learning: Motivation, affect and cognition in interest processes. *Educational Psychology Review* 18 (4), 391–405.

Ainley, M. (2007) Being and feeling interested: transient state, mood, and disposition. In P.A. Schutz and R. Pekrun (eds) *Emotion in Education* (pp. 141–157). Oxford: Elsevier.

Baker, R.S.J.D., D'Mello, S.K., Mercedes, M., Rodrigo, T. and Graesser, A. C. (2010) Better to be frustrated than bored: The incidence, persistence, and impact of learners' cognitive–affective states during interactions with three different computer based learning environments. *International Journal of Human-Computer Studies* 68, 223–241.

Campbell, E. and Storch, N. (2011) The changing face of motivation a study of second language learners' motivation over time. *Australian Review of Applied Linguistics* 34 (2), 166–192.

Csikszentmihalyi, M. (1990) *Flow: The Psychology of Optimal Experience*. New York: Harper & Row.

D'Mello, S. and Graesser, A. (2012) Dynamics of affective states during complex learning. *Learning and Instruction* 22 (2), 145–157.

Dai, D.Y. and Sternberg, R.J. (eds) (2004) *Motivation, Emotion and Cognition: Integrative Perspectives on Intellectual Functioning and Development*. Mahwah, NJ: Lawrence Erlbaum Associates

Dewaele, J.M. (2011). Reflections on the emotional and psychological aspects of foreign language learning and use. *Anglistik: International Journal of English Studies* 22 (1), 23–42.

Dewaele, J.M., Petrides, K.V. and Furnham, A. (2008) Effects of trait emotional intelligence and sociobiographical variables on communicative anxiety and foreign language anxiety among adult multilinguals: A review and empirical investigation. *Language Learning* 58 (4), 911–960.

Dewey, J. (1913) *Interest and Effort in Education*. New York: Houghton Mifflin Company.

Dörnyei, Z. (2005) *The Psychology of the Language Learner: Individual Differences in Second Language Acquisition*. Mahwah, NJ: Lawrence Erlbaum Associates.

Dörnyei, Z. (2009) *The Psychology of Second Language Acquisition*. Oxford: Oxford University Press.

Dörnyei, Z. and Kubanyiova, M. (2014) *Motivating Learners, MotivatingTeachers: Building Vision in the Language Classroom*. Cambridge: Cambridge University Press.

Dörnyei, Z. and Ushioda, E. (eds) (2009) *Motivation, Language Identity and the L2 Self*. Bristol: Multilingual Matters.

Dörnyei, Z. and Ushioda, E. (2011) *Teaching and Researching Motivation* (2nd edn). Harlow: Longman.

Gardner, R.C. (2004) Attitude/Motivation Test Battery: International AMTB Research Project. London, Canada: The University of Western Ontario. See publish.uwo.ca/~gardner/docs/englishamtb.pdf (accessed 12 September 2013).

Hidi, S., Renninger, K.A. and Krapp, A. (2004) Interest, a motivational variable that combines affective and cognitive functioning. In D.Y. Dai and R.J. Sternberg (eds) *Motivation, Emotion and Cognition* (pp. 89–115). Mahwah, NJ: Lawrence Erlbaum Associates.

Hotho, S. (2000) "Same" or "different"? A comparative examination of classroom factors in second language settings. *Foreign Language Annals* 33 (3), 320–329.

Izard, C.E. (2011) Forms and functions of emotion: Matters of emotion-cognition interactions. *Emotion Review* 3, 371–378.

Koizumi, R. and Matsuo, K. (1993) A longitudinal study of attitudes and motivation in learning English among Japanese seventh-grade students. *Japanese Psychologuy Research* 35 (1), 1–11.

Lee Do, S. and Schallert, D.L. (2004) Emotions and classroom talk: Toward a model of the role of affect in students' experiences of classroom discussions. *Journal of Educational Psychology* 96, 619–634.

Lewis, M.D. (2005) Bridging emotion theory and neurobiology through dynamic systems modeling. *Behavioural and Brain Sciences* 28, 169–245.

MacIntyre, P.D. (2002) Motivation, anxiety and emotion in second language acquisition. In P. Robinson (ed.) *Individual Differences in Second Langauge Acquisition* (pp. 45–68). Amsterdam: John Benjamins.

MacIntyre, P.D. and Gardner, R.C. (1994) The subtle effects of language anxiety on cognitive processing in the second language. *Language Learning* 44 (2), 283–305.

MacIntyre, P.D., Dornyei, Z., Clément, R. and Noels, K.A. (1998) Conceptualizing willingness to communicate in a L2: A situational model of L2 confidence and affiliation. *Modern Language Journal* 82 (4), 545–562.

Matthews, G. and Zeidner, M. (2004) Traits, states, and the trilogy of mind: an adaptive perspective on intellectual functioning. In D.Y. Dai and R.J. Sternberg (eds) *Motivation, Emotion and Cognition* (pp. 143–171). Mahwah, NJ: Lawrence Erlbaum Associates.

Mercedes, M. and Rodrigo, T. (2011) Dynamics of student cognitive-affective transitions during a mathematics game. *Simulation & Gaming* 42 (1), 85–99.

Nitta, R. (2013) Understanding motivational evolution in the EFL classroom: A longitudinal study from a dynamic systems perspective. In M.T. Apple, D. DaSilva and T. Fellner (eds) *Language Learning Motivation in Japan* (pp. 268–290). Bristol: Multilingual Matters.

Pawlak, M. (2012). The dynamic nature of motivation in language learning: A classroom perspective. *Studies in Second Language Learning and Teaching* 2 (2), 249–278.

Pekrun, R. Goetz, T. Daniels, L.M., Stupnisky, R.H. and Perry, R.P. (2010). Boredom in achievement settings: Exploring control-value antecedents and performance outcomes of a neglected emotion. *Journal of Educational Psychology* 102 (3), 531–549.

Pekrun, R., Goetz, T., Titz, W. and Perry, R.P. (2002) Academic emotions in students' self-regulated learning and achievement: A program of qualitative and quantitative research. *Educational Psychologist* 37 (2), 91–105.

Poupore, G. (2013) Task motivation in process: A complex systems perspective. *The Canadian Modern Language Review* 69, 1–26.

Schiefele, U. and Csikszentmihalyi, M. (1994) Interest and the quality of experience in classrooms. *European Journal of Psychology of Education* 9 (3), 251–269.

Schutz, P.A. and Pekrun, R. (eds) (2007) *Emotion in Education*. Oxford: Elsevier.

Shernoff, D.J., Csikszentmihalyi, M., Schneider, B. and Shernoff, E.S. (2003) Student engagement in high school classrooms from the perspective of flow theory. *School Psychology Quarterly* 18 (2), 158–176.

Silvia, P. (2005) What is interesting? Exploring the appraisal structure of interest. *Emotion* 5, 89–102.

Swain, M. (2013) The inseparability of cognition and emotion in second language learning. *Language Teaching* 46 (2), 195–207.

Waninge, F., Dörnyei, Z. and de Bot, K. (2014) Motivational dynamics in language learning: Change, stability and context. *The Modern Language Journal*, in press.

15 Once Burned, Twice Shy: The Dynamic Development of System Immunity in Teachers

Phil Hiver

Over the past decade I have met and worked with over 1000 pre- and in-service language teachers in training programmes in which I teach. Each of them unique, they have possessed an almost irrational sense of idealism and hope in equal measure to their agonising and desperation. This experience has been enlightening in some respects, but more than anything it has left me with one burning question: what is the secret to surviving as a teacher? What, in other words, is it that sets those teachers who thrive, despite their unforgiving circumstances, apart from those who stick it out but struggle endlessly and, of course, from the roughly 25%–45% of teachers in the Organization for Economic Co-operation and Development (OECD) countries who give up altogether and walk away from the profession (Parker & Martin, 2009; Watt & Richardson, 2008).

In this chapter I report an exploratory case study that began with qualitative data collected from interviews with language teachers in South Korea. This study captured a snapshot of the developmental process these teachers have gone through in developing their individual patterns of motivation. I briefly examine the literature on teacher motivation and stress before outlining the developmental sequence of self-organisation used in this study. I report how the data revealed a construct I have termed 'teacher immunity', a powerful factor in determining teacher behaviour and responses, and frame my discussion of how this teacher immunity develops and functions from a dynamic systems theory (DST) perspective.

Literature Review

Teacher motivation and stress

Teaching is an occupation fraught with uncertainties and potential stress (Kyriacou & Coulthard, 2000). Low recognition, coupled with the heavy workload and the emotion labour inherent to the job, can take a heavy toll on teachers' psychological and physical well-being. Emotion labour is work that demands a high degree of control over one's emotions, and this is implicit in the expectation for teachers to regulate or manage their own emotions in conjunction with their professional classroom role (Benesch, 2012). Stress has been defined as an affective response to a perceived mismatch between the demands an individual is exposed to and the resources they have available to them to control those demands (Davies & Underwood, 2000; Greenglass, 2000; Jepson & Forrest, 2006). Anyone who has spent some time in a classroom will agree that teachers suffer from an incredible number of demands that are not adequately counterbalanced with the resources to control or cope with those pressures (Ehrman & Dörnyei, 1998).

Teacher stress has been widely-researched in classrooms around the world, and this fact alone suggests that it is both a serious and prevalent phenomenon (Kyriacou, 2001). Teachers report comparable levels of stress to medical professionals, and show astounding rates of emotional exhaustion, cynicism and inefficacy (Farber, 2000). Studies have reported significant relationships between the emotional investment of teaching and burnout (Brouwers & Tomic, 2000; Näring et al., 2006; Skaalvik & Skaalvik, 2010). Some of the core factors at play in teacher burnout include emotional or physical exhaustion resulting from overinvestment in one's work, cynicism towards teaching and detached callousness in responses to others, and feelings of inefficacy and incompetence in work (Freisen & Sarros, 1989). These combine over time, resulting in the high personal and organisational costs that are well-documented in the teacher burnout literature (Maslach & Leiter, 2000).

Despite the increased pressures and deteriorating conditions in contemporary teaching contexts worldwide, the majority of teachers do in fact adapt or survive (Day et al., 2007). This phenomenon is, however, overlooked in the accumulation of research on teacher burnout and attrition. To address this blind spot apparent in much of teacher research, we need to focus on strength, fulfilment and mechanisms for thriving (Bullough, 2011). Teachers' occupational well-being is important for more than just philosophical reasons (Nieto, 2003). It plays a substantial role in the quality of instruction and levels of student success in learning (Hakanen et al., 2006; Woolfolk-Hoy, 2008). Understanding how teachers develop a resistance that shields them from stress and emotional overload, and allows them to function productively, may help us to determine how teachers can achieve optimal teaching effectiveness. Principles from DST provide powerful tools that may allow us to do this (Davis & Sumara, 2006; Howe & Lewis, 2005).

Self-organisation: A developmental sequence

In this section I outline a theoretical model of self-organisation that I apply in understanding the data in this study. What is meant by 'self-organisation'?

When dynamic systems change their internal structure or their overall function in response to some external circumstances through a process that we understand is not directed from outside the system, we call this *self-organisation* (Banzhaf, 2009). Determining how it takes place is the primary goal of complexity science (Larsen-Freeman, 1997), yet few frameworks exist for describing this metaphorical process (Holland, 2006). One existing model of self-organisation is Lewis' psychological model (2005). But because it is designed for the sole purpose of plotting the dynamic development of emotional appraisal, transferring it to wider use is difficult. If it is repurposed and adapted slightly by bringing in broader theoretical insights from DST, it will have a more inclusive focus. Four stages stand out as central to the self-organisation process: (1) triggering; (2) coupling; (3) re-alignment and (4) stabilisation. The first two phases are concerned with behaviour and interaction of system components on the local level, while the two latter phases shift up to a system-centred, global level (Jost *et al.*, 2010).

Triggering

In the triggering stage, a *perturbation* causes a system disturbance similar to the ripples caused by a pebble thrown into still water. Because individual elements in a system adjust and reorder themselves in response to changing conditions, instability is a generic mechanism that is beneath most self-organised pattern formation (Kelso, 1995). As disturbances are essential to destabilise a dynamic system, the process of self-organisation can only proceed if there is a trigger, such as a perturbation (Kiel, 1991). One key consideration is that the size of a perturbation and the size of its effect are seldom in a direct linear relationship (Kra, 2009): huge forces may have relatively little impact on a system, whereas other relatively minor glitches can lead to outcomes that are both unforeseen and catastrophic (Dooley, 1997). If a perturbation is to impact a dynamic system's elements, it must trigger a response or it will simply be absorbed into the system (Straussfogel & Von Schilling, 2009). Disturbances in a dynamic system can follow two possible paths: through *amplifying* they increase in strength to destabilise a system, or they can be subdued when subject to a *damping* force (Strogatz, 1994). Dynamic systems theorists refer to the path of amplification as positive feedback and that of damping as negative feedback (Boschetti *et al.*, 2011).

Coupling

During the process of self-organisation we observe behaviour in which the system actively tries to turn what is happening to its advantage (Manson, 2001). This is when two or more elements interact in a way that develops intelligently (Reitsma, 2003). This element-to-element interaction is called *coupling* (Dooley, 1997). Coupling involves an exchange of energy or information in ongoing feedback loops. These allow new system-wide patterns of behaviour that push the system away from chaos to emerge (Haken *et al.*, 1995). *Feedback loops* are a two-way flow of energy or information that is necessary to direct growth and change, and because of this they have been called the central nervous system of dynamic systems (Newman, 2009). Positive feedback reinforces the local perturbations until they impact the entire system while, simultaneously, negative feedback reins in unsustainable or run-away growth (O'Sullivan, 2009). It is because of this recursive feedback mechanism that dynamic systems are often referred to as adaptive and feedback-sensitive in their behaviour (Kauffman, 1995).

Realignment

As a dynamic system adapts its internal structure, it eventually crosses a threshold where the coupling produces enough coherence and structure, and the system begins to reconfigure itself towards stability (Thelen & Bates, 2003). This return to stability takes place in the realignment stage through the development of new higher-order patterns (Kiel, 1991). When the outcome pattern of the dynamic system that has emerged in the realignment stage is different in some of its main qualities from what we started with, we call this new state a *major phase change*. The key to understanding changes such as these is that they are a result of a system's adaptive self-organisation and do not rely on any one component or on any linear process (Juarrero, 1999). Because these changes and new patterns in the dynamic system appear to have simply come about by themselves spontaneously, we say that they have *emerged* (Kauffman, 1995). Although self-organisation at times appears to be random, there are in fact many pre-existing constraints that steer the path of the emerging stability (Goldstein, 2011). We call these *control parameters* in order to remind ourselves that nothing is random, and that there are pre-existing boundaries that the dynamic system must stay within (Gorochowski et al., 2011).

Stabilisation

Once the new pattern of stability is firmly consolidated in the dynamic system, it transforms itself into a new meta-component that buffers the system from future disturbances and allows it to avoid vulnerability to sudden instability (Tkačik & Bialek, 2009). As it now begins to influence and determine future cycles of self-organisation, we call this emergent meta-component that is a result of the self-organisation process an *order parameter* (Abraham & Shaw, 1992). Order parameters spread and restrict the future behaviour of a dynamic system through what we call *enslavement* (Haken, 1997, 2009a). Because of enslavement, notions of causality are flipped on their head: the behaviour of the internal parts causes the stable pattern in the dynamic system to form, and the stable pattern now begins to drive the behaviour of the parts (Juarrero, 1999). We refer to this simultaneous top-down and bottom-up causation as *reciprocal causality* (Lewis, 2005). In this stage we can see evidence that dynamic systems have memory of the past and are able to learn from it to help guide their actions (Prigogine & Stengers, 1984). Because they are able to remain stable and functional by responding to continuing disturbances based on their past experience of self-organisation, in DST terms these self-organised systems are *hysteretic* (Kelso, 1995).

Method

Participants

Four language teachers, all in the 35–50-year-old age bracket, participated in this study. Because I wanted to include teachers from three different strata that make up the most typical language teaching situations in South Korea (Coolahan *et al.*, 2004) – the private sector, the public sector and tertiary education – these four teachers differed in age, length of service and classroom context[1]. All four teachers showed a strong commitment to the profession and a steady motivation to teach. Below is a brief introduction to these individuals.

Hanna is the most experienced of the four and has been teaching or training teachers in private language schools one way or another for over two decades. At the time of the study she was completing a PhD in applied linguistics. While her first language is Korean, she is multilingual and has lived and worked for extended periods in several countries worldwide. Hanna has a unique mix of professional responsibilities, and her role as a teacher-trainer often requires her to deal with a variety of administrative duties.

Yumi teaches in a large public middle school in a blue-collar, urban area of Korea and has close to 15 years of teaching experience in public secondary schools. She took the teacher certification exam immediately after graduating from university and was just finishing an MA in English Language Teaching (ELT) before this study took place. The vast majority of other English teachers in Korean public schools are likely to have followed a similar path into the profession as Yumi.

Soojin became a language teacher relatively late, and has just under a decade of teaching experience. Unlike most public school English teachers in Korea who majored in education and then passed the teachers' licensing exam in order to immediately begin teaching, Soojin dropped out of college and began a career in corporate real estate. But despite several successful years in sales, she became dissatisfied and ultimately returned to school where she very quickly gained the qualifications needed to become an English teacher in the public sector.

Wilbur began teaching English in Korea in the early 2000s in order to be nearer to a close friend who had also expatriated to Korea. Wilbur spent some time teacher training before transitioning into teaching in credit-bearing English classes at a medium-sized private university in a suburban area. As this study got underway, Wilbur was in the process of converting his ELT qualifications into the credentials needed to become a licensed teacher in his home country because he and his wife planned to move back eventually.

Procedures

Data were collected through multi-session, in-depth, semi-structured interviews with these four participants. Each participant had three or four 90-minute, one-to-one interviews that took place over the spring and summer of 2012. Interviews were conducted solely in English and the interview data were concurrently transcribed and analysed as they were collected in order to feed into subsequent interviews. A mindmap was drawn up before each interview to identify topics for exploration (Wheeldon & Faubert, 2009), and rough questions were scripted from this during the interview (e.g. *What do you do to hold yourself together on a bad day or when things go wrong?*).

Data analysis

The first stage of data analysis followed the grounded theory (GT) sequence of open coding, focused/axial coding and selective coding using *NVivo 9* software. Memoing, which is a core activity during GT data analysis (Merriam, 1998), took place simultaneously to coding, to write up ideas about the codes' meanings and their relationships. During open coding, segments of the data were coded line-by-line in gerunds to gain a strong sense of action and sequence (Charmaz, 2006). Axial coding followed the schematic categories of (1) conditions; (2) actions/interactions and (3) consequences (Strauss & Corbin, 1998). During selective coding, the extensive memos written previously were used to integrate nodes around the emerging concept of 'immunity'. Saturation (Yin, 2008) was reached fairly rapidly because of the typical sampling used in conjunction with the data collected iteratively from in-depth, semi-structured interviews. Signals of this included repetition of information within and across individual data sets, and gradual confirmation of emerging conceptual categories during coding and memoing (Strauss & Corbin, 1994).

Qualitative comparative analysis (QCA) (see Appendix 15.1) was used as a follow-up, top-down procedure of validation to confirm the reliability of findings from the first stage of data analysis. In order to mirror the earlier GT analysis, the independent variables used for the input conditions in computing the *cs*QCA truth tables were factors that had come out from the GT data coding procedures (e.g. experiences motivational disturbances). This stage of data analysis borrowed the following steps from Rihoux and Lobe (2009): defining the outcome of interest; selecting the causal conditions; truth table exploration; minimisation; and finally, interpretation and generalisation.

For this stage of analysis I used the QCA software package *QCA 3*. I first applied the Truth Table Algorithm for crisp set analysis. Because the parsimonious minimal formula was obtained in the very first instance (i.e. the data showed good definition), a further crisp-set analysis of the model was run using a complementary algorithm (the Quine-McKluskey Algorithm) to try to streamline the causal conditions. Solution coverage of the model's configuration was 1.0 (i.e. perfect coverage), while the solution consistency was also 1.0 (i.e. perfect consistency). There were no causal contradictions to solve, no logical remainders that could be omitted, nor prime implicants that could be further minimised.

While it would be atypical to get such results with an intermediate-to-large-N case set, the invariance of the causal conditions linked to the outcome can be attributed to the uncharacteristically small-N sample selected through typical sampling. Ragin (2006) cautions that as the number of cases in the case-set decreases, there is a corresponding increase in homogeneity, which may complicate the task of meaningfully determining causal conditions. Although QCA is seldom used with extremely small-N case studies, I hoped to use it in this study to establish causality from the qualitative data collected.

A Developmental Sequence of Teacher Immunity

Because I had an extensive corpus of data, the analysis produced many angles to look at it from. What was missing was some form of organising principle, until it became clear that one reading of my data points to an interesting four-phase sequence, outlined earlier, which captures the emerging pattern of these teachers' individual experiences and the paths they have followed.

Triggering stage

In the triggering stage, an initial stimulus that acts as a disturbance dislodges the teacher from his or her motivational comfort zone. This trigger causes a disturbance similar to the ripples caused by a pebble being thrown into still water and it results in a major upheaval or interference in the system. This is in accordance with Kubanyiova's (2012) idea of the need to create dissonance in order for conceptual change to take place in teachers, an idea I return to below. The actual disturbance can involve a range of things, for example disruptive behaviour by a student, a critical comment by a colleague or even the introduction of a new coursebook, but they all originate from events, concerns or realities that teachers deal with in their daily practice. The following comment by Hanna illustrates the kind of disturbances that were experienced by all the teachers in this study:

> Sometimes I get evaluations with terrible remarks. (...) There are some people who say things that are very, very harmful and those evaluations influence me, definitely, and disturb me, and make me very unhappy.

Sometimes a student says 'I didn't learn anything in class this semester'. That is very, very discouraging. (Hanna, I1, P3)

This feeling of vulnerability and instability that Hanna describes is essential in order for the teachers to register a need to act on the disturbances. It would simply be pointless and the teachers would become unable to function if the systems were merely dislodged and disturbed. Thus, in order to have any developmental effect on the system's modus operandi, the disturbance must trigger a heightened awareness so that the teacher becomes conscious of the need to do something about it.

We can see how these disturbances both destabilise the system and get the system moving when Yumi tells us:

I wasn't just being cynical when I said that teaching only takes up 30% of my job. We English teachers often joke that we come to work to deal with paperwork and students' life, and then when we have time we go and teach.(. . .) However hard I try there are many things I can't change, so sometimes I feel betrayed and angry. (Yumi, I3, P6)

The goal-oriented endeavour of language teaching provides frequent performance feedback (Dörnyei & Ushioda, 2011), not all of which is guaranteed to be positive. Factors that shake teachers up and destabilise them have been central to most research findings in the second language (L2) teacher motivation literature as far back as the 1990s (Pennington, 1991; Pennington & Riley, 1991). If we frame these factors in a developmental sequence from a DST perspective, we can see that when they are amplified, destabilising factors may allow the teachers to adapt and reconfigure in response to upheavals.

While we may think that all disturbances will end up dislodging the teacher from stability in their practice, automatically assuming that a disturbance will result in a consequence of equal magnitude is a risky proposition. Many times teachers ignore or brave hardships. At other times they take small slights to heart that then shake them up to the core of their teacher being (Bullough, 2005). For example, the feeling that his creative initiative is rejected registers strongly with Wilbur, and as a result he feels an incredible need to act on being rebuked by his superiors to avoid ever experiencing this again:

I could always just phone it in, you know, come in with the book and say 'open to page 13; today we're going to cover the present participle. But when I (. . .) do something that represents hours of thought and planning, and then I'm punished for it and my job is in jeopardy, that is strong, strong discouragement from trying it again. Once burned, twice shy. Right? (Wilbur, I2, P8)

In cases when teachers experience disturbances that shake the system up in a way that is considerably larger than the initial stimulus, we can see that cause and effect are not simple and linear. Like the echo of a shout in a cave that expands and travels outward, in DST terms we say that the disturbance has been amplified.

Coupling stage

Coupling, the generating of a specific response or coping mechanism that matches these disturbances, follows the triggering stage. The coupling stage introduces coping behaviours, such as in the example given by Soojin below, that the teachers use to try to make sense of the disturbances they experience.

> Give up and go home. (laughs) No, but it's true. I mean I don't know if someone's going to tell you I go home and punch pillows or I go into a room alone and scream, or something. (...) I think sometimes I do dramatic stuff. But, sometimes it's better to just let out my feelings when I'm having a bad day. (Soojin, I2, P5)

The coupled components here are the disturbances and the strategic reactions to the disturbances that we can see the teachers using to try to move back in a safe direction and resettle the system. These making-sense-of-disturbance behaviours interact in cycles with the disturbances themselves and the success of these cooperative interactions allows the teachers to absorb difficulties and challenges, and thus enables the system to cope with the initial shake up. Previous research has examined how teachers can channel their responses in order to counter stressors (Griffin *et al.*, 1999). However, when viewed from this developmental sequence, the data in this case study suggest that strategic responses to disturbances are channelled by the coupling of an adaptive coping response that matches these disturbances.

Along with adapting to their environment, humans also have a profound desire to control it so they can re-align towards internal stability (van Geert & Steenbeek, 2005). Teachers generally desire to maximise their functionality and instructional performance in the classroom; they want to perform the best they know how (Day *et al.*, 2007). These teachers' ways of trying to control the disturbing circumstances with which they come into contact begin with reacting to them as Yumi does:

> How did I deal with it? In my previous job I just gritted my teeth and did it. I kept trying new things and tried to be explicit about why I was doing them. (Yumi, I2, P9)

Because coupling involves recursive feedback loops, as the participants continue to experience disturbances over time, like Hanna below, they begin adapting to them:

> Another thing is always try to look on the bright side. For example if a bad thing happens I try not to choose the negative way of looking at things, and that mindset gives me a kind of peace and probably helps me survive hectic situations sometimes. (Hanna, I2, P4)

And, because memory is a form of feedback, when these teachers adapt their responses to the disturbances based on previous intelligence or experience they progress to pre-empting them like Soojin.

> Even though you may fail, there's no reason to get frustrated and disappointed. Of course I don't ignore my problem students, but I ignore my insecurities. Sometimes I feel if I can do that I can get over a lot of issues. (Soojin, I3, P7)

The participants continuously modify their reactions in response to the ongoing disturbances they experience and, just like with mutualism between biological species, when these dynamic interactions take place during coupling the exchange results in an overall benefit for the system (Banzhaf, 2009).

Realignment stage

Eventually the teachers develop the ability to make sense of these disturbances, and come to grips with them and even control them. This is the realignment stage. When the teachers find a way of dealing with the disturbances they experience and regain their productivity, it is because they have applied strategies that seem to work to bring the system back under control of stability. The following quote by Hanna illustrates how she believes this is done:

> Even though sometimes I felt that I was wasting some years teaching, now I feel it was worth it. It would have been better if I had minimised the problems. But at the same time things that are not experienced will never be learned, so in that sense it was a good experience (. . .) and almost all these experiences were worth going through. (Hanna, I3, P10)

We may be forgiven for thinking that the natural or default state of a dynamic system is one of stability, but we would be mistaken because when equilibrium does occur in a dynamic system it is situational (Dooley, 1997). More importantly, however, just as in the process these teachers have gone through, stability always emerges through self-organisation (Thelen & Bates, 2003).

It is also important to remember that stability is dynamic. In DST terms, this means that it results from opposing forces of growth and decay that exert an equal strength on the system (Haken, 2009b). In this realignment stage, the opposing forces that have resulted in this novel outcome of stability are the coupled disturbances and the teachers' strategic responses to them. Wilbur's thoughts about how this new stability emerges show that these teachers were well aware that this is not an accidental stability.

> I think that makes you a stronger teacher. I recommend that teachers in general experience these challenges, and I know this sounds a bit unfortunate for new teachers, but it's almost something you should go through to become a teacher at a different level. (Wilbur, I3, P5)

This emergent stability is developed, not from a single interaction, but from the accumulated adaptation of the system to the disturbances. Because of its origin it is not fixed or permanent, but is in fact prone to constant tweaking in response to contextual interests and demands (Thelen, 2005).

Almost every participant explained at length in their interviews how facing adversity in their teaching career has led them to gain greater stability, and this illustrates something that can be traced through all the participant-cases: settled teachers are made and not born:

> It may sound strange, but as a teacher having only good students would make my life that much easier, but (...) even those disruptive students, thanks to them I experienced a lot and learned a lot so that I can get richer as a teacher. If I hadn't experienced dealing with those students I wouldn't have been pushed to find solutions. (Soojin, I3, P1)

The data suggests that working through difficulties and hardships by using the kinds of strategic behaviours noted earlier leads to a stability that does not come built-in, but is emergent.

Stabilisation stage

In the final stage of stabilisation, the teachers accept and solidify this residue of experience as a new aspect of their identity. The teachers have now added a layer of residual experience to themselves that will go on to affect the way they react to future disturbances, almost as if a layer of wisdom was added to their repertoire of dealing with disturbances. This kind of implicit experiential knowledge is largely an inevitable consequence rather than the product of conscious self-reflection, but it is also what makes good practitioners so precious: they've seen it all and done it all:

> Whenever I'm in the classroom my worries disappear and I just concentrate on the things that happen in that moment in the classroom. I guess that's one thing I've developed as a teacher over time. When I'm in the classroom I easily forget things that are happening all around me and I just concentrate on the classroom setting. (Hanna, I1, P4)

This new outcome that has emerged can be regarded as *teacher immunity*. This teaching immunity develops much like our biological immunity, whose primary purpose is to protect the system behind it. We are all probably familiar with teachers who we describe colloquially as being 'thick-skinned' owing to their decades of experience and accumulated expertise. Immunity is a more precise word that allows us to indicate that initially this outcome was always part of a defensive reaction to a disturbance.

Just as humans are rarely ever born innately immune to viruses, no single participant entered the teaching profession with this immunity. As Yumi reflects below, they all went through periods when they became infected so to speak and lost systemic integrity and coherence before gradually developing this immunity:

> When I was younger I was less stable. But now I'm more formed and optimistic so that's why I can reflect on my lessons or stories to other people I come in contact with. I feel now that I'm more settled and optimistic and all those things I've been through have helped me to be more solid. (Yumi, I3, P8)

Even though these teachers now continue to experience disturbances that may cause minor fluctuations in their immediate day-to-day stability, this immunity acts as a buffer. This buffer overrides the effect of continuing disturbances on the entire system and allows the teachers to continue to function instructionally in the classroom, and emotionally and psychologically over the course of their careers (Thelen, 2005).

> Nowadays I still have frustrations, yes. Of course at the beginning, it was much worse. But nowadays I feel less nervous (...) and less insecure. (Hanna, I2, P5)

Teaching is one of the most stressful professions that exist (Kyriacou, 2001), and when teachers are in a classroom with 30 or 40 adolescents they must remain constantly on red-alert. Making even one silly mistake means the teacher is apt to be caught out. But, just like in the example given by Hanna above, the teaching immunity that each participant develops allows them to avoid vulnerability to the high-stress levels and the emotional strain inherent to the profession, and thus control and respond to shifts that threaten their equilibrium.

What Does Teacher Immunity Do?

How exactly does this teacher immunity function? Teacher immunity must always be defined as a resistance to something because, like the body's immune system, it develops as a reaction to disturbances. Just like the body's immune system is an effective barrier that prevents against certain infections and pathogens, the experiences of these teachers suggest that teacher immunity acts as a line of defence to the demands placed on teachers, and the often traumatic experiences they encounter that result in emotional exhaustion and burnout. This immunity has different guises – with the potential to be either positive or negative – and it affects almost everything that teachers do in their careers.

Regardless of how it manifests itself in their persona, the first thing it allows all teachers to do is to survive and remain within the profession in the long run. Teachers who do not develop this immunity are likely to be vulnerable to commonplace working circumstances, such as a lack of preparation time for classes, requirements for excessive amounts of paperwork, routinely teaching oversized classes with inadequate assistance and being excluded from decision making (Greenglass, 2000). Because of this primary function of ensuring the system's survival, developing a productive and robust resistance to hardship appears to be a prerequisite to becoming a competent teacher (Bullough, 2005; Kelchtermans, 2011). A productive immune system may enable teachers not to be susceptible to stress, failure or burnout. Soojin explains some of the benefits she feels now that she has developed this productive self-defence mechanism:

> It's been only 8 years since I started teaching, and I came to this field a little later than others. There are some really senior teachers who in a playful way call me a senior teacher already. So in terms of teacher wealth I hope I'm in the middle class now and I'm trying to get richer. But I think I've finally found my niche. (Soojin, I3, P1)

Owing to the protective armour of this immunity, teachers like Soojin are able to ignore disturbances and deal with stress productively, and in turn to experience higher levels of commitment, engagement and career satisfaction.

In order to be maximally effective this immunity must also be robust. In DST terms, this measure of strength is called *resilience* (Newman, 2009). We know that an immune system is resilient (1) when virtually no amount of upheaval can unsettle the system and (2) when this stabilising effect lasts over an extended period of time (Strogatz, 1994). Yumi's anecdote shows how a robust immunity functions to support teachers when they deal with disturbances:

> I helped this troublemaker graduate from middle school, but there were many other kids who were influenced by him, so he was like a school scoundrel. Actually my colleagues at school thanked me for that because if he had to come back next year it would've been big trouble for them, but because he graduated I got a reputation for solving tough problems. (Yumi, I1, P6)

Not having this productive and robust teaching immunity is likely to result in low teacher morale, motivation and self-esteem. Teachers will eventually burnout and leave the profession. However, as the data in this study illustrates, teachers who have developed a productive and robust resistance will be able to function and even thrive in the profession despite these adverse conditions (Klusman *et al.*, 2008).

Counterproductive autoimmunity

Just as, nutritionally, there is good cholesterol and bad cholesterol, the teacher immunity identified here can manifest itself as a positive resistance, or as a counterproductive teacher autoimmunity. Teacher autoimmune disorder occurs when the residue of experience solidifies into a permanent, maladapted and fossilised resistance that can be expressed, as Wilbur does below, in the more commonplace terms we use to describe teachers such as 'thick-skinned', 'resigned', 'cynical', 'uncaring' or the well-known 'I'm-just-doing-it-to-pay-the-bills' attitude.

> I have met people who sort of just go through the motions and teach the kids that are shovelled at them. To me they're teaching but they're not teachers. (...) They're teaching just to kill time or just for a paycheck. (Wilbur, I3, P5)

Because teacher immunity develops in reaction to disturbances, if we look at the body's immune system we find a further parallel that justifies the use of this metaphor. While the body's immune system is an efficient self-defence mechanism against certain sicknesses and infections, aberrant and harmful immune system responses can occur (Maier *et al.*, 1994). This autoimmunity, such as when the immune system attacks healthy cells or the host body itself, can have an unintended and debilitating impact. In teaching terms, autoimmunity can manifest itself through undesirable consequences such as excessive rigorousness and settledness, conservatism in pedagogy, and reluctance to change or show any openness to new ideas (Bullough & Hall-Kenyon, 2011), resulting in those clever dinosaurs not uncommonly found in the teaching profession.

In addition to this, from a DST perspective, the excessive stability that accompanies teachers' 'autoimmune disorder' will work against further self-organisation in the system because it suppresses system dynamics. This highlights a DST principle that is often overlooked. We should never assume that a dynamic system's degree of settledness is in a direct linear relationship with its degree of effectiveness (Thelen & Bates, 2003). From the system's perspective, immunity is convenient as it allows the system to survive. But excessive stability over time may lead to the maladapted outcome of counterproductive autoimmunity (Holland, 1992). From the students' point of view, this teacher autoimmune disorder can be disastrous if they have a teacher who resists all innovation and has done the exact same thing for 30 years. Hanna's insightful comment reflects this:

> In many ways experience does not equal a better teacher. (...) Think about people working in other sectors. There is no other industry that allows you not to progress and still survive or keep your job. Why do teachers believe they can stagnate and not improve like everyone else is required to in any other field? (Hanna, I3, P7)

Kelly offered the well-cited observation that, because of our tendency to analyse things and implicitly construct an understanding of the world, human beings are naive scientists (Friedman & Schustack, 2010). If this naturally developing teacher immunity is accompanied by metacognitive thinking, it can lead to a maladapted and fossilised narrative that consciously prevents any response in the system (McAdams, 2006): we may even observe teachers who not only fail to respond, but are proud of this. While the productive version of teacher immunity can lead to increased confidence and a stronger commitment and engagement (Bullough, 2005; Kelchtermans, 2011), its counterproductive doppelgänger can be disastrous because it results in teachers we all know who have stubbornly stuck to the same classroom methods for three decades despite the detriment to their students (Meister & Ahrens, 2011).

Influencing the Development of Immunity

As a broad concept teacher immunity has substantial implications, and it is my hope that the existence of teacher immunity and the various ways it materialises will resonate with others. With a clearer understanding of how its developmental process takes place, we will be able to raise important questions about the more immediate consequences. Too often we see that the developmental process ends up in a negative outcome of counterproductive autoimmunity, and this highlights the issue of how we can alter the outcome and introduce elements that will move the system into the other direction. Because a dynamic system cannot be shut down and self-organisation cannot be paused (Johnson, 2009), the most effective interventions are likely to take place during the formation of counterproductive immunity. The secret to successful intervention is tweaking the system during self-organisation, and to do this we will need to understand how teacher immunity becomes productive and resilient.

Narrative formation

One way this might happen is through individuals building narratives to make sense of their life experiences (McAdams & Pals, 2006). Most people would probably agree that addressing problems head-on and working towards a positive resolution of the negative event leads to better understanding and increased well-being than repressing, denying or dissociating from those experiences does (Lundberg, 2000). When individuals try to come to terms with negative life events by constructing general meaning to their existence based on particular episodic experiences, we call this *autobiographical reasoning* (McAdams, 2008). Generally speaking, negative experiences tend to produce more thought, causal reasoning and exploration of consequences through narrative construction than positive episodes do. Because of this, the negative experiences that are a routine part of many teachers' lives demand an explanation if the teachers are to gain insight from them and move past them productively and maturely (Kyriacou, 2001). By providing supportive frameworks for teachers to think about how their negative experiences came about and what consequences they could have, we may be able to influence the formation of narratives and help them to commit to a positive resolution of that event (McAdams, 2006; Schultz & Ravitch, 2013). This in turn will steer their teacher immunity in a productive and resilient direction while it is still in the developmental stages and allow only the productive and robust variation of immunity to become part of these teachers' transportable, core identities (Hiver & Dörnyei, under review).

Cognitive dissonance

Looking at the research into language teacher cognition, a literature that covers what teachers know, think and believe (Borg, 2006), may provide us with other ideas for altering the formation of counterproductive immunity. Kubanyiova's (2012) theoretical model of Language Teacher Conceptual Change (LTCC) proposes that, among others, two reasons teachers remain resistant to change are (1) because of the lack of dissonance between their actual and possible selves and (2) because the threat to their sense of self is too much to handle. Research using the LTCC model has shown that conceptual change will not happen unless there is a major disturbance (i.e. dissonance) to trigger it (Kubanyiova, 2009, 2012). These past findings suggest that teachers who have developed the solid shell of counterproductive immunity need to have things shaken up significantly in order to dislodge them from the rut they are entrenched in (Dörnyei & Kubanyiova, 2014). In order to break through the detrimental effects of autoimmunity so that the teacher can develop as a professional and as a human being, dissonance must be introduced that will suppress the hard shell of this counterproductive autoimmunity.

While Kubanyiova's (2012) LTCC model does not provide extended reasons why dissonance is needed, the concept of teacher immunity I propose here might offer one explanation of why there is a need for disturbance. Take for instance the analogous process of immunosuppression in the human body. In immunosuppression, the protective function of the physical immune system is purposely diminished in order to bypass potentially unwanted effects (e.g. when someone has received an organ transplant and the doctors administer immunosuppressant drugs to prevent the body from rejecting the new organ) (Folds, 2008). If we are to redirect the developmental path of this counterproductive teacher autoimmunity, we must find the equivalent switch in the mechanism that allows us do this (Hiver & Dörnyei, under review).

Ultimately, future development of teacher immunity is concerned with the question of motivating language teachers so that they can thrive in the profession. It is unlikely that we could simply come in from the cold and do certain magical things to teachers that will inspire and energise them. Rather, in a profession as stressful as language teaching, teachers are engaged in an ongoing immunisation process. Simply approaching teachers out of the blue and saying some bright things that they might find interesting will have little impact, because rarely will they be able to connect it to the developmental process they are currently involved in. Instead, good motivational practice will involve understanding this developmental process and working within it by targeting its elements so that we can steer it to a desirable and positive outcome – an outcome that this study suggests teachers' very survival in the profession depends on. Thus, we have more to learn about the teacher immunity process and how to influence it.

Conclusion

This exploratory study was an initial step to investigate the motivational dispositions and outcomes of four language teachers in South Korea, and the data analysis highlighted a process these participant teachers followed in developing, what I have argued can be regarded as, a unique teacher immunity emerging as a result of disturbances. My findings suggest that the primary function of this teacher immunity is to allow teachers to survive within the profession. Furthermore, if this immunity develops as a productive and robust outcome it may enable teachers to thrive in the profession. Perhaps not surprisingly, however, there are few guarantees that teacher immunity will develop into the productive and robust variety, and teacher immunity can manifest itself equally in a counterproductive form. The thick callous of this counterproductive autoimmunity causes teachers to plateau and fossilise, avoid responding even when it is necessary, and resist positive change throughout their careers. I examined potential ways in which the outcome could be guided along its developmental path into a positive outcome. These included narrative formation, an idea that originates from the well-established fields of psychology and coping, and a concept taken from the theoretical model of LTCC, introducing dissonance to suppress the resistance effect of the fledgling counterproductive autoimmunity.

Because we are dealing with complex dynamic systems that are human beings, there may be a temptation to describe the immunity that emerged as a personality trait or some other individual property (Boschetti *et al.*, 2011). It may be convenient to attribute the motivational immunity of these teachers to their personalities or the unique set of experiences they have each come through in their careers (Malmberg, 2006). However, as with similar emergent properties, it seems more compelling to see it as resulting from the self-organisation of the system (van Geert, 1998, 2009). The fact that these four teachers all have varied backgrounds and distinct personalities, followed multiple paths to the profession and teach in different instructional contexts, is evidence that the shared structure and function of their teacher immunity, and the motivational synchrony they exhibit, are a result of patterns developing qualitatively through self-organisation (Haken, 1985).

Reflecting on the design of this study, it became clear that one of the difficulties of carrying out DST-inspired research is that nothing is likely to emerge spontaneously from pure data or objective technique. It is also entirely possible to conduct a study designed meticulously on the principles of a particular research methodology and still produce findings that may be conceptually insignificant or trivial (Corbin & Strauss, 1990). The jury is still out on precisely what a DST approach brings to researching motivation that is entirely new. Self-organisation is one of the major contributions of DST to research methodology (Byrne, 2002, 2009a). The fact that non-representative qualitative research has been able to offer kernels of truth to our field is precisely because it taps into self-organised commonalities (Laws & McLeod, 2004). If we continue to exploit this feature in a principled way we can approximate universally applicable or broadly applicable tenets (Larsen-Freeman, 2012). In the end, DST's staying power in the second language acquisition (SLA) field will be determined by how well it allows us, not just to say the same things over again in a different way, but to actually discover new things that we could not have said or discovered without it.

Note

(1) Casing, that is deciding on the category to which something belongs, is something deeply rooted in dynamic systems logic (Byrne, 2009b; Harvey, 2009), and while the casing I used in this study was more intuitive and experiential than scientific, other methods, such as Dörnyei's (2014) Retrodictive Qualitative Modelling (see also Chan et al., this volume), devote an entire research phase to collecting external evidence in order to define the archetypes. Because of the exploratory nature of this project, I drew on my own experience with these teachers, as I have known and worked closely with each of them for close to seven years in Korea.

References

Abraham, R. and Shaw, D. (1992) *Dynamics: The Geometry of Behavior* (2nd edn). Redwood City, CA: Addison-Wesley.

Banzhaf, W. (2009) Self-organizing systems. In R. Meyers (ed.) *Encyclopedia of Complexity and Systems Science* (pp. 8040–8050). New York: Springer.

Benesch, S. (2012) *Considering Emotions in Critical English Language Teaching: Theories and Praxis*. New York: Routledge.

Borg, S. (2006) *Teacher Cognition and Language Education: Research and Practice*. London: Continuum.

Boschetti, F., Hardy, P., Grigg, N. and Horowitz, P. (2011) Can we learn how complex systems work? *Emergence: Complexity & Organization* 13 (4), 47–62.

Brouwers, A. and Tomic, W. (2000) A longitudinal study of teacher burnout and perceived self-efficacy in classroom management. *Teaching and Teacher Education* 16, 239–253.

Bullough, R. (2005) Teacher vulnerability and teachability: A case study of a mentor and two interns. *Teacher Education Quarterly* 32 (2), 23–40.

Bullough, R. (2011) Hope, happiness, teaching, and learning. In C. Day and J.C.K. Lee (eds) *New Understandings of Teacher's Work: Emotions and Educational Change* (pp. 15–30). New York: Springer.

Bullough, R. and Hall-Kenyon, K. (2011) The call to teach and teacher hopefulness. *Teacher Development* 15 (2), 127–140.

Byrne, D. (2002) *Interpreting Quantitative Data*. Thousand Oaks, CA: SAGE.

Byrne, D. (2009a) Case-based methods: Why we need them; what they are; how to do them. In D. Byrne and C.C. Ragin (eds) *The SAGE Handbook of Case-Based Methods* (pp. 1–10). London: SAGE.

Byrne, D. (2009b) Complex realist and configurational approaches to cases: A radical synthesis. In D. Byrne and C.C. Ragin (eds) *The SAGE Handbook of Case-Based Methods* (pp. 104–111). London: SAGE.

Charmaz, K. (2006) *Constructing Grounded Theory: A Practical Guide Through Qualitative Analysis*. Thousand Oaks, CA: SAGE.

Coolahan, J., Santiago, P., Phair, R. and Ninomiya, A. (2004) *Attracting, developing and retaining effective teachers: Korea. Organization for Economic Co-operation and Development, Directorate for Education and Training Policy Division*. See http://www.oecd.org/korea/31690991.pdf (accessed 17 November 2013).

Corbin, J. and Strauss, A. (1990) Grounded theory research: Procedures, canons, and evaluative criteria. *Qualitative Sociology* 13, 3–21.

Davies, M. and Underwood, G. (2000) Cognition and stress. In G. Fink (ed.) *Encyclopedia of Stress* (pp. 478–483). San Diego, CA: Academic Press.

Davis, B. and Sumara, D. (2006) *Complexity and Education: Inquiries into Learning, Teaching and Research*. Mahwah, NJ: Lawrence Erlbaum Associates.

Day, C., Sammons, P., Stobart, G., Kington, A. and Gu, Q. (2007) *Teachers Matter: Connecting Lives, Work and Effectiveness*. New York: McGraw-Hill.

Dooley, K. (1997) A complex adaptive systems model of organization change. *Nonlinear Dynamics, Psychology, and Life Sciences* 1 (1), 69–97.

Dörnyei, Z. (2014) Researching complex dynamic systems: 'Retrodictive qualitative modelling' in the language classroom. *Language Teaching* 47 (1), 80–91.

Dörnyei, Z. and Kubanyiova, M. (2014) *Motivating Learners, Motivating Teachers: Building Vision in the Language Classroom*. Cambridge: CUP.

Dörnyei, Z. and Ushioda, E. (2011) *Teaching and Researching Motivation* (2nd edn). Harlow: Pearson Education.

Ehrman, M. and Dörnyei, Z. (1998) *Interpersonal Dynamics in Second Language Education: The Visible and Invisible Classroom*. Thousand Oaks, CA: SAGE.

Farber, B. (2000) Treatment strategies for different types of teacher burnout. *Journal of Clinical Psychology* 56, 675–689.

Folds, J. (2008) An overview of immunity. In M. O'Gorman and A. Donnenberg (eds) *Handbook of Human Immunology* (2nd edn) (pp. 1–28). Boca Raton, FL: CRC Press.

Freisen, D. and Sarros, J. (1989) Sources of burnout among educators. *Journal of Organizational Behavior* 10 (2), 179–188.

Friedman, H. and Schustack, M. (2010) *Personality: Classic Theories and Modern Research* (5th edn). New York: Pearson.

Goldstein, J. (2011) Probing the nature of complex systems: Parameters, modeling, interventions. *Emergence: Complexity & Organization* 13 (3), 94–121.

Gorochowski, T., di Bernardo, M. and Grierson, C. (2011) Evolving dynamical networks: A formalism for describing complex systems. *Complexity* 17 (4), 18–25.

Greenglass, E. (2000) Teaching and stress. In G. Fink (ed.) *Encyclopedia of Stress* (pp. 571–574). San Diego, CA: Academic Press.

Griffin, J., Steptoe, A. and Cropley, M. (1999) An investigation of coping strategies associated with job stress in teachers. *British Journal of Educational Psychology* 69, 517–531.

Hakanen, J., Bakker, A. and Schaufeli, W. (2006) Burnout and work engagement among teachers. *Journal of School Psychology* 43, 495–513.

Haken, H. (1985) Synergetics – an interdisciplinary approach to phenomena of self-organization. *Geoforum* 16 (2), 205–211.

Haken, H. (1997) Visions of synergetics. *Journal of the Franklin Institute* 334B (5/6), 759–792.

Haken, H. (2009a) Synergetics: basic concepts. In R. Meyers (ed.) *Encyclopedia of Complexity and Systems Science* (pp. 8926–8946). New York: Springer.

Haken, H. (2009b) Introduction to synergetics. In R. Meyers (ed.) *Encyclopedia of Complexity and Systems Science* (pp. 8946–8948). New York: Springer.

Haken, H., Wunderlin, A. and Yigitbasi, S. (1995) An introduction to synergetics. *Open Systems and Information Dynamics* 3 (1), 97–130.

Harvey, D. (2009) Complexity and case. In D. Byrne and C.C. Ragin (eds) *The SAGE Handbook of Case-Based Methods* (pp. 15–38). London: SAGE.

Hiver, P. and Dörnyei, Z. (under review) Language teacher immunity: A double-edged sword.

Holland, J.H. (1992) Complex adaptive systems. *Daedalus* 121 (1), 17–30.

Holland, J.H. (2006) Studying complex adaptive systems. *Journal of Systems Science and Complexity* 19, 1–8.

Howe, M. and Lewis, M. (2005) The importance of dynamic systems approaches for understanding development. *Developmental Review* 25, 247–251.

Jepson, E. and Forrest, S. (2006) Individual contributory factors in teacher stress: The role of achievement striving and occupational commitment. *British Journal of Educational Psychology* 76, 183–197.

Johnson, N. (2009) *Simply Complexity: A Clear Guide to Complexity Theory*. Oxford: Oneworld Publications.

Jost, J., Bertschinger, N. and Olbrich, E. (2010) Emergence. *New Ideas in Psychology* 28, 265–273.

Juarrero, A. (1999) *Dynamics in Action: Intentional Behavior as a Complex System*. Cambridge, MA: MIT Press.

Kauffman, S. (1995) *At Home in the Universe: The Search for the Laws of Self-organization and Complexity*. Oxford: OUP.

Kelso, J. (1995) *Dynamic Patterns: The Self-organization of Brain and Behavior*. Cambridge, MA: MIT Press.

Kelchtermans, G. (2011) Vulnerability in teaching: The moral and political roots of a structural condition. In C. Day and J.C.-K. Lee (eds) *New Understandings of Teacher's Work: Emotions and Educational Change* (pp. 65–82). New York: Springer.

Kiel, L. (1991) Lessons from the nonlinear paradigm: Applications of the theory of dissipative structures in the social sciences. *Social Science Quarterly* 72 (3), 431–442.

Klusman, U., Kunter, M., Trautwein, U., Lüdtke, O. and Jürgen, B. (2008) Teachers' occupational well-being and quality of instruction: The important role of self-regulatory patterns. *Journal of Educational Psychology* 100 (3), 702–715.

Kra, B. (2009) Introduction to ergodic theory. In R. Meyers (ed.) *Encyclopedia of Complexity and Systems Science* (pp. 3053–3055). New York: Springer.

Kubanyiova, M. (2009) Possible selves in language teacher development. In Z. Dörnyei and E. Ushioda (eds) *Motivation, Language Identity and the L2 Self* (pp. 314–332). Bristol: Multilingual Matters.

Kubanyiova, M. (2012) *Teacher Development in Action: Understanding Language Teachers' Conceptual Change*. Basingstoke: Palgrave Macmillan.

Kyriacou, C. (2001) Teacher stress: directions for future research. *Educational Review* 53 (1), 27–35.

Kyriacou, C. and Coulthard, M. (2000) Undergraduates' views of teaching as a career. *Journal of Education for Teaching* 26 (2), 117–126.

Larsen-Freeman, D. (1997) Chaos/complexity science and second language acquisition. *Applied Linguistics* 18 (2), 141–165.

Larsen-Freeman, D. (2012) Complex, dynamic systems: A new transdisciplinary theme for applied linguistics? *Language Teaching* 45 (2), 1–13.

Laws, K. and McLeod, R. (2004) Case-study and grounded theory: sharing some alternative qualitative research methodologies with systems professionals. *Proceedings from System Dynamics Society* 2004 (pp. 1–25). Oxford: Wiley.

Lewis, M. (2005) Bridging emotion theory and neurobiology through dynamic systems modeling. *Behavioral and Brain Sciences* 28, 169–245.

Lundberg, U. (2000) Workplace stress. In G. Fink (ed.) *Encyclopedia of Stress* (pp. 684–692). San Diego, CA: Academic Press.

Maier, S., Watkins, L. and Fleshner, M. (1994) Psychoneuroimmunology: The interface between behavior, brain, and immunity. *American Psychologist* 49 (12), 1004–1017.

Malmberg, L. (2006) Goal-orientation and teacher motivation among teacher applicants and student teachers. *Teaching and Teacher Education* 22, 58–76.

Manson, S. (2001) Simplifying complexity: a review of complexity theory. *Geoforum* 32, 405–414.

Maslach, C. and Leiter, M. (2000) Burnout. In G. Fink (ed.) *Encyclopedia of Stress* (pp. 358–362). San Diego, CA: Academic Press.

McAdams, D. (2006) The role of narrative in personality psychology today. *Narrative Inquiry* 16 (1), 11–18.

McAdams, D. (2008) Personal narratives and the life story. In O.P. John, R.W. Robins and L.A. Pervin (eds) *Handbook of Personality Theory & Research* (3rd edn) (pp. 242–262). New York: Guilford.

McAdams, D. and Pals, J. (2006) A new big five: Fundamental principles for an integrative science of personality. *American Psychologist* 61 (3), 204–217.

Meister, D. and Ahrens, P. (2011) Resisting plateauing: Four veteran teachers' stories. *Teaching and Teacher Education* 27, 770–778.

Merriam, S.B. (1998) *Qualitative Research and Case Study Applications in Education*. San Francisco, CA: Jossey-Bass.

Näring, G., Briët, M. and Brouwers, A. (2006) Beyond demand-control: Emotional labour and symptoms of burnout in teachers. *Work and Stress* 20 (4), 303–315.

Newman, L. (2009) Human–environment interactions: complex systems approaches for dynamic sustainable development. In R. Meyers (ed.) *Encyclopedia of Complexity and Systems Science* (pp. 4631–4643). New York: Springer.

Nieto, S. (2003) *What Keeps Teachers Going?* New York: Teachers College Press.

O'Sullivan, D. (2009) Complexity theory, nonlinear dynamic spatial systems. In R. Kitchin and N. Thrift (eds) *International Encyclopedia of Human Geography* (pp. 239–244). Oxford: Elsevier.

Parker, P. and Martin, A. (2009) Coping and buoyancy in the workplace: Understanding their effects on teachers' work-related well-being and engagement. *Teaching and Teacher Education* 25, 68–75.

Pennington, M. (1991) Work satisfaction and the ESL profession. *Language, Culture and Curriculum* 4, 59–86.

Pennington, M. and Riley, P. (1991) A survey of job satisfaction in ESL: ESL educators respond to the Minnesota Satisfaction Questionnaire. *University of Hawaii Working Papers in ESL* 10 (1), 37–56.

Prigogine, I. and Stengers, I. (1984) *Order Out of Chaos*. New York: Shambhala.

Ragin, C. (1989) The logic of the comparative method and the algebra of logic. *Journal of Quantitative Anthropology* 1, 373–398.

Ragin, C. (2006) Set relations in social research: Evaluating their consistency and coverage. *Political Analysis* 16, 291–310.

Ragin, C. (2009a) Qualitative comparative analysis (QCA) as an approach. In B. Rihoux and C. Ragin (eds) *Configurational Comparative Methods: Qualitative Comparative Analysis (QCA) and Related Techniques* (pp. 1–18). Thousand Oaks, CA: SAGE.

Ragin, C. (2009b) Reflections on casing and case-oriented research. In D. Byrne and C.C. Ragin (eds) *The SAGE Handbook of Case-Based Methods* (pp. 523–534). London: SAGE.

Reitsma, F. (2003) A response to simplifying complexity. *Geoforum* 34, 13–16.

Rihoux, B. and Lobe, B. (2009) The case for qualitative comparative analysis (QCA): Adding leverage for thick cross-case comparison. In D. Byrne and C.C. Ragin (eds) *The SAGE Handbook of Case-Based Methods* (pp. 222–242). London: SAGE.

Schultz, K. and Ravitch, S. (2013) Narratives of learning to teach: Taking on professional identities. *Journal of Teacher Education* 64 (1), 35–46.

Skaalvik, E. and Skaalvik, S. (2010) Teacher self-efficacy and teacher burnout: a study of relations. *Teaching and Teacher Education* 26, 1059–1069.

Strauss, A. and Corbin, J. (1994) Grounded theory methodology: An overview. In N. Denzin and Y. Lincoln (eds) *Handbook of Qualitative Research* (1st edn) (pp. 273–285). London: SAGE.

Strauss, A. and Corbin, J. (1998) *Basics of Qualitative Research: Techniques and Procedures for Developing Grounded Theory* (2nd edn). Thousand Oaks, CA: SAGE.

Straussfogel, D. and Von Schilling, C. (2009) Systems theory. In R. Kitchin and N. Thrift (eds) *International Encyclopedia of Human Geography* (pp. 151–158). Oxford: Elsevier.

Strogatz, S. (1994) *Nonlinear Dynamics and Chaos: With Applications to Physics, Biology, Chemistry and Engineering.* New York: Westview Press.

Thelen, E. (2005) Dynamic systems theory and the complexity of change. *Psychoanalytic Dialogues* 15 (2), 255–283.

Thelen, E. and Bates, E. (2003) Connectionism and dynamic systems: Are they really different? *Developmental Science* 6 (4), 378–391.

Tkačik, G. and Bialek, W. (2009) Cell biology: Networks, regulation and pathways. In R. Meyers (ed.) *Encyclopedia of Complexity and Systems Science* (pp. 719–741). New York: Springer.

van Geert, P. (1998) We almost had a great future behind us: The contribution of nonlinear dynamics to developmental-science-in-the-making. *Developmental Science* 1 (1), 143–159.

van Geert, P. (2009) Complex dynamic systems of development. In R. Meyers (ed.) *Encyclopedia of Complexity and Systems Science* (pp. 1872–1916). New York: Springer.

van Geert, P. and Steenbeek, H. (2005) Explaining after by before: Basic aspects of a dynamic systems approach to the study of development. *Developmental Review* 25, 408–442.

Watt, H. and Richardson, P. (2008) Motivations, perceptions, and aspirations concerning teaching as a career for different types of beginning teachers. *Learning and Instruction* 18, 408–428.

Wheeldon, J. and Faubert, J. (2009) Framing experience: Concept maps, mind maps, and data collection in qualitative research. *International Journal of Qualitative Methods* 8 (3), 68–83.

Woolfolk-Hoy, A. (2008) Commentary: What motivates teachers? Important work on a complex question. *Learning and Instruction* 18, 492–498.

Yin, R. (2008) *Case Study Research: Design and Methods* (4th edn). Thousand Oaks, CA: SAGE.

Appendix 15.1

Qualitative comparative analysis (QCA) is a relatively unfamiliar method in the SLA field. I briefly describe it below to offer further clarification of the methods used in this study. QCA is a case-based approach to researching complexity that originated in the work of the sociologist Charles Ragin. QCA describes a collection of techniques spanning sampling, to data analysis and interpretation (Ragin, 2009b). It assumes two very important things about research rarely entertained by other qualitative methods: first, the aim of all research is to provide generalisable findings; secondly, causality can be systematically investigated through qualitative data if we analyse the right type and number of cases (i.e. usually in the double digits) (Ragin, 1989). QCA begins by defining the outcome of interest and casing the outcome (i.e. recruiting a typical sample that will guarantee relevant data about that phenomenon). In order to develop a causal explanation of an outcome, data about the conditions thought to influence the outcome are needed. This is called selecting the causal conditions. Conditions are roughly equivalent in purpose to the term variables that we normally use, and QCA uses the ones and zeros of Boolean algebra to code these conditions. In crisp set QCA

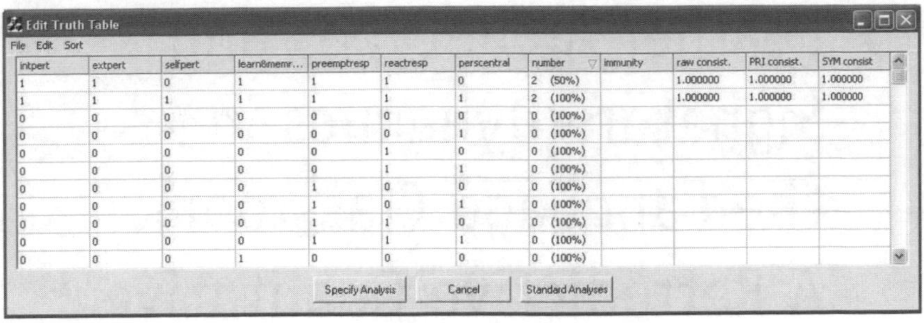
Edit Truth Table

File Edit Sort

intpert	extpert	selfpert	learn&memr...	preemptresp	reactresp	perscentral	number	immunity	raw consist.	PRI consist.	SYM consist
1	1	0	1	1	1	0	2 (50%)		1.000000	1.000000	1.000000
1	1	1	1	1	1	1	2 (100%)		1.000000	1.000000	1.000000
0	0	0	0	0	0	0	0 (100%)				
0	0	0	0	0	0	1	0 (100%)				
0	0	0	0	0	1	0	0 (100%)				
0	0	0	0	0	1	1	0 (100%)				
0	0	0	0	1	0	0	0 (100%)				
0	0	0	0	1	0	1	0 (100%)				
0	0	0	0	1	1	0	0 (100%)				
0	0	0	0	1	1	1	0 (100%)				
0	0	0	1	0	0	0	0 (100%)				

Specify Analysis Cancel Standard Analyses

Figure A15.1 Screenshot of a truth table from my data analysis

(*cs*QCA), used for discrete variables, all the cases are assigned one of two possible crisp membership values for each condition or set included in a study: 1, membership in the set; 0, non-membership in the set (Ragin, 2009a). The results are summarised in truth table rows (Figure A15.1) to determine which causal conditions, or combinations of conditions, are necessary or sufficient for the outcome being investigated.

By solving contradictions and minimising the causal conditions in order to keep the fewest possible causes that still result in the outcome, the researcher will obtain the parsimonious minimal formula. If the formula holds for all of the cases being compared, the consistency (i.e. the number of cases that share this combination of conditions and also display the outcome of interest) is 1.0. Consistency scores, in general, should be as close to 1.0 as possible (Ragin, 2006).

16 Learner Archetypes and Signature Dynamics in the Language Classroom: A Retrodictive Qualitative Modelling Approach to Studying L2 Motivation

Letty Chan, Zoltán Dörnyei and Alastair Henry

This study explores the use of 'retrodictive qualitative modelling' (RQM), a novel approach to second language (L2) research proposed by Dörnyei (2014) that involves the identification of learner archetypes and motivational patterns through empirical investigation. The method reverses the traditional way of conducting research; it first examines outcomes – that is, the end-states – and then traces back the developmental trajectories leading to these outcomes. Situated in a Hong Kong secondary school, we started our project by first asking a teacher focus group to identify salient learner archetypes in their classrooms (Years 7 to 9) and, on the basis of these descriptions, we then conducted in-depth interviews with a prototypical learner from each group. As a result, we gained insights into the 'signature dynamics' of the motivational system associated with each prototype. Our focus in this chapter is on evaluating RQM in action. First we report on the processes in which teachers identified learner archetypes and thereafter offer an in-depth analysis of the system dynamics of one of these students. In the final discussion, we list the main methodological lessons that we have learnt from applying RQM.

Complex Dynamic Systems and RQM

As has been pointed out in several chapters in Part 1 of this volume, we face serious methodological challenges when we conduct empirical research within a dynamic systems vein. At the most general level, the fundamental issue is that the outcomes of the operation of dynamic systems – particularly ones that involve human beings – are difficult to predict as it is virtually impossible to know in advance how the various factors will interact with one another (Haggis, 2008). This has been explicitly highlighted by Diane Larsen-Freeman and Lynne Cameron (2008: 75) who draw attention to the fact that 'the behaviour of a complex system is not completely random, but neither is it wholly predictable'. Limited predictability and the inability to enumerate potentially relevant factors in advance of conducting research pose very real problems for researchers. It was against this backdrop that Dörnyei (2014) proposed RQM as a possibly meaningful way forward. He suggested that researchers can capitalise on the system's *self-organising capacity* – the propensity to increase the orderly nature of the initially transient, fluid and nonlinear system behaviour – summarising this basic assumption in the following way:

> As a result of this self-organisation process, many – if not most – complex systems display a few well-recognisable outcomes or behavioural patterns (e.g. crystallised types, skills, schemas or achievement configuration) rather than the unlimited variation that we could, in theory, anticipate in an erratic system. The existence of these systematic outcome patterns, in turn, opens up a meaningful avenue for researching dynamic systems by means of *'retrodictive qualitative modelling'*. (Dörnyei, 2014: 84–85)

Although 'self-organisation' may sound like an abstract concept, the actual phenomenon is in fact likely to be familiar to classroom practitioners; whereas system dynamics could in principle produce indefinite variability in a classroom, with an infinite range of emerging learner types, in reality we tend to find a certain degree of predictability and a limited range of patterns in most situations. So, for example, even if we visit a classroom in a very different learning context from the one we are used to, before long we will start to recognise familiar learner behaviours and attitudes. These recurring patterns are related to the fact that systems tend to self-organise components into a few preferred modes of behaviour or functionally useful units. Van Geert (2008) has neatly illustrated this idea using the fictional characters Alice and the Queen from the children's story *Through the Looking Glass*. Although there is an infinite number of possibilities for Alice to walk to the Queen, some paths will become more salient as they will be trodden more often and, over time, the number of possible paths to the Queen will be reduced to a small number of trajectories actually used. Indeed, this limited variability has recently been highlighted by Byrne and Callaghan (2014: 197) as a major consideration in analysing complex systems:

> The key aspect of complex systems which gives us some purchase on resolving this dilemma [of how to predict future outcome states in complex systems] is that they do not have an infinite set of possible future states but rather a limited set of more than one but less than too many to comprehend.

Thus, RQM utilises the regulating force of self-organisation that makes system behaviour predictable and therefore researchable. The key word is *retrodiction*, in that RQM reverses the traditional way of conducting research; first we identify the end-states (or outcome-states/prototypes) in system behaviour and then work *backwards* in a retrospective manner to uncover the developmental trajectories that led to those settled states. Thus, instead of the usual forward-pointing 'pre-diction', we pursue 'retro-diction' by tracking back to the reasons why the system might have ended up with a particular outcome, thus producing a retrospective qualitative model of its evolution.

In an attempt to operationalise the concept of RQM for classroom investigations, Dörnyei (2014) has proposed a three-step research template. The first step involves the identification of salient student types in the classroom, which are equated with attractor states in the system's overall phase space. There are several possible ways to identify such prototypes, including the statistical procedures of cluster analysis (cf. Byrne & Callaghan, 2014: 160) and Q methodology (cf. Irie & Ryan, this volume). In this study we followed a qualitative approach that employed teacher focus groups. We asked the participants to brainstorm salient student types and create a rich description of each archetype with a list of characteristics containing cognitive, emotional and motivational components (e.g. motivated + low-proficiency + unconfident). In doing so teachers engaged with *social categorisation* processes. In social psychology, 'social categorisation' is understood as the creation of social categories by 'putting some people into one group based on certain characteristics and others into another group based on their different characteristics' (Aronson *et al.*, 2013: 379). The process is highly useful – one could argue, indispensable – when educators have to interact with numerous language learners in large classes on a regular basis, because such categorical thinking can simplify the person perception process (Allport, 1954). Thus, instead of viewing individuals in terms of their unique attributes and characteristics, teachers can construe them in categories according to the information stored in long-term memory (Macrae & Bodenhausen, 2000), helping them therefore to make sense of the demanding and complex environment of educational settings.

Once a set of relevant prototypes has been established, we need to iden-tify actual students who would fit each archetype, a process that is usually referred to as *critical case sampling* (Dörnyei, 2007). If the identification of the prototypes involves an initial quantitative survey, with data subsequently processed by, for example, cluster analysis, it is possible to select students from the statistically distinct groupings (provided of course the question-naires contained identification data). This approach was adopted, for exam-ple, by Henry (2011) in investigating third language acquisition in Sweden, with a special emphasis on analysing the interference of the L2 (English). In the current study, we followed an alternative process whereby we asked the students' teachers to nominate candidates for each prototype (an issue we will return to in the final discussion). Following this initial nomination process, in a second phase, selected students are invited to take part in a semi-structured interview – or a set of interviews – to obtain a rich descrip-tion of the prototypical cases. Finally, in the third phase, the transcribed interviews are subjected to qualitative data analysis in order to identify the significant components of the classroom's motivational setup and to shed light on the main underlying dynamic patterns – or the system's *signature dynamics* – that produced the observed system outcomes. The current study draws on this three-stage template to examine how RQM methodology works in actual practice and to provide insights into the analytical process that underlies the model's key element: the identification of a motivational system's signature dynamics.

Methodology

Participants

The research took place in a Hong Kong secondary school. In the first stage of the study – the identification of learner archetypes – the participants were six English teachers (one male and five females). In the second stage – identifying the components and signature dynamics of motivational systems for individual students fitting these archetypes – the participants were seven Chinese students (five boys and two girls). The students were all born and brought up in Hong Kong and were all native speakers of Cantonese. At the time of the study the students were enrolled in Years 7 to 9 and between 13 and 14 years old. The school they attended is an aided secondary school[1] where the use of English is greatly encouraged in various ways, including using English in morning assemblies and announcements, organising English drama workshops, international exchange days and immersion programmes abroad. There were two strands in the English instruction – the 'elite' and the 'normal' stream – and students could move between strands, up as well as down, depending on their progress.

Data collection

After obtaining necessary consent to conduct the research, in the first phase of the study a number of English teachers were invited to take part in a focus group interview. The teachers were informed of the procedures and that their identities would not be revealed in subsequent reporting of the research. Six teachers agreed to participate in the focus group interview, which was held in March 2011. Here they identified seven salient learner archetypes among the students in the school (Years 7 to 9). Having done this, they then nominated typical students for each archetype.

Drawing on this list of names, students from Years 7 to 9 were invited to take part in semi-structured interviews (these cohorts not being under the immediate pressure of public exams). Each student was interviewed on two occasions, the initial, longer interview being followed by a shorter interview where, drawing on brief analyses of the data, the aim was to verify whether the findings were in agreement with the participants' experiences and viewpoints (Hesse-Biber & Leavy, 2011). The interviews, which were conducted in Cantonese by the first author (designated 'LC' in the excerpts below) took place in a quiet meeting room and lasted for between 30–90 minutes. The digital audio-recordings were transcribed and subsequently translated into English by the first author.

Besides asking broad questions about the interviewees' experience of learning English at school, their changing attitudes and motivation, their L2 learning habits, the influences of their family and their imaginary view of the English speaker/user they would like to become, students were also asked to plot their motivation on a simple graph. This was designed to help them to indicate the levels of motivation at various points in their learning history and to give them an opportunity to focus on possible underlying reasons for their motivational evolution (cf. Henry, Chapter 19, this volume).

Data analysis

To ensure the accuracy of transcription, the interview corpus (of approximately 145,000 words) was listened to twice. The translated transcripts were then read several times by the authors as a means of gaining familiarity with the data (Harding, 2013). Analysis of the data was carried out in two stages. In the *first stage*, we read the transcripts making brief notes, identifying keywords, highlighting important points and through these processes, generating ideas. Having obtained a general idea of the data, we carried out a content analysis to examine the various factors that affected each participant's L2 motivation in different phases of their academic lives, including environmental, social and personal factors. Relevant parts were highlighted and coded into different categories, and then the interaction between the categories was further examined. We have also looked at the commonalities and differences across participants (Gibson & Brown, 2009) to identify overarching patterns and possible links between learner types.

The current chapter focuses on the *second stage* of the data analysis, which involved a close-grained examination of a single case with the aim of identifying the corresponding signature dynamics. This analysis was carried out using an interpretive approach similar to that outlined by Smith and Eatough (2007) (see also Henry, Chapter 19, this volume). In analysing the transcript of our focal participant, we used the abstractions of self-determination theory (Noels *et al.*, 2000) and complex systems theories (Larsen-Freeman & Cameron, 2008) as a compass, transforming our initial notes into theoretically resonant themes, in particular identifying instances indicating shifts from one attractor state to another, perturbations triggering these shifts and features of emergence.

Results

Phase one: Identifying learner archetypes

At the beginning of the teacher focus group, the first author introduced the aims of the study, its method and the schedule of the session to the teacher participants. In order to facilitate the identification of learner archetypes, a list of adjectives in English (both positive and negative) was presented as a set of illustrative descriptors designed to reflect learners' emotions, cognition, motivation and behaviour. A specific example of a possible learner archetype was also provided and the participants were encouraged to think of typical students representative of this type. After the introduction, the teachers were first asked in pairs, and then in the whole group, to brainstorm and come up with other possible archetypes. The descriptions of the seven learner archetypes generated by the teacher focus group are as follows.

(1) *A highly competitive and motivated student, with some negative emotions.* According to the teachers' focus group, students in this archetype are intelligent, motivated individuals with a noticeable competitive edge. They tend to have high expectations of their teachers and expect to be given new and challenging activities and materials in class. They reflect on things to a great degree and tend to be somewhat nervous.

(2) *An unmotivated student with lower-than-average English proficiency.* This archetype is unique in a way because, although these students are placed in an elite English class, their proficiency in English is not comparable with their peers and they tend to be lower achievers in general. They are described as quiet, sombre and lacking confidence. In comparison to their elite class peers, they are perceived to be 'lazy', 'not hardworking' and that their schoolwork tends to be rather 'slapdash'.

(3) *A happy-go-lucky student with low English proficiency (usually found in the Year 7 remedial classes)*. The teachers' focus group described this archetype as represented by someone who is highly motivated in general and enjoys going to school, but someone who at the same time struggles with English and keeps having to ask questions in order to understand what is going on in the class. Although their grades are relatively poor, their emotional stability and happy-go-lucky disposition allow them to move beyond their failures. As a result, setbacks in their schoolwork do not seem to frustrate them.

(4) *A mediocre student with little L2 motivation*. According to our teacher informants, this is a very common archetype. Despite having the abilities to achieve, students belonging to this category will often only do the minimum required of them owing to a lack of motivation. In English classes they are receptive, well-behaved and can function well without any problems. They nearly always pass their tests. Nonetheless, they are perceived as not taking their learning particularly seriously and not possessing clear expectations for themselves. They are stable in their emotions, tending to be calm and placid.

(5) *A motivated yet distressed student with low English proficiency*. This archetype was described as being largely represented by quiet female students who tend to be hardworking, diligent and motivated. Students in this group tend to complete the tasks teachers ask them to do, submit all their homework on time and take comprehensive notes in class. However, they are also slow and rather rigid in their learning. What few learning strategies they have (e.g. their methods of revising for tests) tend to be ineffective. Consequently, these learners are unhappy with their work in that it fails to produce any enduring results. It is not uncommon for students in this archetype to be brought to tears when receiving a test paper and realising that the considerable effort they have invested in their studies has not borne fruit.

(6) *A 'perfect' English learner*. Teachers saw this archetype – usually found in the elite classes of the school – as the L2 student who is intelligent, independent and focused. Such learners have a great sense of responsibility and are willing to carry out the tasks assigned to them; they are the type of students who, the teachers say, will readily give them a set of notes when the teacher has misplaced his or hers. They are confident, highly motivated, emotionally stable, have a genuine interest in the subject and engage eagerly in autonomous learning (e.g. they keep a vocabulary log, write grammar notes and keep a journal in English).

(7) *An unmotivated student with poor English proficiency*. This student type is very similar to the second of the archetypes in several respects, including being reserved, withdrawn, lazy and lacking motivation. Students belonging to this category are also said to be unhappy and lack confidence in their abilities. Teachers see them as difficult and their work as

substandard. What makes them different from the second archetype is that they have lower-than-average language learning abilities even in a regular (i.e. non-elite) class.

Phase two: Identifying students for each archetype

Having identified the learner archetypes, teachers were given a list of the names of students in the English classes they were teaching at the time of the study and invited to nominate students (a) who best represented each archetype, and (b) others who resembled the prototypical learner (to act as reserves in cases where the best candidate might not be willing to participate in the interviews). During this phase, the teachers discussed the possible candidates among themselves and reviewed the suitability of their selections. Between two and nine learners were selected for each prototype, with one or two identified as the most prototypical learners. Table 16.1 provides descriptive information on the final student sample comprising three proto-typical (Chris, Alex and Rex) and four prototype-resembling learners (Helen, Mary, Saki and Danny).

Phase three: Mapping motivational trajectories and identifying signature dynamics

The final phase of RQM aims to produce two related outcomes: a set of signature dynamics associated with the initially identified archetypes and, based on this set, a dynamic overview of the learning environment under investigation. The second objective goes beyond the scope of this chapter and therefore the focus below will be on the first aim, generating a retrospective account of the system dynamics of a single student typical of one of the teacher-generated archetypes. Although for this purpose we could have selected any of the seven students, our choice was Chris, a student identified by his teachers as being in the *'highly competitive and motivated student, with some negative emotions'* archetype (and also one of the three best-fit prototypical students). Even though the archetypes that teachers identify may vary somewhat from one class to the next (each class being a unique dynamic system), and may differ substantially from one cultural context to another, Chris, we feel, is a student that many teachers will recognise. We begin by offering a *thumbnail portrait* of Chris and his family background. We then describe his *motivational trajectory* from his first encounters with English, moving on to finally identifying the *signature dynamics* of his motivational system.

A thumbnail portrait

Chris, who was aged 14 at the time of the interviews, lives with his grandparents in an urban residential area with mainly public housing estates in the part of Hong Kong known as the New Territories. His parents and

Table 16.1 Emerging learner types in a teachers' focus group discussion

Prototype (pseudonym)	Motivation	Cognition	Emotion	Behaviour	Quotes
A highly competitive and motivated student, with some negative emotions (Chris)	Motivated	High ability in English, has a lot of expectations of teachers and of themselves	Anxious, not cheerful, negative in their way of thinking	Loves comparing self with others, likes competition	'I really wanted to be the best. I was combative and I had a desire to compete and win.'
An unmotivated student with lower-than-average English proficiency (Helen)	Not hardworking, not particularly motivated	Low in ability especially when compared with students in a good class	Reserved, not happy, not confident in English or any other subjects, proud to be in an elite class, inferiority complex	Insufficient engagement, careless with her homework	'When I have to concentrate on something that is relatively boring, I will become stiff. I really need to relax my brain at that moment.'
A happy-go-lucky student with low English proficiency (Alex)	Motivated generally and also in English	Less able, low proficiency	Cheerful	Asks many questions, inflexible, active, needs clear guidelines	'The worst fear is not having any friends. Sometimes, when I am revising and this comes to my mind, I'm quite scared.'

Archetype				
A mediocre student without much L2 motivation (Rex)	Learns only when pushed, does not do his homework seriously	Mediocre in achievement	Neutral in emotions, gentle, lucid	Obedient, attention-seeking, would try to make some jokes in class, funny	'To put it bluntly, I do my work superficially. I only work hard in front of others, but I won't when they are not there.'
A motivated yet distressed student with low English proficiency (Mary)	Hardworking, motivated, will learn autonomously	A weak learner	Empathetic, sad after receiving a test paper	Quiet, obedient, rigid, responsible, fossilised in their learning strategies	'In the last test, I cried. It was also because I was scared to be told off by my parents.'
A 'perfect' English learner (Saki)	Has intrinsic interests in learning English, serious approach to learning	Good memory, has acquired various learning strategies	Emotionally stable, confident	Detail-minded, organised, independent in everything, capable of handling most tasks, helpful, well-behaved	'I would learn five new words and I read English every day. I would always have something with me to read.'
An unmotivated student with poor English proficiency (Danny)	Not hardworking, not particularly motivated, withdrawn	Low in ability even in a regular class	Reserved, not happy, not confident in English or any other subjects, proud to be in an elite class, inferiority complex	Insufficient engagement, careless with his homework	'I didn't want to do my homework, but I had no choice.'

younger brother live in Tung Chung, a town on one of Hong Kong's islands. Perhaps because of the pressure of raising two children, his parents decided that Chris should be brought up by his grandparents. Although Chris does not mention any contact with his parents, he has, in addition to his grandparents, a close relationship with an uncle, who, along with his grandmother, has been instrumental in his education and development. While his grandmother *'has been telling me off since I was young'*, his uncle offers more constructive advice, functioning as an important role model. In particular his uncle has advised Chris to read as many books in English as he can. Similar advice has been received by another important adult in Chris's life, his personal tutor, whom he has had since Year 3. Like his uncle, she advocates the importance of reading: *'Her advice is to read widely. She says the reason why English proficiency is so low among students is because they don't read extensively. They only care about what is required from the school'*. Like many boys of his age the world over, Chris enjoys playing digital games, sometimes at the expense of other activities, such as reading books and doing homework. Sometimes, he says, *'I just want to read everything quickly so that I can play computer games. There's a sense of addiction'*. He is musical, playing both the piano and the guitar, from which he gets particular pleasure, saying that *'when you have loads of homework to do, if you can play the guitar, you will feel less pressurised'*. From a young age he has been attending private English classes run by the British Council.

Chris's motivational trajectory

From our interview data, we present five extracts that illustrate not just the motivational trajectory over time, but also the interactions between different system components. Chris suggests that, as the years have gone by, his motivation has increased continuously:

[Extract 1]

In primary school, I felt bored when I had to read long passages. But because I have built a strong foundation, I naturally didn't think it was that difficult in secondary school. I feel increasingly more interested and my motivation keeps growing.

Although giving the impression of a steady increase – and it is here worth noting that the upward line he drew on the graph (Figure 16.1) has an increase/plateauing pattern – this general trend is somewhat belying. Looking more closely at the interview data it becomes clear that both the intensity of his motivation and its sources have fluctuated over the years.

Chris's first encounters with English were, he recalls, not particularly positive. Reading in class was not something he enjoyed, *'my concentration was not so good, so when I had to read a long passage, I felt really tired'*, he says. At home his grandparents' attempts to expose him to English – *'I remember that*

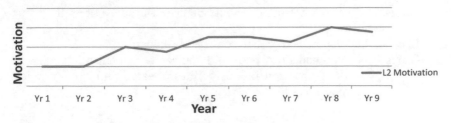

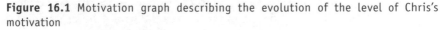

Figure 16.1 Motivation graph describing the evolution of the level of Chris's motivation

my family forced me to watch some foreign cooking programmes' – were not met with enthusiasm. Despite the lack of appeal of TV cookery shows and the boredom he experienced in primary school, Chris nevertheless describes to the interviewer that this point in his life was the start of an interest for English. It is also back in primary school where he believes his *'strong foundation'* developed. Contrasting his learning in and outside of school in these early days, Chris reflects on the fact that he felt much more motivation in the classroom. This, he explains, was because it was here that he had an opportunity to compete:

> [Extract 2]
> **Chris:** I was OK in class, but my learning motivation was extremely low at home.
> **LC:** Extremely low.
> **Chris:** It was a lot higher at school. . . . There were competitions with classmates. Because there were competitions, there was no reason why I should just sit and do nothing, so I became more attentive.

This competitive streak, Chris remembers, blossomed in Year 3 when the teacher began to give regular quizzes. Not only would Chris and his classmates compete to get the best marks, there was also competition to see which of them could complete the tests in the shortest time. This self/peer-generated competition, Chris says, was very enjoyable, far more so than the less intense but more boring lessons in Years 1 and 2:

> [Extract 3]
> **Chris:** Then, we would try to finish the questions as quickly as possible.
> **LC:** You had to compete against time? This started from Year 1?
> **Chris:** No, from Year 3.
> **LC:** What do you think about this?

Chris: It was really fun! You could practise the speed of your writing.

LC: Did you have to do this on the blackboard?

Chris: No, you had a notebook and you wrote ... continuously. Working on it continuously. But in Years 1 and 2, it was a lot more relaxed.

As Chris explains, his level of motivation continued on its upward trajectory during Years 4, 5 and 6. Although in Years 3 and 4 he enjoyed the competitive environment of the classroom, invariably earning top marks on the tests, his real interest lay in computer gaming. Consequently he did not devote too much time to his studies. Even though he did not have a lot of homework at this time – meaning that there was more time for gaming – English homework was still an unenjoyable chore. A turning point however came when he was in Year 4/5. Normally at the top of the class rankings in English, Chris's perception of himself as the class's star performer received a blow when on an exam several of his peers gained better marks:

[Extract 4]

Chris: I remember that I failed my exam once in Year 4 or 5.

LC: How did that affect you?

Chris: It wasn't that bad actually. I was previously ranked either first, first runner-up or second runner-up in Years 4 and 5. It was like.... in one exam, if I can remember...I fell behind and was ranked sixth or seventh. ... So I started reflecting whether I was on the right track with regard to the way I studied.

LC: I see. How did you feel?

Chris: When I got my exam report, I remember crying for a little while.

LC: Oh! You were feeling unhappy, right?

Chris: Yes. Then, I started regretting why I had played computer games before; why wasn't I hardworking and so on...

LC: I see. How did this reflection affect you?

Chris: In Years 5 to 6, I remember that I started to become really hard-working. I paid attention in every single lesson.

A sobering experience, Chris goes on to explain how, pretty much from this time onwards, he has focused much more on learning English. As he explains, the disappointing exam result impacted not just on his approaches in class, but across a range of learning behaviours. He tells how he began to self-monitor his learning, to focus much more on what was going on in the classroom, reading much more out of class and, as a consequence, developing greater self-confidence.

Continuing in this new found study mode, Chris talks about how his motivation increased again when, in Year 7, he transferred to a new English-medium secondary school:

[Extract 5]

LC: This is an English school. Were there any big changes when you started studying in a secondary school?

Chris: When I was in Year 6, I didn't know whether I would be able to adapt in secondary school. But when I came here, and then I realised that it wasn't so hard to adapt. And I didn't really have the desire to compete in Year 7. ... And my family said, 'Now that you are in secondary school, if you can be ranked under the twentieth, you are doing really well'. So, I was taking it easy and not trying my best. I didn't really have to fight to be number one. So, I was taking it easy and was relaxed. I didn't have much pressure.

LC: You didn't have much pressure. Would you say that you weren't really paying a lot of attention? Really taking it easy?

Chris: I was really taking it easy, but since ... but since I came first in a few of the subjects, I started to be scared.

LC: That was Year 8 at that time?

Chris: Year 7 ...

LC: How many subjects did you come first? When did that start?

Chris: Since the first term.

LC: Since the first term, you were ranked first in some of the subjects?

Chris: So ...

LC: Is this the ranking of the whole year?

Chris: My year. So, I started to be scared at that point. I hadn't imagined that I would get such high marks.

LC: Really? Right. I want to ask you ... when you got good grades, how did you feel?

Chris: I haven't thought about it.

LC: Were you surprised? Would that be it?

Chris: I couldn't believe that when I started studying in secondary school, everyone was a Band One student, and I could still get the highest mark. That was really incredible. Since then, I was studying seriously.

Levelling off at a high level for the remainder of Year 8, Chris says that recently – now in Year 9 – his motivation suffered again, momentarily at least, when he did not come top of the class on an exam and how, as before, it caused him to reflect on his approach to learning and the effectiveness of the different strategies he employs.

System components and signature dynamics

Having traced the nature and intensity of Chris's motivation, we now turn our attention to the system's dynamics. The essence of the RQM approach involves uncovering the critical underlying mechanisms associated with typical system outcomes, that is to say, the system's signature dynamics (Dörnyei, 2014). Shedding light on the dynamics of Chris's motivational system, our account begins with an examination of initial conditions.

Initial conditions

Simply put, initial conditions are the state that the system is in at the time the investigation begins (MacIntyre & Gregersen, 2013; Verspoor, this volume). In our case, this means identifying the attractor state the motivational system occupies at the time Chris started English in Year 1. As we can see in Extract 1, Chris does not recall his early encounters with English as being particularly enjoyable. Dutifully ploughing through long passages in class and being forced to watch cookery programmes at home, he describes feeling *'really bored at that time'*. Extrinsically motivated, Chris's approach to learning is characteristic of forms of introjected regulation where, even though the pressure to put in effort is internally generated, it takes the form of a need to live up to external evaluative standards (Noels *et al.*, 2000). For Chris, the imperative is to do that which his family (grandparents, uncle and teachers) expect of him.

As Verspoor (this volume) makes clear, the impact of initial conditions on the system's future development will be dependent on whether or not it is in an attractor state. If, at a given starting point, the system is lodged in a deep-sided attractor basin, initial conditions can have an enduring impact on subsequent development. In Chris's case, at the start of school his motivation to learn English (and, we suspect, other subjects too) is strongly rooted in the desire to maintain self-esteem by conforming to socially derived normative standards. Indeed, one of the most striking things to emerge from the interviews is that, other than providing a route into higher education and prestigious employment (Chris has various notions of becoming a university professor or a writer), he gives no expression to ideas about speaking English in social situations in the future. Nor do we find any examples of intrinsic motivation of the type where the individual engages in an activity for the pleasure and satisfaction of understanding something new, satisfying their curiosity or exploring the world (Vallerand, 1997). While the journey of the motivational system across the state space is one of fluctuations, the initial conditions continue to have a strongly determining effect, the system tending regularly to gravitate back to the powerful attractor state of living up to externally imposed, internally accommodated evaluative standards.

An essential underlying mechanism: The periodic movement between different attractor states

Even though, as we have seen, Chris's motivation changes across the period, with sometimes changes in motivated behaviour being quite marked, a pattern seems to emerge where the system moves between a particular group of attractor states.

(a) *Movement to a new attractor state: The introduction of quizzes in Year 3.* A change in Chris's motivation is evident in Year 3 (Extract 3). From this point onwards, rather than a duty, learning becomes fun. However, it is not the learning activities in class that appear as more engaging or personally meaningful. Nor does Chris mention the teacher's approach as having any particular impact on his motivation. Rather, it is the introduction of assessment in the form of in-class quizzes and the competitive environment to which they give rise, which together have a perturbing effect, pushing the system into another part of the state space.

The paradox of testing bringing about increased pressure and fun at the same time can be linked to what German psychologist Karen Horney (1937: 188–189) has termed *hypercompetitiveness* (or neurotic competitiveness). As Horney explains, a hypercompetitive individual 'measures himself against others, even in situations which do not call for it'. Not only do these individuals want to accomplish more than others, they also desire to be exceptional and attempt to achieve these ends even when this might involve harm to others or to themselves. Although Chris is not competitive to the extent of being neurotic, his disposition is not unlike what has been termed *academic hypercompetitiveness* (cf. Bing, 1999). He engages with English because of the excitement generated by the challenge of a test, and the satisfaction and sense of accomplishment in surpassing his peers, both in terms of accuracy and response speed. From this time onwards, the system periodically shifts into and out of this attractor state, a part of the state space embodying two of the fundamental characteristics of intrinsic motivation, namely achievement (engaging in an activity for the satisfaction of accomplishment) and stimulation (engaging in an activity to experience pleasant sensations) (Vallerand, 1997).

However, it is important to note that even though the emergent behaviour following on from the phase shift triggered by the introduction of quizzes has an enduring quality, competitiveness being the hallmark of Chris's motivation, this does not mean that the desire to live up to family/social expectations – the system's initial condition – is overridden. Rather, as we can see in the interviews, the stimulus of competition and the desire to maintain self-esteem by conforming to family/social expectations, function as twin cyclical attractors between which the system moves. As Larsen-Freeman and Cameron (2008) and Hiver (Chapter 3, this volume) point out, in some cases systems will periodically move between a number of different attractor states. Known variously as *periodic, cyclical, closed loop* or *limit-cycle* attractors, these states represent areas in the state space between which the system regularly oscillates in a periodic loop. Consequently, as Hiver (Chapter 3, this volume) explains, 'patterns emerge when events or behaviours repeat themselves at regular intervals'.

(b) The emergence of a new cyclical attractor: The fear of failure. Although throughout the period the system oscillates between the twin attractor states of *stimulation* (deriving from competition) and *self-esteem maintenance* (the need to live up to family and social expectations), at various points other phase-shift triggering perturbations take place creating new patterns of movement across the state space.

Chris identifies two particular events as having an impact on motivated behaviour prominently linked to reactions to failure. At a point in time in Year 4 or 5 (he can't remember exactly when) he recalls the experience of 'failing' an exam (Extract 4). The other experience was, when switching school to the English-medium secondary school in which he is now enrolled, he realises that success – coming top of his year in this larger, more challenging environment – can be a double-edged sword in that it generates new and more demanding expectations to live up to (Extract 5). In both cases these experiences function as perturbations that jolt the system into another part of the state space. Downstream from these perturbing events new behaviours – the self-monitoring of learning, reductions in the amount of time spent playing computer games, reading more widely and focusing more in class – begin to emerge.

While these new forms of motivated behaviour indicate that a phase shift has taken place, the attractor states to which the system gravitates do not represent radically different areas of the state space. Indeed, the attractors themselves bear a close resemblance to those already identified. Moreover, as the interviews reveal, the shift to these attractor states is not permanent and at various times the system reverts back to the attractor states previously occupied. This is particularly evident when Chris talks about how his uncle became more important in his life in the period during Years 8 and 9, and how he has tried to model his approach on his uncle's advice; in these instances the system appears to revert back to the self-esteem maintenance attractor.

Signature dynamics

To sum up, the signature dynamics we observe can be seen as the movement of the system between three cyclic attractors; *self-esteem maintenance* (the need to live up to family and social expectations by being a good student), *stimulation* (deriving from processes of competition) and *fear of failure* (not achieving at a level both he and others have come to expect). The movement between these cyclic attractors seems to take the form of a closed loop of periodic movement (Larsen-Freeman & Cameron, 2008) between states that represent two of the most fundamental forces in motivation, namely approach and avoidance drives. As MacIntyre and Serroul (this volume) explain, desires to approach situations that trigger positive emotions and to avoid those that generate negative affect are basic human tendencies; these tendencies underpin the system dynamics we have identified here.

Discussion

The primary objective of this study was to carry out an empirical investigation using the RQM approach. Therefore, the discussion will be structured according to the three phases of the RQM template, first addressing the question of learner archetypes and then examining issues concerning the student interviews and the identification of signature dynamics.

Learner archetypes

A key aspect of RQM is the assumption that even complex systems, such as a learner group in a language class, display a limited number of patterns owing to the system's self-organising capacity. One of the central issues in this respect is whether learner archetypes exist in teachers' minds. The answer is affirmative: the ease with which teachers in the focus group agreed on a number of seemingly well-known learner types indicates that, instead of thinking of 30+ unique cases in a class of 30+ students, they perceived the student body along a smaller number of categories, thereby confirming the existence of settled attractor states. This is in line with the general process of social categorisation mentioned earlier and it is also likely to resonate with many classroom practitioners' intuitive awareness of 'familiar' types of students, even when they start working in a new learning environment; indeed, as Dörnyei (2014: 90) pointed out, 'there is wisdom in the saying that an experienced practitioner has "seen it all"'. However, we should note that some of the seven learner prototypes produced in this study appear to be idiosyncratic to the specific sample, which raises the question of how much the specific categorisation process applied in our study influenced these outcomes.

Having interviewed learners associated with each archetype, we have found that the students nominated by the teacher focus group did not always neatly fit the description of the archetypes. This mainly reflects a methodological concern that the prototypical participants nominated by the teachers did not always agree to be interviewed (and we had to resort to 'prototype-resembling' students). Furthermore, we found that even one of the prototypical students did not match the archetype description, which could to be a function of the *actor-observer effect*, according to which 'attributions differ as a function of the perspective of the attributor' (Robins *et al.*, 1996: 375). Since students and teachers have different roles and perspectives, they may have access to different types of information from which to construct perceptions and form attributions.

A further issue regarding the archetypes concerns their stability. While dynamic systems are never fully static, they tend to settle into temporary attractor states (cf. Hiver, Chapter 3, this volume). The research potential of focusing on archetypes lies in this relative stability in that it can provide a certain degree of predictability. Our data show, however, that even within a period of a year, some learners belonging to one archetype shifted into another state as a result of a restructuring of the attractor basin relevant to the particular person. As Byrne and Callaghan explain, such relocations to another domain – that is, phase shifts – can be seen as characteristic features of the overall evolution of a complex system: 'Change is change of *kind*' (Byrne & Callaghan, 2014: 59; emphasis ours).

The observation of phase shifts may not necessarily be bad news for researchers, because studying these movements might constitute a fruitful direction for understanding the dynamic motivational tapestry of the classroom. Examining the shifts may also lead to the understanding of how archetypes can be intentionally 'manipulated' – in our case by motivating learners – to change the system's makeup. Indeed, the finding that individuals are not fixed in a particular in-class archetype, but can shift to another state, may serve as an encouragement for educators who are dealing with demotivated and struggling L2 learners, because it suggests that they can be moved into a re-motivated state if appropriately principled guidance is provided.

Finally, let us return to the question as to the extent to which the emerging archetypes are generalisable. Even given the various reservations concerning the nature and stability of archetypes mentioned above, it seems to us that defining archetypes as the first phase of RQM did indeed fulfil the role of producing purposive sampling for the subsequent qualitative interviews. It was reassuring to find that when we looked at each selected learner's case in detail, we soon arrived at generic topics and issues that have received a great deal of attention in the literature, thereby providing evidence that the archetypical learners represented generalisable phenomena.

Student interviews and signature dynamics

One of the important lessons of the study is that it proved to be more difficult than expected to identify prototypical students for every archetype. Because the focus group assigned only one or two typical students for each archetype, we had to sometimes resort to examining slightly less typical students. This is one of the reasons why we have found that the students nominated by the teacher focus group did not always provide a close match with the description of the archetypes. We can conclude, in retrospect, that it would have been useful to have spent more time in the field with the aim of identifying and verifying the prototypical students. An important task for future research in this respect may be to explore whether teacher-defined archetypes differ from the 'learner types' identified by the students themselves.

If we look back at the interview process in general, it seems that the qualitative interviewing phase relied primarily on the students' accounts. (Although we did interview two further teachers at this stage, our focus there was on general issues concerning the classrooms without trying to obtain specific data to complement the interviewed students' stories.) It is likely to be the case that a more balanced picture would have been achieved by integrating learner and teacher accounts, particularly regarding the performance of academically less successful students. In a similar vein, triangulating the data by conducting classroom observations, as well as examining more than one student associated with each archetype, might be beneficial in producing a thicker description of the attractor states in the system.

Regarding the nature of signature dynamics, we found that defining the exact nature of what constitutes a 'signature dynamic' raised some important questions. Should we, for example, restrict a signature dynamic to some crucial aspect of a case – for example, as was the case with Chris, the matching of a competitive classroom structure with a competitively oriented student who wishes to prove himself – or should we perceive a signature dynamic more like a trajectory that indicates the ongoing direction of system behaviour? Alternatively, would it perhaps be more fruitful to describe signature dynamics through the characterisation of the attractor basin associated with a student's motivational makeup? In other words, Dörnyei's definition of signature dynamics as 'main underlying dynamic patterns' (Dörnyei, 2014: 87) leaves open the question of *patterns of what?* Indeed, it may be that investigating dynamic patterns from various perspectives can lead to a more sophisticated understanding of learners' signature dynamics.

At this point we may also ask a further, critical question: would it have been possible to understand the composition of, and fluctuations in, Chris's motivation *without* adopting a dynamic systems approach? In other words, can a complex dynamic systems approach generate insights that other methodologies cannot? While we recognise that a single study can offer only limited basis for generalisation, our answer to these questions is affirmative. Without an appropriate toolkit (cf. MacIntyre & Serroul, this volume) and an understanding of the functions of attractor states – particularly the ways in which a complex dynamic system oscillates between cyclic attractor states within a closed loop of periodic movement – we would not have been able to identify and conceptually account for the changes Chris describes in his account of his evolving motivation. It is exactly because complex dynamic systems theory enables us to *identify* and *conceptualise* such systematic patterns and periodic fluctuations in learner dispositions that we see it as a powerful framework for future L2 motivation research.

Finally, an implicit assumption in Dörnyei's (2014) proposal of RQM was the belief that each archetype can be matched with one dynamic pattern, hence the term 'signature' dynamic. It is, however, also conceivable that there are several well-worn pathways leading to the same broad outcome. Here, too, only further research involving multiple interviewees linked to an archetype can offer an answer. Nevertheless, the generic nature of the dynamics identified in Chris's case suggests that even if there *is* more than one pattern leading to an attractor state, or limited number of attractor states between which a systems oscillates, the total number is likely to be small; an assumption that is in accordance with our earlier argument concerning the limited variability in complex systems.

Conclusion

The application of RQM in the present study reveals both its strengths and its limitations. On the positive side, the RQM template generated a systematic research process, resulting in rich data that shed light on the underlying issues from various angles. There is no doubt that we gained a close understanding of the specific learning context and its dynamic characteristics. On the other hand, however, we have also encountered methodological challenges in identifying the principal attractor states and the corresponding learners. Nonetheless, as Dörnyei argues, one of the least convincing aspects of qualitative methodology is the justification of the broader relevance of qualitative results in terms of some vague 'resonance' with readers' experiences, and it is in this area where, at its best, RQM can offer improvement; the template can be useful in highlighting aspects of system dynamics that are so essential that they can reasonably be expected to be echoed in other situations. In other words, as Dörnyei (2014: 90) states, RQM offers a research template for deriving essential dynamic moves from idiosyncratic situations in a systematic manner; it 'utilises the basic emerging commonalities in the dynamically changing social world'. Thus, although our study has not implemented the original ideas to the full, the good news is that the results and experiences we have gained still maintain the possibility that RQM can fulfil its potential in future research.

Note

(1)   This was a Band 1 EMI (English as a medium of instruction) school and ones in the first banding (out of three bandings) have the best in-take of students.

References

Allport, G.W. (1954) *The Nature of Prejudice*. Reading, MA: Addison-Wesley.
Aronson, E., Wilson, T.D. and Akert, R.M. (2013) *Social Psychology* (8th edn). New Jersey, NJ: Pearson Education.
Bing, M.N. (1999) Hypercompetitiveness in academia: Achieving criterion-related validity from item context specificity. *Journal of Personality Assessment* 73 (1), 80–99.

Byrne, D. and Callaghan, G. (2014) *Complexity Theory and the Social Sciences: The State of the Art*. New York: Routledge.

Dörnyei, Z. (2007) *Research Methods in Applied Linguistics*. Oxford: Oxford University Press.

Dörnyei, Z. (2014) Researching complex dynamic systems: 'Retrodictive qualitative modelling' in the language classroom. *Language Teaching* 47 (1), 80–91.

Gibson, W.J. and Brown, A. (2009) *Working with Qualitative Data*. London: SAGE.

Haggis, T. (2008) Knowledge must be contextual: Some possible implications of complexity and dynamic systems theories for educational research. *Educational Philosophy and Theory* 40 (1), 158–176.

Harding, J. (2013) *Qualitative Data Analysis from Start to Finish*. London: SAGE.

Henry, A. (2011) Examining the impact of L2 English on L3 selves: A case study. *International Journal of Multilingualism* 8 (3), 235–255.

Hesse-Biber, S.N. and Leavy, P. (2011) *The Practice of Qualitative Research* (2nd edn). Thousand Oaks, CA: SAGE.

Horney, K. (1937) *The Neurotic Personality of Our Time*. New York: W.W. Norton & Company.

Larsen-Freeman, D. and Cameron, L. (2008) *Complex Systems and Applied Linguistics*. Oxford: Oxford University Press.

MacIntyre, P.D. and Gregersen, T. (2013) An idiodynamic approach to studying language learning and use. Paper presented at the American Association of Applied Linguistics annual conference, Dallas, TX.

Macrae, C.N. and Bodenhausen, G.V. (2000) Social cognition: Thinking categorically about others. *Annual Review of Psychology* 51, 93–120.

Noels, K.A., Pelletier, L.G., Clément, R. and Vallerand, R.J. (2000) Why are you learning a second language? Motivational orientations and self-determination theory. *Language Learning* 50, 57–85.

Robins, R.W., Spranca, M.D. and Mendelsohn, G.A. (1996) The actor–observer effect revisited: Effects of individual differences and repeated social interactions on actor and observer attributions. *Journal of Personality and Social Psychology* 71 (2), 375–389.

Smith, J.A. and Eatough, V. (2007) Interpretive phenomenological analysis. In E. Lyons and A. Coyle (eds) *Analysing Qualitative Data in Psychology* (pp. 35–50). London: SAGE.

Vallerand, R.J. (1997) Toward a hierarchical model of intrinsic and extrinsic motivation. In M.P. Zanna (ed.) *Advances in Experimental and Social Psychology* 29 (pp. 27–360). San Diego: Academic Press.

van Geert, P. (2008) The dynamic systems approach in the study of L1 and L2 acquisition: An introduction. *The Modern Language Journal* 92 (2), 179–199.

17 'I Can See a Little Bit of You on Myself': A Dynamic Systems Approach to the Inner Dialogue between Teacher and Learner Selves

Tammy Gregersen and Peter D. MacIntyre

'To teach is to learn twice'.
Joseph Joubert, French Essayist and moralist, 1754–1824

Few veteran teachers and experienced learners would argue with the idea that, generally speaking, motivated teachers beget motivated learners and vice versa – an idea supported by a handful of research studies (Atkinson, 2000; Radel *et al.*, 2010; Roth *et al.*, 2007). The relationship between student and teacher motivation is interactive and synergistic, sometimes for better and sometimes for worse. Self-determination theorists, such as Deci *et al.*, (1997: 68), point out that learners influence teachers' motivation and behaviour just as teachers do for learners. They admonish teachers to 'engender in students the enthusiasm that facilitates a positive rather than a negative cycle'. There are a large number of studies devoted to practical strategies that teachers can use to motivate students (for a review see Gregersen & MacIntyre, 2014). But is it appropriate to place so much responsibility for student motivation on the shoulders of the teacher? On the one hand, positive motivational synergy can sometimes be difficult to establish, students arrive to most language classes with established motivational systems that can be problematic (see Chan *et al.*, this volume), and demotivated students have the capacity to affect everyone in a language class (Papi & Abdollahzadeh, 2012). On the other hand, no matter how teachers may personally be affected, the learners' lack of enthusiasm does not liberate a teacher from the obligation to teach to the best of her/his ability. This argument raises complex questions about the relationship between teacher and learner motivation. But how does the conversation play out when the teacher and learner is one-and-the-same person? The present study uses complex dynamic systems (CDS) theory to interpret the motivational processes described in the self-related discourse of a group of English as a Second Language (ESL) teachers who are themselves learning English.

Across the globe, particularly in foreign language settings, the target languages being taught by teachers are not their first languages (Maum, 2002), creating the hybrid 'teachers-as-learners'. The teacher in the teacher-as-learner amalgamation likely feels some responsibility for the motivation of her or his students. Does that sense of the teacher's role in motivating students extend to the learner in the teacher-as-learner? Surprisingly little research has been done on the interplay of teacher motivation and learner motivation, and we know even less about the synergy of teacher and learner motivation when embodied in the same person.

Possible Selves and Ideal L2 Selves Research

The complex, dynamic nature of identity, and its relationship to the self and second language (L2) motivation, is a cornerstone of what Dörnyei (2005) labelled 'The L2 Self System'. Building on the possible selves model of Markus and Ruvolo (1989) and Higgins (1987, 1996), Dörnyei proposed a broad construct composed of three dimensions: the Ideal L2 Self, which incorporates the future vision one has of oneself and is the person we would like to become; the Ought-to L2 Self, which focuses on duties obligated by external forces and is the persona created to meet expectations and avoid possible negative outcomes; and the L2 Learning Experience, which relates to the immediate learning environment and considers factors such as the teacher, curriculum, peer group and previous experience with success. Motivation to learn the language is enhanced because of the learner's psychological desire to reduce the discrepancy between current and possible future selves (Ushioda & Dörnyei, 2009). Dörnyei (2009: 18) lists five specific conditions followed by strategic implications that enrich or thwart the motivational force of the ideal and ought-to selves. We used these strategies, outlined in the following text, as a guide for developing the classroom activities used in the present study.

Creating the vision

Individuals tap into their previous ambitions, dreams and yearnings while simultaneously intensifying their awareness about the significance of ideal selves. This creative process draws upon individuals' past to create visions for their futures and to explore potential identity alternatives without committing to only one of them. Ideal L2 self-seekers use their imaginations to think of themselves in ways that will capitalize on their current strengths and avoid problematic areas as they project into the future (Dörnyei, 2009).

Strengthening the vision

Individuals implement 'methods of imagery enhancement' to strengthen ideal L2 self-images. Dörnyei (2009: 34) argued, 'even if a desired self-image exists, it may not have a sufficient degree of elaborateness and vividness in some learners to be effective'. He advises that guided imagery techniques might capitalize on students' active imaginations to trigger their visualizations and to make their visions more meaningful.

Substantiating the vision

Individuals anchor their self-images in reality. Because positive motivation is stimulated by visions that can actually be achieved, individuals must really believe that the ideal L2 self is attainable. In this step, individuals attempt to increase their perceptions of the likelihood of being able to accomplish their visions (Dörnyei, 2009).

Operationalizing the vision

Individuals develop a set of tangible action plans that contain not only their ideal visions, but also specific plans and goal-setting strategies for their successful completion (Dörnyei, 2009).

Counter-balancing the vision

Individuals activate the visions of a feared self to exploit the collective power of both approach and avoidance desires. That is to say, a person's ideal self will be more active when compared with the selves that are feared. Dörnyei (2009) postulates that regular activation of the feared self may be an effective deterrent against it becoming an actual self.

The present study examines the interplay of teacher and learner motivation within the same persons. Motivation is linked to an individual's 'possible selves' identity and the dynamics inside a multifaceted teacher–learner L2 self can be complex and entangled with antagonistic and synergistic processes. We propose a CDS approach to provide a lens through which to examine the richness of what happens within participants who are simultaneously learner and teacher.

Dynamic Systems Theory

Much of the literature on individual differences in second language acquisition (SLA) has isolated variables, such as anxiety, beliefs, cognitive abilities, learning strategies and styles, willingness to communicate and motivation (Robinson, 2012). However, from a dynamic perspective, the term 'variables' takes on an expanded meaning, reflecting any influence on the ongoing processes of a system. References to variables in the system include familiar, traditional individual differences in motivation, anxiety or aptitude, but also changeable features of the context, such as the behaviour of the teacher or classmates, progress made during the lesson plan or changing demographics in the community. The many influences on the thought, feelings and behaviour of an individual, whether teacher or learner, are in perpetual flux and often result in emergent, nonlinear, unpredictable outcomes. If the complexity found within each individual is impressive, the dynamism between individuals paired in a communicative process is even more so. Their interaction becomes like a dance:

> The interaction in dyads is multimodal: voice, rhythm and facial expression interact to create mutual understanding and agreement on steps to take. There is constant adaptation and change, but it is often unclear which partner is the initiator of change. Perfect dancers show what in developmental studies has become known as *interactional synchrony*, the seamless understanding between partners that are mutually attuned to the interactional process. Like in all other forms of communication, dancers go through waves of synchrony and asynchrony, and they are constantly adapting to repair asynchrony. (de Bot *et al.*, 2007: 9)

de Bot *et al.* (2007) likely had two people in mind when they described the development of the dance. Yet, the roles played by one individual can sometimes feel like a dance between two different partners. According to Dörnyei (2014: 3), we have to look at 'the overall constellation of the system components' and figure out how all the significant elements function collectively; essentially looking at the L2 self system through a magnifying glass. The present research is not designed to predict outcomes, but rather uses CDS theories to interpret qualitative data from individual teachers-as-learners as they envision their ideal L2 possible selves. CDS theories provide a lens through which we can interpret the salient patterns and underlying processes that created them.

To this end, we selected eight tenets from CDS theory (de Bot *et al.*, 2007; Larsen-Freeman, 2012; MacIntyre, 2013) to guide our interpretation of data. The tenets are described more fully later in the chapter, but can be summarized as follows.

(1) Variables in the system are innumerable, inter-connected and in constant change.
(2) The system changes over time and is composed of multiple interacting timescales.

(3) Dynamic systems settle into attractor states.
(4) Perturbations in the system lead to development and change.
(5) Qualities in the system emerge in an *ad hoc* fashion and moment-by-moment changes coalesce in somewhat unpredictable ways to create something unique.
(6) Nonlinear minor changes in the system can generate large effects while major alterations might not even cause a ripple.
(7) The system can accommodate contradictory conditions through unstable, soft assembly of opposite states.
(8) Each state of a system evolves from a previous state. Systems are continuous; new states of the system emerge from previous ones rather than being created *de novo*.

Although some previous investigations have touched upon the interplay of teacher and learner motivation (Deci *et al.*, 1997; Radel *et al.*, 2010) and the use of a possible selves model as a tool for increasing motivation (Dörnyei, 2005; Dörnyei, 2009), no study has applied a CDS framework to examine the teacher–learner duality within the L2 self system. The present qualitative study examines participants' inner dialogues as they moved between their teacher and learner voices, that is, the words and expressions they use when contemplating themselves as teachers or as learners. The journal responses of teacher–learners were written in response to participating in a series of 'ideal L2 self' activities. We attempt to answer the question: What does a study of the internal dialogues of teachers-as-learners tell us about the L2 self system of teacher–learners, interpreted through a dynamic systems framework?

Method

Participants

Eighteen adult learners, all L1 Spanish-speaking in-service English teachers enrolled in an Applied Linguistics Master's Degree Program at a large metropolitan university in Santiago, Chile, participated in the research. Each participant effectively characterizes the teacher–learner. They balance the identities of being lifelong learners of English as a foreign language who also teach that language. All of them, ten females and eight males ranging in ages from 24 to 40, had completed under-graduate programmes in areas related to the English language and were currently serving as in-service teachers in classrooms ranging from early childhood to adult education. The range of teaching experience for the majority of teacher–learners was between three and five years, with the exceptions being two participants, one who had taught for eight years and one with 18 years of teaching experience.

Procedure

Participants were members of an intensive graduate course, taught by one of the authors of this study that met four nights a week for four weeks. Six activities, presented in Appendix 17.1, were chosen from Gregersen and MacIntyre's (2014) text, *Capitalizing on Language Learners' Individuality: From Premise to Practice*, with the purpose of stimulating the teacher–learners to envision their L2 ideal selves, juxtaposing their learner selves with their teacher selves with each set. To visualize, strengthen, substantiate, operationalize and counter-balance their ideal L2 selves, teacher-learners carried out each of the six activities twice: the first time envisioning themselves as learners and the next as teachers. The tasks were presented as warm-up activities at the beginning of each classroom session. Some were videotaped for later analysis. Participants first responded through their learner lens in their dialogue journals. They then participated as teachers in the same activity during the subsequent class period. Following participation as a teacher, they re-read their learner responses through their teacher lens and responded to their own comments. At the end of the course, participants wrote a final essay in which they provided feedback concerning the interaction between their teacher and learner selves, and whether the process was a productive endeavour. All participants in the course gave informed consent for their data to be used in this study.

The dialogue journals and final essays later were analysed independently by three raters who were familiar with the literature on the L2 self system and CDS. The raters were asked to look for participant commentary related to the eight CDS tenets outlined above. Each of the tenets was assigned a different colour for coding. Only those sections that appeared on two or more raters' scripts are included in the analysis. To maintain the integrity and authenticity of the teacher–learners' voices, we inserted the excerpts and responses exactly as they had been written, with no grammatical or spelling changes. When journal responses are cited, we provide the participant number, the activity and whether the responses had been written as the learner or teacher self. If we quote from participants' final summative essays, we identify them as 'essay excerpt'.

Results and Discussion

To frame the results, we present each of the eight CDS tenets listed in the introduction along with excerpts from participants' journals that represent motivationally salient features of participants' ideal L2 selves. The inner dialogues and final essays showed the dynamic complexity of simultaneously negotiating the roles of teacher and learner.

Variables in the system are innumerable, inter-connected and in constant change

According to Larsen-Freeman (2012: 205), complex systems are 'open and dynamic' and 'operate under conditions that are not in equilibrium'. The innumerability of variables means that one cannot specify a complete list of relevant influences on a system. The various relevant factors are interconnected and change over time, making a system complex and dynamic. If one variable changes, all the other parts in the system can be impacted (de Bot *et al.,* 2007). As variables in the system are altered through interaction with the environment and internal self-reorganization, their continual interrelatedness nevertheless maintains meaning and order. However, even though there is no master plan, script or prescriptive solution for the behaviour of the variables in a system, they are NOT fully random and disconnected (MacIntyre, 2013).

In Excerpts 1A through 1C, participants credit the interconnectedness of the teacher and learner sides of themselves for empowering positive attitudes and a search for knowledge:

Excerpt 1A: My motivation as a learner has paved my way to become a laborious teacher and has helped me to be aware of what my students may expect from me. I think I play two roles at the same time, with two different types of motivation that are not necessarily opposites, instead the combination of both has empowered my attitude towards what I do and it has definitely worked quite well so far. (Participant 7, Essay excerpt)

Excerpt 1B: My current teacher and learner status 'force' me to be in a constant search for knowledge. Also, being a teacher and a student at the same time get your students closer to you since the usual gap between 'trainer' and 'apprentice' is not that strong as in other subjects and students regard you as a role model for them and that can be really motivating and challenging for a teacher. As a conclusion, I would dare to state that the relationship between my learner and teacher motivation is cyclic and they are in constant interaction. (Participant 11, Essay excerpt)

Excerpt 1C: Finally, I really think that both my learner and teacher motivation not only interact but also they provide feedback to each other and help me to improve as a student and as an English teacher. (Participant 14, Essay excerpt)

All three of these excerpts refer to the teacher self and learner self as interconnected. In Excerpt 1A, the respondent suggests that the interaction between teacher and learner motives produces a uniquely empowering combination. Excerpt 1B hints at the ongoing changes that occur when the person negotiates both teacher and learner roles, leading to a constant search for knowledge. The final excerpt refers to a mutually beneficial feedback process between the two selves.

Change takes place when the teacher and learner selves interact. Excerpts 1D and 1E below show how being self-critical and self-reflective as teachers places the respondent in the role of learner and produces positive change. Excerpts 1F and 1G provide evidence of influence in the opposite direction; participants' learner selves engender improvements in their teacher selves:

Excerpt 1D: . . . my conception of a teacher is that of a person who never stops learning. In this sense, I see the teacher as someone who has a dual role, someone who must never stop seeing himself as a learner too. I am very critical of my own performance and what I do in the classroom. I always end up my lessons by thinking of what were the things I did right and the improvements I should apply. When I work on all these improvements my role as a learner puts itself into practice, that is the point when I see myself as a leaner who is trying to investigate about many things, correcting, editing, improving, getting new information. (Participant 16, Essay excerpt)

Excerpt 1E: I've been a teacher for 16 years and I've taught from nursery students to adults and just now I've made a stop and start a reflection about motivation and this is because my possible L2 selves that we worked on in this class, by giving me the chance to talk to my student self as a teacher and vice versa, to be able to express my feelings, fears and insecurity. All the things mentioned before helped me understand my students better and identify myself with them; it has helped me to understand how my student may feel about their English class, about their classmates and about being a student again after so many years . . . which happens to be the same process I'm going through too. (Participant 16, Essay excerpt)

Excerpt 1F: From my point of view, my learner motivation always interacts with my teacher motivation since my experiences and goals as a learner influence the decisions I make in order to teach. This does not mean I teach the way I would like to learn, but that I always try to provide different tools to my students so they can meet their own goals, depending on their personal styles and interests. This is because as a learner, I can easily understand the fact that a learner may have different areas he or she would like to develop, so as a teacher, I am responsible for providing a variety of teaching and assessing techniques that may help them see if they are reaching those goals or not. (Participant 5, Essay excerpt)

Excerpt 1G: There are many reasons why a person wants to start learning a second language, so in this scenario we can find people who are prone to learn a second language due to working interests, academic challenges, or simply because they are highly motivated to master another language. With this in mind, it is needed to notice that learners have to deal with factors such as anxiety, work, and even money issues. In addition to this, there is another set of complicated aspects that learners have to take into account, for example: the development of skills such as speaking, writing, reading, and listening. In this sense, it is a tough thing for learners to realize that learning a second language is something beyond a simple, 'I like English', but it involves to be proficient in the skills already mentioned. (Participant 5, Essay excerpt)

Each of the four excerpts has a sense of being somewhat open-ended in the process by which teacher and learner influence each other, investigating 'many things' (1D) or emphasizing 'variety' (1F). In Excerpt 1G, Participant 5 describes motivations individuals have for originally pursuing a target language and then how the system is affected by a wide variety of influences, some language-related and others more general. The generic influences can be highly idiosyncratic and difficult to predict, yet they are relevant to the interactions among learner variables once the learning process is underway. All of the above excerpts imply an ongoing process of development and change as the teacher and learner selves interact.

The system changes over time and is composed of multiple interacting timescales

The element of time and timescales are hallmarks of CDS. According to Larsen-Freeman (2012: 206), 'Complex systems display behavior over a range of time-scales and at different levels of complexity—the latter are nested, one within the other'. Measuring phenomenon across multiple timescales – whether assessing in minutes, hours, days, years or decades – provides a more exhaustive conception of the countless influencing factors in a highly contextualized manner (MacIntyre, 2013). For example, in language classrooms we would have vastly different results if we measure learning a few minutes after the presentation of a new grammatical concept, a week later after the learner has taken opportunities to practice and a year later after the concept has been automatized.

Responses 2A through 2E highlight the saliency of time and timescales in the inner dialogues. In the excerpts within this section we have used underlining to emphasize all of the references to time that were coded by raters. We note that each response has a minimum of three direct references to time within passages that range from only 35 to 167 words. The variability of verb tenses used by participants, often within the same response, further illustrates the variability in timeframes that are relevant to the participants' sense of self. The respondents seamlessly speak with voices from the past, present and future:

Response 2A: Present/Past
Well, now that you already know the place you are as a learner and where you'd like to be, you should start setting some <u>short-term</u> goals and <u>long-term goals</u>. Ask yourself what kind of learner you want to be <u>at the end of the year</u> and maybe <u>when you got your master degree</u>. It will help you to set reasonable objectives and change them if it is necessary. I think setting <u>short-term</u> goals will help you to deal with your lack of strength towards frustration. (Teacher 15, Activity 1)

In this response (2A) we see the juxtaposition of time-related pairs like 'short-term' and 'long-term', and 'at the beginning' and 'at the end'. Teacher 15 projects years into the future when she discusses her goal planning during the first L2 ideal self envisioning activity. Her goal-setting process is incremental, beginning now and extending over future years to the completion of her graduate degree. She intuitively connects short-term goals with overcoming frustration, a suggestion consistent with previous research on goal setting (Locke & Latham, 1990, 2002). The idea that different types of goals operate on different timescales also is consistent with CDS theories.

The next response shows the fairly rapid evolution of the participant's affective reaction, using a timeframe of minutes. In the second part of this response, Participant 13 responds as her 'teacher' self to the same activity (Response 2B, second section), acknowledging that the learning process is 'endless', implicating a long-term timescale:

Response 2B: Past/Present/Future
This was the <u>first time</u> I've done this kind of activity. <u>At the beginning</u>, I was nervous because I didn't know exactly what the teacher wanted us to do and I was worried of listening the instructions carefully. <u>After the</u>

first two letters (and their corresponding answers) I felt
more secure and I knew I was able to fulfil the task
successfully. At the end, I enjoyed the activity as it had to
do with feelings and emotions, a subject that I really love.
(Learner 13, Activity 2)

I found myself in an endless process of learning. I don't
know whether I'm going to be a 'dictionary' one day
(formal, precise, tidy). I don't know if I'm going to be an
'answer' instead of a question ... probably I don't want
to. If I were those 'perfect' things, I would have ended
with my learning process. I believe I can be as humble as
I can with my knowledge and in that way I may teach
from the heart. (Teacher 13, Activity 2)

The time-related phrases 'endless' and 'one day' set the stage for an ill-
defined and enduring timescale that other participants articulated frequently
with words and phrases such as: 'a long time', and 'the whole life' (2C); 'given
with experience' and 'longer' 'in the end' (2D); 'a lot of time' and 'one day' (2E).
Interestingly, these vague, continuous timescales are used by both learner and
teacher participants, but are only apparent when participants responded to
the last two activities in the study. de Bot (this volume) suggests that rapid
fluctuations in short term timescales are embedded within longer term, slower
developing processes, such as the ones described in the second paragraph of
Excerpt 2B above:

Response 2C: Past/Present/Future
When learning English, first it was a dream to speak a
second language, because although I had a high degree of
motivation, some aspects can be hard to attain. In this
sense, fluency and pronunciation are the biggest issues
when facing this process. As a matter of fact, reaching an
appropriate and accurate proficiency level to sound an
accurate learner. This academic challenge has taken a
long time to be carried out (actually, the whole life) since
as a second language student we need to be quite alert to
so many details when learning English, because a second
language is another code that we need to cope with.
(Learner 5, Activity 5)

Response 2D: Past/Present/Future
My classmates and I decided that many of the things we
wrote are going to be given with experience. So perhaps
we take longer but in the end we are going to achieve
those things. (Teacher 13, Activity 5)

Response 2E: Past/Present/Future
For me, it was motivating in order to build an action plan. It wasn't that difficult, but in order to put this plan into action I will need a lot of time and since I have many things to do this seems as an utopian reality. (Learner 11, Activity 6)
Well, Rome wasn't built in only one day. You have to organize your thoughts and build a plan in order to achieve your goals. You are really good, so you already have what you will need. Keep going! (Teacher 11, Activity 6)

The use of an indeterminate timescale seems to reflect participants' awareness of the life-long developmental nature of language learning and teaching. It is understandable that they are reticent to delineate time markers for ultimate language proficiency or teaching mastery – they avoid even defining benchmarks along the way. Most importantly, this long-term timescale emerges in responses at the end of the L2 envisioning process for the ideal self, suggesting that participants become increasingly appreciative of the complexity and enduring nature of language learning and teaching. Rather than fostering frustration, the emerging appreciation of the interminable language learning and teaching process seemed to engender realism, even optimism.

Dynamic systems settle into attractor states

Although the dynamic systems lens emphasizes change and complexity, subsystems can settle into attractor states – a label that can be somewhat misleading. In CDS, the 'attract' in 'attractor' does not mean pleasant, desirable and appealing (or even good-looking), but rather attractive in the sense of 'to draw toward'. An attractor state will tend to draw together system variables to settle into a stable system state (Hiver, Chapter 3, this volume). The next two entries show that, with experience, the self-system settles into 'teacher' mode:

Response 3A: When we were given this task, I found it difficult to associate the concepts said by the teacher with my current state as a learner. I think this was so because I tend to see myself more as a teacher than a learner since during the last two years I've spent most of my time teaching. (Learner 1, Activity 2)

Response 3B: It makes me feel anxious, and sort of frustrated to think of my weaknesses because I would really like to have a better level of English. However, I've got to admit that it is difficult to see myself as a separate entity; that means

as a learner and as a teacher, because I always tend to
think of myself as a teacher who must be flawless.
(Learner 3, Activity 2)

Movement out of the attractor state associated with the teacher role can
occur; after all, both responses above are written from the learner role (3A
and 3B). In some cases, it would seem that moving away from the teacher
role does not seem to be an easy transition for the respondents. This suggests
that the self-system can settle into a comfortable attractor basin associated
with being a teacher. In the next excerpt, the teacher self is frustrated by
continuing struggles with proficiency as a learner:

Excerpt 3C: The contrary effect happens to a learner if s/he notices that
his/her learning does not improve after being exposed to it
for several years. For example, after being exposed to the
target language, trying hard or applying several techniques
for around five years, your fluency, pronunciation and
grammar construction remain the same. This conveys
frustration which affects your teacher motivation. So there
will be moments where you will desire to be a learner and
not a teacher. (Participant 5, Essay excerpt)

The comments in Excerpt 3C suggest that the strength of the attractor state
is contingent on context. The stability of the system over a longer period of
time (five years is suggested by the participant) is a source of frustration if
associated with a lack of change in key language areas. Here we see that the
passage of time works to move the system away from the comfort zone of
the 'teacher' mode, as we saw in Responses 3A and 3B. Further, the discussion in Excerpt 3C can be seen as an example of an unpleasant attractor state.
    Responses from the next two participants describe learners who have
settled into pleasant attractor states that show greater congruence between
learner and teacher selves:

Response 3D: It is probably quite difficult to achieve my goals as a
language learner, but not something impossible. I feel I
am doing what I have to do in order to improve my L2
skills. Besides I feel this second language is my own now.
Something no one can take away from me and a language
that provides huge opportunities of new life experiences.
It was an activity that asked goals and dreams of your
ideal self. A person I have been thinking a lot about
lately. (Learner 4, Activity 5)

Response 3E: Wonderful! I think it's just wonderful the importance
you are giving to the fact of always being a learner. Do

not be afraid of not having that role 24/7 printed on your
forehead. As long as you give yourself some time to think
about it, especially your needs and goals, the rest is OK.
Once you have figured those out, because of your
interest, the results would come out naturally. (Teacher 8,
Activity 6)

The first learner (3D) developed a pattern of feeling ownership over her target
language that allowed her to embrace the ideal self and reduce perceived
distance between the present and ideal self. Response 3E is written from the
perspective of teacher self, encouraging her learner self to continue to embrace
a learner role. The attractor states described in Responses 3D and 3E highlight the ways in which stability in the system, over a long period, can feel
natural and even progressive toward an ideal state. The combination of all five
responses in this category shows that the self-system settles into attractor
states that can be pleasant or unpleasant.

Perturbations in the system lead to development and change

The preceding section focused on the 'settled' notion of attractors by
examining inner dialogues for relative stability. But change is to be expected, even from attractor states. Various forms of perturbations or disturbances pressure the system to change, settling into the same or different
attractor states:

Response 4A: As a learner I'm always looking for role models on people
and for this activity, I would really love to work on my
speaking ability. Some time ago, I suffered from a
traumatic experience that left me literally speechless and
from that day on, it is really hard for me to speak in
public. Some people say they can't tell from what they
see or listen. But I can realize of my nervousness or
my weak accent when I'm speaking. (Learner 11,
Activity 3)

This response (4A) is perhaps the clearest example in the present data set of
a participant writing about a specific perturbation of the system, an unspeci-
fied traumatic event that continues to have ripple effects. In some sense, the
self-reflective activities in the present study were designed to cause perturbations in their self-systems, to move participants out of their comfort zones,
even temporarily, to examine and possibly change their motivational state as
a result of participating in the activities.

The roles of teacher and learner themselves carry implications beyond
the primary tasks involved in learning and teaching. At times, the

expectancies and activities that go along with a specific role can cause disturbances of their own. The following response describes tension introduced by the administrative requirements of the teacher role:

Excerpt 4B: Nevertheless, teaching is not only language instruction. Assessing students, planning lessons, learning student's own goals, their family conditions, and administrative tasks are also part of the business. My learner's motivation has nothing to do with those duties and my teacher's persona hates them. As a teacher, I love teaching, but I hate checking the attendance, forcing students to work if they do not want to, show them how to behave and have good manners, or interviewing parents that say they can hardly bear their own child. Those responsibilities I have because of my current job are killing my teacher's motivation and the learner's motivation shouts I desperately need a change ... This exercise brought up others' concerns about my own language learning experience; which reminded me I do not live alone in this world. It also helped me focus on becoming my ideal self by keeping away from my feared self practices. One thing I do not want is to become self-indulgent. (Participant 4, excerpt)

Both the response and excerpt in this section highlight perturbations that caused the self-systems of the respondents to change. The first response highlights a single, traumatic event as the source of enduring changes in the participant's affect and language behaviour. The second excerpt highlights the effect of small daily hassles that have a cumulative effect, creating a 'desperate' need for change. Participants with different backgrounds and experiences likely would point to different types of perturbations of the system, and the effect of any specific perturbation will depend on the system conditions at the time.

Qualities in the system emerge in an *ad hoc* fashion and moment by moment changes coalesce in somewhat unpredictable ways to create something unique

Larsen-Freeman (2012: 205) suggests that complexity is emergent: 'It is not built into any one element or agent, but rather arises from their interaction'. The six responses below demonstrate participants' acceptance of language learning as an emerging, unpredictable journey. The first four participants (5A, 5B, 5C and 5D) specifically use the metaphor of going on a journey wherein one enjoys the unfolding process. These responses reveal that the unpredictability of the development of a new sense of self is to be embraced and encouraged:

Response 5A: I think you should follow your dreams but first find out in what direction you plan on going. Maybe at the beginning, you won't have a clear idea bout through the journey you'll discover where you are going. Good luck! (Teacher 10, Activity 1)

Response 5B: More important than where you are is where you are headed to. Keep going to your ideals and don't fall into 'taking for granted.' (Teacher 2, Activity 2)

Response 5C: That's why I like the term of 'DaVinci' because it's what describes me best. I think that how you construct your knowledge, I mean, every step is what leads you to a whole. (Learner 14, Activity 2)

Response 5D: Difficulties are a great motivation for me coz I have always thought that the most interesting part of any journey is the road, not the end. (Learner 12, Activity 5) It is very important to enjoy the journey of learning but you always have to have in mind where you want to go and what you want to achieve. (Teacher 12, Activity 5)

Response 5E: Although every teacher knows why they decided to become teachers, it was a little bit hard to define how my ideal teacher 'possible self' would be. I think this is probably because in every new place I work, every student I teach, I realize I'd never stop discovering new things I need to develop to meet their needs. (Teacher 8, Activity 1)

Response 5F: Start by doing little tasks. You shouldn't be thinking on the success of your activities. Focus on what you do and go step by step. Know your abilities and likes and take them to your life. Put them into practice. Organize and don't be afraid of making mistakes. Share your experience and knowledge and doubts with others. (P6 Teacher, A2)

These six responses share an understanding that the fullness of the journey of self-development includes murky waters, moments of difficulty and mistakes along the way. The participants appear to be embracing the ways in which dealing with adversity enhances the sense of self.

Nonlinear minor changes in the system can generate large effects while major alterations might not even cause a ripple

The unpredictability of the self-development journey also is reflected in what has been called the 'Butterfly Effect', which occurs when a small alteration in the initial conditions of a system produces large consequences down the road, or when a significant amount of input impacts the system with relatively few long-term effects. Initial conditions of a system are key to understanding the effect of external inputs (de Bot *et al.*, 2007; Verspoor, this volume). We looked for evidence of brief or long-ago events that continued to affect the respondents years later. The following two responses refer to the importance of early childhood experiences in the present motivational quality of these participants:

Response 6A: Through this activity I recalled one of the main reasons why I wanted to be able to speak English when I was a child: to travel to an English speaking country and to successfully communicate with English native speakers. When I was twelve (still a child but a little bit older), I had the opportunity to travel to Canada and I remember me feeling very happy about it since I was going to be able to communicate with people whose mother tongue was English. Guess what happened. , ,Since my level of English was too low, I couldn't achieve my goal. It was very difficult for me to understand English and it was even more difficult to make my mouth utter a word. When I came back, I started to pay more attention to my English teacher, and became very motivated about improving my English skills. I haven't stopped since then and hope I never will. (Learner 1, Activity 1)
Dear learner: How interesting it is to see how experiences that we would perceive as 'negative' end up being good ones. And I say this because not being able to accomplish one of your dreams as a child didn't make you happy, but this situation made you realize about the importance that effort has got when improving in life. Today you taught me something new: never give up even when circumstances don't seem very friendly. Thank you! (Teacher 1, Activity 1)

Response 6B: As a learner, our motivation came up from I was a child, because I used to sing songs in English and also I used to read stories. Honestly, I did not understand anything about it, but that was the seed that I needed it to reach years later the English level that I have. In addition, I had affective factors to learn a second language, since my mother was always a source of motivation to learn English and discover the good things of speaking a second language. Thus, as learners we have to find out how much important and stunning is the fact of speaking a second language, not only to be hired in a good company or make a lot of money, but to incorporate a new way of thinking to understand and be witness of other cultures and far away societies. (Learner 5, Activity 3)

It is likely that many other individuals have encountered much the same initial conditions (language difficulty during travel or not understanding songs and stories) but proceeded along a different trajectory. In both of these cases, it would have been difficult to predict the effects of the childhood events described. Yet, in retrospect, the participants have traced current learning activities to events in their childhood. The activities selected for this group of learners were not designed to test specifically for events that had a disproportional effect on the language learning process. This would be an interesting avenue for future research into the dynamics of L2 self system development.

The system can accommodate contradictory conditions through unstable, soft assembly of opposite states

The 'Butterfly Effect' is counter-intuitive in the sense that small events can exert a disproportionately large effect on the system. This, however, is not the only apparent contradiction that emerges in dynamic systems. Seemingly incongruous elements of a system can coexist in a temporary, 'soft-assembled' state, for example feeling simultaneous desire to approach and avoid (MacIntyre, 2007, 2013). Whereas being a teacher and a learner are not inherently *contradictory,* they often are cast as opposing roles, setting up the potential for a complex interplay of incongruous effects.

To explore this CDS tenet, we examined the inner dialogues for evidence of dichotomies or contradictory conditions described by participants, looking for a sense of tension between the expectations for teacher and learner. The following are five responses selected for their varying degrees and types of tensions or incongruities:

Response 7A: As my classmate's said, I don't want to lose my 'human characteristics' as I am teaching my students. I guess that having a lot of knowledge does not mean having the reason. Therefore I'd like to be a humble person sharing this knowledge rather than the teacher who possesses the truth! (Teacher 13, Activity 1)

Response 7B: ... it would be a fake dichotomy to set apart both, especially in such a humanized learning field you're in. Keep up that balance between traditional beliefs and innovation and self-criticism. (Teacher 2, Activity 2)

Response 7C: Remember that to have a role model does not mean losing yourself and trying to be someone else. Instead, you've got to get inspiration from that person. Believe in yourself, you've got the strength to achieve anything you want to. Go ahead! (Teacher 3, Activity 3)

Response 7D: It's so nice you're considering your strengths as a starting point when thinking about you're weaknesses. Probably just because I can see a little bit of you on myself, especially with issues related to self-confidence, so I can tell you to keep up with that positive idea ... time has told me you always improve as long as he goes by. (Teacher 8, Activity 3)

Response 7E: It also helped me to discriminate which are the most and least attainable tasks for me. In relation to that, both my classmates and I agree on the fact that the most difficult to attain tasks are the ones we are more interested in and they are highly time-consuming. (Learner 3, Activity 5)

Dichotomies such as these present a challenge to the integration and sense of cohesion in the self. Henry (Chapter 9, this volume) describes the ways in which the concept of the self is assembled, from information about the self gathered through self-perception, social comparison and self-appraisal, and the ways in which that information is processed. In the above responses we see our respondents actively trying to deal with self-related inconsistencies by invoking overarching beliefs (e.g. one should be humble) or encouraging more elaborate processing (e.g. to avoid a fake dichotomy). This is the nature of a soft-assembled, temporary state, one whose resolution can lead to insight and alterations of the self-guides (Henry, Chapter 9, this volume). We do not propose a 'third person in the mix' refereeing a conflict between learner and teacher selves; rather we find an active process of self-construction going on, a process that sometimes is challenged to deal with temporary inconsistencies in self-view. We see that the process of resolving these contradictions, or at least working toward a resolution by writing the responses to the activities of the present study, provides motivational impetus that alters the larger self-system.

Each state of a system evolves from a previous state. Systems are continuous, new states of the system emerge from previous ones rather than being created *de novo*

So far we have discussed how interconnected variables and processes emerge in an *ad hoc* fashion, coalescing in unpredictable ways and changing on multiple timescales. Our discussion of perturbations and 'Butterfly Effects' added an even greater sense of indeterminacy. Given these observations, is it meaningful to talk about a 'system' at all? CDS suggests that the state of a system changes as part of development. New states of the system must emerge from previous states. Howe and Lewis (2005: 249) note that '(d)ynamic systems pervade our everyday life and include examples as mundane as altering the temperature in one's home (e.g. the energy required to raise the temperature by 10 degrees at time t depends on the ambient temperature at time t-1)'. This idea points to the inherent developmental quality of systems – they grow from one state to another (like a tree) rather than being assembled from component parts (like an automobile). The continuity of systems, as new states building on previous states, was a common thread in participants' inner dialogues:

Response 8A: Every exercise and activity should allow you to grow from where you are now to where you want to be in the future. (Teacher 4, Activity 2)

In Response 8A, Teacher 4 states the issue as clearly as anyone who has written about it. Change must first be grounded in present realities.

The next two responses (8B and 8C) show teacher selves giving pep talks to learner selves. In both cases they choose to ground their encouragement in the stable inner strength of themselves as learners. Although that inner strength varies and might waver at times, it does not seem to vanish:

Response 8B: You have to read, you have to keep your goals in vision. Don't worry! Maybe you can get lost sometimes but you're strong enough to be back in your path to become yourself. (Teacher 6, Activity 1)

Response 8C: It's so nice you're considering your strengths as a starting point when thinking about you're weaknesses. Probably just because I can see a little bit of you on myself, especially with issues related to self-confidence, so I can tell you to keep up with that positive idea ... time has told me you always improve as long as he goes by. (Teacher 8, Activity 3)

Both of these responses show how an individual can use positive self-talk to promote growth. One can imagine that the same 'pep talk' would have differential effects on students brimming with confidence versus those riddled with self-doubt. Applying the CDS principle of system continuity during growth (Howe & Lewis, 2005; Thelen & Smith, 2000), we suggest that the relative effectiveness of affirmations such as these will depend, to a large degree, on the initial conditions of confidence and resiliency of the teacher–learners.

Self-systems were not the only systems that respondents described. Formal, institutionalized systems, such as the education system in which teachers and learners operate, can be even more resistant to change than the human beings involved. The final response is one that will be familiar to most experienced teachers who have had to work within a formal education system:

Response 8D: I would love to change teaching system or the ideas of the Ministry but I know I won't be able to do it alone but I can make a difference. It is the same with you students: wish/think big but start from the beginning, from the very beginning. Good luck to both of us. (Teacher 16, Activity 5)

This is a most poignant example of system continuity, in spite of pressures to change. The response also reflects the understanding that systems are nested within one another; in this case the respondent's beliefs about how teaching should be done, contrast with how the education system currently operates, leading to commentary on how the process of change takes place with the cooperation among persons.

Conclusion

Teachers who also are learners are in a unique position to describe the development of the L2 self system. In the discussion above, we see that tenets of CDS theory can be applied to the self as a system. The specific influences on the system are innumerable because external factors are idiosyncratic and unpredictable across a group of individuals. The L2 self system is constantly undergoing changes over time, partly as a result of the learning process moving the learner along the bumpy road toward the unattainable ideal self. This journey takes place on multiple interacting timescales, from moment-by-moment changes to progress gained over years of effort. Especially on the larger timescales, we see how the system reacts to perturbations and disturbances by settling into patterns, as when the teacher self explicitly encourages the learner self, drawing strength from the dual role, but retaining a sense of a core inner self system. We see also that both pleasant and unpleasant stable attractor states can emerge from tensions between the learner and teacher roles. There are a number of apparent contradictions and opposing states, dichotomies and false dichotomies that must be negotiated as part of the self-development process. This process can lead to somewhat unpredictable, ambivalent, unique states of the system within the teacher–learners. Participants in the present study seem to understand, accept and even enjoy the indeterminate timescale on which they act as both teacher and learner. Yet the structure of their L2 self systems can be maintained even as its components change dramatically, reflecting the process of development of the self rather than an assemblage of constituent parts.

We opened this chapter by quoting Joseph Joubert, 'To teach is to learn twice'. Perhaps we are coming to appreciate that for many ESL educators, to teach is to be twice – to function as two interdependent selves. The dynamics of motivation and L2 self-development within the teacher–learner suggest that teachers accept a great deal of responsibility for the motivation of learners, but that the sometimes difficult process of working toward L2 self-development is an inextricably shared endeavour.

References

Atkinson, E.S. (2000) An investigation into the relationship between teacher motivation and pupil motivation. *Educational Psychology* 20 (1), 45–57.
de Bot, K., Lowie, W. and Verspoor, M. (2007) A dynamic systems theory approach to second language acquisition. *Bilingualism: Language and Cognition* 10, 7–21.
Deci, E.L., Kasser, T. and Ryan, R.M. (1997) Self-determined teaching: Opportunities and obstacles. In J.L. Bess (ed.) *Teaching Well and Liking it: Motivating Faculty to Teach Effectively* (pp. 57–71). Baltimore, MD: Johns Hopkins University Press.
Dörnyei, Z. (2005) *The Psychology of the Language Learner.* New York: Routledge.
Dörnyei, Z. (2009) The L2 motivational self system. In Z. Dornyei and E. Ushioda (eds) *Motivation, Language Identity and the L2 self* (pp. 9–42). Bristol: Multilingual Matters.
Dörnyei, Z. (2014) Researching complex dynamic systems: 'Retrodictive qualitative modelling' in the language classroom. *Language Teaching* 47, 80–91.
Gregersen, T. and MacIntyre, P.D. (2014) *Capitalizing on Language Learners' Individuality: From Premise to Practice.* Bristol: Multilingual Matters.
Higgins, E.T. (1987) Self-discrepancy: A theory relating self and affect. *Psychological Review* 94, 319–340.
Higgins, E.T. (1996) The 'self-digest': Self-knowledge serving self-regulatory functions. *Journal of Personality and Social Psychology* 71 (6), 1062–1083.
Howe, M.L. and Lewis, M.D. (2005) The importance of dynamic systems approaches for understanding development. *Developmental Review* 25 (3–4), 247–251.
Larsen-Freeman, D. (2012) Complex, dynamic systems: A new transdisciplinary theme for applied linguistics? *Language Teaching* 45 (2), 202–214.
Locke, E.A. and Latham, G.P. (1990) *A Theory of Goal Setting and Task Performance.* Englewood Cliffs, NJ: Prentice-Hall.
Locke, E.A. and Latham, G.P. (2002) Building a practically useful theory of goal setting and task motivation: A 35-year odyssey. *American Psychologist* 57, 705–717.
MacIntyre, P.D. (2007) Willingness to communicate in the second language: Understanding the decision to speak as a volitional process. *Modern Language Journal* 91 (4), 564–576.
MacIntyre, P.D. (2013) The dynamics of sexual relationship development. In R.S. Stewart (ed.) *Talk about Sex: A Multidisciplinary Discussion* (pp. 67–83). Sydney, NS: CBU Press.
Markus, H. and Ruvolo, A. (1989) Possible selves: Personalized representations of goals. In L.A. Pervin (ed.) *Goal Concepts in Personality and Social Psychology* (pp. 211–241). Hillsdale, NJ: Lawrence Erlbaum Associates.
Maum, R. (2002) Nonnative-English-speaking teachers in the English teaching profession. Washington, DC: Center for Applied Linguistics. Retrieved from ERIC database (EDO-FL-02-09).

Papi, M. and Abdollahzadeh, E. (2012) Teacher motivational practice, student motivation, and possible L2 selves: An examination in the Iranian EFL context. *Language Learning* 62 (2), 571–594.

Radel, R., Sarrazin, P., Legrain, P. and Wild, T.C. (2010) Social contagion of motivation between teacher and student: Analyzing underlying processes. *Journal of Educational Psychology* 102 (3), 577–587.

Robinson, P. (2012) *The Routledge Encyclopedia of Second Language Acquisition*. New York: Routledge.

Roth, G., Assor, A., Kanat-Maymon, Y. and Kaplan, H. (2007) Autonomous motivation for teaching: How self-determined teaching may lead to self-determined learning. *Journal of Educational Psychology* 99 (4), 761–774.

Thelen, E. and Smith, L.B. (1994) *A Dynamic Systems Approach to The Development of Cognition and Action*. Cambridge, MA: Bradford/MIT Press.

Ushioda, E. and Dornyei, Z. (2009) Motivation, language identities and the L2 self: A theoretical overview. In Z. Dornyei and E. Ushioda (eds) *Motivation, Language Identity and the L2 Self* (pp. 1–8). Bristol: Multilingual Matters.

Appendix 17.1

Activities

The following activities were extracted from Gregersen and MacIntyre (2014). Participants responded to these activities as both a learner and a teacher.

Activity 1: Creating the vision (Part I) of the ideal self through miming gifts

Participants paired up to interview each other using the following prompt, 'What Possible Selves—representing the ideal language learner/teacher that you would like to become—have you entertained in the past?'. They were instructed to ponder views held by others (such as parents, peer groups or the media) and from within themselves. The first time they considered their 'learner' selves and the second time, their 'teacher' selves. Results from these interviews were written on Post-It Notes. Then participants used their partner's previous visions of possible L2 selves to create personalized 'mimed gifts' that would allow their partner's vision to be realized. The imagined gifts were presented to their partners in a gift-giving ceremony later in the same class period.

Activity 2: Creating the vision of the ideal self (Part II) through capitalizing on existing strengths and avoiding weaknesses

Participants were given two alternative metaphors read aloud by the researcher. The task was to choose the one option that best described them *at this moment in their language learning/teaching journey*. The researcher then repeated the pair of alternatives, but in this instance, participants were asked to consider the *language learner/teacher they would ideally like to become*. Consistent with all of the other activities, participants responded as learners during the first rendering and as teachers during the second.

Activity 3: Creating the vision of the ideal self (Part III) through invoking role models

Participants, responding as learners, received a graphic organizer that included instructions to:

(A) Brainstorm your individual strengths and weaknesses;
(B) Articulate the specific qualities you would like to improve;
(C) Define the role model who best emulates each quality;
(D) Clearly and vividly describe each desired behaviour;
(E) Devise a plan to practice those behaviours.

Participants were cautioned against limiting their role model choices to a single person who displayed all of the character traits in their L2 ideal self, but rather to choose three different inspiring individuals who exhibited the three specific qualities they desired to improve. Upon completion of the graphic organizer as learners, participants-as-teachers repeated the same procedures.

Activity 4: Strengthening the vision of the ideal self through guided imagery

This activity had two phases. Using the Post-It Notes from the mimed gifts activity that had been scattered on the floor, participants used only nonverbal communication to organize them into natural categories and come up with a label for each. They then formed a small group with the other individuals whose Post-It Notes were in the same category and wrote a 'Guided Imagery Script' using their combined L2 ideal selves. Each group led the class through their scripts, allowing participants to get comfortable on the floor, close their eyes and visualize. The whole process was done first as learners and then again as teachers.

In the second phase, groups were formed using their Role Model Graphic Organizers from Activity Three. Participants found the categories in their chosen role models and worked with others with similar visions to write another Guided Imagery Script that focused on the small details that this L2 ideal person exuded. Groups again led the class through their second scripts.

Activity 5: Who am I?: Substantiating the vision of the ideal self

Participants were instructed to respond in writing to ten questions. Then, ten consecutive times they were asked the question: 'Who is my ideal L2 (learner/teacher) self?'. At the end of the 'quiz', participants-as-learners (and later participants-as-teachers) were told to think about the attainability of each of their responses and to cross off the three items that seemed furthest out of reach. After a minute, they were asked to eliminate three more. Next, in small groups, participants shared the visions they had for their ideal L2 self. They described how it felt to eliminate specific items, beliefs about why the ones crossed off were less attainable than those remaining and whether the difficulties in the eliminated items diminished their motivation to pursue the ideal self. Finally, they shared their impressions about whether the remaining items were achievable.

Activity 6: Operationalizing and counter-balancing the vision of the ideal self through developing action and goal plans

Each participant was given an empty two-part grid containing both an 'Action Plan' and a 'Goal Plan', where participants listed attributes of the ideal L2 selves they would like to attain as well as those of their 'feared selves' that they wanted to avoid. They created a concrete plan for its completion and strategized using timelines, benchmarks and measures to maintain dedication.

18 Understanding EFL Learners' Motivational Dynamics: A Three-Level Model from a Dynamic Systems and Sociocultural Perspective

Tomoko Yashima and Kumiko Arano

English is a required subject in almost all high schools and universities in Japan. Reflecting the concerns of practitioners facing the challenge of motivating students, motivation research in Japan has heretofore been conducted mostly in required English as a foreign language (EFL) contexts. While acknowledging the importance of addressing this issue, investigating learners' motivation to take a non-required class will shed new light on second language (L2) learning motivation. For this reason, this study focuses on Japanese university students who choose to take non-credit courses at an on-campus learning centre. Specifically, through retrospective semi-structured interviews, we attempt to spotlight the psychological processes that led students to continue (or discontinue) taking courses over eight semesters. By doing so, we hope to capture the dynamics of motivation and motivated behaviour in this context.

This study integrates complex dynamic systems perspectives (DST) (Larsen-Freeman & Cameron, 2008a, 2008b) with Valsiner's (2007) cultural psychological approach to focus on the dynamics of motivational development. Cultural psychology (or sociocultural approaches, as they are more commonly referred to in applied linguistics) and DST have similarities in that both make 'a strong connection between mind and sociocultural context' (Larsen-Freeman & Cameron, 2008a: 35). Both regard the individual and the context as inseparable and boundaries between them as 'blurred and changing'. Both conceive of humans as dynamic, open systems. However, a difference may be that 'to describe the blurring of these boundaries', sociocultural theory emphasises mediation by cultural tools, including signs, whereas DST incorporates 'various environmental or contextual factors as system parameters' (Larsen-Freeman & Cameron, 2008a: 35).

In this chapter, we first present Valsiner's three-level model of human development and how it can be combined with DST to capture L2 learning motivation. We then describe the method of investigation, discuss the results and implications, and finally explore the usefulness of this framework for a deeper understanding of L2 learning motivation.

Theoretical Frameworks

Microgenetic, mesogenetic and ontogenetic processes of human development

We believe that Valsiner's (2007) three-level model of human development is useful in considering motivation as operating along three timescales. Taking a semiotic perspective in cultural psychology, Valsiner presents a three-level model of human experiencing, represented in Figure 18.1 (our adaptation). According to Valsiner (2007: 301), human experiencing is regulated socioculturally through signs encoded 'at different levels of generalisation and in three mutually embedded domains of continuous experiencing: microgenetic, mesogenetic and ontogenetic'. He regards the immediate human living experience as primarily microgenetic, 'occurring as the person faces the

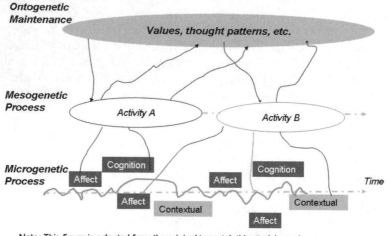

Note: This figure is adapted from the original to match this study's analyses. For example, affect, cognition and contextual in boxes are our addition.

Figure 18.1 Microgenetic, mesogenetic and ontogenetic processes of mutually embedded domains of continuous experiencing (adapted from Valsiner, 2007: 302)

ever-new next time moment in the infinite sequence of irreversible time'. Crucially, this process is affective as we make sense of our experiences in the world through our feelings. Feelings, in turn, are culturally organised through the creation of signs, and as we reflect upon and relate these to the world with emergent signs, our experiences are also reflexive and cognitive. Valsiner (2007: 302) states that the emergent signs are 'tools for creating subjective stability' against a background of 'inevitable uncertainties of experiencing'. Through this process, microgenetic experiences are culturally structured into collectively defined activity frames that operate at the mesogenetic level. This consists of relatively repetitive, situated activity frames, 'such as praying, or going to school, or to a bar', or recurrent frames for human action that structure subjective experiencing as a culturally meaningful activity (Valsiner, 2007: 302). These mesogenetic processes represent socioculturally structured activities, in which socially and contextually embedded human activity is most clearly visible.

Finally, the ontogenetic domain relates to 'the most enduring aspect of human cultural life', or 'the development of the person through the whole life course'. As Valsiner (2007: 302) goes on to observe, our experiences, either directly from the microgenetic domain or through recurrent mesogenetic activities, 'become transformed into relatively stable meaning structures that guide the person within one's life course'. Among examples of this process are religious and other deeply felt values, logical thinking, aesthetic standards and literacy (Valsiner, personal communication, 2012). Once internalised into the ontogenetic domain, these are likely to be maintained. However, as Figure 18.1 indicates, there is no one-to-one correspondence between the three levels. As Valsiner (2007: 303) notes, 'Some microgenetic events – one-time, unexpected events in one's life that are not guided by the mesogenetic collective-cultural framing – may have a major impact on the ontogenetic level'.

For the purpose of our study of L2 motivation, we adapt this three-level analysis of human experiencing and combine it with DST perspectives. In our adaptation, the microgenetic process refers to immediate human experiences that create daily (even momentary) fluctuations in motivation, including feeling physically unfit on a winter morning, being encouraged by a friend to attend class with her or finding a teacher funny. Here, the mesogenetic level refers to the field of meaning where relatively repetitive situated activities, such as enjoying certain activities in a language class, crystallise in the personal, yet socioculturally structured meaning of attending the class, which might sustain motivation. Thus, the recurrent mesogenetic process may mediate the ontogenetic internalisation of L2 learning, leading to lasting motivation. Here it should be noted that the ontogenetic process refers to 'experiences transformed into relatively stable meaning structures' (Valsiner, 2007: 302) (e.g. values, thought patterns) that guide the person. Once ontogenetically internalised, these values, thought patterns or habits guide learning behaviours, maintaining a long-term effort level despite daily fluctuations in motivation, unless, that is, something drastic takes place that halts the ontogenetic maintenance. In this study we hope to capture psychological processes operating at these three levels and representing different times-cales, a process that may illuminate changes in L2 learners as they adapt to an ever-changing environment.

Dynamic systems theory (DST)

DST (Larsen-Freeman, 2006, 2007; Larsen-Freeman & Cameron, 2008a, 2008b) forms the main theoretical pillar in this study. We regard dynamic system behaviour as involving the interlinked cooperation and interaction of a number of components, conditions and factors, which in turn results in outcomes that, in many cases, cannot be described using traditional individual differences paradigms. Larsen-Freeman and Cameron (2008a: 41) suggest that researchers can start 'the process of thought modelling a dynamic system' by applying the following steps: (i) identifying the different components of the system, including agents, processes and subsystems, (ii) identifying the timescales and levels of social and human organisation on which the system operates; (iii) describing the relations between and within components; (iv) describing how the system and context adapt to each other; and (v) describing the dynamics of the system, that is, how the components, as well as how the relations among the components, change over time (Larsen-Freeman & Cameron, 2008a: 41). Further steps include (vi) identifying 'contextual factors that are working as part of the system'; and (vii) 'including processes of co-adaptation with other systems' (Larsen-Freeman & Cameron, 2008a: 70).

In relation to the first of these points, we regard individuals interacting with the environment as systems, and we focus on observable system behaviours (here, attending or not attending non-credit classes, as well as learning behaviour) that result from interactions between the context and subsystems whose boundaries are in fact 'blurred' (Larsen-Freeman & Cameron, 2008a: 35). These subsystems include cognition, affect and motivation (or conation) as components of the system, which interact with each other and the context in the process of organising human behaviours. As regards the second point, a system and its subsystems can be considered as operating at two different levels. In addition, the context and the human system interact and thus create another system, with multiple systems operating simultaneously and influencing each other. In this study, we adapt Valsiner's (2007) three-level model of microgenetic, mesogenetic and ontogenetic processes as representing different time scales.

In analysing the data, we attempt to follow stages (iii)–(vii). Crucially, we need to be conscious that by focusing on these components in the process of conducting research, we inevitably simplify a multitude of nested, mutually embedded and interacting dynamic systems in the real world.

Cognitive, affective and conational components of mental functioning as represented by the learner

As previously mentioned, in analysing our interview data from a DST perspective, we take a componential view of human mental functioning. According to Dörnyei (2009b), even though 'individual differences in mental functions typically involve a blended operation of cognitive, affective and motivational components', one way of justifying proposing the macro-structuring of these separate functions in human psychology is to adopt a phenomenological view. Further he states that, 'people can phenomenally distinguish three areas of mental functioning – cognition, motivation and affect (or emotions)' (Dörnyei, 2009b: 234). Analysing interviews usually requires a phenomenological reading of participants' experiences, and in this study, we pay attention to how learners talk about their experiences. For example, does a participant talk about an experience as an affective reaction, or does he or she present it as an appraisal of a learning situation? Because the entire process of talking about one's learning is reflexive and cognitive, what we analyse here are 'psychological components', as represented by the learners.

The components (or subsystems) identified through interviews constantly interact not only with each other, but also with the environment of which the system is a part. In this respect, de Bot et al. (2007: 14) argue that the learner has his or her own cognitive ecosystem, which is 'related to the degree of exposure to language, maturity, level of education and so on, which in turn is related to the SOCIAL ECOSYSTEM, consisting of the environment with which the individual interacts' (capitalisation in the original). The learner and the environmental (or social and physical) context in which the learner is embedded, adapt to each other because the learner and the context are inseparable (Larsen-Freeman & Cameron, 2008a, 2008b). In studying changes in a dynamic system, we need therefore to examine changing relationships between components and contexts in terms of 'a phase shift' that brings about a qualitatively different state from an earlier state, as well as 'self-organisation', or 'emergence', which refer here to a phenomenon that, when change occurs on one level or scale, 'leads to a new mode on another level' (Larsen-Freeman & Cameron, 2008b: 202). In this study, we assume that the psychological components – that is microgenetic-level experiencing – interact with contexts and operate as a whole when they generate a cultural and personal meaning the learner attaches to an activity at the mesogenetic level.

Another important aspect of a DST-based study is the need to identify attractor states, or patterned outcomes toward which a system trends or approaches over time (Hiver, Chapter 3, this volume). In motivation studies, an example of an attractor state in university language classes in Japan can be the tendency for the learners not to exert extra effort beyond what is required to pass the course unless a force, such as a strong incentive or a vision of the future, encourages them to do otherwise. As regards an individual as a system, psychological components (cognition, affect and conation) interact with contexts (e.g. approaching tests or a chance to study abroad) and may self-organise into an attractor state that manifests fairly stable study behaviour. Dörnyei (2009b) argues that 'future research should try and take a systemic approach by identifying higher level amalgams or constellations of cognition, affect and motivation that act as wholes' (Dörnyei, 2009b: 235). Ideal and ought-to selves, or representations of goals as future self images (e.g. Dörnyei, 2005, 2009a) that sustain motivation at a higher level generate, as it were, attractor states into which a system self-organises. Thus, attractor states that sustain learning behaviour are emergent through microgenetic and mesogenetic processes and, once internalised, may ontogenetically sustain learning behaviours.

Context of the Study

This study focuses on participants in a semester-long non-credit English programme (mostly oral-aural) offered by N University in Japan in an on-campus language institute (hereafter called LC) open to all students wishing to take extra English lessons. In Japanese universities, students study for eight semesters before graduation and thus have opportunities to enrol in LC classes on eight separate occasions, as enrolment is renewed each semester. Although attendance does not incur any extra cost, enrolment nevertheless tends to drop off in the middle of a programme, probably because it is not part of a degree trajectory. In this LC, a total of 42 English classes accommodate 1000 students (20 to 30 in each class), or approximately 3.5% of the student body of the university. According to an LC official, the completion rate is around 20% to 40%, depending on the class. This study focuses on those students who chose to take some courses at the university's LC.

As an alternative English learning facility, N University also operates a coffee lounge (hereafter called 'e-café') where several native speakers (NS) of English can always be found as conversational partners. According to a university official, about 900 students visit the e-café every day.

Research Questions

(1) How do learners explain the factors and processes that resulted in their decision to take (or not to take) LC classes semester by semester?
(2) How do they explain the ebbs and flows in their motivation over the eight semesters?
(3) How can these experiences be understood within the theoretical framework of DST and Valsiner's theory?

Method

Participants

The participants consisted of ten students (five females and five males) who took and completed LC courses during their four years on campus before graduating (one fourth-year undergraduate student, one graduate student and the others having just graduated from the university at the time of the interviews) and two undergraduate students (one female and one male) who were currently taking LC classes. They were contacted using a snowball sampling method and agreed to participate in this study.

Procedure

Semi-structured interviews lasting 30–70 minutes were conducted with the participants in Japanese. They were recorded with the interviewees' permission and transcribed for analysis. Ten participants were interviewed by the second author, who was a student of N University at the same time as some of the participants and who, at the time, was also taking some LC courses herself. Thus, the second author's interviews elicited the candid voices of the learners, with the conversational style being that of friends rather than that of formal interviews. Subsequently, the first author interviewed the two undergraduate participants who were enrolled in the LC classes at the time of the research to capture the real time views of those who were taking the course. Prior to the interviews, each participant was asked to draw a line on a graph indicating his or her motivational trajectory over the eight semesters (or fewer for two undergraduate students) and to indicate whether they completed at least one LC class in each semester. Although interview guides were prepared, these were not followed strictly. In particular, we paid attention to how the learners themselves explained the factors and processes that resulted in their decision to take (or not to take) classes and how they accounted for the perceived motivational fluctuations represented on their graphs.

Results and Discussion

Participants' attendance profile

In Table 18.1 a matrix indicating whether each participant (represented with a pseudonym) took a class in each of the eight semesters is presented. Although the result section will discuss three of these ten participants in detail, all ten learners' profiles were analysed and reviewed for comparison and for better understanding of motivational dynamics.

Table 18.1 Participants' attendance profiles at LC

	1st year		2nd year		3rd year		4th year	
	Spring	Fall	Spring	Fall	Spring	Fall	Spring	Fall
Aya	✓	✓	✓	-[SA]	✓	-	-	-
Keiko	✓	✓	✓	-	✓	✓	Italian	✓
Ken	-	-	✓	-	-	-	-	-
Masa	-	✓	✓ English & Chinese	-[SA]	✓ English & Chinese	✓△ English (dropped out) & Chinese (continued)	✓△	✓
Miyabi	✓	✓	✓	✓	✓	✓	✓	✓
Naoya	-	✓△	✓△	-	-	✓	✓	✓
Natsume	✓	✓	✓	-[SA]	✓	✓	✓	-
Tae	✓	✓	-	✓	-	-	-	-
Toma	-	✓	✓	✓	✓	✓	✓	✓
Yuta	-	-	-	-	✓	✓	✓	✓
Kayo	-	✓	✓	-	✓	✓ (Currently a 3rd year student)		
Ots	✓	-	✓	✓ (Currently a 2nd year student)				

Notes: ✓: completed the class
✓△: registered but dropped out
-: not taking English (other languages being taken during this semester are shown)
[SA]: participated in study-abroad that semester

Coding

First, an analytical procedure called Trajectory Equifinality Model (or TEM, developed by Valsiner & Sato, 2006; Sato, 2009) was applied by the second author to analyse the processes and factors leading to the decisions the participants made about whether or not to attend LC classes. In this procedure, all the utterances elicited through interviews were coded and arranged in chronological order, because in TEM the concept of 'irreversible time' is vital. The results support Dörnyei and Ottó's (1998) process model in that all the participants went through the stages of choice, execution and reflection phases repeatedly (Arano, 2013). In the second stage, the first author reanalysed the transcribed data in line with the theoretical framework of Valsiner's model and DST, as discussed in the previous section. Finally, both stages of the analysis were reviewed by the two co-authors jointly. This chapter focuses mostly on this second-stage analysis.

The interview data were first open-coded, and preliminary results indicated that they comprised various cognitive, affective, social, contextual, physical, contingent, psychological and physiological experiences. We then reanalysed these experiences into categories: (1) affective reactions; (2) desire and will (conation); (3) appraisal of LC as a learning situation and appraisal of learners' needs; (4) metacognition of learning and (5) social and contextual factors (see Tables 18.2–18.4 for examples in which categories are entered in bold italics). Here it should be noted that it was often difficult to place some experiences into specific categories, in particular as regards the distinction between appraisal and affect. In such cases, we entered the experience under both categories.

Analyses using Valsiner's three domains

Next, we used Valsiner's (2007) model to situate each coded experience in the microgenetic, the mesogenetic or the ontogenetic domain. Most of the learners' experiences, which were often superficial and contingent, were placed in the microgenetic domain, as we explain below using a series of examples. As mentioned earlier, we hypothesise that these experiences interact through the blended operation of 'cognition, affect and motivation that act as wholes' (Dörnyei, 2009b: 235), adapting to social and contextual factors and amalgamating into a personal meaning regarding attending LC classes, which we placed at the mesogenetic level. At the same time, other factors emerge as having equally vital personal and cultural meanings, including job hunting, romance, etc. (In Tables 18.2–18.4 they are entered in bold italics.)

Finally, if an L2 learning and using self is internalised as an ontogenetic meaning structure, it may function as a value, or as deeply internalised thought patterns or habits that direct the individual's learning behaviours for

Table 18.2 Results of interview analyses: Tae

	Spring semester		Fall semester	
	Coded interview data	Category	Coded interview data	Category
1st year	**Microgenetic**		**Microgenetic**	
	• I was attracted by the pamphlet	*Affect*	• It would be helpful for getting a job in the travel industry	*Appraisal*
	• It was fun, like an extra-curricular activity	*Affect*		
	• I needed to study something to please my parents instead of taking a teacher training course	*Contextual*	• I wanted to get a TOEIC score that would exempt me from taking a regular class	*Contextual, Appraisal*
	• I like oral/aural classes more than lectures	*Affect*	• I wanted to have fun	*Affect*
	• I was attracted to foreign life and cultures	*Affect*	• I wanted to meet friends	*Social*
	• I had fun talking with foreigners	*Affect*	• I wanted to communicate with foreigners and learn about foreign cultures	*Desire*
	• I wanted to maintain the level of English I acquired in high school	*Desire*		
	• I wanted to raise the level of my English competence	*Desire*		
	Mesogenetic		**Mesogenetic**	
	• *Personal meaning of LC as a learning context*		• Personal meaning of LC as a learning context	

Year				
2nd year	**Microgenetic**		**Microgenetic**	
	• I wanted to talk to an NS teacher (of a regular class) I liked	*Desire, Affect*	• I kept studying for a travel-related qualification exam	*Contextual*
	• I wanted to participate in a regular class and discuss more	*Desire*	• I frequented the e-cafe for its flexibility	*Appraisal*
	• I wanted to be trained to participate in discussions	*Appraisal, Desire*		
	• I met an LC teacher on campus, who invited me to join	*Social*		
	• I started studying for a travel-related qualification exam	*Contextual*		
	Mesogenetic			
	• *Personal meaning of LC as a learning context*			
3rd year (to 4th year)	**Microgenetic**		**Microgenetic** (Spring and fall semesters, 4th year)	
	• Job hunting was more important than English	*Contextual*	• I got a job offer at a retailer (not an English-using job)	*Contextual*
	• I passed the travel-related qualification exam	*Contextual*	• I was busy with different activities: part-time work, graduation thesis, taking a driving test	*Contextual*
	• My schedule did not work out	*Contextual*	Desire to enjoy the last semester of student life	*Desire*
	• I wanted to maintain my level of English	*Desire*	**Mesogenetic**	
	• I reset my target English proficiency level lower for a specific job I had in mind	*Appraisal*	• *Personal and cultural meaning of job hunting*	
	Mesogenetic			
	• *Personal and cultural meaning of job hunting*			

Table 18.3 Results of interview analyses: Aya

	Spring semester		Fall semester	
	Coded interview data	Category	Coded interview data	Category
1st year	**Microgenetic**		**Microgenetic**	
	• Ideal self using English in future occupation	*Cognitive, Affective*	• I felt uncomfortable with an awkward class atmosphere with a lot of silence	*Affect*
	Mesogenetic		• I applied for SA and then decided	*Contextual*
	• *Ideal L2 self*		• My desire to learn was boosted after I decided about SA	*Desire*
	Microgenetic		• I was worried about my inability to use English	*Affect*
	• There was no extra cost	*Appraisal*	• I perceived the need to improve my English	*Appraisal, Metacognitive*
	• I wanted to talk to foreigners	*Desire*	**Mesogenetic**	
	• I thought it was a good opportunity to improve my English	*Appraisal*	• *Ought-to L2 self*	
	• It was a place where I can find my weakness in the L2	*Metacognitive*	**Microgenetic**	
	• It was a place where I could practice speaking	*Appraisal*	• I can get a lot of materials at LC	*Appraisal*
	• The teacher created an 'easy to talk' atmosphere	*Appraisal, Affect*	• Regular class scheduling permitted me to take LC classes	*Contextual*
	• The teaching method was helpful and caring (e.g., the teacher taught phrases that helped us speak up)	*Appraisal*	• I always attended LC with good friends	*Social*

	Mesogenetic • *Personal meaning of LC as a learning context*	**Mesogenetic** • *Personal meaning of LC as a learning context*	
2nd year	**Microgenetic** • I perceived a sense of improvement • I perceived the development of my listening ability • I gained knowledge of what I can do and what I cannot • The teachers give me advice for improvement • I used LC and e-café for different purposes • I was afraid to go to e-café alone • I became a familiar face at e-café • I got to know LC teachers well • It's a place where I can ask teachers questions	**Microgenetic** • I wanted to be a more fluent speaker • I wanted to make more NS friends • I enjoyed communicating	*Desire* *Desire* *Affect*
	Metacognitive *Metacognitive* *Metacognitive* *Appraisal* *Appraisal* *Affect* *Social* *Social* *Appraisal*	**Mesogenetic** • *L2-using self*	
	Mesogenetic • *Personal meaning of LC as a learning context*		

(Continued)

Table 18.3 (Continued)

	Spring semester, 3rd year		Fall semester, 3rd year to 4th year	
	Coded interview data	Category	Coded interview data	Categor
3rd year (to 4th year)	**Microgenetic** • I didn't feel comfortable in the LC class with people who were not actively participating • We spent too much time watching movies, which I can do by myself • I wanted to have discussions • There are things that I can learn at LC that I cannot learn at e-café • My friends didn't influence my decision to attendclasses • My schedule clashed with LC classes • LC is a place where I ask teachers questions • I started considering going to graduate school • I wanted to maintain the English level I reached during SA	*Affect, Appraisal* *Appraisal, Affect* *Desire* *Appraisal* *Desire* *Contextual* *Appraisal* *Contextual* *Desire*	**Microgenetic** • I liked the lively atmosphere of e-café • My class schedule got busier • University life got busier with job hunting activities • I was immersed in e-café for its flexibility • English became more important in my major(law), leading to more constant use • I wanted to learn English for my own sake • I was learning how to write a thesis in English • I perceived a sense of development as an L2 writer	*Affect* *Contextual* *Contextual* *Contextual* *Contextual* *Desire* *Metacognitive* *Metacognitive*
	Mesogenetic • *Personal meaning of LC as a learning context (getting weaker)*		**Mesogenetic** • *Personal meaning of e-café as a learning context* **Ontogenetic** • *Meaning of English in life* • *L2-using self*	

Table 18.4 Results of interview analyses: Miyabi

	Spring semester		Fall semester	
	Coded interview data	Category	Coded interview data	Category
1st year	**Microgenetic** • I can make use of time when I do not have classes	*Appraisal*	**Microgenetic** • I was excited at the start of a new semester	*Affect*
	• I hated wasting time just chatting when there was no class	*Affect*	• I felt physically unfit on winter mornings	*Physiological*
	• There was no cost or economic benefit	*Appraisal*	• I lost a sense of being myself	*Affect*
	• I like conversing in English	*Affect*	• I appreciated LC as a place where I felt I could improve	*Appraisal*
	• I felt tired because of my new life in university	*Affect, Physiological Contextual*		
	• Many activities kept me busy in university			
	• I drew satisfaction from the sense of improving myself	*Affect*		
	Mesogenetic • *Personal meaning of LC as a learning context*		**Mesogenetic** • *Personal meaning of LC as a learning context*	

(Continued)

Table 18.4 (*Continued*)

	Spring semester		Fall semester	
	Coded interview data	*Category*	*Coded interview data*	*Category*
2nd year	**Microgenetic**		**Microgenetic**	
	• I felt excited to make a new start in a new semester	*Affect*	• There was a good community, which sustained motivation	*Social*
	• I like the good class content, good group members, and a good teacher	*Appraisal*	• A good community of lovers of English motivated each other	*Social*
	• The class content was interesting	*Appraisal*	• Stimulated by classmates' eagerness to learn	*Affect*
	• There was an atmosphere that invited participation	*Appraisal*		
	• I was stimulated by classmates' eagerness to learn	*Affect*		
	• I felt tired after being so enthusiastic	*Affect*		
	• One LC class was not as enjoyable as the other class I was taking	*Affect*		
	Mesogenetic		**Mesogenetic**	
	• *Personal meaning of LC as a learning context*		• *Learning community*	
			• *Personal Meaning of LC as a learning context*	

Year	Time scale	Statement	Code
3rd year	**Microgenetic**	Job hunting activities started	*Contextual*
		Preoccupied with romance	*Contextual, Affect*
		I was less attracted to LC with only a fewer classmates remaining	*Affect*
		I like learning and using English	*Affect*
		I like e-café as a place to talk	*Affect*
		I used LC and e-café for different purposes	*Appraisal*
		I appreciated e-café as a stress reliever	*Appraisal*
		E-café is a place to experience the pleasure of speaking English	*Appraisal*
		I had a strong desire to communicate	*Desire*
	Mesogenetic	*Personal meaning of e-café as a learning context*	*Contextual*
		L2-using self	
	Microgenetic	I became busier with job hunting	*Contextual*
		I got depressed because of an unrewarding romance	*Affect*
		I lost a sense of being myself	*Affect*
	Mesogenetic	*Personal and cultural meaning of job hunting*	
		Personal and cultural meaning of romance	
4th year	**Microgenetic**	I started learning Italian at LC as well as English to regain my sense of self	*Will, Agency to change herself*
		I got a job offer	*Contextual*
		I regained the sense of being myself and a person who likes speaking English	*Affect*
	Mesogenetic	*Personal and cultural meaning of job hunting*	
		L2-using self	
	Microgenetic	I was happy with myself because I was making use of my time doing things I like	*Affect*
	Ontogenetic	*L2-using self*	
		Belief in self-development	

an extended period regardless of the daily ebbs and flows of motivational forces. It is difficult to judge just from the interviews whether a learner has internalised such a meaning structure. However, when the analysis of the interview data yielded codes suggesting the possibility of ontogenetic internalisation, we took behavioural patterns, motivational curves and other available information into consideration to judge whether or not the meaning structure could be placed in the ontogenetic domain. (In Tables 18.2–18.4, these are shown in bold italics and underlined.) Thus, participants' experiences, as we understood them through their own words, were reconstructed using our theoretical frameworks.

Individuals' unique motivational trajectories

In this section, we present interview data analyses for three individuals; Tae, Aya and Miyabi (all pseudonyms). These participants were chosen because (a) we could elicit a relatively large amount of data from them, and (b) we regard them as representing specifically distinct motivational trajectories. In addition, the data from a fourth participant, Naoya will be partially presented to aid the interpretation of the main three participants' data. In reporting this, we hope to demonstrate how motivational fluctuations and behavioural choices over the eight semesters are accounted for by microgenetic experiencing, as well as by socioculturally structured activities and their personal meaning at the mesogenetic level, and by the internalisation of L2-related values at the ontogenetic level. The main findings are summarised in Tables 18.2–18.4 and in Figures 18.2–18.4.

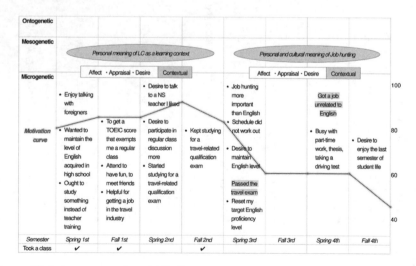

Figure 18.2 A summary of analysis: Tae

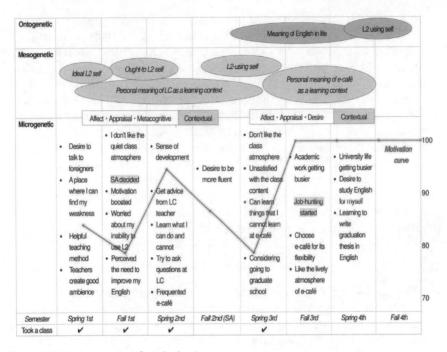

Figure 18.3 A summary of analysis: Aya

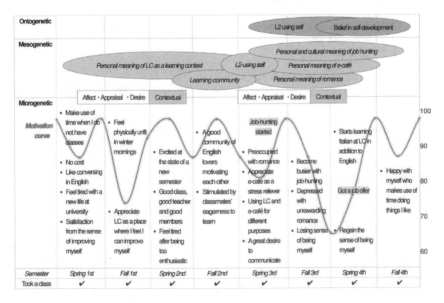

Figure 18.4 A summary of analysis: Miyabi

Figures 18.2–18.4 were designed to present the following information: (1) whether or not the participant took a class in each of the eight semesters; (2) a motivational trajectory for the eight semesters as drawn by each participant; and (3) the results of interview data analyses arranged along a timeline and in three layers corresponding to Valsiner's (2007) three-level model. At the bottom of each figure are eight boxes representing eight semesters placed along a timeline with a check mark indicating that the participant took (and completed) an LC class that semester. The curve is a reproduction of the motivational trajectory as drawn by the participant. Some of the coded interview data are placed along the timeline, mostly in the microgenetic domain (see Tables 18.2–18.4 for all codes). Depending on the results of the analyses, emergent categories are entered in the mesogenetic and ontogenetic domains. Insights gained from interviews with the other five students will be incorporated into the final discussion from a DST perspective.

Tae

The results of the interview data analyses are summarised in Table 18.2 along with coded experiences, with psychological categories in bold italics. As indicated in Figure 18.2, Tae took LC courses during three of the four semesters in her first and second years, but stopped taking classes altogether beyond that point. In a sense, she represents typical LC students, who are motivated enough to take a non-credit class at first and continue to learn English during the two years during which English is a required subject, but discontinue once the requirement is over and they become busier with their major and other activities.

At the beginning, Tae's attitude toward LC classes struck us as rather casual, taking advantage of the fun element of the LC, as represented by her remark, 'I enjoy talking with foreigners' (Affect), and 'It was fun, like an extra-curricular activity' (Affect). However, her interview transcripts also show different psychological processes at work, that is, she thought that 'It would be helpful for getting a job in the travel industry' (Cognitive appraisal of a learning context), and 'I wanted to maintain the level I reached in high school by studying hard and hopefully raise the level of my English' (Desire). Also, her comment 'I needed to study something to please my parents instead of teacher training courses, which I gave up' (Contextual) reveals that at the same time, she was trying to accommodate her family's wishes. At that point, these different thoughts (represented in different psychological categories) worked in harmony to direct her toward taking the LC course.

In conformity with our theoretical framework, our analysis shows that a blend of several psychological experiences, such as those shown above, interact with and adapt to contextual requirements and merge into the socio-culturally structured and personal meaning of LC as a learning context at the mesogenetic domain. Figure 18.2 shows that cognition, affect and conation work together, interacting with and adapting to contextual factors. While there are a multitude of pulls and pushes, as long as the positive meaning remains strong enough, it can generally lead the learner to continue taking a class. Even if a learner is not particularly eager to learn the L2, a combination of other factors – such as the attractiveness of a social gathering, a favourable class schedule that allows the learner to attend or a 'pretty girl' in the class (all revealed in the interview data) – the learner may remain in the class for a while. Conversely, even though a learner is motivated to learn the L2, a schedule conflict often prevents him or her to take a class. Thus, this analysis framework can explain a learner's behaviour that self-claimed motivational intensity alone cannot. While cognitive appraisal of the merit of taking a class takes place, positive affect and desire to learn may override a negative appraisal, or vice versa.

Also placed at the mesogenetic level is the socially structured personal meaning that job hunting has for Tae. Tae was interested in working for a travel agency, for which she thought English competence would be useful. She therefore started studying for a travel-related qualification in her second year in college, which kept her too busy to attend LC in the spring semester. However, she had an NS teacher in her required English class whom she really liked, and as she wanted to talk to him and take a more active part in class discussion, this, through interactions with other social and contingent factors (e.g. meeting an LC teacher she met accidentally in the street who encouraged her to join), contributed to her decision to take an LC class in the fall of the same year. However, in the third year, job hunting became more important in her life. Although she still had a desire to maintain her English level, her schedule that semester did not work out. Although she passed the travel qualification exam, she found by talking to people working in the travel industry that this type of job does not in fact require very high English competence, which seemed to lower her motivation somewhat. In the fourth year, she got a job not in a travel agency, but in a retail outlet, in which she would not need much English. Meanwhile, her university life became busier and full of different activities, including part-time work, a graduation thesis and taking a driving test. Under these circumstances, the relative importance of English in her life waned. For Tae, the significance she placed on job hunting drew her away from L2 learning, and with other commitments in her life, her motivation to learn English plunged, stabilising at a low level.

Finally, we found no L2-related meaning in her comments that could be placed in the ontogenetic domain.

Aya

Aya's comments, coded and categorised, are summarised in Table 18.3. Figure 18.3 shows her attendance at the LC and her motivational curve, with open-coded comments placed along the timeline.

Aya's comments include a large amount of metacognitive talk, which shows that she constantly checks her learning and the progress she has made. In the spring semester of her first year in college, she regarded the LC as a place where she could practice speaking and identify her weak points in her English (Appraisal, Metacognitive). She also appreciated the teaching method as well as the way the teacher made it easier for the participants to speak up by sometimes switching to Japanese (Appraisal, Affect). She decided to apply for a study abroad (SA) programme in October of her first year, and later that year she was selected to be a member of such a group (Contextual). This decision boosted her motivation but also made her worry about her English level, as can be seen in her comments, 'I was shocked to find myself unable to write a sentence properly' (Affect), and 'I found myself unable to speak or listen to English' (Metacognitive). This realisation motivated her to study hard, her attendance at the LC triggered by her ought-to L2 self. This ought-to L2 self was categorised in the mesogenetic domain together with the personal meaning of LC as a learning place.

With the ought-to self emergent at the mesogenetic level, her seriousness about learning is reflected in her metacognitive comments, which increased in frequency in the spring semester of her second year. Also, effort seemed to begin to pay, as seen in her comments: 'I was able to say a sentence in response to questions', and 'I was able to understand what the teacher was asking'. As regards the different functions of LC and e-café, she said, 'I learn what I can do and what I cannot do at LC. I can ask teachers questions and the teachers give me advice for improving further. I then put the advice into practice at e-café'. She gradually frequented e-café more often and became a familiar face there.

Aya is one of the most highly motivated learners among the interviewees. She is also the one who seemed to have at least some vague vision of her ideal L2 self even at an early stage. She related an episode in her high school days about meeting an NS instructor working in the school where her mother was an English teacher. Although she was not able to say much, she remembers the encounter as the frustrating but joyful experience of trying to communicate in English. This episode sowed a seed of desire to communicate in English fluently, and this has remained with her ever since. Her dream in high school was to work for an international organisation, such as the World Health Organization. This early image of her future self, combined with her mother's influence (among other factors), helped her self-organise her learning behaviour toward taking LC classes and applying for study abroad. We therefore entered the ideal L2 self, formed at an early stage in her learning, in the mesogenetic domain.

Figure 18.3 shows that Aya's self-perceived motivation rose in the fall of her third year to the maximum possible level and was maintained at that level, indicating that the motivational system might be in an attractor state. Nevertheless she stopped attending LC classes. In her third year, following the period of SA, her appraisal of the LC became rather negative, as her comments reveal: 'I didn't feel comfortable with the atmosphere in the LC class because many students were just waiting to be called upon' (Affect), 'In the class, we just watched movies and we were asked questions about the phrases used in the movie, which I thought I could do by myself' (Appraisal and Affect (dissatisfaction)), and 'I would rather have discussions' (Desire). After returning from SA, the LC lost significance for Aya. Instead, the e-café emerged as an alternative that filled the gap between her needs and what the LC could offer, even though she perceived that in some LC classes there were discussion sessions on given topics, something e-café did not offer. Thus, we entered the personal meaning of e-café in the mesogenetic domain in Figure 18.3. Comparing the two learning contexts, there was constant appraisal of what was being taught and how useful it was to her. Here, we see her agency in maintaining an optimum learning environment, a learner able to cultivate learning contexts and adapt her learning in ways she believes to be appropriate.

Aya's SA experience seems to have qualitatively changed her attitude toward English, resulting in greater motivation to further improve her English writing and speaking through a realisation that 'I was not good enough' and a feeling of a 'desire to learn English coming from within myself'. In her third year, she chose to enrol in a seminar in the law faculty that required her to write a thesis in English. This gave her renewed interest in learning academic English and made her realise that there was a great deal to learn, wishing to 'learn English for my own self, not because I had to'. Thanks to advice from good English teachers, she felt a sense of improvement as an L2 writer. Attending this seminar and interacting with teachers in this learning situation changed her outlook on learning English as she learned in greater depth about the language and its structure. Thus, we feel that the meaning of English, or her L2-using self, solidified in her life. We therefore placed it in the ontogenetic domain (Figure 18.2) in part because we sense that this L2 self will remain with her as a meaning structure that will guide her to study and use English for some time to come, possibly throughout her life.

Miyabi

Miyabi is the only student among the 12 who continued to take and complete classes at the LC during all eight semesters. Miyabi's comments and coding and categorising are summarised in Table 18.4 and include a much larger proportion of affect than was the case for the other two focal students. Figure 18.4 shows her attendance at the LC and her motivational curve, along with open-coded comments placed along the timeline.

From the beginning, Miyabi impressed us as someone who was extremely talkative and would make the most of what is available, illustrated by repeated comments such as, 'I can make use of the free time between classes instead of wasting time chatting with friends in the cafeteria' and 'I can take the classes for free, ... you can't find such a good story anywhere'. She also wanted to do something, she says, 'to develop myself'. Apart from this appraisal of the merit of the LC, her reaction to it is predominantly affective, with occasional mood fluctuations. We sensed that she really likes speaking English and has a strong desire to seize opportunities to do so. On the other hand, she explained the dent in the curve she drew in the spring semester of her first year by saying, 'I felt tired facing the new life on campus after a while'. As regards the dip in her motivation in the fall semester, she said, 'I didn't feel physically fit on winter mornings'. The same pattern was repeated in the spring of the second semester as she felt tired after the initial excitement following making a new start. Thus, her mood, desire, cognitive appraisal and physiological condition interacted with contextual factors to give rise to motivational fluctuations.

She talked very positively about a class she took at LC in her second year as having 'good class content, good group members, and a good teacher'. She says that it was 'easy to participate, and I made good friends, who I still have contact with...Everyone was interested in English and wanted to improve.... so I was stimulated'. Those class members who were eager to learn English stayed in the class in the fall semester, thus sustaining each other's motivation. These comments describe the learning community as a dynamic system comprising individual learners with emergent collective motivation. Socioculturally structured, the personal meaning of the LC as a learning context was entered in the mesogenetic domain, in which the learning community as a dynamic system played an important role.

In the third year, job hunting started, which kept Miyabi busy in the fall semester. At the same time, she told us that she was preoccupied with a romantic attachment. Miyabi talked only briefly about this and it seemed to end unhappily. Considering the cultural significance of romance for university students in general and its personal significance for Miyabi, we placed this dimension in the mesogenetic domain. Because of these external preoccupations, Miyabi was no longer as attracted to the LC as before, especially with fewer classmates remaining, indicating that the learning community disbanded. However, her liking for English and her desire to communicate led her to keep on taking LC classes and visiting the e-café, which had different functions for her. As she explains, 'the e-café is a place where I can relieve stress by speaking English' and 'a place where I can experience the pleasure of speaking English'. The personal meaning of the e-café thus emerged and, for this reason, it was entered in the mesogenetic domain (see Figure 18.4). In the fall semester, Miyabi became much busier with job hunting activities as well as becoming depressed at the unhappy end of her romance. This, and the mounting stress of job hunting, made her 'lose the sense of being herself'.

With job hunting activities being stagnant in the spring of her fourth year, she started studying Italian because she decided that she needed a new challenge to regain a sense of herself by doing something she liked instead of letting herself give in to stress. Here, we see her agency in changing her circumstances in order to recover her sense of self. Subsequently during this semester, she received a job offer. She attributed her success to recovering her self-confidence, which, she says, 'made me shine'. As she says, 'The key is making yourself a person people would like to work with'.

For Miyabi, job hunting required a great deal of adaptation and self-organisation. The socioculturally structured personal significance of job hunting was therefore entered in the mesogenetic domain. For Miyabi, 'the sense of being myself' means 'being a person who likes to speak English'. She repeatedly states that she 'loves conversing in English', and adds that 'I don't like to study so much, but I like communicating, and in order to communicate I need to acquire English to some extent'. By the end of the interviews, we learned that her experience of interacting with American friends who were international students in high school was the seed of her desire to communicate in English. This intrinsic desire to communicate (in both Japanese and English), that is, her embodied English-speaking self, is at the core of her taking LC classes and frequenting the e-café. It seems that she feels excited, almost 'high' when speaking English. Thus, we placed this dimension in the ontogenetic domain because we sense that this feeling is with her all the time. At the same time, the belief in self-development, often found in her comments, might have motivated her to take classes to the end as a core value, and we thus entered it in the ontogenetic domain.

General Discussion

The study reveals the complexity of human motivation as it fluctuates in learners' lived contexts. In this section, we spotlight the aspects of human motivation that are relevant to L2 learning. As mentioned earlier, Naoya's data will be presented as part of this discussion because contrasting him with the other three focal participants makes it easier to reveal the differences in how learners' adaptation to similar contextual changes results in different behaviours.

The interaction of psychological operations and system behaviour

As the analyses of the three participants presented in the previous section demonstrated, each participant, each with a different combination of psychological operations interacting with the environment in which he or she was placed, produced a unique motivational trajectory and unique learning behaviours. However, we cannot claim any causal links between the behaviour of one individual (a system) and psychological operations (subsystems) because a simple linear link was not found. For example, the single fact of finding a class enjoyable does not necessarily cause the learner to continue taking the class. Appraisals such as how the class content matches the learner's requirements, and contextual factors such as schedules, human relations and other commitments, combine to generate a personal meaning for attending the class, which might lead to a particular behavioural pattern. What we find is an interaction of factors through which a system negotiates and self-organises into certain behavioural patterns or attractor states. To understand how such a system self-organises, we can gain some insights from the three-level analyses. Microgenetic-level experiencing, such as physiological condition, affective reaction to the atmosphere, teachers and friends, the desire and will to speak English, and a cognitive appraisal of one's needs to learn, the teaching method and teacher's teaching style or the perceived usefulness of a task, together with other contingent contextual factors, all result in short-term fluctuations in motivation. If a blend of these reactions converges to a degree of personal meaning of the LC as a learning context at the mesogenetic domain, the learner is likely to continue taking the class. This process may gradually generate a lasting value at the ontogenetic level to sustain motivation. Alternatively, even if we did not see this in our data, a one-time life changing event can have a major impact on the ontogenetic level. Further, as Aya's case demonstrates, one's perceived motivational intensity does not necessarily correspond to taking (or not taking) the LC class, and the three-level analyses illustrate why this is the case.

For a learner to keep taking non-credit English classes, or to keep on learning English beyond requirements in a Japanese university, he or she needs strong incentives, such as participation in a SA programme or career-related goals – often with ideal and ought-to L2 visions – that self-organise into learning behaviours or attractor states. For university students, job hunting often draws participants away from learning an L2 or taking LC classes through a combination of a lack of time, loss of interest or friends leaving the class. In this sense, job hunting, a socially structured activity that requires the learner to adapt to new contextual demands, can trigger a phase shift. For example, for Tae, after she secured a position with a retailer, the meaning of learning English changed and she stopped learning English and decided to enjoy the rest of her university life. This we can contrast with Naoya's case to show that job hunting does not necessarily cause a learner to stop learning; because he was busy preparing for a highly competitive test with a view to becoming a civil servant, Naoya dropped out of LC class for two consecutive semesters. Yet, his failure in the test made him decide to study English instead. With an alternative career in mind, he started planning for a gap year abroad. Having made up his mind, he adapted to a new learning behaviour and started attending LC classes again and working hard, as if he had shifted gear.

Of all the interviewees, Aya and Miyabi are among the minority who, we assumed, internalised L2-related ontogenetic meaning structures. As we showed in the analyses, ontogenetic meanings emerged through interactions between desire, emotional reactions, cognitive appraisals and adaptation to contextual changes, giving rise to learning behaviours, a process that was partly agentive and partly afforded by the environment. From our interviews with Aya, we sense that L2 learning seems to be ontogenetically internalised as an academic exploration to which she is attracted and that she will pursue. By contrast, for Miyabi, although studying English is not something she will continue as an academic exploration, she internalised the excitement and joy of communicating in English, which she values, and therefore we feel that she will continue to find ways of using English. Once using the L2 for communicative purposes had been truly ontogenetically internalised and using it has become a valued and natural part of the person's daily life, with vivid L2 self-images embedded in the learner's living contexts, the motivation to learn and communicate in the L2 will be sustained despite daily fluctuations in mood, affect, appraisal or desire. At this stage, learning English becomes quite inseparable from using it, as was observed in both Miyabi's and Aya's cases. At this stage, English is not something learners encourage themselves to sit down to and study as a school subject. Rather, they find themselves naturally taking opportunities to use the language as a form of self-expression. In other words, the learner's L2-self has become a natural self.

Salience of English at matriculation

Obviously, those who chose to enrol in LC classes needed to be aware of its existence, visit the facility and make a decision to exert extra effort in addition to taking required English classes. Through interviews, we found that English had already become somewhat salient in all but one of the interviewees' lives at the time of matriculation. This psychological readiness enabled them to become aware of the LC and of the classes offered there (a necessary process) before deciding to enrol. The reasons why this became salient vary and include intercultural experiences, meeting a good English teacher who was truly enthusiastic, English being a subject the student studied intensely and did well in or an episodic event such as meeting a foreigner and not being able to communicate well.

L2 learning attractor states

University life is full of excitement and many students juggle different requirements, responsibilities and interests. Unless strong L2-related incentives such as SA, a mandatory TOEIC (Test of English for International Communication) score as an objective and other factors in combination help a system self-organise toward stability (anchored in an L2-learning attractor state), it is likely to be drawn towards non-L2-related commitments. Such activities, including job hunting, other academic requirements or a romantic attachment – and which can be of great sociocultural significance and often appear as more immediately urgent – push a system progress toward a non-L2-learning attractor states. As a consequence, learners move away from taking extra non-credit English classes, or even from studying at all.

Phase shift, adaptation to the context and self-organisation

With the personal meaning of attending LC emergent at the mesogenetic level, the learners adapt to changes in requirements (academic work, job hunting, etc.) or conditions (teachers, classmates, schedules, etc.) and transform themselves as self-organising adaptive systems. For some students, such as Naoya, abrupt changes take place. Although not all changes are as radical as in Naoya's case, some participants, such as Aya, seem to move into a different phase after an intercultural contact experience, which often brings about qualitative changes in their outlook and attitudes toward learning and using English. As the three-level analyses suggest, deeply held values attached to L2 learning, or an embodied and solidified L2-using self, may emerge through continuous learning behaviour, along with adaptive self-organisation.

Sign mediation (signs as prompters): A sociocultural perspective

Sociocultural approaches, including the framework proposed by Valsiner (2007), place a strong emphasis on sign mediation in human motivation and development as individuals self-regulate their behaviours. The significance the learner attaches to L2 learning, or, socioculturally speaking, assembled signs in the mesogenetic and ontogenetic levels, regulates learning behaviours. Unlike L1 acquisition, L2 learning – and in particular instructed L2 learning – is a conscious process learners constantly reflect upon and can talk about. Based on these reflections, they create visions of expected future experiences.

Limitations and future possibilities

This study, being preliminary and experimental, has many limitations. First of all, as soon as we take a componential view and focus on certain aspects, we run the risk of simplifying the nature of DST. Second, in methodological terms, retrospective interviews have limitations of their own as learners may not represent their experiences accurately. A more fruitful approach might be to have real-time interviews with each participant, each semester, in order to capture the dynamics of the focal systems. Third, although we believe that the study of motivation is useful in itself, when conducting a DST-informed second language acquisition study, it would be desirable, in order to grasp the nature of the system more accurately, to incorporate language development either through standard test scores or oral proficiency levels, and to analyse the interaction between motivation and linguistic development. Fourth, in order to spotlight the nested nature of a dynamic system, in addition to observing a focal system, its subsystems and the social and contextual environment and interactions among them through learners' eyes, as we did in this study, we need to ethnographically observe how a group of individuals interact to create motivation in a larger system (such as for example in a learning community, as in Yashima *et al.*, forthcoming). The current study attempts to model the intra-individual psychological subsystems as they adapt to the environment and manifest themselves in the observable behaviour of the system. This methodological constraint therefore forces us to concentrate on certain aspects of DST at a given time. Nevertheless, we believe that this approach has the potential to illuminate complex psychological operations as well as changes in the motivational development of EFL learners.

Conclusion

We have shown that DST-inspired, three-level analyses can help illuminate the complexity and dynamics of motivation to learn an L2. Considering motivation to learn an L2 along three time scales offers a way of addressing the enigma of why some people continue to learn while others do not. It unveils short-term, medium-term and long-term motivational operations, that is, how the microgenetic (the learner's moment-to-moment experiences) interact with contextual challenges and generate the meaning the learner attaches to the learning activities (e.g. through instruction) at the mesogenetic level, which may or may not lead to the emergence of a long-lasting ontogenetic trend or to deeply held values attached to learning the L2. At the same time, once values become ontogenetically emergent, they can sustain the activities at the mesogenetic level and influence how learners process microgenetic experiences. Thus, it allows us to consider the generation of motivation on different time scales as a way of accounting for various puzzling phenomena (e.g. discrepancies between short-term and long-term commitment), and thus has the potential to lead to a comprehensive understanding of language learning motivation.

Through the lens of DST, we analysed a phenomenon, not as a set of linear causal relations among variables, but as it unfolds through the dynamic interactions of multi-level subsystems and parameters. We see individuals as systems, each of which has unique characteristics and experiences that interact with the environment and organise themselves toward certain learning (or non-learning) patterns. With this powerful theoretical tool, we should be able to more closely examine each of the three levels and show how individuals as systems, psychological components as subsystems and contexts as macro systems, adapt to each other to organise emergent motivated (or unmotivated) behavioural tendencies. Eventually, we may be able to offer short-term, medium-term and long-term forecasts of learning behaviours, based on research into how a set of learner characteristics, parameters and contexts is likely to generate particular patterns along different time scales. Thus, DST-informed motivation research has tremendous potential for helping us understand why people do what they do. This is not only a promising, but also an intriguing way to understand human beings.

References

Arano, K. (2013) Motivational fluctuation among Japanese English learners: An analysis using the Trajectory Equifinality Model. Unpublished master's thesis, Kansai University, Osaka, Japan.

de Bot, K., Lowie, W. and Verspoor, M. (2007) A dynamic systems theory approach to second language acquisition. *Bilingualism: Language and Cognition* 10 (1), 7–21.

Dörnyei, Z. (2005) *The Psychology of the Language Learner: Individual Differences in Second Language Acquisition.* Mahwah, NJ: Lawrence Erlbaum Associates.

Dörnyei, Z. (2009a) The L2 motivational self system. In Z. Dörnyei and E. Ushioda (eds) *Motivation, Language Identity, and the L2 Self* (pp. 9–42). Bristol: Multilingual Matters.

Dörnyei, Z. (2009b) Individual differences: Interplay of learner characteristics and learning environment. *Language Learning* 59 (1), 230–248.

Dörnyei, Z. and Ottó, I. (1998) Motivation in action: A process model in action. *Working Papers in Applied Linguistics 4*, Thames Valley University, 43–69.

Larsen-Freeman, D. (2006) The emergence of complexity, fluency, and accuracy in the oral and written production of five Chinese Learners of English. *Applied Linguistics* 27 (4), 590–919.

Larsen-Freeman, D. (2007) On the complementarity of Chaos/Complexity Theory and Dynamic Systems Theory in understanding the second language acquisition process. *Bilingualism: Language and Cognition* 10 (1), 35–57.

Larsen-Freeman, D. and Cameron, L. (2008a) *Complex Systems and Applied Linguistics.* Oxford: Oxford University Press.

Larsen-Freeman, D. and Cameron, L. (2008b) Research methodology on language development from a complex systems perspective. *The Modern Language Journal* 92 (2), 200–213.

Sato, T. (2009) *TEM de hajimeru shitsuteki kenkyu [Qualitative Research Using TEM].* Tokyo: Seishinshobo.

Valsiner, J. (2007) *Culture in Minds and Societies.* Thousand Oaks, CA: SAGE.

Valsiner, J. and Sato, T. (2006) Historically structured sampling (HSS): How can psychology's methodology become tuned into the reality of the historical nature of cultural psychology? In J. Straub, C. Kölbl, D. Weidemann and B. Zielke (eds) *Pursuit of Meaning: Advances in Cultural and Cross-cultural Psychology* (pp. 215–251). Bielefeld, Germany: Transcript Verlag.

Yashima, T., Ikeda, M. and Nakahira, S. (forthcoming) The dynamic interplay between context and the language learner. In J. King (ed.) *Context and the Learner in Second Language Learning.* Hampshire: Palgrave Macmillan.

19 The Dynamics of L3 Motivation: A Longitudinal Interview/Observation-Based Study

Alastair Henry

Learning a third language (L3) in school is a common experience for students in countries all over the world, particularly in Europe (Lasagabaster & Huguet, 2007) where a central aim of European Union educational policy is the development of multilingualism (Cenoz & Jessner, 2000; European Commission, 2005, 2008). Common language combinations, as for example in the Scandinavian countries, are English as the initial instructed foreign language (the L2) with French, German or Spanish (the L3) introduced at a later stage. The simultaneous learning of more than one foreign language (FL) has begun to attract the interest of motivation researchers, with findings pointing to the popularity of English (Csizér & Dörnyei, 2005; Csizér & Lukács, 2010) and indicating that, comparatively, motivational trajectories for L3s show a markedly steeper decline (Henry, 2009). There is also evidence that L3 motivation is prone to greater fluctuation, both gradual and dramatic (Mercer, 2011), and that in competition for the learner's time and resources, L2 English can have negative effects on L3 motivation (Henry, 2010, 2011, 2014; Mercer, 2011).

As Cameron and Larsen-Freeman (2007: 227) note, complexity theory approaches that reject linear scenarios and focus on the webs of interactions taking place within and between dynamic systems, seem to resonate with 'the problem spaces of applied linguistics'. One particular 'problem space' where complex dynamic systems (CDS) theories can usefully be applied is in L3 acquisition. The acquisition of an L3 involves greater degrees of complexity than in situations when only one new language is in focus, as it is necessary to account for the interactions between different language systems in the learner's mind (Herdina & Jessner, 2002; Jessner, 2006, 2008). This means that, in addition to all the individual difference factors recognized in

315

second language acquisition (SLA), in L3 acquisition the evolution of a language system will also be dependent on the development and behaviour of other parallel language systems (Jessner, 2008).

With the aim of examining the motivational dynamics of six Swedish students learning French as an L3, this chapter reports on findings from a series of semi-structured interviews and classroom observations conducted over a nine-month period. The chapter begins with an overview of some of the CDS concepts used when engaging with the data and concludes with a reflection on some of the methodological challenges encountered in this type of research.

Understanding Change in Complex Systems

'Complexity theory is fundamentally about change' (Larsen-Freeman, 2011: 52) and in any complex system growth and decline are normal developmental phenomena, the direction of change dependent on the impact of mutually interacting internal and external resources (Herdina & Jessner, 2002). The key concern of dynamic systems approaches is, therefore, to identify and examine changes in a system that lead to the appearance of new features or behaviours, meaning that CDS studies tend to have a prominent longitudinal element (Dörnyei, 2009a). In CDS theories, a series of important metaphors are used to describe processes of change that, in an SLA context, have been comprehensively examined by Larsen-Freeman and Cameron (2008) in their book-length coverage of the topic.

Attractor states and perturbations

Having defined the system under investigation (a necessary precondition when carrying out CDS research), the researcher needs to embark on a process of mapping. This involves charting the territory or the 'landscape of possibilities' (Larsen-Freeman & Cameron, 2008: 49) across which the system will roam, identifying the system's *phase* or *state space*. Within the multidimensional landscape of a system's state space, there are certain regions, or *attractor states*, to which the system gravitates (Hiver, Chapter 3, this volume; Nowak *et al.*, 2005). When the system moves into a strong attractor state, represented in the state space topography as a steep-sided valley, it exhibits modes of behaviour that appear as relatively stable. However, when attractor states are weaker (i.e. where the valley slopes are less steep), changes in system behaviour are more likely to take place. These can be the result of external influences or changes in one of the system's control parameters (Larsen-Freeman & Cameron, 2008). *Perturbations* are events that disrupt periods of stability in a system's development. As Howe and Lewis (2005: 249) explain, they can originate externally, such as for example war, famine or abuse, or can occur internally, for example hormonal changes, depression or a heart attack. In, for example, the complex system of language assessment, Larsen-Freeman and Cameron (2008) describe how the introduction of a new test might have a disrupting impact. Similarly, the spraining of an ankle could slow down or temporarily bring a halt to a programme of working-out at a gym. Thus, in terms of its resilience in the face of perturbations (i.e. the magnitude of the 'push' needed to disrupt the currently pertaining equilibrium), assessments can be made about the strength of the attractor state and the overall stability of the system (Larsen-Freeman & Cameron, 2008).

Phase shifts and emergence

When a *phase shift* occurs, one or more of a system's components changes in ways, such as to alter the state of the larger system. If a threshold has been passed, the system leaves the attractor state previously occupied, eventually ending up in another, newer state (Howe & Lewis, 2005). A phase shift can be recognized as having taken place when the system's modes of behaviour are observably different either side of the transition. Downstream from a phase shift a system may *self-organize* into a new period of stability and cohesiveness (Larsen-Freeman & Cameron, 2008). Self-organization captures the idea that in complex systems it is the system's own dynamics – as opposed to any external governing/organizing forces – that bring about new periods of stability. As de Bot *et al.* (2007: 14) explain, a system's 'multiple interacting components produce one or many self-organized equilibrium points'. On some occasions a phase shift can lead to something that is quite different from before. This is known as *emergence*, which Larsen-Freeman and Cameron (2008: 59) illustrate by pointing to 'a-ha moments' in learning, where older (imperfect) knowledge can be replaced by completely new (more sophisticated) understandings.

Co-adaptation

Just as components within a system are interrelated, with changes in one potentially affecting all the others, so too are different systems. Nested in complex webs, the impact of changes can be both vertical (up, as well as down) and horizontal. *Co-adaptation* describes the ways in which a complex system changes as a result of its interaction with another/other related systems (Larsen-Freeman & Cameron, 2008). As Dörnyei (2009a: 107) describes it, this involves processes of 'negotiation and adjusting' between systems, each changing in response to the other. When interactions between complex systems take place, the state spaces of the individual systems will inevitably alter. In the context of multilingual acquisition, where account needs to be taken of the interactions between different language systems, co-adaptation is of particular importance, Jessner (2008) making the point that, in a multilingual system, the behaviour of each individual language system will depend on the behaviour of the other systems with which it co-exists. Thus, when researching L3 systems, changes that are observed need to be considered in the context of changes that may be taking place in related systems.

System identities

Even when a system appears to be in a stable mode, the equilibrium pertaining at any particular point in time will be the product of the continuous adaptation to changes in the surrounding environment and in other related systems. Never entirely stable, a dynamic system can be understood as having greater or lesser resistance to outside influences and, in the face of fluctuation and change, as more or less successful in maintaining an *overall identity* (Larsen-Freeman & Cameron, 2008: 33). While recognizing that instability is the defining feature of complex adaptive systems, it is also important – not least in terms of knowing when to intervene (Larsen-Freeman & Cameron, 2008) – to be aware of situations where major changes take place. This means that when carrying out CDS research it becomes necessary to distinguish between, on the one hand, the types of day-to-day adaptation continually taking place as a response to changes in the environment and in other parallel systems, and, on the other, major shifts where the system moves from one part of its state space to another, its overall identity changing in the process.

The Role of Context and the Setting of the Current Study

In CDS the 'here and now' of context is never separate from the system. Rather, it is a part of the dynamics that determine the directions and forms the system takes (Larsen-Freeman & Cameron, 2008; Ushioda, this volume). Not only are contextual factors highly implicated in all types of change to the system, but in CDS physical and cultural factors are inseparable from social and cognitive factors. At the same time, it is not possible in any single study to devote an equal depth of scrutiny to all of the possible contextual factors that affect the system (even if they could be identified). Thus, when designing a study, it is necessary to make pragmatic decisions about the relative importance of different contextual factors (Larsen-Freeman & Cameron, 2008). In the current study, two contextual factors that may have particular importance to the motivational systems under investigation can be identified; the reward of extra credits for L3 learning and the status of L2 English.

The reward of extra credits for L3 learning: An important system parameter

In the here-and-now of L3 learning in upper secondary education in Sweden, grades are likely to form an important system parameter. As a response to increasing numbers of students dropping L3s entirely or, in upper secondary school, switching from the L3 they spent 4 years learning in secondary school to a new, beginner-level language, the Swedish government has recently taken measures to 'reinstate interest and motivation' and to 'provide a clear signal that upper secondary students who chose advanced courses should be rewarded' (Swedish Government, 2006: Bill 2006/07:107: 24) (my translation). Thus, from the Autumn Term 2010, students who continue with the L3 they studied in secondary school and gain at least a passing grade can get additional credits, substantially enhancing their final grade point average (GPA) (for a fuller discussion see Henry, in press).

For students with higher education as an intended destination and who find learning an FL demanding, this policy places them in an 'all-or-nothing' situation. If they gain a passing grade, extra GPA-enhancing credit points are generated. There is however a risk; a passing grade is by no means guaranteed. Thus, their GPA would be doubly affected. Not only would the student lose out on the extra credits, but the GPA would be lowered by the loss of the regular credits attaching to the course grade. For such students, the less demanding option of starting a new L3 from scratch would provide a safer course of action. Nevertheless, many upper secondary students are now opting to continue with their L3 from secondary school (Henry, in press). For these students, the availability of GPA-enhancing extra credits is likely to form an important parameter with a determining influence on the state space of the motivational system.

The status of L2 English: Cross-referencing and co-adaptation

As in many other countries, in Sweden the status of English has undergone considerable change. From a generation ago, being a foreign language where production/interaction largely took place in school, English is now part of a basic social literacy and a medium of expression used extensively in day-to-day life, particularly among young people. In the process of being remoulded into a fundamental educational priority alongside first language literacy and mathematics, the status of English as a *foreign* language is, here as elsewhere, being called into question (Dörnyei *et al.*, 2006; Dörnyei & Ushioda, 2011).

In Sweden, young people currently spend large amounts of time in English-language environments outside the classroom. In a recent study, Olsson (2011) showed that 9th-grade students spent on average over 20 hours per week in English language environments; boys spending more time in English-mediated environments than girls. Sundqvist (2009) found similar results. Further, as Sylvén and Sundqvist (2012) and Henry (2013) have drawn attention to, students' encounters with English outside of school will not only often involve greater levels of individual investment, but, in the case of, for example, digital gaming, can offer highly creative and personally meaningful experiences. Given that students' L2 and L3 motivational systems are interlinked as part of an overall multilingual system (Jessner, 2008), and that cross-referencing between them is likely to take place (Henry, 2010, 2011, 2014), changes to both systems can be anticipated.

Purpose and Overview

Paying particular attention to the function of the GPA-enhancing credits as a system parameter and possible co-adaptive effects resulting from interactions with the L2 English motivational system, the purpose of the study was to investigate the motivational dynamics of six upper secondary students studying French over the course of two semesters. To this end, a series of regularly spaced, semi-structured interviews were carried out. These interviews, which took place at the end of French lessons, were preceded by observations of students' behaviours during the class. In the interviews, students were invited to reflect on their learning behaviours and on the learning/social events that had taken place in the immediately preceding period.

Method

The participants

In Sweden, most upper secondary students learn French, German or Spanish as an L3, the latter being most popular[1]. Here, the six participants (four females and two males) came from a class of 22 first-year students (f = 12; m = 10) studying CEFR A2.2 French. The class was taught by a male teacher in his thirties with ten years of professional experience, who, when younger, had spent a year living in France. The class had two 75 minute lessons per week. In selecting participants the aim was to generate a sample with a broad variation (Dörnyei, 2007). Selection involved three stages.

Stage One

In the first stage (mid-October 2011) an interview was conducted with the class teacher, the purpose being to categorize students' learning behaviours and motivational profiles (cf. Dörnyei, 2014; Chan et al., this volume). The focus of the interview was on differences in students' approaches and attitudes to learning French. From the discussion, three characteristics emerged upon which the teacher felt that most of the students differed in noticeable ways. The characteristics identified by the teacher were aptitude and ability, learning behaviour and language anxiety. Using these parameters, the teacher went through the class register creating a learning profile for each learner (with the exception of two students whom he felt he could not easily categorize). Three profile types emerged:

(1) Higher aptitude and ability/focused learning behaviour/lower anxiety.
(2) Higher aptitude and ability/focused learning behaviour/higher anxiety.
(3) Lower aptitude and ability/less focused learning behaviour/higher anxiety.

Stage Two

In the second stage (end of October), students completed a single open-ended questionnaire item, asking them to list the things that made them (i) motivated and (ii) less motivated to learn French. Students were additionally invited to rank order the items in terms of their impact on motivation.

Stage Three

Cross-referencing the learning profiles assessed by the teacher with the students' own motivational profiles, I selected two students for each of the three learning profile types. In these pairs, the first student was selected because she/he had given a liking of French and a desire to use the language outside of the instructional context a high ranking and, additionally, had not listed the GPA-enhancing credits as a major motivational source. The second student was selected because she/he had ranked the opportunity to gain the additional credits as the single strongest source of motivation[2]. These six students were then invited to participate in the interviews. Identified by pseudonyms, and with the students primarily motivated by the extra credits listed second, they were; *Profile 1* Jonna and Freya, *Profile 2* Tim and Cilla, and *Profile 3* Emil and Siri.

Data collection

Between November 2011 and June 2012, a series of semi-structured individual interviews were carried out. Emil, Jonna and Siri were interviewed on six separate occasions, while Cilla, Freya, and Tim were interviewed five times[3]. The interviews, which lasted for between 10 and 25 minutes, would normally take place towards the end of a lesson. First I would observe the initial 30–40 minutes of the class, and then carry out two, or on occasion, three interviews in an adjacent glass-fronted group room, accessed from the classroom by an adjoining door. This meant that we could talk about things that had just happened while looking out at the activities still continuing in the classroom. Spending time in the classroom I adopted a nonparticipant role, taking an active part in events only if a student happened to ask a question. Observing the events unfolding, making notes about what took place and the behaviour of the six students, I did not though use the type of observation schedule typically used in classroom research (cf. Dörnyei, 2007).

By first observing classroom behaviours and then carrying out the interview, the aim was to increase the ecological validity of the study. As an important principle of CDS theories, context, rather than merely functioning as a backdrop against which behaviours take place, is seen as inseparable from the system being investigated (Larsen-Freeman & Cameron, 2008; Ushioda, this volume). Thus, to reduce the degree to which, in the interview, the learner becomes detached from the social, cultural and pedagogical context of the learning environment, the rationale was to engage participants in discussions about their motivation in a context as close as possible – physically and temporally – to the actual learning situation. In addition, as for example Kvale (1996) and Bryman (2008) both argue, research that relies exclusively on interviewing can lack the depth that complementary observations can provide. As Kvale (1996: 104) explains, 'if you want to study people's behaviour and their interaction with their environment, the observations of field studies will usually give more valid knowledge than merely asking subjects about their behaviour'. Thus, when analysing the data, I was able to relate things the students said with their behaviours in the classroom.

When conducting the interviews, an important aim was to structure parts of the discussion around things that had taken place on the other side of the glass immediately before. In this way, consistent with the commitment of interpretive phenomenological analysis (IPA) to first-order (participant) sense-making (see below), the students were able to reflect on their behaviour and state of mind in the context of a particular event. On two occasions I complemented this technique with specific elicitation strategies designed to stimulate more extended retrospection. First, in the series of interviews following students' return from the spring break, I once again gave them a blank sheet of paper with the headings, 'things that make me motivated to learn French', and 'things that make me less motivated to learn French'. Asking them first to list the different factors, I then invited them to compare these responses with those from October and to reflect on any differences/similarities. The second technique, used in the June interview, involved giving students a blank graph. On the X axis were months from August 2011 to June 2012, and on the Y axis motivation, quantified simply in terms of 'high' and 'low'. After inviting students to plot motivational trajectories, I then asked them to comment on the line they had drawn. Both strategies were conceived as ways of stimulating retrospection and, with the past as a reference, a means of enabling students to consider and evaluate the nature and strength of their current motivation (Gass & Mackey, 2000; see also MacIntyre & Legatto, 2011). All of the interviews were conducted in Swedish. Digital recordings were made and verbatim transcripts produced.

Method of analysis

When analysing the data, an interpretive approach inspired by Ricoeur's (1970) notion of the 'double hermeneutic' and drawing on techniques associated with IPA (Smith & Osborn, 2003) was employed. The double hermeneutic involves the combination of an empathic and a critical standpoint. Thus, while trying to arrive at a point where the researcher's understanding is attuned as closely as possible to that of the participant, analysis also involves taking a step back, adopting a critical position and actively deploying explanatory concepts.

As a methodology, IPA has cognition as a central analytic concern and emphasises processes of sense-making on the part of both the participant and the researcher. Because many participants in studies of language learning motivation cannot be presumed to have previously reflected much, if at all, on motivational processes, interpretive approaches such as IPA can be of value in that there is explicit recognition that, during an interview, participants are actively engaged in processes of sense-making. Here the empathic dimension involved finding out how, in the context of the learning and social events of the classroom, a packed schedule of other school subjects, the societal prestige of English, attainment ambitions and envisioned future FL use, the student experienced the demands of learning French. The critical element involved the use of CDS (de Bot *et al.*, 2007; Larsen-Freeman & Cameron, 2008) and self discrepancy theories (Dörnyei, 2005, 2009b; Markus & Nurius, 1986) to interpret these experiences.

The analysis was conducted in three stages using an approach similar to that outlined by Smith and Eatough (2007). The first stage involved separately reading through the sets of transcripts for each student several times, making notes of interesting features. In a second stage, the transcripts were re-read, this time using the abstractions of CDS and possible selves theories as a compass, transforming the initial notes and ideas into theoretically resonant themes. Finally, in a third stage, connections were sought and the themes grouped together in categories concordant with the purpose of the study, that is to say examples in the data indicating possible changes to contingent stabilities. These included indications of changes in attractor states, perturbations, phase shifts, co-adaptation between the L3 and L2 systems and features of emergence.

Results and Discussion

All of the six students were enrolled on programmes where, in their first year, taking an L3 was compulsory. All had received good grades in French in their previous schools. As experienced learners with a track record of success, patterns of behaviour with outward signs of stability might be expected. Indeed, it would not be unreasonable to assume that, at this stage in their learning, their motivational systems would have settled in strong attractor states to which, following any perturbation, the system would re-gravitate (Nowak *et al.*, 2005). This would be like the way that while an unusually strong ocean wave (a perturbation) might swamp a fibreglass dinghy or cause a fishing trawler to veer off course, the same wall of water would have hardly any impact on the passage of a steel-hulled super-tanker. On the other hand, even though the course is a continuation of previous studies with a similar syllabus, the transition to upper secondary school – with its new social and learning environments, new teachers, higher cognitive demands and the need for greater individual responsibility – can create conditions under which system-level changes might be likely. Further, the availability of the GPA-enhancing credits functions as a new system parameter meaning that, in these new circumstances, system behaviours may alter.

Employing Larsen-Freeman and Cameron's (2008) 'overall identity' metaphor, the results are divided into two sections. In the first I examine different types of continuous system dynamism and the effects of a particular external perturbation (the receipt of test results) that do not trigger any enduring changes to overall system identities. Thereafter in the second section, staying with test results, I consider their role in a process in which, over a longer timescale, a transformation to the overall identity of the motivational system of one of the students occurs. I conclude this second section by identifying a sequence of phase shifts that take place in the system of another student, triggered by decisions relating to a period of study abroad. Here I focus on emergent behaviours downstream from these shifts, examining the system's movements across its state space.

System fluctuations over shorter timescales

In CDS theories, the fundamental recognition that even apparently stable systems are in a constant state of flux, chimes well with the findings of motivation research that have shown how motivation can differ, from one day to another, over the course of a lesson and during particular activities (Dörnyei, 2000; Ushioda, 2006). Such flux is particularly true of institutionalized learning environments, especially those where, as Dörnyei (2000: 523) points out, students have little influence on instructional contexts and where 'many of the decisions and goals are not really the learners' own products but are imposed on them by the system'. Consequently, across the shorter timescale of a lesson, or over the course of a particular activity, the generation and maintenance of effortful learning behaviour can fluctuate dramatically (cf. Ushioda, 1996).

Fluctuations from one day to another

That motivation can differ from one lesson to the next, with no two days being exactly the same, was something recognized by all the students. When at the outset of each interview I would ask them to gauge their motivation, responses would often be along the lines of, 'well today...', students implicitly comparing their level of engagement in the events unfolding in the French classroom with that of previous occasions. The way that motivation differs substantially from one day to another appears to be a function of a range of internal and external factors (cf. Ushioda, this volume). This is neatly summed up by Jonna (Interview 5), who describes how motivation 'goes in waves' (cf. MacIntyre, 2012), and how it 'depends on what task you get, how difficult it has been, what happened immediately before, what kind of mood you are in and so on'. Elaborating further on day-to-day differences, Jonna explains how the negative impact of things she finds particularly difficult – pronunciation and grammar – can differ substantially from one lesson to another:

> Oh...And I haven't actually got this here but it depends a little bit on when I wrote it, because that is what I thought then, but now I wrote it based on today and today things went well. If I had written it when it felt that things were going pretty bad, I might have come up with more negative things, but this was how it kind of felt today. And it is still a little bit hard with pronunciation and a little hard with grammar, but it wasn't you know anything I felt made me less motivated today[4].

As seen in these extracts, initial conditions (see Verspoor, this volume), which include affective factors (the mood she is in), cognitive factors (the level of difficulty she experiences doing a particular task) and social factors (what happened in class immediately before), determine Jonna's motivation at any particular point in time. However, as her response suggests, even though these factors constantly differ, across a longer timescale an enduring stability has evolved. Across its state space, the trajectory of Jonna's L3 motivational system seems, over her years of learning, to have settled into a stable attractor state where all of the system's major components (the ideal and ought-to L3 selves and the L3 learning experience) converge in a mutually complementary manner.

Fluctuations during the lesson

Frequently I would invite students to plot their motivation over the preceding period of the lesson. Typically, as the following extract from an interview with Siri shows, students would describe how the intensity of motivated behaviour would vary. Talking about a dictation and translation back into Swedish, Siri's response provides an indication of how rapidly motivation can fluctuate:

I: How was this lesson?
S: Er....I think it was quite fun....I think it is more fun to work with tasks and stuff. ... much more fun than that which we've got to do now, translation.
I: How did it feel when you got the news that it should be translated back into Swedish?

S: Er...well...you don't get so motivated, you....get tired and get your phone out...and...almost just give a damn in it...but you have to...[sighs] that's how it is...(Interview 3)

Siri's motivational system seems to be lodged in a deep-sided ought-to self dominated attractor state, self-regulated behaviour driven by the desire to pass the course and secure the GPA-enhancing credits. While this has a strong impact on executive decisions, such as attending lessons and doing what is asked – 'you have to' she says – any sense of additionally needing to live up to others' expectations of being good at French, seems entirely lacking. So too is any counterbalancing sense that French might be personally meaningful or a skill she wants to develop for use in the future. Thus, more so than students like Jonna – for whom all three motivational self-system components converge in a deep basin of attraction, thus limiting system movement – for Siri changes in parameters, such as the nature of tasks, are much more likely to trigger shifts across the state space. Sequences in the lesson taken up with activities she finds boring, and periods when the teacher is occupied with other students, create contextual parameters that can stimulate movement out of the ought-to self attractor state and into a different area of the state space (e.g. a preference for social interaction). Thus, because there would be periods during lessons when she would become distracted (without direct interaction with the teacher Siri would often spend time absorbed with her phone or engaged in conversation with her study partner), for her, more so than for a student such as Jonna who has self-relevant reasons for learning, the nature of the classroom activity appears as having a determining influence on the trajectory of the system.

Seating as an initial condition

Since the interviews were conducted towards the end of lessons, it was possible to observe the students' social interaction over the preceding period. Jonna, Cilla, Siri and Freya would nearly always sit with the same study partner(s). For Emil (on some occasions) and Tim (quite frequently) seating patterns were more fluid. Sitting sometimes with students with generally focused learning behaviours, and at others with those who, given the opportunity, would often spend time talking among themselves or Net-surfing on their laptops and phones, there did not seem to be a set place in the classroom to which Tim gravitated; as he says, 'I work with different people, usually'. Reflecting on this tendency to sit with different people, Tim feels that who he sits next to probably both reflects and contributes to the state of his motivation:

T: Well, like I say, it differs. Different people. Which person I sit with. If I sit with those who work, then you work more yourself. It's easily like

that. Others... maybe talk more and work less, then you get
drawn into that too. That's definitely how it is.

I: Do you think how you feel influences who you sit with?

T: Well it isn't pure chance, it certainly isn't. I don't think so.
You sit down anyway .... you, well ... it is some form of,
you know who they are... so you sit down... so of course
there is some thought behind it. I think so. That's how it is.
(Interview 2)

In a complex system change is continuous, the result of a constant interaction between cognitive, affective, social and environmental factors (Ellis,
2007). In explaining the choices he makes in terms of who to sit next to,
Tim's response reveals the interrelationship of these factors. As a result of his
cognitive/affective state at the start of the lesson, on entering the classroom
Tim makes a choice about where and with whom to sit. This choice functions as an initial condition (Verspoor, this volume) that would appear to
have a determining influence on the trajectory of the system over the subsequent period.

Co-adaptation

Complex systems do not exist in isolation and in a school setting each
subject forms a discrete cognitive/affective/social system nested in the larger
school education system. Because these systems are interrelated, changes in
one are likely to impact on the others. When changes in one system trigger
changes in another adjacent system, this is known as co-adaptation. When
co-adaption occurs, changes can take place to the state spaces of both systems (Larsen-Freeman & Cameron, 2008).

Without exception, all of the students in the study speak of the pressure
of simultaneously studying a range of different subjects (seven or eight), and
the unavoidability of constantly having to decide where to channel time and
cognitive resources. 'Having to prioritize' is something mentioned time and
again and, with the exception of Jonna, in these dilemmas French seems to
be consistently deprioritized (see Henry, in press). As Mercer (2011) suggests,
through processes of self-regulation, learners allocate resources to different
competing demands, inevitably prioritizing certain activities over others (see
also Oyserman, 2007). The constant demands of other subjects – tests to be
studied for and assignments to be handed in – are often provided as a reason
for not having enough time for French. For example, a forthcoming maths
exam, and the concerns it might generate, may impact on adjacent systems,
triggering movement out of certain attractor states. For French it might
mean that plans to work on future tenses have to be postponed or even
abandoned.

All of the students see French as a demanding subject. For some though,
particularly Freya, Siri and Cilla, deprioritizing French appears as a very

active strategy. For others, such as Emil and Tim, the choice often seems less deliberate:

> It feels like French isn't exactly the subject I think about first, it's rather more that it comes afterwards somehow. Actually, I don't really know why this is. (Tim, Interview 1)

The perception that French is hard, resource-intensive and difficult to put to use, and the consequent diverting of resources to other subjects, can risk ending up as a self-fulfilling prophesy. As Siri explains, there is a paradoxical logic to the necessity of focusing more on other subjects:

> **S:**   There is an awful lot to do in school right now. So it feels as if you prioritize French last of all. Because it feels that you don't know enough. So then you do the other stuff first, to get it out of the way, and then there's no time left for French. And then ... it takes a long time to learn a language. So it feels like I just haven't got the time right now.
> **I:**   Why do you think you prioritize French last?
> **S:**   Umm ... well ... the others feel more important somehow. French is more ... you know ... what can you say? (Interview 1)

When reflecting on their motivation to learn French, students frequently express their feelings in terms of comparisons with the other subjects they learn. As Siri explains, 'In history you learn something and then you know it' (Interview 1). French, however, is somehow different. This, according to Tim, is because 'it is difficult to see if you get better' (Interview 1), and to Siri, because 'you feel that you are not getting anywhere' (Interview 1). Similarly, there is also recognition that, for French, achievement expectations need to be recalibrated. At the outset of the course, Jonna, for example, says that although, as in other subjects, she should be aiming for an A, she would in fact be happy with a B (her final grade as it turns out) or even a C. Freya, Siri and Cilla, who in other subjects regularly get As and Bs, and just the occasional C, are, at the end of the course, relieved simply to have passed. As Freya explains, knowing that, compared with other subjects, you are not as good in French can be an unsettling experience:

> Umm ... ah ... it's like well, you know I get more stressed I suppose ... um ... I am actually pretty used to ... um ... being quite good in the other subjects ... so there it is more the case that it's me who is helping them .... but here it's like the opposite, so it gets you a bit stressed. (Interview 2)

Similar to the disillusionment and anxiety experienced when not achieving the type of results they are capable of in other subjects, several of the students also speak of frustration when comparing their level of communicative competence in French with friends studying German or Spanish. Students learning these languages, they say, seem to have come much further:

> You notice it when you are sitting in class and someone says something, like, 'what is it in German?' and they always know it and we just ... and so ... of course it's hard for them too, but they feel like they have a base and it feels that we don't have any real base in French that we can build upon. (Cilla, Interview 1)

Comparisons between, on the one hand, the multifacetedness of learning, resource-demands and the paucity of progress indicators associated with French and, on the other, school subjects where knowledge seems more tangible, learning goals are more clearly defined, progress is easier to track and learning outcomes (grades) are better, can mean that at times motivated behaviour is difficult to sustain. In that each subject can be conceptualized as a discrete, yet interlinked, complex system, changes in one can have implications for the others. For example, the effects of students' comparisons of knowledge development and progress indicators can mean that while in a parallel system (history, taking Siri's example) the strength of governing attractor states is enhanced, for French, because evidence of achievement is elusive and progress difficult to quantify, the strength of the system's attractor states may be weakened (see Henry, Chapter 9, this volume; Nowak *et al.*, 2005). This would make movement of the system to other areas of the state space – and fluctuations in motivation – more likely.

Although, as I have suggested, the motivational systems of all subjects are likely to interact, changes to one having implications for the others, co-adaptation is particularly likely to take place between the motivational systems for L3 French and L2 English. Language systems are closely related to one another in the mind of the learner and in constant interaction. Working with the L3, the learner often utilizes linguistic resources from the L2 as an important source of supply and support (Hammarberg, 2009; Jessner, 2006, 2008), meaning cross-referencing between the different language systems is likely to be extremely frequent (Henry, 2014; Jessner, 2006, 2008).

Like the student in Mercer's (2011) study, when talking about motivation to learn French the students here make frequent comparisons with English. Not only is English regarded by the students (although not Jonna or Emil) as more enjoyable but, not surprisingly, it is also seen as more important, not least in the context of desired futures that include travel, higher education and professional careers. As for example Freya explains, in the face of the communicative potential of English, learning French can sometimes seem a little pointless:

> One thing I have thought about is that if you speak English so well, because.... well, it feels a little unnecessary to learn French...because English is of course an international language. It is. You can speak to everybody. Ahh ... so you can get a little less motivated to learn French, because it's not so useful ... um ... and learning English makes you feel good too because you can talk to absolutely anybody and understand almost anything. (Interview 1)

Again with the exception of Jonna and Emil, similar thoughts are expressed by all of the other students. Seen as a language that functions all around the globe – including France – perceptions of a greater use–value for, and self-competence in, English appear to have an impact on the three different components in the French Motivational Self System. As students' responses reveal, there can be an impact on the ideal French-speaking/using self (because English functions much better I can't visualize myself ever actually using French, even in France), on the ought-to French-speaking/using self (other than passing and boosting my GPA, nobody expects me to be able to speak French) and, for Cilla, Tim, Freya and Siri, on the learning experience (learning French is not as enjoyable/rewarding as learning English).

Reflections on the relative future utility, need to learn and learning enjoyment of the two languages are likely to have the effect of a gradual weakening of the attractor states to which the French motivational system can gravitate. Moreover, in that processes of co-adaptation are dyadic, the strength of counterpart attractor states in the English motivational system may consequently be enhanced. Indeed, these processes can have a dynamically spiralling effect. Any change in one of the two closely related systems is likely to prompt changes in the other, which in turn can have a reciprocal impact.

Test results: Perturbations that do not lead to longer-term identity-changing effects

Perturbations are system-external factors (Howe & Lewis, 2005) that can bring about changes to a system's phase space by disturbing an attractor state (Larsen-Freeman & Cameron, 2008). Testing – and the cognitive/affective state surrounding it – can be one such perturbing factor, jolting students' motivational systems out of settled attractor states. In the first term, apart from an initial test perceived as largely diagnostic, no other tests were held. Either side of the winter break, in the absence of any tests or other forms of assessment, students talked about a sense of worry, not knowing 'how I am doing', as many expressed it. Uncertainty about the final grade they were likely to achieve caused concerns, and several talked about how this could sometimes make it difficult to know what to focus on, and how this was unsettling. When the students did finally get an indication of their performance, the impact on motivational systems was noticeable.

The only student for whom the results did not seem to have a perturbing impact is Jonna. Coming off the back of a longer period of uncertainty about her performance and the grade she was likely to get at the end of the course, her almost perfect score provided, as she says, evidence 'that you are actually quite good anyway' (Interview 5). Although Jonna did not speak about being more motivated as a consequence of the test results, nor was it possible to observe any perceptible changes in her approach to learning, this long-awaited summative feedback is likely to have confirmed to her that she was 'on track', her efforts to reduce the gap between her current and ideal L3 selves demonstrably having an effect. This, conceivably, could trigger an upward revision of her ideal L3 self, the effect being to further stabilize the system in its attractor state, further increasing its resilience to change (see Henry, Chapter 9, this volume).

For all of the other students, being an early indicator of a likely final grade, the test results appeared to trigger periods of increased instability, with systems showing signs of entering into repeller states. By nature, unstable, repeller states often reflect a period of transition where the system moves from one attractor state to another. Consequently the system is unlikely to remain in a repeller state for any extended period of time (MacIntyre, 2013).

Getting her test paper back at the beginning of a lesson, Siri seemed thereafter overcome by a sense of despondency, unable to focus, spending long periods of the following hour or so surfing/texting on her phone and talking to her friend. Like Siri, Emil seemed to find it difficult to concentrate after getting his test score. In the period leading up to our interview he spent the first 30 minutes or so talking with his friends, later moving to another desk, sitting on his own with the test paper, a textbook and a pad upon which, by the hour mark, very little had been written. While on the one hand dejected, thoroughly disgusted with himself for getting 'my first ever F', he also expresses a determination to use the setback to generate motivation anew:

> ...Right now I don't even want to be in school. I just want to go home. Sort of try and put all this behind me and like try even harder. But it....of course it makes me disappointed and angry. (Interview 5)

While for both Siri and Emil receiving test results appears to push their motivational systems into a repeller state of turmoil and flux, evidenced by an almost total lack of focus and preferences for activities wholly unrelated to language learning, this period of heightened instability does not endure. Not long afterwards their systems appear to revert more or less back to the areas of the state spaces previously occupied. Emil, perhaps in an attempt to overcome his anger and frustration, says that he wants to use this setback as a means to immediately re-focus his energies. Siri, although despondent about what has happened, says she is not going to give up. Rationally appraising her performance, in our interview she goes through her test paper, providing explanations as to why she 'missed' certain parts, for example the sections on future tenses. Elsewhere in our interviews, Siri talks about how she knows she has the capacity to continue with goals, even when faced with adversity or a lack of willpower (see also Henry, in press). Like Emil, she too musters the energy to keep going with French. When an opportunity to re-take the test comes round, both pass. Moreover, both gain passing grades at the end of the course and continue with French the following year.

Perturbations with an impact on overall system identities

Test results contributing to the weakening of the strength of attractor states

In all of the examples so far discussed, the system seems to respond to changes or disruptions and, although never returning to exactly the same place as previously, overall identities nevertheless seem to be maintained. In this final section, beginning with the continued examination of the perturbing impact of test results, I look at situations where movements to new areas of the state space appear to be more enduring, and where the system's overall identity seems to change.

For Tim, finding out that he passed the test appears to have a positive effect, generating a sense of achievement. However, the results, moderate by his standards, also serve to illustrate the enormity of the task of learning a new language:

> Well of course it's like nice to know that it went well, but if you think about learning French, to be good at it at least, then it's no great achievement. That's how it feels. It … it depends on how you look at it … but um … but of course it's … it's such a huge thing learning a language. There is so incredibly much that you have to take in. (Interview 4)

Having previously decided not to continue with French after the end of the current term, noticeable shifts take place in Tim's learning behaviour during the remaining weeks (see also Henry, in press). Lacking the same degree of focus during lessons as previously, in our interviews he also gives expression to a waning interest in speaking the language in the future; 'It will be English that … English that you use … of course it's not a disadvantage … basic French … but I don't think I am going to use it much'

(Interview 5). In a sense Tim appears to be in the process of preparing to finish with French:

> I am not so motivated in French right now. Not at all. No. It's just not particularly motivating in any way. It comes last basically all the time. The last subject like. (Interview 5)

Seen in this light, his interpretation of the test results confirms that he has made the right choice. As his goals, and his future French-speaking/using self-concept become downwardly revised (see Henry, Chapter 9, this volume), the system's attractors – the ideal and ought-to L3 selves and, most importantly for Tim, the L3 learning experience – seem progressively to weaken. As a consequence, the system has limited power to capture and maintain cognitive energy in the face of competition with other, preferred, activities. This is clearly noticeable in Tim's increasingly cavalier approach to classroom work in the final two months of the term and preferences for participating in discussions with friends about TV programmes, football, working-out at the gym and digital gaming (all of which took place for extended periods in final two lessons I observed).

Perturbations that bring about phase shifts

In the second example I look at, perturbations trigger a process in which two identity-transforming phase shifts take place in one student's L3 motivational system. At the very beginning of our first interview (November 2011), Cilla tells me that choosing French has been a mistake: 'I chose it mostly because I thought it was the nicest language', she says. 'Now I think I would have chosen German'. Indeed, the following autumn, Cilla switches to German, telling me in our final interview (September 2012)[5] how she is enjoying it and that 'it is pretty good actually'.

Cilla gives the impression of being a conscientious student. In most lessons she focuses intently on the activities the class has been assigned. Rarely though does she display any outward signs of enthusiasm. Nor, to any great extent, does she contribute to whole class or group discussions. In our first interview she makes it clear that not only does French hold little personal attraction for her, but it is not a subject she particularly enjoys. She feels that many of the students in the class are better than she is, and is worried about her inability, as she describes it, to put her knowledge of grammar, syntax and vocabulary 'into a language'. Unable to conceive of herself in situations when she would actually use French, she makes it clear that motivation lies simply in the desire to get a passing grade and maximize her GPA:

I: How important is French for you now?
C: Now it is not so important. Now it's just about getting my credits and so on. No, I don't think I am going to have any use for it. Maybe go to

France on holiday, but then I would use English I think. They speak so incredibly quickly the French.

However, around the time when she has to decide on the subjects she will take the following autumn, changes take place to the identity of her motivational system. Moving out of an ought-to L3 self anchored attractor state – the need to get the credits – the system shifts into a new area of the state space and an attractor state centered around the ideal L3 self. When, in our second interview (January 2012, the day after she has registered her electives for the coming year), I ask about her motivation, she responds in a way that differs considerably from the previous interview:

C: Well…it actually feels quite good. I like French more now than I did before. So it was…
I: When you say 'than I did before' do you mean last term or…?
C: Well, before. Round October there   It feels that…that things have settled a little, that I am not so much behind…so it feels good to start again.

Continuing, she goes on to explain that, irrespective of any additional GPA-enhancing credits that might be available, she has chosen French as her elective for the following year. 'I thought', she says, 'that I needed the extra credits, but actually I don't. But I am going to continue with it'.

When I ask her to elaborate a little on the reasoning behind this decision, Cilla tells how, over the winter break, she discussed the choice of electives at home with her parents. Her mother had surprised her by suggesting that she should perhaps spend some time in France in the summer. As the idea of a study abroad trip to France materialized in her mind, she began, she says, to have second thoughts about dropping French. Although she admits that the prospect of travelling alone and spending time in France feels extremely daunting (she has never spent time away from her family before), it is also exciting.

The decision to continue with French appears to have a perturbing effect on the system, bringing about a phase shift. Like the student in Mercer's (2011) study, for whom a period spent in a target language (TL) country had a major perturbing effect, for Cilla the prospect of a period of study abroad triggers movement across the state space, the system entering into a different area, leading, as a consequence, to the emergence of new behaviours. As Larsen-Freeman and Cameron (2008: 59) point out, downstream from a phase shift emergent behaviour has a recognizable 'wholeness'; it is more than just 'the sum of its parts'. For Cilla, this emergent behaviour not only involves new (or possibly renewed) self-relevant reasons for learning, but also changes in self-perceived competence, in her affective state, and in her approach to in-class activities. Some of the performance anxiety (on tests and in class/group/pair work) she has previously spoken of seems to have dissipated. She is more engaged in learning and, she says, things are easier now, not least because she has come to realize that she is not the only one who has trouble formulating sentences and difficulty with pronunciation. She is also much more engaged, knowing, she says, that she will soon find herself in situations using the language:

> I am in any event more motivated. To start by going over the basics in old notes, so that I've got this with me. And learning so that I have directions and things, going over that stuff again. Ah, I am more motivated to study now ... because I am going there. (Interview 2)

However, as Larsen-Freeman and Cameron (2008: 59) make clear, emergent stabilities of behaviour are themselves contingent, open to further change and surrounded by 'different degrees of variability and flexibility'. A further change in Cilla's motivation – a second phase shift – can be detected already in our next interview (Interview 3, February 2012). It transpires that, rather than travelling to France in the summer and learning French, she is instead thinking of spending time in Scotland, studying English. Her mother, she says, has a friend there. Justifying the possible switch in her plans, she points out that she is in any event going to speak much more English in the future, and that a period of time spent in Scotland would therefore be of greater value. Although it would seem that she has not entirely given up hope of a trip to France – 'there is a chance of maybe going to France' – she nevertheless constructs a rationale that, in the context of our interview at least, helps her to come to terms with this lost opportunity:

I: This text today, it's about a girl who spends a period of time in France. Did you think, 'that could have been me'?

C: But it's about coming to France. She was there a whole year. So you need to be in France quite a long time to be able to.... start ... to understand it

I: And she says in the text that it was hard in the beginning...

C: Yes, exactly. You would need to reckon on being there for a few months. And it's hard to be down there in France for so long

I: You don't think it would have been enough with three weeks?

C: Well, it would give you a little boost but at the same time, well, you don't even have all the basics, and it...with an easier language being there three weeks when you've got all the basics, you can build on that, but now you have to fill in all the many gaps, so I think ... you'd certainly get a better appreciation of the language ... but I don't think there would be a great difference in three weeks.

Having, in our previous interview, given the impression of looking forward to the trip, having a confidence in her abilities and a desire to succeed with

French – 'I want to complete French properly. So that I can get up to a decent level, actually' (Interview 2) – Cilla once again focuses on her shortcomings and 'all the many gaps' (Interview 3).

The next time we meet (Interview 4), as in our initial interview the previous November, Cilla gives expression to a sense of frustration with French. She says she feels she is not making any progress and is uncertain about the grade she is likely to get. She is anxious about participating in the oral interaction work taking place in the class on the day of the interview, and says that, generally, she feels a lack of commitment. Moreover, and unusually for her, she seems easily distracted. In the two lessons I observe that week, she spends periods of time absorbed with her smartphone. When, for example, I ask her how she has experienced the period immediately prior to our interview, she replies:

C: It's been OK. But really you don't do that much. Like first you need to work out what you've got to do, and that was OK, but after that I didn't really know what we were supposed to do, and so then it's easy to lose focus and start doing something else.
I: So what did you do?
C: I had my phone out for a bit and checked out other things in the book. And checked a little, we have presentations in Swedish today so I was checking that too...well...

Unfortunately I did not meet Cilla again that term; on my visits to the class in May she was ill, and by June had already left for her study abroad period (in Scotland). When I met her again in September she was taking beginner level German. Asking her to cast her mind back to the previous term and reflect on her motivation in the final weeks of the French course she says, with laughter in her voice, 'Well, it wasn't high. All I wanted to do was to get it over with. And basically I let it go and just worked with the other subjects. And was just hoping for a pass'. Moreover, just as in our very first interview, she again expresses a sense of regret that, back in the sixth grade of secondary school, she did not chose German.

Attempting to understand the changes taking place to the system during the first few months of the year, it is tempting to conclude that, following the decision to switch location of the study abroad from France to Scotland – the perturbation that triggers the second phase shift – her motivational system reverted to the part of the state space it had occupied prior to the initial phase shift. This, however, would be to oversimplify things. The learning behaviour I observed later in the spring was noticeably different to that back in November. Her level of engagement and commitment seemed to be much lower than was the case prior to the winter break, and she was noticeably more easily distracted than before, indicating that the strength of the system governing the ought-to L3 self attractor state had weakened and that the system had gravitated to a different part of the state space. Some aspects of this new, emergent, behaviour are likely to stem from interactions with the adjacent L2 English motivational system. As a consequence of the process of weighing up summer destinations, the L2 English and L3 French motivational self-systems will have come into close contact and, through the process of co-adaptation, each will have exerted an influence on the other. This can be seen when, reflecting on the fact that she would not be going to France, Cilla explains how 'with an easier language being there three weeks when you've got all the basics, you can build on that'. Contrasting languages in this way, we can see how the L2 system impacts on processes in the L3 system. Specifically, attractor states in the L3 system gradually lose their strength and the system's resistance to external influences decreases.

Methodological Reflections and Conclusions

Using a CDS approach to examine processes of change in motivational systems, it becomes clear how, even in systems that over longer timescales appear relatively stable (for example Jonna and Emil), across shorter timescales considerable fluctuation and variation will take place. Thus, even though certain parameters (for example the GPA-enhancement) and robust attractor states might appear to have determining influences on motivation, in any learning situation there is a need to be alert to system movement and non-enduring periods of instability (such as the entry into and out of repeller states) and the changes in the context that might trigger such movements. As we have seen, momentary shifts in these students' motivation could be brought about by a range of different factors including perceptions relating to the enjoyment/meaningfulness/relevance of a particular activity, the impact of perturbing factors, such as receiving the results of a test, and the constant interaction with other complex systems, here for example comparisons with L2 English.

While in a CDS-inspired study, the importance of taking full account of context as part of the system under investigation (Ushioda, this volume) and the need to be alert to relationships and interactions (between system components, with those of other systems and across different timescales) cannot be understated, this can generate considerable methodological challenges. In trying to identify changes taking place across the shortest timescales, and attempting to relate these to longer-term motivational trends, each interview in the series was preceded by observations of the behaviour and interactions taking place in the classroom. This meant that not only were the students able to reflect on their motivation in relation both to what they had said in previous interviews, as well in the context of the immediately preceding learning activities, but also that it was possible to identify and zoom in on particular events, thus giving the opportunity to uncover possible interactions across the shortest of timescales. This having been said, the study is not without its methodological problems. Reflection on these may offer pointers for future CDS-inspired motivation research employing longitudinal qualitative designs.

(i)   Although providing valuable contextual framing for the interviews and revealing how motivated behaviour differed across both shorter and longer timescales (de Bot, this volume), the observations fall short of the 'thick descriptions' of patterns of behaviour generally characteristic of ethnographic study (Duff, 2008; Dörnyei, 2007). Not only was the amount of time spent in the classroom insufficient to achieve this type of descriptive depth, but attention necessarily shifted between the six individuals. For this reason, in future research using an interview/observation approach, it might be important to limit the number of focal learners in order to make it practicably possible to combine interviewing with finer-grained observations of behaviour and interaction patterns.

(ii) A single-case approach, as for example in Mercer's (2011) study of learner agency, or a study with fewer participants, may offer advantages in allowing for a greater number of interviews. This would make it possible to probe changes in focal constructs in greater depth, especially if interviews and observations were combined with some of the idiodynamic approaches described by MacIntyre (MacIntyre & Legatto, 2011; MacIntyre & Serroul, this volume).

(iii) Another distinct advantage with a single/limited subject design would be that the frequency of interviews/observations could be adjusted to correspond with the degree of observed system variability. Greater flexibility in the spacing of data collection intervals would greatly facilitate a more responsive approach to changes in system trajectories; spread out if the system(s) in focus appear stable, but more tightly spaced if periods of volatility are detected (Larsen-Freeman & Cameron, 2008). Reflecting on the findings of the current study it seems clear that, while the strategy of having a relatively uniform spacing of data collection points might have been adequate to track changes in most of the students' systems, for Cilla, more frequent interviews/observations around the identified phase shifts would have been extremely valuable. This would have enabled a more effective probing of the 'wholeness' of newly emergent behaviours.

(iv) Consideration should be given to the investigation of other relevant complex systems. This is particularly important when a student is learning more than one language simultaneously. While it is possible to identify situations when co-adaptation might take place between related systems and, via interviews and observations, to consider their effects on the target system, unless a similar approach is adopted in relation to the other systems, the ways in which this also changes can only be guessed at. Thus, in terms of the current design, interviewing Cilla about her motivation to learn English and observing her behaviour in English classes on a simultaneous basis could have provided important insights into the ways in which co-adaptation between the L2 and L3 motivational systems might have taken place.

(v)   Finally, in a single/limited subject design involving multiple interviews and observations, ethical issues need to be very carefully considered, not least the question of unreasonably taking up students' time with interviews that may lack personal relevance and benefit. There is a limit to the amount of learning time it is reasonable to expect school-aged students to give up (cf. the teacher education student in Mercer's study), especially those who only have a few hours of class-time per week and for whom the focus of the research might have little salience.

Like many of the studies reported on in other chapters, the current study shows how a CDS approach, because it emphasises time and change (Larsen-Freeman & Cameron, 2008), can shed light on the ways in which, in a language learning task, during a lesson or over a school semester, motivation constantly fluctuates. To be sure, many of the motivational shifts identified here would have surfaced even if the data had been analysed without the benefit of a CDS lens. However, by adopting a complexity approach (Verspoor, this volume), it means that we conceptualize the objects of our enquiry – the classroom, the students and their motivation – as systems that are *by nature* dynamic. And, because dynamic systems are never self-contained and are in constant interaction with the contexts in which they are embedded and with other systems, we become alerted to these interactions in ways that we might not otherwise have been. Sensitivity to these interactions in turn enables us to understand how motivational fluctuations – the system's movement into and out of attractor and repeller states – are triggered, and how the novel behaviours that emerge as a result of changes in the system's trajectory come about. As Ushioda notes, the investigation of motivation using a CDS approach means that we constantly shift our analytical perspective between learner/system-external and learner/system-internal contexts. Echoing Ushioda (this volume), it is as a result of these iterations that we can 'deepen our understanding of the person, her motivation and her behaviour, and the interconnected contextual factors involved'.

Notes

(1)   Other languages can be offered provided the school has the teaching resources and there is sufficient interest.
(2)   In cases where there were more than two students to choose from, I sought advice from the teacher as to which of the students he felt would be most likely to be comfortable being interviewed.

340   Part 2: Empirical Studies

(3) Two of the final interviews, with Cilla and Emil, took place in September 2012 as both students had been absent from class in June.
(4) Jonna is comparing the two motivational profiles she had drawn.
(5) Cilla was absent when the other students were interviewed in June.

References

Bryman, A. (2008) Social Research Methods. Oxford: Oxford University Press.
Cameron, L. and Larsen-Freeman, D. (2007) Complex systems and applied linguistics. International Journal of Applied Linguistics 17 (2), 226–240.
Cenoz, J. and Jessner, U. (2000) English in Europe: The Acquisition of a Third Language. Clevedon: Multilingual Matters.
Csizér, K. and Dörnyei, Z. (2005) Language learners' motivational profiles and their motivated learning behaviour. Language Learning 55, 613–659.
Csizér, K. and Lukács, G. (2010) The comparative analysis of motivation, attitudes and selves: The case of English and German in Hungary. System 38, 1–13.
de Bot, K., Lowie, W. and Verspoor, M. (2007) A dynamic systems theory approach to second language acquisition. Bilingualism: Language and Cognition 10, 7–21.
Dörnyei, Z. (2000) Motivation in action. Towards a process-oriented conceptualisation of student motivation. British Journal of Educational Psychology 70, 519–538.
Dörnyei, Z. (2005) The Psychology of the Language Learner. Mahwah, NJ: Lawrence Erlbaum.
Dörnyei, Z. (2007) Research Methods in Applied Linguistics. Oxford: Oxford University Press.
Dörnyei, Z. (2009a) The Psychology of Second Language Acquisition. Oxford: Oxford University Press.
Dörnyei, Z. (2009b) The L2 motivational self system. In Z. Dörnyei and E. Ushioda (eds) Motivation, Language Identity and the L2 Self (pp. 9–42). Bristol: Multilingual Matters.
Dörnyei, Z. (2014) Researching complex dynamic systems: 'Retrodictive qualitative modelling' in the language classroom. Language Teaching 47 (1), 80–91.
Dörnyei, Z. and Ushioda, E. (2011) Teaching and Researching Motivation (2nd edn). Harlow: Longman.
Dörnyei, Z., Csizér, K. and Németh, N. (2006) Motivation, Language Attitudes and Globalisation: A Hungarian Perspective. Clevedon: Multilingual Matters.
Duff, P.A. (2008) Case Study Research in Applied Linguistics. Mahwah, NJ: Lawrence Erlbaum.
Ellis, N. (2007) Dynamic systems and SLA: The wood and the trees. Bilingualism: Language and Cognition 10, 23–25.
European Commission (2005) A New Framework Strategy for Multilingualism (Report 596). Brussels: Commission of the European Communities.
European Commission (2008) Multilingualism: An Asset for Europe and a Shared Commitment (Report 566). Brussels: Commission of the European Communities.
Gass, S.M. and Mackey, A. (2000) Stimulated Recall Methodology in Second Language Research. Mahwah, NJ: Lawrence Erlbaum.
Hammarberg, B. (2009) Processes in Third Language Acquisition. Edinburgh: Edinburgh University Press.
Henry, A. (2009) Gender differences in compulsory school pupils' L2 self-concepts: A longitudinal study. System 37, 177–193.
Henry, A. (2010) Contexts of possibility in simultaneous language learning: Using the L2 motivational self system to assess the impact of global English. Journal of Multilingual and Multicultural Development 31, 149–162.

Henry, A. (2011) Examining the impact of L2 English on L3 selves: A case study. *International Journal of Multilingualism* 8, 235–255.

Henry, A. (2013) Digital games and ELT: Bridging the authenticity gap. In E. Ushioda (ed.) *International Perspectives on English Language Teaching: Motivation* (pp. 133–155). Houndmills: Palgrave Macmillan.

Henry, A. (2014). The motivational effects of crosslinguistic awareness: Developing third language pedagogies to address the negative impact of the L2 on the L3 self-concept. *Innovation in Language Teaching and Learning* 8, 1–19.

Henry, A. (in press) Rewarding foreign language learning: Effects of the Swedish grade point average enhancement initiative on students' motivation to learn French. *The Language Learning Journal.* DOI: 10.1080/09571736.2013.853823.

Herdina, P. and Jessner, U. (2002) *A Dynamic Model of Multilingualism: Changing the Psycholinguistic Perspective.* Clevedon: Multilingual Matters.

Howe, M.L. and Lewis, M.D. (2005) The importance of dynamic systems approaches for understanding development. *Developmental Review* 25, 247–251.

Jessner, U. (2006) *Linguistic Awareness in Multilinguals.* Edinburgh: Edinburgh University Press.

Jessner, U. (2008) A DST model of multilingualism and the role of metalinguistic awareness. *Modern Language Journal* 92, 270–283.

Kvale, S. (1996) *An Introduction to Qualitative Research Interviewing.* Thousand Oaks, CA: Sage.

Larsen-Freeman, D. (2011) A complexity theory approach to second language development/acquisition. In D. Atkinson (ed.) *Alternative Approaches to Second Language Acquisition* (pp. 48–72). New York: Routledge.

Larsen-Freeman, D. and Cameron, L. (2008) *Complex Systems and Applied Linguistics.* Oxford: Oxford University Press.

Lasagabaster, D. and Huguet, A. (eds) (2007) *Multilingualism in European bilingual contexts: Language use and attitudes.* Clevedon: Multilingual Matters.

MacIntyre, P.D. (2012) Currents and waves: Examining willingness to communicate on multiple timescales. *Contact* 38, 12–22.

MacIntyre, P.D. (2013) The dynamics of sexual relationship development. In R.S. Stewart (ed.) *Talk About Sex: A Multidisciplinary Discussion* (pp. 67–83). Sydney, NS: CBU Press.

MacIntyre, P.D. and Legatto, J.J. (2011) A dynamic system approach to willingness to communicate: Developing an idiodynamic method to capture rapidly changing affect. *Applied Linguistics* 32, 149–171.

Markus, H.R. and Nurius, P. (1986) Possible selves. *American Psychologist* 41, 954–969.

Mercer, S. (2011) Understanding learner agency as a complex dynamic system. *System* 39, 427–436.

Nowak, A., Vallacher, R. and Zochowski, M. (2005) The emergence of personality: Dynamic foundations of individual variation. *Developmental Review* 25, 351–385.

Ricoeur, P. (1970) *Freud and Philosophy.* New Haven, CT: Yale University Press.

Olsson, E. (2011) *Everything I Read on the Internet is in English: On the Impact of Extramural English on Swedish 16-year-old Pupils' Writing Proficiency.* Gothenburg: Gothenburg University Press.

Oyserman, D. (2007) Social identity and self-regulation. In A.W. Kruglanski and E.T. Higgins (eds) *Social Psychology: Handbook of Basic Principles* (2nd edn). New York: Guildford Press.

Smith, J.A. and Eatough, V. (2007) Interpretive phenomenological analysis. In E. Lyons and A. Coyle (eds) *Analysing Qualitative Data in Psychology* (pp. 35–50). London: Sage.

Smith, J.A. and Osborn, M. (2003) Interpretive phenomenological analysis. In J.A. Smith (ed.) *Qualitative Psychology. A Practical Guide to Research Methods* (pp. 51–80). London: Sage.

Swedish Government (2006) *Vägar till Högskolan för Kunskap och Kvalitet.* [Paths to university for knowledge and quality] 2006/07:107.

Sundqvist, P. (2009) *Extramural English Matters: Out-of-school English and its Impact on Swedish Ninth Graders' Oral Proficiency and Vocabulary.* Karlstad: Karlstad University Studies.

Sylvén, L.K. and Sundqvist, P. (2012) Similarities between playing World of Warcraft and CLIL. *Apples – Journal of Applied Language Studies* 6, 113–130.

Ushioda, E. (1996) Developing a dynamic concept of motivation. In T. Hickey and J. Williams (eds) *Language, Education and Society in a Changing World* (pp. 239–245). Clevedon: Multilingual Matters.

Ushioda, E. (2006) Language motivation in a reconfigured Europe: Access, identity, autonomy. *Journal of Multilingual and Multicultural Development* 27, 148–161.

20 Study Abroad and the Dynamics of Change in Learner L2 Self-Concept

Kay Irie and Stephen Ryan

The origins of this chapter lie in our ongoing attempts as classroom teachers to make sense of some of the great changes we frequently observe in those learners who venture abroad to study a language. We often hear comments from teachers, and we have probably made similar comments ourselves, about how certain students appear to come back from a period of study abroad 'a completely different person'. Our primary aim here is to unpack this observation in a way that may help us to integrate the idea of 'abroad' more effectively into the home classroom.

We began this research with what we considered to be a single-mindedly 'practical', atheoretical outlook. We were both probably at a stage in our careers where we felt an urge to get back to our classroom roots and our initial attitude was that we were, above all, language teachers looking for practical solutions to concrete problems, and that we had neither the time nor the inclination to deal with the finer points of academic theory. However, as we started writing this chapter we became increasingly aware of an inadvertent subplot running through our narrative, one concerned with how teachers relate to academic theory. The story of how we became oriented towards a complexity perspective is one that we feel illustrates some of the misgivings, misunderstandings and missed opportunities that occur when theory and practice fail to engage with each other, and also some of the possibilities when the two are in harmony.

Study Abroad and Learner Motivation

There is a widespread, popular belief (Freed, 1995, 1998) that study abroad remains the most effective way to learn, or 'pick up', a language and this belief is especially pronounced in language learning contexts where learners have little or no opportunity for contact with second language (L2) speakers (Yashima, 2013). In such contexts, 'abroad' can loom as an invisible presence in the home language classroom. 'Abroad' can motivate students and it may also de-motivate them; it can authenticate learning, and it can (de)legitimise language use. For some students, the prospect of going abroad may give focus to or energise their language learning, making it seem more meaningful; while other learners who have never been abroad, or see little prospect of ever doing so, may feel insecure about their own language use, that it is somehow deficient in comparison with those who have acquired 'real' language in a natural setting (Ryan & Mercer, 2011). Experience of language use abroad, or a lack of it, can represent a significant part of individuals' L2 self-concept, how they regard themselves as language learners/ users and how they approach learning.

The primary focus of much research into study abroad experiences has been, unsurprisingly, on the various gains in competence made by learners (for example, Barron, 2006; Segalowitz & Freed, 2004). Other interesting areas of inquiry have been changes in learners' identity construction during study abroad (Benson et al., 2013; Jackson, 2006, 2008) and in their beliefs about the nature of language learning (Amuzie & Winke, 2009). Though something of a simplification, a common approach throughout much of this research has been to look at learners prior to departure in comparison with how they are at the end of the period of study abroad. In this chapter, we prefer to see learners' ideas about themselves in respect to going abroad, both their anticipation and their subsequent processing of the experience, as part of a continuous process of change within the L2 self-concept, an ongoing internal narrative that is constantly being revised and retold. We take the view that the study abroad experience does not begin in the minds of learners at the airport departure gate, nor does it cease to inform the self concept of those learners once they have returned through the arrivals lobby. Preparing to study abroad, even merely considering the possibility, affects how they see themselves and how they approach learning before they go away, and in a similar fashion, the experience of study abroad can also have profound effects on how these learners then approach learning upon their return. A further vital consideration for teachers is that the behaviour and experiences of learners who go abroad can also have an impact on those around them.

Complex Dynamic Systems Theory and Messy, Unpredictable Practice

We would like to reflect upon why we turned to a complex dynamic systems perspective in our attempt to understand study abroad experiences. The various discussions we had before finally deciding to adopt this approach highlight some of the issues facing teachers when confronted with complex, dynamic descriptions of learning and learners, both some of the reservations they may have about such an approach and some of its attractions. Our interest in this chapter is not so much with complex dynamic systems theory itself (see the chapters in the first section of this volume for insightful discussions of key concepts), but with exploring its links to classroom practice and practitioners.

Much of the impetus for this research came from a perceived need to explore processes of change, rather than identifying or describing specific states or outcomes, and, looking back, a complex dynamic systems perspective seems an obvious approach for such a research project. However, this was not immediately apparent to us. Of course we were aware of the growing interest (see de Bot *et al.*, 2005; Larsen-Freeman, 2011; Larsen-Freeman & Cameron, 2008) in applying complexity perspectives to applied linguistics, but, certainly in the initial stages of our research design, this was something that we regarded, however intriguing, as separate from our everyday classroom concerns. As classroom teachers, our interest was more with pragmatic solutions than theoretical purity and our earliest encounters with complex dynamics systems theory suggested more of the latter than the former. We would describe ourselves at the outset of this research as reluctant passengers on the 'complexity bandwagon' (Mercer, 2011), but we believe that this 'reluctance' is worthy of some consideration as it appears to flag up some key issues about the role of theory and research in the professional lives of teachers (Johnson, 1996).

It was only really when we reverted into our academic researcher roles that the relevance of a complexity perspective became apparent. Of course, in an ideal world the 'classroom teacher' and the 'academic researcher' would share similar concerns and outlooks, but the fact that this gap existed between our respective perspectives as teachers and researchers is indicative of a failure on both sides to engage with each other. Our initial wariness towards a complex dynamics systems approach suggests that the merits of such an approach are not immediately clear to practising teachers and that it is incumbent upon researchers and theorists to make a more attractive, compelling case to classroom practitioners.

Teachers, much like people in other professional fields, are persuaded by accounts that both resonate with their own experience and hold out the promise of helping them perform more effectively. Accounts of human behaviour vary in the degree to which they either attempt to be comprehensive or tend towards reductionism (Dörnyei & Ushioda, 2011). Reductionist accounts, which are usually based around a limited number of static concepts, can be attractive to teachers in that they offer simplicity and clarity; they offer the promise of clearly identifiable solutions. On the other hand, accounts that aim at comprehensiveness can be unwieldy and such accounts can at times appear unhelpful or even intimidating to teachers. It was this 'unhelpful' aspect that was a common theme running through our early conversations with teachers about complex dynamic systems and language education. In a discussion of the role of complex dynamic systems within applied linguistics, de Bot *et al.* (2005) employ the memorable phrase 'the ultimate so what' to warn against expecting too much too soon from dynamic systems theory and this phrase neatly captures some of our own initial reservations about adopting a complex dynamics systems approach. In this case, our 'so what' comes from teachers who already know all too well that learners and learning are complex, dynamic and unpredictable; teachers may well feel somewhat underwhelmed by accounts that emphasise complexity and unpredictability, as they often turn to research in search of order and ways in which to make their working environments more predictable. Our biggest reservation concerned the practical value of a complex dynamic systems approach: does it really have anything to offer practising teachers beyond a new set of terminology?

Our interest in complex dynamic systems originates more than anything in our frustration with other approaches to theory and research, approaches that fail to capture the whole picture of the learning experience and seem to deny the reality of our experiences as teachers. Our own early encounters with second language acquisition (SLA) theory as practising teachers had left us acutely aware that neat, linear theoretical models can seem irrelevant amidst the reality of messy, unpredictable classrooms. Since learners and their learning rarely fit smoothly into linear, causal models, the disparity between theory and classroom practice can cause teachers to question the relevance of that theory. It was our own experiences of feeling alienated from established theoretical models, and hearing other teachers express similar views, that persuaded us that a theoretical framework which allows for unpredictability and complexity may be one that actually resonates with teachers.

Our own position as authors of this chapter provides a timely reminder of how very little within language teaching and research is neatly ordered. It would be very convenient for us at this point in the chapter if we could build a straw man in the form of competing and conflicting interests between teachers and researchers. However, this would be misleading, perhaps even slightly dishonest, as we are, like so many involved with L2 education research, simultaneously teachers and researchers. When wearing our teachers' hats, our principal interest is in research with immediate, practical value; however, as researchers our prime concern is not always with the direct classroom application of our findings. This inherent tension between a desire for theoretical integrity and the need for practical relevance is one of the things that makes applied linguistics a simultaneously frustrating and fascinating discipline. In the current study, our approach was guided by two core guidelines. First, we wanted our research to have an uncompromisingly practical focus and not to lose sight of our original goal of exploring change in learners' L2 self-concepts with the aim of integrating study abroad more effectively into the home classroom. Furthermore, we wanted to present our findings in a way that other teachers may abstract from and apply to their own teaching situations, to 'go beyond a merely descriptive analysis of the particular research sample' (Dörnyei, 2014: 9). Our goal was to make our research, very much grounded in a specific context, relevant to others outside that immediate context, without falling into the trap of oversimplification and reductionism.

Researching the complex and the dynamic

A further factor behind our initial reluctance to embrace a complex dynamic systems perspective was a feeling of helplessness when confronted with the realities of actually researching something that is, by definition, complex and in a constant state of flux. For many of us, this represents a fundamental challenge to our researcher's 'instincts'. Those instincts, or perhaps it would be more accurate to say 'training', encourage us to isolate, to freeze in time, to look at how individual parts affect a system, rather than deal with that system as a whole. In many ways, it feels like we are entering relatively uncharted waters. This sense of entering unknown territory was reinforced through contact with a growing body of literature, and attending numerous conference presentations, in which the potential of a complex dynamic systems approach was described in exciting terms, but almost inevitably qualified with a sheepish admission of a lack of adequate means to empirically research any of these stimulating ideas. This state of affairs is neatly summed up by Pigott's (2013: 362) observation that complexity theory represents 'a new-fangled tool that nobody really understands how to use yet'.

The first real concrete proposal of how to apply a complex dynamic systems perspective to SLA research that we were aware of, was Dörnyei's Retrodictive Qualitative Modelling (RQM) approach (Dörnyei, 2014; Chan *et al.*, this volume) and this formed a rough template for our early research design. At the same time, we were also reading about the potential of Q methodology as a systematic means of investigating individual subjectivity. Our solution was to combine the two and employ the essential RQM template using Q methods to identify typical dynamic outcome patterns. For the analysis of these patterns, we then turned to the interpretative side of Q in order to explore what these patterns may be contingent upon.

Q is a research methodology with origins in early 20th-century psychology. The initial appeal of Q, for us, was that it offered the prospect of integrating qualitative elements, such as interviews and the interpretation of narratives, within a rigorous quantitative framework, in the form of an inverted factor analysis procedure. Our experience as researchers had taught us that these qualitative elements were necessary to investigate subjective notions, such as viewpoints and beliefs, but that attempts to obtain qualitative data required a principled, systematic basis.

The theory underpinning Q methodology is a fascinating area for discussion, but not really the concern of this chapter. Instead, we provide a brief sketch of some of the basic principles and techniques associated with Q in Appendix 20.1. Readers interested in learning more about this approach are advised to consult the dedicated literature, such as Brown (1980) or Watts and Stenner (2012) for a detailed discussion and visit the website (http://qmethod.org) hosted by the International Society for the Scientific Study of Subjectivity (ISSSS).

The Study

Participants

A total of 19 Japanese university students (14 female, 5 male, age 19–22), who participated in various study-abroad language programmes through their university in Tokyo, voluntarily took part in our longitudinal study. Their majors were English and American literature (11), Economics (5) and one student each majoring in Marketing, Information Science and European History. The host countries of the programmes included Australia, New Zealand, the United States, Ireland and Germany. The length of stay varied from five months to one year, depending on the individual programmes.

Instrument

In order to create a set of statements (Q set), we drew upon ideas from the literature and established questionnaires that have been used in previous L2 motivation and other related research (i.e. MacIntyre et al., 2009; Rivers, 2012; Ryan, 2009; Taguchi et al., 2009; Yashima et al., 2004). The selection of items is crucial in any Q study and it is fair to say that this was an area that caused much soul-searching in the early stages of our research design. In this study, we were working with an unfamiliar methodology within a new theoretical approach, and as a consequence we decided that we needed the reassurance and security of links with established L2 motivation research and this strongly influenced our decision to work with items used in previous research. Looking back, a bolder approach would have been to make a clean break with previous L2 motivation research and to have generated original Q statements from our pilot interviews with learners.

Since our interests were principally with the role study abroad plays in the motivation to learn a language and in the development of learner self-concept, our selection of items was heavily biased towards research within the L2 motivational self (Dörnyei, 2005, 2009) framework. We initially generated 127 statements and then reduced this item pool, mainly through piloting, to a set of 50, eliminating overlaps and redundancy. Each of the 50 statements in the Q set was printed on a card in both English and Japanese. The whole set of cards was then to be sorted by the participants. We chose an 11-point (–5 to +5) distribution (see Figure 20.1 in Appendix A20.1) as recommended for Q sets numbering 40–60 items (Brown, 1980; Watts & Stenner, 2012). The relatively flattened distribution was expected to help the participants to make discriminations among the statements and contribute to the identification of distinctive viewpoints (Watts & Stenner, 2012). A total of 20 students sorted the 50 cards as part of the first round of sorts in March 2012 (Time 1), immediately before their departure. One student was unable to participate in the second round (Time 2), which occurred in late November/early December 2012. The absence of this student at Time 2 meant that we had to discard her sort from Time 1, so we were working with a total of 19 participants across both rounds.

The students were first asked to roughly sort the 50 cards into three piles: statements they generally agree with, do not agree with or feel relatively neutral about. Then they were asked to rank the statements and place them following the numbers for each score ranging from –5 to +5 based on the condition of instruction for the study: *How descriptive is this statement about your view of L2 learning and L2 use?* For Time 2, the same procedure was repeated employing an online version of the instrument created by the software, FlashQ (Hackert & Braehler, 2007).

Results

The two sets of 19 sorts (Time 1 and 2) were independently intercorrelated and analysed according to the principles of Q's inverted factor analysis, using the dedicated software PQ Method 2.20 (Schmolck, 2011). For Time 1, seven factors were extracted and rotated through centroid varimax rotation, which together explained 63% of the variance. Since all the students significantly loaded (± 0.44, $p < 0.05$) on to one factor and this factor alone accounted for 45% of the variance, a one-factor solution was chosen.

For Time 2, seven factors were again extracted and rotated, which together explained 62% of the variance. This time a three-factor solution was chosen, using the guideline of an eigenvalue above 1.00. These three factors together accounted for 14 of the 19 sorts, 55% of the variance. Eight sorts significantly loaded on Factor 1, two on Factor 2 and another two on Factor 3 (± 0.44, $p < 0.05$). The sorts that significantly load on to a factor are considered to be exemplars of that factor.

In order to facilitate the interpretation of the factors, the next step is to produce what are known as factor arrays. A factor array can be considered as an exemplary Q sort for a particular factor; in other words the most typical or representative distribution of responses for that factor. The factor arrays for the four factors we discuss in this study are shown in Table 20.1. What we see in this table is the ranking assigned to each statement in the exemplary sorts. Thus, if we look at Statement 1, we see that the exemplary sort for Factor 1 at Time 1 would have given this statement a ranking of +2, as would the exemplary sort for Factor 1 at Time 2; but when we look at Factors 2 and 3 at Time 2, we see that Statement 1 would be given a ranking of –2. The figures in bold are the highest (+5 and +4) and lowest (–5 and –4) rankings that would be assigned to each of the statements and these statements can be considered as the most characteristic statements for the view represented by each factor. These are the statements that form the core of our interpretation of each factor.

Of course, all the individuals significantly loading on to a factor do not have exactly the same set of responses. Some exemplars have a higher factor loading than others, and this is how the factor array is calculated. Exemplars with the higher factor loading are given more weight, therefore, their contributions to the averaging process differ accordingly (for details of weighted average, see Brown, 1980: 241–242, or Watts & Stenner, 2012: 132–133). The factor array is produced when the re-calculated or averaged ranking scores are aligned and replaced with the scores used in the original Q sort activity, in this case from –5 to +5. The factor array provides us with an indication of how an individual typical of a particular factor is likely to have responded, and this then serves as the basis for our subsequent qualitative interpretation.

Interpreting the data: Understanding the individuals

It is at the next stage where Q really starts to become exciting. Conventional factor analysis works by focusing on the relationships among variables rather than the individuals who are measured on these variables. In contrast, Q looks at the correlations among individuals, not items, allowing us to analyse the data without breaking up each individual's pattern of responses. The numerical data are then used, with the support of interview data, to develop a narrative account of a particular subjective viewpoint. In effect, we are composing a holistic picture of recognisable human beings, yet doing so in a principled and systematic fashion.

In this next section, we will offer our interpretation of what we observed within this particular group of learners. We will restrict our illustration of each viewpoint to six definitive statements, the three statements that the learners felt were most applicable (+) to them and the three that were considered least applicable (–). For a more complete picture, readers are encouraged to refer back to Table 20.1.

Table 20.1 Factor arrays

	Statement	Time 1 Factor 1	Time2 Factor 1	Time2 Factor 2	Time2 Factor 3
1	I would like to try living in a foreign country in the future.	2	2	-2	-2
2	Whenever I think of my future career, I imagine myself being able to use English.	2	-1	0	-1
3	I will be able to use English effectively in the future.	1	-5	1	0
4	I can imagine speaking English comfortably with foreign friends in the future.	1	-2	1	0
5	I want to play an active role in a globalised society.	5	0	0	-1
6	I would like to be able to express my opinions in English.	4	-4	2	-2
7	I want to be respected because I speak English fluently.	2	-1	4	0
8	I've wanted to speak English fluently since I was very young.	-1	0	-2	-1
9	English will expand my possibilities in the future.	3	-1	1	-3
10	If I could speak English I would be a much cooler person.	0	-3	2	-3
11	I must learn English in order to become an educated person.	-1	-5	0	0
12	Learning English is necessary because it is an international language.	0	3	0	1
13	I am expected to be able to function in English after I graduate.	0	1	-1	4
14	In order to get a good job I will need to be able to use English well.	0	3	-4	1
15	I need to be fluent in English to do the job I want to do.	2	-1	-4	-3
16	I study English to enjoy travel abroad.	-1	0	0	-3
17	I will feel happy spending a lot of time studying English.	0	2	1	-1
18	My goal is to be able to speak English like a native speaker.	3	2	1	2

(Continued)

Table 20.1 (continued)

Statement	Time 1 Factor 1	Time2 Factor 1	Time2 Factor 2	Time2 Factor 3
19	I will continue studying English after university.	3	-4	0	0
20	I enjoy encountering new ideas in my English study.	3	-4	4	-1
21	I have an English learner role model.	-1	-2	-4	-5
22	Becoming fluent in English is one of the most important things in my life right now.	5	0	1	-2
23	To be honest, I have no idea why I'm learning English.	-5	4	-1	5
24	I like learning languages in general not only English.	1	-2	1	-1
25	I am a proactive English learner.	1	-3	0	2
26	I regularly study English in my own time.	1	-2	2	-1
27	I enjoy films or TV programmes in English.	2	4	2	3
28	I enjoy reading newspapers, magazines or websites in English.	0	0	-1	1
29	Interacting with foreign people in English is fun for me.	4	-1	4	2
30	I like myself when I'm speaking English.	1	1	2	1
31	I feel comfortable in the casual style of communication in English.	-1	-3	5	-2
32	I feel like I'm a different person when I speak English.	-2	1	-5	3

33	I feel good when speaking English.	1	-3	3	-3
34	I am appreciated by my family because I speak English.	-1	1	-2	0
35	People around me are not interested in the progress of my English learning.	-2	0	-2	0
36	Some of my family or friends may feel let down if I fail to learn English well.	-3	1	-1	5
37	I have close friends that speak English as an L2.	-1	0	3	4
38	People around me don't understand how important learning English is for me.	-4	1	-3	-5
39	I think I'm naturally quite good at learning languages.	-2	-1	-1	1
40	I'm too shy to speak English well.	-2	3	-2	0
41	I don't have the right personality for learning English.	-3	5	-1	1
42	No matter how hard I try, I don't think I'll ever be able to master English.	-5	4	-5	3
43	I'm just not smart enough to learn English well.	-4	3	-2	4
44	If I make more effort, I am sure I will be able to master English.	4	1	3	-4
45	For people around me learning English doesn't really matter that much.	-3	5	3	-4
46	Speaking English is a part of my everyday life.	-2	2	-3	1
47	I have friends I communicate with in English.	-3	0	5	2
48	I'm the only person I know who is serious about learning English.	-4	2	-4	3
49	These days I feel like English is at the centre of my everyday life.	0	-1	-1	2
50	I don't have opportunities to use English in my everyday life.	0	-2	-3	-4

Time 1

Immediately prior to departure we found a clearly dominant shared viewpoint among the 19 learners, which we refer to as the *naive optimist* (Table 20.2).

The *naive optimist* is an individual full of purpose and belief. S/he appears gung-ho yet perhaps a little unrealistic about what lies ahead. Language learning success appears to be assured. In the process of successfully learning a language, this individual is also going to become a better person and have had fun doing so. Immediately prior to departure, feelings of hope and anticipation about the upcoming adventure appear to override all feelings of uncertainty or anxiety.

Time 2

The second Q sort was conducted roughly six months after the initial sort. This means that the learners had spent around five months overseas and we found that the original dominant viewpoint had diverged considerably. Here we focus on the three most salient viewpoints. We refer to them as *the shell-shocked doubter* (Table 20.3), *the comfortable user* (Table 20.4) and *the duty-bound learner* (Table 20.5).

This *shell-shocked doubter* learner appears to have been hit very hard by the realities of the study abroad experience. The initial optimism and enthusiasm have completely disappeared, being replaced by something close to despair about ever being able to learn the language successfully. It is interesting to note that in trying to make sense of the study abroad experience, the *shell-shocked doubter* looks to aspects of their basic personality for explanations, something that may be considered fixed and outside their locus of control. This accentuates the overall picture of helplessness and the feeling that this is somebody very close to giving up altogether.

Table 20.2 The naive optimist

Definitive statements (+)	Becoming fluent in English is one of the most important things in my life.
	I want to play an active role in a globalized society.
	Interacting with foreign people in English is fun for me.
Definitive statements (−)	I'm the only person I know who is serious about learning English.
	To be honest, I have no idea why I'm learning English.
	No matter how hard I try, I don't think I'll ever be able to master English.

This *comfortable user* appears to be having an altogether more productive experience. This person seems to be realising all the dreams of the *naive optimist,* comfortable and at ease with language learning and use. The learner has made friends and enjoys communicating with them in the L2. S/he still believes in the possibility of achieving a high level of proficiency and appears to feel secure as both a learner and user of English. In many ways, this appears to represent the ideal study abroad experience.

Table 20.3 The shell-shocked doubter

Definitive statements (+)	I don't have the right personality for learning English.
	For people around me learning English doesn't really matter.
	No matter how hard I try, I don't think I'll ever be able to master English.
Definitive statements (−)	I will continue studying English after university.
	I must learn English in order to become an educated person.
	I will be able to use English effectively in the future.

Table 20.4 The comfortable user

Definitive statements (+)	I have friends I communicate with in English.
	I feel comfortable in the casual style of communication in English.
	I enjoy encountering new ideas in my English study.
Definitive statements (−)	I have an English learner role model.
	No matter how hard I try, I don't think I'll ever be able to master English.
	I feel like I'm a different person when I speak English.

Table 20.5 The duty-bound learner

Definitive statements (+)	To be honest, I have no idea why I'm learning English.
	Some of my family or friends may feel let down if I fail to learn English well.
	I'm just not smart enough to learn English well.
Definitive statements (−)	If I make more effort, I am sure I will be able to master English.
	People around me don't understand how important learning English is for me.
	I have an English learner role model.

The *duty-bound learner* is clearly struggling with the study abroad experience, but has not reached the same levels of despair we observe in the *shell-shocked doubter*. We employ the term 'duty-*bound*' to allude to both how this learner feels tied down or restricted by feelings of obligation to learn and is also 'bound' as in a sense of direction coming from those feelings of obligation. This is somebody who has not given up on learning in the same way as the *shell-shocked doubter* has, but seems to have lost belief and purpose. For this learner, those initial feelings of optimism and enthusiasm seem to have been replaced by an almost grim determination not to give up, perhaps for fear of letting others down. This person feels under pressure to deliver but is not sure why or how.

Discussion

How can we interpret these changes and, more to the point, how can we interpret them in a way that will help us integrate study abroad programmes more effectively into our classrooms? The first point for us to consider is what makes this approach any different from a conventional longitudinal study. The key distinction is one of focus, in that our interest here is not so much in starting points or eventual outcomes; we are more concerned with what occurs between and how this may help us understand what is occurring in our classrooms. Our interest is primarily in movement and momentum, by understanding the possible trajectories of learners we are better equipped to facilitate their 'soft landing' back into the home classroom.

So how do the various learner types we have identified contribute to an understanding of movement and trajectory? Perhaps we need to qualify any claims we make in this chapter with the reminder that here we only report on data collected at the first two stages of the study abroad experience. At this stage of the research, we think of the picture we provide as a simple outline sketch, still lacking colour and shade. Our hope is that data from subsequent Q sorts at later stages of that study abroad experience will provide a more detailed, nuanced picture, one that more fully captures its volatility and vitality. Nevertheless, we still believe that the picture emerging is one containing enough recognisable shapes to form the basis for a discussion of how learner self-concept changes during study abroad.

In order to illustrate, we will concentrate our discussion on perhaps the most dramatic and important change we observed; the shift from *naive optimist* to *shell-shocked doubter*. We were not too surprised to find that all our learners shared a keen sense of anticipation at the prospect of the impending study abroad experience. This seems normal for young people about to embark on such a momentous event in their lives – it should be borne in mind that for many of these learners it was their first time overseas and their first extended period away from home – and this sense of anticipation appears to exert a powerful organising force on the L2 self system. Using the language of dynamic systems theory, this anticipation functions as a powerful attractor, governing a system that is now in a highly stable attractor state. However, the very act of going abroad removes that sense of anticipation, the attractor, the organising force, shifting the system into an unpredictable, volatile state. While in this volatile state, the system may gravitate towards other attractors as it tries to re-establish some form of equilibrium, and it may do so in a wild and turbulent fashion or it may change at a much slower, gradual rate. In response to the shock of the reality of the study abroad experience – it is probably safe to assume that things have not gone smoothly for this individual and they have probably struggled both in and out of the classroom – various domains of the self-concept, such as academic self-concept, social self-concept and even personality, are being reconsidered and realigned. The analogy we would use here is that of a bungee jump; a bungee jumper does not immediately come to rest after the initial jump, but is thrown in all directions for a while, sometimes dramatically, suddenly and unpredictably. We cannot accurately predict where the jumper will be at any particular point in time after that initial fall, but we can make reasonable assessments as to some of the most likely directions of travel and know that they will eventually come to rest. In the case of the *shell-shocked doubter*, we witness an L2 self-concept based around notions that language learning effort is futile since success is unattainable and this is most likely a function of fundamental personality traits that the individual regards as fixed or unmodifiable. It seems difficult to conceive of a more negative motivational profile. We should emphasise here that we are not implying any cause–effect relationship between the *naive optimist* state and the *shell-shocked doubter*. What we are saying is that the *shell-shocked doubter* attractor state exists and some learners may come under its influence for a very short time, others for much longer, some learners may settle here in a long-term stable attractor state, while others may avoid it altogether.

If we turn our attention to a very different trajectory, the case of the shift from *naive optimist* to *comfortable user* also raises interesting questions. A teacher's initial reaction to encountering such an individual may be to view this as an outright success story – and in many respects it is – and to assume that all will be well with this particular learner. However, a complex dynamic systems perspective requires us to think of the interactions between the individual and context, and in this case the maintenance of the *comfortable user* state may be highly dependent on support from the study abroad environment, upon friends made abroad, upon feelings of achievement in the overseas educational context or a sense of satisfaction from regular use of the target language in a naturalistic setting. What happens if these contextual supports are removed when the individual returns to the home classroom? The simple answer to this question is that we do not know, since a complexity perspective also teaches us that human behaviour is neither entirely predictable nor linear. Although we may not know for sure what will happen when this individual returns, it is still very helpful to have some idea of the trajectory path this learner is on. Understanding something of this trajectory allows teachers to make contingencies, to prepare for possible outcomes. Obviously, the more detail we have and the more we understand about a particular individual's journey, the more prepared we can be.

Although our study only deals with the study abroad experience, it may be that we observe similar patterns of change surrounding other critical events in the language learning experience, such as a key test, a crucial presentation or important social event, where the target language is used. When the anticipation of an event plays a key organisational role in a system and that anticipation is removed, then the system is thrown into a state of volatility and is seeking to regain stability. We have always known that such events can exert a powerful motivational force in initiating effort, but our understanding of how learners sustain efforts and approach learning beyond these events has been less clear. From a motivational perspective, an awareness of how learners re-organise themselves after the removal of anticipation is important as it helps us understand how individuals sustain motivation, how they approach learning beyond these key events.

Pedagogic Applications

We began by stressing the practical focus of our research and we will end by considering some of the ways our findings may be applied to the classroom. These preliminary findings indicate that perhaps the most pressing need is for those involved in designing study abroad programmes to pay greater attention to the management of expectations and goal-setting strategies of learners going to study abroad, perhaps at the pre-departure preparation stage. This may be particularly timely in view of the trend towards shorter study abroad programmes (McMurtrie, 2007); the number of people studying abroad is rising, but the length of time they are spending overseas is getting shorter. In shorter programmes, learners may find themselves returning home at the very point where those feelings of 'shellshock' are at their most intense. The attendant danger is that these feelings of 'shellshock', of negativity and helplessness, may come to play a prominent role in the future development of the L2 self-concept. As learners arrive back in their home classrooms, they are taking measures to re-adapt to this familiar environment, re-assessing where they stand in relation to the people around them, such as classmates and teachers, asking themselves who they are as language learners. In cases where learners return to their home classrooms with feelings of negativity or helplessness from their study abroad experience, these feelings may come to form the basis of how they see themselves as learners in the home classroom too. In the language of complex dynamics systems theory, the system may once again attain a stable condition based around these attractors associated with their perceptions of failure abroad.

There is also a further risk that well-intentioned teachers may exacerbate this situation. In attempting to provide positive feedback to learners return-ing from abroad, teachers may, in fact, be reinforcing those feelings of failure and disappointment. Teachers may need to take greater care with how they communicate their own expectations of learners returning from a period of study abroad.

In other cases, learners may return from abroad triumphant and filled with an empowering sense of achievement, yet much of that sense of achieve-ment may be reliant upon supports available only in the study abroad context. When those supports are no longer available, as they may not be in the home classroom, the system may shift into a volatile state seeking other attractors around which to re-organise. At a classroom level, this could manifest itself in learners who feel frustrated or disenchanted with the home classroom and constantly look back to the study abroad experience. If teachers regard learn-ers and learning as being linear, then they are likely to expect that learners returning after a highly successful study abroad experience will go on to even greater achievements. However, a complex dynamic systems perspective warns us against such simplistic expectations and reminds us of the need to remain aware of the constant interactions between learners and the learning context and how these interactions affect approaches to learning.

For us, the clearest pedagogic implication of this research is that teachers need to consider the integration of the study abroad experience and the home classroom in terms of trajectories and contingencies, not expected or normal outcomes. None of us can accurately predict what may happen to any indi-vidual student when they go abroad, or when they return; there are just too many variables to consider. It is not helpful to think of the study abroad experience in terms of a linear development, that a successful study abroad experience results in tangible gains in L2 proficiency. Instead we need to develop our awareness of possible trajectories and our ability to identify where individual learners may lie on a particular trajectory. Once we can do this, we may be able to design the necessary pedagogic interventions that encourage learners towards more adaptive approaches to language learning.

Conclusion

We began this research as, if not exactly 'complexity sceptics', then certainly guarded in our welcome, yet we conclude this chapter as cautious optimists. Our initial 'so what' attitude has shifted in the direction of 'what if'. What if a complexity perspective offers insights not possible in conventional, linear frameworks? What if a complexity perspective allows us the opportunity to develop a theory of language learning based on patterns and contingencies rather than cause and effect, a theory that prac-tising teachers may find more accessible since it acknowledges the realities of their teaching situations?

Applied linguistics as a discipline is at its most productive when theory and practice are in step, when theory both informs and is informed by prac-tice. It is least effective when theory and research are charging off in one direction with practitioners running away in another. In our view, the extent to which the potential of a complex dynamic systems perspective can be realised is greatly dependent upon the degree to which the theory and prac-tice manage to talk to each other. This does not mean that researchers need to 'talk down' or simplify matters for the benefit of teachers; we simply mean that researchers need to remain aware of the concerns of teachers when conducting and communicating their research. In the early stages of this research, we certainly had our doubts about the relevance of a complex dynamic systems approach to teachers looking to understand actual issues occurring in their classrooms, and some of those doubts still linger. However, our own tentative first steps into a complexity perspective suggest an exci-ting and rewarding journey ahead.

References

Amuzie, G.L. and Winke, P. (2009) Changes in language learning beliefs as a result of study abroad. *System* 37 (3), 366–370.

Barron, A. (2006) Learning to say 'You' in German: The acquisition of sociolinguistic competence in a study abroad context. In M.A. DuFon and E. Churchill (eds) *Language Learners in Study Abroad Contexts* (pp. 59–88). Clevedon: Multilingual Matters.

Benson, P., Barkhuizen, G., Bodycott, P. and Brown, J. (2013) *Second Language Identity in Narratives of Study Abroad*. Basingstoke: Palgrave Macmillan.

Brown, S.R. (1980) *Political Subjectivity: Applications of Q Methodology in Political Science*. New Haven, CT: Yale University Press.

Cooker, L. and Nix, M. (2010) On Q: An appropriate methodology for researching auton-omy? (Part 1). *Learning Learning* 17 (2), 24–30.

Cooker, L. and Nix, M. (2011) On Q: An appropriate methodology for researching auton-omy? (Part 2). *Learning Learning* 18 (1), 31–38.

de Bot, K., Verspoor, M. and Lowie, W. (2005) Dynamic systems theory and applied linguistics: the ultimate 'so what'? *International Journal of Applied Linguistics* 15 (1), 116–118.

Dörnyei, Z. (2005) *The Psychology of the Language Learner*. Mahwah, NJ: Lawrence Erlbaum.

Dörnyei, Z. (2009) The L2 motivational self system. In Z. Dörnyei and E. Ushioda (eds) *Motivation, Language Identity and the L2 Self* (pp. 9–42). Bristol: Multilingual Matters.

Dörnyei, Z. (2014) Researching complex dynamic systems: 'Retrodictive qualitative mod-elling' in the language classroom. *Language Teaching* 47 (1), 80–91.

Dörnyei, Z. and Ushioda, E. (2011) *Teaching and Researching Motivation* (2nd edn). Harlow: Longman.

Freed, B.F. (1995) Language learning and study abroad. In B.F. Freed (ed.) *Second Language Acquisition in a Study Abroad Context* (pp. 3–33). Amsterdam: John Benjamins.

Freed, B.F. (1998) An overview of research in language learning in a study abroad setting. *Frontiers, The Interdisciplinary Journal of Study Abroad* 4, 31–60.

Hackert, C. and Braehler, G. (2007) *FlashQ*. See http://www.hackert.biz/flashq (accessed 19 September 2012).

Irie, K. (2013) Q methodology: A scientifically holistic approach to the study of language learning psychology. *The Bulletin of Foreign Language Center, Tokai University* 33, 1–13.

Jackson, J. (2006) Ethnographic pedagogy and evaluation in short-term study abroad. In M. Byram and A. Feng (eds) *Living and Studying Abroad: Research and Practice* (pp. 134–156). Clevedon: Multilingual Matters.

Jackson, J. (2008) *Language, Identity and Study Abroad: Sociocultural Perspectives*. London: Equinox Publishing.

Johnson, K.E. (1996) The role of theory in L2 teacher education. *TESOL Quarterly* 30 (4), 765–771.

Johnson, R. and Wichern, D. (2007) *Applied Multivariate Statistical Analysis* (6th edn). Upper Saddle River: Pearson Prentice Hall.

Larsen-Freeman, D. (2011) A complexity theory approach to second language development/acquisition. In D. Atkinson (ed.) *Alternative Approaches to Second Language Acquisition* (pp. 48–72). New York: Routledge.

Larsen-Freeman, D. and Cameron, L. (2008) *Complex Systems and Applied Linguistics*. Oxford: OUP.

MacIntyre, P., Mackinnon, S. and Clément, R. (2009) Toward the development of a scale to assess possible selves as a source of language learning motivation. In Z. Dörnyei and E. Ushioda (eds) *Motivation, Language Identity and the L2 Self* (pp. 193–214). Bristol: Multilingual Matters.

McMurtrie, B. (2007) Study-abroad numbers continue to climb, trips are shorter, report says. *The Chronicle of Higher Education* 54 (12). http://chronicle.com/weekly/v54/i12/12a03601.htm (accessed 8 May 2013).

Mercer, S. (2011) The self as a complex dynamic system. *Studies in Second Language Learning and Teaching* 1 (1), 57–82.

Pemberton, R. and Cooker, L. (2012) Self-directed learning: Concepts, practice, and a novel research methodology. In S. Mercer, S. Ryan and M. Williams (eds) *Psychology for Language Learning: Insights from Research, Theory, and Practice* (pp. 305–327). Basingstoke: Palgrave Macmillan.

Pigott, J. (2013). A call for a multifaceted approach to language learning motivation research: Combining complexity, humanistic, and critical perspectives. *Studies in Second Language Learning and Teaching* 2 (3), 349–366.

Rivers, D.J. (2012) Modeling the perceived value of compulsory English language education in undergraduate non-language majors of Japanese nationality. *Journal of Multilingual and Multicultural Development* 33 (3), 251–267.

Ryan, S. (2009) Self and identity in L2 motivation in Japan: The ideal L2 self and Japanese learners of English. In Z. Dörnyei and E. Ushioda (eds) *Motivation, Language Identity and the L2 Self* (pp. 120–43). Bristol: Multilingual Matters.

Ryan, S. and Irie, K. (2014) Imagined and possible self perspectives: Stories we tell ourselves about ourselves. In S. Mercer and M. Williams (eds) *Multiple Perspectives on the Self in SLA* (pp. 109–126). Bristol: Multilingual Matters.

Ryan, S. and Mercer, S. (2011) Natural talent, natural acquisition and abroad: learner attributions of agency in language learning. In G. Murray, X. Gao and T. Lamb (eds) *Identity, Motivation and Autonomy in Language Learning* (pp. 160–176). Bristol: Multilingual Matters.

Segalowitz, N. and Freed, B.F. (2004) Context, contact, and cognition in oral fluency acquisition: Learning Spanish at home and study abroad contexts. *Studies in Second Language Acquisition* 26 (2), 173–199.

Schmolck, P. (2011) *PQMethod*, computer software. See http://schmolck.userweb.mwn.de/qmethod/index.htm (accessed 25 January 2012).

Taguchi, T., Magid, M. and Papi, M. (2009) In Z. Dörnyei and E. Ushioda (eds) *Motivation, Language Identity and the L2 Self* (pp. 120–43). Bristol: Multilingual Matters.
Watts, S. and Stenner, P. (2005) Doing Q methodology: theory, method and interpretation. *Qualitative Research in Psychology* 2(1), 67–91.
Watts, S. and Stenner, P. (2007) Q methodology: The inverted factor technique. *The Irish Journal of Psychology* 28 (1–2), 63–76.
Watts, S. and Stenner, P. (2012) *Doing Q Methodological Research: Theory, Method and Interpretation.* London: SAGE.
Yashima, T. (2013) Individuality, imagination and community in a globalizing world: An Asian EFL perspective. In P. Benson and L. Cooker (eds) *The Applied Linguistic Individual: Sociocultural Approaches to Identity, Agency and Autonomy* (pp. 46–58). Sheffield: Equinox Publishing.
Yashima, T., Zenuk-Nishide, L. and Shimizu, K. (2004) The influence of attitudes and affect on willingness to communicate and second language communication. *Language Learning* 54, 119–152.

Appendix 20.1

General overview of Q methodology

Q methodology is a mixed-methods package of philosophy, concepts, data collection, statistical analysis and data interpretation used to identify and categorise the subjective viewpoints of a group of people in a specific context. It is a methodology that is being increasingly employed in various fields in the social sciences and humanities as it offers the advantages of both quantitative and qualitative research. It has only recently begun to attract attention within applied linguistics (Cooker & Nix, 2010; Cooker & Nix, 2011; Irie, 2013; Pemberton & Cooker, 2012; Ryan & Irie, 2014). Our purpose here is to outline the principal characteristics of Q methodology to guide beginners through their first encounters with Q and answer some questions that readers may have regarding the methodology used in the study described in this chapter. It is not intended to be a manual; researchers looking to carry out their own Q study really do need to consult the relevant literature.

Q methodology was originally developed by a British psychologist, William Stephenson, in the 1930s, in reaction to the conventional factor analysis technique, which was at that time forming the basis of the psychometric tradition of individual differences research (Brown, 1980). Stephenson's concern was that the use of factor analysis offers only general information about how a particular group of tests or variables have displayed a similar pattern of variation in a given population, therefore, failing to provide the absolute characteristics or views of individuals (Watts & Stenner, 2007: 65). According to Stephenson (cited in Watts & Stenner, 2007), even factor loadings of individuals do not give a holistic picture of any individual, as they only represent the differences entered into a factor and the responses that individuals gave are pulled apart and aggregated together with the responses of all the other people in the sample.

How does, then, Q methodology treat participants' opinions and views statistically but holistically? Typically, Q studies involve a group of participants sorting a sample of statements (Q set) into a configuration that expresses the degree of personal agreement with the statements. This step is referred to as a Q sort. Q sorts from a number of participants, or sorts from the same participant, are statistically analysed to generate factors, each of which identifies a highly inter-correlated group of Q sorts, a shared point-of-view on the topic addressed by the statements. This procedure is called *inverted factor analysis,* as Stephenson originally proposed to flip the columns and rows of the correlation matrix used in conventional factor analysis: scores of a single variable or an item in a column to a full set of responses given by a single person in a column. While conventional factor analysis is based on test-by-test (or variable-by-variable) correlations to identify a smaller number of latent variables, the inverted factor analysis in Q methodology is based on person-by-person correlations, allowing the researchers to observe associations between people's views encapsulated in each Q sort. Each factor, representing a shared view held by some participants, can be then studied and narrated through careful interpretation of the exemplary ranking of the all items. The process of interpretation is akin to that of other qualitative research methods, such as ethnography or narrative studies (Watts & Stenner, 2005).

Many readers may be reminded of cluster analysis, as this is also used to identify the grouping of people using quantified responses to the statements provided by researchers. Q methodology and cluster analysis are similar on one level in that they both make no assumptions regarding the number of groups or the membership of those groups a priori. Since cluster analysis is an umbrella term that covers a variety of grouping techniques, such as hierarchical and non-hierarchical clusters, based on some measure of similarity, including correlation coefficients (Johnson & Wichern, 2007), it is difficult, almost pointless, to make statistical comparisons between Q methodology and cluster analysis. On another level, they are quite different procedures and this reflects the purpose of research. The most fundamental difference between the two approaches is the kinds of grouping they do. The aim of cluster analysis is to identify the grouping of items or people based on the similarities between the measurements of variables preselected by the researchers. Therefore, in cluster analysis, groups and their structure are predetermined by the researcher. For example, in marketing, cluster analysis is often used to identify segments or groups among the users of a certain product, or within a target market, by gathering demographic information such as income, geographical location or gender, as well as attitudinal or behavioural data. For example, a hotel may be interested in finding out more about its guests and ask those guests to fill out a questionnaire, perhaps asking about the reason for choosing the hotel, the length and purpose of the stay, facilities used and a rating for those facilities and services. Since the researchers are explicitly looking for information about these categories, the groupings that they find are very much a function of the questions that they are asking. Contrary to this, a Q study does not impose such restrictions; the researcher does not make these fundamental assumptions about the views or behaviour of participants. Instead, in a Q study, participants are simply asked to sort a diverse set of statements relating to a particular topic; referring back to the hotel case, this set could be developed from comments typically made by hotel guests. The statements should be as diverse as possible in order to allow participants the freedom to express their own subjective views and opinions. In this respect, Q methodology requires participants' active engagement with the task, as it only after the statements have been sorted that the various viewpoints emerge.

If we continue with the example of the hotel, a conventional study would look at, for example, data pertaining to use of the hotel restaurant in isolation, what kind of people are using the restaurant, how often and when, and the same process may be adopted to find out about the use of other facilities, such as, say, the fitness centre. In a Q study, we do not look at the use of these various facilities separately; in a Q study the approach taken is to look at the person as a whole, to look at the person who enjoys spending time in the hotel restaurant as being the same person with no interest at all in using the fitness facilities. The rankings of statements in a Q study tell stories that are almost infinite and the data, statistical analysis and interpretation ensure a holistic picture of distinctive perspectives held by the individuals.

Procedures

There are five stages that are integral to a sound Q study: (1) defining a research question; (2) developing a Q set; (3) administrating Q sorts; (4) carrying out statistical analysis; (5) interpreting the results.

Defining a research question

In Q methodology, *condition of instruction* refers to the question or instruction given to the participants to evaluate the statements that express their view on a certain topic and this should correspond to the research question. Q methodological research questions are usually (a) identification of representative viewpoints in the culture, community or society; (b) understanding personal meanings of a thing or issue; and (c) discovering opinions about an issue (e.g. what should be done about something) (Watts & Stenner, 2012). In the study described in this chapter, we defined our condition of instruction to be *'How descriptive is this statement about your view of L2 learning and L2 use?'*, as our goal was to trace the change in their L2 self, how learners perceived L2 learning and use in relation to themselves.

Developing a Q set

Once the question is set, the next stage is to gather statements. Since the purpose of the questionnaire in most survey-based quantitative studies is to obtain measurements, it is important to collect similar items to increase the reliability of the construct. However, the purpose of a Q set is to have a broad enough range of value-free statements for participants to express their views so that prototype views are identified (Watts & Stenner, 2012: 64–65). These statements can be compiled from interviewing the target group of individuals, consulting with experts and the literature, as well as previously created Q sets. For example, in the study described in this chapter, we used items taken from various questionnaires used in previous L2 motivation studies and other language learning psychology literature.

Administrating Q sorts

The Q sort is an item/card-sorting task by ranking the statements according to the condition of instruction, by placing the items along a continuum ranging between two extremes (i.e. most descriptive to least descriptive) in the form of a quasi-normal distribution grid (see Figure A20.1). In order to gain further information to facilitate the interpretation of the statistical analysis in the next stage, many Q practitioners interview the participants after the task by asking them to reflect on the sort and the topic.

Carrying out statistical analysis

The statistical analysis of the data collected through Q sorts is an inverted factor analysis usually carried out through the use of dedicated

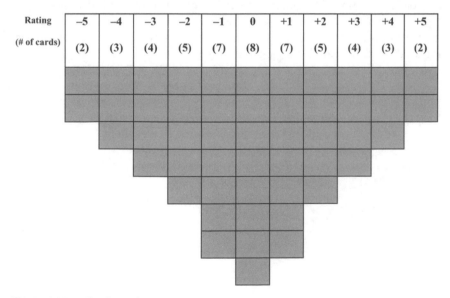

Rating (# of cards)	−5 (2)	−4 (3)	−3 (4)	−2 (5)	−1 (7)	0 (8)	+1 (7)	+2 (5)	+3 (4)	+4 (3)	+5 (2)

Figure A20.1 Fixed quasi-normal distribution used for the 50-card sorts

software (e.g. PCQ, www.pcqsoft.com; PQMethod, www.rz.unibw-munchen.de/~p41bsmk/qmethod). In an inverted factor analysis, groupings are based on the ranking of all items in relation to one another, not the similarity of independent responses to each item, which is usually the case for Likert-scale-type questionnaires. Therefore, the extracted factors represent groups of people who share similar viewpoints. People load on factors, not items. Once factors are extracted and rotated appropriately, *factor arrays* are prepared for interpretation, in which Q sorts loaded on a factor are merged to form a single ideal-typical Q sort (see Table 20.1).

Interpreting the results

A summary table of factor arrays, such as Table 20.1, sketches out the configurations of statements for the factors extracted. The items with both the highest and lowest scores serve as the basis for a description of the subjective view represented by that factor, along with all the other statements. The outlined viewpoint must be fleshed out by the researchers by looking at the statistically structured factor array and using other sources of information, including demographic and interview data. This final process of interpretation and development of narrative accounts is what characterises Q methodology as a qualitative research method.

In short, Q methodology is an approach to explore subjective views of any topic that allows for a range of different points of view. Its methodological design ensures the expression of individual subjectivity and the statistical rigour on which the narrative construction can be grounded. The methodology marks a clear departure from the currently dominant quantitative approaches in applied linguistics, particularly in the area of individual differences. It is an attractive alternative that can respond to the call for more situated studies to capture the uniqueness and specifics of the minds of learners rather than universality and generalisability.

21 Self-Regulation in the Evolution of the Ideal L2 Self: A Complex Dynamic Systems Approach to the L2 Motivational Self System

Ryo Nitta and Kyoko Baba

Research on second language (L2) motivation at the beginning of the 21st century has been dominated by an influential model proposed by Dörnyei (2005, 2009a), the L2 Motivational Self System (see e.g. chapters in Apple *et al.*, 2013; Dörnyei & Ushioda, 2009; Murray *et al.*, 2011). This comprehensive model is comprised of the *ideal L2 self*, the *ought-to L2 self* and *L2 learning experience*, and offers a reinterpretation and extension of the former dominant dichotomy in the field, *integrative and instrumental orientation/motivation* (Gardner & Lambert, 1972). A number of empirical studies have tested and validated the important role played by the ideal L2 self in influencing learners' motivation and behaviours within various learning contexts (e.g. Csizér & Kormos, 2009; Ryan, 2009; Taguchi *et al.*, 2009).

Another important recent theoretical development in the area has been the introduction of a complex dynamic systems approach to researching L2 motivation (e.g. Dörnyei, 2009b, 2009c, 2014; Dörnyei & Ushioda, 2011; MacIntyre & Legatto, 2011). A complex dynamic system refers to a system consisting of many interacting components, with the micro-level interaction between the components changing their properties and creating properties on a macroscopic level over time (van Geert, 2011). As a consequence of dynamic interactions between various microscopic components (e.g. the teacher, peer students, textbooks and tasks) students' motivation on a macroscopic level within the English as a foreign language (EFL) classroom context may emerge, change and vary in elaboration.

Despite the emerging importance of views on complex dynamic systems, only a limited number of empirical studies have so far researched L2 motivation from this perspective (see e.g. Nitta, 2013). Most studies on the L2 Motivational Self System have investigated the linear relationships between the three components and certain criterion measures, and have paid little attention to how the ideal L2 self and L2 learning experience influence each other. The third component of the construct, the L2 learning experience, has in previous research been conceptualised in rather abstract and generalised terms, and more specific and systematic approaches are needed. Research on *task motivation* (e.g. Dörnyei, 2002) or investigations into motivational and self-regulatory processes at a task-specific level can shed important light on this issue, and the present study has been designed with this in mind. A complex dynamic systems approach not only allows us to investigate both macro- and micro-levels, but also to integrate these different levels of L2 motivation.

This chapter is aimed at tackling this overarching question from a complex dynamic systems theory approach, with a broad aim of discovering 'how such self images [ideal L2 selves] develop and evolve in interaction with the complex constellations of internal and contextual processes shaping engagement in learning, represented as a third component (L2 learning experience) in the L2 Motivational Self System' (Ushioda & Dörnyei, 2012: 401). We investigated how the ideal L2 self in an EFL classroom develops through repeated engagements in language learning tasks over one year by adopting self-regulation as a construct for characterising L2 learning experience. From analysing changes in students' self-regulation and L2 writing, we found that the ideal L2 self evolves co-adaptively with the development of micro-level functioning of self-regulation.

Research Background

A micro-perspective on L2 motivation

In his theorisation of the L2 Motivational Self System, Dörnyei (2009a) argues that when one envisions an ideal L2 self, this self-image is tangible and represented with the same imagery and semantics as the here-and-now self. This representation of a future ideal image influences one's motivation and behaviours by enhancing the desire to reduce discrepancies between the actual self and the projected behavioural standards of the ideal self (Higgins, 1987). While much previous research tended to test and validate the motivational roles of the ideal L2 self on L2 learning, it is also important to pay attention to the functions of the projected standards of the ideal L2 self and to explore the interaction between the ideal L2 self and everyday learning experience. That is, learners could monitor and reflect on their own performance and self-evaluate how much they had changed from the past self, and how far they had moved towards achieving the ideal future self by referring to such standards offered by the ideal self image. More importantly, it has been argued that the continuous functioning of such *self-regulatory* processes are necessary to maintain one's motivation in everyday learning environments over sustained periods of learning (Dörnyei & Ottó, 1998). Dörnyei and his colleagues (e.g. Dörnyei, 2002; Dörnyei & Kormos, 2000; Dörnyei & Tseng, 2009) assumed in a series of studies on task motivation that the motivational dynamics of learning tasks is influenced by how learners execute their performance (task execution), how they perceive the motivational stimuli (task appraisals) and how they activate necessary strategies (action control).

Task execution refers to the learners' engagement in task-based learning according to an action plan that has been provided either by the teacher or a task designer (Dörnyei & Tseng, 2009). Because this is an initial condition for any L2 processing to take place (Dörnyei, 2002), task execution is a central issue in instructed second language acquisition (SLA), as has been researched in the area of task-based language teaching (e.g. van den Branden *et al.*, 2009).

Various self-regulatory processes come into play while engaging in tasks, involving the learners' own strategic efforts to manage their own achievements through specific processes (Zimmerman & Rinsenberg, 1997). *Task appraisal* refers to learners' continuous processing of the multitude of stimuli arriving from the environment concerning their progress towards achieving the action outcome, and their comparing the actual performance with the predicted or likely performance (Dörnyei & Tseng, 2009). There have been various attempts in educational psychology to account for how appraisals function in the learning process. For example, Boekaerts and Niemivirta (2000) claimed that appraisals (either primary or secondary) were key indicators of intra-individual responsiveness to learning situations. Primary appraisal refers to learners' emotional reactions to the situation and the personal significance of the present learning is estimated in terms of their wellbeing. On the other hand, secondary appraisal refers to the learner's mental representation of the objective characteristics of a learning situation; here the prerequisites for dealing with the situation and how learners handle a task under present conditions are in focus (Boekaerts, 1996). For example, students may engage in tasks not only because performance is in itself enjoyable (i.e. primary appraisal), but also because they recognise that the present activities will lead to improvements in their L2 skills (i.e. secondary appraisal). Thus, primary appraisal usually occurs as a natural response to the learning situation, whereas secondary appraisal plays a greater part in learning by encouraging learners to connect the task at hand to their specific learning goals.

Action control, involving learners' conscious efforts to regulate their own learning, needs to operate for effective performance and learning in response to their appraisals of the on-going performance. Wolters (2003) claims that students need to react with deliberate and purposeful attempts to influence their level of task motivation by setting purposeful goals as part of their overall *motivational self-regulation*. He found, for example, that college students faced with difficult tasks indicated that they would break them down and make them more manageable to sustain their efforts at completing them (Wolters, 1998).

Although such task-specific regulatory processes are assumed to take place within the performance of a task, they could also be extended to longer periods of classroom learning. In the self-regulation literature (e.g. Zimmerman, 1998) the learning sequence is represented in an open-ended cyclical model of the forethought, performance and self-reflection phases. The forethought phase concerns processes and beliefs preceding efforts to learn, followed by the performance phase that concerns processes that occur during performance; the self-reflection phase involves processes that occur after the performance phase and they influence forethought after subsequent learning opportunities. In line with the construct of task motivation, one's task execution in the performance phase is self-observed and self-evaluated in the self-reflection phase. Thereafter, specific learning goals are set in the following forethought phase, before executing tasks in the performance phase. These processes are cyclically repeated and continue to influence the subsequent phases during the course of learning.

Towards the integration of the ideal L2 self and task-specific motivation

Micro-level motivational processes are likely to influence the formation and evolution of the ideal L2 self in the self-regulation cycle from one task to another. When learners recognise that what they engage in will lead to their future ideal self, this sense of connectedness might provide a virtuous cycle of learning; that is, engaging actively in the immediate task is likely to increase the perceived possibility of achieving the ideal L2 self, and this self-efficacy may promote the elaboration and specifications of their future possible selves (cf. also Dörnyei *et al.*, Chapter 10, this volume). Elaborating the ideal L2 self is one important condition for motivational capacity (Dörnyei, 2009a), because vague, general possible selves lacking behavioural strategies neither provide a specific picture of one's goals, nor a roadmap of how to reduce discrepancies between present and future possible selves (Oyserman *et al.*, 2004). A series of *proximal* learning goals needs to be established in the immediate learning in this respect with a view to pursuing the ideal L2 self. According to Oyserman and James (2009), learning needs to be linked to outcomes in the future for distal possible selves to matter via proximal goals, because these proximal goals can serve as evidence that progress is being made and as key indicators that help learners to decide whether their current effort is sufficient or needs to be increased, or whether their overall plans of action need to be revised for the distal ideal goal to be attained.

The ideal L2 self thus needs to be integrated into the system of self-determined goals using students' own reference norms (Miller & Brickman, 2004), through setting and revising their own proximal learning goals and evaluating their own learning in relation to these standards. Rheinberg *et al.* (2000) reported that students who were encouraged to estimate the probability of success based on their own reference norms, rather than on social reference norms, were more likely to use activity-related incentives in a learning situation. Goals set by the students themselves, rather than those set by a teacher or task designer, were more likely to increase their task engagement (Lock & Latham, 2002). That is, students need to transform a task provided by a teacher into a series of self-set learning goals, which will eventually lead to their achieving a realisation of their ideal L2 self.

Complex dynamic systems approach to researching L2 motivation

Although research on the ideal L2 self and on micro-level, task-specific, motivation has developed along different lines, adopting a complex dynamic systems perspective to viewing L2 motivation may cause them to coalesce, in that this perspective focuses both on the interaction between macro- and micro-level components (van Geert, 2011). While most previous research on the L2 Motivational Self System has focused on the ideal L2 self from a macro-perspective using a variable-centred approach, using a complex dynamic systems approach, the present study was aimed at exploring how the ideal L2 self and task-specific motivation dynamically interact or *co-adapt*.

The relationship between the ideal L2 self and task-specific motivation can be considered co-adaptive within the framework of the L2 Motivational Self System. Co-adaptation refers to 'the interaction of two or more complex systems, each changing in response to the other' (Larsen-Freeman & Cameron, 2008a: 67). In other words, it describes 'a kind of mutual causality in which change in one system leads to change in another system connected to it, and this mutual influencing continues over time' (Larsen-Freeman & Cameron, 2008b: 202). Co-adaptive phenomena are widely observed in various situations; for example, when a child in a child–caregiver conversation does not respond verbally, the caregiver is likely to interpret the child's non-verbal behaviour and continues the conversation accordingly, leading thus to an iterative process with each adjusting to the other over and over again (Larsen-Freeman & Cameron, 2008a). Furthermore, not only does co-adaptation occur between individual organisms, but also *within* the organism (Oyama *et al.*, 2001); for example, cancer cells in the human body may mutate or multiply in response to *perturbations* such as those that result from surgery or taking anticancer drugs. Similarly, the ideal L2 self and self-regulation processes are co-adaptive in a sense that the ideal L2 self functions as an evaluative standard for self-regulation, while self-regulatory processes influence the formation and revision of the ideal L2 self.

A complex dynamic system, as suggested by the co-adaptive process, also involves the *iterative* character of the process (van Geert, 2009). Repeated operations take the result of the preceding iteration as input for the next one and produce a result that again serves as input for yet other iterations (van Geert *et al.*, 2011). More importantly, such iterative and cyclical patterns take place on interdependent timescales. That is, processes on short-term (or micro-development) and long-term (or macro-development) timescales influence processes on the other timescales (de Bot, this volume; Lewis, 2005; Thelen & Smith, 1994). For example, teacher–student conversation is regarded as being co-adaptive as each response constructs a feedback loop between the participants (Larsen-Freeman & Cameron, 2008a). The short-term timescale of classroom talk in such situations will affect a student's long-term L2 learning, whereas his/her current L2 level will determine certain limitations on the kind of L2 performance that can be retained (van Geert *et al.*, 2011). Understanding macro-development through reiterated micro-developmental sequences is important in EFL classroom contexts where instruction is regularly provided (usually weekly). That is, the relation of one lesson to the next is iterative and cyclical with the next, including the effect of the preceding one to some extent (van Geert *et al.*, 2011).

Another important dimension of the perspective on complex dynamic systems is its emphasis on individual cases rather than groups of learners (see Nitta & Baba, in press, who investigated a group of students by regarding a class as a system). Past research on individual differences has typically focused, not so much on differences between individuals, as on averages or aggregates that group people together who share certain characteristics; in doing so, it has foregrounded the group's central tendency that may not be true of any particular person in the participant sample (Dörnyei, 2009b; Larsen-Freeman, 2006; Ushioda, 2009). When, though, our focus is on an individual person as an organised whole, we cannot expect generalised findings to explain the complex multiplicity of internal, situational and temporal factors that may impinge on individual motivation (Dörnyei & Ushioda, 2011).

Detailed analysis of changes in individual learners within contexts has been suggested as one promising direction for research on complex dynamic systems. Dörnyei (2009b) emphasised the significance of individual level variations in the characteristics and contextual circumstances of the learner. This would be in accordance with what Ushioda (2009) calls a *person-in-context relational view of motivation*, emphasising the importance of an evolving network of relations among relevant features, phenomena and processes, and of viewing motivation as an organic process that emerges through this complex system of interrelations (cf. also Mercer, Chapter 8, this volume; Ushioda, this volume). Citing studies by Richards (2006) and Legenhausen (1999), Ushioda (2009) suggests that data drawn from students who 'speak as themselves' provide valuable evidence to illustrate emergent motivation from the complex relations between a person and his/her context. Ushioda (2009) claims in connection with the notion of possible selves that the person-in-context relational view of motivation may, through micro-level analysis of relevant discourse data, facilitate or constrain students' engagement with future possible selves.

In our own research, we have explored patterns in the development of L2 writing fluency over one year (Baba & Nitta, 2014) by using a case-based method taken from a perspective of complex dynamic systems (Byrne & Ragin, 2009). We identified discontinuous changes, called *phase transitions*, in two EFL learners using various analyses of multi-level data. Although both students (with similar L2 proficiencies) experienced phase transitions during the year, they followed unique developmental paths under the same learning conditions. The findings confirmed the effectiveness of the case-based method for exploring various patterns of changes in the L2 system and elaborating what was happening at different points in time in each developmental pattern.

Building on relevant research in the areas of educational psychology and L2 motivation, as well as applications of a case-based methodology, the present longitudinal study was aimed at investigating how the ideal L2 self evolved over one year in interaction with language learning tasks. Two main research questions guided our investigation:

- What self-regulatory processes do students equipped with an ideal L2 self employ over one year through language learning tasks?
- How do the ideal L2 self, task execution and self-regulation in individual students interact in an EFL classroom over one year?

Methods

Setting

The data were collected from first year Japanese university students in an EFL class ($n = 26$) for one academic year (two semesters and 30 weeks in total). The class was taught by the first author for both semesters. Students in the class were exposed to various oral and written tasks in order to develop their English skills. The present project was conducted as part of this task-based learning course. Students were given an informed consent form on the first day of the class and all of them agreed to participate in the present research project.

Participants

For the purpose of the current study we selected two students from the class group, Aki and Chika (both female; pseudonyms), based on the amount and degree of change in their task engagement (see below). They shared a similar educational background: six years of formal English education and no experience of living abroad before they began classes at the university. All the students in the class took a TOEIC (Test of English for International Communication) test at the beginning and end of the academic year. The class average scores were 414.42 at the beginning and 476.73 at the end. The scores for Aki were 505 (beginning) and 555 (end), and those for Chika were 395 (beginning) and 415 (end); thus, they were placed towards the two contrasting ends of the overall distribution curve.

Tasks and procedures

Tasks should be challenging and meaningful to promote learners' self-regulatory processes so that learners view their motivation as emanating from within themselves and view themselves as agents in regulating it (Ushioda, 2006). The specific activities and conditions in our study were devised to incorporate these motivational conditions. The tasks involved timed writing, in which students wrote a composition in English on a topic of their choice for 10 minutes. They were given a list of three different topics each time. For example, they could choose from: (1) *What is your favourite game or sport and explain why you enjoy it*; (2) *What foreign country would you like to visit, and why would you like to go there?* and (3) *What is your main purpose in studying at this university?* The aim of offering three alternatives was to compensate for differences in the students' individual experiences and preferences. We tried to select writing topics that were personal and required little background knowledge. The same list of three writing topics was used for two weeks, and the students were told to write on the same chosen topic twice. Then, a new topic list was presented to them the following week.

After the students had finished writing their compositions, they were asked to count the number of produced words that they had written and to record this. They then filled out a reflection sheet in Japanese immediately. We assumed that these opportunities for recording word counts and reflecting on their writing were likely to encourage self-regulatory processes. There were three sections on the reflection sheet: (1) comments on that day's composition; (2) comments comparing that day's composition with previous compositions and (3) goals for future writing. There were four subsections in the first section, (a) grammar and vocabulary; (b) organisation and expression; (c) content and (d) writing processes and strategies, and the students wrote about how they had performed in terms of each aspect. It usually took about 10 minutes for the students to complete the reflection sheet.

The instructor wrote some encouraging comments on all the compositions and returned them the following week (after the students had finished writing their new compositions). Because the aim of the feedback was to create a sense of audience and to maintain students' motivation to write every week, errors were not corrected. At the end of the academic year, the instructor interviewed some of the students who had volunteered to participate in the study. Interviewed students were asked how they thought their writing had improved, what goals they had in performing the tasks and what long-term future goals (or the ideal self) they had. The interviews were conducted in Japanese, and all the interview excerpts in this chapter were translated into English by the authors.

Analysis

Although group-level analysis is useful in finding general trends in a population, the present study adopted a case-based method (Byrne & Ragin, 2009) that analysed intra-individual variability. We examined the students' L2 compositions (i.e. timed writing tasks) and L1 reflective writing to understand changes in the students' use of self-regulation and their ideal L2 self. First, we analysed students' reflections written in Japanese to understand how proactively students were engaged in the tasks and what self-regulatory processes they employed. The number of Japanese characters used in these reflections constituted a quantitative index of the degree of the students' *task engagement* or proactive attitudes towards the task. This section was written in their L1, so language problems did not hinder their writing, and because the writing task was provided at the end of each class, students were allowed to leave when they had finished writing their reflections. Some students concentrated on writing their reflections right up to the end of the 90-minute class, while others seemed to try to finish them earlier. Thus, the amount they wrote was likely to indicate the extent to which they engaged with the tasks. Because this measure was obtained each time, it was also expected to reflect changes in the degree of engagement over the year. While some students displayed relatively similar amounts of reflective writing throughout the year, others changed the degree of engagement more drastically at some point in time.

The two participants in our study were selected on the basis of their task engagement indices. Aki demonstrated high levels of task engagement throughout the year; her average task engagement (measured by the total number of Japanese characters, divided by the number of task occasions) placed her second highest of all the students in the class, and she was rated as having the highest value for task engagement among the interviewed students. The second participant, Chika, was chosen because she manifested a clear change in task engagement during the observation period. Changes in students' task engagement values were identified through change point analysis (Steenbeek et al., 2012), which identifies points at which sudden changes occur in time series data. The actual calculations were carried out using specialist computer software (Taylor, 2000) by setting a 95% confidence interval with 10,000 bootstraps without replacement (see Baba & Nitta, 2014, for details on how to identify phase transitions using change point analysis). The change point in Chika's trajectory at Week 17 (Figure 21.1) was highlighted by the program as the most salient change in all the trajectories in the class group. While Chika was not interviewed (because we had not examined the collected data at the time of the interviews and had not determined which students we would choose for analysis), all interviewed students displayed high values in task engagement. Thus, we decided to present Aki as a representative case.

We coded the reflections according to three key self-regulatory processes to analyse the qualitative aspects of L1 reflections: goal-setting, self-observation and self-evaluation. Of the three sections on the reflection sheet (see *Tasks and procedures* above), goal-setting was coded from the third section (i.e. goals for future writing), whereas self-observation and self-evaluation were coded from the first two sections (i.e. comments on that day's composition and comments comparing that day's composition with previous compositions). Self-observation in the present analysis concerned students' impressionistic descriptions of their thoughts or actions, often containing somewhat superficial descriptions of their own writing. On the other hand, self-evaluation required evaluative comments that involved several cognitive processes, such as specifying, reasoning, analysing or comparing reflections. Table 21.1 presents and illustrates the main categories, broken down to further subcategories, that were generated through repeated reading of reflections.

Changes in the linguistic aspects of L2 writing were measured in terms of fluency (number of words per composition), syntactic complexity (average sentence length) and lexical complexity (the measure of textual lexical diversity; McCarthy & Jarvis, 2010), all of which are indicative of the quality of task execution. The trajectories of the three measures were plotted in altitude lines graphs (van Geert & van Dijk, 2002; see the Results section) for the whole class, thus enabling observation of the selected two students' progression relative the other students' performance.

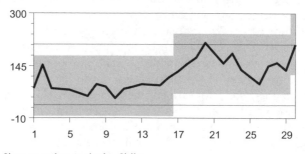

Figure 21.1 Change point analysis: Chika

Table 21.1 Identified self-regulatory processes

Self-regulatory processes	Examples
Self-observation	
1. Language	'I couldn't use simple vocabulary.'
2. Content	'The topic was relatively easy for writing.'
3. Composition processes	'I focused on writing well without stopping.'
4. Overall quality	'I finished writing that was worse than the last time.'
5. Effort	'I made an effort to increase the word count.'
Self-evaluation	
1. Language	'I tried to include expressions regarding relative nouns, but I couldn't manage to do it.'
2. Content	'I thought I couldn't explain reasons in my previous writing due to the structure of sentences, so I wrote my composition this time with the aim of making readers clearly understand my reasons.'
3. Composition processes	'Because I exhausted my topic sooner than the last composition, I jumped to the conclusion, and eventually became stuck.'
4. Organisation	'I think it would be easier to read my composition if I could write paragraphs.'
5. Overall quality	'Because I didn't write English during the winter vacation, my writing ability declined.'
Goal-setting	
1. Language	'Even though I make mistakes, I want to improve my knowledge of grammar and vocabulary and I want to be able to write long sentences.'
2. Content	'I want to be able to describe what I am thinking about more accurately.'
3. Composition processes	'I want to be able to write more fluently.'
4. Organisation	'I want to be able to write compositions so that they transition from 'general' to 'specific'.'
5. Overall quality	'I want to write more words. Even if I make grammatical mistakes, I want to write many more words.'
6. Learning-orientation	'I need to pay attention to how vocabulary and grammar are used not only when I write in English, but also when I read English texts.'

We also observed the content of L2 writing and identified *ideal L2 self-related episodes* to explore how the ideal L2 self was represented and changed over time. Because many writing topics were related to personal issues and students could choose the topic they wanted to write on, over 70% of the compositions included ideas involving either their interests or their future ideal selves. Owing to the iterative nature of the study, students repeatedly wrote about their future goals, and their descriptions were likely to be elaborated on and specified through repetition in accordance with changes in their writing skills and their self-set proximal goals. While the interviews were aimed at eliciting the students' explicit thoughts and ideas about their ideal L2 selves, future self-images emerged in the compositions without students having to be directly asked. Thus, we examined the content of their compositions as constituting 'speak as themselves' (Ushioda, 2009) data.

Results

Self-regulation in L1 reflections

Figure 21.2 presents the trajectories of task engagement (number of Japanese characters) in Aki (above) and Chika's reflections (below) within the altitude lines graph (van Geert & van Dijk, 2002) for the whole class, which plotted the 75th, the 50th and the 25th percentiles. The figures allowed for the visual inspection of the altitude and steepness, and thus to investigate transitions of states and identify variation ranges. For example, a shift from around the 25th percentile line to above the 75th percentile line can be interpreted as evidence for development over time relative to the other students. As can be seen in the figures, the values in the whole class were relatively stable over the academic year, while the two individual cases presented dynamic fluctuation. The specific trajectories also identified distinctive characteristics for each case. While Aki, despite occasional drops, continued to achieve values above the 50th percentile line, Chika changed from relatively low values – even below the 25th percentile line in the beginning – to higher values in the latter half of the year. We now present an overview of the different self-regulatory processes each student utilised and how they changed during the year.

Aki

Figure 21.3 presents the evolution of Aki's self-regulatory processes. Each value represents the number of themes identified in the reflections for each week. The diagram indicates that she tended to focus on self-evaluation processes and made limited use of self-observation throughout the year. The first six weeks in particular involve numerous identified processes, and afterwards the frequency of identified processes stabilised around four for the rest of the period. Although the overall frequency of identified processes is not

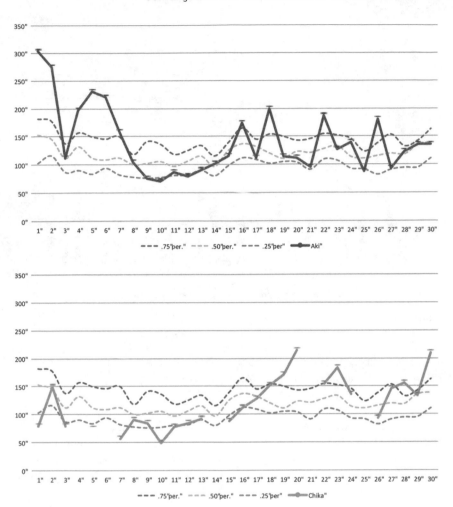

Figure 21.2 Changes in task engagement

extensive, they include specific evaluative statements as exemplified by the following self-evaluation extracts:

> I tried to incorporate expressions like relative clauses, but I couldn't write them well. (Self-evaluation: language, Week 3)

> I wrote about sports, but I couldn't give specific examples as I had planned. (Self-evaluation: content, Week 1)

> I planned to write a sequential organisation of ideas such as 'reason one, reason two ...' before actually starting to write so that readers could follow the flow of writing. (Self-evaluation: composing processes, Week 2)

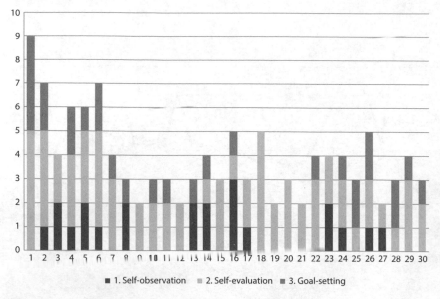

Figure 21.3 Changes in self-regulatory processes: Aki

I created paragraphs beginning from first, second . . . to make the content more easily understood in terms of organisation. (Self-evaluation: organisation, Week 4)

Table 21.2 provides a detailed breakdown of the range of Aki's self-evaluation processes throughout the year. As can be seen, the number of identified goals was very limited, but the types of goals were widely distributed. That is, while many students initially tended to concentrate on linguistic goals, Aki set goals for various aspects from the opening weeks.

Chika

The diagram in Figure 21.4 suggests that the number of Chika's self-regulatory processes did not display any clear distinction from the beginning towards the end of the academic year, but her focus shifted from self-observation in the first half, to self-evaluation in the second half of the year. In addition, the specificity of her reflections also shifted from a lack of tangibility to more elaborate and detailed explanations. For example, in the beginning weeks she wrote:

I could only use simple words. (Self-observation: language, Week 1)

I can write it in Japanese but I can't write it in English. (Self-observation: composing processes, Week 2)

I need to increase my vocabulary. (Goal-setting: language, Week 3);

Table 21.2 Summary of self-regulatory processes: Aki

Week	1	2	3	4	5	6	7	8	9	10	11	12	13	14	15	16	17	18	19	20	21	22	23	24	25	26	27	28	29	30	Total
1. Self-observation	0	1	2	1	2	1	0	2	0	0	0	0	2	2	0	3	1	0	0	0	0	0	2	1	0	1	1	0	0	0	22
language		1				1		2						2		1										1	1				9
content			2	1	1								1			1							1	1							7
composing process													1			1							1								3
overall quality					1											1	1														3
effort																															0
2. Self-evaluation	5	4	2	3	3	4	3	0	2	2	2	2	0	1	3	1	2	5	2	3	1	3	1	2	1	2	0	2	4	3	68
language	2	2	1	1	1	1	1		1	1	1	1			1		1	2	1	1	1			1	1			1	1		24
content	1	1	1	1	1	1	1		1	1	1	1		1		1	1	2	1	1		1	1	1		1		1		1	24
composing process	2	1			1	1	1								1			1				1				1			1	1	12
organizational				1		1									1							1							1	1	6
overall quality																				1									1		2
3. Goal-setting	4	2	0	2	1	2	1	1	0	1	1	0	1	1	0	1	0	0	0	0	1	1	1	1	2	2	1	1	0	0	28
language	2	2		2		1					1			1							1				1		1	1			13
content					1	1		1																							3
composing process										1						1								1	1	1					5
organizational																						1									1
overall quality																							1			1					2
learning-orientation	2						1						1																		4
Total	9	7	4	6	6	7	4	3	2	3	3	2	3	4	3	5	3	5	2	3	2	4	4	4	3	5	2	3	4	3	118

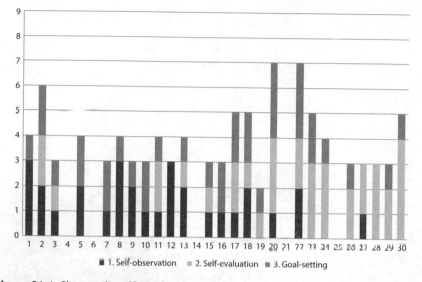

Figure 21.4 Changes in self-regulatory processes: Chika

In the final weeks, however she wrote:

I might not have used 'not only – but also' before, but I'm satisfied that I could use it this time. (Self-evaluation: language, Week 28)

I couldn't complete both strengths and weaknesses, but now I'm satisfied that I could write them. (Self-evaluation: content, Week 30)

I think the number of times I checked the dictionary decreased, and as I feel like sufficiently increasing my vocabulary, I will try to do this more. (Goal-setting: language, w29)

Table 21.3 confirms the change in Chika's focus from self-observation to self-evaluation. It also indicates that her focus on linguistic goal setting in the first half shifted to various goals in the second half of the year. Another interesting characteristic is the frequent occurrence of positive emotional comments on her writing in the final weeks, for example, *I really enjoyed myself today because I felt writing on today's topic was easy'* (Week 24) and *'I was happy because I could write very well'* (Week 30). As these comments were not observed in the beginning weeks, these affective reactions were assumed to have emerged through repeated engagements in the task.

Task execution and the ideal L2 self in L2 writing

Aki

Figure 21.5 plots change in the linguistic measures of Aki's compositions (i.e. fluency, syntactic and lexical complexity). While the percentile lines for

Table 21.3 Summary of self-regulatory processes: Chika

Week	1	2	3	4	5	6	7	8	9	10	11	12	13	14	15	16	17	18	19	20	21	22	23	24	25	26	27	28	29	30	Total
1. Self-observation	3	2	1	0	2	0	1	3	2	1	1	3	2	0	1	1	1	2	0	1	0	2	0	0	0	0	1	0	0	0	30
language	1							1				1						1													4
content	1	1	1		1			1	1		1	1			1	1						1					1				12
composing process	1	1			1		1	1	1			1	1					1		1		1									11
overall quality										1			1				1														3
effort																															0
2. Self-evaluation	0	2	1	0	0	0	0	0	0	2	2	0	1	0	1	0	2	1	1	3	0	2	3	1	0	2	2	3	2	4	35
language		1	1							1	1						1	1		1		1	1			1	1	1	1	1	14
content		1									1						1			1		1	1			1		1	1	1	10
composing process										1			1		1				1	1			1	1			1	1		1	10
organizational																														1	1
overall quality																															0
3. Goal-setting	1	2	1	0	2	0	2	1	1	2	1	1	1	0	1	2	2	2	1	3	0	3	2	1	0	1	0	0	0	1	34
language	1	1	1		1		1	1		1	1				1	1	1	1		1		1	1								15
content																1								1							2
composing process		1			1		1		1			1	1					1	1	1		1	1			1					12
organizational																															0
overall quality																	1			1											2
learning-orientation										1												1								1	3
Total	4	6	3	0	4	0	3	4	3	3	4	3	4	0	3	5	5	5	2	7	0	7	5	4	0	3	3	3	3	5	99

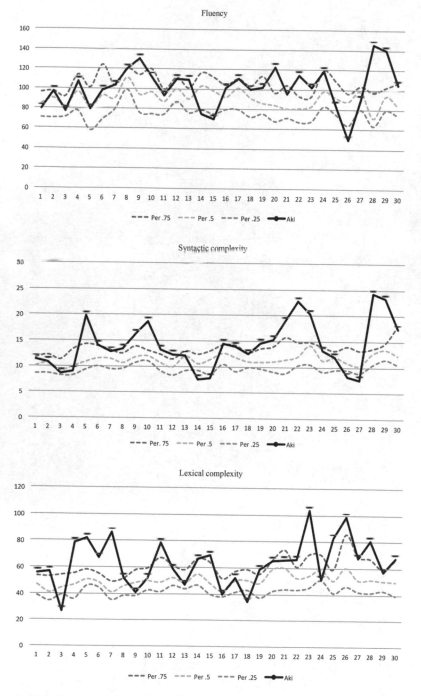

Figure 21.5 Changes in L2 writing: Aki

the whole class are suggestive of relative stability over the observed period, the two focal students display very different trajectories. Aki's linguistic measures in the first few weeks had relatively low values (around the 50th percentile line) but then increased above the 75th percentile line for most of the weeks. The final weeks in particular recorded very high values for these measures.

Regarding the content of the compositions, the following extracts from her compositions evidence the fact that Aki's ideal L2 self became more elaborated over time through repeated writing opportunities. She most frequently selected music as a writing topic (eight times out of 30), and her descriptions of music became increasingly elaborate and detailed. While the initial weeks involved rather superficial references to music, later accounts included more detailed descriptions of her strong desire to be a musician and to work in the music industry. When she first mentioned music as a topic in Week 3, she only described somewhat commonplace aspects, such as her favourite types of music. (All compositions are presented below without any errors being corrected.)

> When I'm unhappy, I listen to music. I like listening to music for example, rock or pop – music. When I listen to it, I can forget everything. If I want listening, I listen to music with loud volume.

> When I'm unhappy, I also talk with my friends or meet my friends. When I talk about it, my mind becomes happier and warmer. I'm here because of my friends. I really thank to my friends. (Week 3: fluency – 77; syntactic complexity – 8.556; lexical complexity – 26.667)

In addition, the compositions lacked consistency, because she moved onto an issue unrelated to music in the second paragraph.

Her writing seemed to have improved in Week 7 in terms of elaborating on the topic and making it more consistent. After briefly introducing the topic in the first paragraph, she explained how much she loved her favourite band by identifying specific names of the band members. Her composition included parts of speech specifying the content, such as the conjunctions *and* and *or*, as well as introductory phrases such as *for example*:

> If I was alone for a week, I select to listen to my favourite bands or artist music. I love foreign music very much, so I can spend a wonderful time alone with listening to music for hours, days or weeks.

> My favourite band is a kind of emotional rock or punk rock. For example, "Fall Out Boy" who are very famous American band, their music makes me comfortable. And recently, I listen to "the HIATVS" who are Japanese band included Takeshi Hosomi. He has great talents about singing, playing and writing music. He belonged to "ELLEGARDEN" few months ago.

"ELLE GARDEN" is (Week 7: fluency – 103; syntactic complexity – 12.875; lexical complexity – 86.418)

Aki further developed ideas about her favourite musician in Week 29. She explained how she was excited by his songs, and imagined what she would do if she met him. It is also noticeable that she used multiple emotional words (e.g. amazing, excited and relax), which made her composition more expressive and lively:

> If I can have a conversation with a famous living person, I want to choose Takeshi Hosomi.
>
> He is a famous rock singer who was belong to ELLEGARDEN for ten years and now is belong to the HIATUS. His amazing songs are express-ing my mind every time. When I listened to his music on TV, I was very excited and could relax more and more. Since then I am served by his songs day by day, so if I can talk with him, I really want to say thanks to him, hear his idea about his life style as a rock musician and ask his future and dreams. Because I have been to his band's live concert of the HIATUS but I never have been to ELLEGARDEN one, I want to him to act again as ELLEGARDEN's vocalist. (Week 29: fluency – 140; syntactic complexity – 23.333; lexical complexity – 57.384)

Her linguistic measures according to her conceptual development over time increased from 77 to 140 in fluency, 8.556 to 23.333 in syntactic complexity and 26.667 to 57.384 in lexical complexity, which suggest that her descrip-tions of the ideal L2 self become more developed with her improved L2 writ-ing skills.

While the above extracts are suggestive of her as a person externally situ-ated from her ideal self, the following extracts show the internalisation of a figure in her ideal L2 self, indicating that her strong desire to join the music industry is closely related to her future ideal goal. Writing about her future goal as an international person in Week 5 ('My future is to be an interna-tional person who know foreign languages, culture') was repeated and elabo-rated on in Week 6, connecting the goal of becoming an international person to the ideal self situated in the music industry:

> (...) First, I want to work at foreign countries because dream is to be a international person who know about different cultures or languages, and so on. (...) Third, I want to work in the music cultures of foreign countries because I respect foreign music very much. There are those factors, I'll satisfied my job or career. (Week 6)

That is, these extracts suggest that Aki's ideal self emerged through her increased interest in foreign music and the singer she idolises, further evolving through being integrated with her international orientations. That is, the emerged ideal self was continuously energised and further specified by her recognition of its connection to other things she was interested in. In addition, she not only had an elaborate and vivid future self-image, but also had a belief that her current learning efforts would lead to realisation of her future ideal self, as represented in the following composition:

> If I could take back any deed I have done, I would want to change my mind when I was eighteen years old at high school. It is a reason that I didn't think seriously about my future, for example my college life. If I have thought about it more in those days, I could try to study hard or decide my future early. I thought that I studied hard every time, but it was wrong. Because of my wrong feeling, I couldn't enter another college which I wanted to go.

> There are a lot of things which I want to take back any deed, but I must go ahead. So I tried to study and learn hard in XYZ University for my future. (Week 15)

Chika

Chika's compositions frequently involved sports (5 times out of 25) and music (6 times out of 25). Like Aki, she had a dream of working in a music company. Figure 21.6 plots changes in the three linguistic measures of her writing. Similar to Aki, Chika's writing seems to improve over time, but what is noticeable is that the values for the second half of the year are distinctly better in fluency and lexical complexity than those for the first 15 weeks.

Initially, Chika clearly stated that she was interested in music but was unsure of how she could accomplish her dream:

> Now, I'm 18 years old. After 10 years I'll be 28 years old. I'll imagine in my future. I want to be a person concerned of music. So while I attend in this university, I want to experience a part-time job. But I don't know where I go. I'll ask my friend. Through my experience, I want to work at music ground until 28 years old. (Week 7: fluency – 71; syntactic complexity – 8.875; lexical complexity – 37.5)

However, on returning to the same topic in Week 8, her future possible self-image seemed to emerge with some specifications (i.e. becoming an acoustic engineer):

> Now, I have a dream in the future. But I think that it is very difficult for women to do it. What I want to be is a acoustics engineer. For that, I have to have a skill so that I can dream come true. Until graduating from this

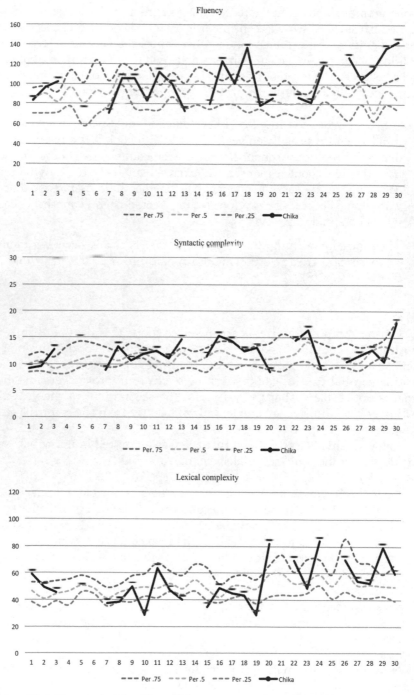

Figure 21.6 Changes in L2 writing: Chika

university, I want to have a skill, so I think that try to work as a acoustics engineer at live house and so on. Then I will have a enough skill, I will stick out until 28 years old. And it will be continue it forever. I only stick out so that I can dream come true. (Week 8: fluency – 106; syntactic complexity – 13.25; lexical complexity – 38.254)

It is less clear how consciously she linked her everyday English learning to her future goals stated in Weeks 7 and 8, but her experience of studying abroad for one month in the summer (between Weeks 15 and 16) seemed to change her overall attitude towards learning English, as stated in her reflection in Week 16 ('*After returning from Canada, I reviewed textbooks and vocabulary note which I used at high school. I wish I could improve my English*'). The composition in Week 29 includes very detailed descriptions of her favourite musician and her linguistic measures are superior to those in Week 8 (i.e. from 106 to 136 in fluency and 38.254 to 79.609 in lexical complexity). Frequent use of emotional expressions (e.g. cry, refresh and impressed) reflects her strong admiration for this person as well as her improved L2 writing skills.

If I could speak a famous person, I chose Motoo Fujiwara. He is a member of BUMP OF CHICKEN and a vocalist and guitarist. He writes all the words and compose all songs. I respect him because he can play guitar, bass, dram and piano. I'm helped by his words when I'm in very low spirits. Sometimes, I cry listening to their music and then I feel refresh. I have gone to their concert with my friend three times. At first, I met them closely in small live house. At second, I met them in big house, it's Gaishi-Hole. At last, I met them in Osaka despite my leg was in a cast. All lives were wonderful and I was impressed by them. I wanna say to them that thank you. No BUMP. (Week 29: fluency – 136; syntactic complexity – 10.462; lexical complexity – 79.609)

Discussion

To summarise the findings, Aki employed self-evaluation processes and set a wide range of goals while elaborating on her future goals and internalising them as her ideal L2 self through the repetition of the writing tasks. For Chika, self-regulatory processes and the quality of L2 writing showed marked contrasts in the first and second halves of the year, presumably as a function of her experiences in studying abroad. Her ideal L2 self emerged and became more elaborate in tandem with these changes. The most important theoretical implications of the findings fall into two categories: (a) self-regulatory capacity as a component of individual differences and (b) co-adaptation between the ideal L2 self, task execution and self-regulation.

Self-regulatory capacity as a component of individual differences

Although investigations into self-regulation have been rather neglected in L2 motivation research (for a valuable exception, see Tseng & Schmitt, 2008), the present findings suggest that self-regulatory capacity should be regarded as an important factor in individual differences, with a potent impact on the student's immediate performance and long-term development when linked to their ideal future selves. While task engagement values describe the degree of a student's proactive attitude towards learning tasks, self-regulatory processes provide more detailed information on motivational task processing. Within the broad rubric of self-regulation, self-evaluation processes seem to play a more important role in relation to L2 writing than self-observation processes.

In addition, setting a wide range of goals, rather than exclusively focus-ing on linguistic aspects, might be another underlying function to develop L2 writing skills. The interview protocol with Aki, in terms of the impor-tance of focusing on a wide range of goals, complements her self-regulatory capacity with clear learning goals in mind (all interview extracts were trans-lated from Japanese):

Aki: I tried to use various grammatical structures, and not just structures junior high school students can understand. I tried to make long sentences and connect explanations by using grammar like that in relative clauses.

I: Did many of your goals concern grammatical aspects?

Aki: Yes, and as writing many words gave the readers more information, I tried to write a number of words quickly.

Despite her initial focus on fluency, her goals shifted to making her composi-tions more understandable for readers:

Aki: I continued to have fundamental goals. As we were given different topics every week, I don't remember what specific goals I had each time, but I always thought about how I could make my writing more easily understood.

I: Did you have this goal from the beginning of the year?

Aki: No, I initially didn't have this goal. I just tried to write as many words as possible. Then, I started to think that I had to write comprehensible sentences not only for myself but also for everyone. For example, what connecters should I use here? At the beginning, I only looked at my writing at a single sentence level, but then I realised I had to look at the whole and create paragraph structures.

Aki's initial focus on writing fluency can be regarded as a natural course of development, also observed in many other students, as the goal to achieve fluency was primed by the task instruction to count written words immediately after writing had been completed. Although some other students continued to pursue this fluency goal throughout the year, Aki wondered how she could more effectively make her ideas understood and thus shifted her goals into other aspects of writing. In other words, she self-set her own goals in engaging in writing, and as she self-evaluated her own compositions, she revised her writing goals as she became more skilled in L2 writing. Thus, it is acknowledged that, despite students' repeated engagement in the same tasks, the tasks generated variability in the self-regulation processes that accompanied their performance (cf. Coughlan & Duff, 1994).

Co-adaptation between the ideal L2 self, task execution and self-regulation

The results concerning the second research question regarding the relationship between the ideal L2 self, task execution and self-regulation have demonstrated that, in both observed cases, the ideal L2 self evolved through repetition of the writing tasks over time. It should be emphasised that the evolution of the ideal L2 self was attained by employing efficient self-regulatory processes, which seemed to be closely related to the development of L2 writing. The interview with Aki supports this observation. In retrospect, Aki explained that she started listening to English songs because she found that her favourite Japanese singer who was working overseas (mentioned in the cited compositions above) was a competent English user. Her desire for approaching him is well represented in the following extract:

I: What triggered you to study more English?
Aki: I found that my favourite artist was a good English communicator
        who privately travelled overseas alone, introduced people he met,
        and enjoyed himself by uploading his photos on his blog. I thought
        I wanted to get acquainted with him. It may be simply
        admiration, but I always thought I wanted to be a person who
        could use English well. In addition, as I wanted to study abroad, I
        thought I needed to continue to study English even harder to
        achieve this.

The last part of this excerpt tells us that her admiration for the singer oriented her to study English in a more focused manner. As she aspired to become a proficient English communicator like her idol, she decided to make exerted efforts to be selected as a foreign exchange student in her university's programme to study abroad. This proximal goal further encouraged her to continue her everyday learning. It is clear here that a virtuous cycle occurred – having an ideal L2 self (i.e. a person working in the international music industry) led her to set a proximal goal (i.e. studying abroad), which then spurred her efforts to learn English. Her strong desire to approach her idol influenced her choice of a future job:

I: Is English needed for the job you would like to do in the future?
Aki: Yes, it is. Although I haven't yet decided, I would like to produce music. I want to do a job that allows me to bridge Japan and overseas countries.

The extent to which these two students developed their ideal L2 selves seems closely related to how actively they engaged in the tasks, as suggested by the changes in task engagement (Figure 21.2). While Aki constantly demonstrated relatively high values in task engagement, Chika exhibited high values during the second half of the year, probably as a consequence of studying abroad in the summer. The measure of task engagement can be a useful indicator of the students' proactive attitudes, and our findings underscore the positive relationship between relatively high values in task engagement (in the second half of the year) and developmental trends in the L2 writing measures.

As has been discussed thus far, complex co-adaptive processes between the ideal L2 self and task-specific motivation, as well as their dynamic evolution, could be clearly observed in two individual cases both from a macro- and micro-perspective. While co-adaptation between individual organisms, such as children and caregivers (van Geert et al., 2011) and students and teachers (Larsen-Freeman & Cameron, 2008a), has been the subject of some research in applied linguistics, the present study highlights co-adaptation *within* the organism (Oyama et al., 2001), that is, concerning the ideal L2 self, self-regulation and L2 writing performance for specific individual students. Even if students are equipped with an ideal L2 self-image at the beginning, the initial state of motivation associated with this image may not be sustained for extended periods if they do not continue to develop and elaborate these ideal L2 selves. Key motivational issues within the classroom context involve maintaining assigned goals, elaborating on subgoals and exercising control over other thoughts and behaviours (Dörnyei & Ottó, 1998) and it is important to emphasise that the ideal L2 self plays an important role in energising this task-specific motivation and providing students with self-evaluative standards. As the self-regulatory capacity develops, it promotes the initial state of the ideal L2 self into becoming more elaborate and tangible, which then provides even more functional and refined evaluative standards. In other words, learners need to generate a coherent system of proximal subgoals to guide action towards attaining personally valued future goals (Miller & Brickman, 2004). In the present study, Aki was equipped with relatively specific subgoals to accompany her ideal L2 self even during the initial weeks of the project. Our results indicate that these proximal subgoals played the role of self-evaluative standards to improve her writing. As particular subgoals were accomplished and the system of subgoals became refined over time, the degree of commitment to the future goal grew stronger. That is, the repetition of tasks seemed to maximise the initial conditions over time, and, as a result, Aki elaborated her ideal L2 self in conjunction with her improved self-regulatory capacity over time.

While we believe that the present study has provided useful insights into the evolution of the dynamics of possible selves and L2 motivation, the investigation admittedly has some limitations. First, we selected two cases on the basis of their pattern of task engagement; there are however other meaningful ways of sampling individual students, for example according to their initial proficiency levels. It may also be instructive to investigate cases with limited self-regulatory capacity and explore what factors that make them *amotivated*. Second, one academic year might not have been long enough to observe the full evolution of their ideal L2 selves. Collecting data over longer periods of time (e.g. from enrolment at a college to graduation), or at critical stages of students' learning experiences, such as studying abroad, may provide a different and possibly more comprehensive picture.

Conclusion

We have explored how the ideal L2 selves of two particular students emerged and evolved over time in interaction with classroom-based tasks using a complex dynamic systems perspective. We conceptualised the relationship between the ideal L2 self and L2 learning experience as being co-adaptive within the context of the EFL classroom, displaying interrelated changes. The present study revealed that students' self-regulatory processes played an important role in facilitating the development of the ideal L2 self and L2 writing.

The present study adopted a longitudinal approach and employed a range of analytical methods: visual analysis of linguistic changes, quantifying task engagement and self-regulatory processes, statistical analysis of change points, qualitative analysis of the content of L2 compositions, written L1 self-reflections and retrospective interviews. Using these varied methods of exploring multi-level data depicted the landscape in L2 motivation as a rich but complex terrain. In contrast to the dominant manner of previous research on the L2 Motivational Self System that has involved administering questionnaires to large samples, our study indicates that a focus on a limited number of individuals and the use of 'speak as themselves' (Ushioda, 2009) data are useful ways of describing how language learners navigate in this motivational state space. However, because the methods of investigation adopted in the present study were rather exploratory, our findings need to be corroborated by future studies involving other cases within other contexts.

References

Apple, M., Da Silva, D. and Fellner, T. (eds) (2013) *Language Learning Motivation in Japan*. Bristol: Multilingual Matters.

Baba, K. and Nitta, R. (2014) Phase transitions in the development of writing fluency from a complex dynamic systems perspective. *Language Learning* 64 (1), 1–35.

Boekaerts, M. (1996) Personality and the psychology of learning. *European Journal of Personality* 10, 377–404.

Boekaerts, M. and Niemivirta, M. (2000) Self-regulated learning: Finding a balance between learning goals and ego-protective goals. In M. Boekaerts, P.R. Pintrich and M. Zeidner (eds) *Handbook of Self-Regulation: Directions and challenges for future research* (pp. 417–450). San Diego, CA: Academic Press.

Byrne, D. and Ragin, C.C. (2009) *The SAGE Handbook of Case-Based Methods*. Los Angeles, CA: SAGE.

Coughlan, P. and Duff, P. (1994) Same task, different activities: Analysis of a SLA task from an Activity Theory perspective. In J.P. Lantolf and G. Appel (eds) *Vygotskian Approaches to Second Language Research* (pp. 173–194). Westport, CT: Ablex.

Csizér, K. and Kormos, J. (2009) Learning experiences, selves and motivated learning behaviour: A comparative analysis of structural models for Hungarian secondary and university learners of English. In Z. Dörnyei and E. Ushioda (eds) *Motivation, Language Identity and the L2 Self* (pp. 98–119). Bristol: Multilingual Matters.

Dörnyei, Z. (2002) The motivational basis of language learning tasks. In P. Robinson (ed.) *Individual Differences and Instructed Language Learning* (pp. 137–158). Amsterdam: John Benjamins.

Dörnyei, Z. (2005) *The Psychology of the Language Learner: Individual Differences in Second Language Acquisition*. Mahwah, NJ: Lawrence Erlbaum.

Dörnyei, Z. (2009a) The L2 Motivational Self System. In Z. Dörnyei and E. Ushioda (eds) *Motivation, Language Identity and the L2 Self* (pp. 9–42). Bristol: Multilingual Matters.

Dörnyei, Z. (2009b) Individual differences: Interplay of learner characteristics and learning environment. *Language Learning* 59 (1), 230–248.

Dörnyei, Z. (2009c) *The Psychology of Second Language Acquisition*. Oxford: Oxford University Press.

Dörnyei, Z. (2014) Researching complex dynamic systems: 'Retrodictive qualitative modelling' in the language classroom. *Language Teaching* 47 (1), 80–91.

Dörnyei, Z. and Kormos, J. (2000) The role of individual and social variables in oral task performance. *Language Teaching Research* 4 (3), 275–300.

Dörnyei, Z. and Ottó, I. (1998) Motivation in action: A process model of L2 motivation. *Working Papers in Applied Linguistics, Thames Valley University, London* 4, 43–69.

Dörnyei, Z. and Tseng, W.T. (2009) Motivational processing in interactional tasks. In A. Mackey and C. Polio (eds) *Multiple Perspectives on Interaction* (pp. 117–134). London: Routledge.

Dörnyei, Z. and Ushioda, E. (eds) (2009) *Motivation, Language Identity and the L2 Self*. Bristol: Multilingual Matters.

Dörnyei, Z. and Ushioda, E. (2011) *Teaching and Researching Motivation* (2nd edn). Harlow: Longman.

Gardner, R.C. and Lambert, W.E. (1972) *Attitudes and Motivation in Second Language Learning*. Massachusetts: Newbury House.

Higgins, E.T. (1987) Self-discrepancy: A theory relating self and affect. *Psychological Review* 94, 319–340.

Larsen-Freeman, D. (2006) The emergence of complexity, fluency, and accuracy in the oral and written production of five Chinese learners of English. *Applied Linguistics* 27 (4), 590–619.

Larsen-Freeman, D. and Cameron, L. (2008a) *Complex Systems and Applied Linguistics.* Oxford: Oxford University Press.

Larsen-Freeman, D. and Cameron, L. (2008b) Research methodology on language development from a complex systems perspective. *Modern Language Journal* 92 (2), 200–213.

Legenhausen, L. (1999) Autonomous and traditional learners compared: The impact of classroom culture on attitudes and communicative behavior. In C. Edelhoff and R. Weskamp (eds) *Autonomes Fremdsprachenlernen* (pp. 166–182). Ismaning: Hueber.

Lewis, M.D. (2005) Bridging emotion theory and neurobiology through dynamic systems modeling. *Behavioral and Brain Science* 28, 169–245.

Lock, E.A. and Latham, G.P. (2002) Building a practically useful theory of goal setting and task motivation: A 35-year Odyssey. *American Psychologist* 57 (9), 705–717.

MacIntyre, P.D. and Legatto, J.J. (2011) A dynamic system approach to willingness to communicate: Developing an idiodynamic method to capture rapidly changing affect. *Applied Linguistics* 32 (2), 149–171.

McCarthy, P.M. and Jarvis, S. (2010) MTLD, vocd-D, and HD-D: A validation study of sophisticated approaches to lexical diversity assessment. *Behavior Research Methods* 42, 381–392.

Miller, R.B. and Brickman, S.J. (2004) A model of future-oriented motivation and self-regulation. *Educational Psychology Review* 16 (1), 9–33.

Murray, G., Gao, X. and Lamb, T. (eds) (2011) *Identity, Motivation and Autonomy in Language Learning.* Bristol: Multilingual Matters.

Nitta, R. (2013) Understanding motivational evolution in the EFL classroom: A longitudinal Study from a dynamic systems perspective. In M.T. Apple, D. Da Silva and T. Fellner (eds) *Language Learning Motivation in Japan* (pp. 268–290). Bristol: Multilingual Matters.

Nitta, R. and Baba, K. (in press) Task repetition and L2 writing development: A longitudinal study from a Dynamic Systems Perspective. In H. Byrnes and R.M. Manchón (eds) *Task-Based Language Learning: Insights from and for L2 Writing.* Amsterdam: John Benjamins.

Oyama, S., Griffith, P. and Gray, R. (eds) (2001) *Cycles of Contingency, Development Systems and Evolution.* Cambridge, MA: The MIT Press.

Oyserman, D. and James, L. (2009) Possible selves: From content to process. In K.D. Markman, W.M.P. Klein and J.A. Suhr (eds) *Handbook of Imagination and Mental Simulation* (pp. 373–394). NY: Psychology Press.

Oyserman, D., Bybee, D., Terry, K. and Hart-Johnson, T. (2004) Possible selves as roadmaps. *Journal of Research in Personality* 38, 130–149.

Rheinberg, F., Vollmeyer, R. and Rollett, W. (2000) Motivation and action in self-regulated learning. In M. Boekaerts, P.R. Pintrich and M. Zeidner (eds) *Handbook on Self-Regulation: Directions and challenges for future research.* San Diego, CA: Academic Press.

Richards, K. (2006) 'Being the teacher': Identity and classroom conversation. *Applied Linguistics* 27 (1), 51–77.

Ryan, S. (2009) Self and identity in L2 motivation in Japan: The ideal L2 self and Japanese learners of English. In Z. Dörnyei and E. Ushioda (eds) *Motivation, Language Identity and the L2 Self* (pp. 120–143). Bristol: Multilingual Matters.

Steenbeek, H., Jansen, L. and van Geert, P. (2012) Scaffolding dynamics and the emergence of problematic learning trajectories. *Learning and Individual Differences* 22, 64–75.

Taguchi, T., Magid, M. and Papi, M. (2009). The L2 Motivational Self System among Japanese, Chinese and Iranian Learners of English: A comparative study. In Z. Dörnyei and E. Ushioda (eds) *Motivation, Language Identity and the L2 Self* (pp. 66–97). Bristol: Multilingual Matters.

Taylor, W.A. (2000) *Change-point analysis: A powerful new tool for detecting changes*. See http://www.variation.com/cpa/tech/changepoint.html (accessed 29 November 2012).

Thelen, E. and Smith, L.B. (1994) *A Dynamic Systems Approach to the Development of Cognition and Action*. Cambridge, MA: MIT Press.

Tseng W.T. and Schmitt, N. (2008) Toward a model of motivated vocabulary learning: A structural equation modeling approach. *Language Learning* 58 (2), 357–400.

Ushioda, E. (2006) Language motivation in a reconfigured Europe: Access, identity, and autonomy. *Multilingual and Multicultural Development* 27 (2), 148–161.

Ushioda, E. (2009) A person-in-context relational view of emergent motivation, self and identity. In Z. Dörnyei and E. Ushioda (eds) *Motivation, Language Identify and the L2 Self* (pp. 215–228). Bristol: Multilingual Matters.

Ushioda, E. and Dörnyei, Z. (2012) Motivation. In S. Gass and A. Mackey (eds) *The Routledge Handbook of Second Language Acquisition* (pp. 396–409). New York: Routledge.

van den Branden, K., Bygate, M. and Norris, J. (2009) *Task Based Language Teaching: A reader*. Amsterdam: John Benjamins.

van Geert, P. (2009) Complex dynamic systems of development. In R.A. Meyers (ed.) *Encyclopedia of Complexity and System Science, Vol.2: Applications of Physics and Mathematics to Social Science* (pp. 1872–1916). Berlin: Springer.

van Geert, P. (2011) The contribution of complex dynamic systems to development. *Child Development Perspectives* 5 (4), 273–278.

van Geert, P. and van Dijk, M. (2002) Focus on variability: New tools to study intra-individual variability in developmental data. *Infant Behavior & Development* 25, 340–374.

van Geert, P., Steenbeek, H. and van Dijk, M. (2011) A dynamic model of expert-novice co-adaptation during language learning and acquisition. In M.S. Schmid and W. Lowie (eds) *Modeling Bilingualism: From Structure to Chaos* (pp. 235–266). Amsterdam: John Benjamins.

Wolters, C.A. (1998) Self-regulated learning and college students' regulation of motivation. *Journal of Educational Psychology* 90, 224–235.

Wolters, C.A. (2003) Regulation of motivation: Evaluating an underemphasized aspect of self-regulated learning. *Educational Psychologist* 38 (4), 189–205.

Zimmerman, B. (1998) Developing self-fulfilling cycles of academic reflection: An analysis of exemplary instructional model. In D.H. Schunk, and B.J. Zimmerman (eds) *Self-Regulated Learning: From Teaching to Self-reflective Practice* (pp. 1–19). New York: Guilford Publications.

Zimmerman, B. and Rinsenberg, R. (1997) Becoming a self-regulated writer: A social cognitive perspective. *Contemporary Educational Psychology* 22, 73–101.

22 The Dynamics of L2 Imagery in Future Motivational Self-Guides

Chenjing (Julia) You and Letty Chan

Over the past five years, a great deal of research on second language (L2) motivation has focused on the theoretical construct of the L2 Motivational Self System (Dörnyei, 2005, 2009), which comprises L2-specific facets of future self-guides, that is to say, the ideal L2 self, the ought-to L2 self and the L2 learning experience. As such, L2 learners' identities have been at the centre of attention as motivation is seen as a function of the individual's imagined selves in a future state. Although within this new approach imagery is a crucial component of learners' self-guides (Dörnyei, 2014; Dörnyei & Chan, 2013), few studies so far have investigated the evolving nature of L2 imagery and its relationship with L2 motivation. Using a mixed-method approach, the present study aims to fill this gap by examining the dynamic impact of L2 imagery on future self-guides.

Definition of Mental Imagery

As a common everyday experience, imagery is defined as the 'internal [representations] of a perception of the external world in the absence of that external experience' (Hall *et al.*, 1990: 28). It is a product of imagination that can be vivid and colourful, somewhat analogous to a type of water-colour of the mind's eye (Ravenscroft, 2012). It can lead to unlimited possibilities and to moments and places that are beyond our physical constraints. As suggested by Wenger (1998: 176), 'imagination refers to a process of expanding our self by transcending our time and space and creating new images of the world and ourselves'. Indeed, we do not necessarily need to experience something in order to imagine (Morris, 2010) and imagery allows us to predict both an imminent or distant possible future based on past experience (Moulton & Kosslyn, 2009). Although imagery tends to involve visual images, auditory imagery and tactile imagery are also important.

Imagery in L2 Motivation

In the field of L2 motivation, mental imagery has been introduced through theoretical and empirical channels. Theoretically, Dörnyei's (2005, 2009) L2 Motivational Self System draws on the motivating power of L2-specific facets of future self-guides, themselves a product of learners' vision and imagery. Future self-guides, also referred to as possible selves (Markus & Nurius, 1986) '[reflect] a dynamic, forward-pointing conception that can explain how someone is moved from the present toward the future' (Dörnyei, 2014: 8). Dörnyei's motivational framework has three constituents; (a) the *Ideal L2 Self*, which, as a central concept, concerns a desirable self-image of the language user we would like to become in the future, (b) the *Ought-to L2 Self*, which reflects the attributes that one believes one ought to possess in order to meet expectations and to avoid possible negative outcomes in the process of L2 learning, and (c) the *L2 Learning Experience*, which represents situated and executive motives related to the immediate learning environment and experience. This three-component model has been validated in a wide range of L2 learning contexts including China (Taguchi *et al.*, 2009), Germany (Busse, 2013), Hungary (Csizér & Kormos, 2009; Csizér & Lukács, 2010), Indonesia (Lamb, 2012), Iran and Japan (Taguchi *et al.*, 2009), Pakistan (Islam *et al.*, 2013), Saudi Arabia (Al-Shehri, 2009) and Sweden (Henry, 2009, 2010, 2011). These diverse datasets generate cumulative empirical evidence in verifying the motivational power of the model's three constructs generally, and of the ideal L2 self in particular.

For the purposes of the present study, it is important to reiterate that the imagined visualisation of the learner's future L2 identity is seen as a central characteristic of motivation within this construct. In many ways, future L2 selves are similar to the dreams and visions people have about their future lives in that learners can 'see' and 'hear' their future selves (Dörnyei, 2009). Furthermore, imagining a possible self as being successful also contributes to improved performance on persistence and effort tasks (such as in L2 learning). Not only does envisioning success generate images of positive desired end-states, but it can also lead to the development of plans and strategies necessary for achieving success in various domains (Ruvolo & Markus, 1992). A clear vision in a future state will help individuals to access future-relevant cues, which can facilitate selective processing in attaining desired states, thereby improving goal-related performance.

The past few years have seen a small but growing body of research on language imagery, primarily in terms of the quantitative examination of the relationships between distinct future L2 self-guides, learning styles and motivated L2 behaviour. Al-Shehri's (2009) initial research along these lines considered whether learners who prefer a visual learning style would be more likely to have a stronger capacity for visual imagery and imagination, and thus develop a stronger ideal L2 self. Confirming this hypothesis, the results showed significant correlations between the ideal L2 self, visual learning style, imagination and motivated L2 behaviour. Other studies (Dörnyei & Chan, 2013; Kim, 2009; Kim & Kim, 2011) concerning the multisensory dimension of future identities have similarly revealed that both visual and auditory sensory modalities are incorporated in the development of learners' future self-guides. These converging findings indicate that if learners have established a vivid and elaborate image of themselves as an effective L2 user, this can act as a powerful driving force in their L2 learning.

Other researchers have investigated the impact of visualisations and possible selves on L2 motivation (Fukada *et al.*, 2011; Jones, 2012; Magid, 2011; Magid & Chan, 2012; Sampson, 2012). After conducting a focused motivational intervention programme, Fukada and his colleagues (2011) identified a significant increase in the correlations between students' possible selves and their investments in L2 learning, both in and outside the classroom. In Magid and Chan's (2012) intervention study, the researchers found that, after an initial training programme, the learners were more motivated to learn English and their linguistic self-confidence also increased. The participants in Sampson's research (2012) reported that activities that focused on ideal and feared L2 selves were particularly motivating. Moreover, the typical finding in such research has been that the majority of the learners not only benefit from, but also enjoy working with, image-enhancing visualisation as an in-class activity (Chan, 2014).

The Dynamics of Future Self-Guides and Imagery

In social psychology, instead of viewing the self-concept as a monolithic structure that is stable across time, possible selves are typically regarded as constituents of a differentiated, dynamic self-system (Markus & Wurf, 1987) that is 'linked to the dynamic properties of the self-concept – to motivation, to distortion, and to change, both momentary and enduring' (Markus & Nurius, 1986: 954). Along with other self-concepts and self-knowledge, possible selves can undergo change (see Henry, Chapter 9, this volume), these changes impacting on the overall self-concept. This dynamic aspect of the self-concept is addressed by Markus and Nurius in their description of the 'active' or 'working' self-concept:

> Not all self-knowledge is available for thinking about the self at any one time. The working self-concept derives from the set of self-conceptions that are presently active in thought and memory. It can be viewed as a continually active, shifting array of available self-knowledge. (Markus & Nurius, 1986: 957)

In the field of L2 motivation, changes in future L2 self-guides have been investigated both longitudinally and in the short-term, momentary context of the working self-concept by Henry and colleagues (e.g. Henry, 2009, 2010, 2011; Henry & Apelgren, 2008). For example, in one study Henry (2009) found an emerging gender gap at the end of secondary school where, while the ideal L2 selves of girls' increased in strength, those of boys' decreased. Further, the findings also suggested that students' ideal L2 self-guides were significant predictors of the amount of effort they were willing to put into L2 learning. In addition, Henry (2011) found that in the working self-concept, possible L2 and L3 selves could compete with one another, suggesting specifically that an ideal L2 English-speaking/using self might have a negative impact on L3 learning motivation.

Purpose

The research reported in this chapter was conducted in China, where proficiency in English is seen as important, both for the individual and, in the current era of economic globalisation, for Chinese society as a whole. Consequently English is a compulsory subject learnt by Chinese students from primary school all the way up to the end of the second year of university for all non-English major students.

The purpose of this exploratory mixed-method study was to investigate how changes in L2-relevant self-imagery might affect L2 learning behaviours. In our research, four particular issues were addressed: (a) whether there are any transformations in Chinese students' L2-relevant mental imagery; (b) how any transformations might impact L2 learning behaviour; (c) the kind of changes in imagery that might be involved; and (d) how these changes interact with various L2 learning variables. In evaluating the findings, a dynamic systems theory (DST)-inspired approach was used, in that complexity theory 'offers theory and methods for understanding systems in change' (Larsen-Freeman & Cameron, 2008: 25). Therefore, adopting a DST perspective seems to be well suited for this purpose.

Methodology

The study's design

In order to investigate the shifting nature of the L2 imagery of future self-guides, we used a mixed-method design, employing both surveys and in-depth interviews (Dörnyei & Ushioda, 2011). In the first stage, a questionnaire survey was carried out to establish whether the use of L2 imagery is a recognisable phenomenon among our sample of learners. In the second stage, interviews were then conducted to explore the nature of any changes in learners' uses of L2 imagery.

Participants

Our sample consisted of two separate sub-samples: 208 students who participated in the questionnaire survey and 20 informants who took part in the in-depth interviews (see Table 22.1 for detailed demographic information). For the questionnaire survey, the participants were (i) first- and second-year undergraduate students majoring in engineering and required to attend a compulsory and credit-bearing English course; and (ii) secondary school students in their first and second-year of high school (the equivalent of years 11 and 12 in the UK system). All of these students had been studying English as a foreign language since the age of eight. For the interviews, apart from two informants who were students studying at a British university, all of the other interviewees were students studying in China. All of these students had backgrounds similar to those of the survey participants. In all cases pseudonyms have been used when the results are reported.

Instruments

For the quantitative part of the study, a questionnaire measuring students' L2-related future self-guides, the L2 imagery connected to these self-guides, changes in L2 imagery, as well as other variables (such as learners' attitudes towards English learning) was used. The items were partly adapted from previous studies of L2 imagery (e.g. Dörnyei & Chan, 2013; Kim, 2009; Kim & Kim, 2011) and from the questionnaire on the L2 Motivational Self System developed by Taguchi and colleagues (2009) (see also Dörnyei, 2010). Additionally, a number of items measuring the dynamic changes of L2 imagery

Table 22.1 Number of respondents by student types and gender

	Student type	No. of participants	Age	Mean age
Survey	University students	109 (59 males, 48 females, 2 missing)	18–22	20.2
	High school students	99 (42 males, 54 females, 3 missing)	15–18	16.4
	Total	208 (101 males, 102 females, 5 missing)	15–22	18.4
Interview	University students	11 (5 males, 6 females)	18–21	19.9
	High school students	9 (2 males, 7 females)	15–18	16.7
	Total	20 (7 males, 13 females)	15–21	18.5

Table 22.2 Information about the multi-item scales

Variables	No. of items	Cronbach alpha	Sample items
Vision of the ideal L2 self	5	0.91	I can imagine myself in the future having a discussion with foreign friends in English.
Vision of the ought-to L2 self	3	0.71	My dreams of how I want to use English in the future are the same as those of my parents.
Vividness and elaborateness of imagery	5	0.92	When I'm imagining myself using English skilfully in the future, I can usually have both specific mental pictures and vivid sounds of the situations.
Intended effort	5	0.82	I would like to spend lots of time studying English.
Visual style	5	0.74	I use colour coding (e.g. highlighter pen) to help me as I learn.
Readiness of using vision and imagery	6	0.90	I think I have a natural ability to visualise myself using English successfully in the future.
Dynamic nature of the ideal L2 self image	5	0.74	My image or dream of myself using English has changed over the past year.

were specially designed. A summary of the variables is given in Table 22.2. The self-report items were assessed using 6-point Likert-type scales, ranging from strongly disagree (1), to strongly agree (6). The instrument, which was originally in English, was translated into Chinese by the first author. Thereafter a back translation were carried out by a professional Chinese/English translator, modifications being made when appropriate. Finally it should be noted that the items measuring 'Readiness of using vision and imagery' and 'Dynamic nature of the ideal L2 self image' were only completed by the respondents if they reported imagining themselves using English in the future.

Data collection and processing

Questionnaire

The questionnaire was administered to the two high school and three university classes by their respective English teachers and took approximately 15 minutes to complete. Students were informed about the study and its purposes in advance. The quantitative data were processed using

SPSS 19.0. The Likert item scales rendered satisfactory reliability coefficients, all of which were above the recommended 0.70 threshold (see Table 22.2).

Interview guide

For the qualitative part of the study, semi-structured interviews, each lasting approximately 25 minutes, were conducted by the first author in Mandarin and audio-recorded. An interview guide comprising questions on the dynamic changes in L2-specific imagery was used. Examples of the interview questions employed are listed as follows.

Ideal L2 Self

- Do you sometimes imagine yourself being a competent learner in the future?
- Can you imagine a clear situation in the future when you are a successful speaker of English? Who would you be speaking to? Where and when? What would you be using English for?
- How has your image or dream of yourself using English in the future changed over the past few years/three months? Why?
- What are the sources of the change?

Ought-to L2 Self[1]

- Do you have a sense of what you ought to become as an English speaker/writer in the future? Can you see, hear or feel who you ought to become as an English speaker/writer in the future?
- Do your parents put pressure on you to study English? Are your dreams for how you want to use English in the future in any way different from those of your parents'?
- How has your image of who you ought to become as an English speaker/writer in the future changed over the past few years/months? Why?
- What are the sources of the change?
- Are you afraid of not becoming a successful user of English in the future? Why? What will it cause? Are you scared when you think of it?
- How does this feeling affect your English learning?
- How has the fear of not becoming a successful user of English in the future changed over the past few years/months? Why?
- What are the sources of the change?

The interview data were translated into English, yielding a corpus of approximately 36,000 words. The data were analysed multiple times, the aim being to identify emerging themes as well as patterns concerning the dynamics of the learners' L2 imagery.

Results and Discussion

Findings generated from the quantitative data

Previous findings reported in the literature have established strong, positive correlations between future self-guides and a number of variables including learners' effort in English and visual style (e.g. Al-Sheri, 2009; Dörnyei & Chan, 2013; Kim & Kim, 2011; Taguchi *et al.*, 2009). Our results are consistent with these findings. As shown in Table 22.3, we have identified strong, positive correlations between future self-guide images (both ideal and ought-to L2 selves), the learners' intended effort and two variables related to imagery. The correlations are high, explaining between 23%–67% of shared variance, and the findings also indicate that, generally, these learners had more vivid, specific and richer imagery for the ideal L2 self than for the ought-to L2 self.

In order to further investigate L2 imagery, particularly regarding its impact on other variables, the sample was divided into two groups; those who responded to the items in the final section, thereby indicating active engagement in visualisation ($N = 164$), and those who had not completed these items ($N = 44$). The questionnaire items in this section are set out in Table 22.4.

Independent-samples *t*-tests were computed to assess the differences between the two groups in terms of the variables previously analysed. As can be seen in Table 22.5, there were significant differences between the two groups in favour of the engagement group (marked as 'vision-yes' in the table) on all the measures, further confirming that imagery has an impact on motivated L2 behaviours.

Transformations of L2 imagery

Research on L2-specific vision and imagery has taken a rather static approach to date, primarily investigating the role of imagery as a constant target to reach for. An example of this approach is the study conducted by

Table 22.3 Correlations between vision and imagery of future self-guides and various variables

	Vision of the ideal L2 self	Vision of the ought-to L2 self
Vividness and elaborateness of imagery	0.82***	0.59***
Intended effort	0.61***	0.67***
Visual style	0.54***	0.48***

***$p < 0.001$

Table 22.4 Questionnaire items related to 'Readiness of using vision and imagery' and 'Dynamic nature of the ideal self image'

Readiness of using vision and imagery
- Sometimes images of myself using English successfully in the future come to me without the slightest effort.
- I find it easy to 'play' imagined scenes and/or conversations in my mind.
- It is easy for me to imagine how I could successfully use English in the future.
- I think I have a natural ability to visualise myself using English successfully in the future.
- I have always found it easy to visualise imagined situations.
- When I'm thinking of myself using English fluently in the future, I often have visual and/or auditory images rather than thoughts in my mind.

Dynamic nature of the ideal L2 self image
- My image or dream of myself using English has changed over the past year.
- My image or dream of myself using English used to be simple, but it has now become more specific.
- My image or dream of myself using English has now become more vivid than it used to be.
- In the past I couldn't imagine myself using English in the future, but now I do imagine it.
- I used to have rich imaginations of myself as a successful English user in the future, but now I don't.

Table 22.5 Descriptive analyses of the main motivational dimensions and independent-samples *t*-test statistics comparing the scores of vision-yes and vision-no groups

	M	SD	M		t-value
			Vision-yes	Vision-no	
Vision of the ideal L2 self	3.67	1.15	3.82	3.12	3.66***
Vision of the ought-to L2 self	3.65	1.00	3.74	3.31	2.58*
Vividness and elaborateness of imagery	3.66	1.08	3.84	3.00	5.56***
Intended effort	4.01	.86	4.08	3.71	2.56*
Visual style	3.56	.84	3.65	3.22	3.10**

*$p < 0.05$; **$p < 0.01$; ***$p < 0.001$

Magid and Chan (2012) in which certain imagery-training and possible selves-promoting tasks were employed with the aim of enhancing L2 learners' motivation. The objective was for people to acquire firm, vivid and elaborate images, which in turn act as a 'magnet' drawing them towards a goal (van der Helm, 2009). In contrast to this static conception, our data suggest that, for many participants, the use of imagery may be something that evolves dynamically during the learning process. Thus, in the second part of our study, we wanted to look at the ways in which L2 imagery might have evolved during the period when our informants had been learning English.

Findings generated from the qualitative data

Key patterns in the dynamics of imagery

In the first part of our study we established that many of the participants made use of imagery in their L2 learning. Although it is a reasonable assumption that this imagery developed over the course of their language learning histories, our cross-sectional data cannot however reveal *how* these changes occurred, or the *types* of change that took place. Thus, the next step involved asking a number of similar learners to reflect on their years learning English and inviting them to identify: (i) points in time when various types of mental imagery might have begun to evolve; and (ii) changes that might have taken place. Of the 20 participants, 19 reported that their mental imagery evolved at times they regarded as critical stages in their L2 learning process. In this respect two major trends were observed: changes involving the *nature and content* of their L2 imagery and changes concerning the *elaborateness*, the *frequency of generation* and *fluctuations* in their L2 imagery.

Changes in the nature and content of L2 imagery

Ten of the participants reported experiencing qualitative changes in the visualisation of future L2 self-guides, either within their ought-to L2 self, or as experiencing shifts from the ought-to L2 self to the ideal L2 self and vice versa. In interpreting our data we conceptualise the L2 Motivational Self System (Dörnyei, 2009) as a complex dynamic system where the respective self-guides are sub-systems. When describing the changes we observe, we make use of the DST concepts of 'state space' and 'attractor states'. In DST, the state space is the landscape through which the learner's system moves. In the state space of these learners' L2 motivational systems, the different future self-guides (the ideal L2 self, the ought-to L2 self and the feared L2 self) form various attractor states. As Hiver (Chapter 3, this volume) explains, attractor states are preferred states, which systems or sub-systems settle into, revealing their long-term tendencies or behaviours.

Changes in the ought-to L2 self

Two high-school students reported changes in the imagery associated with the ought-to L2 self. Katie indicated that her visualisation of the ought-to L2 self and feared L2 self had both been dominant in the past. Changes had however taken place and new images developed at various points over the years as a result of changes in her self-perception and perceptions about her future life. As revealed in the following interview extract, a shift took place in her sense of a social obligation to learn English:

> In the past, I learned English only for my parents. I often imagined I couldn't get a high score in an English test [in the future] and that they would be very depressed and sighed. Now I imagine that a foreigner is speaking English to me and I can't talk to him [in English]. I feel I am humiliating to us Chinese people! And the image of our nation will be ruined by me. I can't do that!

Dynamic systems are, by nature, nested in complex webs of other systems (Larsen-Freeman & Cameron, 2008). Here, regarding the overall motivational system, the change we observed does not involve the type of phase shift where it moves to another part of the state space. Rather, the change takes place within the basin of attraction in which the system is currently lodged, as the nature of the direction of social obligation at the heart of the ought-to L2 self shifts from Katie's parents to the wider Chinese society. However, if we conceptualise the ought-to L2 self as a dynamic system in its own right, then a major traverse across the state space seems to have taken place, the system lodging in a different attractor state (societal obligation) than previously (parental obligation).

Changes in the ideal L2 self

As seen above, even when the system is lodged in the same attractor basin, different mental imagery and imaginary scenarios can develop, and this we have also found in the case of the ideal L2 self. Kyle, who was an exchange student studying in the UK, had, at one stage, had the dream of settling for a longer period and working in Britain. However recent experiences had caused him to reconsider whether such a dream was a realistic prospect. As the following extract reveals, this triggered a process in which the nature and content of the imagery underpinning his ideal L2 self undergoes a transformation:

> My English is still far from enough for me to find a job here [in the UK]. This has made me consider my future use of English in China. I imagine I am working in a large joint venture in China. I am sharing the findings from my project with those experts in the world, and I'm speaking perfect English to them.

Here we see how the possibly unrealistic nature of Kyle's dream (working in the UK) and the accompanying visual imagery seem to have undergone (or are undergoing) a process of revision in the direction of a new, more feasible vision of being back home in China. Thus, it seems as if we are here witnessing a phase shift in his ideal L2 self as a consequence of these insights with the system moving to a new part of the state space.

A similar process of revision of the ideal L2 self can also be seen in another interview with Bruce, a student who was interviewed at his university in China:

> In my secondary school, I imagined I would be a famous entrepreneur, like the richest Chinese entrepreneur, Li Ka-Shing, negotiating business in English with foreign businessmen. Now, I just imagine I can speak English to foreigner people for basic communicative purposes. (Why?) Gradually I find English has become harder and harder and we seldom use English in our daily life except for English classes, so it is not so easy to realise my ambition.

Bruce's previous vision of becoming a highly proficient and sophisticated speaker of English, like billionaire Li Ka-Shing, may have had 'the flavour of fantasy' (Lamb, 2012: 1018), tempting him to mentally enjoy the desired future in the here and now (Oettingen & Thorpe, 2006), rather than developing 'the kind of hard-edged ambition that might promote self-regulated learning' (Lamb, 2012: 1018). Nevertheless it seems as if the vision of his future English-speaking self – seeing himself speaking English with undefined foreigners 'for basic communicative purposes' – is decidedly less glamorous. The shift we witness here, where the image conjured up although more mundane is also more realistic, seems to be an example of the downward revision of Bruce's ideal L2 self. As Henry (Chapter 9, this volume) explains, downward revisions can take place when an individual receives negative feedback on progress, or experiences that progress towards an ideal self is not going as well as anticipated. This means that doubts can be created as to the credibility or the 'possibility' of the desired self, meaning that 'an alternative, less desirable, but perhaps more realistic "ideal" self may appear as more attractive' (Henry, Chapter 9, this volume). When a downward shift takes place, this can mean that, because the distance between the actual and ideal selves has diminished – the ideal L2 self becoming more likely and the discrepancy more manageable – the strength of the attractor weakens. No longer taking the form of a desire to emulate the language skills of a prominent member of the Chinese elite, Bruce is now happy to conceptualise a more realisable future state, meaning that the basin of attraction around the ideal L2 self may have become shallower and the system thus more easily disrupted.

Shifts from the ought-to L2 self to the ideal L2 self

For a number of our participants, the self-guide imagery they talked about seemed to change from a sense of social obligation (an ought-to L2 self), to a more personalised future vision (an ideal L2 self). This seemed to be owing to a number of reasons, such as indirect contact with the target language and culture. A typical example is Harry, whose system shifted in the state space from an attractor state of an ought-to L2 self, driven by a sense of parental obligation, to an attractor state where the ideal L2 self is central. The main source of this shift in the system's trajectory was a developing intrinsic interest in learning English, initiated by contact with English literature:

> My parents hoped [that] I could use my English to help develop their business in domestic chemical. So I imagined I could communicate fluently with foreign businessmen in English. But this summer, after reading those English novels, I imagine working as an English editor in a large publisher, editing and revising a draft of an English news report.

Although perceptions of his obligations to his parents may not vanish easily (suggesting that the ought-to L2 self attractor still exerts an influence on the system), it is probable that Harry's motivational system has been drawn to a different part of the state space by a powerful ideal L2 self attractor.

A similar shift can be seen in Ivory's motivational system. Previously anchored in an attractor state centred on an internalised ought-to L2 self – the social obligation related to supporting her parents' company – the system shifts to an attractor state in which her ideal L2 self – and even also an ideal L3 self – have powerful roles:

> Now I often imagine that I am a successful sales girl doing business with foreigners and speaking English to them fluently. I also speak Spanish skilfully to businessmen from South America about our business contract … I think the reason now is that I have come to like English.

In our data we consistently observed how the participants' parents attributed great importance to the knowledge of English, all but one mentioning that their families placed a high value on being able to communicate fluently in English. For Candy a shift took place in her motivational system after she went to university. Because she could detach herself somewhat from her family, she experienced her parents' expectations as becoming less intense. From an attractor state that revolved around the visualisation of a feared L2 self (generated by a fear of not matching up to parental expectations) the system appears to move to a new ideal L2 self attractor state:

> After I went to university, my parents just wanted me to get good attainment in my studies of English and to pass the tests. Now I feel more relaxed. I can imagine the situation where I'm introducing my project in English to foreign clients [in the future].

Shifts in the other direction: From an ideal L2 self to an ought-to L2 self

For one of our interviewees, however, the motivational system appears to have moved in a different direction to the shifts we have so far identified. For Ruby, movement of the system seems to have taken place from, when she was younger, being lodged in an ideal L2 self attractor state to a position where it is now in an ought-to L2 self attractor state. As Ruby explains, the imagery associated with her imagining finding employment in a joint venture stems from a growing feeling of responsibility to her family:

> When I was a primary school student and I watched some Chinese people speaking English to foreigners fluently on TV, I would imagine myself speaking English successfully like them. Now I have come to imagine that I find a job in a Sino joint venture, so that I can support my family [in the future].

So, to sum up, while for many of our interviewees system movement tends to have been from ought-to to ideal L2 self attractor states, other system movements, such as in Ruby's case, can also be detected.

Changes in the elaborateness and frequency of generation of L2 imagery

Besides changes in the imagery content of L2 self-guides, our data also point to other types of transformations of the learners' imagery, namely in its elaborateness and in the frequency that visualisations of future L2 selves are generated.

Increasingly elaborate ideal L2 self imagery

Many of our participants reported that, as time progressed, the images they generated of themselves in future English-speaking/using situations had greater clarity, were more specific, more elaborate and happened more frequently. Indeed, for half the participants, recollections of visualisations of the L2 self were almost non-existent in the initial stages of their L2 learning, such imagery only developing later on. The experience described by Lucy is typical of many of the other students:

> In the past I didn't imagine this since I had to prepare for the entrance examination to high school. After I finished the exam, I began to watch [English] movies and videos online. I think their English is perfect, so I admire them and imagine I can speak English like them [in the future].

Some of the learners developed L2 self imagery from scratch, gradually acquiring a general visualisation of a future English-speaking self and developing more specific future-oriented L2 images as they matured, both educationally and in terms of their language proficiency:

> I didn't have such image at my junior school since I had no idea of what English was used for. In high school, I did imagine that I could one day communicate with foreigners freely. Now, I imagine that after my graduation from university, I need to do a market survey [in English] for a factory. I am talking to those participants in English fluently so that real and in-depth information can be collected. (Kyle)

Reflecting on the sources of such incremental developments, the interviewees mentioned various role models (teachers and peers, as well as English native speakers and various celebrities), direct contact with foreigners, indirect contact with English-speaking cultures (e.g. through watching English movies or reading novels), as well as positive learning experiences. This latter factor – also documented by Lamb's (2012) recent study in Indonesia – highlights the relevance of the educational environment, well illustrated by Ruby's account of how the mental images she has of her future English-speaking self first materialised:

> I started to imagine [myself using English successfully in the future] when I was a primary school student. I imagined myself speaking English successfully like those Chinese people speaking English on TV. Now, I think my imagination is wider in scope. You know, my English has always been the best [in my class] since my primary school. I often imagine that I am reading very difficult English articles deeper. And I imagine I am working as a customs officer [with English being my working language]. I can also imagine that in the future I am a simultaneous interpreter working at conferences on international business and trade.

Developing imagery associated with a feared self

Changes in the nature of participants' visions were also observed in relation to images of feared selves. Six participants reported that although, initially, they had tended not to visualise a feared L2 self, or tended to visualise a rather simple vision, later, owing to the pressure from English tests or soon-to-begin job hunting, they had generated pronounced feared-self visions. An example of this was described by Emma, whose visualisation of a feared L2 self develops after starting university and has been triggered by her fear of having to hunt for a job:

> Before I entered university, I just had the fear of failing in English exams. After I became a university student, I have my own major and I want to

develop it well and sustainably. ... I imagine being interviewed in English for a job, I cannot answer the questions and I fail to get the job. I feel scared when imagining this.

An increasing frequency in visualising an ideal L2 self

Even when a motivational system is lodged in an ideal L2 self attractor state, meaning a contingent stability has been attained, the frequency with which learners visualise future language use can still differ. As Jemima explains, after she realised the important role that English would play in her future she began to visualise herself in English-speaking situations more frequently:

> I did imagine those ... but not that often, maybe once or twice [at my junior school]. After I entered high school, I have come to know that English is a *Lingua Franca* and is really important to my future. So, now I often imagine that I can speak English like those people who are successful in speaking English.

Thus, even though the position of the system in the state space does not change, because these visions occur with increasing frequency, the system becomes more deeply rooted in its attractor state, the system's resilience to change (assessed in terms of the force required to dislodge it) being even greater than before. For another student, Manny, the increasingly frequent occurrence of ideal L2 self imagery was owing to the influence of one of her peers who helped to raise her awareness of the importance of English:

> In the past I didn't think much about it. But now it's different. (Why?) It's mainly because, after I entered high school, my roommate told me many times about the importance of English. I have been inspired by her words. You know, she is so good at English. ... So I began to imagine it more and more often.

Like Manny, as learners come across situations and stimuli that are congruent with the ideal L2 self, in these contexts future scenarios of language in use will be conjured up. In the extract presented above, when, in various ways, the importance of English is highlighted (e.g. 'my roommate told me many times'), Manny's vision of her ideal L2 self develops and occurs with increasing frequency.

Fluctuations in the frequency of L2 imagery in future self-guides

Several of the participants talked about fluctuations in the imagery surrounding their ideal L2 selves that took place at different stages in their learning. Reflecting on these changes Candy recalls that:

> At my primary school, I could imagine that some foreigners asked me (in English) for help in a street ... At high school, I studied hard to pass

tests and didn't imagine anything. Now, I feel less burdened. I can imagine that I am introducing my project in English to foreign clients [in the future].

Harry reports how the vision of a feared L2 self, once generated, although developing into a strong vision, has weakened as time has moved on:

I didn't imagine the fearful scenes that I used to in the past. Now, I do have some. Three months ago, my fear was much stronger than it is now since I chose English as my major. Thinking of the [future] failure made me feel scared indeed. [Now], I imagine I am rejected in a job interview. But the feeling will disappear in a few days. I think I should still believe in my own potential.

For Harry, it was prevention-oriented instrumentality (i.e. the desire to avoid failure in learning English) that fuelled the vision of a powerful feared L2 self. What we can also see here is the way in which fluctuations occur across different timescales (see de Bot, this volume). As is evident in Harry's account, change can take place both across longer timescales – 'I didn't imagine the fearful scenes that I used to in the past', he says. 'Now, I do have some' – and shorter timescales – 'the feeling will disappear in a few days'.

The dynamic interplay of imagery, motivation, language learning behaviour and L2 proficiency

Up to this point, we have primarily identified system shifts between one self-guide attractor state and another, and changes in the strength of self-guide attractor states stemming from changes in the mental imagery clothing self-guides. We have also looked at the ways that, as targets, self-guides can be reassessed and downwardly revised. However, in this final section of our investigation of the dynamics of L2 imagery we turn to look at the interaction of imagery with other factors. In particular, we examine dynamic interactions with three key variables related to L2 learning; motivational intensity, L2 learning behaviour and L2 proficiency. Of course, as would be expected in any dynamic system, these factors are inextricably interrelated, meaning that it is beyond the scope of our limited investigation to study these interrelationships in any depth. Rather, our aim is to identify three particular types of interaction we regard as central in understanding the functioning of imagery. These are, respectively, the interactions between imagery and increasing motivation, the interactions between imagery and language learning behaviour and the interactions between imagery and language proficiency.

An interaction between imagery and increasing motivation

The first pattern we observed is well established in the literature (see e.g. Dörnyei & Kubanyiova, 2014), indicating that imagery is related to L2 motivation. When a change in visualisation functions as the initiator of the imagery–motivation interaction – that is to say when someone becomes better at, or gains practice in, visualisation skills – this can bring about an increased level of motivation and, consequently, increased effort in language learning behaviour. As Katie explains 'The more I dream of it, the happier I become. Then I feel I'm full of drive and I learn English harder'.

However, our data also revealed an opposite pattern; sometimes changing imagery is not the beginning, but the outcome of the process. An increase in motivation can also act as an initiator, triggering a change in visualisation. It is this pattern that we see emerging in the interview with Quintus:

> Now, it is more specific. I imagine that I'm attending a conference in my company with many foreigners there, and that I am explaining something to them in English. It is because I have become more interested in English, which motivates me to learn it harder.

An interaction between imagery and language learning behaviour

The second pattern we observed concerns an interrelationship between imagery development and changes in language learning behaviour. For example, Kyle described various changes in his behaviours that took place as the imagery clothing his ideal L2 self began to evolve, pointing to the fact that, as new images develop, this may lead in turn to the setting of new goals and to matching goal-oriented L2 learning behaviours:

> Later I entered university in China... I imagined I could one day study abroad, so I studied hard to get ready for IELTS or TOEFL tests. Now, I often imagine that I could one day work in a joint-venture [in China]. So I'm now trying hard to learn the skills for the job interviews [in English].

The powerful impact that imagery can have on language learning behaviours is underscored when, in his interview, Andy explains that 'every time I have those images, the next day I will get up very early at 6 am to learn English'.

On the other hand, we have seen earlier that language learning behaviour – for example, when learners have to take tests or prepare extensively for exams – can also function as a catalyst triggering the development of self-relevant L2 imagery.

Interactions between imagery and language proficiency

The link between imagery and L2 proficiency was found to be the third salient dynamic pattern. The established pattern is that the use of L2-relevant mental imagery leads to increased L2 proficiency, either indirectly through the mediation of motivation or learning behaviours, or directly as a consequence of mental rehearsals. Our data, however, also reveal examples of the reversed pattern, namely when participants' increased L2 proficiency, allows them to revise their ideal L2 self-images, for example, by opening up more possibilities of future career choices related to English. That is, imagery content can be altered according to perceptions of proficiency. For example, while Jessica explains that 'I have been improving my English these years. I think my images have been changing as well', Manny says: 'Now I imagine it more often and in a richer way. (Why?) ... Because I'm better at English now'. Interestingly, Jessica further reports that, after she came to study in the UK, it can also be the perception of low proficiency that makes her conjure up a rich visualisation of an ideal L2 self as a way of generating motivation to reduce the discrepancy between the current (undesired) level of proficiency and that which is hoped for in the future:

> I imagine that I am talking to [English] people I meet in a supermarket or at a railway station in English fluently. (Why?) Because I think my English is not good enough and I hope to reach the proficiency I have imagined.

Reflections on the dynamic interactions

In previous second language acquisition research, imagery has mainly been discussed in connection to future L2 self-guides. It is therefore noteworthy that our study indicates that visualisation is also related to other factors, such as, as discovered here, motivational intensity, language learning behaviour and language proficiency. Furthermore, as seems to emerge from our data, patterns not only differ, but can also be reversed, thus pointing to the operation of interlinked components in the motivational system. The relationship between imagery and the other three variables that we looked at would appear to be bi-directional, that is to say that, in some cases, the change in imagery seemed to have an impact on the other variables, while at other times the evolution of imagery appeared to be triggered by changes in these other variables. In that this is an exploratory study, based on a series of single 25–minute interviews, we cannot hope to provide a comprehensive illustration of the full functioning of any of the learners' motivational systems. Nevertheless, the fact that we observed patterns with differing trajectories is indicative of systemic functioning, in that it suggests that whenever one component of a motivational system changes, it can, potentially, impact on all the others.

Conclusion

In this study, we have suggested that mental imagery in the form of L2 self-guides is not static and is likely to change during the process of L2 learning. The changes in self-relevant L2 imagery experienced by the learners we interviewed relate to changes in content and changes in elaborateness, as well as changes in the frequency with which such images are cognitively invoked. Although this was an exploratory study and we were not able to achieve a depth of analysis that would normally be needed in a DST-inspired interview-based study (see e.g. Mercer, 2011), it is nevertheless noteworthy that we identified possible dynamic interactions between imagery and three other factors, namely, motivational intensity, language learning behaviour and language proficiency. These interactions point to the operation of the interlinked components of motivational systems.

Research on future self-guides has, until now, treated possible selves and their underpinning imagery content as fixed 'targets' or 'goalposts' that learners strive to reach for. The dominant message in the various theoretical and practical publications has been that producing such solid goals or targets can enhance L2 learners' motivation and performance. However, our findings show that imagery is more dynamic than has perhaps previously been perceived. As learners start approaching these goalposts (i.e. mental images of possible selves), the goalpost may not always remain constant (see Henry, Chapter 9, this volume). Rather, it can start shifting, movement which can trigger chains of dynamic interactions. In other words, imagery not only affects the process of L2 learning, but is itself affected by the process. This, however, places Higgins' (1987) theory of self-discrepancy theory – that is, the belief that motivated behaviour is fuelled by the tension of the perceived discrepancy between actual and desired future self images – in a new light, in that the size and nature of the gap also interacts with the process. Thus, although in some cases the gap is reduced by forward movement, in other cases it can be reduced by bringing the goalpost nearer.

Note

(1) Questions related to the feared L2 self imagery are subsumed under the category of ought-to L2 self.

References

Al-Shehri, A.S. (2009) Motivation and vision: The relation between the ideal L2 self, imagination and visual style. In Z. Dörnyei and E. Ushioda (eds) *Motivation, Language Identity and the L2 Self* (pp. 164–171). Bristol: Multilingual Matters.

Busse, V. (2013) An exploration of motivation and self-beliefs of first year students of German. *System* 41, 379–398.

Chan, L. (2014) Effects of an imagery training strategy on Chinese university students' possible second language selves and learning experiences. In K. Csizér and M. Magid (eds) *The Impact of Self-Concept on Language Learning.* Bristol: Multilingual Matters.

Csizér, K. and Kormos, J. (2009) Learning experiences, selves and motivated learning behavior: A comparative analysis of structural models for Hungarian secondary and university learners of English. In Z. Dörnyei and E. Ushioda (eds) *Motivation, language Identity and the L2 Self* (pp. 98–119). Bristol: Multilingual Matters.

Csizér, K. and Lukács, G. (2010) The comparative analysis of motivation, attitudes and selves: The case of English and German in Hungary. *System* 38, 1–13.

Dörnyei, Z. (2005) *The Psychology of the Language Learner: Individual Differences in Second Language Acquisition*. Mahwah, NJ: Lawrence Erlbaum.

Dörnyei, Z. (2009) The L2 Motivational Self System. In Z. Dörnyei and E. Ushioda (eds) *Motivation, Language Identity and the L2 Self* (pp. 9–42). Bristol: Multilingual Matters.

Dörnyei, Z. (2010) The relationship between language aptitude and language learning motivation: Individual differences from a dynamic systems perspective. In E. Macaro (ed.) *Continuum Companion to Second Language Acquisition* (pp. 247–267). London: Continuum.

Dörnyei, Z. (2014) Future self-guides and vision. In K. Csizér and M. Magid (eds) *The Impact of Self-Concept on Language Learning*. Bristol: Multilingual Matters.

Dörnyei, Z. and Chan, L. (2013) Motivation and vision: An analysis of future L2 self images, sensory styles, and imagery capacity across two target languages. *Language Learning* 63 (3), 437–462.

Dörnyei, Z. and Kubanyiova, M. (2014) *Motivating Learners, Motivating Teachers: Building Vision in the Language Classroom*. Cambridge: Cambridge University Press.

Dörnyei, Z. and Ushioda, E. (2011) *Teaching and Researching Motivation* (2nd edn). Harlow: Longman.

Fukada, Y., Fukuda, T., Falout, J. and Murphey, T. (2011) Increasing motivation with possible selves. In A. Stewart (ed.) *JALT 2010 Conference Proceedings* (pp. 337–349). Tokyo: JALT.

Hall, E., Hall, C. and Leech, A. (1990) *Scripted Fantasy in the Classroom*. London: Routledge.

Henry, A. (2009) Gender differences in compulsory school pupils' L2 self-concepts: A longitudinal study. *System* 37, 177–193.

Henry, A. (2010) Contexts of possibility in simultaneous language learning: Using the L2 Motivational Self System to assess the impact of global English. *Journal of Multilingual and Multicultural Development* 31 (2), 149–162.

Henry, A. (2011) Examining the impact of L2 English on L3 selves: A case study. *International Journal of Multilingualism* 8 (3), 235–255.

Henry, A. and Apelgren, B.M. (2008) Young learners and multilingualism: A study of learner attitudes before and after the introduction of a second foreign language to the curriculum. *System* 36, 607–623.

Higgins, E.T. (1987) Self-discrepancy: A theory relating self and affect. *Psychological Review* 94, 319–340.

Islam, M., Lamb, M. and Chambers, G. (2013) The L2 Motivational Self System and national interest: A Pakistani perspective. *System* 41, 231–244.

Jones, K. (2012) Visualising success: An imagery intervention programme to increase two Students' confidence and motivation in a foreign language. Unpublished MA dissertation, University of Nottingham.

Kim, T.Y. (2009) Korean elementary school students' perceptual learning style, ideal L2 self, and motivated behavior. *Korean Journal of English Language and Linguistics* 9 (3), 461–486.

Kim, Y.K. and Kim, T.Y. (2011) The effect of Korean secondary school Students' perceptual learning styles and ideal L2 self on motivated L2 behavior and English proficiency. *Korean Journal of English Language and Linguistics* 11 (1), 21–42.

Larsen-Freeman, D. and Cameron, L. (2008) *Complex Systems and Applied Linguistics*. Oxford: Oxford University Press.

Lamb, M. (2012) A self system perspective on young adolescents' motivation to learn English in urban and rural setting. *Language Learning* 62 (4), 997–1023.

Magid, M. (2011) *A validation and application of the L2 motivational self system among Chinese learners of English*. PhD thesis, University of Nottingham.

Magid, M. and Chan, L. (2012) Motivating English learners by helping them visualize their Ideal L2 Self: Lessons from two motivational programmes. *Innovation in Language Learning and Teaching* 6 (2), 113–125.

Markus, H. and Nurius, P. (1986) Possible selves. *American Psychologist* 41, 954–969.

Markus, H. and Wurf, E. (1987) The dynamic self-concept: A social psychological perspective. *Annual Review of Psychology* 38, 299–337.

Mercer, S. (2011) Understanding learner agency as a complex dynamic system. *System* 39, 427–436.

Morris, T. (2010) Imagery. In S. J. Harahan and M. B. Anderson (eds) *Routledge Handbook of Applied Sport Psychology: A Comprehensive Guide for Students and Practitioners.* (pp. 481–499). New York: Routledge.

Moulton, S.T. and Kosslyn, S.M. (2009) Imagining predictions: Mental imagery as mental emulation. *Philosophical Transactions of the Royal Society B* 364, 1273–1280.

Oettingen, G. and Thorpe, J. (2006) Fantasy realization and the bridging of time. In L.J. Sanna and E.C. Chang (eds) *Judgments Over Time: The Interplay of Thoughts, Feelings, and Behaviors* (pp. 120–144). New York: Oxford University Press.

Ravenscroft, I. (2012) Fiction, imagination and ethics. In R. Langdon and C. Mackenzie (eds) *Emotion, Imagination, and Moral Reasoning.* New York: Psychological Press.

Ruvolo, A.P. and Markus, H.R. (1992) Possible selves and performance: The power of self relevant imagery. *Social Cognition* 10 (1), 95–124.

Sampson, R. (2012) The language-learning self, self-enhancement activities, and self perceptual change. *Language Teaching Research* 16 (3), 317–335.

Taguchi, T., Magid, M. and Papi, M. (2009) The L2 motivational self system among Japanese, Chinese and Iranian learners of English: A comparative study. In Z. Dörnyei and E. Ushioda (eds) *Motivation, Language Identity and the L2 self* (pp. 66–97). Bristol: Multilingual Matters.

van der Helm, R. (2009) The vision phenomenon: Towards a theoretical underpinning of visions of the future and the process of envisioning. *Futures* 41, 96–104.

Wenger, E. (1998) *Communities of Practise: Learning, Meaning, and Identity.* Cambridge: Cambridge University Press.

23 Conclusion: Hot Enough to be Cool: The Promise of Dynamic Systems Research

Peter D. MacIntyre, Zoltán Dörnyei
and Alastair Henry

Not long ago, in a special issue of the journal *Child Development Perspectives*, Marc Lewis' (2011) paper 'Dynamic Systems Approaches: Hot Enough? Cool Enough?' took stock of 20 years of dynamic systems research in the field of child development. He concluded that 'the DS paradigm must continue to be "cool" enough to attract developmental psychologists with its fresh insights and novel techniques yet strive to become "hot" enough to deliver robust findings, consistently and convincingly, through powerful analytical tools' (Lewis, 2011: 283). His analysis noted that dynamic systems proponents writing in the journal found research progress to be slower than they had hoped, yet Lewis offered an impressive list of significant contributions to understanding child development that are tied to a dynamic perspective.

Now it is our turn. To conclude the present volume we would like to summarise the main lessons that we have learned in the process of putting together this collection, informed by experience in allied disciplines. Editing this anthology has been a real learning experience, as noted in the Introduction chapter. In many ways, the field itself might be thought of as a dynamic system, constantly changing and subject to perturbations. Seminal works in the field, such as Larsen-Freeman and Cameron (2008) and Verspoor *et al.* (2011), have disturbed the status quo in L2 motivation research, and we hope that the findings and insights offered in this anthology will provide momentum for future research that will lead to a new equilibrium.

Will Complex Dynamic Systems be a Cool but Fringe Methodology?

The advent of complex dynamic systems in language research has sprung a new type of conceptual and methodological language on the field, and we are grateful to the authors of the conceptual pieces in Chapters 2–10 for helping to clarify some of the key issues. The dynamic perspective presented in these chapters yields a unique and perhaps unfamiliar way of approaching research questions. The papers foreground concepts and subject matter rarely encountered elsewhere in second language acquisition (SLA) research in such an explicit manner, such as, for example, the question of free will, the significance of timescales, the nature of equilibrium and attractor states, the organism's sensitivity to initial conditions, as well as different types of self-organising processes within the system, such as emergence, coupling, realignment, etc. These concepts are interesting in their own right but, admittedly, do not connect easily to more familiar concepts in this research area.

The novelty of the dynamic perspective is both a good and a bad thing. As the new kid on the block, by promising to do things differently from the mainstream practice, dynamic approaches offer new and different ways of understanding the processes of SLA and development (de Bot *et al.*, 2013), potentially shedding light on as yet unresolved issues and providing inroads into unchartered areas. However, not being part of the mainstream in research brings its own set of problems. To start with, even the research questions themselves are usually substantively different from the majority of prior literature. Novel types of questions present a challenge, especially for new researchers in the field, such as those doing studies as part of a Master's or PhD programme. Many of the contributors to this volume would gladly testify to the difficulty involved in developing a dynamically oriented mindset. We have learnt from hard-won experience that working with dynamic systems competently and confidently has a high learning threshold. Once the threshold is crossed, the toolkit becomes genuinely profitable, but most SLA students in universities at present would find few opportunities for training that can help them to get close to this threshold. This is in stark contrast with books and courses on conventional statistics and research methods that are readily available.

Does the present situation foreshadow a future whereby adopting dynamic systems principles may remain a cool but fringe methodology, chosen to be employed by a selected few 'initiated' scholars? The purpose of producing this anthology has been exactly to avoid such a marginalised fringe position, and in the rest of this conclusion we shall summarise some key maxims and recommendations that we hope will encourage researchers to 'take the plunge'. Let us, however, first state here why we think that adopting complex, dynamic system principles is integral to the language processes we study and therefore cannot remain optional. To put it plainly, the social world around us *is* dynamic and, as one of the contributors to this volume astutely pointed out, 'once a researcher understands the complexity worldview, in a sense there is a transformation in thinking. Everything you observe and experience from then on – whether it involves personal relationships, parenting concerns, events unfolding in contemporary society, to say nothing of SL classroom phenomena – is nothing if not complex and dynamic. This understanding leads to the conviction that there are certain things that can only be uncovered from a dynamic systems perspective' (Hiver, personal communication). This point reiterates Thelen and Smith's (1994) conclusion to their classic work on the topic – *A Dynamic Systems Approach to the Development of Cognition and Action* – two decades ago:

> Once we began to view development from a dynamic and selectionist approach, we found the ideas so powerful that we could never go back to other ways of thinking. Every paper we read, every talk we heard, every new bit of data from our labs took on new meaning. We planned experiments differently and interpreted old experiments from a fresh perspective. Some questions motivating developmental research no longer seemed important; other, wholly new areas of inquiry begged for further work. (Thelen & Smith, 1994: 341)

Terminology

We have already indicated in the Introduction that one of the main difficulties in adopting a complex, dynamic approach is the fact that it comes with a language of its own. Most of this terminology is imported from other disciplines. Even choosing a title for the overall dynamic approach itself differs among leading scholars. Depending on which feeder discipline a scholar has been influenced by most, the new dynamic approach has been referred to under at least four different terms: complexity theory, dynamic or dynamical systems theory, chaos theory and emergentism. In most cases, but not always, these have been used interchangeably, converging in the same general nonlinear systems approach. Some authors in this volume followed Larsen-Freeman and Cameron (2008) in referring to the theory underlying their approach as 'complexity theory', others adopted the practice of developmental psychology as conveyed by de Bot *et al.* (2007) by using 'dynamic systems theory', and we also find the compromise: 'complex dynamic systems theory' (CDS – a term used in this Conclusion to remain inclusive).

Once scholars have got their heads round the issue of the overall labelling of the field, they will soon encounter a more serious challenge; the terminology applied to the processes under study. As already pointed out in the Introduction chapter, most of the technical terms used in dynamic systems approaches are rooted in mathematical representations of processes and phe-nomena. There is some difficulty in trying to map this terminology onto our social reality in a meaningful way. Qualitative researchers have faced a simi-lar challenge trying to work with the constraints of terms originating in the quantitative tradition, such as validity, reliability or generalisability. This is not a trivial issue because the process of disseminating research requires that all the actors in the field – authors, reviewers, etc. – share at least some common ground.

The CDS term 'attractor' is perhaps the best illustration of the issue of terminology. Attractors have special significance in CDS because the concept offers a way of focusing on predictable aspects of a system, the states in which a system is most likely to settle for some period of time, even taking into account the unpredictable, chaotic elements of system behaviour. This preferred system behaviour – or equilibrium – has been referred to as an attractor state. But the term immediately raises a question; what are the 'attractors' in relation to this state? Can they be described as magnets that attract the system's behaviour? If so, can attractors be equated with 'vari-ables'? The simple answer would be no, because these questions suggest straightforward linear causation (as if attractors cause specific system behav-iour). In a discussion of this topic during the editing process, Kees de Bot (personal communication) categorically stated that 'Attractors do not attract, they simply are. Attractors are not magnets'. David Byrne (personal com-munication) went even further when he concluded, 'An attractor is very dif-ferent from a variable. The term "attractor" is simply used to describe a possible state of a system. As such we can think of it as a domain in the possible (state) space'. Gregersen and MacIntyre (this volume) explicitly note that the term attractor in everyday language might mean 'pleasant, desirable and appealing (or even good-looking)'. But in CDS terminology, attractor states are not necessarily pleasant; they just have to be stable over a specific time frame. Consequently, we have come to think of attractors exclusively as system outcome states, an understanding developed more fully in Phil Hiver's summary of the concept (this volume, Chapter 3).

While restricting the scope of 'attractors' to refer only to states makes the term less ambiguous, at the same time it reveals the absence of straightfor-ward terminology in CDS approaches for conceptualising the specific influ-ence that some factors – such as some kind of an input – exert on the system. According to Byrne (personal communication), 'For an individual considered as a system, an input to that system – a reward, etc. – is just that, an input ... it is still not a variable as we would normally conceptualize it'. For example, a specific analgesic drug (input) might relieve pain, have no effect or be lethal depending on the system (body) into which the input is introduced. The impact that an input has on the system can be understood in different ways. An input can be approached as a co-adaptation process between two sys-tems. In the language of synergetics (cf. Haken, 2009), an input to the system can refer to the influence of a control parameter, which is an existing external principle that constrains the possibilities of the system's behaviour. It may well be the case that, from a mathematical perspective, these variations merely amount to variant equations, but when we try to apply our metaphors in a phenomenologically transparent manner, we need to come up with socially accurate definitions and representations. We see that the perception of the term 'attractor' illustrates a broader issue; the difficulties inherent in developing phenomenological understandings of CDS terminology when they are applied in conceptualising and empirically investigating different SLA phenomena.

A Set of Dynamic Principles

CDS theories have been instrumental in drawing attention to the fact that to understand the reality of phenomena in the social world we need to internalise in our worldviews certain dynamic principles. While it is often difficult to pin down this 'worldview' in terms of specific methodological propositions, it is possible to draw up a set of powerful and universally relevant maxims that are now all but indispensable for first-class research. Such key principles include the following (see also Larsen-Freeman, this volume).

- *Open system*: Studies of motivation in SLA are examining an open, inherently continuous system that involves fluctuations from one state to another with constant interference from additional motives and other processes in an ongoing, evolving and iterative basis.
- *Self-organisation and nonlinearity*: Motivation has adaptive and self-organising properties, with feedback loops that continuously integrate internal and external contexts and act as reinforcing or counteracting forces, creating nonlinear changes in levels of motivated behaviour.
- *Multicausality and soft assembly*: Motivation is multi-determined, so that no single element, input or force controls or causes change. Instead, motivational processes and outcomes are softly assembled (i.e. elements of the system interact in different ways depending on the task, context, etc.), rather than hardwired.
- *Timescales*: Language development itself occurs continuously on multiple simultaneous timescales with particular processes tied to specific timescales, meaning that conclusions about motivation are tied to the timescale on which they occur. In other words, the ongoing ebbs and flows of motivation, or the emerging cycles or repeating patterns, can be observed and described using various starting points and over various timescales.
- *Levels of abstraction of the 'system'*: The motivational patterns that we observe in SLA can be described alternatively at different levels of abstraction by focusing on the interrelationships among processes in a more

abstract sense (e.g. how vision plays a role in the formation of an ideal L2 self), processes within an individual (e.g. why an initially unsuccessful language learner will not give up), or processes at a group level (e.g. why competition within a class is productive at times, yet detrimental to motivation at others).

Some Advice on How to Conduct Research in a Dynamic Vein

One of the fundamental lessons we drew from reviewing the submissions to this anthology is that the vast majority of the studies that were originally initiated in a non-CDS framework could not be reanalysed to yield valuable CDS insights. Many of the papers that were submitted could best be described as traditional qualitative, longitudinal or correlational studies with an introduction that focused on CDS theory. In such cases, we typically observed a disconnect between the assumed theoretical framework and the details of the research methods; quite simply the latter were not designed to produce the density of data required to study the iterative process of change. Therefore, the most basic research methodological advice we can offer someone wishing to adopt a CDS approach is that applying a dynamic perspective should begin right at the design stage, by considering the dynamics of a well-defined system.

In practical terms, operationalising the 'dynamics' part is easier; it means examining the interplay among factors and the iterative processes involved. Defining the 'system' under study might, however, be trickier than it sounds. Of particular importance is the need to consider the level of the system we wish to study, a process that is often referred to as 'casing' in the CDS literature (e.g. Carter & Sealey, 2009). The selected domain of reality in focus could be an individual person or, if we move in an upward direction, a dyad, a classroom, a social group, a culture or a subculture. Moving in the opposite direction, the system could be the cognitive or emotion system of a person, or for example, the coordination of the anxiety-arousal system. We usually can examine an issue at multiple levels, making it particularly important to 'case' the system under investigation in unambiguous terms by putting specific limits around what we study.

Identifying the focal system and the level at which it operates is only the beginning. A dynamic system is never isolated from other systems; rather, it is in continual interaction with different systems at different levels. Consequently, at the design stage of any CDS study, processes of mapping need to take place. Other systems that might interact with the focal system need to be identified, with a particular need to be alert to the ways in which the focal system might adapt as a response to the interaction. Accordingly, building in opportunities for studying such between-system interactions becomes an important aspect of CDS study design.

Framing a suitable research question might be one of the crucial phases of the process and the one that can prove to be most difficult in the CDS area. Developing research questions from a dynamic perspective requires questions about *process* rather than product; it really is a different way of thinking. For example, conventional research might ask about the correlation between two variables (e.g. *'What is the correlation between motivation and L2 course grades?'*); there is value in doing this research, and studies dating back to Gardner and Lambert's (1959) work have found that L2 motivation is reliably correlated with grades in a language course. Although traditional research questions such as this can lead to significant contributions, the process that connects motivation to language behaviour and outcomes has to be inferred. Adopting a CDS approach, fruitful research questions can be thought of in terms of describing a process in motion. Thus, examples of CDS research questions would be: *'What makes motivation rise and fall during a conversation/lesson/unit/semester?'*, or *'How does a learner vacillate between approaching and avoiding a native speaker?'*, or *'How does a specific encounter with a native speaker in the past feed back into the motivation system years later?'*

A research question phrased in CDS-terms needs to be married to an appropriate methodology for research to proceed. Conventional quantitative studies are best conducted with a large sample, reliable measures and statistical procedures to assess the probability of observing patterns of relationships, group differences or change over time in variables under investigation. Qualitative studies typically offer an in-depth examination of a small number of persons, often using retrospective interviews or focus group techniques that reflect the respondents' memory and understanding of prior events. CDS methods should offer something different, which in turn means that dynamic accounts of motivation necessitate the development of new and/or altered methodologies. Van Dijk *et al.* (2011: 62) neatly capture the idea of the data necessary to study dynamics: 'if we really want to know how an individual (or group) develops over time we need data that is dense (i.e. collected at many regular measurement points), longitudinal (i.e. collected over a longer period of time), and individual (i.e. for one person at a time and not averaged out)'. The continuing acceptance of mixed methods research (see e.g. Dörnyei, 2007) bodes well with respect to CDS studies, especially if it allows unanticipated factors into the mix. However, a mixed methods study is *not* inherently dynamic in nature, and neither does qualitative data automatically meet van Dijk *et al.*'s (2011) criteria.

The studies in the current anthology have been conducted using a variety of methods, some of which will be new to readers and might even have been used for the first time in the study of SLA motivation. These methods, and others yet to be developed, will allow future research to explore CDS questions (see Table 23.1).

Without any doubt this is a promising start, but at the same time we see it as an imperative that these and other dynamic methods be further developed

Table 23.1 Examples of CDS methods used in this anthology

Method	Examples in chapters by ...
Two-stage qualitative interview design	Waninge (Ch. 14)
Longitudinal qualitative interview design	Henry (Ch. 19); Yashima & Arano (Ch. 18)
Qualitative interview design gathering data on multiple timescales	Mercer (Ch. 12)
Qualitative comparative analysis (QCA)	Hiver (Ch. 15)
Mixed methods research/Triangulation of multiple data sources	Gregersen & MacIntyre (Ch. 17); Nitta & Baba (Ch. 21); You & Chan (Ch. 22)
Cluster analysis	Piniel & Csizér (Ch. 13)
Q methodology	Irie & Ryan (Ch. 20)
Idiodynamics	MacIntyre & Serroul (Ch. 11); Mercer (Ch. 12)
Retrodictive qualitative modelling	Chan, Dörnyei & Henry (Ch. 16)
Latent growth modelling	Piniel & Csizér (Ch. 13)
Change point analysis	Nitta & Baba (Ch. 21)
Variability analysis	Piniel & Csizér (Ch. 13)
Trajectory equifinality model	Yashima & Arano (Ch. 18)

and refined if the field is to move forward along the dynamic path. It will be necessary to adjust the criteria for evaluating research methods in order to accommodate the dynamic turn; in this respect a future article that draws up parallels between research terms used in traditional closed systems and dynamic open systems – for example by specifying the CDS equivalent or meaning of terms such as significance, generalisability, cause-effect relations, purposive sampling, reliability, validity, etc. – would be particularly welcome.

Positive Examples: Issues That Could Not Have Been Studied as Meaningfully Without a CDS Approach

We believe that the field already has moved past the question of whether a CDS perspective is relevant to the study of motivation in SLA – it is. By means of illustration, we have dipped into the current collection to extract some of the most telling insights into motivational processes that we believe would have not been possible without this specific toolkit. Reflecting on some of the most important findings to emerge from Chapters 11–22 we can see how:

- MacIntyre and Serroul used the idea of soft assembly of incompatible states to show how learners can react with both approach motivation and high anxiety at the same time, documenting the effects of L2 vocabulary retrieval on a temporary repeller state in the affective domain.

- Mercer used the notion of multiple timescales to capture the nuances of self-development in a set of nested concepts that showed considerable variation across levels, reinforcing the importance of explicitly taking timescales into account.
- Piniel and Csizér identified patterns of change in the relationships of L2 self-related variables over an academic term, using advanced quantitative modelling of change processes.
- Waninge used a series of short interviews to identify four salient attractor states (interest, boredom, neutral attention and anxiety) with an emphasis on the transitions and variability among states as well as the interaction of motivation, cognition and emotion.
- Hiver was able to show that the notion of a self-organising system, rather than personality traits, can be a more appropriate way to conceptualise the development of teacher immunity among his participants.
- Chan, Dörnyei and Henry observed the back and forward shifting between different sources of motivation, which would have been difficult to explain without the aid of cyclic/closed-loop attractors.
- Gregersen and MacIntyre used a triangulation of qualitative data to show a dynamic, iterative process within the self-system of teachers/learners that is best understood using properties of a dynamic system.
- Yashima and Arano were able to consider dense data on motivation over three different timescales to account for what they deem puzzling phenomena and inconsistencies in emerging motivation.
- Henry documented the sometimes rapid changes into and out of attractor and repeller states, showing the sensitivity of the motivation system to a variety of influences, some of which would not have been anticipated prior to the study, reflecting the properties of an open system.
- Irie and Ryan use the conflicted messages encountered in their understanding of motivation from their dual perspective as teachers and researchers, settling on the idea of attractor states to capture differences among types of study abroad experiences of students, along with the variability (and unpredictability) in the trajectories that students follow.
- Nitta and Baba used multi-level data to describe the complex, adaptive relationship among L2 self elements and L2 motivation.
- You and Chan identified and documented how dynamic changes in imagery develop complex patterns of self-development and L2 motivation.

These results, and the more detailed ones to be found in the chapters themselves, point to the beginnings of several new research directions. As with virtually every study in the literature, the research can be refined and new questions developed; we hope that future studies will build upon the lessons described in the preceding chapters in further developing both CDS conceptualisations of motivational processes and the methods to address them.

Concluding Thoughts: Although a Road That May Not be Widely Travelled, DST is Not a Cul-De-Sac!

It is said that 'the perfect is the enemy of the good'. As editors, we have learned that the expression is prescient when applying a CDS perspective to language learning motivation. Future researchers, including graduate students and their advisors, must not be dissuaded by the seemingly impossible standards demanded in some publications in this area. A CDS approach might offer imperfect metaphors adopted from the natural sciences, but even in its incompleteness it has important implications for understanding language learning and development. We do not see the CDS perspective as a theory in a strict sense, but rather a way of thinking about the world and a way of addressing questions that differs from traditional approaches. Because of the complexity of the processes under investigation, CDS, to be honest, is more difficult to apply than traditional methods of data collection and analysis. However, as a counterbalance, a CDS approach can be more rewarding in the sense of the feeling gained that the study is closer to describing events as they actually occur. Moreover, as the contributions to this anthology reveal, it also allows for genuinely new insights and understandings.

Just as they have not supplanted traditional longitudinal studies in developmental psychology, CDS methods are unlikely to replace other approaches to research in our field. Correlations, analysis of variances, interviews, classroom observation schemes and other methods will continue to have their place in the literature for the foreseeable future. Alongside these methods, filling in some of the blanks left by the focus on product, will be studies of dynamic processes. Each strand will inform the other. As John Schumann noted in the Foreword, a dynamic perspective will 'value variation as strongly as states', and that really is a new development for our field.

The state-of-the-art research collected in the current anthology is a sign that some researchers have found the CDS approach both 'cool' enough to explore in a research project and 'hot' enough to inspire new ideas. Of course only time will tell what impact the studies in this volume will have on understandings of motivation in SLA in the years to come. Nevertheless, we are optimistic. Looking into the future, we envisage current trends continuing, the pace of CDS research into L2 motivation gradually gaining momentum, the dynamic toolbox expanding (and with time becoming more useable) and, as a consequence, the emergence of genuinely new insights.

References

de Bot, K., Lowie, W. and Verspoor, M. (2007) A Dynamic Systems Theory approach to second language acquisition. *Bilingualism: Language and Cognition* 10 (1), 7–21.

de Bot, K., Lowie, W., Thorne, S.L. and Verspoor, M. (2013) Dynamic Systems Theory as a theory of second language development. In M. Mayo, M. Gutierrez-Mangado and M. Adrián (eds) *Contemporary Approaches to Second Language Acquisition* (pp. 199–220). Amsterdam: John Benjamins

Carter, B. and Sealey, A. (2009) Reflexivity, realism and the process of casing. In D. Byrne and C.C. Ragin (eds) *The SAGE Handbook of Case-based Methods* (pp. 69–83). London: Sage.

Dörnyei, Z. (2007) *Research Methods in Applied Linguistics: Quantitative, Qualitative and Mixed Methodologies.* Oxford: Oxford University Press.

Gardner, R.C. and Lambert, W.E. (1959) Motivational variables in second language acquisition. *Canadian Journal of Psychology* 13, 266–272.

Haken, H. (2009) Synergetics: Basic concepts. In R.A. Meyers (ed.) *Encyclopedia of Complexity Science* (pp. 8926–8945). New York: Springer.

Larsen-Freeman, D. and Cameron, L. (2008) *Complex Systems and Applied Linguistics.* Oxford: Oxford University Press.

Lewis, M.D. (2011) Dynamic systems approaches: Cool enough? Hot enough? *Child Development Perspectives* 5 (4), 279–285.

Thelen, E. and Smith, L.B. (1994) *A Dynamic Systems Approach to the Development of Cognition and Action.* Cambridge, MA: MIT Press.

van Dijk, M., Verspoor, M. and Lowie, W. (2011) Variability and DST. In M.H. Verspoor, K. de Bot and W. Lowie (eds) *A Dynamic Approach to Second Language Development: Methods and Techniques* (pp. 55–84). Amsterdam: John Benjamins.

Verspoor, M., de Bot, K. and Lowie, W. (2011) *A Dynamic Approach to Second Language Development: Methods and techniques.* Amsterdam: John Benjamins.